SOCIAL COMPARISON THEORIES

Key Readings in Social Psychology

General Editor: ARIE W. KRUGLANSKI, University of Maryland at College Park

The aim of this series is to make available to senior undergraduate and graduate students key articles in each area of social psychology in an attractive, user-friendly format. Many professors want to encourage their students to engage directly with research in their fields, yet this can often be daunting for students coming to detailed study of a topic for the first time. Moreover, declining library budgets mean that articles are not always readily available, and course packs can be expensive and time-consuming to produce. *Key Readings in Social Psychology* aims to address this need by providing comprehensive volumes, each one of which will be edited by a senior and active researcher in the field. Articles will be carefully chosen to illustrate the way the field has developed historically as well as current issues and research directions. Each volume will have a similar structure to include:

- an overview chapter, as well as introduction to sections and articles
- questions for class discussion
- annotated bibliographies
- full author and subject indexes

Published Titles

The Self in Social Psychology	Roy F. Baumeister
Stereotypes and Prejudice	Charles Stangor
Motivational Science	E. Tory Higgins and Arie W. Kruglanski
Emotions in Social Psychology	W. Gerrod Parrott
Social Psychology and Human Sexuality	Roy F. Baumeister
Intergroup Relations	Michael A. Hogg and Dominic Abrams
The Social Psychology of Organizational Behavior	Leigh L. Thompson
Social Psychology: A General Reader	Arie W. Kruglanski and E. Tory Higgins
Social Psychology of Health	Peter Salovey and Alexander J. Rothman
The Interface of Social and Clinical Psychology	Robin M. Kowalski and Mark R. Leary
Political Psychology	John T. Jost and James Sidanius
Close Relationships	Harry T. Reis and Caryl Rusbult
Social Neuroscience	John T. Cacioppo and Gary G. Berntson
Social Cognition	David L. Hamilton
Small Groups	John M. Levine and Richard L. Moreland

Titles in Preparation

Attitudes	Richard E. Petty and Russell Fazio
Persuasion	Richard E. Petty and Russell Fazio
Language and Communication	Gün R. Semin

For continually updated information about published and forthcoming titles in the Key Readings in Social Psychology series, please visit: **www.keyreadings.com**

SOCIAL COMPARISON THEORIES
Key Readings

Edited by

Diederik A. Stapel
Tilburg University, The Netherlands

Hart Blanton
Texas A&M University, USA

Psychology Press
Taylor & Francis Group

NEW YORK AND HOVE

Published in 2007
by Psychology Press
270 Madison Avenue
New York, NY 10016
www.psypress.com

Published in Great Britain
by Psychology Press
27 Church Road
Hove, East Sussex BN3 2FA
www.psypress.co.uk

Psychology Press is an imprint of the Taylor & Francis Group, an informa business

Typeset in Times by Macmillan India, Bangalore, India
Printed in the USA by Sheridan Books, Inc., Ann Arbor, MI, on acid-free paper
Paperback cover design by Hybert Design
Paperback cover image "How to compare apples and apples" by Marie-Anne Stapel

10 9 8 7 6 5 4 3 2 1

Library of Congress Cataloging in Publication Data
Social comparison theories : key readings / edited by Diederik A. Stapel, Hart Blanton.
    p. cm. – (Key readings in social psychology)
  Includes bibliographical references and index.
  ISBN-13: 978-1-84169-090-2 (hardback : alk. paper)
  ISBN-10: 1-84169-090-2 (hardback : alk. paper)
  ISBN-13: 978-1-84169-091-9 (pbk : alk. paper)
  ISBN-10: 1-84169-091-0 (pbk : alk. paper) 1. Social perception. 2. Social
comparison. 3. Self-perception. 4. Comparison (Psychology) I. Stapel, Diederik A. II.
Blanton, Hart, 1967–

BF323.S63S635 2006
302'.12–dc22
                                        2006024731

ISBN 13: 978-1-84169-090-2 (hbk)
ISBN 13: 978-1-84169-091-9 (pbk)

ISBN 10: 1-84169-090-2 (hbk)
ISBN 10: 1-84169-091-0 (pbk)

Contents

About the Editors

Diederik A. Stapel is Professor of Consumer Science and Director of the Tilburg Institute for Behavioral Economics Research (TIBER) at Tilburg University, in the Netherlands. He is associate editor of *Psychological Science*, the *Personality and Social Psychology Bulletin*, a former associate editor of the *British Journal of Social Psychology*, and has served on the editorial boards of *Self and Identity*, the *European Journal of Social Psychology*, and the *Journal of Personality and Social Psychology*. For his research on knowledge accessibility effects, he earned the Jos Jaspars Award of the European Association of Experimental Social Psychology. Stapel's publications concern judgment and decision making and unconscious affective and evaluative processes.

Hart Blanton is Associate Professor of Psychology at Texas A&M University. He is associate editor of the *Journal of Experimental Social Psychology*; on the editorial boards for *Personality and Social Psychology Bulletin* and *Self and Identity*; and has served on the editorial board of *Psychology and Health*. For his work on Deviance Regulation Theory, a comparison-based theory of behavioral self-regulation, he received the 2002 Theoretical Innovation Award from the Society of Personality and Social Psychology. Blanton's publications concern individual and group comparison processes, behavioral self-regulation, normative social influence, research methods, and the measurement of implicit attitudes.

Acknowledgments

The editors and publisher are grateful to the following for permission to reproduce the articles in this book:

Reading 1: Festinger, L. (1950). Informal social communication. *Psychological Review*, *57*, 271–282. Copyright © 1950 by the American Psychological Association. Reprinted with permission.

Reading 2: Festinger, L. (1954). A theory of social comparison processes. *Human Relations*, *7*, 117–140. Copyright © 1954 by Sage Publications, Inc. Reprinted with permission.

Reading 3: Goethals, G. R., & Darley, J. M. (1977). Social comparison theory: An attributional approach. In J. M. Suls & R. L. Miller (Eds.), *Social comparison processes: Theoretical and empirical perspectives* (pp. 259–278). Washington, DC: Hemisphere.

Reading 4: Brickman, P., & Bulman, R. J. (1977). Pleasure and pain in social comparison. In J. M. Suls & R. L. Miller (Eds.), *Social comparison processes: Theoretical and empirical perspectives* (pp. 149–186). Washington, DC: Hemisphere.

Reading 5: Taylor, S. E., & Lobel, M. (1989). Social comparison activity under threat: Downward evaluation and upward contacts. *Psychological Review*, *96*, 569–575. Copyright © 1989 by the American Psychological Association. Reprinted with permission.

Reading 6: Tesser, A. (1999). Toward a self-evaluation maintenance model of social behavior. In R. F. Baumeister (Ed.), *The self in social psychology* (pp. 446–460). Philadelphia: Psychology Press. Copyright © 1999 by Psychology Press. Reprinted with permission.

Reading 7: Buunk, B., Collins, R., Taylor, S., Dakof, G., & Van Yperen, N. (1990). The affective consequences of social comparison: Either direction has its ups and downs. *Journal of Personality and Social Psychology*, *59*, 1238–1249. Copyright © 1990 by the American Psychological Association. Reprinted with permission.

Reading 8: Lockwood, P., & Kunda, Z. (1997). Superstars and me: Predicting the impact of role models on the self. *Journal of Personality and Social Psychology*, *73*(1), 91–103. Copyright © 1997 by the American Psychological Association. Reprinted with permission.

Reading 9: Alicke, M. D., LoSchiavo, F. M., Zerbst, J. I., & Zhang, S. (1997). The person who outperforms me is a genius: Maintaining perceived competence in upward social comparison. *Journal of Personality and Social Psychology*, *73*, 781–789. Copyright © 1997 by the American Psychological Association. Reprinted with permission.

Reading 10: Gibbons, F. X., Benbow, C. P., & Gerrard, M. (1994). From top dog to bottom half: Social comparison strategies in response to poor performance. *Journal of Personality and Social Psychology*, *67*(4), 638–652. Copyright © 1994

Reading 11: Weinstein, N. D. (1980). Unrealistic optimism about future life events. *Journal of Personality and Social Psychology, 39*, 806–820. Copyright © 1980 by the American Psychological Association. Reprinted with permission.

Reading 12: Klein, W. M. (1997). Objective standards are not enough: Affective, self-evaluative, and behavioral responses to social comparison information. *Journal of Personality and Social Psychology, 72*(4), 763–774. Copyright © 1997 by the American Psychological Association. Reprinted with permission.

Reading 13: Moore, D. A., & Kim, T. G. (2003). Myopic social prediction and the solo comparison effect. *Journal of Personality and Social Psychology, 85*(6), 1121–1135. Copyright © 2003 by the American Psychological Association. Reprinted with permission.

Reading 14: Schroeder, C. M., & Prentice, D. A. (1998). Exposing pluralistic ignorance to reduce alcohol use among college students. *Journal of Applied Social Psychology, 28*, 2150–2180. Copyright © 1998 by the American Psychological Association. Reprinted with permission.

Reading 15: Nosanchuck, T. A., & Erickson, B. H. (1985). How high is up? Calibrating social comparison in the real world. *Journal of Personality and Social Psychology, 48*(3), 624–634. Copyright © 1985 by the American Psychological Association. Reprinted with permission.

Reading 16: Marsh, H. W., & Hau, K.-T. (2003). Big-fish–little-pond effect on academic self-concept: A cross-cultural (26-country) test of the negative effects of academically selective schools. *American Psychologist, 58*(5), 364–376. Copyright © 2003 by the American Psychological Association. Reprinted with permission.

Reading 17: Hagerty, M. R. (2000). Social comparisons of income in one's community: Evidence from national surveys of income and happiness. *Journal of Personality and Social Psychology,* 78(4), 764–771. Copyright © 2000 by the American Psychological Association. Reprinted with permission.

Reading 18: Tiedens, L. Z., & Fragale, A. R. (2003). Power moves: Complementarity in dominant and submissive nonverbal behavior. *Journal of Personality and Social Psychology, 84*(3), 558–568. Copyright © 2003 by the American Psychological Association. Reprinted with permission.

Reading 19: Tajfel, H., & Turner, J. C. (1986). The social identity theory of intergroup behavior. In S. Worchel & G. A. Williams (Eds.), *Psychology of intergroup relations* (pp. 7–24). Chicago: Nelson-Hall. Copyright © 1986 by Burnham Inc., Publishers. Reprinted with permission.

Reading 20: Miller, D. T., Turnbull, W., & McFarland, C. (1988). Particularistic and universalistic evaluation in the social comparison process. *Journal of Personality and Social Psychology, 55*, 908–917. Copyright © 1988 by the American Psychological Association. Reprinted with permission.

Reading 21: Crandall, C. S. (1988). Social contagion of binge eating. *Journal of Personality and Social Psychology, 55*, 588–598. Copyright © 1988 by the American Psychological Association. Reprinted with permission.

Reading 22: Major, B. & Forcey, B. (1985). Social comparisons and pay evaluations: Preferences for same-sex and same-job wage comparisons. *Journal of Experimental Social Psychology, 21*, 393–405. Copyright © 1985 by Academic Press, Inc. Reprinted with permission.

Reading 23: Blanton, H., Christie, C., & Dye, M. (2002). Social identity versus reference frame comparisons: The moderating role of stereotype endorsement. *Journal of Experimental Social Psychology, 38*, 253–267. Copyright © 2002 by Elsevier. Reprinted with permission.

Reading 24: Gilbert, D. T., Giesler, R. B., & Morris, K. A. (1995). When comparisons arise. *Journal of Personality and Social Psychology, 69*, 227–236. Copyright © 1995 by the American Psychological Association. Reprinted with permission.

Reading 25: Stapel, D. A., & Koomen, W. (2001). I, we, and the effects of others on me: How self-construal level moderates social comparison effects. *Journal of Personality and Social Psychology*, *80*, 766–781. Copyright © 2001 by the American Psychological Association. Reprinted with permission.

Reading 26: Mussweiler, T., & Strack, F. (2000). The "relative self": Informational and judgmental consequences of comparative self-evaluation. *Journal of Personality and Social Psychology*, *79*, 23–38. Copyright © 2000 by the American Psychological Association. Reprinted with permission.

Introduction to the History of Social Comparison

Hart Blanton and Diederik A. Stapel

With few exceptions, social psychologists regard their discipline as an attempt to understand and explain how the thought, feeling, and behavior of individuals are influenced by the actual, imagined, or implied presence of other human beings.

Gordon Allport (1954, p. 5)

When the above quote appeared in the *Hand-book of Social Psychology*, Gordon Allport introduced a succinct but inclusive definition that nonetheless captured the whole of what was then the field of social psychology. Given the many scientific advances that have occurred since the *Handbook* was published, it is reasonable to ask if Allport's definition can cover the breadth of the discipline today. We suspect it cannot. The past two decades have seen the rise of many hybrid versions of social psychology—sub-disciplines that trace their lineages to anthropology, sociology, cognitive science, neuropsychology, and psycho-physiology. Applied areas have also broken off from the mainstream and helped researchers to predict behaviors with relevance to health, political, organizational, and consumer outcomes.

We view the expansion of social psychology beyond Allport's original definition as a sign of intellectual growth, but we also share the concerns expressed by many social psychologists who bemoan the loss of "the social" in our branch of psychology. To adapt Allport's phrase, it is at times hard to find the presence of others—actual, imagined, or even implied—in much of what is now considered to be social-psychological research. Perhaps the field stopped focusing on the individual when it began placing priority on mechanism over meaning or processes over content. Perhaps the need for scientific rigor has led researchers to focus on smaller, more clearly defined problems; problems that lend themselves to experimental control and replication. Whatever the reason, social psychology nowadays is probably less social (interpersonal) and more psychology (mechanism) than it has ever been.

In this book of readings, we draw attention to a sub-discipline of social psychology where the presence of others remains an indispensable and defining attribute. In fact, we would go so far as to argue that Allport's (1954) definition of social psychology remains accurate and complete, as long as it has the more circumscribed goal of defining this

1

one area of inquiry. *Social comparison* is a field of research that examines psychological phenomena initiated by the presence of at least one "other." This other can be an actual other, as when a positive role model inspires a student to succeed in school (Lockwood, Marshall, & Sadler, 2005). This other can be an imagined other, as when a cancer patient constructs a worse-off other in her head to help her cope with her fears (Wood, Taylor, & Lichtman, 1985). Or this other can be an implied other, as when a research psychologist finds evidence that comparison standards become accessible in working memory when research participants are asked to reflect on the self (Stapel & Tesser, 2001).

The fact that social comparison today could co-opt what was once the definition of an entire field reveals that social comparison is a very broad area of inquiry. This breadth can be seen in the wide range of topics that have been studied from a social comparison perspective. Social comparison researchers have shown how perceptions of other people can influence subjective well-being, life satisfaction, physical health, and self-esteem, and help them improve. Social comparison researchers have also uncovered biases that influence our perceptions of others, and shown how these biased perceptions can then go on to influence our behavioral decisions. They have also examined the cognitive processes underlying social comparisons, in order to map out how mental systems organize, process, and interpret social events. The readings in this book touch on all of these topics—and others as well.

A Victim of Its Own Success?

A dazzling array of psychological events has been viewed as social comparison phenomena and so, when we began compiling the articles we would include in this book, we found it exciting to think of the many subjects that we could include in a reader on social comparison. We have to confess, however, that as we continued to survey the terrain this volume might cover, an awkward concern began to emerge. We found ourselves wondering if the field of social comparison is now too big for its own good. The range of psychological events

that can be given the label "social comparison" is now so broad, so inclusive, and at times so overwhelming, that the social comparison label may fail to confer any meaning (see also Wood, 1989, 1996). Conceivably, human actions that range from helping to hurting another, from liking to disliking another, or from approaching to avoiding another, can be (and have been) viewed through social comparison glasses.

To explain how we resolved this issue and made Allport's definition manageable, we must first review how social comparison became a subdiscipline within social psychology. This discussion reveals a field of study that began with a single theoretical statement that was ambitious and provocative, and yet equally flawed. As we will explain, however, the many shortcomings of this original theory have made the field healthier today and they are largely responsible for the unusual breadth we now must grapple with in compiling a list of social comparison readings.

Social Comparison: A Good, Bad, and Ever-Expanding Theory

Social comparison is one of the rare domains in social psychology that has a clear and agreed starting point. It would be hard to identify a single originating source for modern theories of attitudes, stereotyping, group processes, or emotions. But social comparison springs from a single well.

Festinger's (1954) paper is the seminal work on social comparison, and it remains a monument to bold thinking. Adopting the rhetorical style and logical structure that might be expected in the writings of John Locke or David Hume, Festinger presented his social comparison theory in the form of nine hypotheses, eight corollaries, and eight deviations. In the current era of theorizing, where psychologists now lament that our theories are no longer exact, no longer internally consistent, and no longer falsifiable (Birnbaum, 1984; Wallach & Wallach, 1994), Festinger's paper on social comparison stands as an example of an ambitious theory that makes clear and testable predictions. His theory was all this—and it was less. Festinger's paper also had key deficiencies. In an interesting and thoroughly unpredictable way, however, the limitations built into this original document have done as much to promote a vibrant social comparison literature today as did the theory's strengths.

What were the deficiencies in Festinger's (1954) article? For one, his terminology was vague. Although his theory was logical in its structure and derivations, it employed a vocabulary that was hard to penetrate and this led to considerable confusion. As a primary example, consider the "similarity hypothesis," around which most predictions centered. In Hypothesis III Festinger argued that people prefer comparisons with similar others. This would seem straightforward enough, but Festinger introduced ambiguity to his theory by never defining what he meant by similarity. In many of his examples, he implied that two people will only compare their abilities and opinions if they are similar to one another on the ability or opinion being compared. But how would a person know that another person has similar opinions and abilities without first making a social comparison on that dimension? Thus, at least one reasonable interpretation of the term "similarity" introduced a paradox that defied empirical analysis. Other aspects of his theory were equally vague. In particular, his notion of a "unidirectional drive upward" has at times been interpreted to mean that we seek contact with slightly superior others (i.e., upward comparison; Berger, 1977; Gruder, 1977; Mettee & Smith, 1977) and at other times it has been interpreted to mean that we seek contact with slightly inferior others (i.e., downward comparison; Hackmiller, 1966; Wheeler *et al.*, 1969). We discuss likely interpretations of these and other confusing parts of his theory in the next section. For now, we simply note that Festinger's paper often lacked conceptual clarity.

Festinger's theory was also deficient in its depiction of human motives. Festinger focused his attention on a single orienting concern that he thought drove the need to compare. This was the need to reduce uncertainty. Festinger's theory of social comparison painted the portrait of an individual who wants to hold an accurate view of the world. This rational actor who can be found in Festinger's (1954) theory of social comparison bears little resemblance to the motivated and irrational actor who appeared three years later in Festinger's (1957)

theory of cognitive dissonance. Both of these individuals are too extreme to capture the complexity of human actors, but many researchers found the rational social comparison seeker far less interesting and far less plausible than the irrational dissonance reducer. If one surveys the breadth of social comparison research today, it is amazing to think that this broad domain originates in single theory (Festinger, 1954) that explored how a single human motivation (the desire to resolve uncertainty) could be satisfied by a single response (seeking comparisons with similar others).

And how is it that such an evolution could have taken place? One view is simply that the positives in the original theory overcame the negatives. Festinger's ambitious theorizing and the importance of the topic might have been sufficient to overcome the theory's initial missteps. In our view, however, the shortcomings of his original theory played pivotal roles in the theory's success. One clear effect they had was that they stimulated research. Consider the conceptual ambiguity in Festinger's similarity hypothesis and the paradox that one cannot detect similarity unless comparisons have already been made. In response to this, researchers developed research methods by which similarity between self and other is only *implied*, and they then tested if people would seek comparisons with people who they expected to be similar (e.g., Pyszczynski, Greenberg, & LaPrelle, 1985; Thornton & Arrowood, 1966; Wheeler *et al.*, 1969). Theoreticians also revised the similarity hypothesis to state that people seek comparisons with others who are similar on non-focal or background dimensions—that is, on dimensions related to the dimension being compared—rather than comparisons with those who are similar on the focal dimension (e.g., Goethals & Darley, 1977; C.T. Miller, 1984; D.T. Miller, Turnbull & McFarland, 1988). Each of these approaches made the similarity hypothesis viable and stimulated new research and theory.

Investigators also expanded the list of the motivations that might drive interest in social comparisons. A cursory review of the comparison literature will reveal the motive to maintain positive self-esteem (Tesser, 1988), to distinguish oneself from others (Snyder & Fromkin, 1977), to improve skills and performances (Collins, 1996), to validate opinions

and beliefs (Goethals & Darley, 1977), and to maintain harmonious social interactions (Brickman &
Bulman, 1977). As researchers added new concerns
to the social comparison drive, Festinger's once
rational actor was replaced with a person who possessed a far more complex and multifaceted motivational system than was ever considered by the
cognitive dissonance literature. Certainly, the motivational system underlying dissonance has undergone evolution as well, but it is rare to find theories
of cognitive dissonance that focus attention on
more than one motivational concern (cf., Stone &
Cooper, 2001).

In short, the field of social psychology responded
to the weakness of social comparison theory, not by
abandoning it but by expanding it. Festinger's original vision was still important, however, because it
kept a wide range research of questions bundled
together under a single label. It did this, even while
the need to overcome the weaknesses of his original
vision inspired a complexity of thought that might
easily have confounded a single label. But is this
history so unique in the field of social psychology?
One might argue, after all, that all influential theories start out with more promise than they can
deliver. Perhaps this is all that happened with social
comparison. We contend that something unusual
did happen, however, and that the negatives in social
comparison theory had a positive effect that would
have been hard to predict early in the history of this
discipline. We draw attention to cognitive dissonance theory to argue this point.

Festinger (1957) wrote cognitive dissonance theory just three years after his comparison paper and
it, too, has gone on to define a well-contained field
of inquiry. The conventional wisdom is that cognitive dissonance proved to be the more powerful
and influential of the two theories (Jones, 1998).
We concede that cognitive dissonance theory was
a less qualified success at its inception. Like social
comparison theory, cognitive dissonance was bold
and provocative, but it also exhibited a conceptual
clarity and a predictive power that social comparison lacked. Researchers who incorporated this
theory into their work were rewarded with clear
(and often accurate) predictions. With dissonance
theory, Festinger found his voice and it was

received more warmly by the research community
than his paper on social comparison processes.

We would argue, however, that the original
appeal of Festinger's (1957) cognitive dissonance
theory contributed to its downfall, and that the
inadequacies of Festinger's (1954) social comparison theory protected it from this same fate. This can
be seen by comparing how researchers responded
when they found problems with one theory or the
other. Unlike with social comparison theory, when
researchers found limitations of the original cognitive dissonance theory, they did not try to expand
it. They sought to own it. When researchers found
limitations of the original (which many did), the
overwhelming tendency was to advance a *new*
version of cognitive dissonance theory that could
encapsulate Festinger's original statement (and
also account for a new set of discrepant findings).
This process repeated itself over and over again,
and the result was that social psychology journals
filled with competing cognitive dissonance theories. At various points in the field's history, there
have been as many as half a dozen theories vying
for the title of *the* cognitive dissonance theory.
There is no equivalent history in the social comparison literature. There certainly have been papers
that have sought to revise earlier theoretical
assumptions or claims, but at no point in the history
of the field has there been a fight or debate over
which researcher or which set of researchers can lay
claim to the social comparison theory of the day.

Why did social psychologists approach dissonance theory by trying to seize it, but did not do
the same with social comparison theory? Part of
the answer probably is that dissonance theory was
counter-intuitive and so it inspired the imagina-
tion of the field in a way that any theory of social
comparison processes could not. Dissonance theory also served an important function in social
psychology, in that it gave the field a unique perspective that could be used to loosen behaviorism's
grip on psychology. In these ways, dissonance was
a bigger fish, and so this might be enough to explain
why people responded to it in the way they did.
We think, however, that any account of why these
two theories engendered different responses must
look not just to the factors that made cognitive

dissonance a desirable possession; it must also look to the factors that diminished proprietary grabs for social comparison theory. And this is where social comparison theory's negatives came into play.

To put it plainly, social comparison was not treated as a prize to be had, because it was never a prize to begin with. Certainly social comparison theory did inspire researchers to try to expand upon it, but no researcher was able to provide a succinct statement on how to clean it up or make it whole again. In contrast, dissonance theory came as a fully formed and functioning package, and so it was easy to co-opt with a stroke of the pen. With one change in the nature of dissonance motivation (from viewing it as a need for consistency to a need for self-esteem, or from viewing it as a need for self-esteem to a need for public approval), a researcher could introduce a powerful new theory into the literature. The ease with which one could update and thereby lay claim to dissonance theory had important effects on the intellectual climate in the dissonance literature, a climate that was much different than it was in social comparison.

As entirely new revisions of cognitive dissonance began to accumulate, researchers began constructing critical tests that would pit their own prized versions of cognitive dissonance theory against their most formidable competitors. In contrast, the social comparison literature plodded along with little controversy, little drama, and far fewer critical tests. The result was that the social comparison field began expanding into a set of non-conflicting statements about how, why, and to what effect people compare, whereas cognitive dissonance became a contest to write the definitive work on dissonance motivation.

And so, from Festinger's two great works, we see two distinct models of how a theory can evolve within the psychological literature. Cognitive dissonance theory was a relatively complete piece that was greeted with a great deal of early enthusiasm, and this sparked competitive theory testing. Social comparison was a more qualified success early on, and this encouraged a communal exchange. The standard prediction is that the stronger initial theory and the resulting competitive theory testing would have made cognitive dissonance the more powerful of the two (Lakatos, 1978), but history tells a different story. Although the clarity of the original dissonance theory resulted in early enthusiasm for the topic, critical testing of the theory ultimately drove researchers away. Perhaps excitement over competition could not be sustained or perhaps the reliance on critical testing made dissonance researchers explore less ambitious or risky tests of their theories (see McGuire, 1973). It is hard to say what went wrong, but enthusiasm for cognitive dissonance dwindled over time, while interest in social comparison theory only grew.

The contrasting histories of these two theories can be seen in Figure I.1. This graph shows the life course of social comparison and cognitive

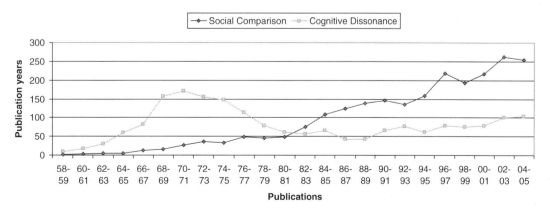

FIGURE I.1 ■ The life course of social comparison and cognitive dissonance: The graph was made "by counting the number of PsychInfo citations that indexed the terms 'social comparison' and 'cognitive dissonance'."

dissonance (adapted from Blanton & Christie, 2003). It charts the number of papers that were indexed in PsychInfo under cognitive dissonance and social comparison theory in the years since each of Festinger's original publications. This analysis reveals that cognitive dissonance theory burned more brightly than social comparison theory at first, but ultimately the dissonance flame diminished and it now burns about as brightly as it did in 1980. In contrast, social comparison theory has only become brighter over time. We are hesitant to express a general principle about the nature of theoretical process from our analysis of cognitive dissonance and social comparison theories, but we think Figure I.1 illustrates the value of a "good bad" theory in psychology. Festinger's (1954) social comparison theory was good enough to pique interest, to generate testable predictions, and to jumpstart a new area of study, but it was bad enough to require a cooperative exchange between many individuals for the field to move forward.

And this is how the field of social comparison grew to be so big.

But Is It Too Big?

This returns us to the question that started our analysis: Is social comparison literature now too big for its own good? In some ways, we think maybe so. With the continued expansion of social comparison in the literature, researchers now place so few boundaries on the events they might label as "social comparison" that far less is gained than in Festinger's day by employing this explanatory framework. In fact, social comparison analyses can at times reveal imprecision in thinking, rather than precision. The two of us see this shortcoming at times in our own thinking (though certainly not in the other's). As comparison researchers, we often find ourselves declaring that a psychological event we have observed illustrates a social comparison principle in action, but such can be said of most any social event that we might observe. So, we have to admit that there is something about these pronouncements that at times lacks intellectual heft.

A Resolution

This was the dilemma we faced in choosing readings for our book. Although we felt that social comparison is a vibrant and healthy field of study today, we also feared that a book of readings that accurately captured its breadth might fail to cohere as a single topic. We needed more direction than we could get from Allport's definition alone, no matter how appropriate it may be to describe our topic. Our way out of this dilemma can be found by returning to Figure I.1.

Recall that we constructed this figure by counting the number of articles that were indexed under the term "social comparison." How is it that these articles (and not others) were given this label, when so many other articles in PsychInfo could speak to social comparison processes? We suspect that these articles were indexed in this way because the authors themselves made connections between their own research topic and the social comparison literature. We imagine that many of these authors cited Festinger (1954) and other "classics" in the social comparison literature. Thus, the articles in Figure I.1 qualified as articles on social comparison because the researchers who wrote them construed them as such. Of course, any number of other articles in the PsychInfo database *could* have been couched in social comparison terms. In many instances, if they had done so they could have incorporated a literature that would have allowed them to see further. But they did not, and so their articles were not comparison articles.

Outline of Our Selected Articles

This analysis of what does and does not qualify as a comparison article inspired the current choice of articles. When selecting readings, we imposed two strict standards. First, we looked for readings that revealed how the presence of others (real, imagined, or implied) influenced (the thoughts, feelings, and actions of) the individual. Second, we only considered articles in which the authors themselves integrated their theory or their findings with the larger literature on social comparison. In this way, we would not simply reveal social comparison "effects" that might be of interest, but we could also show the power of a social-psychological analysis of social phenomena. We believe that the current articles are useful in this way. Some focus on concerns that were originally highlighted in Festinger (1954), some show the collective spirit with which researchers tried to repair his original theory, others highlight ways in which social comparison expanded into applied areas, and still others highlight psychological mechanisms that drive social comparisons. The breadth of this book remains far greater than anything that can be found in Festinger's (1954) theory, but we hope our readers will still see signs of the original vision that began with this paper. We also hope that readers will begin to see new links between their own work and the social comparison literature. The result is that they may couch their work in these terms and the field of social comparison will grow even broader than it is today. And we would view this as a good thing.

We have decided to present these 26 readings in seven sections. In each section, a certain aspect or theme that we think is important in social comparison research is made salient. The first section ("Festinger") introduces Festinger's original social comparison theory and places it in context by discussing the importance of an earlier theory on social communication. As we will show, many of the limitations of the original can perhaps be found in Festinger's attempt to adapt his earlier paper rather than start afresh. In the second section ("Comparison motives: Classic statements") we have collected a number of readings that reflect important turning points in the theory away from Festinger's thinking, and that continue to influence the field today. Together, these first two sections lay the foundations for those that follow. In "Threats and Inspiration" we discuss how people regulate their comparisons in response to threats, and how comparison activities themselves can be a source of threat or inspiration. If this section promotes a view that social comparison is used by individuals to help them adapt to their environments, the next ("Breakdowns in Comparison") considers what might be viewed as flaws in the social comparison process. It shows that people often draw comparative inferences from limited information and rely on comparison information

when they should not. The next two sections ("Implications in Everyday Life") and ("Social Identity and Reference Group Comparisons") consider social comparisons from two perspectives. The first considers how individuals rely on comparisons to navigate their own personal worlds in everyday life, and the second considers how group membership can structure and limit the ways social comparisons are used. The final section ("Social Cognition") focuses on the most recent trend in social comparison research, and this is the pursuit of cognitive mechanisms underlying comparison phenomena. Combined, we hope that this collection of readings shows the wide range of topics that concern social comparison researchers and also the shared beliefs that bind them together.

REFERENCES

Allport, G. W. (1954). The historical background of modern social psychology. In G. Lindzey, *Handbook of social psychology* (Vol. 1, pp. 3–56). Reading, MA: Addison–Wesley.

Berger, S. M. (1977). Social comparison, modeling, and perseverance. In J. M. Suls & R. L. Miller (Eds.), *Social comparison processes: Theoretical and empirical perspectives* (pp. 209–234). Washington, DC: Hemisphere.

Birnbaum, M. H. (1984). Philosophical criteria for psychological explanation. *Bulletin of the Psychonomic Society, 22*(6), 562–565.

Blanton, H., & Christie, C. (2003). Social comparison: Everybody's personal theory. Review of J. Suls and L. Wheeler (2002), "Handbook of Social Comparison." *Contemporary Psychology, 48*(3), 311–313.

Brickman, P., & Bulman, R. J. (1977). Pleasure and pain in social comparison. In J. M. Suls & R. L. Miller (Eds.), *Social comparison processes: Theoretical and empirical perspectives* (pp. 149–186). Washington, DC: Hemisphere.

Collins, R. L. (1996). For better or worse: The impact of upward social comparison on self-evaluations. *Psychological Bulletin, 119*(1), 51–69.

Festinger, L. (1954). A theory of social comparison processes. *Human Relations, 7*, 117–140.

Festinger, L. (1957). *A theory of cognitive dissonance.* Stanford, CA: Stanford University Press.

Goethals, G. R., & Darley, J. M. (1977). Social comparison theory: An attributional approach. In J. M. Suls & R. L. Miller (Eds.), *Social comparison processes: Theoretical and empirical perspectives* (pp. 259–278). Washington, DC: Hemisphere.

Gruder, C. L. (1977). Choice of comparison persons in evaluating oneself. In J. Suls & R. L. Miller (Eds.), *Social comparison processes: Theoretical and empirical perspectives* (pp. 21–42). Washington, DC: Hemisphere.

Hackmiller, K. L. (1966). Need for self-evaluation, perceived similarity, and comparison choice. *Journal of Experimental Social Psychology, Suppl. 1,* 49–54.

Jones, E. E. (1998). Major developments in five decades of social psychology. In D. T. Gilbert, S. T. Fiske, & G. Lindzey (Eds.), *The handbook of social psychology* (Vol. 2, 4th ed., pp. 3–57). New York: McGraw-Hill.

Lakatos, I. (1978). *Mathematics, science, and epistemology.* Cambridge, UK: Cambridge University Press.

Lockwood, P., Marshall, T. C., & Sadler, P. (2005). Promoting success or preventing failure: Cultural differences in motivation by positive and negative role models. *Personality and Social Psychology Bulletin, 31,* 379–392.

McGuire, W. J. (1973). The yin and yang of progress in social psychology: Seven koan. *Journal of Personality and Social Psychology, 26,* 446–456.

Mettee, D. R., & Smith, G. (1977). Social comparison and interpersonal attraction: The case for dissimiliarity. In J. M. Suls & R. L. Miller (Eds.), *Social comparison processes: Theoretical and empirical perspectives* (pp. 69–101). Washington, DC: Hemisphere.

Miller, C. T. (1984). Self-schemas, gender, and social comparison: A clarification of the related attributes hypothesis *Journal of Personality and Social Psychology, 46,* 1222–1229.

Miller, D. T., Turnbull, W., & McFarland, C. (1988). Particularistic and universalistic evaluation in the social comparison process. *Journal of Personality and Social Psychology, 55,* 908–917.

Pyszczynski, T., Greenberg, J., & LaPrelle, J. (1985). Social comparison after success and failure: Biased search for information consistent with a self-servicing conclusion. *Journal of Experimental Social Psychology, 21,* 195–211.

Snyder, C. R., & Fromkin, H. L. (1977). Abnormality as a positive characteristic: The development and validation of a scale measuring need for uniqueness. *Journal of Abnormal Psychology, 86,* 518–527.

Stapel, D. A., & Tesser, A. (2001). Self-activation increases social comparison. *Journal of Personality and Social Psychology, 81,* 742–750.

Stone, J., & Cooper, J. (2001). A self-standards model of cognitive dissonance. *Journal of Experimental Social Psychology, 37,* 228–243.

Tesser, A. (1988). Toward a self-evaluation maintenance model of social behavior. In L. Berkowitz (Ed.), *Advances in experimental social psychology (Vol. 21,* pp. 181–227). New York: Academic Press.

Thornton, D. A., & Arrowood, A. J. (1966). Self-evaluation, self-enhancement, and the locus of social comparison. *Journal of Experimental Social Psychology, Supplement, 1,* 40–48.

Wallach, L., & Wallach, M. A. (1994). Gergen versus the mainstream: Are hypotheses in social psychology subject to empirical test? *Journal of Personality and Social Psychology, 67,* 233–242.

Wheeler, L., Shaver, K., Jones, R., Goethals, G. R., Cooper, J., Robinson, J. E. *et al.* (1969). Factors determining choice of a comparison other. *Journal of Experimental Social Psychology, 5,* 219–232.

Wood, J. V. (1989). Theory and research concerning social comparisons of personal attributes. *Psychological Bulletin, 106,* 231–248.

Wood, J. V. (1996). What is social comparison and how should we study it? *Personality and Social Psychology Bulletin, 22,* 520–537.

Wood, J. V., Taylor, S. E., & Lichtman, R. R. (1985). Social comparison in adjustment to breast cancer. *Journal of Personality and Social Psychology, 49,* 1169–1183.

Discussion Questions

A common view of psychological theories is that the "strongest survive." This view argues for critical tests of two or more competing theories to ensure that weak theories are dropped in favor of stronger alternatives. How does this logic fall down in the comparison between the relative successes of dissonance theory and social comparison theory? What role did the negative aspects of Festinger's (1954) social comparison theory play in this success?

Suggested Readings

Blanton, H. (2001). Evaluating the self in the context of another: The three-selves model of social comparison assimilation and contrast. In G. B. Moskowitz (Ed.), *Cognitive social psychology: The Princeton Symposium on the Legacy and Future of Social Cognition* (pp. 75–87). Mahwah, NJ: Lawrence Erlbaum Associates Inc.

Buunk, B., & Gibbons, F. X. (Eds.). (1997). *Health, coping, and well-being: Perspectives from social comparison theory*. Mahwah, NJ: Lawrence Erlbaum Associates Inc.

Markman, K. D., & McMullen, M. N. (2003). A reflection and evaluation model of comparative thinking. *Personality and Social Psychology Review, 7,* 244–267.

Suls, J., & Miller, R. L. (Eds.). (1977). *Social comparison processes: Theoretical and empirical perspectives*. Washington, DC: Hemisphere.

Suls, J., & Wills, T. A. (Eds.). (1991). *Social comparison: Contemporary theory and research*. Hillsdale, NJ: Lawrence Erlbaum Associates Inc.

Suls, J., & Wheeler, L. (Eds.). (2000). *Handbook of social comparison: Theory and research*. Dordrecht, The Netherlands: Kluwer Academic Publishers.

Wood, J. V. (1989). Theory and research concerning social comparison of personal attributes. *Psychological Bulletin, 106,* 231–248.

Wood, J. V. (1996). What is social comparison and how should we study it? *Personality & Social Psychology Bulletin, 22,* 520–537.

PART 1

Festinger

It is widely accepted that social comparison theory became a formal area of study with the publication of Leon Festinger's (1954) paper, *A Theory of Social Comparison Processes.* However, Festinger clearly stated in this work that he viewed his social comparison theory as a "further development" of a 1950 paper he had written, titled *Informal Social Communication.* We thus present both of these papers in their entirety in this section. We believe that much can be learned by understanding the context that the first paper provided for the second. Given the claims we made in the Introduction, that both the positives and the negatives of Festinger's theory of social comparison have been essential to its success, we feel it is useful in our analysis not simply to view all of Festinger's "updates" as improvements.

We argue here that Festinger's earlier theory had some desirable qualities that are missing in his later work, and we suggest that Festinger's attempts to make his social theory compatible with his theory of social communications at times held his new theory back. We think it important to recognize, however, that any failings we point out in Festinger (1954) must be put in their proper context. Given that this work has inspired more than five decades of research on social comparison, we can only view it as a great achievement. We nonetheless view it as useful to critique this theory and to discuss its origins in an earlier work. Our analysis begins by highlighting a number of key features in Festinger's (1950) *Informal Social Communication.* We then discuss how this theory shaped *A Theory of Social Comparison Processes*, for both good and bad.

A Theory of Informal Social Communication

Festinger's theory of social communication was written in the language of Lewin's (1951) field theory to consider a set of social forces that operated on the individual. This work was not concerned with social comparison per se, but with the "forces" that cause people to communicate with one another and, in particular, with pressures to achieve uniformity of opinions. Festinger (1950) argued that people are motivated to view their own opinions as valid, and that one of the primary ways in which they infer validity is by observing that their own views are shared by others. When others disagree, he argued, people engage in communications that will pressure greater uniformity.

This original theory drew heavily on the contemporary concept of the *reference group* (Hyman, 1942; Hyman & Singer, 1968; Sherif & Sherif, 1964; Newcomb, 1950). A reference group was a set of real or implied individuals whose opinions and beliefs are valued by individuals and incorporated into their own self-evaluations. By orienting his theory around the concept of the reference group, Festinger showed his appreciation of the fact that people do not try to align their opinions with the opinions of all other people. Festinger did not elaborate in great detail how we decide that a person is a referent, but he appeared to understand that this status can be gained from identification with an in-group, from friendship bonds, and the simple admiration one person can have for another person. Even when someone is a referent, however, Festinger argued that we do always feel it is important to share all referent opinions. He noted that some beliefs are important to the functioning of groups or to the attainment of group goals, and so uniformity pressure will most likely form in groups when these features are present.

The theory of informal social communications has gone on to influence research on groups and social influence, but its largest contribution to the field of social psychology was probably the way in which it shaped Festinger's own social comparison theory. We turn to this second theory now. Our major premise is that Festinger's attempt to build social comparison theory from this earlier work, rather than develop an entirely new theory, led to many of the weaknesses we noted in the Introduction.

A Theory of Social Comparison Processes

A careful reading of Festinger (1950) can give insight into the concerns that Festinger must have grappled with while he was developing his theory of comparison processes. One can see, for instance, that Festinger retained an interest in how opinions are socially constructed (an interest that remained in Festinger's 1957 paper on cognitive dissonance). His social comparison theory was more ambitious, however, in that he wanted to consider not just how opinions are constructed, but also how perceptions of abilities are shaped through contact with others. This move to considering both opinions and abilities was important to the success of Festinger's (1954) theory of social comparison.[1] But this move did present numerous difficulties.

In a sense, Festinger's decision to build a theory of ability perception out of a theory of social communication put him in the position of having to "retrofit" an old theory for a new purpose. One key change that Festinger needed to make was to abandon his focus on the pursuit of validity. Although it is meaningful to ask if one's opinions are valid, it is not so meaningful to ask this same question of one's abilities. Abilities can be good or bad, but there is nothing inherently "valid" about, say, a fast running speed or a low IQ. Festinger thus oriented his theory of social comparisons around a concern that he viewed as more universal than the need for validity, and this was the need to *evaluate*. Festinger stated that:

> Hypothesis I: *There exists, in the human organism, a drive to evaluate his opinions and his abilities.*

There has been some debate over what Festinger meant by arguing for a need to evaluate, but the view that fits most interpretations is that social comparisons is a theory about *uncertainty reduction.* When Festinger stated that we have a need to "evaluate," he was arguing that we have a need to know with some degree of certainty what opinions we hold and what abilities we possess. Through social comparisons, he argued, we gain a greater sense of true qualities (whether they are good or bad, valid or invalid).

The focus on uncertainty reduction helped Festinger move past his original concern for validity, but it created many new problems as well. For one, it oriented Festinger around a single comparison motive, when many other motives would be needed to create an inclusive theory of social comparison. Psychologists have long argued that Festinger's focus on just one motivational concern showed that he had a limited view of the motives that might drive social comparisons. We agree with this to a point, and we will return to the issue of other motivations shortly. For now we simply note that, at least originally, Festinger's decision to focus on an uncertainty reduction motive showed that he knew he needed to *broaden* his theoretical framework, not restrict it. This one change from his earlier theory allowed him to consider a broad concern that would be relevant to both the perception of opinions and the perception of abilities.

The move away from validity and towards evaluation was thus an important move, but it was not the only one. Of course, the most significant change Festinger made was that his new theory focused on the forces that cause people to compare with one another, not the forces that cause them to communicate with one another. The shift to social comparison made Festinger's new theory less interpersonal than his earlier effort, and it drew greater attention to psychological mechanisms that occur in people's heads. Because the theory of social communications focused attention on reference groups, it encouraged researchers to consider the type of relationships people form, the nature of group identities, and the pressures that people exert

---

[1] In general, social comparison researchers have been more interested in identifying how social comparisons shape ability perceptions, rather than how they shape opinions. The greater interest in ability perceptions probably reflects the simple fact that social psychologists often orient their theories around variables that predict self-esteem and positive self-evaluations. Abilities perceptions have clear links to feelings of self-worth, whereas the link from opinions is more tenuous.

between one another to reach consensus. To be sure, there are times in Festinger's theory of social comparison where he expressed interest in similar interpersonal dynamics, but this discussion on these topics was muted in his new theory, relative to their volume in his earlier work.

Festinger's move to a theory that focused on cognitive mechanisms and ability perceptions had other ramifications as well. In particular, the role of referent others became less important. This is because even non-referent others can create useful comparison standards. To illustrate, consider a non-referent other that was discussed by Festinger (1950). Festinger noted that a Ku Klux Klanner probably will not worry if his opinions are not shared by a northern liberal. The Ku Klux Klanner can feel valid, even in the absence of such support, because he does not care for the opinions of northern liberals. However, if a northern liberal of the same age and physical build were to run faster than the Ku Klux Klanner, then this comparison might make the Klanner feel slow.

Although the concept of the reference group was no longer important for the concept of abilities, Festinger did need a variable that could play a similar role in his new theory. Festinger appreciated that people do not compare their abilities with everyone— any more than they concern themselves with the opinions of everyone. His solution was to replace the reference group concept with a variable that could be relevant to both the comparison of abilities and the comparison of opinions. This new variable was similarity:

Hypothesis III: *The tendency to compare oneself with some other specific person decreases as the difference between his opinion or ability and one's own increases.*

Corollary III A: *Given a range of possible persons for comparison, someone close to one's own ability or opinion will be chosen for comparison.*

By shifting his new theory away from reference group and towards similarity, Festinger retained much of the spirit of his original theory, while giving it a slight "tweak" that could help it achieve broader goals. Unfortunately, and as we noted in the Introduction, the meaning of similarity was not made clear in Festinger (1954), and this led many researchers to try to clarify what Festinger meant or should have meant (e.g., Goethals & Darley, 1977). This shift to similarity also resembled other shifts, in that it too had the effect of making the theory of social comparison processes less social than the theory of social communications. To put it simply, similarity can help a person draw descriptive inference about their opinions and abilities, but reference group status can help a person draw inferences about the broader social meaning of opinions and abilities. To adapt an observation by Miller and Prentice (1996), comparisons with a similar other can help people determine if their abilities are high and if their opinions are extreme, but communications with referent others can help people determine if their abilities are high *enough* to merit praise or if their opinions are *too* extreme and likely to generate criticism.

In summary, Festinger's social comparison theory was inspired by and, in some ways, constrained by his earlier theory on social communications. The key adaptations were that social comparison theory (a) considered the social construction of both opinions and abilities, (b) replaced the need for validity with the need to reduce uncertainty, (c) focused on social comparisons rather than social communications, and (d) emphasized the importance of similar others in shaping descriptive perceptions, rather than the role of referent others in shaping subjective evaluations. These changes made social comparison theory broader in its scope and increased its appeal to social psychologists more generally, but it also resulted in a theory that was less social than the one it replaced. We would also argue that Festinger's approach to theory development, i.e., retrofitting an old theory to create a new one, caused social comparison theory to make a range of predictions that might strike modern readers as strange. We turn to these now.

Some Curious Qualities of "A Theory of Social Comparison Processes"

Social comparison has many curious features that we suspect it would not have had if Festinger had created it from the whole cloth, rather than patching it together from a previous piece. As one example, we again point to the paradox surrounding similarity. Festinger argued that individuals only seek comparisons with similar others, but a person can only know if someone is similar if a comparison already has been made (cf., Gilbert, Giesler, & Morris, 1995). We think that such a glaring problem as this would have been noticed and resolved, had Festinger not been trying to find a comparison variable that could stand in for an old communication variable.

As another example, we return to the limited set of motivations that Festinger built into his theory of social comparison processes. It is a common criticism that Festinger over-estimated the role that uncertainty reduction plays in motivating people to compare, but we think the more provocative issue is just how far Festinger pushed this one motive as an explanatory framework. Consider Festinger's argument that people exert pressures on themselves to have their abilities and opinions conform to those of others (Derivations DI through D3). There is something reasonable in these predictions, but the motivation that drives these tendencies stretches intuition.

Consider as an example a liberal woman who tempers her opinions after she develops a new set of friends who are slightly less liberal than she is. Or consider a runner who works hard to run faster, because all of his teammates run faster than he does. Although both outcomes seem reasonable, it is important to remember *why* these changes would occur, under a strict reading of Festinger (1954). If a certainty-reduction motive drives comparisons, then the answer to this question is a curious one.

Specifically, the liberal does not change her attitudes because her new friends have persuaded her to change her views, or because she has internalized the opinions of her new friends, or because she wants to be liked by these women. Rather, the liberal is simply changing her views because she would be uncertain of her own opinions if she were to remain extremely liberal while in the company of moderates. This explanation is not terribly intuitive. Now consider the running example. A strict reading of social comparison theory in this instance would argue that the runner is not training to become faster because he feels slow. He is training to become faster because he will not know how fast he is until he begins to catch up with his friends.[2]

Clearly, the uncertainty reduction motive that social comparison theory posits as an account for these two case studies would strike many as unlikely. We think that the odd manner in which Festinger might explain two phenomena shows how hard he strained to adapt his old theory to a new cause. Had he not felt a need to replace the desire for validity with a concern that could also be relevant to ability perceptions, we think that Festinger might have looked at the above situations and realized that he needed to build his new theory around a broader set of motives.

At the risk of being too critical, we see other points of strain that seem worth noting. We find it odd, for instance, that Festinger's social comparison theory says almost nothing about the *effects* social comparisons will have on the individual—other than reducing certainty. It is interesting to consider, for instance, that at a time when research was moving to consider when perceptions will generate perceptual assimilation or contrast effects (Helson, 1947; Lewin, Tamara, Festinger, & Sears, 1944; Sherif, Taub, & Hovland, 1958; Volkmann, 1936), Festinger (1954) gave this issue no attention at all. One thus cannot use Festinger's social comparison theory to predict when social comparisons will make liberals feel more or less liberal, or make runners feel more or less fast. His theory can only tell us when a liberal thinker will feel certain that she is liberal, and when a slow runner will feel certain that he is slow.

It is possible, however, that Festinger assumed the effects of comparison on perceptions would be obvious to readers and so he did not elaborate upon them in print. There are hints of this in his writing. For instance, it seems in places as if Festinger believed that the social comparisons of abilities would be contrastive, as when he argued that the desire to perceive one's abilities as good will lead people to try to be slightly better than others. It also appeared at times that Festinger thought the social comparisons of opinions would be assimilative, as when he argued that people want to find evidence that their opinions are shared by others. But Festinger never stated such views explicitly.

As a final example of curious theory making, we find it interesting that Festinger's theory of social comparison process did not identify any clear end state. That is, he did not describe any psychological outcome that will cause people to be "satisfied" to feel certain enough in their abilities and opinions to stop comparing. For point of contrast, consider the end state that was built into the 1950 paper on social communications. Although it was not described in these terms, this paper really was a theory about discrepancy reduction and so an end state was outlined. Festinger argued that the need for communication "increased monotonically" with

---

[2]Festinger identified two psychological forces that would cause a slow runner to try to speed up. The one that was the primary focus of social comparison theory was the desire to evaluate abilities (or to reduce uncertainty). Festinger also thought that people would want to have superior abilities when compared to others, and so the slow runner might try to speed up in order to affirm his speed. Although this second motive provides an intuitive reason that slow runners might speed up, it is important to note that this "unidirectional drive upward" was a less universal need than was the need to evaluate. Festinger even speculated that this latter motive was "culturally determined, and hence culturally variable" (p. 34).

increases in opinion discrepancies and that people would respond to discrepancies either by (a) trying to get others to conform to one's own opinions, (b) by conforming one's own opinions to those of others, or (c) by rejecting those who disagree. Whichever method was pursued, Festinger predicted that the pressure to communicate would cease once opinion discrepancies were eliminated. In essence, conformity of opinion resulted in a state of quiescence.

One possible reading of *A Theory of Social Comparison Processes* is that people achieve a similar state of quiescence once certainty is achieved. At times, Festinger alluded to such an outcome, particularly in the sections where he discussed the comparison of opinions in ways that were reminiscent of his earlier theory. However, a strict reading of his hypotheses argues a contrary view, i.e., that social comparison pressures only lead to greater social comparison pressures. This is because, whereas *Informal Social Communication* proposed that the need to communicate increases with increasing discrepancy, *A Theory of Social Comparison Processes* argued for greater comparison with decreasing discrepancy. It is true that the desire for greater certainty should cause people to work to reduce attitude and opinion discrepancies, much like in the earlier theory (see Derivation DI and D2). However, the tendency to *compare* with another was thought to increase with increasing similarity (Hypothesis III and Corollary

IIIA) and to diminish with increasing discrepancies (Derivation D3). Thus, people should be oriented to reduce discrepancies (DI through D3), which should increase comparisons (III and IIIA). It appears that individuals can then become locked into a comparison dynamic from which they cannot escape.[3] We think, again, that the lack of a clear outcome was an oversight reflecting the fact that this theory was developed out of another theory. The fact that states of quiescence were hinted at in the descriptions, but argued against in the formal features of the theory, suggests once again that the theory tried to do too much.

Summary

We also acknowledge that our analysis puts us in a somewhat odd position. We are devoting a book of readings to a field of inquiry that originated in Festinger's theoretical writings, but we are arguing that these writings were not always so strong. We think, however, that we would be doing readers a disservice if we simply stated that Festinger was an important figure, who often got things right. The ambiguities of his original theory, the decisions that led to them, and the effects they had on the literature that followed, are important parts of any scholarly analysis of social comparison. If Festinger at times showed that he was mortal and capable of a misstep, then this only makes him more useful to other mortals who also would like to make their own lasting contributions to this field.

---

[3] At times, Festinger appears to argue that quiescence will occur for opinions but not for abilities. Here, however, he links the continued volatility in ability comparisons to the unidirectional drive upward. We thus think that Festinger may have meant to argue that the tendency to compare would diminish with greater certainty, and that it is only the drive to feel superior that leads a person to continue comparing. Unfortunately, it is hard to find a justification for this view from the hypotheses, corollaries, and deviations built into Festinger's (1954) theory of social comparison.

REFERENCES

(Asterisks indicate Key Readings in this section.)

* Festinger, L. (1950). Informal social communication. *Psychological Review, 57,* 271–282.

* Festinger, L. (1954). A theory of social comparison processes. *Human Relations, 7,* 117–140.

Festinger, L. (1957). *A theory of cognitive dissonance.* Stanford, CA: Stanford University Press.

Gilbert, D. T., Giesler, R. B., & Morris, D. A. (1995). When comparisons arise. *Journal of Personality and Social Psychology, 69,* 227–236.

Goethals, G. R., & Darley, J. M. (1977). Social comparison theory: An attributional approach. In J. M. Suls & R. L. Miller (Eds.), *Social comparison processes: Theoretical and empirical perspectives* (pp. 259–278). Washington, DC: Hemisphere.

Helson, H. (1947). Adaptation-level as a frame of reference for prediction of psychophysical data. *American Journal of Psychology, 60,* 1–29.

Hyman, H. H. (1942). Psychology of status. *Archives of Psychology, 269,* 5–28.

Hyman, H. H., & Singer, E. (Eds.) (1968). *Readings in reference group theory and research.* New York: Free Press; London: Collier-Macmillan Ltd.

Lewin, K. (1951). *Field theory in social science; selected theoretical papers* (D. Cartwright, Ed.), New York: Harper & Row.

Lewin, K., Tamara, D., Festinger, L., & Sears, P. (1944). Level of aspiration. In J. McV. Hunt (Ed.), *Personality and the behavior disorders* (Vol. I, pp. 333–378). New York: Ronald Press.

Miller, D. T., & Prentice, D. A. (1996). The construction of social norms and standards. In E. T. Higgins & A. W. Kruglanski (Eds.), *Social psychology: Handbook of basic principles* (pp. 799–829). New York: Guilford Press.

Newcomb, T. (1950). *Social psychology.* New York: The Dryden Press, Inc.

Sherif, M., & Sherif, C. (1964). *Reference groups.* New York: Harper & Row.

Sherif, M., Taub, D., & Hovland, C. I. (1958). Assimilation and contrast effects of anchoring stimuli on judgments. *Journal of Experimental Psychology, 55,* 150–155.

Volkmann, J. (1936). The anchoring of absolute scales. *Psychological Bulletin, 33,* 742–743.

Discussion Questions

1. What are the key differences between social communication and the theory of social comparison processes?
2. In what ways did the former paper guide the second and what effect did this have?
3. Which of the two statements Festinger wrote on comparison processes (Informal communication and Social comparison theory) do you like best and why?

Suggested Readings

Festinger, L., Gerard, H. B., Hymovitch, B., Kelley, H. H., & Raven, B. H. (1952). The influence process in the presence of extreme deviates. *Human Relations, 5,* 327–340.

Festinger, L., Schachter, S., & Back, K. (1950). *Social pressures in informal groups: A study of a housing project.* New York: Harper.

Festinger, L., & Thibaut, J. (1951). Interpersonal communication in small groups. *Journal of Abnormal and Social Psychology, 46,* 92–99.

Schachter, S. (1959). *The psychology of affiliation: Experimental studies of the sources of gregariousness.* Stanford, CA: Stanford University Press.

Informal Social Communication

Leon Festinger*

The importance of strict theory in developing and guiding programs of research is becoming more and more recognized today. 'Yet there is considerable disagreement about exactly how strict and precise a theoretical formulation must be at various stages in the development of a body of knowledge. Certainly there are many who feel that some "theorizing" is too vague and indefinite to be of much use. It is also argued that such vague and broad "theorizing" may actually hinder the empirical development of an area of knowledge.

On the other hand there are many who express dissatisfaction with instances of very precise theories which do exist here and there, for somehow or other a precise and specific theory seems to them to leave out the "real" psychological problem. These persons seem to be more concerned with those aspects of the problem which the precise theory has not yet touched. From this point of view it is argued that too precise and too strict theorizing may also hinder the empirical development of an area of knowledge.

It is probably correct that if a theory becomes too precise too early it can have tendencies to become sterile. It is also probably correct that if a theory stays too vague and ambiguous for too long it can be harmful in that nothing can be done to disprove or change it. This probably means that theories,

when vague, should at least be stated in a form which makes the adding of precision possible as knowledge increases. It also probably means that theory should run ahead, but not too far ahead, of the data so that the trap of premature precision can be avoided. It certainly means that theories, whether vague or precise, must be in such a form that empirical data can influence them.

This article is a statement of the theoretical formulations which have been developed in the process of conducting a program of empirical and experimental research in informal social communication. It has grown out of our findings thus far and is in turn guiding the future course of the research program.[1] This program of research concerns itself with finding and explaining the facts concerning informal, spontaneous communication among persons and the consequences of the process of communication. It would seem that a better understanding of the dynamics of such communication would in turn lead to a better understanding of various kinds of group functioning. The theories and hypotheses presented below vary considerably in precision, specificity and the degree to which corroborating data exist. Whatever the state of precision,

* Research Center for Group Dynamics, University of Michigan.

[1] This research program consists of a number of coordinated and integrated studies, both in the laboratory and in the field. It is being carried out by the Research Center for Group Dynamics under contract N6onr–23212 NR 151–698 with the Office of Naval Research.

however, the theories are empirically oriented and capable of being tested.

Since we are concerned with the spontaneous process of communication which goes on during the functioning of groups we must first differentiate the variety of types of communication which occur according to the theoretical conditions which give rise to tendencies to communicate. It is plausible to assume that separating the sources or origins of pressures to communicate that may act on a member of a group will give us fruitful areas to study. This type of differentiation or classification is, of course, adequate only if it leads to the separation of conceptually clear areas of investigation within which communication can be organized into statable theoretical and empirical laws.

We shall here deal with those few of the many possible sources of pressures to communicate in which we have thus far been able to make theoretical and empirical progress. We shall elaborate on the theory for regarding them as giving rise to pressures to communicate and on specific hypotheses concerning the laws of communication which stem from these sources.

I. Pressures Toward Uniformity in a Group

One major source of forces to communicate is the pressure toward uniformity which may exist within a group. These are pressures which, for one reason or another, act toward making members of a group agree concerning some issue or conform with respect to some behavior pattern. It is stating the obvious, of course, to say that these pressures must be exerted by means of a process of communication among the members of the group. One must also specify the conditions under which such pressures toward uniformity arise, both on a conceptual and an operational level so that in any specific situation it is possible to say whether or not such pressures exist. We shall, in the following discussion, elaborate on two major sources of pressures toward uniformity among people, namely, social reality and group locomotion.

1. *Social reality*: Opinions, attitudes, and beliefs which people hold must have some basis upon which they rest for their validity. Let us as a start abstract from the many kinds of bases for the subjective validity of such opinions, attitudes, and beliefs one continuum along which they may be said to lie. This continuum we may call a scale of degree of physical reality. At one end of this continuum, namely, complete dependence upon physical reality, we might have an example such as this: A person looking at a surface might think that the surface is fragile or he might think that the surface is unbreakable. He can very easily take a hammer, hit the surface, and quickly be convinced as to whether the opinion he holds is correct or incorrect. After he has broken the surface with a hammer it will probably make little dent upon his opinion if another person should tell him that the surface is unbreakable. It would thus seem that where there is a high degree of dependence upon physical reality for the subjective validity of one's beliefs or opinions the dependence upon other people for the confidence one has in these opinions or beliefs is very low.

At the other end of the continuum where the dependence upon physical reality is low or zero, we might have an example such as this: A person looking at the results of a national election feels that if the loser had won, things would be in some ways much better than they are. Upon what does the subjective validity of this belief depend? It depends to a large degree on whether or not other people share his opinion and feel the same way he does. If there are other people around him who believe the same thing, then his opinion is, to him, valid. If there are not others who believe the same thing, then his opinion is, in the same sense, not valid. Thus where the dependence upon physical reality is low the dependence upon social reality is correspondingly high. An opinion, a belief, an attitude is "correct," "valid," and "proper" to the extent that it is anchored in a group of people with similar beliefs, opinions, and attitudes.

This statement, however, cannot be generalized completely. It is clearly not necessary for the validity of someone's opinion that everyone else in the world think the way he does. It is only necessary that the members of that group to which he refers this opinion or attitude think the way he does. It is not necessary for a Ku Klux Klanner that some northern liberal agree with him in his attitude toward Negroes, but it is eminently necessary that there be other people who also are Ku Klux Klanners and who do agree with him. The person who does not agree with him is seen as different from him and not an adequate referent for his opinion. The problem of independently defining which groups are and which groups are not appropriate reference groups for a particular individual and for a particular opinion or attitude is a difficult one. It is to some extent inherently circular since an appropriate reference group tends to be a group which does share a person's opinions and attitudes, and people tend to locomote *into* such groups and *out of* groups which do not agree with them.

From the preceding discussion it would seem that if a discrepancy in opinion, attitude, or belief exists among persons who are members of an appropriate reference group, forces to communicate will arise. It also follows that the less "physical reality" there is to validate the opinion or belief, the greater will be the importance of the social referent, the group, and the greater will be the forces to communicate.

2. *Group locomotion*: Pressures toward uniformity among members of a group may arise because such uniformity is desirable or necessary in order for the group to move toward some goal. Under such circumstances there are a number of things one can say about the magnitude of pressures toward uniformity.

(a) They will be greater to the extent that the members perceive that group movement would be facilitated by uniformity.

(b) The pressures toward uniformity will also be greater, the more dependent the various members are on the group in order to reach their goals. The degree to which other groups are substitutable as a means toward individual or group goals would be one of the determinants of the dependence of the member on the group.

We have elaborated on two sources of pressure toward uniformity among members of groups. The same empirical laws should apply to communications which result from pressures toward uniformity irrespective of the particular reasons for the existence of the pressures. We shall now proceed to enumerate a set of hypotheses concerning communication which results from pressures toward uniformity.

II. Hypotheses About Communication Resulting from Pressures Toward Uniformity

Communications which arise from pressures toward uniformity in a group may be seen as "instrumental" communications. That is, the communication is not an end in itself but rather is a means by which the communicator hopes to influence the person he addresses in such a way as to reduce the discrepancy that exists between them. Thus we should examine the determinants of: (1) when a member communicates, (2) to whom he communicates and (3) the reactions of the recipient of the communication.

(1) Determinants of the magnitude of pressure to communicate:

Hypothesis la: *The pressure on members to communicate to others in the group concerning "item x" increases monotonically with increase in the perceived discrepancy in opinion concerning "item x" among members of the group.*

Remembering that we are considering only communication that results from pressures toward uniformity, it is clear that if there are no discrepancies in opinion, that is, uniformity already exists in the group, there will be no forces to communicate. It would be plausible to expect the force to communicate to increase rapidly from zero as the state of affairs departs from uniformity.

Hypothesis lb: *The pressure on a member to communicate to others in the group concerning "item x" increases monotonically with increase in the degree of relevance of "item x" to the functioning of the group.*

If "item x" is unimportant to the group in the sense of not being associated with any of the values or activities which are the basis for the existence of the group, or if it is more or less inconsequential for group locomotion, then there should be few or no forces to communicate even when there are perceived discrepancies in opinion. As "item x" becomes more important for the group (more relevant), the forces to communicate when any given magnitude of perceived discrepancy exists, should increase.

Corroborative evidence for this hypothesis is found in an experiment by Schachter [8] where discussion of the same issue was experimentally made relevant for some groups and largely irrelevant for others. It is clear from the data that where the discussion was relevant to the functioning of the group there existed stronger forces to communicate and to influence the other members. Where the issue is a relevant one the members make longer individual contributions to the discussion and there are many fewer prolonged pauses in the discussion.

Hypothesis 1c: *The pressure on members to communicate to others in the group concerning "item x" increases monotonically with increase in the cohesiveness of the group.*

Cohesiveness of a group is here defined as the resultant of all the forces acting on the members to remain in the group. These forces may depend on the attractiveness or unattractiveness of either the prestige of the group, members in the group, or the activities in which the group engages. If the total attraction toward the group is zero, no forces to communicate should arise; the members may as easily leave the group as stay in it. As the forces to remain in the group increase (given perceived discrepancies in opinion and given a certain relevance of the item to the functioning of the group) the pressures to communicate will increase.

Data from an experiment by Back [1] support this hypothesis. In this experiment groups of high and low cohesiveness were experimentally created using three different sources of attraction to the group, namely, liking the members, prestige attached to belonging, and possibility of getting a reward for performance in the group activity. For each of the three types of attraction to the group the more cohesive groups were rated as proceeding

at a more intense rate in the discussion than the corresponding less cohesive groups. In addition, except for the groups where the attraction was the possibility of reward (perhaps due to wanting to finish and get the reward) there was more total amount of attempted exertion of influence in the highly cohesive groups than in the less cohesive groups. In short, highly cohesive groups, having stronger pressures to communicate, discussed the issue at a more rapid pace and attempted to exert more influence.

(2) Determinants of choice of recipient for communications:

Hypothesis 2a: *The force to communicate about "item x" to* A PARTICULAR MEMBER *of the group will increase as the discrepancy in opinion between that member and the communicator increases.*

We have already stated in Hypothesis 1a that the pressure to communicate in general will increase as the perceived non-uniformity in the group increases. In addition the force to communicate will be strongest toward those whose opinions are most different from one's own and will, of course, be zero towards those in the group who at the time hold the same opinion as the communicator. In other words, people will tend to communicate to those within the group whose opinions are most different from their own.

There is a clear corroboration of this hypothesis from a number of studies. In the previously mentioned experiment by Schachter [8] the distribution of opinions expressed in the group was always as follows: Most of the members' opinions clustered within a narrow range of each other while one member, the deviate, held and maintained an extremely divergent point of view. About five times as many communications were addressed to the holder of the divergent point of view as were addressed to the others.

In an experiment by Festinger and Thibaut [5] the discussion situation was set up so that members' opinions on the issue spread over a considerable range. Invariably 70 to 90 percent of the communications were addressed to those who held opinions at the extremes of the distribution. The curve of number of communications received falls off very rapidly as the opinion of the recipient moves away from the extreme of the distribution. The hypothesis would seem to be well substantiated.

Hypothesis 2b: *The force to communicate about "item x" to* A PARTICULAR PERSON *will decrease to the extent that he is perceived as not a member of the group or to the extent that he is not wanted as a member of the group.*

From the previous hypothesis it follows that communications will tend to be addressed mainly toward those with extreme opinions within the group. This does not hold, however, for any arbitrarily defined group. The present hypothesis, in effect, states that such relationships will apply only within *psychological* groups, that is, collections of people that exist as groups psychologically for the members. Communications will tend not to be addressed towards those who are not members of the group.

The study by Schachter [8] and the study by Festinger and Thibaut [5] both substantiate this hypothesis. In Schachter's experiment those group members who do not want the person holding the extremely divergent point of view to remain in the group tend to stop communicating to him towards the end of the discussion. In the experiment by Festinger and Thibaut, when the subjects have the perception that the persons present include different kinds of people with a great variety of interests, there tends to be less communication toward the extremes in the last half of the discussion after the rejection process has had time to develop. In short, communication towards those with different opinions decreases if they are seen as not members of the *psychological* group.

Hypothesis 2c: *The force to communicate "item x" to a particular member will increase the more it is perceived that the communication will change that member's opinion in the desired direction.*

A communication which arises because of the existence of pressures toward uniformity is made in order to exert a force on the recipient in a particular direction, that is, to push him to change his opinion so that he will agree more closely with the communicator. If a member is perceived as very resistant to changing his opinion, the force to communicate to him decreases. If it seems that a particular member will be changed as the result of a communication so as to increase the discrepancy between him and the communicator, there will exist a force not to communicate to him. Thus under such conditions there will be tendencies *not* to communicate this particular item to that member.

There is some corroboration for this hypothesis. In a face to face verbal discussion where a range of opinion exists, the factors which this hypothesis points to would be particularly important for those members whose opinions were near the middle of the range. A communication which might influence the member at one extreme to come closer to the middle might at the same time influence the member at the other extreme to move farther away from the middle. We might then expect from this hypothesis that those holding opinions in the middle of the existing range would communicate less (because of the conflict) and would address fewer communications to the whole group (attempting to influence only one person at a time).

A number of observations were conducted to check these derivations. Existing groups of clinical psychologists who were engaging in discussions to reconcile their differences in ratings of applicants were observed. Altogether, 147 such discussions were observed in which at least one member's opinion was in the middle of the existing range. While those with extreme opinions made an average of 3.16 units of communication (number of communications weighted by length of the communication), those with middle opinions made an average of only 2.6 units of communication. While those with extreme opinions addressed 38 percent of their communications to the whole group, those with middle opinions addressed only 29 percent of their communications to everyone.

(3) Determinants of change in the recipient of a communication:

Hypothesis 3a: *The amount of change in opinion resulting from receiving a communication will increase as the pressure towards uniformity in the group increases.*

There are two separate factors which contribute to the effect stated in the hypothesis. The greater the pressure towards uniformity, the greater will be the amount of influence exerted by the communications and, consequently, the greater the magnitude of change that may be expected. But the existence of pressures toward uniformity will not only show itself in increased attempts to change the opinions of others. Pressures toward uniformity will also produce greater readiness to change in the members of the group. In other words, uniformity may be achieved by changing the opinions of others and/or by changing one's own opinions. Thus we may expect that with increasing pressure towards uniformity there will be less resistance to change on the part of the members. Both of these factors will contribute to produce greater change in opinion when the pressure toward uniformity is greater.

There is evidence corroborating this hypothesis from the experiment by Festinger and Thibaut [5]. In this experiment three degrees of pressure towards uniformity were experimentally induced in different groups. Irrespective of which of two problems were discussed by the group and irrespective of whether they perceived the group to be homogeneously or heterogeneously composed, the results consistently show that high pressure groups change most, medium pressure groups change next most, and low pressure groups change least in the direction of uniformity. While the two factors which contribute to this effect cannot be separated in the data, their joint effect is clear and unmistakable.

Hypothesis 3b: *The amount of change in opinion resulting from receiving a communication will increase as the strength of the resultant force to remain in the group increases for the recipient.*

To the extent that a member wishes to remain in the group, the group has power over that member. By power we mean here the ability to produce real change in opinions and attitudes and not simply change in overt behavior which can also be produced by means of overt threat. If a person is unable to leave a group because of restraints from the outside, the group can then use threats to change overt behavior. Covert changes in opinions and attitudes, however, can only be produced by a group by virtue of forces acting on the member to remain in the group. Clearly the maximum force which the

group can successfully induce on a member counter to his own forces can not be greater than the sum of the forces acting on that member to remain in the group. The greater the resultant force to remain in the group, the more effective will be the attempts to influence the member.

This hypothesis is corroborated by two separate studies. Festinger, Schachter and Back [4] investigated the relationship between the cohesiveness of social groups in a housing project (how attractive the group was for its members) and how effectively a group standard relevant to the functioning of the group was maintained. A correlation of 72 was obtained between these two variables. In other words, the greater the attractiveness of the group for the members, the greater was the amount of influence which the group could successfully exert on its members with the result that there existed greater conformity in attitudes and behavior in the more cohesive groups.

Back [1] did a laboratory experiment specifically designed to test this hypothesis. By means of plausible instructions to the subjects he experimentally created groups of high and low cohesiveness, that is, conditions in which the members were strongly attracted to the group and those in which the attraction to the group was relatively weak. The subjects, starting with different interpretations of the same material, were given an opportunity to discuss the matter. Irrespective of the source of the attraction to the group (Back used three different types of attraction in both high and low cohesive conditions) the subjects in the high cohesive groups influenced each other's opinions more than the subjects in the low cohesive groups. In short, the greater the degree of attraction to the group, the greater the amount of influence actually accomplished.

Hypothesis 3c: *The amount of change in opinion resulting from receiving a communication concerning "item x" will decrease with increase in the degree to which the opinions and attitudes involved are anchored in other group memberships or serve important need satisfying functions for the person.*

If the opinion that a person has formed on some issue is supported in some other group than the one which is at present attempting to influence him, he will be more resistant to the attempted influence. Other sources of resistance to being influenced undoubtedly come from personality factors, ego needs and the like.

Specific evidence supporting this hypothesis is rather fragmentary. In the study of social groups in a housing project by Festinger, Schachter and Back [4], the residents were asked whether their social life was mainly outside the project or not. Of those who conformed to the standards of their social groups within the project about 85 percent reported that their social life was centered mainly within the project. Less than 50 percent of those who did not conform to the standards of the project social group, however, reported that their social life was centered mainly in the project. It is likely that they were able to resist the influences from within the project when their opinions and attitudes were supported in outside groups.

The experiments by Schachter [8] and by Festinger and Thibaut [5] used the same discussion problem in slightly different situations. In the former experiment subjects identified themselves and verbally supported their opinions in face-to-face discussion. In the latter experiment the subjects were anonymous, communicating only by written messages on which the sender of the message was not identified. Under these latter conditions many more changes in opinion were observed than under the open verbal discussion situation even though less time was spent in discussion when they wrote notes. This difference in amount of change in opinion is probably due to the ego defensive reactions aroused by openly committing oneself and supporting one's opinions in a face-to-face group.

(4) Determinants of change in relationship among members:

> Hypothesis 4a: *The tendency to change the composition of the psychological group (pushing members out of the group) increases as the perceived discrepancy in opinion increases.*

We have already discussed two of the responses which members of groups make to pressures toward uniformity, namely, attempting to influence others and being more ready to be influenced. There is still a third response which serves to move toward uniformity. By rejecting those whose opinions diverge from the group and thus redefining who is and who is not in the psychological group, uniformity can be accomplished. The greater the discrepancy between a person's opinion and the opinion of another, the stronger are the tendencies to exclude the other person from the psychological group.

There is evidence that members of groups do tend to reject those whose opinions are divergent. In the study of social groups within a housing project Festinger, Schachter and Back [4] found that those who did not conform to the standards of their social group were underchosen on a sociometric test, that is, they mentioned more persons as friends of theirs than they received in return. Schachter [8] did an experiment specifically to test whether or not members of groups would be rejected simply for disagreeing on an issue. Paid participants in the groups voiced divergent or agreeing opinions as instructed. In all groups the paid participant who voiced divergent opinion on an issue was rejected on a postmeeting questionnaire concerning whom they wanted to have remain in the group. The same paid participants, when voicing conforming opinions in other groups, were not rejected.

> Hypothesis 4b: *When non-conformity exists, the tendency to change the composition of the psychological group increases as the cohesiveness of the group increases and as the relevance of the issue to the group increases.*

We have previously discussed the increase in forces to communicate with increase in cohesiveness and relevance of issue. Similarly, these two variables affect the tendency to reject persons from the group for non-conformity. Theoretically we should expect any variable which affected the force to communicate (which stems from pressures toward uniformity) to affect also the tendency to reject non-conformers in a similar manner. In other words, increases in the force to communicate concerning an item will go along with increased tendency to reject persons who disagree concerning that item.

The previously mentioned experiment by Schachter [8] was designed to test this hypothesis by experimentally varying cohesiveness and relevance in club groups. In this experiment the more cohesive groups do reject the non-conformer more than the less cohesive groups and the groups where the issue is relevant reject the non-conformer more than groups where the issue is not very relevant to the group functioning. Those groups where cohesiveness was low and the issue was not very relevant show little, if any, tendency to reject the deviate.

III.   Forces to Change One's Position in a Group

Another important source of forces to communicate are the forces which act on members of groups to locomote (change their position) in the group, or to move from one group to another. Such forces to locomote may stem from the attractiveness of activities associated with a different position in the group or from the status of that position or the like. Thus a new member of a group may wish to become more central in the group, a member of an organization may wish to rise in the status hierarchy, a member of a business firm may want to be promoted or a member of a minority group may desire acceptance by the majority group. These are all instances of forces to locomote in a social structure.

It is plausible that the existence of a force acting on a person in a specific direction produces behavior in that direction. Where locomotion in the desired direction is not possible, at least temporarily, there will exist a force to communicate in that direction. The existence of a force in a specific direction will produce behavior in that direction. One such kind of behavior is communication. This hypothesis is not very different from the hypothesis advanced by Lewin [6] to account for the superior recall of interrupted activities.

An experiment by Thibaut [9] tends to corroborate this theoretical analysis. In his experiment he created two groups, one of high status and privileged, the other of low status and under-privileged. These two groups, equated in other respects, functioned together so that the members of the high status group could play an attractive game. The low status group functioned merely as servants. It was clear that forces were acting on the members of the low status group to move into the other group. As the privilege position of the high status group became clearer and clearer the amount of communication from the low status team to the high status group increased. The number of communications from members of the high status group to the low status group correspondingly decreased. When, in some groups, the status and privilege relationship between the two teams was reversed toward the end of the experimental session, thus reducing the forces to locomote into the other group, the number of communications to that other group correspondingly decreased.

Further corroboration is found in a preliminary experiment, mainly methodologically oriented, conducted by Back *et al.* [2]. In this experiment new items of information were planted with persons at various levels in the hierarchy of a functioning organization. Data on transmission of each of the items of information were obtained through cooperators within the organization who were chosen so as to give adequate coverage of all levels and all sections within it. These cooperators recorded all instances of communication that came to their attention. Of seventeen acts of communication recorded in this manner, eleven were directed upwards in the hierarchy, four toward someone on the same level and only two were directed downwards. The existence of forces to move upward in such a hierarchical organization may be taken for granted. The great bulk of the communications recorded went in the same direction as these forces to locomote.

In considering communication among members of differentiated social structures it is important also to take into account restraints against communication.

Infrequent contact in the ordinary course of events tends to erect restraints against communication. It is undoubtedly easier to communicate a given item to a person whom one sees frequently or to a person to whom one has communicated similar items in the past. The structuring of groups into hierarchies, social clusters, or the like, undoubtedly tends to restrict the amount and type of contact between members of certain different parts or levels of the group and also undoubtedly restricts the content of the communication that goes on between such levels in the ordinary course of events. These restrictions erect restraints against certain types of communication.

There are some data which tend to specify some of the restraints against communication which exist. In the study of the communication of a spontaneous rumor in a community by Festinger, Cartwright *et al.* [3] it was found that intimacy of friendship tended to increase ease of communication. Persons with more friends in the project heard the rumor more often than those with only acquaintances. Those who had few friends or acquaintances heard the rumor least often. At the same time this factor of intimacy of friendship was not related to how frequently they relayed the rumor to others. In other words, it was not related to forces to communicate but seemed to function only as a restraint against communicating where friendship did not exist.

There is also some evidence that the mere perception of the existence of a hierarchy sets up restraints against communication between levels. Kelley [7] experimentally created a two-level hierarchy engaging in a problem-solving task during which they could and did communicate within levels and between levels. Control groups were also run with the same task situation but with no status differential involved between the two subgroups. There was more communication between subgroups under these control conditions than where there was a status differential involved.

It seems that, in a hierarchy, there are also restraints against communicating hostility upwards when the hostility is about those on upper levels. In the same experiment by Kelley there was much criticism of the *other group* expressed by both high status and low status members. The proportion of these critical expressions which are directed upward by the low status group is much less, however, than the proportion directed downward by the high status groups.

IV.   Emotional Expression

An important variety of communications undoubtedly results from the existence of an emotional state in the communicator. The existence of joy, anger, hostility and the like seems to produce forces to communicate. It seems that communications resulting from the existence of an emotional state are consummatory rather than instrumental.

By an instrumental communication we mean one in which the reduction of the force to communicate depends upon the effect of the communication on the recipient. Thus in communication resulting from pressures toward uniformity in a group, the mere fact that a communication is made does not affect the force to communicate. If the effect has been to change the recipient so that he now agrees more closely with the communicator, the force to communicate will be reduced. If the recipient changes in the opposite direction, the force to communicate to him will be increased.

By a consummatory communication we mean one in which the reduction of the force to communicate occurs as a result of the expression and does not depend upon the effect it has on the recipient. Certainly in the case of such communications the reaction of the recipient may introduce new elements into the situation which will affect the force to communicate, but the essence of a consummatory communication is that the simple expression does reduce the force.

Specifically with regard to the communication of hostility and aggression, much has been said regarding its consummatory nature. The psychoanalytic theories of catharsis, in particular, develop the notion that the expression of hostility reduces the emotional state of the person. There has, however, been very little experimental work done on the problem. The previously mentioned experiment by Thibaut in which he created a "privileged–underprivileged" relationship between two equated groups has some data on the point. There is evidence that those members of the "underprivileged" groups who expressed their hostility toward the "privileged" groups showed less residual hostility toward them in post-experimental questionnaires. There is, however, no control over the reactions of the recipients of the hostile communications nor over the perceptions of the communicators of what these reactions were. An experiment is now in progress which will attempt to clarify some of these relationships with both negative and positive emotional states.

V. Summary

A series of interrelated hypotheses has been presented to account for data on informal social communication collected in the course of a number of studies. The data come from field studies and from laboratory experiments specifically designed to test the hypotheses.

Three sources of pressures to communicate have been considered:

1. Communication arising from pressures toward uniformity in a group. Here we considered determinants of magnitude of the force to communicate, choice of recipient for the communication, magnitude of change in recipient and magnitude of tendencies to reject nonconformers.
2. Communications arising from forces to locomote in a social structure. Here we considered communications in the direction of a blocked locomotion and restraints against communication arising in differentiated social structures.
3. Communications arising from the existence of emotional states. In this area data are almost

completely lacking. Some theoretical distinctions were made and an experiment which is now in progress in this area was outlined.

BIBLIOGRAPHY

1. Back, K. The exertion of influence through social communication. *J. abn. soc. Psychol.*, 1950 (in press).
2. ———, Festinger, L., Hymovitch, B., Kelley, H. H., Schachter, S., & Thibaut, J. The methodological problems of studying rumor transmission. *Human Relations*, 1950 (in press).
3. Festinger, L., Cartwright, D., *et al.* A study of a rumor: its origin and spread. *Human Relations*, 1948, 1, 464–486.
4. ———, Schachter, S., & Back, K. *Social pressures in informal groups: a study of a housing project.* New York: Harper & Bros., 1950.
5. ———, & Thibaut, J. Interpersonal communication in small groups. *J. abn. soc. Psychol.* (in press).
6. Lewin, K. Formalization and progress in psychology. In *Studies in Topological and Vector Psychology I., Univ. Ia. Stud. Child Welf.*, 1940, 16, No. 3.
7. Kelley, H. H. Communication in experimentally created hierarchies. *Human Relations* (in press).
8. Schachter, S. Deviation, rejection, and communication. *J. abn. soc. Psychol.* (in press).
9. Thibaut, J. An experimental study of the cohesiveness of underprivileged groups. *Human Relations*, 1950, 3.

Received March 6, 1950 ■

A Theory of Social Comparison Processes

Leon Festinger*

In this paper we shall present a further development of a previously published theory concerning opinion influence processes in social groups [7]. This further development has enabled us to extend the theory to deal with other areas, in addition to opinion formation, in which social comparison is important. Specifically, we shall develop below how the theory applies to the appraisal and evaluation of abilities as well as opinions.

Such theories and hypotheses in the area of social psychology are frequently viewed in terms of how "plausible" they seem. "Plausibility" usually means whether or not the theory or hypothesis fits one's intuition or one's common sense. In this meaning much of the theory which is to be presented here is not "plausible". The theory does, however, explain a considerable amount of data and leads to testable derivations. Three experiments, specifically designed to test predictions from this extension of the theory, have now been completed [5, 12, 19]. They all provide good corroboration. We will in the following pages develop the theory and present the relevant data.

Hypothesis I: There exists, in the human organism, a drive to evaluate his opinions and his abilities.

* The development of this theory was aided by a grant from the Behavioral Sciences Division of the Ford Foundation. It is part of the research program of the Laboratory for Research in Social Relations.

While opinions and abilities may, at first glance, seem to be quite different things, there is a close functional tie between them. They act together in the manner in which they affect behavior. A person's cognition (his opinions and beliefs) about the situation in which he exists and his appraisals of what he is capable of doing (his evaluation of his abilities) will together have bearing on his behavior. The holding of incorrect opinions and/or inaccurate appraisals of one's abilities can be punishing or even fatal in many situations.

It is necessary, before we proceed, to clarify the distinction between opinions and evaluations of abilities since at first glance it may seem that one's evaluation of one's own ability is an opinion about it. Abilities are of course manifested only through performance which is assumed to depend upon the particular ability. The clarity of the manifestation or performance can vary from instances where there is no clear ordering criterion of the ability to instances where the performance which reflects the ability can be clearly ordered. In the former case, the evaluation of the ability does function like other opinions which are not directly testable in "objective reality". For example, a person's evaluation of his ability to write poetry will depend to a large extent on the opinions which others have of his ability to write poetry. In cases where the criterion is unambiguous and can be clearly ordered, this furnishes an objective reality for the evaluation of one's ability so that it depends less on the opinions of other persons and depends more on actual comparison of one's performance with the performance of others. Thus, if a person evaluates his running ability, he will do so by comparing his time to run some distance with the times that other persons have taken.

In the following pages, when we talk about evaluating an ability, we shall mean specifically the evaluation of that ability in situations where the performance is unambiguous and is known. Most situations in real life will, of course, present situations which are a mixture of opinion and ability evaluation.

In a previous article [7] the author posited the existence of a drive to determine whether or not one's opinions were "correct". We are here stating that this same drive also produces behavior in people oriented toward obtaining an accurate appraisal of their abilities.

The behavioral implication of the existence of such a drive is that we would expect to observe behavior on the part of persons which enables them to ascertain whether or not their opinions are correct and also behavior which enables them accurately to evaluate their abilities. It is consequently necessary to answer the question as to how persons go about evaluating their opinions and their abilities.

Hypothesis II: To the extent that objective, non-social means are not available, people evaluate their opinions and abilities by comparison respectively with the opinions and abilities of others.

In many instances, perhaps most, whether or not an opinion is correct cannot be immediately determined by reference to the physical world. Similarly it is frequently not possible to assess accurately one's ability by reference to the physical world. One could, of course, test the opinion that an object was fragile by hitting it with a hammer, but how is one to test the opinion that a certain political candidate is better than another, or that war is inevitable? Even when there is a possible immediate physical referent for an opinion, it is frequently not likely to be employed. The belief, for example, that tomatoes are poisonous to humans (which was widely held at one time) is unlikely to be tested. The situation is similar with respect to the evaluation of one's abilities. If the only use to which, say, jumping ability was put was to jump across a particular brook, it

would be simple to obtain an accurate evaluation of one's ability in this respect. However, the unavailability of the opportunity for such clear testing and the vague and multipurpose use of various abilities generally make such a clear objective test not feasible or not useful. For example, how does one decide how intelligent one is? Also, one might find out how many seconds it takes a person to run a certain distance, but what does this mean with respect to his ability—is it adequate or not? For both opinions and abilities, to the extent that objective physical bases for evaluation are not available, subjective judgments of correct or incorrect opinion and subjectively accurate assessments of one's ability depend upon how one compares with other persons.

Corollary II A: In the absence of both a physical and a social comparison, subjective evaluations of opinions and abilities are unstable.

There exists evidence from studies on "level of aspiration" which shows clearly the instability of evaluations of abilities in the absence of comparison with other persons [13, 15, 20, 21, 23]. The typical situation in an experiment designed to study "level of aspiration" is as follows: a person is given a task to perform which is serial in nature. This may be a series of trials of throwing darts at a target or a series of information tests or a series of puzzles or the like. After each trial the person is told what he scored (how many points he made or how many correct answers or how long it took) and is asked to state what score he expects to get or will try for on the next trial. These experiments have previously been interpreted in terms of goal directed behavior. If we examine the situation closely, however, it is apparent that the individual's stated "level of aspiration" is actually a statement of what he considers a good performance to be. In other words, it is his evaluation, at that time, of what score he should get, that is, his evaluation of his ability. The data show clearly that if the person scores as well as he said he expected to do, he feels he has done well (experiences success) and if he scores less than his "aspirations" he feels he has done poorly (experiences failure) [17].

Let us examine, then, the stability of these evaluations in a situation where the person performing the task has no opportunity for comparison with others. The data from these studies show that the "level of aspiration" fluctuates markedly as performance fluctuates. If the person makes a score better than his previous one, then what was formerly considered a good performance is no longer good and his "level of aspiration" goes up. If his performance drops, his "level of aspiration" drops. Even after a person has had a good deal of experience at a task, the evaluation of what is good performance continues to fluctuate.

Similar instability is found in the case of opinions. When, using the autokinetic effect, persons are asked to make judgments of how far the point of light moves, these judgments continue to fluctuate before there are any comparison persons.[1]

To the extent, then, that there are relevant data available, they tend to confirm *Corollary II A* concerning the instability of evaluations in the absence of comparisons.

> *Corollary II B*: When an objective, non-social basis for the evaluation of one's ability or opinion is readily available persons will not evaluate their opinions or abilities by comparison with others.

Hochbaum [18] reports an experiment concerning the effect of knowledge of others' opinions on one's own opinion which corroborates *Corollary II B*. Half of the subjects in this experiment were persuaded by the experimenter that they were extremely good at being able to make correct judgments concerning things like the issue they were to discuss. The other half of the subjects were made to feel that they were extremely poor in making such judgments. They were then asked to write their opinions down and were handed back a slip of paper presumably reporting to them the opinions of each other person in the group. In this way the subjects were made to feel that most of the others in the group disagreed with them. Those subjects who were given an objective basis for feeling that their opinion was likely to be correct did not change their opinions very often in spite of the disagreement

with others in the group. Those who had an objective basis for feeling their judgments were likely to be poor changed their opinion very frequently upon discovering that others disagreed with them.

> *Hypothesis III*: The tendency to compare oneself with some other specific person decreases as the difference between his opinion or ability and one's own increases.

A person does not tend to evaluate his opinions or his abilities by comparison with others who are too divergent from himself. If some other person's ability is too far from his own, either above or below, it is not possible to evaluate his own ability *accurately* by comparison with this other person. There is then a tendency not to make the comparison. Thus, a college student, for example, does not compare himself to inmates of an institution for the feeble minded to evaluate his own intelligence. Nor does a person who is just beginning to learn the game of chess compare himself to the recognized masters of the game.

The situation is identical with respect to the evaluation of opinions. One does not evaluate the correctness or incorrectness of an opinion by comparison with others whose opinions are extremely divergent from one's own. Thus, a person who believes that Negroes are the intellectual equals of whites does not evaluate his opinion by comparison with the opinion of a person who belongs to some very anti-Negro group. In other words, there is a selfimposed restriction in the range of opinion or ability with which a person compares himself.

> *Corollary III A*: Given a range of possible persons for comparison, someone close to one's own ability or opinion will be chosen for comparison.

There is some evidence relevant to this corollary from an experiment by Whittemore [24]. The purpose of the study was to examine the relation between performance and competition. Subjects were seated around a table and given tasks to work on. There was ample opportunity to observe how the others were progressing. After the experimental session, in introspective reports, the subjects stated that they had almost always spontaneously selected someone whose performance was close to their own to compete against.

---

[1] Although published material on the autokinetic effect does not present the data in this form, it is clearly shown in special analysis of data from an experiment by Brehm, J. W., "A quantitative approach to the measurement of social influence", Honors thesis, Harvard University, 1952.

Corollary III B: If the only comparison available is a very divergent one, the person will not be able to make a subjectively precise evaluation of his opinion or ability.

There is evidence supporting this corollary with respect to abilities but no relevant evidence in connection with opinions has been found.

Hoppe [20] in his experiment on level of aspiration reports that when subjects made a score very far above or very far below their level of aspiration they did not experience success or failure respectively. In other words, this extremely divergent score presented no grounds for self evaluation. Dreyer [5] performed an experiment in which high school children were made to score either: very far above the reported average for boys like themselves; at the reported average; or very far below the reported average. After a series of trials they were asked, "How well do you feel you did on the test?" There were five possible categories of response. The top two were good or very good; the bottom two were poor or very poor. In the middle was a noncommittal response of fair. Both those who scored very far below and those who scored very far above the reported group average gave the response "fair" significantly more often than did those who scored at the reported group average. Also, on the average, the persons who had scored at the reported average felt they had done better than did those scoring far above the group. Again the data support the hypothesis.

We may then conclude that there is selectivity in comparison on abilities and opinions and that one major factor governing the selectivity is simply the discrepancy between the person's own opinion or ability and that of another person. Phenomenologically, the appearance of this process is different for opinions and for abilities but conceptually it is exactly the same process. In dealing with opinions one feels that those with whom one does not compare oneself are different kinds of people or members of different groups or people with different backgrounds. Frequently this allegation of difference, to support the non-comparability, is made together with some derogation. In the case of abilities, the phenomenal process is that of designation of status inferior or superior to those persons who

are noncomparable to oneself. We will elaborate on this later.

Derivation A (from I, II, III): Subjective evaluations of opinions or of abilities are stable when comparison is available with others who are judged to be close to one's opinions or abilities.

Derivation B (from I, II, III): The availability of comparison with others whose opinions or abilities are somewhat different from one's own will produce tendencies to change one's evaluation of the opinion or ability in question.

There are also data to show the effect which knowledge of group opinions or group abilities have on the person's evaluations which were initially formed privately. If the evaluation of an opinion or an ability formed in the absence of the possibility of comparison with others is indeed unstable, as we have presumed, then we would expect that, given an opportunity to make a comparison with others, the opportunity would be taken and the comparison would have a considerable impact on the self evaluation. This is found to be true for both abilities and opinions. "Level of aspiration" experiments have been performed where, after a series of trials in which the person is unable to compare his performance with others, there occurs a series of trials in which the person has available to him the knowledge of how others *like himself* performed on each trial [1, 4, 6, 17]. When the "others like himself" have scores different from his own, his stated "level of aspiration" (his statement of what he considers is good performance) almost always moves close to the level of the performance of others. It is also found that under these conditions the level of aspiration changes less with fluctuations in performance, in other words, is more stable. When the reported performance of others is about equal to his own score, the stability of his evaluation of his ability is increased and, thus, his level of aspiration shows very little variability. Dreyer, in an experiment specifically designed to test part of this theory [5], showed clearly that the variance of the level of aspiration was smaller when the subject scored close to the group than when he scored far above or far below them. In short, comparison with the performance of others specifies what his ability should be and gives stability to the evaluation.

Festinger, Gerard, *et al*. [10] find a similar situation with respect to opinions. When a person is asked to form an opinion privately and then has made available to him the consensus of opinion in the group of which he is a member, those who discover that most others in the group disagree with them become relatively less confident that their opinion is correct and a goodly proportion change their opinion. Those who discover that most others in the group agree with them become highly confident in their opinion and it is extremely rare to find one of them changing his opinion. Again, comparison with others has tended to define what is a correct opinion and has given stability to the evaluation. This result is also obtained by Hochbaum [18].

We may then conclude that *Derivations A and B* tend to be supported by the available data.

> *Derivation C (from I, III B)*: A person will be less attracted to situations where others are very divergent from him than to situations where others are close to him for both abilities and opinions.

This follows from a consideration of *Hypothesis I* and *Corollary III B*. If there is a drive toward evaluation of abilities and opinions, and if this evaluation is possible only with others who are close enough, then there should be some attraction to groups where others are relatively close with respect to opinions and/or abilities. There are data confirming this for both opinions and abilities.

Festinger, Gerard, *et al*. [10] report an experiment in which after each person had written down his opinion on an issue he was handed back a slip of paper presumably containing a tabulation of the opinions in the group. Some in each group were thus given the impression that most of the others in the group held opinions close to their own. The rest were given the impression that most others in the group held opinions quite different from their own. After the experiment they were each asked how well they liked the others in the group. In each of the eight different experimental conditions those who thought that the others held divergent opinions were less attracted to the group.[2]

The previously mentioned experiment by Dreyer [5] has as one of its main purposes the testing of this derivation in connection with abilities. He used a "level of aspiration" situation and falsified the scores he reported to the subjects so that some thought they were scoring very far above the group, some thought they were scoring very far below the group, while others thought they were scoring about at the same level as the average of others like them. After each trial they were asked whether they wanted to continue for another trial or whether they would prefer to stop. The reasoning was that if those scoring well above or well below the group average were not able to evaluate their ability accurately, the situation would be less attractive to them and they would stop sooner. On the average, those scoring very much above the group stop after the fifth trial, while those scoring below or at the average of the group stop after the ninth trial.[3] There is no difference between those scoring at and those scoring well below the average of the group. The derivation in the case of abilities seems confirmed for deviation from the group in one direction then but not in the other. This is probably due to the presence of another pressure which we shall discuss in detail later, namely, the value placed in our culture on being better and better with the result that the subjects scoring below the group wanted to, and felt that they might, improve and achieve comparability with the group average.

This result from the experiment by Dreyer [5] is also corroborated in the previously mentioned experiment by Hochbaum [18]. It will be recalled that half the subjects were made to feel that their ability in judging situations of the kind they were to discuss was extremely good and very superior to the abilities of the others in the group. The other half of the subjects were made to feel that their ability was poor and considerably worse than the ability of the others in the group. At the end of the experiment all the subjects were asked whether, if they returned for another session they would like to be in the same group or a different group.

---

[2] This result is not reported in the article cited. It was obtained by analyzing the data for this particular purpose.

[3] It is interesting to note that on this point, the usual theory of level of aspiration [21] would lead to a quite different prediction, namely, that those scoring consistently below the group would stop earliest.

Of those who felt they were very much above the others in the group, only 38 percent wanted to return to the same group. Of those who felt that they were considerably inferior to the others, 68 percent wanted to return to the same group.

With the qualification concerning the asymmetry with regard to abilities the derivation may be regarded as confirmed. We will discuss the unidirectional drive upwards for abilities, which produces the asymmetry, in more detail later.

> *Derivation D (from I, II, III)*: The existence of a discrepancy in a group with respect to opinions or abilities will lead to action on the part of members of that group to reduce the discrepancy.

We have stated in *Hypotheses I, II, and III* and in the corollaries to these hypotheses that there is a drive to evaluate accurately one's opinions and abilities, that this evaluation is frequently only possible by comparison with others and that the comparison tends to be made with others who are close to oneself on the particular ability or opinion in question. This implies that the drive to evaluate one's ability or opinion will lead to behavior which will produce for the person a situation where those with whom he compares himself are reasonably close to him, in other words, there will be action to reduce discrepancies which exist between himself and others with whom he compares himself.

Before we can discuss the data relevant to this derivation it is necessary to point out two important differences between opinions and abilities which affect the behavioral manifestations of the action to reduce discrepancies. We will state these differences in the form of hypotheses.

> *Hypothesis IV*: There is a unidirectional drive upward in the case of abilities which is largely absent in opinions.

With respect to abilities, different performances have intrinsically different values. In Western culture, at any rate, there is a value set on doing better and better which means that the higher the score on performance, the more desirable it is. Whether or not this is culturally determined, and hence culturally

variable, is an important question but one with which we will not occupy ourselves here.[4]

With respect to most opinions, on the other hand, in the absence of comparison there is no inherent, intrinsic basis for preferring one opinion over another. If we thought of opinions on some specific issue as ranging along a continuum, then no opinion in and of itself has any greater value than any other opinion. The value comes from the subjective feeling that the opinion is correct and valid.

> *Hypothesis V*: There are non-social restraints which make it difficult or even impossible to change one's ability. These non-social restraints are largely absent for opinions.

If a person changes his mind about something, deserts one belief in favor of another, there is no further difficulty in the way of consummating the change. It is true that there are sometimes considerable difficulties in getting someone to change his mind concerning an opinion or belief. Such resistance may arise because of consistency with other opinions and beliefs, personality characteristics that make a person lean in one direction or another and the like. But the point to be stressed here is that once these resistances are overcome, there is no further restraint which would make it difficult for the change to become effective.

There are generally strong non-social restraints, however, against changing one's ability, or changing one's performance which reflects this ability. Even if a person is convinced that he should be able to run faster or should be more intelligent, and even if he is highly motivated to improve his ability in this respect, there are great difficulties in the way of consummating the change.

We may now examine the implications of *Derivation D*. Considering *Hypothesis IV* it is clear that the action to reduce the discrepancy which exists is, in the case of opinions, a relatively uncomplicated pressure towards uniformity. When and if uniformity of opinion is achieved there is a state of social quiescence. In the case of abilities, however, the action to reduce discrepancies interacts

---

[4]There is some evidence, for example, that among the Hopi Indians this preference for better performance is absent [2].

with the unidirectional push to do better and better. The resolution of these two pressures, which act simultaneously, is a state of affairs where all the members are relatively close together with respect to some specific ability, but not completely uniform. The pressures cease acting on a person if he is just slightly better than the others. It is obvious that not everyone in a group can be slightly better than everyone else. The implication is that, with respect to the evaluation of abilities, a state of social quiescence is never reached.

Competitive behavior, action to protect one's superiority, and even some kinds of behavior that might be called cooperative, are manifestations in the social process of these pressures which do not reach quiescence. We shall now elaborate this further in considering the specific nature of the social action arising from pressures toward uniformity. There are three major manifestations of pressure toward uniformity which we shall list below together with the relevant data.

Derivation D_1: When a discrepancy exists with respect to opinions or abilities there will be tendencies to change one's own position so as to move closer to others in the group.

Derivation D_2: When a discrepancy exists with respect to opinions or abilities there will be tendencies to change others in the group to bring them closer to oneself.

Considering *Hypothesis V* in relation to the above two subderivations we can see that a difference is implied between the resulting process for opinions and for abilities. Since opinions are relatively free to change, the process of changing the positions of members of a group relative to one another is expressed in action which is predominantly socially oriented. When differences of opinion exist, and pressures toward uniformity arise, these pressures are manifested in an influence process. Members attempt to influence one another, existing opinions become less stable and change occurs. This process of social influence, as we have mentioned before, ceases if and when uniformity of opinion exists in the group.

When pressures toward uniformity exist with respect to abilities, these pressures are manifested

less in a social process and more in action against the environment which restrains movement. Thus, a person who runs more slowly than others with whom he compares himself, and for whom this ability is important, many spend considerable time practising running. In a similar situation where the ability in question is intelligence, the person may study harder. But, needless to say, movement toward uniformity may or may not occur. Even if it occurs, it will take much, much longer than in the case of opinions.

This process would, of course, not be competitive if it were not for the simultaneous operation of the unidirectional push upward which is stated in *Hypothesis IV*. Because of this unidirectional push and the pressure toward uniformity, the individual is oriented toward some point on the ability continuum slightly better than his own performance or the performance of those with whom he is comparing himself. If uniformity concerning an ability were reached this would not lead to a cessation of competition as long as the unidirectional push upward is operating.

There are data which corroborate the two derivations with regard to both abilities and opinions. Back [3], Festinger and Thibaut [9], Festinger, Gerard, *et al.* [10], and Gerard [14] have shown clearly that the presence of disagreement in a group concerning some opinion leads to attempts to influence others who disagree with them and also to tendencies to change own opinion to agree more with the others in the group. The effect of this process is to have the group move closer and closer to agreement. In groups where uniformity concerning some issue is reached the influence process on that issue ceases.

In the case of abilities the evidence is less direct for a number of reasons. First, there have been fewer studies conducted relevant to this point. Second, since the process resulting from pressure to reduce discrepancies concerning abilities is not clearly shown in a social process, and since it is complicated by the drive to do better and better, it is harder to identify. Some evidence is available from the literature on level of aspiration [21]. It has been shown that in most situations, an individual's level of aspiration is placed slightly above his performance.

When told the average performance of others like himself, the level of aspiration is generally set slightly above this reported group average. These results are what we would expect if the resolution of the simultaneous unidirectional drive upward and the pressure towards uniformity is indeed a drive to be slightly better than the others with whom one compares oneself. These data can then be viewed as an indication of the desire to change one's position relative to others.

An experiment by Hoffman, Festinger, and Lawrence [19] specifically designed to test parts of the present theory, shows this competitive process clearly. In a performance situation where one of three persons is scoring considerably above the other two, these two can and do act so as to prevent the high scorer from getting additional points. Thus, when the situation is arranged such that the performance of each person is controllable by the others in the group, action is taken to change the position of the members to reduce the discrepancies which exist.

Let us also examine what we would expect of the behavior of someone whose performance is considerably higher than the other members of the group and who has no other possible comparison group to turn to for his evaluation of this ability. Since the others are considerably poorer, they will not effectively serve as a comparison for his own evaluation. The pressure acting on him toward comparability can manifest itself in two ways. It is possible that under these conditions his performance will actually deteriorate slightly over a period of time. It is also possible that he will devote considerable time and effort to trying to improve the performance of the others in the group to a point where at least some of them are close to, but not equal to, him. This could take the form of helping them practice, coaching them, motivating them to improve and the like. Once comparability has been achieved, however, the process should change to the familiar competitive one.

There is some indirect corroboration of this from experimental evidence. Greenberg [16] reports a study in competition in which pairs of children, seated together at a table, were to construct things out of "stones" (blocks) which were initially all in one common pile. Grabbing blocks from the pile was one of the indications of competition while giving blocks to the others was taken as one indication of lack of competition. The author reports the case of two friends, E. K. and H. At a time when E. K.'s construction was clearly superior to that of H., H. asked for "stones" and was freely given such by E. K. Subsequently E. K. asked H. whether or not she wanted more "stones". At the end of the session, although privately the experimenter judged both constructions to be nearly equal, when the children were asked "whose is better?" E. K. said "mine" and H., after a moment, agreed.

From many such pairs the author summarizes as follows: "Sometimes when a child gave another a 'stone', it was not at all an act of disinterested generosity, but a display of friendly competition and superior skill."

Derivation D_3: When a discrepancy exists with respect to opinions or abilities there will be tendencies to cease comparing oneself with those in the group who are very different from oneself.

Just as comparability can be achieved by changing the position of the members with respect to one another, so can it also be achieved by changing the composition of the comparison group. Thus, for example, if pressures toward uniformity exist in a group concerning some opinion on which there is a relatively wide discrepancy, there is a tendency to redefine the comparison group so as to exclude those members whose opinions are most divergent from one's own. In other words, one merely ceases to compare oneself with those persons.

Here again we would expect the behavioral manifestation of the tendency to stop comparing oneself with those who are very divergent to be different for opinions and for abilities. This difference arises because of the nature of the evaluation of opinions and abilities and because of the asymmetry introduced by the unidirectional push upward for abilities. We will consider these in order.

It will be recalled that opinions are evaluated in terms of whether or not subjectively they are correct while abilities are evaluated in terms of how good they seem. In other words, the existence of someone whose ability is very divergent from one's own, while it does not help to evaluate one's ability, does not make, in itself, for discomfort or unpleasantness. In the case of opinions, however, the existence of a discrepant opinion threatens one's own opinion since it implies the possibility that one's own opinion may not be correct. *Hypothesis VI*, which we will state below, leads us then to expect that the process of making others incomparable (ceasing to compare oneself with others) will be accompanied by hostility or derogation in the case of opinions but will not, generally, in the case of abilities.

Hypothesis VI: The cessation of comparison with others is accompanied by hostility or derogation to the extent that continued comparison with those persons implies unpleasant consequences.

Thus, in the case of opinions we expect the process of making others incomparable to be associated with rejection from the group. In the case of abilities, this may or may not be the case. It would be plausible to expect that there would rarely be derogation in making those below oneself incomparable. When making those above oneself incomparable, the presence of unidirectional push upward might lead to derogation in some instances.

The asymmetry introduced in the case of abilities is another difference we may expect to find. While in the case of opinions, deviation on either side of one's own opinion would lead to the same consequences, in the case of abilities there is a difference. The process of making others incomparable results in a "status stratification" where some are clearly inferior and others are clearly superior.

Corollary VI A: Cessation of comparison with others will be accompanied by hostility or derogation in the case of opinions. In the case of abilities this will not generally be true.

Festinger, Schachter, and Back [8] and Schachter [22] have shown that when there is a range of opinion in a group there is a tendency to reject those members of the group whose opinions are very divergent from one's own. This rejection tends to be accompanied by a relative cessation of communication to those who are rejected. This is undoubtedly

another evidence of the cessation of comparison with those persons.

There are data relevant to this point in connection with abilities from the experiment by Hoffman, Festinger, and Lawrence [19]. In this experiment, one out of a group of three persons were made to score very much higher than the other two on a test of intelligence. When the nature of the situation allowed, the two low scoring subjects ceased to compete against the high scorer and began to compete against each other. When they did this they also rated the intelligence of the high scorer as considerably higher than their own, thus acknowledging his superiority. In those conditions where they continued to compete against the high scorer they did not rate his intelligence as higher than their own. In other words, when the situation allowed it they stopped comparing their scores with the score of someone considerably higher than themselves. This cessation of comparison was accompanied by an acknowledgment of the others' superiority. A number of sociometric questions showed no hostility toward or derogation of the high scorer.

Having discussed the manifestations of the "pressure toward uniformity" which arises from the drive to evaluate opinions and abilities, we will now raise the question as to the factors which determine the strength of these pressures.

Derivation E (from I, II and III): Any factors which increase the strength of the drive to evaluate some particular ability or opinion will increase the "pressure toward uniformity" concerning that ability or opinion.

Hypothesis VII: Any factors which increase the importance of some particular group as a comparison group for some particular opinion or ability will increase the pressure toward uniformity concerning that ability or opinion within that group.

To make the above statements relevant to empirical data we must of course specify the factors involved. The corollaries stated below will specify some of these factors. We will then present the data relevant to these corollaries.

Corollary to Derivation E: An increase in the importance of an ability or an opinion, or an increase in its relevance to immediate behavior, will increase the pressure toward reducing discrepancies concerning that opinion or ability.

If an opinion or ability is of no importance to a person there will be no drive to evaluate that ability or opinion. In general, the more important the opinion or ability is to the person, the more related to behavior, social behavior in particular, and the more immediate the behavior is, the greater will be the drive for evaluation. Thus, in an election year, influence processes concerning political opinions are much more current than in other years. Likewise, a person's drive to evaluate his intellectual ability will be stronger when he must decide between going to graduate school or taking a job.

The previously mentioned experiment by Hoffman, Festinger, and Lawrence [19] corroborates the Corollary to *Derivation E* with respect to abilities. It will be recalled that this experiment involved groups of three persons who took an "intelligence test". The situation was arranged so that one of the subjects (a paid participant) started out with a higher score than the other two. From then on the two subjects could completely control how many points the paid participant scored. The degree to which they prevented him from scoring points was taken as a measure of the extent to which they were competing against him and hence as an indication of the strength of the pressure toward uniformity acting on them. Half of the groups were told that this test which they were to take was an extremely valid test and hence a good measure of intelligence, an ability which these subjects considered important. The other half of the groups were told that it was a very poor test and the research was being done to demonstrate conclusively that the test was no good. For these subjects their performance was consequently not important. The results showed that the competition with the high scorer was significantly greater for the high importance than for the low importance condition.

Unfortunately there are no relevant data from experiments concerning opinions. The Corollary to *Derivation E* applies to opinions also, however, and is testable.

The data which we have presented refer to changing the position of members in the group. As the pressure toward uniformity increases there should also be observed an increase in the tendency to cease comparison with those who are too different from oneself. Specifically, this would mean that the range within which appreciable comparison with others is made should contract as the pressure toward uniformity increases. This leads to an interesting prediction concerning abilities which can be tested. The more important an ability is to a person and, hence, the stronger the pressures toward uniformity concerning this ability, the stronger will be the competition about it and also the greater the readiness with which the individuals involved will recognize and acknowledge that someone else is clearly superior to them. And just as in influence processes, where, once rejection has taken place there tends to be a cessation of communication and influence attempts toward those who have been made incomparable [10, 22], so we may expect that once inferior or superior status has been conferred, there will be a cessation of competition with respect to those who have been thus rendered incomparable.

Thus, for example, let us imagine two individuals who are identical with respect to some particular ability but differ markedly in how important this ability is to them personally. The prediction from the above theory would say that the person for whom the ability is more important would be more competitive about it than the other; would be more ready to allocate "inferior status" to those considerably less good than he; and would be more ready to allocate "superior status" to those considerably better than he. In other words, he would be more competitive within a narrower range.

Corollary VII A: The stronger the attraction to the group the stronger will be the pressure toward uniformity concerning abilities and opinions within that group.

The more attractive a group is to a member, the more important that group will be as a comparison group for him. Thus the pressure to reduce discrepancies which operate on him when differences of ability or opinion exist will be stronger. We would expect these stronger pressures toward uniformity to show themselves in all three ways, increased tendency to change own position, increased effort to change the position of others, and greater restriction of the range within which appreciable comparison is made.

There are a number of studies which corroborate *Corollary VII A* with regard to opinions. Back [3] showed that in groups to which the members were highly attracted there were more attempts to influence others than in groups to which the members were less attracted. This greater exertion of influence was accompanied by more change of opinion in the highly attractive groups. Festinger, Gerard, *et al.* [10] showed a tendency for members of highly attractive groups to change their opinions more frequently than members of less attractive group upon discovering that most others in the group disagreed with them. This change of opinion was before any influence had actually been exerted on them by other members of the group. They also found that there was more communication attempting to influence others in the high than in the low attractive groups.

Schachter [22] showed that this same factor, attraction to the group, also increased the tendency to cease comparison with those who differed too much. Members of his highly attractive groups rejected the deviate significantly more than did members of the less attractive groups.

Festinger, Torrey, and Willerman [12] report an experiment specifically designed to test *Corollary VII A* with respect to abilities. If, given a range of performance reflecting some ability, the comparison, and hence the competition, in highly attractive groups would be stronger than in less attractive groups, then this should be reflected in the feelings of having done well or poorly after taking the tests. If *Corollary VII A* is correct we would expect those scoring slightly below others to feel more inadequate in the high than in the low attractive groups. Similarly we would expect those scoring equal to or better than most others to feel more adequate in the high than in the low attractive groups. Groups of four persons were given a series of tests supposed to measure an ability that these persons considered important. One of the subjects was caused to score consistently slightly below the others. The other three were made to score equally well. Those members who were highly attracted to the group, and scored below the others, felt they had done worse than similar persons who were not attracted to the group. Those who were attracted to the group and had scored equal to the others felt that they had done better than did similar persons who were not attracted to the group. Thus the results of the experiment corroborate the corollary for abilities.

> *Corollary VII B*: The greater the relevance of the opinion or ability to the group, the stronger will be the pressure toward uniformity concerning that opinion or ability.

The conceptual definition of relevance of an opinion or an ability to a group is not completely clear. There are, however, some things one can state. Where the opinion or ability involved is necessary or important for the life of the *group* or for the attainment of the satisfactions that push the members into the group, the need for evaluation in that group will be strong. Groups will thus differ on what one may call their "realm of relevance". A group of men who meet every Friday night to play poker, and do only this together, will probably have a narrow "realm of relevance". The abilities and opinions for which this group serves as a comparison will be very restricted. The members of a college fraternity, on the other hand, where the group satisfies a wider variety of the members' needs will have a wider "realm of relevance".

In spite of the conceptual unclarity which is involved it is possible to create differences in relevance of an issue to a group which are clear and unambiguous. Thus Schachter [22] created high and low relevance conditions in the following manner. Groups which were to discuss an issue relevant to the group were recruited specifically for that purpose. Other groups were recruited ostensibly for very different kinds of things and on a pretext were asked to discuss the particular issue in question. They were promised this would never happen again in the life of the group thus making this issue of low relevance to that particular group. Schachter found, confirming *Corollary VII B*, that the tendency to reject deviates was stronger in the high relevance condition than in the low relevance condition.

No other evidence bearing on *Corollary VII B* has been located.

Thus far we have discussed only factors which, in affecting the pressure toward uniformity, affect all three manifestations of this pressure in the same direction. There are also factors which affect the manifestations of pressure toward uniformity differentially. We will discuss two such factors.

Hypothesis VIII: If persons who are very divergent from one's own opinion or ability are perceived as different from oneself on *attributes consistent with the divergence*, the tendency to narrow the range of comparability becomes stronger.

There is evidence supporting this hypothesis with respect to both abilities and opinions. In the previously mentioned experiment by Hoffman, Festinger, and Lawrence [19] half the groups were told that the three persons in the group had been selected to take the test together because, as far as could be determined, they were about equal in intelligence. The other groups were told that one of the three was very superior to the others. This was reported in a manner which made it impossible for either of the subjects to suppose that he himself was the superior one. In the "homogeneous" condition the subjects continued to compete against the paid participant who was scoring considerably above them. In the condition where they thought one of the others was clearly superior they competed considerably less with the paid participant and tended to compete with each other. In other words, when there was the perception of a difference consistent with the fact that the paid participant was scoring above them, they ceased comparison with him.

There is additional evidence on this point from level of aspiration experiments. Festinger [6] reports an experiment where, on an intellectual task, subjects (college students) were told they were scoring considerably above another group which they ordinarily considered inferior to themselves (high school students) or were told they were scoring considerably below a group which they considered superior to themselves (graduate students). In these circumstances there is practically no effect on the level of aspiration. Thus, the knowledge of

this other group's being divergent in a direction consistent with the label of the group had no effect on their evaluation. It is interesting to note in this same experiment that if the reported direction of difference is inconsistent with the level of the group this destroys the incomparability and the effect on the level of aspiration is very great.

The evidence concerning opinions relating to *Hypothesis VIII* comes from experiments reported by Gerard [14] and Festinger and Thibaut [9]. In both of these experiments discussions were carried on in a group of persons with a considerable range of opinion on the issue in question. In each experiment, half of the groups were given the impression that the group was homogeneous. All the members of the group had about equal interest in and knowledge about the issue. The other half of the groups were given the impression that they were heterogeneously composed. There was considerable variation among them in interest in and knowledge about the problem. In both experiments there was less communication directed toward those holding extremely divergent opinions in the heterogeneous than in the homogeneous condition. In other words, the perception of heterogeneity on matters related to the issue enabled the members of the groups to narrow their range within which they actively compared themselves with others.

It is interesting, at this point, to look at the data from these two experiments in relation to *Hypothesis III* which stated that the tendency to compare oneself with others decreased as the divergence in opinion or ability increased. In both the Gerard experiment [14] and the Festinger and Thibaut experiment [9] it was found that most communication was directed toward those whose opinions were most different from the others. Since we have just interpreted a reduction in communication to indicate a reduction in comparison with others, it is necessary to explain the over-all tendency to communicate most with those holding divergent opinions in the light of *Hypothesis III*.

From *Hypothesis III* we would expect comparison to be made mainly with those closest to oneself. This is indeed true. The support one gets for one's opinion is derived from those close to one's own. However, it will be recalled that, in the case of opinions, comparison with others who are divergent represents a threat to one's own opinion. It is for this reason that communication is directed mainly toward those most divergent but still within the limits where comparison is made. This communication represents attempts to influence them. Reduction in communication to these extreme opinions indicates that the existence of these extreme opinions is less of a threat to one's own opinion. In other words, one is comparing oneself less with them. In the case of abilities we would not expect to find any such orientation toward very divergent persons. Comparison behavior in the case of abilities would follow very closely the simple relation stated in *Hypothesis III*.

> *Hypothesis IX*: When there is a range of opinion or ability in a group, the relative strength of the three manifestations of pressures toward uniformity will be different for those who are close to the mode of the group than for those who are distant from the mode. Specifically, those close to the mode of the group will have stronger tendencies to change the positions of others, relatively weaker tendencies to narrow the range of comparison and much weaker tendencies to change their own position compared to those who are distant from the mode of the group.

Some data are available to support this hypothesis, with reference to opinions, from experiments by Festinger, Gerard, *et al.* [10] and by Hochbaum [18]. In both of these experiments some persons in each group were given the impression that the rest of the group disagreed with them while others were given the impression that most of the group agreed with them. In both experiments there was considerably more change of opinion among the "deviates" than among the conformers. In both experiments there were considerably more attempts to influence others made by the conformers than by the deviates. While there exist no adequate data relevant to the tendency to narrow the range of comparison, corroboration is suggested in the experiment by Festinger, Gerard, *et al.* [10]. In this experiment it was found that the deviates actually communicated less to those holding most divergent opinions than to those somewhat closer to their own position. The

conformers showed the more familiar pattern of communicating most to those with extremely divergent opinions in the group.

The question may also be raised as to the determinants of the extent to which the group actually does move closer toward uniformity when pressures in this direction exist. In part, the degree of such movement toward uniformity will be dependent upon the strength of the pressures. In part they will be dependent upon other things. In the case of opinions it will be dependent upon the resistances to changing opinions, and upon the power of the group to successfully influence its members. The theory concerning the determinants of the power of the group to influence its members is set forth elsewhere [7]. We will not repeat it here since the power of the group to influence its members is relatively unimportant with regard to abilities. The social process itself, no matter how much power the group has, cannot achieve movement toward uniformity on abilities. The power of the group successfully to influence its members will be effective only insofar as changing members' values concerning a given ability and increasing motivations can be effective. With respect to values and motivations concerning the ability the situation is identical with the social process that goes on concerning opinions.

Implications for Group Formation and Societal Structure

The drive for self evaluation concerning one's opinions and abilities has implications not only for the behavior of persons in groups but also for the processes of formation of groups and changing membership of groups. To the extent that self evaluation can only be accomplished by means of comparison with other persons, the drive for self evaluation is a force acting on persons to belong to groups, to associate with others. And the subjective feelings of correctness in one's opinions and the subjective evaluation of adequacy of one's performance on important abilities are some of the satisfactions that persons attain in the course of these associations with other people. How strong the drives and satisfactions stemming from these sources are compared to the other needs which people satisfy in groups is impossible to say, but it seems clear that the drive for self evaluation is an important factor contributing to making the human being "gregarious".

People, then, tend to move into groups which, in their judgment, hold opinions which agree with their own and whose abilities are near their own. And they tend to move out of groups in which they are unable to satisfy their drive for self evaluation. Such movement in and out of groups is, of course, not a completely fluid affair. The attractiveness to a group may be strong enough for other reasons so that a person cannot move out of it. Or there may be restraints, for one or another reason, against leaving. In both of these circumstances, mobility from one group to another is hindered. We will elaborate in the next section on the effects of so hindering movement into and out of groups.

These selective tendencies to join some and leave other associations, together with the influence process and competitive activity which arise when there is discrepancy in a group, will guarantee that we will find relative similarity in opinions and abilities among persons who associate with one another (at least on those opinions and abilities which are relevant to that association). Among different groups, we may well expect to find relative dissimilarity. It may very well be that the segmentation into groups is what allows a society to maintain a variety of opinions within it and to accommodate persons with a wide range of abilities. A society or town which was not large enough or flexible enough to permit such segmentation might not be able to accommodate the same variety.

The segmentation into groups which are relatively alike with respect to abilities also gives rise to status in a society. And it seems clear that when such status distinctions are firmly maintained, it is not only members of the higher status who maintain them. It is also important to the members of the lower status to maintain them for it is in this way that they can relatively ignore the differences and compare themselves with their own group. Comparisons with members of a different

status group, either higher or lower, may sometimes be made on a phantasy level, but very rarely in reality.

It is also important to consider whether or not the incomparability consequent upon group segmentation is a relatively complete affair. The conferring of status in the case of abilities or the allegation of "different kind of people" in the case of opinions may markedly lower the comparability but may not completely eliminate it. The latter is probably the more accurate statement. People are certainly aware, to some extent, of the opinions of those in incomparable groups. To the extent that perfect incomparability is not achieved, this has important bearing on differences in behavior to be expected from members of minority groups. Members of minority groups, if they are unable to achieve complete incomparability with other groups, should be somewhat less secure in their self evaluations. One might expect from this that within a minority group, the pressures toward uniformity would be correspondingly stronger than in a majority group. The minority group would seek stronger support within itself and be less well able to tolerate differences of opinion or ability which were relevant to that group.

In connection with opinion formation, there is experimental evidence that this is the case [14]. Subgroups which were in the minority within larger experimental groups showed evidence of stronger pressures toward uniformity within the subgroup than did the majority subgroups. In minority groups where particular abilities were relevant, we would, by the same line of reasoning, also expect stronger pressures toward uniformity and hence fiercer competition with respect to that ability than in majority groups.

We may recall that stronger pressure toward uniformity also implies the existence of stronger tendencies to regard as incomparable those who deviate markedly. Since others are made incomparable with respect to opinions by means of rejection from the group, this gives us a possible explanation of the persistent splitting into smaller and smaller factions which is frequently found to occur in minority groups which are under strong pressure from the majority segments of the population.

Consequences of Preventing Incomparability

There are predominantly two kinds of situations in which comparability is forced despite the usual tendencies not to compare oneself with those who deviate markedly. One such situation occurs when the attraction of the group is so strong, for other reasons, that the member continues to wish to remain in the group in spite of the fact that he differs markedly from the group on some opinion or ability. If, together with this state of affairs, he has no other comparison group for this opinion or ability, or if the opinion or ability is highly relevant to that group, then comparability is forced to a great extent. The psychological tendencies to make incomparable those who differ most will still be present but would not be as effective as they might otherwise be.

Under these circumstances where the attraction to the group remains high, the group has power to influence the member effectively and, in the case of opinion difference, we would expect an influence process to ensue which would be effective enough to eliminate the difference of opinion. In short, there would be movement toward uniformity. But what happens in the case of an ability? Here, while the group will probably succeed in motivating the member concerning this ability it is quite likely that the ability itself may not be changeable. We have then created a situation where a person's values and strivings are quite out of line with his performance and we would expect, if he is below others, deep experiences of failure and feelings of inadequacy with respect to this ability. This is certainly not an unusual condition to find.

The other major situation in which comparability is forced upon a person is one in which he is prevented from leaving the group. The theory concerning the effect of this situation on opinion formation is spelt out elsewhere [11]. We will touch on the main points here in order to extend the theory to ability evaluation. In circumstances where a person is restrained from leaving a group either physically or psychologically, but otherwise his attraction to the group is zero or even negative, the group does not have the power to influence him effectively. Uniformity can, however, be forced, in a sense, if the group exerts threats or punishment for noncompliance. In the case of opinions, we may here expect to find overt compliance or overt conformity without any private acceptance on the part of the member. Thus a boy who is forced to play with some children whom he does not particularly like would, in such circumstances, where threat was employed, agree with the other children publicly while privately maintaining his disagreement.

Again, when we consider abilities, we find a difference which arises because abilities may be difficult if not impossible to change on short notice. Here the deviating member who is restrained from leaving the group may simply have to suffer punishment. If he deviates toward the higher end of the ability scale, he can again publicly conform without privately accepting the evaluations of the group. If he deviates toward the lower end of the ability scale this may be impossible. Provided he has other comparison groups for self evaluation on this ability he may remain personally and privately quite unaffected by this group situation. While publicly he may strive to perform better, privately his evaluations of his ability may remain unchanged.

Summary

If the foregoing theoretical development is correct, then social influence processes and some kinds of competitive behavior are both manifestations of the same socio-psychological process and can be viewed identically on a conceptual level. Both stem directly from the drive for self evaluation and the necessity for such evaluation being based on comparison with other persons. The differences between the processes with respect to opinions and abilities lie in the unidirectional push upward in the case of abilities, which is absent when considering opinions and in the relative ease of changing one's opinion as compared to changing one's performance.

The theory is tentatively supported by a variety of data and is readily amenable to further empirical testing. One great advantage, assuming the correctness of the theory, is that one can work back and forth between opinions and ability evaluations. Some aspects of the theory may be more easily tested in one context, some in the other. Discoveries in the context of opinions should also hold true, when appropriately operationally defined, in the context of ability evaluation.

BIBLIOGRAPHY

1. ANDERSON, H. H., and BRANDT, H. F. "Study of Motivation Involving Self-Announced Goals of Fifth Grade Children and the Concept of Level of Aspiration", *Journal of Social Psychology*, 1939, *10*, 209–232.

2. ASCH, S. E. "Personality Developments of Hopi Children", Unpublished manuscript referred to in Murphy, Murphy and Newcomb, Experimental Social Psychology. New York and London: Harper and Brothers, 1931, 1937 (Revised Edition).

3. BACK, K. "The Exertion of Influence Through Social Communication", *Journal of Abnormal and Social Psychology*, 1951, *46*, 9–24.

4. CHAPMAN, D. W., and VOLKMANN, J. A. "A Social Determinant of the Level of Aspiration," *Journal of Abnormal and Social Psychology*, 1939, *34*, 225–238.

5. DREYER, A. "Behavior in a Level of Aspiration Situation as Affected by Group Comparison". Ph.D. Thesis, 1953, University of Minnesota.

6. FESTINGER, L. "Wish, Expectation and Group Standards as Factors Influencing Level of Aspiration", *Journal of Abnormal and Social Psychology*, 1942, *37*, 184–200.

7. FESTINGER, L. "Informal Social Communication", *Psychological Review*, 1950, *57*, 271–282.

8. FESTINGER, L., SCHACHTER, S., and BACK, K. *Social Pressures in Informal Groups*, New York: Harper and Brothers, 1950.

9. FESTINGER, L., and THIBAUT, J. "Interpersonal Communications in Small Groups", *Journal of Abnormal and Social Psychology*, 1951, *46*, 92–100.

10. FESTINGER, L., GERARD, H., *et al.* "The Influence Process in the Presence of Extreme Deviates," *Human Relations*, 1952, *5*, 327–346.

11. FESTINGER, L. "An Analysis of Compliant Behavior", in *Group Relations at the Crossroads*, edited by M. Sherif, New York: Harper and Brothers, 1953.

12. FESTINGER, L., TORREY, J., and WILLERMAN, B. "Self-Evaluation as a Function of Attraction to the Group", *Human Relations*, 1954, *7*, 2.

13. GARDNER, J. W. "Level of Aspiration in Response to a Prearranged Sequence of Scores", *Journal of Experimental Psychology*, 1939, *25*, 601–621.

14. GERARD, H. "The Effect of Different Dimensions of Disagreement on the Communication Process in Small Groups", *Human Relations*, 1953, *6*, 249–272.

15. GOULD, R. "An Experimental Analysis of 'Level of Aspiration' ", *Genetic Psychology Monographs*, 1939, *21*, 1–116.

16. GREENBERG, P. J. "Competition in Children: An Experimental Study", American *Journal of Psychology*, 1932, *44*, 221–248.

17. HILGARD, E. R., SAIT, E. M., and MAGARET, G. A. "Level of Aspiration as Affected by Relative Standing in an Experimental Social Group", *Journal of Experimental Psychology*, 1940, *27*, 411–421.

18. HOCHBAUM, G. M. "Certain Personality Aspects and Pressures to Uniformity in Social Group." Ph.D. Thesis, 1953, University of Minnesota.

19. HOFFMAN, P. J., FESTINGER, L., and LAWRENCE, D. H. "Tendencies Toward Comparability in Competitive Bargaining", *Human Relations*, 1954, *7*, 2.

20. HOPPE, F. "Erfolg und Misserfolg", Pschyol. Forsch., 1930, *14*, 1–62.

21. LEWIN, K., DEMBO, T., FESTINGER, L., and SEARS, P. S. "Level of Aspiration", in *Personality and the Behavior Disorders*, Vol. 1, pp. 333–378. New York: Ronald Press Co., 1944.

22. SCHACHTER, S. "Deviation, Rejection and Communication", *Journal of Abnormal and Social Psychology*, 1951, *46*, 190–208.

23. SEARS, P. S. "Levels of Aspiration in Academically Successful and Unsuccessful Children", *Journal of Abnormal and Social Psychology*, 1940, *35*, 498–536.

24. WHITTEMORE, I. C. "The Influence of Competition on Performance", *Journal of Abnormal and Social Psychology*, 1925, *20*, 17–33.

BIOGRAPHICAL NOTE

Leon Festinger, after taking a bachelor's degree at the College of the City of New York, studied at the University of Iowa under the late Professor Kurt Lewin, there completing his master's degree in 1940 and his doctorate in 1942. For the next two years he worked as instructor in the psychology department of Iowa, and as research associate at the Iowa Child Welfare Research Station. For a year and a half, beginning in 1944, Dr. Festinger was senior statistician of the National Research Council's Committee on Selection and Training of Aircraft Pilots, and instructor in the Department of Education of the University of Rochester, New York. From 1945 until his appointment to the University of Minnesota, he was a member of the staff of the Research Center for Group Dynamics, where he was assistant professor of psychology. He is now Professor of Psychology in the University of Minnesota. Leon Festinger has published numerous papers on statistics, on the effect of group standards and group atmospheres on the level of aspiration, on conflict and decision time, and on motivation and preference. His last paper to appear in this journal [*Human Relations*] was on the subject, "The Influence Process in the Presence of Extreme Deviates", Vol. V, No. 4 (1952), and was written in collaboration with Harold B. Gerard, Bernard Hymovitch, Harold H. Kelley, and Bert Raven.

PART 2

Comparison Motives: Classic Statements

The papers in this section show how social comparison theory has evolved since Festinger's (1954) paper. We introduce four articles that show important turning points in the way that psychologists have thought about the comparison process since Festinger's article. Each of the papers shows a shift in thinking, but they also reveal a perspective that continues to influence how contemporary psychologists think about and study the social comparison process. As one moves through the readings in chronological order, it becomes clear that Festinger's theory has become less central over time. His article was used as a "launching point" in the first two articles, whereas the more recent papers focused on issues that are hard to view as concerns advanced by Festinger. We think this shift shows how social comparison has been an area that stimulates the healthy exchange and expansion of ideas.

The first article, Goethals and Darley (1977), shows an important early "update" on Festinger's (1954) thesis. This paper adopted much of Festinger's original framework, and the primary concern was the similarity hypothesis. Goethals and Darley drew heavily on Festinger's original statement, and even conceded that their position on the similarity hypothesis was "not, strictly speaking, a revision of Festinger's hypothesis, but a restatement in the sense that it is a statement of what Festinger probably meant" (p. 55). As we noted earlier, although Festinger viewed similarity as the primary determinant of social comparison activity, he was not at all clear about what exactly he meant by a "similar" other. At times, he seemed to mean similarity on the *comparison dimension.* Thus, a runner who is trying to gauge her own speed might compare it with another runner of similar speed. At other times, Festinger seemed to mean similarity on *surrounding dimensions.* Thus, a runner who is trying to gauge her ability to run fast might compare her speed with another runner of the same sex, same age, and same general build.

Goethals and Darley argue that Festinger "meant" to define similarity based on surrounding dimensions, and that people are particularly interested in comparing their performances and opinions with other people who are similar on surrounding dimensions that are "related to and predictive of" performances and opinions. Although the authors frame this contribution as a minor restatement of the original, this "related attributes hypothesis" (Wheeler & Zuckerman, 1977) has had far-reaching implications on the social comparison literature. By weaving attribution theory into their related attributes hypothesis, Goethals and Darley were able to show that attention to related attributes allows people to discern when their performances suggest high ability, when their beliefs seem to be correct, and when their personal values appear to be in their best interest. This seemingly minor clarification of what Festinger meant to say has thus revealed a role for social comparison in daily life that is far richer than what can be found from a strict reading of Festinger (1954).

If Goethals and Darley were conservative in their treatment of the similarity hypothesis, they were liberal in their treatment of comparisons goals. Recall that Festinger thought social comparison was a reasoned action that was engaged in by a rational perceiver—someone who wanted to hold certain and accurate perceptions. Goethals and Darley saw a more engaged individual than this. They saw social comparison as a motivated action that was pursued by an invested perceiver—someone who wanted to validate important perceptions. It was because people are often strongly invested in seeing what they want to see (in their abilities, their opinions, and their values) that Goethals and Darley needed to update Festinger. Festinger's impoverished statements regarding similarity were not as problematic when they were paired with an impoverished view of human motivation. But as Goethals and Darley began to consider the other motivations that drive a person to compare, they needed a richer view on what type of similarity is desired and what type is not.

A more dramatic departure from Festinger can be found in Brickman and Bulman. They, too, thought that Festinger had too a narrow view of the motives that drive comparison. However, in direct contradiction of the Festinger's primary hypothesis, that we seek comparisons to reduce uncertainty, Brickman and Bulman argued that we are at times motivated to *avoid* social comparisons. They noted that it can be unseemly to compare with another person and that those who ignore this reality risk uncovering information that is in no one's best interest. As they put it, "If two people compare themselves on a valued dimension, the chances are that one will be superior and the other will be inferior. Someone will feel bad, and both parties or the collectivity must be concerned with coping with these negative feelings" (p. 69).

From this starting point, Brickman and Bulman go on to turn Festinger's similarity hypothesis on its head. They argue that people often seek contact with similar others as a way of *minimizing* social comparisons. When two people are similar in many ways, the differences between them are less likely to jump to the fore of their interactions and conversations. At the same time, however, any comparisons that do occur between similar others will be more diagnostic (in the ways that both Festinger and Goethals and Darley discuss) and thus more painful. For this reason, they argue, people strive to avoid contact with people who are better than them or worse than them, because such contacts can generate comparisons. At the same time, they pursue interpersonal strategies that minimize the likelihood that comparisons will be made with people who are similar to them.

Clearly, Brickman and Bulman thought that we live in a complex social world, fraught with social conflicts and tensions. Taylor and Lobel (1989) placed the individual in a similar world, but they differed from Brickman and Bulman in that they saw an important role for social comparison. Taylor and Lobel began by noting that people who are dealing with major life stressors, such as those receiving cancer diagnoses, have good reasons to seek out both upward social comparisons with people who are coping well and downward social comparisons with people who are adjusting poorly. For a cancer patient, upward comparisons can be inspiring and suggest to them that they can expect a similar outcome in the future. This can result in greater optimism and thus quicker recovery. But downward comparisons with people who are doing poorly can affirm that one is coping well. This can promote positive mood and leave the individual feeling relatively efficacious in how they are handling their crisis (Wills, 1981).

What do people do when they are stressed? Do they compare upward or downward? In a sense, Taylor and Lobel argue that they do both. Taylor and Lobel suggest that people under threat "affiliate upward." That is, they seek contact with people who are coping better than they are with shared stressors. But they also "compare downward." That is, they note the many ways that comparable others are adapting badly with the same stressors. With these two comparison tendencies, people can feel content with their present situations and yet inspired to improve.

However, this analysis begs the obvious question of how people can simultaneously pursue two opposing comparison strategies. It seems that, under stress, people do this by avoiding unwanted comparisons with the upward contacts they make. When people have contact with upward comparison others they draw inspiration from these individuals, even while they avoid making explicit comparisons that might lead them to draw unflattering inferences. Taylor and Lobel's notion that at times we avoid comparisons with people we encounter is consistent in some ways with Brickman and Bulman, but the rest of their analysis is not. Taylor and Lobel also argue that people under threat "compare downward" with others who are doing poorly, even though they try not to come in contact with them. They do this by constructing downward comparisons in their head. Rather than seeking contact with people who are coping badly, they imagine individuals with poor coping skills or they selectively remember past interactions with such people. Thus, Taylor and Lobel take the provocative position that people avoid making comparisons with the people they seek (upward targets), but they make comparisons with the people they avoid (downward targets).

The article by Tesser (1988) is similar to Taylor and Lobel in that it assumes people want comparisons with some people more than others. Tesser also shared their view that social comparisons serve our emotional needs. His model differed from Taylor and Lobel's, however, in that he mapped out the effects that direct comparisons with others can have on our self-evaluations, particularly those that might influence self-esteem.

Tesser suggested that social comparisons take two distinct forms: comparison process and reflection process. When the comparison process is activated, people contrast their performances with comparison others, and they feel best when they encounter downward social comparisons with inferior others. An example of this type of enhancement would be the individual who takes pride in her running ability when she realizes she is a better runner than another woman of her same age. This type of downward comparison in no way makes this runner faster, but it does make her *feel* faster. When the reflection process is activated, people identify with others, and they feel best when they encounter upward social comparisons with superior others. An example of the reflection process would be the father who takes pride in his daughter's running ability. The father in no way feels like a faster runner because of his daughter's success, but his associations with her allow him to enjoy her successes as if they were his own.

To determine when reflection or comparison processes will occur, Tesser considered the interactive influences of three variables (closeness, relevance, and performance). His model is complex and it considers a wide range of dynamic ways in which people can be affected by the comparisons they make. At the same time, his model leads to clear and testable predictions, much in the spirit Festinger (1954) attempted. Tesser's paper and the others in this section thus illustrate that researchers continue to see value in making bold predictions about how, why, and under what conditions people compare with others. This is true, even if the theories that receive the most attention today differ considerably from the one that got the conversation going.

REFERENCES

(Asterisks indicate Key Readings in this section.)

* Brickman, P., & Bulman, R. J. (1977). Pleasure and pain in social comparison. In J. M. Suls & R. L. Miller (Eds.), *Social comparison processes: Theoretical and empirical perspectives* (pp. 149–186). Washington, DC: Hemisphere.

Festinger, L. (1954). A theory of social comparison processes. *Human Relations, 7,* 117–140.

* Goethals, G. R., & Darley, J. M. (1977). Social comparison theory: An attributional approach. In J. M. Suls & R. L. Miller (Eds.), *Social comparison processes: Theoretical and empirical perspectives* (pp. 259–278). Washington, DC: Hemisphere.

* Taylor, S. T., & Lobel, M. (1989). Social comparison activity under threat: Downward evaluation and upward contacts. *Psychological Review, 96,* 569–575.

* Tesser, A. (1988). Toward a self-evaluation maintenance model of social behavior. In L. Berkowitz (Ed.), *Advances in experimental social psychology* (Vol. 21, pp. 181–227). New York: Academic Press.

Wheeler, L., & Zuckerman, M. (1977). Commentary. In J. Suls & R. Miller (Eds.), *Social comparison processes* (pp. 335–357). Washington, DC: Hemisphere Publishing Corporation.

Wills, T. A. (1981). Downward comparison principles in social psychology. *Psychological Bulletin, 90,* 245–271.

Discussion Questions

1. How did Goethals and Darley (1977) alter the concept of "similarity" from Festinger's (1954) view?
2. Did this represent a new conception or a refinement?
3. How do predictions differ for attitudes, beliefs, and opinions?
4. Brickman and Bulman (1977) argue that there are downsides to comparing with upward targets, downward targets, and similar targets. What are these negatives and how do people react, given all these bad options?
5. Taylor and Lobel (1989) argue that there is value in upward comparisons and downward comparisons. Given this, how do people coping with stressors reap both sets of benefits?
6. Tesser (1988) notes that the very people who can be the most threatening to us can also be the very ones who make us feel good. How does he account for this with the three variables of comparison, closeness, and relevance?
7. What can people do to diminish the threat of unwanted comparisons, based on Tesser's model?

Suggested Readings

Gruder, C. L. (1977). Choice of comparison persons in evaluating oneself. In J. M. Suls & R. C. Miller (Eds.), *Social comparison processes: Theoretical and empirical perspectives*, (pp. 21–42). Washington, DC: Hemisphere.

McGuire, W. J., McGuire, C. V., Child, P., & Fujioka, T. (1978). Salience of ethnicity in the spontaneous self-concept as a function of one's ethnic distinctiveness in the social environment. *Journal of Personality and Social Psychology, 36*, 511–520.

Morse, S., & Gergen, K. J. (1970). Social comparison, self-consistency, and the concept of the self. *Journal of Personality and Social Psychology, 16*, 148–156.

Stapel, D. A., & Tesser, A. (2001). Self-activation increases social comparison. *Journal of Personality and Social Psychology, 81*, 742–750.

Thornton, D., & Arrowood, A. J. (1966). Self-evaluation, self-enhancement, and the locus of social comparison. *Journal of Experimental Social Psychology, 2*, 40–48.

Wheeler, L. (1966). Motivation as a determinant of upward comparison. *Journal of Experimental Social Psychology, 1*, 27–31.

Wills, T. A. (1981). Downward comparison principles in social psychology. *Psychological Bulletin, 90*, 245–271.

Social Comparison Theory: *An Attributional Approach*

George R. Goethals* and John M. Darley**

Introduction

The purpose of this chapter is to restate social comparison theory (Festinger, 1954) in terms of some of the insights of attribution theory (Heider, 1944, 1958; Kelley, 1967, 1971, 1972). An attempt will be made to recast a number of Festinger's original propositions in attributional terms and, where possible, to consider some of the evidence for these newly formulated statements. The parts of Festinger's theory that will concern us most directly are Hypotheses I, III, and VIII. These are the propositions concerning the drive in human organisms to evaluate their opinions and abilities, the preference for comparing with similar others, and the tendency to cease comparing with other people who are different on characteristics that are consistent with their differences in ability and opinion. We will omit, for the most part, consideration of the differences between abilities and opinions and the consequences of these differences for comparison processes (Hypotheses IV, V, VI). We will also omit consideration of the implications of the

* Williams College.
** Princeton University.
The research reported here was supported by NIMH Grant 23527 to G. R. Goethals, principal investigator.

preference for comparing with similar others for affiliation and group dynamics (Hypotheses VII, IX). In other words, our main focus will be on the individual's need to evaluate his opinions and abilities and the way he selects other people for comparison purposes.

Festinger's Social Comparison Theory

At the outset, let us review briefly the portions of Festinger's original statement that will concern us most, Hypotheses I, III, and VIII and Corollary IIIA.

> *Hypothesis I*: There exists, in the human organism, a drive to evaluate his opinions and his abilities. (p. 117)

This proposition notes the need to evaluate opinions and abilities. It is a need based on the requirements for effective action in the environment. The person who does not have an accurate appraisal of his abilities and correct opinions is at a serious disadvantage in attempting to behave adaptively. The present restatement of social comparison theory will also assume that the individual has a drive to reduce as much uncertainty as possible about the correctness of his opinions and the adequacy of his abilities. However, the present treatment will also consider how the need to believe positive things about oneself, or the need to hold oneself in high esteem, augments or conflicts with the need for objective self-appraisal.

> *Hypothesis III*: The tendency to compare oneself with some other specific person decreases as the difference between his opinion or ability and one's own increases. (p. 120)

> *Corollary IIIA*: Given a range of possible persons for comparison, someone close to one's own ability or opinion will be chosen for comparison. (p. 121)

These two propositions state the critical "similarity hypothesis" of social comparison theory, the notion that people prefer comparing with similar others. This hypothesis has been the subject of extensive research. An attempt will be made to clarify it in this chapter.

> *Hypothesis VIII*: If persons who are very divergent from one's own opinion or ability are perceived as different from oneself on *attributes consistent with the divergence*, the tendency to narrow the range of comparability becomes stronger. (p. 133, emphasis in original)

This proposition is actually very much part of the similarity hypothesis. It can be read to suggest that people will tend to include in their comparison range those who are similar to themselves on attributes related to opinions or abilities. The restatement of the similarity hypothesis that will be developed below will incorporate Hypothesis VIII.

The Attributional Perspective

One important point highlights the utility of an attributional approach to social comparison and the prominence that attributional processes will play in the restatement to follow. This point is that often what is being evaluated through social comparison are dispositions that cannot be observed directly but must instead be inferred from behavioral manifestations. This observation is more obviously applicable in the case of abilities. While abilities are being evaluated, they cannot be directly observed. Rather, performances are observed. It is important to note that performances are only in part determined by ability (Heider's "can") and that making inferences about ability from

performances can be difficult for this reason. There is always a question as to the role of nonability factors in a performance. These factors include effort, luck, and difficulty (see Weiner, Frieze, Kukla, Reed, Rest, & Rosenbaum, 1971), as well as such factors as age and practice. These nonability factors must be taken into account in any social comparison of performances designed to evaluate abilities. In other words, ability evaluation is an attributional problem. What can be inferred about ability when it is only one of several factors conjointly determining performance?

Opinion evaluation seems to differ from ability evaluation in that opinions or, at least, opinion statements are directly observable and can be directly compared, while this is not true for abilities. However, opinions are also multidetermined, by the person's beliefs about reality, his basic values, his more specific likes and dislikes, and his immediate needs and interests. Furthermore, while a specific opinion may be under consideration, the individual may be more concerned with evaluating his intelligence and judgment or his system of values. The evaluation of these less-observable attributes can be approached by socially comparing opinions on specific issues. However, this kind of evaluation involves complex attributions about the causes of specific persons' opinion statements and equally complex inferences about what their opinions do or do not reveal about their intelligence or values.

In sum, often the attribute to be evaluated through comparison (an ability or a value) cannot be directly observed and the manifestations of these attributes, which can be observed (performances and opinion statements), are complexly determined. These considerations will be important in predicting social comparison processes.

Kelley's Attribution Theory

The basic principles of attribution theory that will concern us have been spelled out in several papers by Harold Kelley (1967, 1971, 1972) and have been summarized in Kelley (1973). Kelley has been concerned with the rules that an observer uses to make attributions of causality for a person's responses, his own, perhaps, or others'. Three major principles will concern us here: the principles of covariation, discounting, and augmentation. These are three of the most important rules that the individual employs to determine whether a response is attributable to the entity in the environment to which the person is responding, or whether it is attributable to something about the person himself.

The covariation principle is stated as follows: an effect is attributed to the one of its possible causes with which, over time, it covaries (Kelley, 1973, p. 108). Kelley's application of this principle in discussing the way a person attributes responses (i.e., effects) to either the person or the environment considers whether the response of a person to an entity is distinctive, consistent, and consensual. A response is distinctive if the individual does not respond to all entities in the way he responded to the present one. It is consistent if the individual responds to the entity in the same way at different times and in different modalities of interacting with the entity. That is, the person likes a movie whenever he sees it, and he likes it whether he sees it on television, in a theatre, or at the drive-in. Finally, a response is consensual if other people respond to the entity in the same way as the individual.

If a response is distinctive, consistent, and consensual, it is attributed to the entity. This is because such a response covaries, as far as can be seen from the available data, almost perfectly with the entity, but it does not covary with the person. Whenever the entity is present, the individual and others emit the response. However, the individual does not always emit the response. When other entities are present, he responds differently. On the other hand, a response that is not distinctive (the individual performs the response in the presence of many other entities), is consistent over time and modality of interaction with the entity, and is not consensual is attributable to the person and not the entity, on the basis of the covariation principle. Such a response occurs consistently in the person, whether or not the entity is present, but the entity does not elicit the response from other people.

The discounting principle is stated as follows: the role of a given cause in producing an effect is discounted if other plausible causes are also present (Kelley, 1973, p. 113). This principle becomes particularly important in the social comparison of abilities. To the extent that nonability causes are present at the time of a performance, the role of ability in producing that performance must be discounted. The operation of this principle in opinion comparison will also be considered.

The augmentation principle is a variation of the discounting principle but actually leads to an opposite inference. This principle states that if there is an inhibitory cause, one that works to suppress an observed effect, then the impression of the force of other causes is increased or heightened. For example, if a person successfully completed a difficult task, the task difficulty would be seen as an inhibitory external cause of the effect (success). It is one that makes the effect less likely to appear. As a consequence, a stronger attribution about the presence of the individual's ability is appropriate than would be the case if the inhibitory cause were less or absent.

Social Comparison and Attribution Theories

A fundamental commonality between social comparison theory and attribution theory is that both discuss phenomena that grow out of a common human need. That is the need, discussed by Heider (1944), for the individual to order and predict his environment so that he can act effectively in it and maximize his outcomes. Whereas attribution theory discusses the general rules that the individual follows in order to make attributions of causality that facilitate the prediction of objects and persons, social comparison theory considers the interpersonal processes that are involved in the individual's efforts to evaluate his predictions about objects and persons (his opinions) and his predictions about his capacity to act effectively with respect to these entities (his abilities).

In addition to their common basis in people's needs to order and predict their environment and their own behavior in that environment, both theories emphasize that one's perceptions of the adequacy of his opinions and abilities is determined by comparing himself with other people. This emphasis is explicit in social comparison theory. We evaluate our abilities by seeing how our performances compare with other people's performances. We evaluate our opinions by seeing whether others agree or disagree. Similarly, Kelley's attribution theory (1967) puts considerable emphasis on the principle that an individual making attributions of causality about his own or others' responses considers the responses of others to the same entities or in the same situations and makes attributions according to the degree of consensus he finds for his responses. If the individual finds that others are responding similarly, he is likely to make an entity attribution. If he finds that others respond differently, then his response is attributed to his own personal characteristics. We will see that Kelley's proposition that responses of high consensus are attributed to the environment while responses of low consensus are attributed to the person are of major importance in social comparison processes.

Social Comparison Theory: An Attributional Statement

It seems that our understanding of social comparison processes would be faciliated by a critical analysis of some of the key propositions in Festinger's original statement of the theory and, where appropriate, a restatement, from an attributional perspective, of some of those propositions.

The Evaluation Drive

Let us begin with Hypothesis I. Festinger (1954) states that there is a drive for the individual to evaluate his opinions and abilities. We have no quarrel with this proposition. What needs to be amended is the implication that all social comparison processes are driven only by this motive. As others have pointed out (e.g., Latané, 1966b), there is a related but sometimes competing motive for the individual to validate rather than evaluate his opinions and abilities. That is, while he may have a need to find out *whether* his opinions and abilities are correct and good, respectively, he also has

a need to discover that they *are* in fact correct and good. It may be apparent already that the needs for evaluation versus validation can lead to divergent social comparison strategies. In any case, this point will be elaborated later in this chapter.

The drive to validate one's opinions and abilities is also related to Festinger's statement of the unidirectional drive upward for abilities. Festinger suggested that while any opinion is as good, a priori, as any other, any ability is not as good as any other. Superior abilities are valued in Western culture. The importance of the unidirectional drive upward in Festinger's original statement is that the need to be better than others often conflicted with the need to be similar to others for purposes of ability evaluation. As a result, the prediction of comparison tactics in a number of instances was complicated. Festinger stated that in general the need to do better and the need to compare with similar others would combine to orient the individual toward some point on the comparison continuum slightly better than his own performance.

An experiment by Wheeler (1966) supported Festinger's prediction. Wheeler showed that subjects who were most motivated to have a high standing on a personality trait compared upward on a performance continuum. Wheeler notes that this comparison tactic seems paradoxical since by comparing upward, the individual is increasing his chances of discovering that he compares poorly. The resolution of this paradox, Wheeler contends, is that people who are motivated to be superior on a particular trait often assume superiority and thus compare upward in the expectation of confirming their superiority. The fact that they are maximizing the objective likelihood of receiving an unfavorable comparison does not seem salient.

The drive to be better than others is relevant at present because it implies that at least in the case of abilities the evaluation process is not totally disinterested. It implies that although the individual *may* objectively seek to find whether his abilities are good, he has a preference for the finding that they *are* good over the finding that they are not. Although it does not necessarily follow that a drive to have good abilities will lead to a need to obtain information that they are good rather than objective information that may indicate that they may be good or bad, such a drive could provide the basis for biased ability evaluations. In any case, we are positing a need for self-validation, related to the unidirectional drive upward, which will play an important role in strategies for social comparison choice and the interpretation of comparison information.

Although there is no unidirectional drive upward for opinions, opinion evaluation is probably not a disinterested process either. The person wants to be correct and he has a preference for comparison information that will show him to be correct, just as he has a preference for comparison information that will indicate that his abilities are a little better than those of others. It can be added, parenthetically, that Jellison and Davis (1973) have shown that some opinion positions are associated with high ability. So that just as people are motivated to give performances that are indicative of high ability, they may also be motivated, other things being equal, to adopt opinion positions that are associated with competence. Again, simply because the individual has a preference for one comparison outcome over the other (i.e., the one showing his opinion to be correct over the one showing it to be incorrect), it does not necessarily follow that he will not objectively seek information about the validity of his opinions. Nevertheless, it seems a reasonable proposition that the individual's social comparison behavior may at times reflect the motive to hold positive beliefs about his opinions and abilities.

In sum, we would like to amend Festinger's original statement that there is a desire to evaluate opinions and abilities by adding that there is also a desire to validate them and to obtain evidence that they are, in fact, correct and good, respectively.

The Similarity Hypothesis

The key proposition in the original statement of social comparison theory is Corollary IIIA, the proposition that people will choose to compare their own opinion or ability with the opinion or ability of someone who has a similar opinion or ability. In much of the research that has been conducted to test this hypothesis, a very literal understanding

of it has been employed. It has been thought that the individual will be interested in comparing his own performance or opinion with that of someone whose performance score or opinion is similar. It is unclear, however, just what information can be gained by examining a group of persons with varying performance levels or opinions and then choosing to compare with those whose scores or opinions are similar. Also, there is the somewhat baffling paradox that presumably the comparison is made in order to find out what the other's opinion or score is, yet prior knowledge of the similarity of his score or opinion is assumed as the basis for comparison.

The difficulties of the literal interpretation of Corollary IIIA were first alluded to by Wheeler, Shaver, Jones, Goethals, Cooper, Robinson, Gruder, and Butzine (1969). They suggested that "we do not merely seek out someone with an opinion similar to ours but rather seek out someone who ought to have, by virtue of similarity to us on attributes related to the opinion issue, a similar opinion" (p. 231). This statement suggests a different but much more meaningful interpretation of Festinger's similarity hypothesis. Our statement below is not, strictly speaking, a revision of Festinger's hypothesis, but a restatement in the sense that it is a statement of what Festinger probably meant. Regardless of what Festinger meant, however, the following seems to be a more accurate and useful statement of preferences for social comparison choice: given a range of possible persons for comparison, someone who should be close to one's own performance or opinion, given his standing on characteristics related to and predictive of performance or opinion, will be chosen for comparison.

In the introduction to this chapter, it was noted that Hypotheses I, III, and VIII would be of central concern in the restatement of social comparison theory. We have considered modifications of Hypotheses I and III. We shall discuss Hypothesis VIII only briefly and note simply that it is entirely consistent with our restatement of Hypothesis III. While Hypothesis VIII is phrased in a negative way, that is, it considers when the tendency to compare decreases, it can be stated positively as follows: when persons are perceived to be similar to oneself on attributes related to an opinion or performance, the tendency to compare with them increases. In fact, if Hypotheses III and VIII are read together, it can be seen that the most economical statement of social comparison preferences is, as we stated above, that the individual will prefer comparing himself with those who are perceived to be similar on attributes that are related to their opinion or performance level.

This restatement of the similarity hypothesis has a certain logic to it in light of several considerations from attribution theory. An attempt will be made at this point to consider in detail the way in which comparison with similar others reduces ambiguity about one's ability or opinion relative to other comparison choices. We will discuss ability comparison first and then opinion comparison.

The evaluation of abilities

Often others who are different on attributes affecting performance are different either in ways that make them likely to perform better or in ways that make them likely to perform worse. That is, their overall standing on nonability attributes affecting performance could be such to make them advantaged with respect to oneself or disadvantaged. Let us take running to be the ability in question. The advantaged other might be younger (or older), more practiced, more knowledgeable about techniques, and might perform on a fast track. Whatever their particular combination of attributes, we can imagine an array of comparison persons who range from having inferior standing on attributes affecting performance, to having equal or similar attributes related to performance, to having a decided advantage over the individual. Let us consider the various comparison choices the individual could make, the possible outcomes of these various comparisons, and the implications for ability these outcomes would have. Then we can consider the individual's needs and identify which comparison choices seem to best serve those needs.

If the individual compared with others who were relatively advantaged on attributes related to performance, the most likely outcome would be that he would perform at a lower level, although it is possible that he would perform equally or better.

In the likely event that his performance was worse, the implications for his ability are ambiguous. Perhaps his ability is low. Low ability is one possible explanation for the inferior performance. But, following Kelley, this cause can be discounted since there is another plausible cause present, namely, the superior nonability attributes of the comparison person. It is equally likely, then, that the individual's ability level is medium or average. If the individual did equally well or better than advantaged others, he could conclude that his ability was quite high, on the basis of the augmentation principle. His relatively low standing on the relevant nonability factors are regarded as inhibitory causes.

If the individual compared himself with others who were similar to him on attributes related to ability, he might expect to perform at an equal level. If he did perform at an equal level, he could conclude that his ability was medium or average. On the other hand, he would have clear evidence that his ability was poor if he performed less well than a similar other, and convincing evidence that his ability was superior if he performed better than the similar other.

If the individual compared with someone who was relatively disadvantaged in terms of the attributes he possessed that were relevant to performance, the individual should expect to perform better. If he did, there would be ambiguity about the meaning of his performance. The performance differential could be attributable to his having superior ability or to his relative advantage in terms of nonability factors affecting performance. Thus the comparison outcome has ambiguous implications for his performance. Perhaps it is good or superior, but perhaps it is only medium. If the individual should only equal, or perhaps do worse than the disadvantaged other, he would be pushed hard toward the conclusion that his ability is low. Again, the discounting and augmentation principles are relevant here.

Given the three comparison choices (with others who are advantaged, equal, or disadvantaged) and the three possible outcomes (the individual performs better, the same as, or worse than the comparison persons) and their likelihood or occurrence, what can we conclude about comparison choice? If we assume that the individual is driven to "evaluate" his ability in the objective sense suggested by Festinger's hypothesis, it seems clear that comparing himself with similar others is the most appropriate comparison. The most likely outcomes of comparing upward or downward (i.e., with advantaged or disadvantaged others) have ambiguous implications for ability. Furthermore, there is no way for the individual to discover conclusively that he is poor if he compares upward and no way to discover convincingly that he is superior if he compares downward. On the other hand, any comparison outcome yields meaningful information if he compares with a similar other. If he is superior, average, or inferior, that state of affairs should be made clear through comparing himself with others who are matched on factors affecting performance.

There is strong support for the similarity hypothesis for ability comparison in a recent study by Zanna, Goethals, and Hill (1975). These investigators were interested in testing Festinger's hypothesis that people prefer comparing with similar others versus the hypothesis that people prefer comparing with others who are best off or standard setters. There has been a considerable degree of support generated for the hypothesis that comparing with best-off others is a top comparison priority. Most of this evidence has come out of the rank-order paradigm developed by Wheeler and others (see Latané, 1966a). Zanna *et al.* suggested that this paradigm does not offer a fair test of what Festinger's Corollary IIIA really seemed to mean. Subjects can compare with others who have similar performance scores, but they are not able to compare with others who are similar on characteristics related to performance score. It is this latter kind of comparison that seems critical in social comparison. The Zanna *et al.* study gave subjects an opportunity to make this kind of comparison and weighed subjects' desire to do so with their tendency to make competing comparisons.

The procedure was fairly straightforward. Male and female undergraduates took a test supposedly designed to measure an underlying ability at which, they were told, either males or females excelled. The test items were actually taken from a practice booklet for the Miller Analogies Test. In the females-excel condition, the test was described as

a one of "verbal acuity," which included testing the ability to understand linguistic relationships as well as testing vocabulary level. It was stated that typically women did better on the test. In the males-excel condition, the test was described as a test of "logical reasoning," including the ability to understand conceptual and abstract relationships. It was stated that men typically performed better on this test. In sum, the design was a 2 (male subjects versus female subjects) × 2 (males excel versus females excel) factorial.

After the subjects took the test, they were given an ambiguous performance score and told that they would have the opportunity to see the performance scores of other groups that had taken the test. The subjects were then given a "Normative Group Data Order Sheet," which listed various groups of students and nonstudents. One column contained seven groups of male students of various majors or professional programs (e.g., male history majors, male prelaw students) as well as seven groups of male nonstudents categorized by their work (e.g., male sales workers, male clerical workers, male service workers). The other column contained the same listings for females. Subjects were told that they could see normative data concerning how well each group had done. They were asked to indicate the group whose test-score distributions they most wanted to see and the group they wanted to see second most.

Of major interest was the extent to which subjects chose to see the scores of members of their own sex and the extent to which they chose to see the scores of members of the standard-setting sex. In conditions where the subjects' own sex excelled, they could compare with both similar others and standard setters by comparing with a group of their own sex. In conditions where the opposite sex excelled, matters were more complicated. Subjects had to choose whether to give priority to comparing with similar others or priority to comparing with standard setters. The similarity hypothesis would suggest that these subjects would compare first with reference groups of their own sex. If, on the other hand, subjects gave first priority to comparing with standard setters, they would compare first with the opposite sex.

The results of the experiment were quite clear. There was an overwhelming tendency, even in conditions in which the opposite sex excelled, to compare with a same-sex reference group. Ninety-seven percent of the subjects (all but two) compared first with a reference group of the same sex. Subjects in the opposite-sex excels conditions did show a secondary preference to compare with standard setters, but it was clear that the first priority was to compare with similar others. Other data supporting the similarity hypothesis were that of the subjects who had a major or occupational plan identical to one on the "order form," 87 percent requested a group with that major or occupational plan on their first choice. All of these subjects who chose to see an opposite-sex reference group on their second choice chose to see the group with that major or career plan. Finally, all but one of the first-choice and one of the second-choice comparisons were with students rather that nonstudents.

Perhaps these results imply something about subjects' conception of ability. One's ability can be defined in either absolute or relative terms. One can consider how well one does compared to all other performers, or one can define one's ability in terms of how well one performs compared to others who are matched on attributes related to performance. The overwhelming prevalence of comparing with similar others suggests that in many instances people define their ability in relative terms. If sex is related to performance, a difference in performance level between oneself and a member of the opposite sex is not ambiguous as far as one's absolute ability level is concerned, but it is ambiguous as to its implications for one's ability relative to others of the same sex. It is the latter that subjects want to evaluate.

The evaluation of opinions

Demonstrating the rationale for comparing with similar others is somewhat more complicated in the case of opinions. Again, we can consider whom the individual might compare with and what the possible outcomes of the comparison might be. Then on the basis of these outcomes and the individual's needs, we can consider what the most useful comparison strategies are.

Before beginning this discussion, it is crucial to recall the familiar distinction in the attitude and opinion literature between a belief (a potentially verifiable assertion about the true nature of an entity) and a value (a preference or liking or disliking for an entity). The processes of social comparison that we will discuss below will differ for the two kinds of opinions.

The treatment of opinions in attribution theory, or at least Kelley's version of the treatment, seems to focus on beliefs rather than values. Kelley suggests that the attributional problem for the naive person is to decide whether his "perceptions, judgments, and evaluations of the world are *correct* or *true*" and that the wise man is he who knows and knows that he knows (emphasis added). Deciding whether an opinion is. "correct" seems relevant only for the evaluation of beliefs. Beliefs, but not values, can be true or false, correct or incorrect.

A quite different evaluational issue is involved in the case of values. The person wants to know whether the entity is one that will better his interests and outcomes. He may tentatively decide that he will enjoy working in a particular city or owning a particular record, and he needs to determine whether that opinion is correct. He is not concerned with whether the city or the record is objectively good. He is concerned with whether he will profit from transaction with that entity and with whether his predictions about what he will enjoy or what will give him positive or negative outcomes are true. Deciding whether a belief is true and deciding whether an evaluation or decision is likely to further one's interests are very different issues and involve different social comparison processes.

Let us first consider the social comparison of beliefs. The individual's need to evaluate the correctness of his beliefs is based on his uncertainty about whether the beliefs are correct. In terms of attribution theory (Kelley, 1967, 1973), he is uncertain as to whether his belief is entity-caused, that is, whether it accurately describes the objects in the environment with which it is concerned or whether, on the other hand, it is person-caused, that is, whether it is a biased appraisal of the environment caused by the individual's needs or values or wishes. In other words, the individual will know that his beliefs are correct if they can confidently make an entity attribution for it (Kelley, 1973, p. 112).

If the individual compared himself with others who were similar on factors affecting the belief, such as their basic values, their interests, and their needs, he would probably expect them to agree. Several studies have suggested that people usually feel confident that their beliefs are correct and expect similar people in particular to agree (e.g., Goethals, 1972). If the similar others do agree, how does this affect the individual's confidence that he can make an entity attribution about his opinion? It seems that the discounting principle that operates to make him less than perfectly confident of his own opinion would operate as well for attributions he makes about the others' agreement. That is, the individual must discount the entity as a cause for his own opinion to the extent that his own needs and values are plausible causes for that opinion. Whatever the plausibility of his own belief being person-caused, the other's belief is equally likely to be person-caused if he is similar. Whatever the possible flaws in his own judgment, they are equally likely to distort the judgments of similar others. If the entity must be discounted as a cause for his own belief, so must it be discounted as a cause for similar beliefs of similar others. Therefore, the individual gains little information about the veridicality of his belief if a similar other agrees.

On the other hand, if the similar other disagrees, the individual must become less confident that his belief is entity-caused. This is based on consensus considerations. If the effect (the person's belief about the entity) does not covary with the entity across persons, it cannot confidently be attributed to the entity. This application of the covariation principle would hold unless there was some way to discount the entity as a cause of the belief of the disagreeing consensus. If some plausible internal cause could be located for the others' belief, the individual might be able to discount the entity as a cause and thus discount the validity of the other's beliefs. However, since he is similar, it will be difficult to account for the belief difference in terms of an internal characteristic that the consensus has but that he does not have. In short, the disagreement of similar persons is fairly persuasive

evidence that the individual is incorrect. Thus we see that the individual who compares with a similar and co-oriented consensus cannot be much more confident if the consensus agrees, but he must reduce his confidence if the consensus disagrees.

What conclusions can the individual draw about the validity of his beliefs on the basis of comparison with dissimilar others? If dissimilar others agree, the individual would seem to be in a position where he can be highly confident of his opinions. The dissimilar others' opinion cannot be attributed to the same potentially biasing characteristics that the individual himself possesses. Also, if the individual assumes that similar others have the same opinion as himself, the indication that different others agree as well supplies evidence suggesting a very broad consensus.

If the dissimilar others disagreed, the person could easily dismiss the other's belief as being due to their personal characteristics. There is no data pattern that would necessarily support this attribution. But the individual would be motivated to account for the disagreement. The others' dissimilar values would seem to be a reasonably plausible explanation for the belief difference. Of course, the individual could also account for the difference by admitting that he is wrong. But, as Heider (1958) notes, there is a tendency for people to assume that their own responses accurately mirror the environment and that others' responses, when they are divergent, are person-caused. This assumption is facilitated when the others are dissimilar.

Given these possible outcomes of comparing oneself with similar and dissimilar others, what can we say about comparison choice? First, it does not seem as clear in the case of opinions as it did with abilities that comparison with similar others is the strategy that maximizes information gain. Agreement from a similar other seems ambiguous, although their disagreement seems informative. Just the opposite is true for dissimilar others. Their agreement seems informative, but their disagreement does not. It seems that if the individual were genuinely concerned with evaluating the correctness of his opinion, or seeing whether it was attributable to the entity, he would have to compare himself with both similar and dissimilar others. On the basis of the present analysis, we cannot predict whether he would give first priority to comparing himself with similar or dissimilar others.

Let us now consider the social comparison of those opinions that include evaluations of entities rather than mere description, that is, values. Suppose the individual is trying to decide which of two novels to take with him on a short vacation. He is familiar with the authors of both books from other works they have published. He makes the tentative evaluation that he would enjoy the book by author A more than the one by author B. If he compared with a similar other and found him to agree, his confidence in his opinion would be strengthened. Since the other has the same values and interests, his opinion that author A is more enjoyable should make the individual considerably more confident that he will enjoy author A's novel more than author B's. If a dissimilar other agrees, the individual learns little, it seems, about the adequacy of his own judgment. The fact that someone with different values related to liking for literature has the same preference seems at best irrelevant to whether or not the individual would prefer the author's work. In fact, the individual may actually reduce his confidence if he finds that someone with divergent values has made the same choice. He may reason that if someone with different values likes author A's work, he himself may find it quite tedious. An experiment by Berscheid (1966) suggests that the individual may actually change his evaluation if he finds that someone with dissimilar values agrees.

This analysis suggests that when the opinion in question is a value, the individual learns relatively little from agreement with a dissimilar other but will find that the agreement of a similar other lends him considerable confidence. In cases where the comparison person disagrees, we would expect to find the individual drawing the same conclusions as he did with belief comparison. The disagreement of a similar other should markedly reduce the individual's confidence. The disagreement of a dissimilar other can easily be attributed to the other's values. In any case, what the dissimilar other likes is not particularly relevant to what the individuals will like. In sum, the opinion of a similar other is informative to the individual whether he agrees or disagrees. The opinion of a dissimilar other is not particularly informative in either case. The implications for comparison choice seem quite clear. If the individual is concerned with evaluating a value (a preference for an entity), he should compare himself with similar others. Given the goal of information maximization, this choice has the higher payoff.

We have been considering a limited class of values, simple statements of one's own liking or preference. There are obviously others. Often, values are statements of what is good or true or beautiful. When making such a statement, one is doing more than stating one's preferences. One is making assertions about the true or actual qualities of entities. It is worth considering the possibility that in terms of social comparison these values work more like beliefs than preferences. For example, consider the value "equality is good" or "equality is more important than freedom." The individual might be interested in finding whether a dissimilar other agreed. If he did agree, the individual could rule out personal bias and know that equality really is important. Therefore, he might show an interest in the values of dissimilar others that seems characteristic of belief comparison but not preference-value comparison.

Most opinions probably represent a rather complex mixture of underlying beliefs, basic values, and simple likes or dislikes. This would seem to be true for opinions such as the following: the space program is a waste of money; the president is doing a good job; busing should be used to achieve racial balance in schools; Robert Redford is good-looking; Chris Evert is an excellent tennis player; Einstein revolutionized physics; abortion is immoral. In the comparative appraisal of these opinions, there can be considerable shifting about as to whether the individual regards them as assertions about the actual qualities of the entities or simply as his statement of his personal evaluation of them. For example, an argument over whether Bergman is a better director than Antonioni may change from one where the issue is defined as being one of facts and objective truth to one that is simply a matter of personal preference.

An exploratory study on social comparison choices for opinions has been conducted by Goethals and Ebling (1975) to try to determine to what extent people would compare their opinions with others who were similar on characteristics that were related to the opinion issue. The subjects were high school seniors. The experimenter explained to them that the study concerned impression formation and the ways people form attitudes about other people. The subjects were first asked to indicate the importance they attached to eight phrases that could be used to describe a person (e.g., is loyal and dependable to friends, reacts spontaneously) by rank-ordering them. The experimenter suggested that he was interested in seeing how different people with different values made judgments about other people.

At this point, the subjects were shown a videotape of two college seniors who discussed various aspects of their college careers, indicating what they had found valuable and enjoyable, as well as speculating about their goals for the future. The subjects were asked to indicate which of the two stimulus persons they liked more or would prefer to have as a friend. Then the subjects were told that they would have an opportunity to see the opinion of another person before making a final decision. The experimenter explained that he had on file the opinions of many other people who had seen the tapes previously. He told them that they could select the person whose opinion they would see by indicating what they wanted the other person's priorities to be on the list of eight characteristics they had ranked before. In other words, they were told to write down a rank order of characteristics that they wanted the other person to have. The experimenter stated that he would get them the opinion of someone who had that rank order or one as close to it as possible.

The procedure used to analyze the data was to calculate the rank-order correlation between the subjects' priorities and the priorities they specified the comparison person to have. The data showed an overwhelming tendency toward comparison with similar others. Forty-nine percent of the subjects had positive correlations between their own rank and the other person's that were significant at the

.01 level. These were correlations of .88 or more. Eighty-two percent of the subjects had correlations of .57 or more, significant at the .10 level. Eleven percent of the correlations did not approach significance, r between .29 and $-.12$. Finally, 6 percent of the subjects indicated a desire to compare with dissimilar others whose rank orders were correlated significantly in the negative direction. In sum, more than 80 percent of the subjects chose to see the opinion of someone whose values were similar to their own as measured by the correlation between them. The remainder chose either to see the opinion of someone whose values were totally independent of their own, or were actually opposite of their own.

In choosing a comparison person, the subjects in this experiment were more concerned with evaluating a preference than a belief. They were not concerned with whether their judgments were objectively accurate. Given this orientation, the strong tendency to compare with similar others makes sense. However, it follows from our discussion of beliefs versus values that a concern with belief accuracy might lead subjects to compare with dissimilar others in an effort to correct their beliefs for bias.

There is some evidence from an experiment by Reckman and Goethals (1973) that when subjects are, in fact, concerned with making accurate judgments, they do show a tendency to compare with dissimilar others. The experimenter explained to the subjects that the ongoing experimental session was preliminary and that a number of them would be asked to return for a second session during which they would join several others in watching and discussing a person on a videotape. The subjects' first task was to complete a fictitious test of interpersonal judgment style, described as a measure of differences in the ways people go about judging each other. Afterward, the experimenter described in some detail the nature of the second session. In the accuracy conditions, he said the subjects would see a tape of a college student discussing several topics with other students. After watching the tape, they would be asked to make specific judgments about the central student. They might be asked to predict his major academic interests, his career plans, or his attitudes on controversial issues. It was emphasized that the experimenter already knew the answers to these questions and he was interested in seeing how accurate the members of each group could be in making individual decisions about such issues after discussing the issues with the group. In the congeniality conditions, the subjects were told that they would discuss questions such as whether the student on the videotape was likable and whether he seemed to be a good leader. The experimenter emphasized that there was no right answer to these questions and that he was not as concerned about the subjects' actual judgments as he was in discovering what factors in the group contributed to congenial discussion and cooperative interaction.

Then the subjects were told that they would have a chance to indicate a preference for the kind of person that they would most like to have in their group during the second session. They were to indicate how similar to or different from themselves they would like that person to be. It was explained very carefully to the subjects that two given profiles from the interpersonal judgment test could differ from each other very slightly or a great deal, indicating similar or different interpersonal judgment styles. They were asked to indicate, on an 8-point scale, how much they wanted the other's profile to differ from their own. The end points of the scale were labeled "highly similar" and "highly dissimilar."

The results indicated that subjects in the accuracy conditions showed a stronger mean preference for comparing with dissimilar others. Furthermore, twelve of seventeen subjects (71%) in the accuracy conditions had a score of 4 or higher on the 8-point similarity scale, indicating a preference for a group member who was at least somewhat dissimilar. Only three of sixteen subjects (19%) had scores as high as 4 in the congeniality condition. This experiment provides some evidence for a tendency to compare with dissimilar others when being accurate is important.

Self-esteem and Social Comparison

Although we discussed earlier the importance of a need to believe that one's opinions are correct and one's abilities are good, thus far we have considered only the need to maximize information gain about one's opinions and abilities as a determinant of social comparison choice. In this section, some consideration will be given to the way in which the need to protect one's self-esteem may affect comparison choices and interpretations of comparison outcomes.

In terms of ability validation, the individual's need to think positively of his performances, and hence his abilities, should push him toward making those comparison choices that will provide him with evidence that his performances are better than those of others. It would seem that the most straightforward way of doing this would be to compare with others who are relatively disadvantaged in terms of their standing on nonability attributes that affect performance. Although no study has demonstrated this kind of downward comparison, another kind has been demonstrated in several studies using the rank-order paradigm. The germinal study, done by Hakmiller (1966), showed that when individuals' evaluations of their standing on a personality trait were threatened, they selected from a range of possible comparison choices persons whose scores were lower than their own. Presumably, they were seeking to find convincing evidence that they were indeed superior to those who were less well off on the trait. Their comparison choices represented an attempt to salvage a positive self-appraisal in a situation in which that view was threatened. They wanted to collect evidence that others were significantly worse. Wheeler (1970) has characterized the subjects' presumed rationale as follows: "Even a hawk is an eagle among crows" (p. 72).

Although Hakmiller's study provided some support for the notion of defensive downward comparison, the attributional approach outlined here raises questions that cannot be answered by his study or by others using the rank-order paradigm. Several additional complexities need to be considered. First, recalling our earlier discussion of the conclusions that the individual might draw from the outcomes of comparing with advantaged, equal, and disadvantaged others, we noted that if the individual compared with advantaged others, he could not draw the conclusion that he is inferior. Even if his score is less than that of a superior other, the interpretation is ambiguous. The differential can be attributed to the comparison person's standing on the nonability factors affecting performance. On the other hand, if the individual compared downward, there would be no conclusive way to decide that he is superior. If his performance score is better, the differential is attributable to nonability factors. Furthermore, if the individual compares downward, he risks obtaining conclusive evidence that he is inferior. If he compares upward, he may find that he is superior. Thus it would seem that the individual has little to gain and much to lose by comparing downward and much to gain and little to lose by comparing upward. How then can we sensibly predict downward comparison?

First, we must recall that the most likely outcome of downward comparison is finding that the other has a lower score. The most likely outcome of upward comparison, especially in the mind of the threatened or insecure individual, is finding that the comparison person has a higher score. Other comparison outcomes are probably not salient. Given these as the most probable comparison outcomes, the individual seems to gain more from comparing downward. He can infer medium or high ability if he scores better, whereas he must infer medium or low ability if he compares upward and finds himself with a lower score. It seems easier for the individual to convince himself that a positive instance of superiority (a higher score) means something than to convince himself that a negative instance (a lower score) means nothing.

Another consideration is that while the meaning of having performed better than a disadvantaged other seems ambiguous, the person concerned with protecting his self-esteem may engage in distorted interpretations of that comparison outcome. His desire, it would seem, would be to convince himself that his higher score really is indicative of a high level of ability. He can do this by distorting the standing of the comparison person on the nonability factors affecting performance. If the individual can perceive disadvantaged others to be more advantaged than they actually are, he can convince himself they are equals when they are actually

inferior. An example might be a father of two young boys who gets a "boost" out of being able to throw a football further than his sons. The more he can distort or minimize their disadvantage in terms of size and experience, the more he can take his relatively superior tosses as evidence of high ability.

The tendency to view others' standing on nonability factors affecting performance as more advantaged than it actually is, is probably a pervasive tendency. It would be useful not only in the case of downward comparison. Whether a person compares upward, downward, or with similars, and whether his performances are better, the same, or worse than those of comparison persons, the interpretations he will place on his performance are always more positive to the extent that he can subjectively enhance the others' standing on nonability factors affecting performance.

This discussion emphasizes the person's assessment of the role of nonability factors that might affect other people's performances. Jones and Nisbett's theory of actor-observer differences in attribution (1971) is relevant here. Jones and Nisbett contended that an observer tends to attribute an actor's responses more to dispositional causes, such as ability, than to external causes, while the actor tends to attribute responses more to external factors, such as task difficulty. Thus it may run counter to the Jones and Nisbett thesis to suggest that the person will give much consideration to nonability factors affecting a comparison person's performance. Their argument would allow for consideration of dispositional nonability factors that affect performance, such as effort, but would clearly exclude external factors. Nevertheless, we believe that as the individual casts about for ways to diminish the other's performance, it will not take him long to think of attributing it to facilitating external causes. The kind of validation-directed social comparison process considered here may be an exception to the rule suggested by Jones and Nisbett.

While in ability evaluation, the individual desires to obtain evidence that his performances are better than those of other people, the individual concerned with validating an opinion is interested in discovering that his opinions are the same as those of others.

The most straightforward way of doing this would be to compare oneself with others who are similar on attributes affecting the opinion. In ability comparison, the evaluation motive seemed to push people toward comparison with similar others, while the validation motive seemed to push them toward comparing downward. With opinion comparison, both the need for accurate evaluation and the need for esteem are likely to be satisfied through comparing with similar others.

One qualification of this statement, discussed above, is that people may want to compare with dissimilar others in objectively evaluating beliefs. Agreement from dissimilar others on beliefs is highly influential. It may be that the person concerned with esteem might also compare with dissimilars in an attempt to obtain their impressive belief cross-validation. Of course, since dissimilars are unlikely to agree, the individual might not take the risk of comparing with them. He might simply extrapolate from the agreement of similar others and conclude that dissimilars agree even though he has no specific evidence for this conclusion.

Another way for the individual to supply himself with the perception that the consensus for his opinion is high would be to distort the similar others' standing on attributes affecting opinion so as to perceive it as less similar to his own standing than it actually is. In general, he would like to view as broad and varied whatever consensus there is supporting his belief, so that discounting the entity as a cause of his and their opinion is not facilitated by there being a plausible internal cause that is present for all of them. In other words, if all who agree are similar on some attribute affecting opinion, it might be easy to discount the entity as a cause of their opinion.

Distorting the diversity of those who agree so as to inflate the perceived consensus for a belief can be accompanied by a related distortion about those who disagree. Essentially, one would like to dismiss the opinions of those who disagree as being person-caused. The individual can more easily attribute those disagreeing opinions to the personal biases of the disagreers if he can find some biasing characteristic that they all share. While he will see the disagreers as quite different from himself, he will perceive them as being quite similar among themselves. Ideally, the individual will perceive one critical biasing characteristic that is a plausible internal cause for the disagreers' opinion. The he can discount the entity as a cause for the disagreers' opinion and feel more confident that his own opinion is appropriately entity-caused.

These positions regarding the distortions of the personal characteristics of others that might be involved in social comparison are speculative. Research is needed to verify them.

REFERENCES

Berscheid, E. Opinion change and communicator-communicatee similarity and dissimilarity. *Journal of Personality and Social Psychology*, 1966, *4*, 670–680.

Festinger, L. A theory of social comparison processes. *Human Relations*, 1954, *7*, 117–140.

Goethals, G. R. Consensus and modality in the attribution process: The role of similarity and information. *Journal of Personality and Social Psychology*, 1972, *21*, 84–92.

Goethals, G. R., & Ebling, T. A study of opinion comparison. Unpublished manuscript, Williams College, 1975.

Hakmiller, K. L. Threat as a determinant of downward comparison. *Journal of Experimental Social Psychology*, 1966, *Supplement 1*, 32–39.

Heider, F. Social perception and phenomenal causality. *Psychological Review*, 1944, *51*, 358–373.

Heider, F. *The psychology of interpersonal relations*. New York: Wiley, 1958.

Jellison, J., & Davis, D. Relationship between perceived ability and attitude extremity. *Journal of Personality and Social Psychology*, 1973, *27*, 430–436.

Jones, E. E., & Nisbett, R. E. *The actor and the observer: Divergent perceptions of the causes of behavior.* Morristown, N.J.: General Learning Press, 1971.

Kelley, H. H. Attribution theory in social psychology. In D. Levine (Ed.), *Nebraska symposium on motivation.* University of Nebraska Press, 1967.

Kelley, H. H. *Attribution in social interaction.* Morristown, N.J.: General Learning Press, 1971.

Kelley, H. H. *Causal schemata and the attribution process.* Morristown, N.J: General Learning Press, 1972.

Kelley, H. H. The process of causal attribution. *American Psychologist*, 1973, *28*, 107–128.

Latané, B. (Ed.). Studies in social comparison. *Journal of Experimental Social Psychology*, 1966, Supplement 1. (a)

Latané, B. Studies in social comparison—Introduction and overview. *Journal of Experimental Social Psychology*, 1966, *Supplement 1*, 1–5. (b)

Reckman, R. F., & Goethals, G. R. Deviancy and group-orientation as determinants of group composition preferences. *Sociometry*, 1973, *36*, 419–423.

Weiner, B., Frieze, I., Kukla, A., Reed, L., Rest, S., & Rosenbaum, R. M. *Perceiving the causes of success and failure*. Morristown, N.J.: General Learning Press, 1971.

Wheeler, L. *Interpersonal influence*. Boston: Allyn & Bacon, 1970.

Wheeler, L. Motivation as a determinant of upward comparison. *Journal of Experimental Social Psychology*, 1966, Supplement 1, 27–31.

Wheeler, L., Shaver, K. G., Jones, R. A., Goethals, G. R., Cooper, J., Robinson, J. E., Gruder, C. L., & Butzine, K. W. Factors determining the choice of comparison other. *Journal of Experimental Social Psychology*, 1969, 5, 219–232.

Zanna, M. P., Goethals, G. R., & Hill, J. F. Evaluating a sex related ability: Social comparison with similar others and standard setters. *Journal of Experimental Social Psychology*, 1975, 11, 86–93.

Pleasure and Pain in Social Comparison

Philip Brickman and Ronnie Janoff Bulman*

Dear Ann Landers: I am the mother of identical twins . . . I never felt that strangers were "picking my kids

to pieces" . . . (but) proud that people cared enough to look for identifying characteristics.

Dear N.O.: You may be the mother of identical twins, but I AM an identical twin and can report first-hand

what it's like to be victimized by well-meaning strangers who are constantly examining twins for

"differences" . . . My original advice still stands. The mother of twins should permit NO comparisons

whatever.—Excerpted from Chicago Daily News, March 10, 1977

From Festinger's paper on social comparison (1954), three general postulates are usually derived: first, that people have a drive to compare themselves with others in order to evaluate their own opinions and abilities; second, that people prefer to compare themselves with similar others because information derived from comparison with similar others is more likely to be useful; and, third, that people prefer to compare themselves with superior others, either because they prefer to see themselves as similar to those who are above them or because information derived from upward comparison is more likely to be useful.

Considerable evidence supports each of these postulates (see Latané, 1966), and it is not our purpose to contest their validity. However, it is our purpose to argue that the opposite of each of these postulates is also true: that people have a desire to avoid social comparison, that they prefer comparison with dissimilar rather than similar others, and that they prefer to compare downward rather than upward. These propositions will be derived from a consideration of the simple fact that comparison involves rather substantial costs for the parties involved.

In considering pleasure and pain in social comparison, we are shifting the traditional focus of social comparison theory. Indeed, for us, the interesting problem of social comparison begins at the point where past research on social comparison has typically seen the problem as ending: when an individual knows both his or her own position and the general distribution of positions in the group. It should not be assumed that merely because people know the distribution of scores in a group (e.g.,

* Northwestern University, USA

test grades in a class) and their own standing in this distribution, they know everything that is to be gained from social comparison. First, they do not yet know their standing relative to particular others, such as their friends, their roommates, people of their own sex versus the opposite sex, people in their quiz section versus other sections. Second, they do not know how their performance compares in detail with those of others—whether their answers to particular items were correct or not, and whether other people did well on similar or different items from the ones they did well on. Finally, no matter what else people know about their current standing relative to others, the question remains as to how they will stand relative to others in a day or a week, or whenever the next occasion for comparison is, and who they would prefer to compare themselves with at that time. In other words, like Radloff (1966), we see social comparison as an ongoing process rather than a need that occurs and is satisfied at a single point in time.

Moreover, we see social comparison as ordinarily taking place through social interaction, and indeed as an almost inevitable element of social interaction, whether it be competition, cooperation, or simple discussion. The interesting question for us is how people seek social comparison information through social interaction of various sorts while at the same time working to avoid the psychological and social costs that are inflicted by social comparison. If we limit ourselves to studying how people seek social comparison without social interaction, we limit ourselves to studying the very special case in which comparison is both highly simplified and virtually cost-free. In the research that follows, we infer a desire to avoid social comparison from a variety of different indicators, including both reports that a person would not enjoy or be satisfied with a situation and indications that the situation has made the person less satisfied with his or her own state.

The present chapter is primarily concerned with how people feel about themselves and their own merits, or the social comparison of abilities, rather than the case in which people compare their attitudes or opinions about third parties or the world in general. It remains for future research to test whether there is also a drive to avoid social comparison of

attitudes and opinions. We suspect there is, however, and not merely from the fact that people will be uncomfortable if they discover disagreement (in France, asking a person's politics may be a very personal question). Attitudes and opinions are also a matter of skill, the end product of complex learning, sometimes called socialization (a word that gives all the credit to the socializing agent and none to the person who masters or improvises appropriate responses). In order to be a radical or a conservative, it is not enough that one has learned simply to check the appropriate ends of various scales. The opinions involved in being a radical (or a vegetarian or a movie fan) are complex and subtle. What they are and when and how they are expressed reveal a lot about how well informed their holders are, how articulate they are, how motivated and committed they are—all positively valued attributes on which people may feel superior or inferior to one another. The social psychology of attitudes would probably be enriched by looking at attitude learning as a matter of skill acquisition rather than simply a question of acquiescence. In any event, to the extent that people are motivated to avoid social comparison of abilities, they will also in many instances be motivated to avoid social comparison of attitudes and opinions.

In this chapter, we first review evidence that people are motivated to avoid social comparison; we then consider what advantages might accrue from a general strategy of minimizing social comparison; and finally we propose a simple balance of forces model for predicting when people will prefer to seek and when they will prefer to avoid comparison.

Norms Concerning Social Comparison

A desire to avoid social comparison can actually serve as an alternative explanation for certain earlier results that have usually been interpreted as evidence of a drive for social comparison, as first pointed out by Brickman and Berman (1971). A condition in which subjects lack definitive information about their own standing is compared to a condition in which subjects have this information (e.g., Gerard, 1963; Singer & Shockley, 1965). It is found that subjects are less likely to prefer the company of another person when they know the meaning of their own test scores than when they do not know. This is usually interpreted as indicating that their desire for social comparison has been satiated through their having been provided with enough information to evaluate themselves, and thus their need to seek out other people to provide this information has been reduced. Suppose, however, that the effect of giving people more information about their own performance is, first, simply to make the performance and the information about it more salient. In this case, the subject may anticipate that the first thing he or she and another person waiting together would do would be to exchange scores and make other social comparisons. If the subject would just as soon not exchange scores (assuming, for example, that one or the other of them would be embarrassed by the results of the comparison), the condition in which this exchange of scores looms as most likely and most definitive would be exactly the condition in which subjects would be most likely to prefer waiting alone rather than waiting in another's company.

How can we account for the fact that this alternative explanation and the desire to avoid social comparison in general have been so conspicuously absent from research and theory on social comparison to date? The most likely explanation is that the research so far has been largely oriented to explore rational information-seeking behavior in humans. One seeks social comparison, according to Festinger, to obtain an accurate appraisal of his or her abilities or opinions. Since more can be learned from similar, slightly superior others, similar upward comparisons will be sought. The motives that oppose social comparison are in the main hedonic and social, rather than matters of rational information seeking. It is somewhat ironic that Festinger's social comparison theory (1954) may be biased in its overemphasis on a rational process, while his dissonance theory (1957) may be biased in the preeminence it gives to an essentially irrational process in human behavior.

A related reason for the prior neglect of avoidance of social comparison may be methodological. Virtually all research testing comparison processes has been conducted in the experimental laboratory, and it can be argued that there exist normative pressures in such an environment that emphasize information seeking, consistency, and rationality (see Rosenthal & Rosnow, 1969; Brickman & Davis, 1975). Subjects' concern for evaluation by the experimenter leads them to place great emphasis on obtaining the information that will enable them to achieve the best possible performance. Furthermore, subjects probably believe that experimenters will evaluate them more favorably if they emphasize their curiosity. This belief may lie behind the fact that in laboratory tests, people indicate that they prefer to hear arguments that are novel or that contradict their own views, while in field studies, listening to a speech is much more likely by people for whom the arguments of that speech will be familiar and supportive of their own views (Freedman & Sears, 1965).

More generally, previous research has tended to make it both impossible and unnecessary to avoid social comparison. In telling subjects that there is an initial distribution of abilities in the group, some higher and some lower than theirs, or an initial distribution of opinions in the group, some similar and some dissimilar to theirs, the experimenter has already made it too late for the subjects to effectively avoid social comparison, since the subjects have already been forced to confront certain uncomfortable discrepancies. Even if people would like to avoid further comparison, they are often not even given this option but simply required to choose which others they would like to compare themselves with. Finally, avoidance of further comparison is made unnecessary by the fact that such comparison often involves no more than seeing someone else's score or reading a pamphlet, with none of the social costs involved in confronting other people who may be embarrassed either for themselves or for the subject.

The essential problem with social comparison may be put very simply. If two people compare themselves on a valued dimension, the chances are that one will be superior and one will be inferior. Someone will feel bad, and both parties or the collectivity must be concerned with coping with these negative feelings. One of us (P.B.) studied for prelims in graduate school with a very good friend. Sharing a certain sense of humor, we enjoyed laughing before the exam about the hypocrisy with which whoever of us happened to do better on the exam would console the one who had done worse. Fortunately, perhaps, our humor was not tested, since we did equally well on the exam.

Ordinarily, not only is comparing difficult, but even talking about comparing, or not comparing, is difficult. Powers (1975), in an article titled "Can Friendship Survive Success?" reports both on his own reluctance to approach friends who had become much more successful than he and on his observation of similar reluctance on the part of old friends to approach him after he had become successful. Moreover, in response to suggestions that people talk about the problems of social comparison, he cannot even imagine how this would be done:

> How would you tell an old friend that you understand why he is tongue-tied with you, that failure has sometimes infected your spirit too, but you like him anyway, you don't care a damn whether he's done the vast things he wanted to do, that you sympathize with his disappointment and understand the shrinkage of his ambition? This would be such an affront, such a condescending insult, such an unmanning attack on a friend's effort to maintain his own dignity that it is (to me at any rate) unthinkable.

When future contact with someone whose success threatens us is unavoidable, as with a spouse, we are apt to avoid discussing the question of social comparison and criticize them instead for talking with their mouth full or neglecting their chores (Viorst, 1975).

To cope with these problems, norms grow up that restrict or prohibit social comparison, even at the cost of depriving people of interesting and potentially valuable information. Here are a couple of examples close to academic home. A young academician, newly arrived at a university, thought he would let other faculty know his background and interests and encourage them to share theirs with him, by circulating his *vita*. The reaction to this was stony and suspicious, with questions raised about whom he was trying to impress, typical of reactions that may be observed when a norm is violated. The episode probably set back his integration into the

department by at least as many months as he had hoped it would be facilitated.

More recently, members of a graduate program in social psychology were asked to consider the idea of filling out an annual report on whatever in the way of teaching or taking courses, completed or anticipated research, or general commentary that they thought others would be interested in. The report would have been filled out by both students and faculty, and the assembled document would have been distributed to all program members. General discussion quickly turned down the proposal, on the grounds that it was nice to think that a small community did not need such formal communication for members to be informed of what everyone was doing. But the proposal had initially been made by a person who naively took at face value remarks by both students and faculty that they did not, in fact, have complete or convenient information about what others were doing. It cannot be maintained that no useful information would have been conveyed by the report. On the contrary, it would appear that the report would have provided too much information (especially for the students, and also for junior faculty) that would have made salient disruptive problems of social comparison.

Our analysis at this point may also help us to understand both why gossip is so prevalent and why it has such a bad reputation. It is prevalent because it provides people with the social comparison information they need. It is in bad repute because it involves violating norms against such social comparison and creates problems for future interactions. Since gossip involves discussing third parties who are not present, each discussant may acquire useful social comparison information without the risks of embarrassment that would accompany mutual direct self-disclosure. In areas where people are traditionally reluctant to disclose their experiences, such as sex or income, gossip may be the primary way of acquiring desperately needed social comparison information. The information may not be accurate, and its unverified character leaves plenty of room for projection. Lawler (1965) found that managers misperceived the pay of those around them in a way that made them less satisfied with their own pay levels, and it would not be surprising if people's misperceptions of others' sexual activity also serves to make them less satisfied with their own state. People's reliance on gossip is impressive testimony to their willingness to tolerate even inaccurate and painful information rather than run the social comparison costs of seeking a more reliable version. When people do spread even moderately personal information about themselves through a social network—such as by sending out a mimeographed Christmas letter detailing their family's fortunes over the past year—the disclosure is viewed by others with great ambivalence, despite their interest in the information itself. They enjoy satisfying their curiosity about what the senders of the letter have been doing, but resent the social comparison pressure they feel the letter implies.

If there are norms against social comparison, we should expect to find that people are more likely to admit engaging in social comparison when questioned in private than when questioned in public, since norm violations are more likely to be admitted in private than in public. Exactly this has been demonstrated by Berman, Murphy-Berman, and Heil (1976). In their experiment, all subjects overheard the test score of another individual. When questioned in private 100 percent of the subjects admitted to having overheard the score, whereas when questioned in public, only 60 percent admitted knowledge of the other's score. This occurred regardless of whether the subject received an inferior or a superior grade on the same task.

If people are reluctant to engage in mutual self-disclosure, there are in theory two possible reasons for this reluctance: they do not wish to disclose their own position, or they do not wish to hear about the other's position. Which of these is more important? Will the inhibitions on social comparison disappear if people are protected from having to disclose their own scores? Will people not mind having to disclose their own scores so long as they remain ignorant of the position of their recipient? In the case of nonreciprocal disclosure, if the person who learns the other's score feels bad through being inferior or feels elated through being superior, he or she can mask these feelings or temporarily suppress them, so that the dyad as a collectivity does not have to cope with someone's negative feelings.

Whether social comparison would be more acceptable under these conditions was the question asked in an experiment carried out by Donald Kessler.

Experiment I: Preference for Nonreciprocal Social Comparison

Philip Brickman and Donald Kessler

Method

Participants. Subjects were 146 students from seven classrooms of a suburban Chicago high school. Each subject was randomly assigned to one of sixteen conditions. Excess subjects in each condition were randomly discarded to equalize cell totals at eight subjects (four males and four females) in each condition. Subjects were run in classroom groups by two male experimenters.

Design. The full design was a $2 \times 2 \times 2 \times 2$ factorial. The first variable was whether or not the subject anticipated having to reveal his or her own test score to various discussion partners later in the experiment. The second variable was whether or not the subject anticipated learning the test scores of their discussion partners during this interaction. Thus subjects anticipated one of the following: (1) mutual disclosure, or reciprocal comparison, (2) self-disclosure without receiving social comparison information, (3) receiving social comparison information without self-disclosure, (4) neither self-disclosure nor receiving information from the other person.

The remaining two variables referred to whether subjects believed that the distribution of scores in their class was positively skewed or negatively skewed and whether their own score in the distribution was relatively high or relatively low. Since neither of these variables produced any effects on the questions of interest, they will not be discussed further.

Procedure. The experiment was introduced as a study attempting to validate the effects of age and sex on the important ability of symbol discrimination. Subjects were first given four tests of their ability to scan an array of numbers or letters and to correctly note rows in which selected targets occurred. The experimenters then left the room, supposedly to correct the tests. When they returned, they gave each subject a sheet on which was sketched a histogram of the group's scores, along with a report of the subject's own score.

Subjects then read: "One of the things we are especially interested in is how people think and feel about this test, both on their own and after they have had a chance to talk with others who have taken the test. In the second part of this study we want to give you a chance to talk about your reactions to the test with each of your classmates. To do this we will play a game, a kind of musical chairs. When we say 'Go,' each of you will find one other person to talk things over with for a minute or two. When we say 'Go,' again, everyone will find a new partner. We will continue this until everyone has had a chance to talk with almost everyone else."

At this point, subjects were asked to fill out a questionnaire that actually contained the dependent measures, after which the experiment was ended and the experimenters initiated a discussion of its true purposes and the reasons for the methods employed. The circulation period was not actually held.

Manipulations. In the condition in which subjects anticipated a mutual exchange of scores, their written instructions suggested that it is hard to talk if each person is wondering whether to ask how the other did or to tell how he or she did, and "therefore, we would like you to begin your discussions by exchanging your scores and go on from there."

In the condition in which subjects anticipated no disclosure of scores by either party, their written instructions suggested that it is hard to talk if each person is wondering what to say about how the other person did or what to say about how he or she did, and "therefore, we would like you *not*, under any circumstances, to reveal your score or to ask the other person what his or her score was."

In the condition in which subjects anticipated nonreciprocal disclosure of scores, their written instructions suggested that it is hard to talk if people are forced into direct, face-to-face comparison with the person they are talking to. Therefore, "in every group we will always have one person who is asked to reveal the score he or she got on the test, while the other person is always asked *not* to reveal his or her score." In half the cases, people learned that the other person would always be the person to tell his or her score to them while they would always be forbidden to tell their score to the other person. In the other half of the cases, people learned that they would always be the ones to tell their score to the other person, while the other person would always be forbidden to tell his or her score to them.

Measures. After a series of cover questions asking subjects about the test, subjects were asked to rate how satisfied they were with their performance on the test and with their score, whether they would enjoy participating in the discussion part of the study, and how much they were looking forward to talking with other people about the test, both in general and specifically with other people who had scored at the same level as they and other people who had scored at a different level from them. Each response was made on a 7-point scale ranging from zero ("not at all") to 6 ("very much").

Results

As shown in Table 4.1, subjects were least likely to think they would enjoy the discussion period if they anticipated mutual disclosure of scores or mutual social comparison. The interaction of whether or not subjects anticipated revealing their own scores and whether or not they anticipated learning other people's scores had an $F(1, 112) = 3.97, p < .05$. If they anticipated that others would be revealing their scores, they much preferred not

TABLE 4.1. Experiment I: Anticipated Enjoyment of a Discussion as a Function of Presence or Absence of Mutual Comparison

Anticipate self will reveal score to others	Anticipate others will reveal scores to self	
	Yes	No
Yes	2.91	3.59
No	3.97	3.44

to reveal their own. If they anticipated that others would not be revealing their scores, they were more or less indifferent as to whether or not they revealed their own and indeed showed a slight trend toward preferring to reveal their own. Thus subjects preferred situations in which social comparison was asymmetrical or nonreciprocal to situations in which it was symmetrical or reciprocal. Similar patterns were significant or approached significance on questions asking how much subjects were looking forward to talking with other people about the test and especially how much they were looking forward to talking with others who had scored at a different level than they had, as well as on questions asking them how satisfied they were with their performance and their score.

Since subjects in the present study had seen a sketch of the overall distribution of scores in their class before discussion with others was to begin, their motivation to acquire information about other people's scores was perhaps less than it would have been if the discussion period were to start with subjects' knowing only their own scores and nothing about the overall distribution. Without this information, we might expect that subjects would in general prefer conditions in which others revealed their scores (column one of Table 4.1) to conditions in which others did not reveal their scores (column two of Table 4.1). However, there is no reason to expect a simple elevation of curiosity about others to remove the interaction in Table 4.1, that people generally anticipate learning other people's scores with more pleasure when they do not have to reveal their own, and anticipate revealing their own scores with more pleasure when they do not have to learn other people's scores.

As in the Berman *et al.* study (1976), there was no difference in the pattern of preferences for people who had done well on the test (and could anticipate that they would be superior to most of the others they would compare themselves with) and people who had done poorly on the test (and could anticipate that they would be inferior to most of the others they would compare themselves with). Both those who anticipated superiority and those who anticipated inferiority preferred nonreciprocal social comparison to reciprocal social comparison.

From a different starting point, Kelley (1951) found that merely introducing a status difference between two experimental subgroups led to a reduction in communication to the other group that could possibly be interpreted as critical of that group. Relative to controls, both subjects who believed their status was superior to the other group and subjects who believed their status was inferior to the other group inhibited critical communications to that group. Further, both Radloff (1966) and Miller (in press) have shown that both highly superior subjects and highly inferior subjects find social comparison information less valuable than subjects whose scores are less extreme. Radloff found that subjects who believed they were very superior or inferior were less able to use the social comparisons available to them to anchor accurate evaluations of their own performance. Miller found that students at the very top and the very bottom of a distribution were more likely to prefer nonsocial to social comparison (information about the absolute number correct rather than information about their standing relative to others) than were students in the middle of the distribution.

All of this evidence suggests that superiority as well as inferiority presents problems for social comparison that people might wish to avoid. Yet it is unlikely that the problems of superiority and inferiority (or even perhaps equality) are the same or that the costs of each are identical. We now turn to an analysis of what the costs might be of inferiority, superiority, and equality, respectively, and to a report of the evidence that people in each of these positions might prefer to avoid social comparison or to emphasize comparison with dissimilar rather than similar others.

Problems of Inferiority

Problems of inferiority in social comparison may be thought of as having two parts, one relevant when comparison is public and one relevant even when comparison is private. The public part concerns coping with and dealing with other people's reactions. The private part concerns coping with one's own feelings about oneself. If the comparison is public, it may be expected that other people will look down on or derogate the less fortunate person, especially if they think that person's ill fortune is his or her own fault (see Kipnis, 1972; Schopler & Mathews, 1965), and sometimes even if they have objective information that the person's ill fortune was the result of random events over which the person had no control (Lerner & Simmons, 1966; Rubin & Peplau, 1973). If the inferior status person is disparaged, avoided, or victimized, this will in turn consolidate the negative attitudes of those who have acted in this fashion as they seek to justify their own behavior (Brock & Buss, 1964). If others are kind and considerate, the person may suspect that they are merely covering less favorable sentiments, and even accepting sympathy means accepting a subordinate status that involves a sacrifice of self-esteem. Privately, the person in the inferior position may feel bad about himself or herself and insecure in interaction even if other people are unaware of his or her standing.

If we could think of a common situation in which people gathered explicitly for the purpose of social comparison, an examination of who chose to come and who chose not to come would shed light on who most preferred to avoid social comparison. There is such a situation: the class reunion. People come specifically to find out how other people have been doing and to let others satisfy similar curiosity about themselves. It is common knowledge among people who organize these affairs that the less successful members of a class are less likely to come. Social comparison is simply too painful for them, perhaps especially if they were once similar or even superior to their classmates, or if they have not lived up to their promise. People whose memories of school were unpleasant are also less likely to come, although there is some tendency for an Ugly Duckling/Dumbo/Rudolph the Red-Nosed Reindeer/Jonathan Livingston Seagull who has made it to return to "show people," even at the cost of reactivating the prior pain. Janis Joplin's going back to her Texas high school reunion, which she later discussed on national television, was a dramatic case of a person enacting this ambivalence. It might be of interest to study the precise relationship between success during school and success later in life to reunion attendance. Interestingly enough, one of the things that people who attend reunions complain about is that all anyone talks about is the good old days, instead of what they have done since or are doing now. Of course, it is easier to talk about the past, since this is what the people have in common. But in light of our present analysis, we also suggest that even among people sufficiently tolerant of social comparison to attend a class reunion, there are inhibitory forces that push them to spend a disproportionate amount of time rehearsing only the information that everyone already knows.

As with social comparison in general, we would expect that people might be more willing to seek comparison with superior others when the comparison could be made privately, without an audience who was aware of the relative standing of the parties, than when the comparison and the relative merits of the parties were public. Wheeler *et al.* (1969) compared the extent to which subjects would choose to compare themselves with the best other in their group under conditions in which they could simply see this person's score versus conditions in which they would have to interact and work with this person. As made clear in the reanalysis carried out by Arrowood and Friend (1969), the prospect of interacting publically with the other person decreased subjects' choice of superior others. Similarly, Wilson and Benner (1971) found that the tendency to compare upward was sharply reduced when the comparison process changed from a private process, done without knowledge of the target or any third parties, to a public competition with the other person.

Even when acquiring the social comparison information does not involve problems of reciprocal disclosure or public impression management, people who expect to do poorly or to occupy inferior positions may be less interested in seeking comparison. Trope (1975) has shown that there is a remarkable difference in how interested people high in achievement motivation and people low in achievement motivation are in seeking precise or diagnostic information about their abilities on particular tasks. Those in the highest quartile of the sample showed a very strong preference for working on test items that would be diagnostic of their abilities over test items that would not be diagnostic. Those in the lowest quartile of achievement motivation were essentially indifferent as to whether they worked on the informative or the uninformative items. The low achievement-motivation subjects showed this lack of interest in diagnostic test items despite the pressures in laboratory settings for subjects to present themselves as rational, curious, and interested in social comparison. In a nonlaboratory setting, we may suspect that low achievement-motivation subjects would actually prefer the test items that provided them with little information to the test items that provided them with a great deal of information about themselves and their standing relative to others. Individuals low in achievement motivation have been shown to have lower expectancies for successful performance and especially for successful performance that can be attributed to their own effort (Weiner & Kukla, 1970; Kukla, 1972).

Similarly, Willerman, Lewit, and Tellegen (1960) found that subjects who were high in fear of failure and were told explicitly that they had low ability showed a greater preference for working under conditions in which they could not obtain clear information about how well they performed. In the Willerman *et al.* study, subjects displayed their preference for avoiding diagnostic feedback by actually choosing to work in groups, rather than alone, since the division of labor in the group situation made it impossible for individuals to take responsibility for success or failure. Friend and Gilbert (1973) found that subjects who were high in fear of negative evaluation were less likely to choose to compare themselves with the best-off other person in their group and more likely to compare themselves with worse-off others. We interpret this as further evidence that people who anticipate that social comparison information will be unfavorable to them are especially reluctant to expose themselves to that information—even when acquiring that information does not involve the problems of reciprocal disclosure.

If people for whom social comparisons are unfavorable can avoid these social comparisons, they will in fact feel better about themselves (even though they may perform less well for having given up the benefits of exposure to superior models). Thus

Eash (1961) and Goldberg, Passow, and Justman (1966) have presented evidence that below-average students feel better about themselves in classrooms with homogeneous ability grouping, where they are exposed only to others of similar modest ability, than in classrooms with heterogeneous ability grouping, though they may perform better in an absolute sense in heterogeneous classrooms. The presence of more-fortunate, superior others reduces their own self-esteem. (Note that this can also occur through the process of being labeled and segregated into "lower" tracks or streams; see Findlay & Bryan, 1970). Similarly, evidence has been collected that integration may in certain cases have occurred at the expense of the self-esteem of black students coming from previously inferior schools (Weber, Cook, & Campbell, 1971).

If people are for any reason self-conscious, anxious, or just sensitive about their own position in a group, we might expect them to be especially interested in avoiding potentially unfavorable comparisons. If people are not self-conscious or sensitive, the prospect of social comparison should matter less to them. People in an inferior position are likely to be especially sensitive if they are alone or in a minority among superiors. Company is reassuring in situations of stress and misfortune, especially if the company shares one's fate (Schachter, 1959). Thus we might expect that people in minority positions would be more concerned to avoid social comparisons in which they were inferior than people in majority positions. An experiment that sheds light on this was carried out by Donald Kessler and Alan Perkins.

Experiment II: Greater Sensitivity of Minorities to Comparison

Philip Brickman, Donald Kessler, and Alan Perkins

Method

Participants. Subjects were 109 students from a suburban Chicago high school. Subjects were randomly assigned to each of ten experimental conditions, with excess subjects randomly deleted to leave seven subjects in each cell. Of the final sample, fifty-one subjects were female and nineteen were male. All subjects were run in classroom groups by two male experimenters.

Design. The design was a $2 \times 2 \times 2$ factorial, with two extra groups, for a total of ten conditions. Subjects were led to anticipate either a series of discussions involving social comparison or a series of discussions not involving social comparison. Subjects received scores that placed them either in the category in which the majority of their group fell or in the category in which the minority of their group fell. The category of the minority was either superior to or inferior to that of the majority. In the two extra conditions, all subjects received equal scores and either anticipated or did not anticipate social comparison. Since these two conditions are not germane to the major ideas being tested by the study and had no significant results, they will not be discussed further.

Procedure. The procedure was the same as in Experiment I.

Manipulations. The manipulation causing subjects to anticipate either mutual disclosure or no disclosure by either party was the same as in Experiment I. Minority subjects each saw a display indicating that their own score, along with a few other scores (the exact number was dependent upon the size of the class), fell into a broad category either above or below the category in which the vast majority of the class had apparently scored. Majority subjects each saw a display indicating that their own score, along with those of most of the class, fell into a broad category either above or below the category in which a small minority of the class had apparently scored. The category of the majority was always labeled "average" and occupied percentiles 41 to 60 on the chart. The majority subject's score was always given as 51. The category of the minority either fell in a range labeled "below average" and occupied percentiles 21 to 40 on the chart, or in a range labeled "above average" and occupied percentiles 61 to 80 on the chart. The minority subject's

score was always either 31 (in the inferior-status condition) or 71 (in the superior-status condition).

Measures. The dependent measures were the same as in Experiment I.

Results

As can be seen from Table 4.2, majorities are virtually indifferent to the presence or absence of social comparison in subsequent discussion. They are slightly more likely to prefer social comparison to no comparison when they are in the superior position, and slightly more likely to prefer no comparison to comparison when they are in the inferior position, but these differences are negligible. Minority subjects, on the other hand, are very sensitive to the presence or absence of social comparison. They strongly prefer comparison to no comparison when they are in the superior position, and no comparison to comparison when they are in the inferior position. The three-way interaction of group membership, position, and the anticipation of social comparison was significant, $F (1, 48) = 13.32$, $p < .01$. A similar pattern of results was significant on questions asking subjects whether they were looking forward to talking with other people about the test, whether they were looking forward to talking with people who had scored at the same level as they had, and whether they would be more certain about their level of ability if they had a chance to talk over the test with others.

These results may be paralleled with those of Kaplan and Olczak (1971), who found that minority subjects cared more than majority subjects whether someone else agreed with them or not. Jellison

TABLE 4.2. Experiment II: Anticipated Enjoyment of Discussion by Majorities and Minorities in Superior and Inferior Positions

Social comparison anticipated	Majority position		Minority position	
	Superior	Inferior	Superior	Inferior
Yes	3.14	2.57	3.28	2.28
No	3.00	2.71	1.57	3.57

and Zeisset (1969) found that members of a superior minority were more strongly attracted to one another than members of a superior majority, while Gerard and Hoyt (1974) found that members of minority groups evaluated each other more favorably relative to outgroup members than did members of majority groups. Our results also appear to have obvious implications for understanding the possibly greater sensitivity of racial and ethnic minority populations to social comparisons and the relative insensitivity of the white majority to the entire issue. The simple fact of being in a minority, rather than any particular history, may account for some of this sensitivity. The simple fact of being in a majority, rather than any particular prejudice, may account for some of this insensitivity.

If people in inferior positions cannot avoid social comparison, they may feel better if they can believe that upward comparisons are made with people who are dissimilar rather than similar to them in abilities, talents, or background. Mettee and Riskind (1974) found that when subjects were defeated by another person, they were most favorable toward this other and least threatened by her when the other person had defeated them decisively and was subsequently reported to be in an entirely different ability class than the subject. Hoffman, Festinger, and Lawrence (1954) found that subjects were least likely to compete against another subject who had established an early lead over them in an intellectual contest when they believed that the person with the early advantage was markedly superior in ability to them. Nadler, Jazwinski, and Lau (1976) found that male subjects who saw another male chosen over them by an attractive female felt worse about themselves and disliked the other male if the other had attitudes similar to their own, but not if the other had dissimilar attitudes. In the dissimilar condition, subjects could presumably attribute their rejection to their dissimilar attitudes, while in the similar condition they had to find another, perhaps more personal, explanation for their loss. In general, by accepting the fact that the other person is dissimilar to them and should not be taken as a basis for comparison, subjects can make their standing relative to this other irrelevant to their self-esteem and take some of the sting out of defeat or inferiority.

Even when the superior other person is helpful to the subject, and when similarity is a matter of having identical or opposite attitudes, subjects feel better about themselves when the other person is dissimilar rather than similar to them. Fisher and Nadler (1974) demonstrated that receiving aid from a similar other had a negative effect on the recipient's situational self-esteem and self-confidence, while receiving aid from a dissimilar donor resulted in an increase in esteem and confidence. When the donor was dissimilar, subjects apparently appreciated and felt good about the aid, without taking the donor as a comparison other whose greater good fortune made their own state look bad or undermined their own self-confidence. When the donor was similar to the subjects, however, the unsolicited gift apparently focused subjects' attention on the discrepancy between their two positions and in consequence caused subjects to feel worse about themselves despite the generosity of the other.

Although another person's success may often make an individual feel worse by comparison, it is also possible that this other's success would be a source of pride to the individual, a success he or she could identify with and one that would thereby enhance rather than diminish the person's estimate of his own chances for success. Under these circumstances, having the other person be similar or comparable to the subject should be a positive feature rather than a negative one, since it would be easier to identify with the success of a similar other than a dissimilar other. The more general question is thus when will somebody else's success make people feel good about themselves (and prefer the other to be similar), and when will it make people feel bad about themselves (and prefer the other to be dissimilar)? One possibility is that this will depend on whether they see the other person as competitive with them, in which case their success would be threatening, or noncompetitive, in which case their success might be encouraging. An important way in which people are either directly competitive with each other or not directly competitive with each other is determined by whether they are members of the same generation or different generations. Someone our own age or just a little older who has done very well may make us uncomfortable about our own achievements and our own chances for success, while someone of a previous generation who has done very well may be a model whose glory we may hope to inherit and can thus admire without ambivalence. These ideas were tested in an experiment carried out by Janice Moore and Garry Melnick.

Experiment III: Preference for Successful Others of Different Generation and Same Background

Philip Brickman, Janice Moore, and Garry Melnick

Method

Participants. Subjects were thirty-two male and thirty-two female seniors at Northwestern University. Eight subjects were randomly assigned to each of the eight experimental conditions. A male and a female experimenter each ran two subjects of each sex in each condition.

Design. The design was a $2 \times 2 \times 2$ factorial. The comparison other was presented as either successful or unsuccessful, of the same generation as the subject or a previous generation, and of a similar background or a different background from the subject.

Procedure. Undergraduates in their senior year of college were approached individually and asked to participate in a study whose purpose was to improve the placement and counseling services, and in particular the quality of the files maintained on the career histories of past Northwestern graduates. The experimenters told students:

> We would like to see these files improved in a way that would make them more useful to current seniors. Ideally, we would like to see a system in which just about every senior could go in and look up the files on past students who had the same major and intended to go into the same field. To be really helpful, we think the file should include not just the bare listing of what job they took, but also a more detailed report of what they have done, what they

achieved, and how they felt about it. Naturally, this would be done only for people who are willing to participate.

> We have collected so far just a sample of about 100 files from alumni and alumnae who have generously agreed to share their successes and failures with us. What we would like to do is to find out whether the information we are collecting is really valuable to Northwestern seniors, and whether the form we are using is convenient and easy to read. We would like to show you an example of such a file and have you rate it for us on a variety of dimensions.

The subject was then asked what his or her major field was and what he or she intended to do after graduation. The experimenter then located a file ostensibly of another person with a similar major and plans. At this point, the experimenter manipulated the subject's perception of the independent variables establishing the identity of the file. Before giving the subject the file, the experimenter said: "First, I'd like to get your opinion on a number of things, uninfluenced by what you read about this person. Knowing your views beforehand will help us understand the reasons for some of your reactions when you read the information I'll give you." The questionnaire containing the dependent measures was then given to the subject, after which the experiment was terminated and the subject was debriefed. No files were actually read.

Manipulations. To establish comparability or noncomparability of background, subjects were orally asked where they were from, what their father did, what their religion was, and how many brothers and sisters they had. In the comparable condition, the experimenter then said that the person had a similar background to theirs. In the noncomparable condition, the experimenter said that the person had a very different background from theirs.

In the same-generation–competitive condition, the experimenter said: "This person will probably be a competitor of yours, in some sense, because he has just recently graduated." In the different-generation–noncompetitive condition, the experimenter said: "This person is obviously not directly competitive with you because he graduated years ago."

To establish an upward comparison, the other person was described as "someone who has been outstandingly successful in his (or her) field. He (or she) has done extremely well financially and has already received a most unusual degree of respect from his (or her) peers and friends." To establish a downward comparison, the other person was described as "someone who has not been outstandingly successful in his (or her) field. He (or she) has not done well financially and has already undergone a series of counseling sessions designed to help him (or her) put things together."

Measures. After a couple of cover questions asking students how satisfied they were with placement and guidance at Northwestern, students were asked seven questions assessing how they felt about themselves and their life chances: how satisfied they were with their education, how well Northwestern had prepared them for their career, how satisfied they were with their future prospects, how satisfied they were with their chances for a successful career, how satisfied they were with what they had accomplished so far, how satisfied they were with their career so far, and whether they felt they would be free to do as they wanted in the future. All responses were made on a 7-point scale running from zero ("not at all") to 6 ("very much"). An index summing subjects' responses to all seven questions comprised the dependent variable analyzed in the study.

Results

The results of the study for upward comparison are shown in Table 4.3. As can be seen, in the same-generation condition, the difference between comparable and noncomparable models parallels the difference in previous research, such as Mettee and Riskind (1974). Subjects felt better about their own state when their successful peer was noncomparable in background rather than comparable. In the previous-generation condition, however, the results are reversed. Subjects felt better about their own state when the successful older person was comparable or similar to them rather than noncomparable or dissimilar. The interaction of model's

TABLE 4.3. Experiment III: Satisfaction with Own State as a Function of Comparison with a Successful Other of Comparable or Noncomparable Background and Same or Different Generation

Generation of model	Background of model	
	Comparable to subject	Noncomparable to subject
Same generation as subject	4.11	4.59
Previous generation to subject	4.55	3.63

generation and model's background was significant, $F(1, 28) = 6.75, p < .015$. For downward comparison, means suggested a slight tendency for subjects to feel better about themselves with dissimilar others, but all differences were insignificant.

Identification with a superior model and withdrawal from direct competition is of course the Oedipal solution to the problems of inferiority. The solution to the related problem of sibling rivalry and envy of peers is a concern for justice and equality—according to Freud (1939), who looks favorably upon this outcome, and Schoeck (1970), who looks unfavorably upon it.

Problems of Superiority

Like the problems of inferiority, the problems of superiority for social comparison have two aspects, one relevant when the comparison is public and one perhaps relevant even when the comparison is private. If the comparison is public, the superior person can anticipate some negative feelings in the less fortunate others, feelings of resentment, envy, or just embarrassment, all of which can make interaction more difficult. Neither being sympathetic and empathic, nor unsympathetic and insensitive to the others can remove these problems of interaction. Privately, the persons in the superior position risk losing their own good feeling if they identify with or empathize with the less fortunate others (see Stotland, 1969). If the superior persons are not secure in their own state, they may find that state assimilated to rather than contrasted with the state of the less fortunate others. The superior persons may simply fear that the position of the less fortunate others may be contagious, either through direct taking of goods from the more fortunate by the less fortunate, or through transmission of feeling from the disadvantaged. Thus the reasons that advantaged persons might wish to avoid social comparison are quite different from the reasons that disadvantaged persons might wish to avoid comparison, and indeed the reasons are complementary. It is not feeling bad, but fear of the others' feeling bad, that is the source of the problems. The result, however, should be the same: a concern to avoid social comparisons, or to minimize their relevance when they occur.

Initial evidence that people are aware of the costs of superiority comes from a study by Brickman and Seligman (1974). In that study, subjects rated a person who disclosed a high expectancy for doing well on an exam as less likable by others than a person who disclosed a low expectancy for the exam. The low-expectancy person was sharply downgraded if he exaggerated his self-presentation to his friends, while the high-expectancy person was not penalized at all if he publically reported an expectancy that was as much as 80 percent less confident than his private expectancy. In support of our more general argument that all social comparison has costs, subjects rated a person who disclosed no public expectancy for his performance as more likable than one who disclosed either a high or a low expectancy.

To some extent, a reluctance by persons with superior outcomes to interact with persons with inferior outcomes may be seen as a special case of the general reluctance to transmit bad news. Tesser and Rosen (1975) have documented that in a wide variety of circumstances people are less willing to tell others that they should call home for unspecified bad news than for unspecified good news. They present evidence that three concerns of the communicators help mediate this effect. These are that the communicators may feel guilty or bad about the fate of the bad-news recipients; that the communicators may fear that the recipients will associate the communicators with the bad news, hold them responsible, and thus dislike them; and that

the communicators may simply become depressed themselves by the act of delivering bad news. Each of these concerns could also characterize superior-status persons in a situation in which their presence or actions may be seen as making salient their own superiority to inferior-status others. It is especially interesting to note that there is less reported guilt and greater transmission of bad news when the communicators believe they are to share the fate of the recipients than when the communicators believe their own position is more fortunate (Tesser & Rosen, 1972), and when the communicators think the recipients believe that they are to share the same fate (Johnson, Conlee, & Tesser, 1974). Thus it is not merely the bad news but the discrepancy between the communicators' and the recipients' states that gives the communicators pause.

Recent work has demonstrated that subjects who are randomly assigned to higher-status positions, especially if these positions involve holding power over lower-status others, will devalue these inferiors. Kipnis (1972) found that subjects given a wide range of supervisory powers over another person's performance gave the person less credit for the performance and rated the person less favorably than did subjects who did not have these supervisory powers. Lerner and Simmons (1966) found that subjects devalued another person who agreed to suffer a series of electrical shocks in the course of an experiment. In a study that received national attention, Zimbardo, Haney, and Banks (1973) discovered that ordinary college students asked to play the role of prison guards in a mock prison put so much psychological distance between themselves and their prisoners, and so feared and devalued the prisoners, that they were enabled to engage in or at least to witness the severe brutalization of these prisoners. The trauma for the prisoners and the implications for the guards and the experimenters were so severe that the experimenters terminated the study after only six days instead of its intended two weeks. Kipnis, Castell, Gergen, and Mauch (1976) report correlational evidence that marriage partners who see themselves as having a great deal of authoritative power over their spouses tend to devalue both their spouses and their marriage relationship.

Even if superior-status persons are confident that they are not vulnerable to the corruption of power and status, they cannot expect that subordinates will share this confidence. Subordinates will be aware that superiors are hard put to avoid looking down on subordinates. Superior-status persons may prefer to avoid interacting with less fortunate others merely to avoid having to cope with subordinates' watchful scrutiny of the superiors' motives and behavior, or to avoid having to maintain a correspondingly rigorous monitoring of their own behavior. In general, where people are more concerned to be liked, they may be more likely to downplay their talents (Hendricks & Brickman, 1974). In the extreme case, where interaction with the less fortunate is unavoidable, superior people may prefer to mask or even degrade their talents, as Radloff (1966) suggests has been the case with intellectually gifted children.

An elegant experiment by Rabbie and Horwitz (1969) provides direct evidence that winners in a competition will prefer to associate with fellow winners, while losers in the competition will prefer to associate with fellow losers. This was true even though the competition was merely the flip of a coin to determine which four of an eight-person group of subjects would receive a set of prizes (transistor radios) allegedly in short supply. Following the coin flip, subjects showed a marked preference for fellow subjects whose status was the same as their own. Rabbie and Horwitz (1969) suggest that this preference was due to the anticipated ease and rewards of interaction with in-group members, and the anticipated difficulty and discomfort of interaction with out-group members:

> Winners who interacted with losers would need to suppress any display of satisfaction with winning, lest they communicate that they were pleased with the others' loss. Losers who interacted with winners would need to suppress their feelings of dissatisfaction with losing, lest they communicate that they were displeased with the others' gain. By contrast, interaction with members of the subjects' own group would be devoid of conflict and, indeed, offer subjects social support for freely expressing their feelings about winning or losing.

Rabbie and Horwitz strengthen the case for this interpretation of their findings by noting that female

winners actually discriminated more strongly against losers than did male winners. Other research has indicated that females usually show more compassion than males (Terman & Miles, 1936) and strive more than males for fair outcomes rather than to win at another's expense (Uesigi & Vinacke, 1963; Vinacke, Mogy, Powers, Langan, & Beck, 1974). If females have more compassion, they would naturally feel even more uncomfortable with people at whose expense they had profited than would males. The authors report that in a subsequent experiment in which winners did not win in direct competition with losers or at losers' expense (because separate coins were flipped for each group), girls showed a greater preference for interacting with the losing out-group. Under noncompetitive circumstances, their own good fortune would not interfere so much with an expression of compassion.

Two other literatures have suggested that females have a greater preference for equality than males (Leventhal & Lane, 1970; Mikula, 1974) and that females are characterized by a greater fear of success than males (Horner, 1970). It now appears that both of these phenomena are manifestations under specific circumstances of a greater concern by females for the problems of superiority. Kidder, Belletirie, and Cohn (1977) carried out three studies all indicating that the greater preference of females for equality in the division of rewards is entirely a matter of public concern. Under anonymous conditions, this sex difference not only disappeared but reversed itself, with females penalizing tardy co-workers more strongly than males. Thus, where females could not be held responsible by the other party for having a superior share of the rewards and perhaps be sanctioned for what might be considered assertiveness inappropriate to their sex role, they were at least as strict or eager to assert their claims as males.

Zuckerman and Wheeler (1975), in reviewing the literature on fear of success, conclude that while there is evidence for fear of success, there is little evidence that females are uniquely characterized by this motivation (males also show fear of success) or that the presence of this motivation can explain avoidance of success by women. One of the few differences they do report fits especially well with our analysis. Female law school students were less likely to reveal high grades to others than were males. Similarly, in one of the best studies on the issue, Peplau (1976) found that females who were both high in their orientation to a traditional feminine sex role and high in fear of success performed less well than other groups in a situation where they were competing individually against males. However, they were not simply less competent than other groups or less willing to work hard and do well in general. In noncompetitive circumstances, this group of females actually did better than the other groups. In sum, they differed from other groups primarily in being more sensitive to the social circumstances of their achievement, and the potential costs of superiority.

It should be noted that in Peplau's study, the females were competing against their boyfriends, and while Peplau found no effects of the boyfriends' attitudes or the quality of the relationship on the females' willingness to compete, it is possible that the effects she did find are specific to the circumstances of competition and social comparison in intimate relationships. It might be hypothesized that people in intimate relationships have an enhanced desire to avoid social comparison with one another except in areas where the order of comparison has been mutually agreed upon (Viorst, 1975). In support of this is the finding by Morgan and Sawyer (1967) that boys who were friends showed less concern with maintaining strict equality in their division of rewards (where this equality would cost one of them a chance for greater reward) than did boys who were strangers. It may be that not only were the friends more likely to want the other person to profit, out of altruism, but that the friends were also better able to relax their social comparison accounting of superiority and inferiority in the situation, and preferred to avoid either generous or invidious comparison.

If social comparison with the less fortunate cannot be avoided, the burden of guilt and fear of contagion will be reduced for those in the superior position if they can see themselves as dissimilar to those below them, or see the differences between them as justified and stable. We have already reviewed studies by Kipnis (1972), Lerner and Simmons (1966), and Zimbardo, Haney, and Banks (1973) indicating that superior-status others see those below them as different. Novak and Lerner (1968) found that people were more attracted to and comfortable with a mentally disturbed other if they believed that other was dissimilar to them, while Taylor and Mettee (1971) found parallel results for a clumsy other. Walster (1966) reported that subjects assign more responsibility to the victim of a serious accident than to the victim of a less serious one, thus enabling them to see themselves as more dissimilar to the victim of the serious accident. Staines, Tavris, and Jayaratne (1974) found that among highly successful career women, those who saw themselves as different from other women more because of chance or lucky circumstances were more likely to empathize with other women and share the goals of the women's liberation movement than were those who saw their own good fortune as due to their own skill and hard work. Jones (1974) found that attributing one's own escape from shock to effort rather than chance tended to make people less willing to help others escape.

If people who believe they were once like the unfortunate are less likely to derogate them, people who believe that they may in the future occupy the same status as the unfortunate are also less likely to derogate them. Thus Chaiken and Darley (1973) and Sorrentino and Boutilier (1974) have shown that if subjects are led to believe that they themselves will eventually be vulnerable to clumsiness or electrical shocks, they are less likely to disparage other subjects who suffer from clumsiness or electrical shocks. One of us (RB) has had the experience of interviewing at great length twenty-nine paraplegic and quadriplegic victims of serious accidents for a study of perception of causality (Bulman & Wortman, in press). One might have expected that the experience would have made the interviewer much more appreciative of the benefits and good furtune of her own life by providing her with such extensive exposure to less fortunate others (see Brickman & Campbell, 1971; Brickman, 1975; Morse & Gergen, 1970), and to some extent this happened. But the net effect, despite the generally strong and cheerful adaptation of these victims, was to depress the interviewer by increasing her sense of the vulnerability of her own life. Her capacity to empathize with the victims was "too great."

Problems of Equality

Equality would appear to be the solution to the problems of social comparison we have reviewed thus far. If everyone is equal, there is no one to feel bad that he or she is inferior and no one to fear that he may lose his superiority, no one to feel bad that he may be either arrogant or awkwardly sympathetic, and no one to fear that he may be derogated or patronized. And indeed there is evidence that people seek equality in part as a solution to these problems. When people are instructed to allocate rewards in a way that will minimize conflict, they are more likely to give everyone an equal share than when minimizing conflict is not a primary concern (Leventhal, Michaels, & Sanford, 1972). Greater concern for the social-emotional costs of social comparison may lie behind females' greater preference for allocating rewards equally (Kidder, Belletirie, & Cohn, 1977; Mikula, 1974). Freud (1939) saw equality as the general solution adopted within families to the intense problems of sibling rivalry. Parents will be familiar with the extreme precision with which something special done for one child must be balanced by something else equally special done for other children. Indeed, the fact that children only gradually relinquish their preference for equality over equity (to each according to his or her individual merits or contributions) as a principle of fairness as they grow older (e.g., Leventhal, Popp, & Sawyer, 1973) may be due in part to the fact that only as children grow older does the intensity of sibling rivalry wane. This analysis would predict that concern for equality would be greatest and last longest in families where social comparison was most intense—among children relatively close in age with only each other to compare with.

However, equality too has problems. First, if everyone is equal, there will no longer be any pleasure from social comparison. It is the positive contrast that people can on occasion make between themselves and others that enables them to feel that they are excellent, distinguished, or special, and these are feelings that people enjoy, even if they also are ambivalent about the fact that they may obtain these pleasures at someone else's expense (Brickman, 1975). Second, if everyone is equal, people may lose the sense that they are distinct, separate, unique individuals, which has also been shown to be important (Fromkin, 1973). If being equal means that everyone is simply average and identical to everyone else, it seems unlikely that people will find equality to be a very satisfying state.

This view, however, essentially treats equality as a single point along a dimension ranging from very inferior to very superior (see Martens & White, 1975). If we consider more than one dimension of comparison, however, or two people comparing their scores on two different tests rather than on a single test, a variety of different kinds of equality are possible. In one case, the two parties may be equal because both have scored at the average on both tests. In another case, the two parties may be equal because each has scored high on one test and low on the other. We would predict that people would be more satisfied with equality if they each had one very favorable comparison than if each had no favorable comparisons because their scores were average and identical on both tests. If the two people did make identical and average scores on both tests, we would then predict that they would be more satisfied if they had at least been tested on different dimensions, thus allowing each person to preserve some sense that the two are distinct and unique individuals. An experiment to test these ideas was carried out by Roxane L. Silver and Grant Petersen.

Experiment IV: Preference for Diverse and Noncomparable Equality

Roxane L. Silver, Philip Brickman, and Grant Petersen

Method

Participants. Subjects were ninety male and ninety female Northwestern University undergraduates who received credit in their introductory psychology course for participation in the experiment. Ten subjects of each sex were randomly assigned to each of the nine experimental conditions. An additional eighteen subjects were randomly eliminated to obtain an equal number of subjects per cell, and one additional female was eliminated because she suspected the true intent of the study. Half the subjects in each condition were run by a male experimenter, the other half by a female experimenter.

Design. There were nine experimental conditions, the nine possible varieties of equality in which two people each receive scores on two of four possible dimensions. The mean of each person's scores was always the same, deriving either from two average scores or from one high and one low score. The full design can be best described through an examination of Table 4.4.

In six conditions, each subject received one high and one low score. These conditions are represented in the first "Pattern of Equality" column of Table 4.4. In two of these conditions, they were tested on the same two dimensions. In the first, they received identical scores on the same dimensions, each scoring high where the other scored high and low where the other scored low. In the second, they received opposite scores, one scoring high where the other scored low, and vice versa. In the next three conditions, they were each tested on one common dimension and one unique dimension. In the first of these, they each had their high score on the common dimension (shared excellence). In the second of

these, they each had their low score on the common dimension (shared incompetence). In the third, one had the high score on the common dimension while the other had the low score on the common dimension. In the sixth condition, they were never tested on the same dimension, so that one had his or her high and low scores on two dimensions and the other had his or her high and low scores on two different dimensions.

In the last three conditions, each subject received two average scores. These conditions are represented in the second "Pattern of Equality" column of Table 4.4. In the first of these, the two subjects were tested on the same two dimensions. In the second, they were each tested on one common dimension and one unique dimension. In the third, they had no dimensions in common, so that one received average scores on two dimensions and the other received average scores on two different dimensions.

Procedure. Subjects were run in same-sex groups of ten, with each of the first nine subjects in a group randomly assigned to one of the nine experimental conditions. The experiment was introduced as one on

> the social circumstances of the test-taking situation. Earlier studies have shown conflicting results on this topic, with several studies finding that one works better on a task when alone in a large group. On the other hand, other studies have found that the best test-taking situation is where one is in the company of another person and is either competing, cooperating, or just working closely side by side. Therefore, this experiment will attempt to resolve this conflict and will be run in two parts. In the first part, you will be working alone on several tasks within this larger group. In the second part, you will be divided into five pairs of two each and will be working on tasks in the company of another person.

Subjects were deliberately not allowed to anticipate whether they would be competing, cooperating, or working side by side in the second part of the experiment. They were told only that their own scores and the scores of their partner would be important to them in the remainder of the experiment. This was done to make comparison salient,

TABLE 4.4. Experiment IV: Satisfaction as a Function of Pattern of Equality and Number of Common Dimensions

Number of common dimensions	Identical score on the same dimension	Pattern of equality	
		High/Low High/Low	Average/Average Average/Average
Two	Yes (both)	3.21	2.61
	No	3.16	
One	Yes (high)	3.45	2.99
	Yes (low)	2.96	
	No	2.94	
None	No	3.46	3.28

but to avoid focusing on specific forms of comparison that might make one or another pattern of scores appear more useful. Subjects had a number placed in front of them, and were allowed to anticipate who their partner would be by being told at the start what their partner's number was.

Test booklets of four different colors and titles were then distributed, with each subject receiving two. The experimenter explained that while the tests were short,

> since we have only an hour of your time and a great many things to ask you to do in this hour, we cannot afford to spend the time asking each of you to take all four tests. Instead, we will be randomly passing out two of the tests to each of you. In this way, in the end, we will get the information we need without having to make any one of you spend the whole time taking all four tests. While these four tests measure different abilities, each test is of equal importance in our study.

In fact, each subject received one quantity-estimation and symbol-discrimination test and one word-formation test. In the quantity-estimation and symbol-discrimination test, each of four items required the subject to scan a page of letters and estimate both the total number of letters on that page and the letter that appeared most frequently. For the word-formation test, each of four items required the subject to scan a line of twelve letters and estimate both the total number of words that could be formed by these letters and the length of the longest word that could be formed. Items varied in difficulty.

While the experimenters were collecting and scoring the tests, subjects worked on a filler questionnaire. The experimenters then gave to each subject a sheet with his or her name, his or her partner's name, and a listing of the four tests. The scores assigned to the subject and the partner were written next to the appropriate tests. Subjects were also asked at this point to fill out a short questionnaire that contained the dependent measures. The alleged second part of the experiment, with subjects working in pairs, was not actually run. After collecting the questionnaires, experimenters initiated a discussion of the experiment and debriefed the subjects.

Manipulations. Scores were reported in percentiles allegedly based on norms from the previous term. People who received one high and one low score were reported to have scored "90 percent or above" on one test and "50 to 59 percent" on the other test. People who received two average scores were reported to have scored "70 to 79 percent" on both tests.

The tests were labeled Digit-Symbol Discrimination Test (blue booklet), Butler-Haigh Perception Inventory (green booklet), RAPH Measure (pink booklet), and Jost Association Inventory (yellow booklet). Subjects could see by looking at their partners whether they had received two booklets of the same color, one of the same and one different color, or two booklets of different colors. In addition, the feedback sheet made it clear which tests if any they had taken in common and which tests only one of them had taken. The association of high and low scores with particular test names was counterbalanced across conditions.

Measures. After subjects were asked several cover questions about their perception of the tests, subjects were asked to rate how satisfied they were with their performance on each of the two tests they took, how satisfied they were with their overall performance on the tests, and how satisfied they were with the relationship between their scores and the scores of their partner. These four questions were summed to form the dependent variable for the study. All ratings were made on scales ranging from zero ("not at all") to 6 ("very much").

Results

The results in Table 4.4. are most easily summarized by noting that the condition in which the two people received identical and average scores on the same two tests was the least satisfying form of equality in the experiment. People were less satisfied with this condition than with the conditions in which the two of them were tested on the same two dimensions but each received one high and one low score, regardless of whether they received the high and low scores on the same dimensions or on opposite dimensions, $F (2, 48) = 4.03$, $p < .03$.

People also tended to be less satisfied with this condition than with the conditions in which the two of them received identical and average scores but in which either one or both of the dimensions they had been tested on were different from those of their partner, $F (2, 48) = 2.55, p < .09$.

There is evidence that besides insisting on equality, siblings also prefer to specialize in different roles or different areas that have the effect of making their achievements less comparable (Leventhal, 1970). Firstborns are overrepresented in intellectual fields and fields in which steadiness and conformity may be virtues (Schachter, 1963), while later-borns are overrepresented in fields involving physical and social-emotional risks (Nisbett, 1968). Even where equality is possible, people may prefer a situation that minimizes social comparison to a situation in which social comparison is always salient and vigilance must be maintained against minor deviations in either direction.

Apart from the fact that it may be unappealing in depriving people of certain genuine pleasures of comparison, equality has another problem: it is unstable. First, even minor differences will be potent because the very state of equality that initially existed or was taken as a goal makes everybody always a relevant comparison for everybody else. Thus, while the general drift toward industrialization in the last century has substantially reduced inequality in Western countries, it has not reduced concern for equality and distress over institutions that appear ineffective in their avowed purpose of promoting equality (Lipset, 1972; Jencks *et al.*, 1972). Second, the pressure for equality may work against natural forces promoting variation and various forms of individual initiative, which in turn may be seen as forces to be controlled by rules and bureaucracies (Kristol, 1972; Moynihan, 1972). Thus the maintenance of equality, like liberty, requires eternal vigilance. This has been the experience of communes that have attempted to make all members equally attractive to one another. China, a country more strongly dedicated to equality than any other in history, is constantly engaged in new campaigns and struggles against the apparent regeneration of class interests, bureaucratic privileges, and other forms of social distinction. Some of these problems might be better dealt with by working for a state in which people are equal but diverse and noncomparable, rather than equal in any narrow sense, and in which social comparison can be highly selective, minimized, or avoided entirely.

Advantages of Minimizing Social Comparisons

The problems associated with inferiority, superiority, and equality would be minimized if social comparisons were minimized. This may or may not be a reasonable goal. First, however, we should recognize this proposition as an implication of our analysis so far, consider what it means, and see if there is any evidence that bears upon it.

A very strong version of the foregoing position would read as follows: As the number of social comparisons people are required to make increases, people's average comfort and satisfaction decreases. In part, this might be due simply to the fact that if five people are comparing themselves to each other in a rank ordering, a smaller proportion of them are occupying what they would consider to be unsatisfactory positions than if fifty people are comparing themselves to each other in a rank ordering. In part, it might be due to the possibility that while the satisfaction of being first or second in a fifty-person group is greater than the satisfaction of being first or second in a five-person group, this gain is more than canceled by the loss of having to deal with forty-nine others who might be ambivalent about one's position instead of four ambivalent others. This would certainly be true if the marginal utility of being superior to an additional person decreases as the number of persons one is already superior to increases (as almost all marginal utilities do; see Samuelson, 1955), while the interpersonal costs of superiority remain constant. In the case of inferiority, the proposition is probably obvious. The more people one is inferior to, regardless of whether they are sympathetic, scornful, or indifferent, the worse one feels.

Even in the case of equality, greater numbers of relevant comparisons can be expected to create problems. Suppose the person is similar to these others. The more others one is similar to, the greater the likelihood of being threatened by the loss of a sense of uniqueness, which people have been shown to value (Fromkin, 1973). Suppose one is different from these others. The more others one is different from, the greater the likelihood of being threatened by the feeling of being deviant, which also makes people uncomfortable (Freedman & Doob, 1968).

Small groups may be better than large ones not only because they involve fewer comparisons but also because small groups are better able to develop norms for minimizing social comparisons, the only alternative to having winners and losers (Mann, 1976). Social comparisons among large numbers of people and especially among strangers are necessarily made through the application of general standards. Social comparisons among small numbers of people who know each other well can be made on an idiosyncratic and ad hoc basis. When many details are known about each person, these details may make every comparison seem like a special case. Comparisons as a series of special cases will have little implication for issues of superiority, inferiority, or equality. Each person in such a group is connected to the others in a manner so intricate that it cannot be described or threatened by a few comparisons. Slater (1974) suggests that rewards in such groups are not distributed to people on the basis of any abstract principle, either equity or equality or need, but on the basis of the perceptions of the unique positions and the connectedness of each individual. It is impossible to give this kind of attention to judgments about other people when the number of people one comes in contact with passes a certain point. The comparisons that then occur are starker and oversimplified, and an effort to avoid them may be one factor contributing to the greater inattention with which others are regarded in cities as opposed to small towns (Milgram, 1970).

One of us (PB) has been strongly impressed over the years at how people who may not seize our attention in larger groups become strikingly attractive in their own right in situations that do not require them to overcome competing stimulation from numerous others. Or, as a college roommate put it,

for the duration of the bus ride, he was in love with the prettiest woman on the bus—whoever she was. Under these circumstances, smaller numbers of people on each bus would obviously result in greater interpersonal rewards for more people. Gerard and Hoyt (1974) have found suggestive evidence that people evaluate more favorably someone else they think is a fellow member of a small group than someone else they think is a fellow member of a larger group. Small fraternities and sororities generally present more satisfying living arrangements than large dormitories, and the small Society for Experimental Social Psychology convention is generally more satisfying than larger meetings—so much so that some people retain their membership in these groups in spite of, rather than because of, the elitism that currently justifies their membership selectivity. The ideal would seem to be combining restricted size with democratic selection so that membership in various small groups would be available to any and all who wanted it.

There is evidence that people do profit from restricting their social comparisons. Young children have a much smaller world of comparisons before they enter school than afterward. Their circle of comparisons widens continually through their school years. Their self-esteem drops continually through the school years (Purkey, 1970). Later on, among students with equal ability, those attending smaller and less prestigious colleges are more likely to rank high in their classes, feel good about themselves, and in consequence go on to do graduate work or other advanced study (Davis, 1966).

In comparison with normal adults, old people and handicapped people have fewer skills and get fewer rewards on many dimensions. Yet, contrary to the stereotyped view, old people and handicapped people (including both the blind and the malformed) do not appear to be less happy than other groups (Cameron, 1972; Cameron, Titus, Kostin, & Kostin, 1973). This is not because these groups are ignorant about the differences between their own lives and those of the rest of the population. Both the old and the handicapped correctly recognize that their lives are significantly more difficult than those of other people. They have, however, profited by restricting the extent to which they compare themselves with other groups, or by recalibrating their standards for judgment in a way that makes their final position no less favorable to finding satisfaction than the position of any other group (see Brickman & Campbell, 1971).

In research on happiness, marital status is probably the most important single predictor (Campbell, 1975), with the married being happier than all other groups. There are of course many reasons for this difference, not the least of which is self-selection of the more able and stable into enduring marriages. However, in line with our present analysis, one possible reason for the positive effect of being married is that being married is traditionally a strong basis for restricting social comparisons. After marriage, one is no longer so actively testing one's attractiveness against same-sex competitors or opposite-sex judges, with highs and lows that correspond to the continuous ebb and flow of new relationships. Also, marriage itself constitutes an important relationship within which social comparison is probably diffused, controlled, or agreed upon (see Viorst, 1975). When a husband and wife work in the same field, an additional reason for the wife's retaining her maiden name is that the separate names will at least reduce the tendencies of outsiders to make ignorant comparisons between them and assumptions about which partner is trading on the other's eminence. The common finding that marital partners perceive themselves to be more similar to each other than they actually are (Levinger & Breedlove, 1966) becomes more interesting if we think of it not merely as a result of friendly distortion but as a consequence of the couple's actively avoiding social comparison in areas that would be uncomfortable.

Interestingly enough, and contrary to the stereotyped view, being unmarried has repeatedly been shown to be harder on males than on females (see Bernard, 1973). This difference too may follow from our social comparison analysis. Unmarried males are more likely to continue comparing themselves with all available others, as swinging bachelors are supposed to do. Unmarried females are more likely to restrict their comparisons and live reasonably happily ever after. Thus it is easy for a male to fall short of the happiness a bachelor is supposed to achieve, and easy for a female to exceed the happiness a spinster is supposed to achieve.

In the cases just considered, social comparison is restricted not by any social planning or social policy intended to have that effect, but either as a spontaneous occurrence or as a result of policies whose explicit purposes have nothing to do with social comparison. Would it be practical to consider controlling social comparisons in particular areas as a matter of policy, and are there any cases in which this has been done? We will treat briefly two possible areas of application: contacts between tourists and natives, and evaluations of teachers and students.

When tourists are few in number and obviously aristocratic, as was the case in the nineteenth century (Cohen, 1972), they present few problems for the native culture. They are obviously not relevant as social comparisons. With the advent of mass tourism in the twentieth century, tourists became a major factor in the economic and social development of many countries, especially small countries in which sun and surf are important natural resources. Tourists are now seen as bringing in Western goods and Western morals and corrupting the native culture. In our terms, tourists now constitute a new social comparison for people in the host culture, negative for the old but positive for many of the young. This may be a threat both to traditional cultures and to revolutionary ones, and countries as different as Burma and Cuba have responded by restricting or even banning tourism. Currently, one of us (PB) is working with Donald Campbell and Nilly Ben-Shakhar to formulate an alternative model of tourism that would have the same economic benefits to the host country without the same social costs. Tourists would be charged the same rates for access to the sun and the sea as they now pay for luxury hotels, but would live under circumstances that contrasted less sharply with the life of the natives around them. Under the name of "resort cooperatives," tourist centers would feature foreign tourists mingling on an equal-status basis with natives on vacation, and spending some part of their vacation days learning, teaching, or doing other work of value to the host culture. Obviously, this form of tourism would have the most appeal for tourists who shared their host countries' concern for problems of superiority and inferiority in social comparison.

If comparisons cannot be controlled, the timing of comparison and the form of comparison can be made more flexible. Controlling the times and the bases on which one is judged may be one of the most important privileges of high status. Students, who have low status, are compared at fixed times (at the end of each term) on fixed tasks (exams). Faculty, who have high status, are compared on the basis of tasks they choose to work on (areas of research) at points when they choose to summarize their progress or release their results (by publication). Faculty also have a much smaller number of peers with whom they can be fairly compared. The system by which faculty are evaluated, the publication model, is certainly rigorous and respectable, and may put quite as much pressure on those involved in it as the system by which students are evaluated, the examination model. Nonetheless, the publication model, which gives people some periods of freedom from comparison and some control over the conditions of their comparison, seems more humane and more in the interests of those being evaluated than does the examination model. Brickman (1976) has recently proposed publication as an alternative model for evaluating both teacher and student performance in the classroom.

A Balance of Forces Model for Social Comparison

We know people seek social comparison, for themselves and for others they care about. A New Jersey elementary school recently tried to replace traditional grades with purely descriptive accounts of what kinds of reading skills or arithmetic problems each child had mastered. Parents rebelled and forced the school to return to the old report cards. What parents wanted to know was whether their child was performing at the level he or she was supposed to perform in comparison with others. Students at colleges that have done away with grades have been reported to engage in elaborate and subtle inquiries designed to learn something

about how they are doing in relation to others. Social comparison is the means by which performance scores are interpreted (see Brickman & Berman, 1971). Our review is not meant to deny that there is a drive for social comparison, but only to substantiate that there is also a drive to avoid social comparison. Thus, to predict when people will seek comparison, we need a model that contains representations both of the forces that push for comparison and of the forces that push against it, and a calculus for determining which will prevail.

If there are forces both promoting and inhibiting social comparison, we might expect to find that the net tendency to approach comparison situations is a curvilinear function of the degree of comparison expected—first increasing, as curiosity is engaged, then decreasing, as the costs of comparison mount. Preliminary evidence in support of this proposition was obtained by Daniel DeWitt (1977) in a master's study carried out at Ball State University. DeWitt had individual subjects (90 males and 90 females) first take a series of novel tests and then randomly assigned them to one of three conditions. In the first, they were scheduled to return alone, to discuss their feelings about the test with the experimenter, but with no possibility of social comparison with other subjects. In the second condition, subjects were scheduled to return with a small group of others, with whom they anticipated an opportunity to discuss their feelings about the tests and to share their scores. In the third condition, they were scheduled to return with a large group of others, with whom they likewise anticipated social comparison. Mean interest in knowing how other people scored was 5.62 in the no-comparison situation, 6.27 in the small-group situation, and 5.69 in the large-group situation, $F(2, 162) = 3.09$, $p < .05$. Mean willingness to tell one's own scores to others was 5.13 in the no-comparison situation, 5.81 in the small-group situation, and 5.46 in the large-group situation, $F(2, 162) = 2.58$, $p < .08$.

We see the conflict between seeking and avoiding social comparison as primarily a contest between adaptive and hedonic forces. Adaptive pressures push people to seek social comparisons as one form of useful information that they can use to improve themselves. To this end, comparison with similar others is more valuable than comparison with dissimilar others, since more valid inferences can be made from similar others. Comparison with superior others, although painful, is more valuable than comparison with inferior others, since more useful information may be acquired by observing superior others. Hedonic pressures push people to avoid social comparisons as situations in which one party or the other will feel bad, threatened by inferiority or insecurity, sensitivity or insensitivity, shame or guilt, loss of uniqueness or sense of deviance. To this end, comparison with dissimilar others is more valuable than comparison with similar others, since less valid inferences can be made from dissimilar others. Comparison with inferior others, although less useful, has greater hedonic value than comparison with superior others.

Previous authors, such as Thornton and Arrowood (1966) and Hakmiller (1966), have also drawn distinctions between two functions of social comparison, a drive to acquire accurate information and a drive to maintain or improve self-esteem. These correspond in good measure to our distinction between adaptive and hedonic functions. However, the idea of an adaptive function is more general than a drive for self-evaluation. Furthermore, other authors have not always seen self-evaluation and self-enhancement as mutually exclusive, while we see the adaptive and hedonic functions as necessarily and invariably conflicting forces whose balance determines social comparison choices, including the choice to avoid comparison entirely.

The competition between adaptive and hedonic forces may be illustrated by comparing positively skewed and negatively skewed distributions, and may also help to explain why the former are more frequently chosen even though the latter are more satisfying. In the simplest case, a positively skewed distribution is one in which a single outcome is much more positive than the general run of outcomes; a negatively skewed distribution is one in which a single outcome is much more negative than the general run of outcomes. There is evidence that outcomes in a negatively skewed distribution are on the average more satisfying than outcomes in a positively skewed distribution (Brickman, 1975; Parducci, 1968). In the negative-skew case, the

extreme negative outcome constitutes a comparison point that makes all the others look good, while in the positive-skew case, the extreme positive outcome is a comparison point that makes all the others look bad.

Any case in which people pursue a single great experience or great accomplishment that occurs infrequently or perhaps not at all—a Holy Grail, an impossible dream, a brilliant model, a great white whale—is a case of a positively skewed distribution in which they may be predicted to be unhappy most of the time. Yet people often put themselves on such schedules, or take for themselves the most superior possible comparison points, and perhaps it is adaptive forces that cause them to do so. In terms of cultural or biological evolution, individuals that accomplish certain breakthroughs may acquire advantages that eventually allow them to outcompete and replace their less restless cousins. People who take an almost impossible goal may have very little chance of reaching that goal, but they may have no chance at all of reaching it if they do not set their sights on it, and they may in addition have a greater chance of accomplishing lesser goals by having initially set their sights so high (see Locke, 1968; Zajonc & Brickman, 1969). They can also make the attributions that the failures that occur are not due to their ineptness but to the difficulty of the task, while any successes are entirely to their credit (Brickman, Linsenmeier, & McCareins, 1976). The distinction between adaptive and hedonic pressures corresponds to the distinction between task leaders (who are always pushing for accomplishment) and social-emotional leaders (who are always working to make interpersonal relationships more pleasant) in groups (Bales, 1958), and perhaps even to the fundamental distinction between sublimation or self-denial in the service of achievement (the Protestant ethic) versus the pursuit of pleasure.

When hedonic concerns are satisfied, people should be better able to pursue their adaptive interests, and vice versa. Thus, when people are confident that others will like them, they are more willing to associate with others who have different attitudes and who can on this account be expected to be more challenging and informative in discussion

(Levinger & Moreland, 1969; Walster & Walster, 1963). When they are not confident of being liked, people are more willing to give up the advantages of meeting dissimilar others in favor of the reassurance of similar others. When people are more concerned with being liked, we have found they prefer competition with others whose pattern of abilities is dissimilar to theirs and thus with whom competition is less likely to be challenging and informative. It is interesting to note that in the case of attitudes, others who are dissimilar to the subject are more likely to be challenging and informative associates, while in the case of abilities, others who are similar to the subject are more likely to be challenging and informative. Why similar others in one domain are preferred under the same conditions that dissimilar others are preferred in the other domain cannot be explained by a preference for similarity or dissimilarity per se, but only by a consideration of the balance between adaptive and hedonic pressures.

The ultimate metaphor for irreconcilable pressures to seek and to avoid social comparison is the figure of Christ. Comparison with Christ is in orthodox Christianity both necessary and impossible, since Jesus is in equal measure human and divine. As human, he is similar to each of us, a source of adaptive information, a fitting though uncomfortable person for us to compare ourselves with and to strive to imitate. As divine, he is different from us in every way, his powers impossible to comprehend, a source of comfort and consolation, awe and terror. Most of the important heresies in the history of Christianity have attempted to resolve this paradox of an impossible comparison by denying either the humanity or the divinity of Jesus (Tillich, 1967). We may no longer treat this paradox as literal truth, but it stands as a metaphor for the profound ambivalence with which we face the prospect of judgment and comparison.

REFERENCES

Arrowood, A. J., & Friend, R. Other factors determining the choice of a comparison other. *Journal of Experimental Social Psychology*, 1969, *5*, 233–239.

Bales, R. F. Task roles and social roles in problem-solving groups. In E. E. Maccoby, T. M. Newcomb, & E. L. Hartley (Eds.), *Readings in Social Psychology.* New York: Holt, Rinehart and Winston, 1958.

Berman, J., Murphy-Berman, V., & Heil, D. Some costs of social comparison. Unpublished manuscript, University of Nebraska, 1976.

Bernard, J. *The future of marriage.* New York: Bantam, 1973.

Brickman, P. Adaptation-level determinants of satisfaction with equal and unequal outcome distributions in skill and chance situations. *Journal of Personality and Social Psychology*, 1975, *32*, 191–198.

Brickman, P. Publication as a model for teacher and student evaluation. *Teaching of Psychology*, 1976, *3*, 31–32.

Brickman, P., & Berman, J. J. Effects of performance expectancy and outcome certainty on interest in social comparison. *Journal of Experimental Social Psychology*, 1971, *7*, 600–609.

Brickman, P., & Campbell, D. T. Hedonic relativism and planning the good society. In M. H. Appley (Ed.), *Adaptation-level theory.* New York: Academic Press, 1971.

Brickman, P., & Davis, S. F. Responses to unexpected outcomes in open and closed atmospheres. Unpublished manuscript, Northwestern University, 1975.

Brickman, P., Linsenmeier, J. A., & McCareins, A. Performance enhancement by relevant success in irrelevant failure. *Journal of Personality and Social Psychology*, 1976, *33*, 149–160.

Brickman, P., & Seligman, C. Effects of public and private expectancies on attributions of competence and interpersonal attraction. *Journal of Personality*, 1974, *42*, 558–568.

Brock, T. C., & Buss, A. H. Dissonance, aggression, and evaluation of pain. *Journal of Abnormal and Social Psychology*, 1964, *68*, 403–412.

Bulman, R. J., & Wortman, C. B. Attributions of causality and coping in the field: Severe accident victims react to their lot. *Journal of Personality and Social Psychology*, in press.

Byrne, D. *The attraction paradigm.* New York: Academic Press, 1971.

Cameron, P. Stereotypes about generational fun and happiness. *Gerontologist*, Summer 1972, *Part I*, 120–123; 190.

Cameron, P., Titus, D. G., Kostin, J., & Kostin, M. The life satisfaction of non-normal persons. *Journal of Counseling and Clinical Psychology*, 1973, *41*, 207–214.

Campbell, A. The American way of mating: Marriage, si, children only maybe. *Psychology Today*, 1975, *8*, 37–43.

Chaiken, A. L., & Darley, J. M. Victim or perpetrator?: Defensive attribution of personality and the need for order and justice. *Journal of Personality and Social Psychology*, 1973, *65*, 268–275.

Cohen, E. Toward a sociology of international tourism. *Social Research*, 1972, *39*, 169–182.

Davis, J. A. The campus as a frog pond: An application of the theory of relative deprivation to career decisions of college men. *American Journal of Sociology*, 1966, *72*, 17–31.

DeWitt, D. J. *Social comparison—A push-pull phenomenon.* Paper presented at the convention of the Midwestern Psychological Association, Chicago, May 1977.

Eash, M. J. Grouping: What have we learned? *Educational Leadership*, 1961, *18*, 429–434.

Festinger, L. A theory of social comparison processes. *Human Relations*, 1954, *7*, 117–140.

Festinger, L. *A theory of cognitive dissonance.* Evanston, Ill.: Row Peterson, 1957.

Findlay, W., & Bryan, M. Ability grouping: 1970. Athens, Ga.: Center for Educational Improvement, University of Georgia, 1970.

Fisher, J. D., & Nadler, A. The effect of similarity between donor and recipient on recipient's reaction to aid. *Journal of Applied Social Psychology*, 1974, *4*, 230–243.

Freedman, J. L., & Doob, A. N. *Deviancy.* New York: Academic Press, 1968.

Freedman, J. L., & Sears, D. O. Selective exposure. In L. Berkowitz (Ed.), *Advances in experimental social psychology* (Vol. 2). New York: Academic Press, 1965.

Freud, S. *Moses and monotheism.* London: Hogarth Press, 1939.

Friend, R. M., & Gilbert, J. Threat and fear of negative evaluation as determinants of locus of social comparison. *Journal of Personality*, 1973, *41*, 328–340.

Fromkin, H. L. *The psychology of uniqueness.* Krannert School of Industrial Administration, Purdue University, Paper No. 438, December, 1973.

Gerard, H. B. Emotional uncertainty and social comparison. *Journal of Abnormal and Social Psychology*, 1963, *66*, 568–573.

Gerard, H. B., & Hoyt, M. F. Distinctiveness of social categorization and attitude toward ingroup members. *Journal of Personality and Social Psychology*, 1974, *29*, 836–842.

Goldberg, M. L., Passow, A. H., & Justman, J. *The effects of ability grouping.* New York: Teachers College Press, 1966.

Hakmiller, K. L. Threat as a determinant of downward comparison. *Journal of Experimental Social Psychology*, 1966, Supplement 1, 32–39.

Hendricks, M., & Brickman, P. Effects of status and knowledgeability of audience on self presentation. *Sociometry*, 1974, *37*, 440–449.

Hoffman, P., Festinger, L., & Lawrence, D. H. Tendencies toward comparability in competitive bargaining. *Human Relations*, 1954, *7*, 141–159.

Horner, M. S. Femininity and successful achievement: A basic inconsistency. In J. Bardwick, E. Douvan, M. Horner, & D. Gutman (Eds.), *Feminine personality and conflict.* Belmont, Calif.: Brooks/Cole, 1970.

Jellison, J. M., & Zeisset, P. T. Attraction as a function of the commonality and desirability of a trait shared with another. *Journal of Personality and Social Psychology*, 1969, *11*, 115–120.

Jencks, C., Smith, M., Acland, H., Bane, M. J., Cohen, D., Gintis, H., Heyns, B., & Michelson, S. *Inequality: A reassessment of the effect of family and schooling in America.* New York: Basic Books, 1972.

Johnson, R. E., Conlee, M. C., & Tesser, A. Effects of similarity of fate on bad news transmission: A reexamination. *Journal of Personality and Social Psychology*, 1974, *29*, 644–648.

Jones, C. *The effects of prior experience on empathy and helping behavior.* Unpublished doctoral dissertation, University of Texas–Austin, 1974.

Kaplan, M. F., & Olczak, P. V. Attraction toward another as a function of similarity and commonality of attitudes. *Psychological Reports*, 1971, *28*, 515–521.

Kelley, H. H. Communication in experimentally created hierarchies. *Human Relations*, 1951, *4*, 39–56.

Kidder, L., Belletirie, G., & Cohn, E. S. Secret ambitions and public performances: The effects of anonymity on reward allocations made by men and women. *Journal of Experimental Social Psychology*, 1977, *13*, 70–80.

Kipnis, D. Does power corrupt? *Journal of Personality and Social Psychology*, 1972, *24*, 33–41.

Kipnis, D., Castell, P. J., Gergen, M., & Mauch, D. The metamorphic effects of power. *Journal of Applied Psychology*, 1976, *61*, 127–135.

Kristol, I. About equality. *Commentary*, 1972, *54*, 42–47.

Kukla, A. Foundations of an attributional theory of performance. *Psychological Review*, 1972, *79*, 454–470.

Latané, B. Studies in social comparison—Introduction and overview. *Journal of Experimental Social Psychology*, 1966, Supplement 1, 1–5.

Lawler, E. E. Managers' perceptions of their subordinates' pay and their superiors' pay. *Personnel Psychology*, 1965, *18*, 413–422.

Lerner, M. J., & Simmons, C. H. Observer's reaction to the "innocent victim": Compassion or rejection? *Journal of Personality and Social Psychology*, 1966, *4*, 203–210.

Leventhal, G. S. Influence of brothers and sisters on sex-role behavior. *Journal of Personality and Social Psychology*, 1970, *16*, 452–465.

Leventhal, G. S., & Lane, D. W. Sex, age, and equity behavior. *Journal of Personality and Social Psychology*, 1970, *15*, 312–316.

Leventhal, G. S., Michaels, J. W., & Sanford, C. Inequity and interpersonal conflict: Reward allocation and secrecy about reward as methods of preventing conflict. *Journal of Personality and Social Psychology*, 1972, *23*, 88–102.

Leventhal, G. S., Popp, A. L., & Sawyer, L. Equity or equality in children's allocation of reward to others persons? *Child Development*, 1973, *44*, 753–763.

Levinger, G., & Breedlove, J. Interpersonal attraction and agreement: A study of marriage partners. *Journal of Personality and Social Psychology*, 1966, *3*, 367–372.

Levinger, G., & Moreland, J. Approach-avoidance as a function of imagined shock threat and self-other similarity. *Journal of Personality and Social Psychology*, 1969, *12*, 245–251.

Lipset, S. M. Social mobility and equal opportunity. *Public Interest*, 1972, *29*, 90–108.

Locke, E. A. Toward a theory of task motivation and incentives. *Organizational Behavior and Human Performance*, 1968, *3*, 157–189.

Mann, R. D. Winners, losers and the search for equality in groups. In G. L. Cooper (Ed.), *Theories of group process.* New York: Wiley, 1976.

Martens, R., & White, V. Influence of win-loss ratio on performance, satisfaction and preference for opponents. *Journal of Experimental Social Psychology*, 1975, *11*, 343–362.

Mettee, D. R., & Riskind, J. Size of defeat and liking for superior and similar ability competitors. *Journal of Experimental Social Psychology*, 1974, *10*, 333–351.

Mikula, G. Nationality, performance, and sex as determinants of reward allocation. *Journal of Personality and Social Psychology*, 1974, *29*, 435–440.

Milgram, S. The experience of living in cities. *Science*, 1970, *167*, 1461–1468.

Miller, R. Preferences for social versus non-social comparison as a means of self-evaluation. *Journal of Personality*, in press.

Morgan, W. R., & Sawyer, J. Bargaining, expectations, and the preference for equality over equity. *Journal of Personality and Social Psychology*, 1967, *6*, 139–149.

Morse, S., & Gergen, K. J. Social comparison, self-consistency, and the concept of self. *Journal of Personality and Social Psychology*, 1970, *16*, 148–156.

Moynihan, D. Equalizing education—In whose benefit? *Public Interest*, 1972, *29*, 69–89.

Nadler, A., Jazwinski, C., & Lau, S. The cold glow of success: Effects of the interpersonal success of a similar or a dissimilar other on the observer's self and other perceptions. Unpublished manuscript, Purdue University, 1976.

Nisbett, R. E. Birth order and participation in dangerous sports. *Journal of Personality and Social Psychology*, 1968, *8*, 351–353.

Novak, D., & Lerner, M. J. Rejection as a consequence of perceived similarity. *Journal of Personality and Social Psychology*, 1968, *9*, 147–152.

Parducci, A. The relativism of absolute judgments. *Scientific American*, 1968, *219*(6), 84–90.

Peplau, L. A. When do women fear successful achievement? *Journal of Personality and Social Psychology*, 1976, *34*, 561–568.

Powers, T. Can friendship survive success? *Ms.*, January 1975, 16–18.

Purkey, W. W. *Self concept and school achievement*. Englewood Cliffs, N.J.: Prentice-Hall, 1970.

Rabbie, J. M., & Horwitz, M. Arousal of ingroup-outgroup bias by a chance win or loss. *Journal of Personality and Social Psychology*, 1969, *13*, 269–277.

Radloff, R. Social comparison and ability evaluation. *Journal of Experimental Social Psychology*, 1966, *Supplement 1*, 6–26.

Rosenthal, R., & Rosnow, R. L. *Artifact in behavioral research*. New York: Academic Press, 1969.

Rubin, Z., & Peplau, A. Belief in a just world and reactions to another's lot: A study of participants in the national draft lottery. *Journal of Social Issues*, 1973, *29*, 73–93.

Samuelson, P. A. *Economics* (8th ed.). New York: McGraw-Hill, 1955.

Schachter, S. Birth order, eminence, and higher education. *American Sociological Review*, 1963, *28*, 757–768.

Schachter, S. *The psychology of affiliation*. Stanford, Calif.: Stanford University Press, 1959.

Schoeck, H. *Envy*. New York: Harcourt, Brace & World, 1970.

Schopler, J., & Mathews, M. The influence of perceived causal locus of partner's dependence on the use of interpersonal power. *Journal of Personality and Social Psychology*, 1965, *2*, 609–612.

Singer, J. E., & Shockley, V. L. Ability and affiliation. *Journal of Personality and Social Psychology*, 1965, *1*, 95–100.

Slater, P. *Earthwalk*. Garden City, N.Y.: Anchor Press, 1974.

Sorrentino, R. M., & Boutilier, R. G. Evaluation of a victim as a function of fate similarity/dissimilarity. *Journal of Experimental Social Psychology*, 1974, *10*, 84–93.

Staines, J., Tavris, C., & Jayaratne, T. E. The queen bee syndrome. *Psychology Today*, January 1974, *7*, 55–60.

Stotland, E. Exploratory investigation of empathy. In L. Berkowitz (Ed.), *Advances in experimental social psychology* (Vol. 4.). New York: Academic Press, 1969.

Taylor, S. E., & Mettee, D. R. When similarity breeds contempt. *Journal of Personality and Social Psychology*, 1971, *20*, 75–81.

Terman, L. M., & Miles, C. C. *Sex and personality*. New York: McGraw-Hill, 1936.

Tesser, A., & Rosen, S. On understanding the reluctance to transmit negative information (the MUM effect): The effect of similarity of objective fate. *Journal of Personality and Social Psychology*, 1972, *23*, 46–54.

Tesser, A., & Rosen, S. The reluctance to transmit bad news. In L. Berkowitz (Ed.), *Advances in experimental social psychology* (Vol. 8.). New York: Academic Press, 1975.

Thornton, D. A., & Arrowood, A. J. Self-evaluation, self-enhancement, and the locus of social comparison. *Journal of Experimental Social Psychology*, 1966, *Supplement 1*, 40–48.

Tillich, P. *A history of Christian thought: From its Judaic and Hellenistic origins to existentialism*. New York: Simon and Schuster, 1967.

Trope, Y. Seeking information about one's own ability as a determinant of choice among tasks. *Journal of Personality and Social Psychology*, 1975, *32*, 1004–1013.

Uesigj, T. K., & Vinacke, W. E. Strategy in a feminine game. *Sociometry*, 1963, *26*, 75–88.

Vinacke, W. E., Mogy, R., Powers, W., Langan, C., & Beck, R. Accommodative strategy and communication in a three-person matrix game. *Journal of Personality and Social Psychology*, 1974, *29*, 509–525.

Viorst, J. The marriage Superbowl: When husbands and wives compete. *Redbook*, April 1975, 9–12.

Walster, E. Assignment of responsibility for an accident. *Journal of Personality and Social Psychology*, 1966, *3*, 73–79.

Walster, E., & Walster, B. Effect of expecting to be liked on choice of associates. *Journal of Abnormal Social Psychology*, 1963, *67*, 402–404.

Weber, S. J., Cook, T. D., & Campbell, D. T. The effect of school integration on the academic self-concept of students. Paper given at 43rd meeting of the Midwestern Psychological Association, Detroit, Mich., 1971.

Wheeler, L., Shaver, K. G., Jones, R. A., Goethals, G. R., Cooper, J., Robinson, J. E., Gruder, C. L., & Butzine, K. W. Factors determining choice of a comparison other. *Journal of Experimental Social Psychology*, 1969, *5*, 219–232.

Weiner, B., & Kukla, A. An attributional analysis of achievement motivation. *Journal of Personality and Social Psychology*, 1970, *15*, 1–20.

Willerman, B., Lewit, D., & Tellegen, A. Seeking and avoiding self-evaluation by working individually or in groups. In D. Wilner (Ed.), *Decisions, values, and groups* (Vol. 1.). New York: Pergamon Press, 1960.

Wilson, S. R., & Benner, L. A. The effects of self esteem and situation upon comparison choices during ability evaluation. *Sociometry*, 1971, *34*, 381–397.

Zajonc, R. B., & Brickman, P. Expectancy and feedback as independent factors in task performance. *Journal of Personality and Social Psychology*, 1969, *11*, 148–156.

Zanna, M., Goethals, G., & Hill, J. Evaluating a sex-related ability: Social comparison with similar others and standard setters. *Journal of Experimental Social Psychology*, 1975, *11*, 86–93.

Zimbardo, P., Haney, C., & Banks, W. C. A Pirandellian prison. *New York Times Magazine*, April 8, 1973.

Zuckerman, M., & Wheeler, L. To dispel fantasies about the fantasy-based measure of fear of success. *Psychological Bulletin*, 1975, *82*, 932–946.

Social Comparison Activity Under Threat: Downward Evaluation and Upward Contacts

Shelley E. Taylor and Marci Lobel

Social comparison processes include the desire to affiliate with others, the desire for information about others, and explicit self-evaluation against others. Previously these types of comparison activity and their corresponding measures have been treated as interchangeable. We present evidence that in certain groups under threat, these comparison activities diverge, with explicit self-evaluation made against a less fortunate target (downward evaluation), but information and affiliation sought out from more fortunate others (upward contacts). These effects occur because downward evaluation and upward contacts appear to serve different needs, the former ameliorating self-esteem and the latter enabling a person to improve his or her situation and simultaneously increase motivation and hope. Implications for the concept, measurement, and theory of social comparison are discussed.

For almost 30 years, social comparison theory has held the dubious distinction of being social psychology's "second favorite theory" (Arrowood, 1978). Nonetheless, as a consequence, it has spawned several hundred empirical investigations (see Suls, 1977, for a review). In recent years, the influence of the theory has extended into clinical and personality psychology, as the importance of

Preparation of this article was supported by National Institute of Mental Health Grant MH 44258 and by Research Scientist Development Award MH 00311 to Shelley E. Taylor. Marci Lobel was supported by National Institute of Mental Health Training Grant MH 15750.

The authors are grateful to Bart van den Borne and Jean Pruyn for the stimulating conversations that prompted the development of this article. We are also grateful to Rebecca Collins, Gayle Dakof, and Joanne Wood for their comments on an early draft of the article.

Correspondence concerning this article should be addressed to Shelley E. Taylor, Department of Psychology, University of California, Los Angeles, 405 Hilgard Avenue, Los Angeles, California 90024-1563.

social comparisons in coping processes has been identified (Wills, 1981). In part as a result of these extensions to coping, it has become increasingly apparent that social comparisons are not purely social, but can also be cognitively manufactured to meet particular motives or goals (S. E. Taylor, Wood, & Lichtman, 1983). As a result, researchers have become interested in the cognitive underpinnings of social comparisons.

With this expanding influence has come the need for theoretical, conceptual, and empirical refinements to the original theory, one of which constitutes the concern of the present article. Festinger's (1954) original conceptualization of comparison activity was relatively broad and included the processes of gathering information from and about other people for the purpose of implicit or explicit self-evaluation. As a consequence, operational definitions adopted by social comparison researchers have been varied and have included choice of others with whom to affiliate, requests for information about others, and more explicit self-evaluations of one's attributes, emotions, opinions, and outcomes in comparison with those of a target. The present analysis suggests that there is now reason to distinguish among these different types of comparison activity because they show divergent empirical patterns under the same psychological conditions and therefore may be differentially responsive to different psychological needs. In particular, we will show that in certain groups under threat, there is a strong preference to evaluate the self against less fortunate others (*downward* evaluations) but a desire for information about and contact with more fortunate others (a pattern we will label *upward* contacts). We will show that these patterns exist simultaneously in the same subjects under the same psychological circumstances and that, as such, they suggest a need for a more precise understanding of different types of comparison activities.

Overview of the Theory

Festinger's (1954) theory of social comparison maintains that people need to have stable, accurate appraisals of themselves. The theory posits that people prefer to evaluate themselves using objective and nonsocial standards, but if such objective information is unavailable, then individuals will compare themselves using other people. Originally the theory stipulated that the preferred source for social comparison is a person who is similar to the self-evaluator on the ability or opinion in question. Comparison with a similar other is maximally informative, according to Festinger, because it provides the person with a more precise, stable evaluation than would a comparison with someone who is very different. Subsequent additions to and modifications of the theory (Goethals & Darley, 1977) have suggested that under some circumstances, people prefer comparison others who are similar on attributes related to the dimension under evaluation. Thus, for example, a junior tennis player might select someone similar in age, experience, and training in order to have a basis for evaluating his or her skill at playing tennis.

Festinger (1954) also hypothesized that there is a unidirectional drive upward, generally interpreted to mean that people strive to be more capable than their current level of performance and more capable than the persons with whom they compare themselves. Some investigators (e.g., Wheeler, 1966) have interpreted the unidirectional drive upward as meaning that people prefer to compare themselves to others whose performance or abilities are slightly better. These social comparisons have been referred to as upward comparisons. Others (see Suls, 1977) have suggested that the drive to improve performance relative to others or to appear more capable involves an ego-enhancing motive that may be better served by making downward comparisons to less fortunate others, enabling the evaluator to deduce that he or she is better off than a worse-off other. Confusion regarding what Festinger meant by the unidirectional drive upward has led to confusion in generated predictions.

A central feature of Festinger's (1954) original proposal concerned the implications that social comparison processes have for interpersonal interaction. That is, the theory was elaborated primarily as a social one, such that the need for self-evaluation under conditions of information ambiguity leads people to affiliate with others in order to better evaluate their opinions and abilities. This theme was given prominence in Stanley Schachter's (1959) book, *The Psychology of Affiliation*. The book presented the results of studies demonstrating that anxiety leads to affiliation with similar others. Schachter maintained that the relationship between anxiety and affiliation derives, at least in part, from the need to socially compare one's emotional state in order to determine its appropriateness.

As a result of these joint origins in cognitive and social processes, several different operational definitions of social comparison activity were adopted in the literature. A large literature on the evaluation of emotional states and abilities adopted the fear-affiliation model and used the desire to affiliate as a dependent measure indicating the desire to socially compare (see Cottrell & Epley, 1977; Rofe, 1984; Suls, 1977, for reviews). Apart from the fear-affiliation studies, other investigators have used preference for affiliation as an indicator of social comparison (Frey & Ruble, 1985; Nosanchuk & Erickson, 1985). Social comparison activity has also been operationally defined as a desire to see relevant individual difference information about selected target others and as a desire for information about others (e.g., Rofe, 1984; Suls, 1977; Wheeler & Koestner, 1984; Wheeler, Koestner, & Driver, 1982). Some research has also explicitly asked subjects to compare their own abilities and outcomes with those of others (e.g., Campbell, 1986; Crocker, Thompson, McGraw, & Ingerman, 1987; Marks, 1984; Tabachnik, Crocker, & Alloy, 1983).

Whether these different measures of social comparison activity can all be considered to be measuring the same process is difficult to evaluate. For the most part, researchers who have used one measure of comparison activity have not included other operational definitions. There is, however, an area within the social comparison literature that has examined desire for information, preference for affiliation, and explicit evaluations of self against target in the same samples evaluating the same outcomes. This is a modest but consistent literature on social comparisons among cancer patients. Of interest is the fact that this literature involves people in field settings experiencing real threat and evaluating the self on dimensions that are important and central to the self-concept. In the next sections, we will review the literature on cancer patients' explicit self-evaluations and desire for contacts with othercancer patients in order to address the question of the functional interdependence of different operational definitions in the social comparison paradigm.

Explicit Self-Evaluations of Cancer Patients

In recent years, there has been substantial research interest in social comparisons under threat, and cancer has been one of the threatening events examined in this context. Before reviewing that literature, it is useful to provide the historical context for examining this research. With the development of Schachter's (1959) fear-affiliation paradigm and the growing literature on social comparison under threat came an important development in social comparison theory, namely the emphasis on motives other than self-evaluation. Several researchers, most notably Hakmiller (1966) and Thornton and Arrowood (1966), suggested that social comparisons can be made for the purpose of self-enhancement as well as for self-evaluation. In a now-classic experiment, Hakmiller (1966) provided subjects who had taken a personality test with threatening feedback, suggesting that they harbored a high level of hostility toward their parents. Subjects who were threatened responded by comparing themselves with someone who had received feedback that they were even more hostile, whereas subjects exposed to little threat compared themselves with someone receiving feedback that they held less hostility. These findings were interpreted to mean that, under conditions of threat, self-enhancement may lead people to make downward comparisons with somebody worse off than themselves.

Since that hypothesis was initially ventured, a large amount of literature has confirmed the finding that, under conditions of threat, individuals typically make downward social comparisons (see Wills, 1981, for a review). For example, laboratory studies have replicated Hakmiller's (1966) initial finding with a variety of threats (e.g., Amabile & Glazebrook, 1982; Pyszczynski, Greenberg, & LaPrelle, 1985; Sherman, Presson, & Chassin, 1984). A conceptually similar body of literature examining negative evaluations of outgroups by threatened persons shows that prejudice is strongest among individuals whose self-esteem is low or whose social status is low (Brewer & Campbell, 1976; Ehrlich, 1973; Stephan & Rosenfield, 1978; D. G. Taylor, Sheatsley, & Greeley, 1978; see also Goethals & Darley, 1986; Holmes, 1978; Wills, 1981). Research on the social comparisons of people under threat reveals a preponderance of downward comparisons (Affleck, Tennen, Pfeiffer, Fifield, & Rowe, 1987; Gibbons, 1985; Schulz & Decker, 1985).

Research on cancer patients consistently shows that cancer patients also evaluate their situation vis-à-vis less fortunate others. A study by Wood, Taylor, and Lichtman (1985) coded the spontaneous social comparisons of cancer patients made during 2-hour interviews across several attributes: physical situation (including state of health and treatments received), coping abilities, personal situation, and overall psychological adjustment. Statements were coded as comparative in nature only if the respondent explicitly evaluated herself against another individual. Overwhelmingly, respondents made downward comparisons to less fortunate others. Frequencies ranged between 60% and 90% of the total comparisons made by the sample within each category. Looking at respondents overall, we found that of 73 respondents, 4 made no free-response comparisons, 1 made more upward than downward comparisons, 5 made an equal number of upward and downward comparisons, and 63 made more downward than upward comparisons. Thus, the preponderance of comparison activity was clearly in the downward direction.

Other studies have elicited self-evaluative activity more directly by asking cancer patients to evaluate their physical situation or coping abilities vis-à-vis others. In a survey study of 668 cancer patients (S. E. Taylor, Falke, Shoptaw, & Lichtman, 1986), respondents were asked to indicate how they felt they were doing in comparison with other cancer patients. The results showed that 93% felt they were coping better than other cancer patients, and 96% felt they were in better health than other cancer patients. In an interview study of 55 cancer patients, Collins, Dakof, and Taylor (1988) asked respondents to indicate whether they evaluated their physical situation, coping abilities, and individual resources against those of other cancer patients. In all three categories, patients showed a strong preponderance of downward comparisons.

To summarize, in studies of cancer patients in which explicit evaluations of one's own abilities or outcomes have either been coded from free responses or cued by questions, a pattern of downward evaluations has been found. As previously noted, these findings are consistent with a large body of literature suggesting that under conditions of threat, people make downward comparisons with less fortunate others (Wills, 1981; 1983).

Preferences for Contacts Among Cancer Patients

In contrast to the downward comparisons observed in the explicit evaluations measures, cancer patients do not appear to seek contact with or information about less fortunate others. Indeed, quite the opposite appears to be the case. There is emerging evidence to suggest that cancer patients seek exposure to other patients who have either overcome their threatening circumstances or adjusted well to them and that they avoid exposing themselves to those who are doing poorly.

In a questionnaire study of 506 cancer patients, Molleman, Pruyn, and van Knippenberg (1986) asked respondents if they would like to interact with fellow patients who were much less, slightly less, similarly, slightly more, or much better off physically. Subjects strongly preferred to interact with a fellow patient who was similarly or slightly better off. Patients were also asked how they experienced their interactions with fellow patients. Interaction with fellow patients who were much worse off was experienced most negatively, followed by interactions with fellow patients who were slightly worse off. Interaction with fellow patients who were similarly or slightly better off was experienced less negatively still, and interaction with fellow patients who were much better off was experienced the most positively.

S. E. Taylor, Aspinwall, Dakof, and Reardon (1988) found evidence suggesting that cancer patients experience information about better-off others positively and worse-off others negatively. They interviewed 55 male and female cancer patients regarding their responses to stories about other cancer patients. The majority reported that most of the stories they were told by others involved cancer patients who were coping poorly, who had physically deteriorated, or who had died. Almost uniformly, the patients found these stories to be unhelpful, often attributing selfish and morbid motives to the storyteller. In contrast, stories that were upbeat, involving long-term survival or successful coping, were experienced as significantly more helpful.

Similarly, in an examination of social support (S. E. Taylor & Dakof, 1988), cancer patients were asked to indicate the most helpful and least helpful actions that they experienced in their interactions with other cancer patients. Three of the most common helpful actions were (a) acting as a good role model, (b) coping well with the cancer, and (c) simply surviving with cancer, implying that cancer patients who were doing well were preferred as interpersonal contacts. The most unhelpful actions reported by cancer patients in their interactions with other cancer patients were (a) acting as a poor role model by coping poorly or (b) continuing to engage in actions that threatened health, implying that those doing poorly were not desired as interpersonal contacts.

In addition to evidence revealing cancer patients' preferences for contact with or information about more fortunate others, there is some evidence that cancer patients prefer not to interact directly with less fortunate others. Collins *et al.* (1988) asked cancer patients how they felt about waiting in the waiting room with other cancer patients to see their physician. More than 70% of the patients

indicated that they found the waiting-room situation to be noxious, and one of the most common reasons given for this reaction was that the presence of others who were so obviously deteriorating physically upset them or made them depressed.

In attempting to understand the patterns of preferences for contact uncovered by these data, it is useful to borrow the upward–downward distinction applied to explicit self-evaluations. Upward contacts may be defined as a preference to interact with or to gain information about individuals who are slightly or much better off, and downward contacts may be defined as a preference to interact with or gain information about others who are worse off. Converging evidence suggests that among cancer patients, upward contacts are preferred over downward ones, whether those contacts involve direct affiliation or simply the opportunity to get information about others.

Because the preference for upward contacts seems to conflict with research on comparison processes under threat, it is useful to consider whether the pattern occurs for a distinctive group of patients who are either well-adjusted, have low informational uncertainty, or who do not meet the conditions under which social comparisons are likely to be invoked. Three points argue against these possibilities. First, there are no factors that distinguish the samples in studies that demonstrate downward evaluations from the samples used in studies that demonstrate preferences for upward contacts. The sample demographics are very similar. Second, and more important, is that downward evaluations exist simultaneously with preferences for upward contacts in at least one sample (i.e., Collins *et al.*, 1988; S. E. Taylor *et al.*, 1988, used the same sample). Third, there is evidence to refute the idea that patients choosing upward contacts have had their informational uncertainty resolved. The study by Molleman *et al.* (1986) found that cancer patients preferred to affiliate with other cancer patients as uncertainty about aspects of their illness and treatment was greater. Therefore, preconditions for demonstrating social comparison activity appear to have been met: Objective information was lacking, and consequent uncertainty was high (see Festinger, 1954;

Gerard, 1963; Gerard & Rabbie, 1961; Singer & Shockley, 1965).

Another possible confounding explanation is that patients express a preference for contact with better-off others because they feel uncomfortable or ambivalent about making downward comparisons. The literature has suggested that downward comparisons create conflict for people because feeling better at another's expense is considered to be a socially inappropriate behavior (e.g., Brickman & Bulman, 1977; Wills, 1981). However, this interpretation seems an unlikely explanation for the observed pattern of data. The preference to affiliate with a worse-off other, if it existed, would seem to be quite socially appropriate, inasmuch as it could be interpreted as showing compassion for others' misfortunes. In contrast, the process of making downward evaluations to less fortunate others might be considered somewhat socially inappropriate. However, precisely the opposite data pattern exists, namely a readiness to make downward evaluations but a preference for upward contacts. Ambivalence over making downward comparisons does not appear to explain the pattern of upward contacts observed in these studies.

Reconciling Downward Evaluations and Upward Contacts

In this section, we highlight some of the problems these divergent data patterns pose for social comparison theory and suggest some interpretations that may serve as a guide to theoretical and empirical refinement in the future. A first question that arises is how cancer patients, and possibly also other victims, make downward evaluations in the absence of contact with less fortunate others. Indeed, our own data suggest that revulsion and fear are often reactions to the prospect of contact with less fortunate cancer patients (e.g., S. E. Taylor et al., 1988). A partial answer is that cancer patients may have enough direct and indirect contacts with less fortunate others to make downward evaluations. Although the media usually feature positive, upbeat cancer stories (Rimer, 1984; S. E. Taylor & Levin, 1976), they do include some stories

that involve poor coping, deterioration, and death (Rimer, 1984), which may provide exposure to less fortunate others and create opportunities for downward evaluation. In physicians' waiting rooms patients are often exposed to fellow patients who are worse off than themselves (Collins et al., 1988; Wood et al., 1985). Family, friends, and acquaintances tell cancer patients stories about other cancer patients who have coped poorly or who have physically deteriorated (S. E. Taylor et al., 1988). Thus, although cancer patients themselves may avoid contacts with less fortunate others, such contacts may be thrust on them nonetheless, making downward evaluations a possibility.

Another part of the answer may be provided by the observation that when cancer patients do not have directly available targets for downward evaluation, they invent them. In a study with breast cancer patients, S. E. Taylor and her associates (S. E. Taylor et al., 1983; Wood et al., 1985) found that sometimes patients manufactured a hypothetical group of less fortunate others with whom to compare themselves. For example, a patient who had undergone a mastectomy might compare her own adjustment favorably to "those other women" who seem to have so much difficulty adjusting (S. E. Taylor et al., 1983, p. 34; see also Schulz & Decker, 1985). By cognitively inventing a less fortunate group, victims may spare themselves direct contact with such a group. In summary, then, cancer patients may be able to make downward evaluations without seeking contact with less fortunate others, first, because they have some unavoidable contacts with less fortunate others and, second, because they invent less fortunate others with whom to compare themselves.

A parallel issue that arises when considering cancer patients' preferences for contacts with well-adjusted others is how patients avoid the negative implications of explicit self-evaluations when compared with such people. One could argue that evaluating one's self against a survivor or an especially good coper would produce ego-deflating consequences (Suls, 1977). One possible answer is that cancer patients may not use their contacts with survivors and good copers for explicit self-evaluation, but rather may use them for some other purpose.

Evidence from the studies assessing preferences for affiliation with more fortunate others suggests that exposure to good copers and long-term survivors may serve both informational and emotional functions. Cancer patients in one study (S. E. Taylor *et al.*, 1988) reported that good copers and long-term survivors acted as role models on whom they could pattern their own coping and efforts to survive. Respondents also reported feeling inspired, optimistic, and hopeful from such contacts. Indeed, evidence from one study that asked patients if they compared themselves with other cancer patients doing better uncovered relatively few direct self-evaluations (Collins et al., 1988).

Overall, what causes explicit self-evaluations and preferences for contacts to diverge in cancer patients and possibly other people under threat? One possibility is that the management of emotional needs is paramount under conditions of threat and that these needs are best satisfied by downward evaluations and upward contacts. Evaluation against a less fortunate other may be ego-enhancing, but actual contact with such people may also be depressing and frightening. Similarly, contact with very well-adjusted targets can be motivating and inspirational, but direct evaluation of one's current status against such targets could be ego-deflating. Consequently, in the interests of maintaining positive affect, upward contacts and downward evaluations may be made without the potential liabilities of downward contacts and upward evaluations.

Another possible explanation seems more compatible with the evidence relating preference for upward contacts to the perceived informativeness of better-off others (Molleman *et al.*, 1986). If one assumes that a highly stressful event like cancer produces both emotional needs (e.g., fear, anxiety) and problem-solving needs (e.g., efforts to eliminate the cancer), then one would expect coping to revolve around these two basic sets of tasks: the regulation of emotional states and problem-solving efforts (Lazarus & Folkman, 1984). Downward evaluations seem to be clear efforts to regulate emotions by making the person feel better in comparison with worse-off others. Upward contacts, however, may be viewed simultaneously as problem-solving efforts, by providing a person with information valuable for potential survival and successful coping, and as a method for meeting emotional needs, by providing hope, motivation, and inspiration. Consistent with the idea that upward affiliations are a valuable source of motivation, inspiration, and hope, a study of 663 lymphoma and breast cancer patients (van den Borne, Pruyn, & van den Heuvel, 1987) found improved mood among cancer patients following contacts with fellow patients. Significantly, increased self-esteem was found only among patients who were the worst off (i.e., who were undergoing a second set of treatments). Those who were better off did not show increased self-esteem as a result of contact with fellow patients. This finding tentatively suggests that upward contacts can be valuable for improving self-esteem.

Consistent with the idea that upward contacts satisfy informational needs and emotional needs simultaneously, a review of 18 articles by van den Borne, Pruyn, and van Dam-de Mey (1986) found that cancer patients' contacts with fellow cancer patients consistently led to a higher level of information, as well as to a reduction in negative feelings (anxiety, fatigue, tension, and confusion; see also Kulik & Mahler, 1987). This finding lends some credence to the idea that contacts with fellow sufferers meet both informational and emotional needs. Unfortunately, none of the studies reviewed assessed whether patients differentially preferred to affiliate with better-off others; consequently, the types of affiliations sought by these patients cannot be assessed, only the outcomes of the affiliations.

Cautions and Limitations Regarding the Present Analysis

Several cautions regarding the present analysis should be raised. One limitation is that the preponderance of evidence comes from one research laboratory. Although this presents a potential point of bias, several factors argue against its significance. First, the data patterns uncovered by the senior author's studies have been confirmed by at least one other investigation in the case of upward contacts and by a preponderance of evidence from individuals under threat in the case of downward evaluations. Second, the divergence of contact and evaluative activities was uncovered gradually in serial investigations, and moreover, the data pattern was unanticipated. Consequently, the likelihood of bias would appear to be small. Finally, the preference for upward contacts and downward evaluations emerged with several different types of data—some free-response, some directed—in each of the two categories of measures (explicit self-evaluations and contacts) and therefore would not appear to be a methodological artifact. Overall, the fact that most of the evidence comes from one laboratory would not seem to have a major impact on the nature of the data, although investigations by other researchers are desirable.

A second caution concerns the fact that the data on evaluations and contacts came from cancer patients, and the points may not generalize to other victimized groups. Consequently, more research on social comparison processes among victims other than cancer patients is needed. Although the tendency for victimized groups to make downward comparisons under threat is well-established (Wills, 1981; 1983), information concerning informational and affiliative preferences among victims is lacking.[1]

When social comparison processes are examined as cognitive processes and as coping processes, several additional implications for social comparison theory emerge. The first concerns how "social" the process is. Festinger's (1954) original formulation assumed, and subsequent research has incorporated the assumption, that the process is fundamentally a social one. When objective information is unavailable for self-evaluation, social information is the next best thing, and so a relatively similar other is selected as a yardstick for self-evaluation. Undoubtedly, there are many circumstances when social comparison occurs in this way. However, the literature on social comparison under threat, including the cancer literature, suggests that making social comparisons can also be a heavily cognitive process. When a similar other is not available, or the right kind of similar other is not available, victims under threat can manufacture comparison others by inventing less fortunate others from whole cloth (S. E. Taylor *et al.*, 1983). As previously noted, these processes are most evident when victims' needs for self-enhancement are paramount, as evidenced by the strong bias toward downward comparisons. But threat may not be the only circumstance in which the social comparison process is cognitive rather than social. For example, people striving toward a goal for which there is no readily available role model may also cognitively assemble such a model from available pieces in the environment. In any case, the heavy involvement of cognitive constructions in social comparisons under threat should alert researchers to the potential role of cognitive construction in social comparison activity under nonthreatening conditions as well.

In conclusion, there is now evidence to suggest that social comparison processes involve a diverse set of social and cognitive activities, including affiliation with others, desire for information about others, and explicit self-evaluation against others. Rather than paralleling each other, these different types of comparison activity diverge, at least under certain conditions of threat. Explicit self-evaluation tends to be downward toward less fortunate others, and preferences for information and affiliation (i.e., contacts) tend in an upward direction. We have suggested and presented some evidence that these processes diverge in part because they address different needs. Downward "comparisons" (or explicit self-evaluations, as we have called them) may meet emotional needs by making people feel fortunate in comparison with others and by raising self-esteem. Upward contacts may serve problem-solving needs by providing role models on whom one can pattern one's own behavior and meet certain emotional needs by providing hope and inspiration. These two patterns (upward contacts and downward evaluations) may

---

[1] We have replicated the finding that people under stress do not like stories about less fortunate others and prefer stories about more fortunate others, with a different population, namely college students facing examinations; thus, the preference for upward contacts and rejection of downward evaluations appears to extend beyond the samples described in this article.

exist simultaneously in the same people without engendering any contradictions, inasmuch as affiliations are social contacts and downward evaluations can be cognitive constructions.

These findings have at least three implications. The first is the need to attend more carefully to operational definitions of social comparison activity in the future—in particular, keeping self-evaluation and measures of preferences for affiliation or information conceptually and empirically distinct. The second implication is the need to reexamine the results and conclusions of previous investigations that have confounded or potentially misinterpreted effects of different types of social comparison activities. The third and most important need is to refine social comparison theory to distinguish among and identify the antecedents and consequents of different kinds of social comparison activity. We offer the present analysis as an effort in this direction.

REFERENCES

Affleck, G., Tennen, H., Pfeiffer, C., Fifield, J., & Rowe, J. (1987). Downward comparison and coping with serious medical problems. *American Journal of Orthopsychiatry, 57*, 570–578.

Amabile, T. M., & Glazebrook, A. H. (1982). A negativity bias in interpersonal evaluation. *Journal of Experimental Social Psychology, 18*, 1–22.

Arrowood, A. J. (1978). Social comparison theory: Retrieved from neglect. *Contemporary Psychology, 23*, 490–491.

Brewer, M. B., & Campbell, D. T. (1976). *Ethnocentrism and intergroup attitudes: East African evidence.* New York: Halstead.

Brickman, P., & Bulman, R. J. (1977). Pleasure and pain in social comparison. In J. M. Suls & R. L. Miller (Eds.), *Social comparison processes: Theoretical and empirical perspectives* (pp. 149–186). Washington, DC: Hemisphere.

Campbell, J. D. (1986). Similarity and uniqueness: The effects of attribute type, relevance, and individual differences in self-esteem and depression. *Journal of Personality and Social Psychology, 50*, 281–294.

Collins, R. E., Dakof, G., & Taylor, S. E. (1988). *Social comparison and adjustment to a threatening event.* Manuscript submitted for publication.

Cottrell, N. B., & Epley, S. W. (1977). Affiliation, social comparison, and socially mediated stress reduction. In J. M. Suls & R. L. Miller (Eds.), *Social comparison processes: Theoretical and empirical perspectives* (pp. 43–68). Washington, DC: Hemisphere.

Crocker, J., Thompson, L. L., McGraw, K. M., & Ingerman, C. (1987). Downward comparison, prejudice, and evaluations of others: Effects of self-esteem and threat. *Journal of Personality and Social Psychology, 52*, 907–916.

Ehrlich, H. J. (1973). *The social psychology of prejudice.* New York: Wiley.

Festinger, L. (1954). A theory of social comparison processes. *Human Relations, 7*, 117–140.

Frey, K. S., & Ruble, D. N. (1985). What children say when the teacher is not around: Conflicting goals in social comparison and performance assessment in the class-room. *Journal of Personality and Social Psychology, 48*, 550–562.

Gerard, H. B. (1963). Emotional uncertainty and social comparison. *Journal of Abnormal and Social Psychology, 66*, 568–573.

Gerard, H. B., & Rabbie, J. M. (1961). Fear and social comparison. *Journal of Abnormal and Social Psychology, 62*, 586–592.

Gibbons, F. X. (1985). Social stigma perception: Social comparison among mentally retarded persons. *American Journal of Mental Deficiency, 90*, 98–106.

Goethals, G. R., & Darley, J. M. (1977). Social comparison theory: An attributional approach. In J. M. Suls & R. L. Miller (Eds.), *Social comparison processes: Theoretical and empirical perspectives* (pp. 259–278). Washington, DC: Hemisphere.

Goethals, G. R., & Darley, J. M. (1986). Social comparison: Self-evaluation and group life. In B. Mullen & G. R. Goethals (Eds.), *Theories of group behavior* (pp. 21–47). New York: Springer-Verlag.

Hakmiller, K. L. (1966). Threat as a determinant of downward comparison. *Journal of Experimental Social Psychology* (Suppl. 1), 32–39.

Holmes, D. S. (1978). Projection as a defense mechanism. *Psychological Bulletin, 85*, 677–688.

Kulik, J. A., & Mahler, H. I. M. (1987). Effects of preoperative room-mate assignment on preoperative anxiety and recovery from coronary-bypass surgery. *Health Psychology, 6*, 525–543.

Lazarus, R. S., & Folkman, S. (1984). *Stress, appraisal and coping.* New York: Springer.

Marks, G. (1984). Thinking one's abilities are unique and one's opinions are common. *Personality and Social Psychology Bulletin, 10*, 203–208.

Molleman, E., Pruyn, J., & van Knippenberg, A. (1986). Social comparison processes among cancer patients. *British Journal of Social Psychology, 25*, 1–13.

Nosanchuk, T. A., & Erickson, B. H. (1985). How high is up? Calibrating social comparison in the real world. *Journal of Personality and Social Psychology, 48*, 624–634.

Pyszczynski, T., Greenberg, J., & LaPrelle, J. (1985). Social comparison after success and failure: Biased search for information consistent with a self-serving conclusion. *Journal of Experimental Social Psychology, 21*, 195–211.

Rimer, I. R. (1984). The mass media and the cancer patient: Some views. *Health Education Quarterly, 10*, 95–101.

Rofe, Y. (1984). Stress affiliation: A utility theory. *Psychological Review, 91*, 235–250.

Schachter, S. (1959). *The psychology of affiliation*. Stanford, CA: Stanford University Press.

Schulz, R., & Decker, S. (1985). Long-term adjustment to physical disability: The role of social support, perceived control, and self-blame. *Journal of Personality and Social Psychology, 48*, 1162–1172.

Sherman, S. J., Presson, C. C., & Chassin, L. (1984). Mechanisms underlying the false consensus effect: The special role of threats to the self. *Personality and Social Psychology Bulletin, 10*, 127–138.

Singer, J. E., & Shockley, V. L. (1965). Ability and affiliation. *Journal of Personality and Social Psychology, 1*, 95–100.

Stephan, W. G., & Rosenfield, D. (1978). Effects of desegregation on racial attitudes. *Journal of Personality and Social Psychology, 36*, 795–804.

Suls, J. M. (1977). Social comparison theory and research: An overview from 1954. In J. M. Suls & R. L. Miller (Eds.), *Social comparison processes: Theoretical and empirical perspectives* (pp. 1–20). Washington, DC: Hemisphere.

Tabachnik, N., Crocker, J., & Alloy, L. B. (1983). Depression, social comparison, and the false-consensus effect. *Journal of Personality and Social Psychology, 45*, 688–699.

Taylor, D. G., Sheatsley, P. B., & Greeley, A. M. (1978). Attitudes toward racial integration. *Scientific American, 238(6)*, 42–49.

Taylor, S. E., Aspinwall, L. G., Dakof, G. A., &. Reardon, K. (1988). *Stress, storytelling, social comparison and social support: Victim's reactions to stories of similar victims*. Manuscript in preparation.

Taylor, S. E., & Dakof, G. A. (1988). Social support and the cancer patient. In S. Spacapan & S. Oskamp (Eds.), *The social psychology of health: The Claremont symposium on applied social psychology* (pp. 95–116). Newbury Park, CA: Sage.

Taylor, S. E., Falke, R. L., Shoptaw, S. J., & Lichtman, R. R. (1986). Social support, support groups, and the cancer patient. *Journal of Consulting and Clinical Psychology, 54*, 608–615.

Taylor, S. E., & Levin, S. (1976). *Psychological aspects of breast cancer: A conceptual overview of the literature and annotated bibliography*. San Francisco: West Coast Cancer Foundation.

Taylor, S. E., Wood, J. V., & Lichtman, R. R. (1983). It could be worse: Selective evaluation as a response to victimization. *Journal of Social Issues, 39*, 19–40.

Thornton, D. A., & Arrowood, A. J. (1966). Self-evaluation, self-enhancement, and the locus of social comparison. *Journal of Experimental Social Psychology* (Suppl. 1), 40–48.

van den Borne, H. W., Pruyn, J. F. A., & van Dam-de Mey, K. (1986). Self-help in cancer patients: A review of studies on the effects of contacts between fellow-patients. *Patient Education and Counseling, 8*, 367–385.

van den Borne, H. W., Pruyn, J. F A., & van den Heuvel, W. J. A. (1987). Effects of contacts between cancer patients on their psychosocial problems. *Patient Education and Counseling, 9*, 33–51.

Wheeler, L. (1966). Motivation as a determinant of upward comparison. *Journal of Experimental Social Psychology* (Suppl. 1), 27–31.

Wheeler, L., & Koestner, R. (1984). Performance evaluation: On choosing to know the related attributes of others when we know their performance. *Journal of Experimental Social Psychology, 20*, 263–271.

Wheeler, L., Koestner, R., & Driver, R. E. (1982). Related attributes in the choice of comparison others: It's there, but it isn't all there is. *Journal of Experimental Social Psychology, 18*, 489–500.

Wills, T. A. (1981). Downward comparison principles in social psychology. *Psychological Bulletin, 90*, 245–271.

Wills, T. A. (1983). Social comparison in coping and help-seeking. In B. M. DePaulo, A. Nadler, & J. D. Fisher (Eds.), *New directions in helping* (Vol. 2, pp. 109–141). New York: Academic Press.

Wood, J. V., Taylor, S. E., & Lichtman, R. R. (1985). Social comparison in adjustment to breast cancer. *Journal of Personality and Social Psychology, 49*, 1169–1183.

Received February 8, 1988
Revision received September 7, 1988
Accepted December 16, 1988 ■

Toward a Self-Evaluation
Maintenance Model of Social Behavior

Abraham Tesser *

This article describes some of the research that has kept me preoccupied over the last six to eight years. The research explores social behavior through something called a Self-Evaluation Maintenance (SEM) model. In the space alloted I briefly describe that model; describe several studies to provide a feel for the kind of research that has been completed in an attempt to explore the predictions of the model; and take a bird's eye view of the research and the model to establish the comprehensiveness of the research, the systemic nature of the model, and the interactive quality of its predictions. Next, the SEM model is fit into the perspective of related work including self-theories, social comparison theory, and Cialdini's BIRGing research. Then I review the epistemological status of the model. Here I hope to show that by focusing more on mediating processes there is something to be learned about emotion and affect. Finally, I conclude by pointing out some of the implications of the research for a variety of areas in psychology.

The Self-Evaluation Maintenance Model

The SEM model assumes

1. persons behave in a manner that will maintain or increase self-evaluation
2. one's relationships with others have a substantial impact on self-evaluation. The SEM model is composed of two dynamic processes. Both the *reflection process* and the *comparison process*

have as component variables the closeness of another and the quality of that other's performance. These two variables interact in affecting self-evaluation but do so in quite opposite ways in each of the processes.

One's self-evaluation may be raised to the extent that a close other performs very well on some activity, that is, one can bask in the reflected glory of the close other's good performance. For example, one can point out her close relationship with her friend "the concert pianist" and thereby

* University of Georgia

increase her own self-evaluation. The better the other's performance and the closer the psychological relationship, the more one can gain in self-evaluation through the reflection process. The intellectual parent of the reflection process is Cialdini's work on BIRGing (Cialdini, Borden, Thorne, Walker, Freeman, & Sloan, 1976; Cialdini & Richardson, 1980).

The outstanding performance of a close other can, however, cause one's own performance to pale by comparison and decrease self-evaluation. Being close to a high-performing other invites comparison and results in one's own performance looking bad, thereby adversely affecting self-evaluation. Again, the better the other's performance and the closer the psychological relationship, the greater the loss in self-evaluation through the comparison process. The intellectual parent of the comparison process comes from social comparison theory (e.g., Festinger, 1954; Goethals, 1984; Suls & Miller, 1977) and is most closely compatible with Wills' (1981) idea of downward comparison.

In both the reflection process and the comparison process, if closeness or the level of the other's performance decreases, the effects of the reflection and comparison processes are attenuated or perhaps even reversed. For example, if the other person has little to do with oneself (i.e., is psychologically distant), one cannot bask in the reflected glory of his/her accomplishments nor is one as likely to engage in comparison processes. Psychological closeness is like unit relatedness (Heider, 1958): friends are closer than strangers, persons with more characteristics in common are closer than persons with fewer characteristics in common, and so on. (See Campbell & Tesser, 1985, for a more complete discussion of the closeness variable.) Similarly, if the performance of the other is mediocre, one cannot increase self-evaluation by reflection nor is one as likely to suffer decreases in self-evaluation by comparison.

It should be apparent from the description that both the reflection and comparison processes depend on the same two variables but have opposite effects on self-evaluation: when closeness and performance are high there is a potential gain in self-evaluation through the reflection process but

there is a potential loss through the comparison process. That being the case, the question arises: when will a close other's outstanding performance raise self-evaluation (via reflection) or lower self-evaluation (via comparison)? To answer this question, the *relevance* variable is introduced.

Individuals can recognize, value, and attend to the performance of others on a large variety of dimensions. However, any individual has a personal stake in doing well on only a small subset of performance dimensions. For example, being a good football player may be important to an individual's self-definition, but being a good speller may be inconsequential. A dimension is important to an individual's self-definition to the extent that he strives for competence on the dimension, describes himself in terms of the dimension, or freely chooses to engage in tasks that are related to the dimension. Another's performance is *relevant* to an individual's self-definition to the extent that the performance is on a dimension that is important to the individual's self-definition and to the extent that the other's performance is not so much better or worse than the individual's own performance that comparisons are rendered difficult.

According to the SEM model the relevance of another's performance to one's self-definition determines the relative importance of the reflection and comparison process. If the other's performance is highly relevant, then the comparison process will be relatively important and one will suffer by comparison to the close other's better performance. If the other's performance is minimally relevant, the reflection process will be relatively important and one can enhance self-evaluation by basking in the reflected glory of a close other's better performance.

Perhaps the best way to illustrate the operation of the model is through an example. Suppose Alice and her good friend Barbara try out for the high school symphonic band and only Barbara is selected. Suppose further that doing well in music is an important part of Alice's self-definition. Relevance is high, so the comparison process should be more important than the reflection process: since Barbara is close and performs better than Alice, there is a potential loss in self-evaluation for Alice. To prevent this loss, Alice can do a variety of things. She can alter the closeness of her relationship with Barbara. She can spend less time around her or focus on ways in which the two of them are different. By reducing the closeness, the impact of Barbara's better performance is reduced. Alice can also change her self-definition. She can spend less time studying music or decide that butterfly collecting is much more interesting. By reducing the importance of music to her self-definition, the relevance of Barbara's performance is reduced. The reflection process becomes relatively more important with the consequence that Alice may actually gain in self-evaluation through her close friend Barbara's good performance. Finally, Alice can attempt to affect Barbara's performance. By reducing Barbara's performance she also reduces the threat of comparison. She can break Barbara's reed or hide her music for the next try-out or she can come to believe that Barbara's good performance was based on luck. Or, she can attempt to alter her own performance by practicing more.

Some Research Examples

We have completed a number of studies now that tend to corroborate each of these strategies. Below I will review several of these studies to give you a feel for the kind of research that has been done. The studies look at changes in relative performance as a function of the relevance and closeness of the other person, changes in closeness as a function of the relevance and performance of the other, and changes in relevance or self-definition as a function of the other's closeness and performance.

The Effects of Closeness and Relevance on Performance

Affecting another's performance

Suppose an individual is able to facilitate or hinder another's performance. Under what conditions will she facilitate the other's performance? Under what conditions will she hinder the other's

performance? The SEM model suggests that the answers to these questions are conditional. That is, helping or hurting another depends on an interactive combination of the relevance of the performance dimension and the closeness of the other. When relevance is high the comparison process is more important than the reflection process. Thus, one will suffer by the other's good performance particularly if the other is close. Therefore, in order to avoid this threat to self-evaluation, when relevance is high the closer the other the less help one would expect the other to be given. On the other hand, when relevance is low, the reflection process is more important than the comparison process. One may bask in the reflection of the other's good performance, particularly if the other is close. In order to enjoy that reflection, then, when relevance is low the closer the other the more help should be given to the other.

To test this set of hypotheses, Jon Smith and I (Tesser & Smith, 1980) designed a laboratory experiment. Male subjects were recruited and asked to bring a friend to the lab with them. Each session was composed of two pairs of friends. The four subjects were individually seated in booths around the experimenter. They were told that they would participate in a verbal task. For half the subjects, the task was described as measuring important verbal skills, leadership, et cetera (high relevance). The remaining subjects were told that the task was not related to verbal intelligence or leadership or anything of importance that we could determine (low relevance). The task was actually based on the game *Password*. Each of the subjects, in turn, was given an opportunity to guess a target word from a set of clues. The clues ostensibly came from the other three participants who chose them from a list. Since the clues were graded in difficulty, the other participant could give clues that would make it easier or more difficult to guess the target word. The first two persons to guess the target word came from each of the two friendship pairs. By experimental arrangement, these two persons were made to perform poorly. It is the subsequent behavior of these two that we keep track of. If they want to help the other perform well (i.e., better than themselves), they could give clues that are easy; if they want to "hurt" the other (i.e., make him perform less well), they could give him difficult clues. The next two persons to perform were both friend and stranger to the former participants.

Common sense suggests (as well as a number of psychological theories) that one should help one's friend. However, the SEM model prediction is not that simple. When relevance is low and one can bask in the reflected glory of another's good performance, then, certainly one should help one's friend more than a stranger. However, this relationship should be attenuated and perhaps even reversed when relevance is high.

We looked at the number of experimental sessions in which the friend was helped more than the stranger and the number of sessions in which the stranger was helped more than the friend. The prediction from the SEM model was strongly upheld. When relevance was low the friend was helped more than the stranger in 10 of the 13 sessions. When relevance was high, the stranger was helped more than the friend in 10 of the 13 sessions.

Now I would like to turn to another laboratory study. This one, conducted with Jennifer Campbell (Tesser & Campbell, 1982), tested the same hypotheses. However, instead of examining a behavioral criterion, it examined cognitions or beliefs about the other's performance as a dependent variable. I think this study is particularly interesting because it has some very definite implications for psychological projection (e.g., Holmes, 1978; Sherwood, 1981). In most studies of projection, an individual is given information that he possesses an undesirable trait or attribute which he previously believed he did not possess. The extent to and conditions under which he attributes that trait to target others, that is, projects it, is then examined. From the present point of view, the feedback can be seen as a manipulation which lowers an individual's performance on a relevant dimension, thus increasing the target's relative performance. Given high relevance, the model predicts that individuals should tend to distort the target's performance downward (i.e., project the negative trait onto the target other). Further, the model predicts that this effect should be more pronounced given a

psychologically close target than given a more distant target.

There is some evidence that such a pattern does occur with the projection of negative attributes (Secord, Backman, & Eachus, 1964; Bramel, 1963; Edlow & Kiesler, 1966). However, the obtained pattern can be explained by assuming that projection is a simple, nonmotivated information-processing strategy. If a person learns something new about himself, he will, to the extent that the other is similar, simply assume that it is also true of the other (Holmes, 1978). This "information-processing" interpretation can be made to confront the SEM interpretation. The information-processing model implies that projection should increase with closeness regardless of the valence of the feedback: if one learns something positive about himself, he should be just as likely to project that as something negative. Furthermore, the information-processing model is mute with respect to the relevance of the feedback for the individual's self-definition. The SEM model makes different predictions. First, it does not necessarily predict any general tendency to project more onto close versus distant targets. Projection should be conditioned by the relevance and valence of the feedback. More positive and less negative feedback (i.e., positivity) should be projected onto a close target when the feedback is on a low-relevance dimension than when it is on a high-relevance dimension. Further, this difference in positivity in projection should be attenuated for a distant target. To explore the informationprocessing and self-evaluation maintenance explanations of social patterning in projection the following procedure was used.

Two pairs of female friends reported for each session. They were told that the study concerned personality and impression formation. Each subject was given an opportunity to describe herself to the others so that they might form impressions of one another. Then each of the participants was individually seated before a microcomputer which administered a number of items purportedly measuring social sensitivity and esthetic judgment ability. For each item, the subject was given two choices. After she chose what she thought was the correct answer and received feedback regarding that answer, she was asked to guess what answer her friend had given to the item or what answer one of the other participants, a stranger, had given to the item. The computer was programmed to provide feedback that the subject was right on half the items and wrong on half the items. Finally, subjects filled out a variety of questionnaires including items which measured the importance or relevance of social sensitivity and esthetic judgment to their own self-definition. In sum, each subject was given an opportunity to estimate the performance of a close (friend) or distant (stranger) other on both more or less relevant performance dimensions.

Recall the SEM prediction. Closeness and relevance should interact in affecting one's beliefs about the other's performance. When relevance is low one should be more charitable toward one's friend than toward a stranger. When relevance is high this effect should be attenuated, perhaps even reversed. Contrast this prediction with one which might be derived from a straightforward information-processing

model. An information-processing model might suggest that one simply projects one's own answers onto one's friend. Since one's friend is more similar to the self that would be the best guess one could make.

We looked first at projection (i.e., the number of answers that the subject said that the other gave that was similar to her own answers). There was not an overall difference as a function of closeness, as predicted by the information-processing model. Let us now consider positivity in perception, or the number of answers the subject guessed the other would get right. On this form of the dependent variable the SEM prediction is upheld. As can be seen in Figure 6.1, when the task is irrelevant, subjects are more charitable toward the friend than toward the stranger. When the task is relevant, however, just the opposite is the case. Subjects are more charitable toward the stranger than toward the friend. Thus, the data appear to support the SEM model's predictions regarding

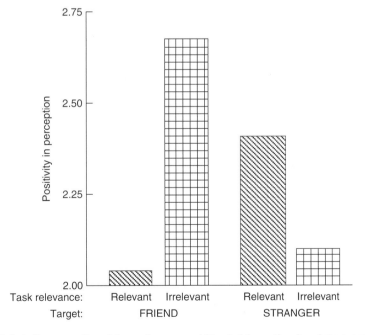

FIGURE 6.1 ■ Positivity in the perception of the performance of friends (close others) and strangers (distant others) on tasks which are relevant or irrelevant to one's self-definition. From Abraham Tesser and Jennifer Campbell, Self-evaluation Maintenance and the Perception of Friends and Strangers. *The Journal of Personality, 50:3,* pp. 261–279. Copyright © 1982 by Duke University Press.

defensive projection rather than predictions derived from the information-processing model.[1]

Some recent work on the false consensus effect (Marks & Miller, 1986; Ross, Green, & House, 1977) seems to support the "projection" aspects of these findings. According to the false consensus hypothesis people have a tendency to assume falsely that others will exhibit the same behaviors, attributes, and values as themselves. There has been a substantial amount of research on this bias and the general finding tends to substantiate the hypothesis (Mullen, Atkins, Champion, Edwards, Hardy, Story, & Vanderklok, 1985). However, the SEM model suggests that when it comes to performance, particularly performance on a relevant dimension, one should not see others as similar but rather as performing less well. In a recent theoretical review, Marks and Miller (1986) conclude that this is the case. For example, Gary Marks (1984) found that when dealing with performance dimensions or ability dimensions rather than a false consensus effect, one obtains a false uniqueness effect. Jennifer Campbell (1986), in a very sophisticated analysis of the accuracy issue in projection and the false consensus effect, similarly found a false uniqueness effect when dealing with performance or ability dimensions. Further, this false uniqueness effect becomes even more pronounced as the performance dimension becomes more self-relevant. Finally, Suls and Wan (1987) found false uniqueness effects on estimates of fear when such estimates could bolster one's perceived self-competence. I think the cross-fertilization among these approaches (psychological projection, false consensus, and the SEM model) will turn out to be a good thing.

Affecting own performance

If one conceptualizes performance in relative terms, then comparison and reflection processes can be affected not only by changing another's performance but by changing one's own performance as well. Let us focus first on relevant performance.

When a close other's performance is relevant to one's self-identification there is a potential for one to suffer lowered self-evaluation via the comparison process. One way to reduce this potential is to increase one's own efforts (behavioral) or facilitatively distort the perception of one's own performance (cognitive).

There is some preliminary evidence consistent with both of these resolutions. Tesser, Campbell, and Campbell (reported in Tesser & Campbell, 1986) looked at own actual performance among high school students. Relevance of school was defined in terms of interest in having additional education. It follows from the model that, given high relevance of school:

1. The better another's performance, the more one will try and, hence, the better one's own performance.
2. This will be particularly true if the other is close (i.e., a friend).

On the other hand, given low relevance:

3. The overall impact of others' performance on one's own should be attenuated.
4. The difference between friends and nonfriends should also be attenuated.

The effects of socioeconomic status, sex, and race were statistically removed from each respondent's own grade point average (GPA). Respondents were divided in terms of high or low interest in school. Within these groups, respondent's own "residualized" GPA was correlated with the GPA of a classmate that the respondent nominated as a friend and a classmate that the respondent did not nominate as a friend. The pattern of correlations conformed to theoretical expectations. The only correlation which was significantly more positive than zero is that among high-relevance respondents and their friends. When school is relevant, i.e., respondents want more education, the difference between the correlations for friends and nonfriends is significant. When school is not relevant, the corresponding difference

---

[1] The SEM hypothesis can also be contrasted with a balance theory hypothesis (Heider, 1958). Since one likes or is in a unit relationship with a friend but not necessarily with a stranger, one should, according to balance theory, attribute good things to one's friend. As noted in the text, this general difference was not obtained. Only in the low-relevance condition was one more charitable to one's friend.

in correlations is not significant. None of the other differences in correlation are significant.

There is also evidence for the distortion of one's own performance. Tesser, Campbell, and Smith (1984) compared performance ratings that fifth and sixth graders made of their own performance, on a relevant activity and on an irrelevant activity, with the ratings made by their teacher. If the teachers' ratings are interpreted as an "objective" benchmark then the students distorted their performance upward on the relevant activity and downward on the irrelevant activity.

Although these studies are consistent with the present viewpoint, they are correlational and there are a number of plausible alternative explanations of the results. What is needed is a more detailed theoretical analysis and more focused research. Generally, I would expect that performance which is important to one's self-definition is well practiced and actually difficult to improve. So it becomes important to specify the conditions under which threat from the comparison process will affect increased efforts to improve own performance. Since it is difficult to improve performance, attempts at actual improvement should be more likely when another's performance is unambiguously better than one's own performance (and difficult to distort) and it is difficult or costly to reduce the level of that close other's performance. Further, if one believes that effort will result in better performance, then increased task effort might be more likely as a result of the threat of comparison.

The good performance of a close other could result in increasing own effort because the other's performance is "inspirational." That is, the good performance of a close other may redefine the possibilities for the self: "If he/she can do it so can I." My guess is that the inspirational effect is most likely when the close other has not outperformed the self in the past and/or the other's better performance relies on a new (to the self) instrumentality. Both conditions define a *possibility* for self-improvement: in the first instance, when someone who has not been better than the actor becomes better than the actor it may suggest that the actor can also improve. The introduction of a new instrumentality, the second condition, also suggests that the actor can improve himself, this time by doing things differently.

To this point we have focused on the conditions under which persons may attempt to increase their own efforts to make their performance better. The SEM model suggests that there are also circumstances under which one may actually perform at a less-than-optimal level. In dealing with the maximization of own performance we focused on the comparison process of the SEM model. People can maintain a positive self-evaluation by the reflection process as well. One can bask in the reflected glory of a close other's outstanding performance if that performance has little relevance to one's self-definition. One way of making another's performance look good is to make one's own (relative) performance look bad. This leads to the prediction that when the performance of another is low in relevance to the self the closer the other the greater the possibility that one will actually perform poorer than he/she would when that other's performance is self-relevant.

Since there is a general tendency for people to want to do well, the prediction of self-handicapping may not seem plausible. Therefore, qualifications of this prediction may be in order. For example, from an intuitive perspective the relevance of the activity to the other person should play a role. If the performance is highly relevant to the other (but low in relevance to the self), there is an added inducement to handicap one's own performance. Under high relevance to the other, one's own poorer performances provide something for the other. That is, while the self is basking in the other's (relative) accomplishment, the other is not threatened by comparison. The closer the relationship with the other person is the greater the impact of relevance-to-other on self's own performance.

Clearly, this line of thinking is speculative. A better understanding of the determinant of own effort on own self-handicapping is important from both a practical and a theoretical perspective. It would seem then that this would be a productive line of research to pursue.

The Effects of Relevance and Performance on Closeness

Now we focus on some research dealing with the effects of relevance and performance on closeness.

How should relevance, or self-definition, interact with another's performance to affect closeness? Let's go back to the basic dynamics of the SEM model to make a prediction. When relevance is high the comparison process is more important than the reflection process and one will suffer by the other's good performance, particularly if the other is close. In order to avoid this potential threat to self-evaluation we would expect that when relevance is high the better the other's performance the less close or the more distance one will put between one's self and the other. On the other hand, when relevance is low and the reflection process is important there is the possibility of basking in the reflected glory of another's good performance, particularly if that other is close. Therefore, in order to experience that potential gain, when relevance is low, the better the other's performance the closer one should put oneself to another.

To test this hypothesis, we (Pleban & Tesser, 1981) returned to the laboratory. When our male subjects showed up they found one other subject already there. Both participants filled out a questionnaire which asked them to indicate how important various areas were to their self-definition. The areas consisted of things like rock music, current events, hunting and fishing, and so on. After finishing the questionnaire, the two subjects competed in a kind of college bowl competition. The experimenter, on a random basis, selected a topic that was either high or low in relevance to the subject's self-definition. The other subject, actually a confederate, had previously memorized the answers to all the questions. When the questioning began, the confederate varied his performance so that he either clearly outperformed the real subject, performed about the same, or was outperformed by the real subject. Following the question-and-answer period the subjects were given feedback about how they did. The subject learned that he had performed about average, near the 50th percentile. The subject also learned that the confederate was clearly better (performing at the 80th percentile), slightly better (performing at the 60th percentile), slightly worse (performing at the 40th percentile), or much worse (performing at the 20th percentile). Thus,

we had manipulated relevance to the subject's self-definition and the relative performance of the other.

In order to measure closeness, we asked the subjects to go into an adjoining room. The confederate sat down first and we simply measured how close or far the subject sat from the confederate. After they were seated, a questionnaire containing alternative, paper and pencil, measures of closeness was administered. Recall our expectations: when relevance is high, the better the other's performance the less close the subject should put himself to the other. When relevance is low, the better the other's performance the closer the subject should put himself to the other.

It should be noted at the outset that level of performance made no difference when the subject outperformed the confederate. However, when the confederate outperformed the subject, each of the expectations from the SEM model was sustained. Let us look first at the behavioral index (see Figure 6.2), the distance the individual sat from the confederate. As can be seen, as the confederate's performance improved from the 60th percentile to the 80th percentile, the subject's distance increased when the topic was one of high relevance; the subject's distance decreased or closeness increased when the topic was of low relevance. Similar effects were obtained with the behavioroid index (Aronson & Carlsmith, 1968), "Would you want to work with this (confederate) again?" and with the cognitive index, "How much are you and this confederate alike?" There were no reliable effects on the affect index, "How attracted are you to this confederate?" Taken together these results offer some nice support for the hypotheses and also suggest that the closeness variable be defined in unit-formation terms rather than affect terms. Both the behavioral and the cognitive indices of closeness showed the predicted effect, while the affective index did not.

Before we take this conclusion too seriously, however, I would like to describe a study by Toni Giuliano and Dan Wegner (personal communication, May, 1985). The study was done for another purpose but seems to have some clear implications for the self-evaluation maintenance model and its

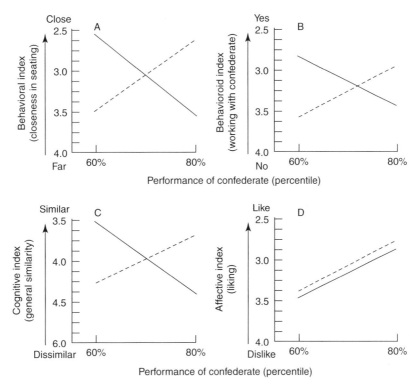

FIGURE 6.2 ▪ The effects of relative performance and relevance on closeness to other as indexed by behavioral, behavioroid, cognitive, and affective indices. Solid lines indicate high relevance; broken lines indicate low relevance. From Pleban and Tesser (1981).

predictions about closeness. The model predicts that we should be close to others who do not outperform us on things that are self-definitional and thereby do not threaten us by comparison, but do outperform us on things that are not self-definitional so that we can bask in their reflected glory. Giuliano and Wegner gave 50 couples a list of topics, including things like restaurants, movies, money and business, phone numbers, famous sculptures, and so on. For each topic, each member of the couple had to indicate which of them was an expert, that they were both experts, or that neither was an expert. Let us assume that areas in which one claims expertise are more relevant than areas in which one does not claim expertise. If one's partner acknowledges one's expertise there is no threat by comparison as a result of closeness. Further, to acknowledge another's expertise in an area in which one does not claim personal expertise (low relevance) is to

provide for the opportunity to bask in the reflected glory of that other, particularly if the other is close.

Giuliano and Wegner computed what they call a differentiation score (i.e., the number of items on which one member of the couple claims expertise and the other member corroborates that claim). The SEM model leads us to expect that the greater the number of such items; that is, the higher the differentiation score, the closer the couple. Giuliano and Wegner correlated the differentiation score with the couple's rated satisfaction with the relationship. The correlation was in the predicted direction and it was substantial, $r = .60$.

Although there are undoubtedly alternative explanations, the Giuliano and Wegner data seem to be consistent with the SEM model. They are also consistent with the notion of complementarity in interpersonal attraction. Couples that show a large number of areas in which there are acknowledged *differences* in expertise are more satisfied with the relationship. The prominent finding in the interpersonal attraction literature is that persons who are *similar* to one another tend to be more satisfied (e.g., Byrne, 1969). Elsewhere (Campbell & Tesser, 1985; Tesser, 1984) we have argued that much of the evidence for similarity leading to attraction concerns similarity on what might be called emotional dimensions. That is, values, opinions, and the like. As noted above, patterns of complementarity or uniqueness are more likely to be associated with closeness on things like ability domains or performance domains.

The Effects of Performance and Closeness on Relevance

Now let us turn to some examples of research on the determinants of self-definition or the relevance parameter. Again, the model makes some very specific predictions. Recall that the relevance parameter directly weights the comparison process and inversely weights the reflection process. Thus, the relevance of an activity increases the importance of the comparison process relative to the reflection process. When another's performance is better than one's own, one should reduce the relevance of that performance dimension. This would permit one to bask in reflected glory rather than suffer by comparison. Further, one's tendency to reduce relevance should be greater the closer the other person. In short, the better another's performance in an activity the less relevant should that activity be to one's self-definition, particularly if the other person is close.

The study to be described here has both behavioral and cognitive measures of relevance or self-definition. The laboratory study was completed in collaboration with Del Paulhus (Tesser & Paulhus, 1983). Pairs of male subjects were told that the experiment concerned the validation of a personality inventory. Half the subjects were led to believe that the two of them were scheduled at the same time because they were very much alike in a number of different ways (the close condition). The remaining subjects were led to believe that they were scheduled at the same time because they were very different from one another (the distant condition).

The subjects were then seated before a microcomputer and worked on a task which they were told measured cognitive–perceptual integration. After working on the task for some time, they were given feedback. Subjects learned that they had outperformed the other subject or that the other subject had outperformed them at cognitive–perceptual integration. Thus, we had manipulated closeness and performance. (The study was actually more involved than this and dealt with the issue of public versus private self-evaluation maintenance. This issue, however, is beyond the scope of this article. See Tesser & Barbee, 1985; Tesser & Moore, 1987; and Tesser & Paulhus, 1983, for discussion.) There were three measures of relevance: an interview measure in which the subjects were asked how important cognitive–perceptual integration was to them; a questionnaire measure, again asking how important cognitive–perceptual integration was; and a behavioral measure. The behavioral measure involved surreptitiously observing the amount of time the subjects spent reading biographies of persons they believed were high in cognitive–perceptual integration versus low in cognitive–perceptual integration.

Each of the measures produced the same pattern of results. They were therefore combined and are displayed in Figure 6.3. Recall our prediction: the better another does relative to the self, the less relevant should be the performance dimension, particularly when that other is close. This is precisely the pattern that was found and the interaction is significant.

Now we leave the laboratory and look at data from a "real world" setting, that of the family. These data have been collected by William Owens, who has over the last several years collected biographical data on a large number of undergraduates at the University of Georgia (e.g., Owens & Schoenfeldt, 1979). One of the questions that he has asked these freshmen is "During the time you spent at home, how successful were your brothers and/or sisters in such things as popularity, skills, possessions, and appearance?" They were able to respond, "The other was more successful," "We were equally successful," or "I was more successful." Thus, there was a measure of relative performance among siblings. But what about a measure of closeness? Certainly siblings are close. While this is true, we

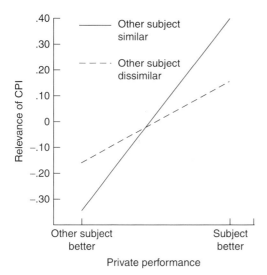

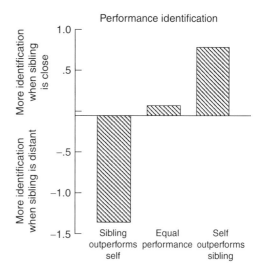

FIGURE 6.3 ■ The effects of relative performance on cognitive–perceptual integration (CPI) and similarity (i.e., closeness) of other on the relevance of CPI to one's self-definition. Relevance is averaged over behavioral, interview, and questionnaire measures. From "The definition of self: Private and public self-evaluation management strategies" by A. Tesser and D. Paulhus, 1983, *Journal of Personality and Social Psychology, 44,* 672–682. Copyright 1983 by the American Psychological Association. Adapted by permission.

FIGURE 6.4 ■ The effects of closeness of age and perceived relative performance of sibling on performance identification with sibling. Data for male subjects only. Data from "Self-esteem maintenance in family dynamics" by A. Tesser, 1980, *Journal of Personality and Social Psychology, 39,* 77–91. Copyright 1980 by the American Psychological Association. Adapted by permission.

(Tesser, 1980) took difference in age as an index of relative closeness. That is, we assumed that siblings separated by less than three years of age were closer than siblings separated by more than three years of age. Now we had measures of relative performance and closeness. What about relevance? Recall that relevance has to do with self-identity. Fortunately, Owens included a couple of items which dealt with identification with the sibling: "How much were you like your brother or sister in skills and ability . . . ways of acting in social situations?" Now we had, if not direct measures, at least proxies for each of the items we needed to

test the hypothesis. We are interested in the interactive effects of closeness and performance on relevance or, in this case, identification with the sibling.

We focused only on the respondents from two sibling families. The data displayed in Figure 6.4 are the effect of closeness. That is, a positive number means more identification when the sibling is close (less than three years apart in age) than when the sibling is distant (more than three years apart in age). A negative number means less identification when the sibling is close than when the sibling is distant.

There were no effects for females.[2] It is the data for males that are displayed, and these data are quite consistent with the model. When the

---

[2] Although SEM predictions have been supported in several studies including females, on the few occasions on which gender effects have been found the SEM effects have been stronger for males than for females. This may mean a variety of things. Perhaps the tasks used had differential relevance for males and females; perhaps the comparison process (competition) is less important for females than for males (Bond & Vinacke, 1961; Gilligan, 1982). It is worth noting in this context that the differences between males and females may also characterize

differences between cultures which may make the model more or less applicable. For example, when the comparison process is presumed to be important, the formulation may work best for people with a desire to enhance their self-evaluation *individualistically*, such as Western or even American society. Societies with a more collectivist orientation, in which individual value is presumably less prized (such as Soviet Russia in theory), might not show the same kind of effects.

respondent believes he is outperformed by his sibling, then the closer (in age) the sibling the less the identification with the sibling. On the other hand, when the respondent believes he outperforms his sibling this closeness effect is reversed: greater closeness (in age) leads to greater identification. Thus, the model appears to have some nontrivial implications for self-identity and for intrafamily relationships.

The implications of the SEM model for family relationships have only begun to be explored. For example, there has been some discussion of the use and development of SEM processes in a family context (Tesser, 1984). And there are some preliminary, archival data bearing on the dynamics of father–son relationships (Tesser, 1980, Study 3). In spite of these beginnings, however, some of the fascinating and fundamental questions about the applicability of comparison and reflection processes in parent–child relationships have yet to be dealt with in any definitive way. [...]

The Model in Perspective

To this point I have given a broad-brush description of the SEM and reviewed a sample of the available evidence to evaluate it. The SEM model draws on a number of research traditions in psychology and sociology. The model is generally related to what might loosely be called self-theory. Its more specific antecedents include social comparison theory and Cialdini's research and theorizing on "BIRGing" phenomena. Below I deal with each of these.

Self-Theory

The self-evaluation model has at its core the assumption that persons behave so as to maintain a positive self-evaluation. Such a notion is not new. William James (1907) discussed it at the turn of the century. While most contemporary psychologists agree that persons tend to see themselves in a positive light (cf. Greenwald, 1980; Taylor & Brown, 1986), whether such positive self-perception is motivated or a cold information-processing strategy is still debatable. Thus, some investigators see self-serving attribution biases as motivated (Bowerman, 1978; Bradley, 1978; Zuckerman, 1979) while others see them as the result of information-processing strategies and biases (Nisbett & Ross, 1980; Miller & Ross, 1975). There is even an emerging literature to suggest that self-serving biases/distortions may be associated with positive mental health (Taylor & Brown, 1986). For example, compared to normals, mildly depressed/low self-esteem individuals are less vulnerable to an illusion of control (e.g., Greenberg & Alloy, 1987) and more accurate (and less optimistic) in estimating future task performance (e.g., Campbell & Fairey, 1985). This is not to say that even nondepressed/high self-esteem persons do not have some negative self-conceptions (e.g., shy, fat; Wurf & Markus, 1983, 1986). The general thrust, however, is toward positivity. Obviously maintenance of positive self-evaluation is central to the SEM model and, therefore, so are these issues.

The relevance parameter of the model deals specifically with the substance of one's self-definition and there are a number of self-theories that address this question as well (cf. Gordon & Gergen, 1968). McGuire (e.g., McGuire, 1987; McGuire, Child, & Fujioka, 1978; McGuire & Padawer-Singer, 1976) has noted that psychological investigations of self-concept have focused very narrowly on self-evaluation or self-esteem. However, when persons are allowed to choose the dimensions that are salient or significant to them, fewer than 10% of their choices deal with self-evaluative dimensions (McGuire & Padawer-Singer, 1976). Although self-evaluation dimensions per se may constitute only a small fraction of spontaneous choices, the large majority of the dimensions chosen are subject to evaluation. For example, attributes such as actor, jogger, bridge player, gardener, expert on baseball, and mother are not in themselves self-evaluative, but performance on these attributes is certainly subject to evaluation. The SEM model suggests that the relevance of these "nonevaluative" attributes for one's self-definition is determined to a large extent by attempts to maintain a positive self-evaluation.

Hazel Markus (1977) has suggested that the substance of one's self inheres in relatively enduring self-schemas. These schemas serve to make pertinent areas of the individual's functioning more salient, easier to remember, and easier to organize. Persons who are self-schematic with respect to a particular attribute in Markus's terms are, in the terminology of the present model, persons for whom that attribute is relevant.[3] Thus, the two bodies of research appear to be complementary. Markus's work details the effects of relevance on information processing (e.g., Markus & Wurf, 1987) and the present work makes some suggestions about the conditions under which self-schemata will change.

From a symbolic interactionist position (Mead, 1934), the self emerges from social interaction (Stryker & Statham, 1985). Thus, Cooley (1902) developed the notion of the looking-glass self. One's view of one's self comes from what one imagines others think of him/her. The present thesis also suggests that others play a crucial role in determining the substance of self but that the actor himself is a more active ingredient in the genesis of imagined (and real) consensus. I have already detailed how others' closeness and performance affect one's self-view. Perhaps the interpersonal aspects of these dynamics lead persons to share the same view of one another. That is, it is to each actor's advantage, especially if they are in a close relationship, to agree on how they see one another. It is to Actor A's advantage to see Actor B as the kind of person who is good at "X" if Actor A is good at "Y," just as it is to Actor B's advantage to see himself as good at "X" if Actor A is good at "Y." By doing this both can take joy in and promote the accomplishments of the other without being threatened by those accomplishments. Thus, one might speculate that persons negotiate their self-identity with those around them (Secord & Backman, 1965; Swann, 1983; Swann & Predmore, 1985). The result of such a process would be a kind of bargain in which the participants agree on a set of complementary identities. The agreement would serve to validate one another's view of self while enhancing one's own view of self.

Social Comparison Theory

[…] Social comparison theory is predicated on the notion that persons want to understand their world. They come together, communicate, and influence one another to gain cognitive clarity, to validate their opinions and to evaluate their skills. The theory does prominently include the notion that there is a unidirectional drive upward with respect to abilities, and a number of subsequent workers have focused on the role of self-evaluation maintenance (e.g., Gruder, 1977; Hakmiller, 1966; Thornton & Arrowood, 1966; Wheeler, 1966; Friend & Gilbert, 1973; Wills, 1981, 1985; Wood, Taylor, & Lichtman, 1985). However, the emphasis of the original theory is clearly on gaining cognitive clarity rather than on self-enhancement. In contrast, the present approach starts at the point at which the person already knows how to evaluate his abilities (and opinions) and deals with the consequences of such knowledge.[4] The motivational emphasis is not on reducing uncertainty but rather on maintaining or enhancing self-evaluation.

Much of the classical research generated by the theory of social comparison processes is only tangentially relevant to the present formulation. The rank-order choice experimental paradigm is an example. In this paradigm, an individual is given feedback (i.e., a score on a particular attribute) and is then asked which other scores in the distribution he would like to examine. A typical finding with this paradigm is that subjects tend to want to see scores of others slightly higher than themselves (e.g., Wheeler, 1966). These findings can be interpreted as supporting both cognitive clarity and self-evaluation maintenance motives (e.g., Gruder, 1977). However, desire for private information about score

---

[3] In the present approach relevant dimensions are dimensions on which persons strive for excellence. According to Markus, people can have self-schemas on nonperformance dimensions—some people have a fat self-schema (Markus, Sentis, & Hammill, 1979). Even here, however, it is possible to think of someone striving to become thin.

[4] Brickman and his colleagues (Brickman & Bulman, 1977; Perloff & Brickman, 1980) have dealt with social comparison-like situations in which persons know where they stand with respect to some ability. The questions they raise and sensitively deal with are as follows: When will an individual avoid or seek comparison? When will he display or withhold information about his own performance?

distributions is not equivalent to affecting the public psychological distance to another. Indeed, these two variables behave quite differently (Wheeler, Shaver, Jones, Goethals, Cooper, Robinson, Bruou, & Butzine, 1969; Wilson & Benner, 1971). The latter is more nearly what is meant by closeness in the present model. Furthermore, none of the studies, to this writer's knowledge, varies the relevance of the performance dimension. Thus, interpretation of the outcomes in terms of the SEM model is only possible if one is willing to make some assumption about relevance. The rank-order choice paradigm is typical of the kind of research generated by social comparison theory. […]

The models are also quite different in their specifics. The "comparison component" of the SEM model comes formally closest to social comparison theory. Recall, however, that the comparison component is only half of the SEM model. The SEM model also includes a "reflection component," the notion that persons can gain in self-evaluation by being close to a high-performing other on a low-relevance dimension. There is no analogous component in the theory of social comparison processes.

Cialdini's BIRGing Research

The reflection component of the model comes closest to Cialdini's research on "Basking in Reflected Glory," or BIRGing (Cialdini *et al.*, 1976). Cialdini and his co-workers have found that persons tend to put themselves into close association with "winners." For example, college students are more likely to wear clothing that identifies their own school following a winning football weekend than following a losing football weekend. Students are more likely to use the pronoun "we" when describing a football game that their school team won than when describing a football game that their school lost. Furthermore, the latter tendency is more pronounced after the students have undergone a failure experience than after they have undergone a success experience. This finding suggests that BIRGing is in the service of self-evaluation maintenance.

Cialdini and Richardson (1980) explain BIRGing in terms of Heider's (1958) balance theory. The argument is that if a person is in a positive unit relation with a positively evaluated entity, then balance forces will lead the person to be positively evaluated. As a further test of this explanation, they reasoned that if a person is in a negative relation with another entity, to the extent that the entity was negatively evaluated, balance forces would cause the person to be positively evaluated. In an experiment designed to test this idea subjects were given either a success or failure experience and were then given an opportunity to rate (compliment or "blast") their own university (positive association) or a rival university (negative association). Consistent with the balance theory prediction, the tendency to compliment one's own university and blast the rival university increased with prior threat to self-evaluation.

The BIRGing research and theorizing is quite consistent with the SEM model. However, the BIRGing research is more generally interpreted in terms of self-presentation rather than private self-evaluation. Further, there is no relevance parameter in the BIRGing approach and it deals only with the reflection half of the SEM model. On the basis of the research reviewed here, I would argue that a more complete picture must include both reflection and comparison processes and a way of weighting these processes, i.e., a relevance parameter. […]

Conclusion

It should be clear that the SEM approach has implications for a variety of areas of concern to psychologists. It has implications for prosocial behavior, the helping and hurting of others to affect their performance. It has implications for one's own personal performance as well. There are implications for interpersonal relationships, attraction, unit formation, and the like (See Campbell & Tesser, 1985, for discussion). It also raises some developmental questions: What is the origin of the self-evaluation maintenance processes? How do they play themselves out in families? (See Tesser, 1984, for discussion.) Lowered self-evaluation and negative affect are the hallmarks of depression. The SEM model provides a social psychological perspective for understanding these symptoms. Each of these implications is worth pursuing, but they are beyond the present discussion.

REFERENCES

Aronson, E., & J. M. Carlsmith. (1968). Experimentation in social psychology. In G. Lindzey & E. Aronson (Eds.), *Handbook of social psychology, social edition* (Vol. 2). Reading, MA: Addison-Wesley.

Bond, J. R., & Vinacke, W. E. (1961). Coalitions in mixed-sex triads. *Sociometry, 24,* 61–75.

Bowerman, W. R. (1978). Subjective competence: The structure, process and functions of self-referent causal attributions. *Journal of the Theory of Social Behavior, 8,* 45–75.

Bramel, D. (1963). Selection of target for defensive projection. *Journal of Abnormal and Social Psychology, 66,* 318–324.

Byrne, D. (1969). Attitudes and attraction. In L. Berkowitz (Ed.), *Advances in experimental social psychology* (Vol. 4) (pp. 36–90). New York: Academic Press.

Campbell, J. D. (1986). Similarity and uniqueness: The effects of attribute type, relevance, and individual differences in self-esteem and depression. *Journal of Personality and Social Psychology, 50,* 281–294.

Campbell, J. D., & Fairey, P. J. (1985). Effects of self-esteem, hypothetical explanations, and verbalization of expectancies on future performance. *Journal of Personality and Social Psychology, 48,* 1097–1111.

Campbell, J. D., & Tesser, A. (1985), Self evaluation maintenance processes in relationships. In S. Duck & D. Perlman (Eds.), *Personal Relationships* (Vol. 1). London: Sage.

Cialdini, R. B., Borden, R. J., Thorne, A., Walker, M. R., Freeman, S., & Sloan, L. R. (1976). Basking in reflected glory: Three (football) field studies. *Journal of Personality and Social Psychology, 34,* 366–375.

Cialdini, R. B., & Richardson, K. D. (1980). Two indirect tactics of image management: Basking and blasting, *Journal of Personality and Social Psychology, 39,* 406–415.

Cooley, C. H. (1902). *Human nature and the social order.* New York: Scribner.

Edlow, D. W., & Kiesler, C. A. (1966). Ease of denial and defensive projection. *Journal of Experimental Social Psychology, 2,* 56–59.

Festinger, L. (1954). A theory of social comparison processes. *Human Relations, 7,* 117–140.

Friend, R. M., & Gilbert, J. (1973). Threat and fear of negative evaluation as determinants of locus of social comparison. *Journal of Personality, 41,* 328–340.

Gilligan, C. (1982). *In a different voice.* Cambridge, MA: Harvard University Press.

Goethals, G. B. (1984). *Social comparison theory: Psychology from the lost and found.* Paper presented at the American Psychological Association, Toronto.

Gordon, C., & Gergen, K. J. (1968). (Eds.), *The self in social interaction* (Vol. 1). New York: Wiley.

Greenberg, M. S., & Alloy, L. B. (1987). Depression versus anxiety: Differences in self and other schemata. In L. B. Alloy (Ed.), *Cognitive processes in depression.* New York: Guilford.

Greenwald, A. G. (1980). The totalitarian ego: Fabrication and revision of personal history. *American Psychologist, 35,* 603–618.

Gruder, C. L. (1977). Choice of comparison persons in evaluating one's self. In J. Suls & R. L. Miller (Eds.), *Social comparison process: Theoretical and empirical perspectives.* Washington, DC: Hemisphere.

Hakmiller, K. L. (1966). Threat as a determinant of downward comparison. *Journal of Experimental Social Psychology, 2* (Suppl. 1), 32–39.

Heider, F. (1958). *The psychology of interpersonal relations.* New York: Wiley.

Holmes, D. S. (1978). Projection as a defense mechanism. *Psychological Bulletin, 85,* 677–688.

James, W. (1907). *The principles of psychology* (Vol. 1). New York: Holt.

Marks, G. (1984). Thinking one's abilities are unique and one's opinions are common. *Personality and Social Psychology Bulletin, 10,* 203–208.

Marks, G., & Miller, N. (1986). Ten years of research on the "False Consensus Effect": An empirical and theoretical review. *Psychological Bulletin, 102,* 72–90.

Markus, H. (1977). Self-schemata and processing information about the self. *Journal of Personality and Social Psychology, 35,* 63–78.

Markus, H., Sentis, K., & Hamill, R. (1979). *Thinking fat: Self-schemes for body weight and the processing of weight relevant information.* Unpublished manuscript, University of Michigan.

Markus, H., & Wurf, E. (1987). The dynamic self-concept: A social psychological perspective. *Annual Review of Psychology, 38,* 300–333.

McGuire, W. J. (1987). Content and process in the experience of self. In L. Berkowitz (Ed.), *Advances in experimental social psychology* (Vol. 20). New York: Academic Press.

McGuire, W. J., McGuire, C. V., Child, P., & Fujioka, T. (1978). Salience of ethnicity in the spontaneous self- concept as a function of one's ethnic distinctiveness in the social environment. *Journal of Personality and Social Psychology, 36,* 511–520.

McGuire, W. J., & Padawer-Singer, A. (1976). Trait salience in the spontaneous self-concept. *Journal of Personality and Social Psychology, 33,* 743–754.

Mead, G. H. (1934). *Mind, self and society.* Chicago: University of Chicago Press.

Miller, D. T., & Ross, M. (1975). Self-serving biases in the attribution of causality: Fact or fiction? *Psychological Bulletin, 82,* 213–225.

Mullen, B., Atkins, J. L., Champion, D. S., Edwards, C., Hardy, D., Story, J. E., & Vanderklok, M. (1985). The false consensus effect: A metananalysis of 155 hypothesis tests. *Journal of Experimental Social Psychology, 22,* 262–283.

Nisbett, R., & Ross, L. (1980). *Human inferences: Strategies and shortcomings of social judgment.* Englewood Cliffs, NJ: Prentice-Hall.

Owens, W. A., & Schoenfeldt, L. F. (1979). Toward a classification of persons. *Journal of Applied Psychology, (Monograph), 64,* 569–607.

Pleban, R., & Tesser, A. (1981). The effects of relevance and quality of another's performance on interpersonal closeness. *Social Psychology Quarterly, 44,* 278–285.

Ross, L., Green, D., & House, P. (1977). The false consensus phenomenon: An attributional bias in self-perception. *Journal of Experimental Social Psychology, 13,* 279–301.

Secord, P. F., & Backman, C. W. (1965). An interpersonal approach to personality. In B. A. Maher (Ed.). *Progress in experimental personality research* (Vol. 2) (pp. 91–125). New York: Academic Press.

Secord, P. F., Backman, C. W., & Eachus, H. T. (1964). Effects of imbalance in the self-concept on the perception of persons. *Journal of Abnormal and Social Psychology, 68,* 442–446.

Sherwood, G. G. (1981). Self-serving biases in person perception: A reexamination of defense. *Psychological Bulletin, 90,* 445–459.

Stryker, S., & Statham, A. (1985). Symbolic interaction and role theory. In G. Lindzey & E. Aronson (Eds.), *Handbook of social psychology* (Vol. I) (3rd ed.) (pp. 311–378). New York: Random House.

Suls, J., & Wan, C. K. (1987). In search of the false uniqueness phenomenon: Fear and estimates of social consensus. *Journal of Personality and Social Psychology, 52,* 211–217.

Swann, W. B., Jr. (1983). Self-verification: Bringing social reality into harmony with the self. In J. Suls & A. G. Greenwald (Eds.), *Psychological perspectives on the self* (Vol. 2). Hillsdale, NJ: Erlbaum.

Swann, W. B., & Predmore, S. C. (1985). Intimates as agents of social support: Sources of consolation or despair? *Journal of Personality and Social Psychology, 49,* 1609–1617.

Taylor, S. E., & Brown, J. D. (1986). Illusion and well-being: Some social psychological contributions to a theory of mental health. Submitted to *American Psychologist.*

Tesser, A. (1980). Self-esteem maintenance in family dynamics. *Journal of Personality and Social Psychology, 39,* 77–91.

Tesser, A. (1984). Self-evaluation maintenance processes: Implications for relationships and development. In J. Masters & K. Yarkin (Eds.), *Boundary areas of psychology: Social and development.* New York: Academic Press.

Tesser, A., & Barbee, A. (1985). *Appearing competent: Self-evaluation maintenance processes.* Unpublished manuscript, University of Georgia.

Tesser, A., & Campbell, J. (1980). Self-definition: The impact of the relative performance and similarity of others. *Social Psychology Quarterly, 43,* 341–347.

Tesser, A., & Campbell, J. (1982). Self-evaluation maintenance and the perception of friends and strangers. *Journal of Personality, 59,* 261–279.

Tesser, A., & Campbell, J. (1983). Self-definition and self-evaluation maintenance. In J. Suls & A. Greenwald (Eds.), *Social psychological perspectives on the self* (Vol. 2).

Tesser, A., & Campbell, J. (1986). A self-evaluation maintenance model of student motivation. In C. Ames & R. Ames (Eds.), *Research on motivation in education: The classroom milieu.* Orlando, FL: Academic Press.

Tesser, A., Campbell, J., & Smith, M. (1984). Friendship choice and performance: Self-evaluation maintenance in children. *Journal of Personality and Social Psychology, 46,* 561–574.

Tesser, A., & Moore, J. (1987). On the convergence of public and private aspect of self. In R. Baumeister (Ed.), *Public self and private self.* Berlin: Springer-Verlag.

Tesser, A., & Paulhus, D. (1983). The definition of self: Private and public self-evaluation management strategies. *Journal of Personality and Social Psychology, 44,* 672–682.

Tesser, A., & Smith, J. (1980). Some effects of friendship and task relevance on helping: You don't always help the one you like. *Journal of Experimental Social Psychology, 16,* 582–590.

Thibaut, J. W., & Kelley, H. H. (1959). *The social psychology of groups.* New York: Wiley.

Thornton, D. A., & Arrowood, A. J. (1966). Self-evaluation, self-enhancement, and the locus of social comparison. *Journal of Experimental Social Psychology, 2* (Suppl. 1), 40–48.

Wheeler, L. (1966). Motivation as a determinant of upward comparison. *Journal of Experimental Social Psychology, 2* (Suppl. 1), 27–31.

Wheeler, L., Shaver, K. G., Jones, R. A., Goethals, G. R., Cooper, J., Robinson, J. E., Gruder, C. L., & Butzine, K. W. (1969). Factors determining choice of a comparison other. *Journal of Experimental Social Psychology, 5,* 219–232.

Wills, T. A. (1981). Downward comparison principles in social psychology. *Psychological Bulletin, 90,* 245–271.

Wills, T. A. (1985). Downward comparison as a coping mechanism. In C. R. Snyder & C. Ford (Eds.), *Clinical and social-psychological perspectives on negative life events.* New York: Academic Press.

Wilson, S. R., & Benner, L. A. (1971). The effects of self-esteem and situation upon comparison choices during ability evaluation. *Sociometry, 34,* 381–397.

Wood, J. V., Taylor, S. E., & Lichtman, R. R. (1985). Social comparison in adjustment to breast cancer. *Journal of Personality and Social Psychology, 49,* 1169–1183.

Wurf, E., & Markus, H. (1983). *Cognitive consequences of the negative self.* Paper presented at 91st annual meeting of the American Psychological Association, Anaheim, CA.

Zuckerman, M. (1979). Attribution of success and failure revisited, or: The motivational bias is alive and well in attribution theory. *Journal of Personality, 47,* 245–287.

PART 3

Threats and Inspiration

Most people like themselves and want to keep it that way. Or, to put it in more psychological terms, most people have positive self-evaluations and work to maintain positive self-images (see Baumeister, 1998; Tesser, 1988). Much of the work that focuses on the maintenance of positive images examines the responses people have to threats, and research suggests that people can differ widely in how they respond to common threats. Consider college students who receive unfavorable evaluations on college exams. Some might respond to this by denying the negative feedback ("No, I did not do that test. That F is not my grade"). Others might respond by questioning the importance or the relevance of the feedback ("That was not a good test," "This test is designed for Americans and I am from Europe"). Still others might respond by attributing the bad performance to external circumstances ("The classroom was hot and I could not concentrate," "The test was multiple choice, and I am better at written exams"). These various strategies may differ in how believable they are, but they illustrate that people have a wide array of options if they wish to maintain positive self-evaluations in the face of threat.

The readings in the present section show that social comparison can also influence how a person responds to threat. But, adding to the complexity, they also show that social comparisons can be a source of threat, as much as a response. Further, they show that the types of social comparisons that can be threatening in certain situations can be inspiring in others. Take as an example how people might perceive upward social comparisons (comparisons with people who are better off). In certain contexts, comparisons with better-off others can lead to negative affect, jealousy, and self-doubt, because these interactions can challenge the goodness of one's own qualities. In different contexts, however, these same comparisons can be uplifting. Consider a man who is struggling to get a promotion at work. Upward comparisons with a successful colleague might inspire him that he can achieve his goals, and increase his confidence that his promotion is under his own control. This same type of analysis can be carried out with downward comparisons (with people who are worse off). Worse-off others can assure us of our own good qualities, but they can also cause us to worry that we might one day suffer their same fate.

The papers we have selected for this section show these and other complex ways in which social comparisons can be both threatening and inspiring. The first article, Buunk *et al.* (1990), reveals some of the circumstances that can determine when different forms of comparisons will be perceived as threatening. Buunk *et al.* report data suggesting that people with low self-esteem perceive social comparisons as having negative consequences. These people are more likely to assimilate to downward comparison targets ("I may become like her") and contrast to upward comparison standards ("I am not as good as she is"). People with high self-esteem respond differently. They see the positive side of things, and thus especially focus on the positive side of social comparisons. Thus, high self-esteem people are more likely to contrast to downward comparison standards ("I am much better than she is") and to

assimilate to upward comparison standards ("I can become like her").

The second paper in this section, Lockwood and Kunda (1997) explores an issue related to Buunk *et al.* (1990), and this is how we respond to people who have achieved great successes. Lockwood and Kunda note that such individuals can act as positive role models who show us what we might achieve one day. At the same time, however, they can be threatening to us, because people who do very well sometimes put our own meager accomplishments in sharper focus. Lockwood and Kunda argued that the key variable that determines how we will respond is *attainability*. When an upward comparison standard's success is viewed as unattainable, he or she is likely to be threatening. When an upward comparison standard's success is viewed as something that can be achieved, he or she is likely to be inspiring.

The papers by Lockwood and Kunda and by Buunk *et al.* complement each other in a number of ways. In a sense, Lockwood and Kunda can be seen as an experimental follow-up of the Buunk *et al.* paper, which relied on correlational data. These two articles are also similar in that they both focus on a key determinant of how people respond to social comparisons that, at its roots, has to do with the amount of control a person perceives over his or her future. Buunk *et al.* show that people with high self-esteem can respond in a positive manner to upward comparisons, just as Lockwood and Kunda show that inspiration follows when a comparison other's successes are perceived as attainable (see also Major, Testa, & Bylsma, 1991). Clearly, people who can envision a bright future for themselves can do better with upward comparisons than those who cannot. But the key difference we see in these two papers goes to the primary theme of this section.

Buunk *et al.* focus on how we respond in a strategic manner to threats as they crop up. They show that threats cause some to look down and others to look up, and that both strategies can serve the goals of specific individuals. In contrast, Lockwood and Kunda focus on inspiration. They show that some people feel encouraged about their own possible successes when they see the successes of another, whereas others only feel demoralized (see also Tesser, 1988).

Whereas the articles by Buunk *et al.* and Lockwood and Kunda focus on how social comparison information can be threatening (or inspiring) and what may determine these effects, the papers by Alicke *et al.* (1997) and Gibbons *et al.* (1994) focus more on how people may use social comparisons or specific aspects of social comparison information to restore their self-images. Thus, while Buunk *et al.* and Lockwood and Kunda point out the ways that social comparison information can affect self-evaluations, Alicke *et al.* (1997) and Gibbons, Benbow, and Gerrard (1994) focus on ways in which specific social comparison can be used as techniques to maintain, restore, or repair thwarted self-views.

In their paper on the so-called "genius effect," Alicke *et al.* (1997) investigate one particular self-repair strategy that people may use when they are outperformed by another. Specifically, social comparers can exaggerate the differences between themselves and upward targets. At a glance, this strategy might seem likely to backfire. After all, it adds even greater elevation to the upward target and thus causes the social comparer to fall even further behind. By exaggerating self–other differences,

however, the social comparer puts the high performer in a "different league" and removes the target as a relevant standard of comparison. Consider as an example a girl who outperforms all of her classmates in math. She would not seem so threatening to the boys if they decide to label her as the "Madame Curie of our class." This new label makes her a less relevant standard for comparison, and this can remove the sting that might result if the boys felt a greater need to compare with her (see also Cash, Cash, & Butters, 1983). We would note that this genius effect follows from Festinger's (1954) similarity hypothesis, but it shows that people are capable of a level of creativity in how they construe comparison others that Festinger's paper did not anticipate.

Gibbons *et al.* (1994) explore a time of transition in a group of adolescents, and show how these individuals shift their comparison frames as a way of minimizing threats. They followed a group of high-school students who participated in a program for gifted students and another group of high-school students who entered college. In both cases, the shift to a new and more competitive academic environment should be a threat to the average student's academic self-concept. This is because students who are used to being the best in their classes (i.e., the "top dogs") will move towards the middle of the distribution in their new schools (see Marsh & Hau, 2003, in the section on *Implications in Everyday Life*). Gibbons *et al.* showed that students respond to this threatening new academic environment by shifting their comparisons downward. They also found that, in such threatening situations, students compared less with others and devalued the importance of the comparison dimension (see Taylor & Lobel, 1989; Tesser, 1988; this volume).

Clearly, the ways that social comparison can threaten and inspire are complex and the way people might respond can change from one context to the next. We suspect for this reason that readers might find this section to be the most challenging. A full discussion of how comparisons influence people is beyond what can be covered here. We thus sum up simply by returning to the organizing principle that began this section: Most people like themselves and want to keep it that way. Social comparisons often serve that goal, and social comparisons often get in its way. Teasing these different effects apart continues to be a challenge that many social psychologists find rewarding to study.

REFERENCES

(Asterisks indicate Key Readings in this section.)

* Alicke, M. D., LoSchiavo, F. M., Zerbst, J. I., & Zhang, S. (1997). The person who outperforms me is a genius: Maintaining perceived competence in upward social comparison. *Journal of Personality and Social Psychology, 73*, 781–789.

Baumeister, R. F. (1998). The self. In D. T. Gilbert, D. T. Fiske, & G. Lindzey (Eds.), *Handbook of social psychology* (4th ed., pp. 680–740). New York: McGraw-Hill.

* Buunk, B., Collins, R., Taylor, S., Dakof, G., & Van Yperen, N. (1990). The affective consequences of social comparisons: Either direction has its ups and downs. *Journal of Personality and Social Psychology, 59*, 1238–1249.

Cash, T. F., Cash, D. W., & Butters, J. W. (1983). "Mirror, mirror, on the wall…?": Contrast effects and self-evaluations of physical attractiveness. *Personality and Social Psychology Bulletin, 9*, 351–358.

Festinger, L. (1954). A theory of social comparison processes. *Human Relations, 7*, 117–140.

* Gibbons, F. X., Benbow, C. P., & Gerrard, M. (1994). From top dog to bottom half: Social comparison strategies in response to poor performance. *Journal of Personality and Social Psychology, 67*(4), 638–652.

* Lockwood, P., & Kunda, Z. (1997). Superstars and me: Predicting the impact of role models on the self. *Journal of Personality and Social Psychology, 73*(1), 91–103.

Major, B., Testa, M., & Bylsma, W. H. (1991). Responses to upward and downward social comparisons: The impact of esteem-relevance and perceived control. In J. M. Suls & T. A. Wills (Eds.), *Social comparison: Contemporary theory and research* (pp. 237–260). Hillsdale, NJ: Lawrence Erlbaum Associates Inc.

Marsh, H. W., & Hau, K-T. (2003). Big-fish–little-pond effect on academic self-concept: A cross-cultural (26-country) test of the negative effects of academically selective schools. *American Psychologist, 58*(5), 364–376.

Taylor, S. T., & Lobel, M. (1989). Social comparison activity under threat: Downward evaluation and upward contacts. *Psychological Review, 96*, 569–575.

Tesser, A. (1988). Toward a self-evaluation maintenance model of social behavior. In L. Berkowitz (Ed.), *Advances in experimental social psychology* (Vol. 21, pp. 181–227). San Diego: Academic Press.

Discussion Questions

1. Will individuals just do anything to defend themselves against threatening social comparison information?
2. Under what circumstances are social comparisons less likely to be threatening?
3. Based on the readings in this section, design an intervention technique that should help people to cope with threatening social comparison information.
4. Can geniuses be inspiring or are they "too far away and out of my league" to act as relevant comparison targets?
5. Discuss the similarities and differences between the following variables: similarity, relevance, closeness, and attainability.

Suggested Readings

Collins, R. L. (1996). For better or worse: The impact of upward social comparison on self-evaluations. *Psychological Bulletin, 119*, 51–69.

Kulik, J. A., & Gump, B. B. (1997). Affective reactions to social comparison: The effects of relative performance and related attributes information about another person. *Personality and Social Psychology Bulletin, 23*, 452–468.

Lyubomirsky, S., & Ross, L. (1997). Hedonic consequences of social comparison: A contrast of happy and unhappy people. *Journal of Personality and Social Psychology, 73*, 1141–1157.

Major, B., Testa, M., & Bylsma, W. H. (1991). Responses to upward and downward social comparisons: The impact of esteem-relevance and perceived control. In J. Suls & T. A. Wills (Eds.), *Social comparison: Contemporary theory and research* (pp. 237–260). Hillsdale, NJ: Lawrence Erlbaum Associates Inc.

Stapel, D. A., & Schwinghammer, S. A. (2004). Defensive social comparison and the constraints of reality. *Social Cognition, 22*, 147–167.

Wood, J. V., Taylor, S. E., & Lichtman, R. R. (1985). Social comparison in adjustment to breast cancer. *Journal of Personality and Social Psychology, 49*, 1169–1183.

READING 7

The Affective Consequences of Social Comparison: Either Direction Has Its Ups and Downs

Bram P. Buunk,* Rebecca L. Collins,** Shelley E. Taylor,***
Gayle A. Dakof,*** and Nico W. VanYperen*

Research on social comparison processes has assumed that a comparison in a given direction (upward or downward) will lead to a particular affective reaction. In contrast, the present two studies proposed and found that a comparison can produce either positive or negative feelings about oneself, independent of its direction. Several factors moderated the tendency to derive positive or negative affect from upward and downward comparisons. In Study 1, cancer patients low in self-esteem and with low perceived control over their symptoms and illness were more likely to see downward comparisons as having negative implications for themselves. Those low in self-esteem were also more likely to perceive upward comparisons as negative. In Study 2, individuals with high marital dissatisfaction and those who felt uncertain about their marital relationship were more likely to experience negative affect from upward and downward comparisons. The implications of these findings for social comparison theory and for the coping and adaptation literature are discussed.

* University of Nijmegen, The Netherlands.
** University of British Columbia, Vancouver, Canada.
*** University of California, USA.

   This research was supported by a grant from The Netherlands Organization for Scientific Research (NWO) to Bram P. Buunk, and by National Cancer Institute Grant CA 36409, National Institute of Mental Health Grant MH 42258, and Research Scientist Development Award MH 00311 to Shelley E. Taylor. Rebecca L. Collins was supported by National Institutes of Health Training Grant MH 15750, and Gayle A. Dakof was supported by a fellowship from the American Cancer Society—California Division. Nico W. VanYperen was supported by a grant from NWO.

   We are grateful to Roberta Falke, Jamie Lee, Laurie Skokan, Ina Smith, and Robyn Steer for their help in data collection; to Patricia Ganz for her help in coding prognosis; and to Monique Cloud for coding the comparison examples. We are also grateful to Darrin Lehman and Joanne Wood for their helpful comments on an earlier version of this article.

   Correspondence concerning this article should be addressed to Shelley E. Taylor, Department of Psychology, University of California, 405 Hilgard Avenue, Los Angeles, California 90024–1563.

In the seminal work on social comparison, Festinger (1954) suggested that when individuals are uncertain about their opinions or abilities, they will compare themselves with others to evaluate their own situation. Schachter (1959) expanded the domain of social comparison activities to include emotions. In a number of experiments, he showed that fear evoked in most subjects the desire to wait with someone else, preferably an individual in the same situation who reacted with a similar degree of emotional intensity. Schachter reviewed a number of explanations for these findings, but, in line with Festinger's theorizing, clearly favored the idea of self-evaluation. More recently, social comparison theory has been expanded to include motives for social comparison other than self-evaluation, including self-enhancement (e.g., restoring one's self-esteem by comparing oneself with others worse off; Wills, 1981), and self-improvement (e.g., seeking a positive example of the domain under evaluation; cf. Wilson & Benner, 1971).

The direction of comparison, namely whether one compares to a better-off or worse-off other (termed upward and downward comparisons, respectively), has been a central part of the theory (Latané, 1966). A great deal of research has substantiated that under conditions in which self-evaluation and self-improvement predominate, individuals prefer to compare their state with that of a slightly better-off other (e.g., Gruder, 1971; Wheeler, 1966; Wilson & Benner, 1971; see also Wheeler et al., 1969). On the other hand, a substantial body of literature indicates that when a comparison is motivated by self-enhancement, as is the case when self-esteem is threatened, the preferred target of comparison is one who is worse off (Crocker, Thompson, McGraw, & Ingerman, 1987; Friend & Gilbert, 1973; Hakmiller, 1966; Smith & Insko, 1987; Wills, 1981, 1987; Wood, Taylor, & Lichtman, 1985).

In this last line of research, differences in comparison target selection have been assumed to derive from differences in the effects of each type of information. In his downward comparison theory, Wills (1981) maintained that, under conditions of threat, downward comparisons are more likely to occur because they generate the positive affect essential for self-enhancement. Downward comparisons appear to boost self-esteem and positive emotion and reduce anxiety (Amoroso & Walters, 1969; Crocker & Gallo, 1985; Gibbons, 1986; Hakmiller, 1966; Kiesler, 1966; Lemyre & Smith, 1985; Morse & Gergen, 1970). Upward comparisons appear to be a useful source of self-evaluative information (Nosanchuk & Erickson, 1985; Wheeler et al., 1969), but seem concurrently to produce negative affect and lower self-evaluations by reminding one that one is inferior (Diener, 1984; Marsh & Parker, 1984; Morse & Gergen, 1970; Salovey & Rodin, 1984; Tesser, Millar, & Moore, 1988; Testa & Major, 1988).

In contrast to the previous literature, the present article proposes that the affective consequences of a comparison are not intrinsic to its direction. Although an upward comparison may serve the purpose of evaluation more readily than a downward one, and a downward comparison may more readily serve the function of self-enhancement, each may not necessarily have this effect. Learning that another is better off than yourself provides at least two pieces of information: (a) that you are not as well off as everyone and (b) that it is possible for you to be better than you are at present. Those able, by virtue of their personalities or circumstances, to focus on the positive aspect of this information may feel better about themselves as a result of an upward comparison. Those who focus on the negative aspect may feel worse. Conversely, learning that another is worse off than yourself also provides at least two pieces of information: (a) that you are not as badly off as everyone and (b) that it is possible for you to get worse. Focusing on the fact that one is better off than others may lead one to feel better about oneself as a result of a downward comparison, but focusing on the possibility of getting worse may produce negative feelings about oneself. Thus, how one feels in response to the information that another person is better off or worse off than oneself may depend on how one interprets the information.

Preliminary evidence suggests that downward comparisons can indeed result in negative feelings. In their studies of victims of chronic illness (a group under threat to self-esteem), both Dakof (1986) and Wood *et al.* (1985) found that these individuals sometimes felt threatened by exposure to others who had the same disease as themselves, but who were more ill. For example, their respondents described the doctor's waiting room as a particularly difficult situation because it forced on them the realization that things could be worse. Downward comparison theory would predict the opposite: These people should feel better about their own state when they see how much better off they are than others (Wills, 1981). Work by Tesser and his colleagues (see Tesser, 1986, for a review) also suggests that downward comparisons can be aversive. When people learn of worse-off others with whom they are "close" (highly similar or emotionally tied) and the comparison dimension is not central to self-definition, they may experience negative affect and arousal. Tesser (1986) and Wood (1984) also found evidence for positive affective consequences of upward comparisons: People who learned that another had done better than they had felt better about themselves as a result of this information. For example, a cancer patient may feel comforted or inspired by exposure to another who has recovered from the illness (Taylor & Lobel, 1989).

Various factors may moderate the affective impact of upward and downward comparisons. Tesser (1986) proposed relevance of the evaluation dimension as a potential moderator. He hypothesized that when one is competing with the comparison target, comparisons will have the effects typically described in downward comparison theory, but that in noncompetitive circumstances (when the evaluation is not self-relevant), downward comparisons will be negative and upward comparisons will be positive.[1] The studies presented here examine additional factors that may produce such outcomes. Study 1 examined the influence of self-esteem, the likelihood of improvement or decline on the attribute under evaluation, and perceived controllability of the attribute being evaluated. Study 2 extended these findings by replicating them in a

second population and examining the moderating roles of uncertainty and dissatisfaction over the dimension under evaluation.

First, the effect of comparing may be dependent on personality characteristics of the individual who is making the comparison. Crocker and her colleagues (Crocker & Schwartz, 1985; Crocker *et al.*, 1987) found that individuals high in self-esteem are more likely to make self-enhancing downward comparisons than are those with relatively low self-esteem. They argued that high self-esteem individuals have positive self-concepts, in part, because they engage in these self-enhancing strategies. Their hypothesis assumes that the meaning derived from a comparison is intrinsic to its direction and that downward comparisons always lead to greater self-esteem and upward comparisons do not. However, a more general version of the hypothesis would be that individuals high in self-esteem make comparisons favorable to themselves, regardless of their objective standing relative to the target. Thus, high self-esteem individuals may be more likely to make self-enhancing downward comparisons than low self-esteem persons and more likely to interpret upward comparisons as self-enhancing as well (cf. Wilson & Benner, 1971). Conversely, those with low self-esteem may be less likely to interpret either an upward or a downward comparison as favorable to themselves.

A second factor that may determine the effect of comparison information is the individual's likelihood of improving or declining on the attribute under evaluation. The importance of the possibility of the comparer attaining the target's level of achievement for comparison processes has been examined previously. Studies testing the related-attributes hypothesis suggest that comparisons are more meaningful when the comparer is similar to the target on dimensions related to that under evaluation (Goethals & Darley, 1977; Wheeler & Zuckerman, 1977). Furthermore, Wheeler (1966) proposed that the comparer's motivation level affects presumed similarity to the target as well, and thus will determine the choice of a comparison other. Both lines of research imply that the meaning derived from a comparison is dependent on the likelihood of finding oneself at the target's level

---

[1] It should be noted that although he uses the same method to assess these two processes, Tesser (1986) refers to the latter as a reflection (rather than comparison) process, and distinguishes between the two.

(Brickman & Bulman, 1977). Thus, if the comparison dimension is a skill acquired through practice or one that increases naturally with maturity, upward comparisons may be uplifting because they provide the comparer with the information that such achievements are within reach. Similarly, an individual who is undergoing a stressful event but whose situation may improve may make an upward comparison and feel good, seeing him- or herself as progressing toward the target's superior state. Conversely, for someone whose situation is likely to decline, an encounter with another who is worse off may be threatening. The information may be interpreted as indicative of a worse future, rather than as reassurance about one's presently superior state.

Third, the degree to which individuals perceive their progress as controllable by themselves or by others may affect comparison responses. Perceived control has been shown to have powerful effects on other aspects of cognition (see Fiske & Taylor, 1984), coping (Taylor, Lichtman, & Wood, 1984; Thompson, 1981), and emotional responses (Thompson, 1981). In terms of the present theory, people in control may feel that they have the means to attain a higher level of functioning or avoid a downfall, and thus neither downward nor upward comparisons would theoretically pose a threat. In fact, upward comparisons should be inspiring to these individuals. Consistent with this point, Testa and Major (1988) found that individuals making upward comparisons reported lower levels of depression and hostility when control was high than did a group with low control. However, they did not have a baseline measure of mood, so it is not clear whether control produced a negative impact in one group, a positive impact in the other, or both.

To summarize, the first study was conducted (a) to demonstrate that comparisons in a given direction can lead to divergent affective responses and (b) to determine how the factors of self-esteem, probability of improvement or decline in outcomes, and control over outcomes influence these responses. The population chosen to examine these issues was cancer patients. Previous research (Wood et al., 1985) has found that the majority of these individuals make social comparisons, suggesting that it is a prevalent coping strategy among them.

This research also found that most comparisons were self-enhancing downward comparisons, as would be predicted by downward comparison theory (Wills, 1981). Consequently, we expected that the majority of comparisons would be self-enhancing, and that most of these self-enhancing comparisons would be made to worse-off others. However, we predicted that when upward comparisons were made, individuals high in self-esteem, those who expected their condition to improve, and those who felt their future was controllable would be more likely to experience them as self-enhancing and less likely to experience them as aversive than would those low in self-esteem, those who expected their condition to decline, or those who perceived their condition as uncontrollable. Similarly, we predicted that persons with high self-esteem, expectations for improvement, and belief in control would be less likely to experience downward comparisons negatively and more likely to experience them positively than would those low in self-esteem, with poor prognoses, and with little sense of control.

Study 1

Method

Subjects. The sample consisted of 55 individuals recruited from a pool of 668 cancer patients who had previously participated in a survey of social support needs among cancer patients (Taylor, Falke, Shoptaw, & Lichtman, 1986).[2] To be eligible for the present study, patients had to be within 5 years of diagnosis or recurrence and between 30 and 70 years of age. Blocks of potential subjects by gender, estimated prognosis (good versus fair/poor), and support group membership (yes or no) were constructed for selection purposes.[3] Subjects were then randomly selected from these blocks and invited to participate in the interview study. Of the subjects contacted, 93% agreed to participate (i.e., 4 subjects declined).

---

[2] In that previous study, the response rate for participation approximated 80%.

[3] Support group membership was a blocking variable because it related to other aspects of the interview that dealt with issues of social support.

The sample included 30 women and 25 men, ranging in age from 30 to 66 with a median age of 54. Eighty-three percent were married, and 84% had children. Fifty-six percent were employed, and the median yearly family income was between $40,000 and $49,000. Ninety-three percent had completed high school, and 29% were college graduates. The sample was 44% Protestant, 25% Jewish, 13% Catholic, and 18% had another or no religious affiliation.

Participants had been diagnosed or had sustained a recurrence an average of 3.2 years prior to the interview ($SD = 1.7$). Twenty percent of respondents were receiving treatment for their cancer at the time of the interview. Using medical chart materials, an oncologist rated prognosis on a 5-point scale ranging from *very guarded or grave prognosis* (1) to *probable cure* (5). Thirty-six patients had cancers that were rated 4 or 5 (in remission), and the remainder (19) had prognostic ratings of 1, 2, or 3 (active cancers). Patients with all sites of cancer participated.

Interview. Respondents were telephoned and the interview was arranged, usually in the home. At the beginning of the structured interview, respondents received an informed consent form, and permission to tape record the interview was obtained. The average interview lasted between 1½ and 2 hr.

The interview covered basic demographic data, the respondent's past and current health status, social support experiences following the cancer diagnosis, perceptions concerning how his or her life had changed following diagnosis, and items relevant to the present investigation, including beliefs about control as well as social comparison processes.

Social comparison items. Four questions concerning social comparisons related to the present study. Because previous research has already documented the prevalence of comparisons in a similar population (Wood *et al.*, 1985), we felt closed-ended questions were appropriate. To avoid leading subjects to report particular affective consequences, however, we presented the possibility of both emotional responses before questioning subjects more

specifically. Downward comparisons were assessed first. Subjects were told:

> Some people have told us that when they see cancer patients who are not doing as well as they are, it makes them feel lucky and grateful that they are not in worse shape themselves. Other people have told us that when they see cancer patients who are not doing as well as they are, it makes them feel worse. For these people, seeing cancer patients who are worse off only increases their fears and anxieties.

Subjects were then asked to rate the frequency with which they had felt lucky or grateful when exposed to worse-off others on a 4-point scale where 1 = *never*, 2 = *rarely*, 3 = *sometimes*, and 4 = *often*. Following this, participants giving a rating greater than 1 were asked to provide an example of a time when they experienced such a comparison. Next, subjects were asked how often they had felt fearful or anxious in response to such people. Subjects indicated their answer on the same 4-point scale, and were again asked for a specific comparison instance. Upward comparisons were assessed next. Subjects were told:

> Some people have told us that when they see cancer patients who are doing better than they are, it makes them feel frustrated or depressed. Other people have told us they feel inspired or comforted when they see other cancer patients who seem to be doing better than they are.

Again, subjects rated the frequency of each of these reactions on the same 4-point scale and were asked to provide examples of them.

Control items. Both personal control and control by external factors were assessed. The items assessing personal control were prefaced by "Some people who suffer from serious illness feel that they have some control over day-to-day symptoms, over the future course of the disease, or over the treatments themselves, whereas others do not." Subjects were then asked two questions regarding personal control: (a) "Now that your cancer has been detected, to what extent do you feel you have control over the amount of fatigue, pain, or other symptoms you experience on a daily basis?" and (b) "To what extent do you feel you can keep the cancer from spreading or coming back?" Subjects indicated their answers on a 5-point scale ranging from *not at all* to *completely*.

Items assessing the control exerted by other factors were prefaced with "Some people believe that someone or something else may have control over day-to-day symptoms, over the future course of disease, or over treatments themselves, whereas others do not." This was followed by two questions: (a) "To what extent do you think someone or something else has control over your day-to-day symptoms?" and (b) "To what extent do you feel that someone or something else can keep your cancer from spreading or coming back?" Each of these items was followed by the same scale ranging from *not at all* (1) to *completely* (5).

Self-esteem. The Rosenberg Self-Esteem Inventory (Rosenberg, 1965) was used as a measure of chronic self-esteem. This questionnaire was left with the patient at the conclusion of the interview, along with measures of adjustment and indicators of cancer-related problems that were part of the larger study. Eighty percent of the respondents returned this questionnaire.

Results

Looking at the number of respondents who had ever experienced each type of comparison paired with each affective consequence, 82% ($n = 42$) of subjects made downward comparisons and felt good, 59% ($n = 28$) made downward comparisons and felt bad, 40% ($n = 19$) made upward comparisons and felt bad, and 78% ($n = 37$) made upward comparisons and felt good.[4] Although a substantial proportion of the sample reported making each type of comparison with each effect, there were differences in the frequency with which each comparison was reported to have occurred. A one-way multivariate analysis of variance (ANOVA) with four

repeated measures of comparison frequency produced a significant effect, $F(3, 135) = 13.87, p < .001$. Downward positive affect comparisons were the most common, as predicted, although upward positive affect comparisons were almost equally common. As expected, downward negative and upward negative affect comparisons occurred less often. Patients reported making comparisons resulting in positive affect, regardless of direction, more frequently than comparisons resulting in negative affect, $t(52) = 6.09, p < .001$. Mean frequency ratings and simple comparisons are presented in Table 7.1.

Two independent raters coded 25% of the cases to determine whether the examples provided by subjects clearly constituted comparisons and were associated with the designated affect. Interrater agreement on these judgments was 88%. Inconsistencies were resolved through discussion, and one rater coded the remaining cases. Results further substantiate the frequency rating data. Eighty-three percent of those who reported experiencing an upward comparison and feeling good (i.e., who responded with a frequency rating greater than *never*) gave a clear example of a time when this had happened to them; 71% did so for downward/ positive affect comparisons. Eighty-two percent of those who had experienced downward negative affect comparisons also provided a clear example of this. Results were less clear for upward comparisons resulting in negative affect: 42% of those who reported experiencing this were able to provide a clear instance of its occurrence.

We also examined the content of these examples. Previous research (Wood *et al.*, 1985) has identified

---

[4] Percentages reported are of subjects responding to the question. A few respondents indicated that they never compared themselves with others, and some indicated that they did not know any cancer patients with whom the comparison could be made.

TABLE 7.1. Mean Frequency Ratings of Upward and Downward Comparisons Paired with Positive and Negative Affective Consequences among Cancer Patients

Type of comparison	Affective consequence	
	Positive	Negative
Upward	2.63a	1.60ab
Downward	2.75b	2.00ab

Note: Means sharing a common subscript are significantly different, $p \le .01$. Scales ranged from 1 (*never*) to 4 (*often*). $N = 55$.

four major dimensions on which cancer patients make social comparisons: prognosis, physical limitations or symptoms, coping and adjustment, and external resources such as finances or social support. Comparisons in a particular direction and with a particular consequence may be more likely to be made on some dimensions than others (e.g., it may be easier to feel good about someone with better adjustment than someone with superior resources to one's own). An independent rater coded each comparison example for the dimension involved so that this possibility could be tested. Interrater reliability (again based on a subset of 25% of the cases coded by an additional rater) for this measure was 90%. We then conducted four Cochran Q tests, one for each comparison/affect item. The Cochran Q tests whether the proportions in dichotomous categories (in this case, mentions versus nonmentions of a comparison dimension) are the same across variables (in this case, across the four dimensions). There were significant differences in the frequency with which each dimension was used. This occurred in response to all four questions (downward/negative affect $Q = 27.07$, $p < .001$; downward/positive affect $Q = 15.40$, $p = .002$; upward/negative affect $Q = 9.00$, $p = .03$; upward/positive affect $Q = 16.67$, $p < .001$). However, examination of the frequencies reveals that the patterns of response were the same for three of the four questions. For all but upward/positive affect comparisons, comparisons of prognosis were the most frequent (ranging from 52% to 67% of each category); comparisons on other dimensions were infrequent and occurred about equally often. In the case of upward comparisons resulting in positive affect, comparisons of prognosis were also most common (50%); however, comparisons of adjustment were nearly as frequent (33%). Comparisons of resources and physical status were, again, infrequent and approximately equal.

It was hypothesized that high self-esteem individuals would make more positive affect and less negative affect comparisons in both directions than would low self-esteem individuals. To test this, the sample was split into two groups, those above and those below the median score on the self-esteem inventory. Four t tests were conducted

comparing the frequency with which each group reported making comparisons in each direction with each affective consequence (upward/positive affect, downward/positive affect, upward/negative affect, and downward/negative affect). There were significant differences in the frequency with which persons high and low in self-esteem reported comparisons resulting in negative affect. Specifically, high self-esteem individuals were less likely to feel bad when comparing upward (M frequencies = 1.25 and 1.95), $t(31) = 2.60$, $p = .007$, one-tailed, and less likely to feel bad when comparing downward (M frequencies = 1.60 and 2.43), $t(39) = 2.50$, $p = .008$, one-tailed, than were low self-esteem individuals. The two groups did not differ in the frequency with which they reported positive affect in response to comparison, both ps (one-tailed) $> .10$.

Prognosis was also hypothesized to influence interpretation of comparison information. Participants were divided into a good prognosis group (ratings of 4 and 5) and a poor prognosis group (ratings of 1 through 3). Four t tests were conducted to test for differences between these groups in the frequency with which they reported each comparison affect and direction. There were no significant differences found, all ps (one-tailed) $> .05$.

Finally, it was hypothesized that individuals who believe they or others have control over their illness would be more likely to report feeling good in response to upward comparisons and less likely to report feeling bad in response to downward comparisons, as compared with those with lower perceived control. Correlations were calculated between each rating of control (personal and other control over daily symptoms and the future course of the illness) and the frequency of each type of comparison. Because prognosis may be related to perceived control, it was partialed out of these analyses. As predicted, the belief that one has personal control over the future course of one's illness and the belief that one has control over daily symptoms were both inversely associated with feeling bad in response to worse-off others (rs = $-.31$ and $-.30$, respectively, both ps $< .05$). Perceived other control was unrelated to this measure, and no type of control was associated with the frequency of upward positive affect comparisons.[5]

Discussion

The present study produced four sets of results that have relevance to social comparison theory. First, in contrast to much previous theorizing and empirical emphasis, the data revealed that upward and downward comparisons are not intrinsically linked to particular affective outcomes. Instead, as predicted, we found that people may construe both upward and downward comparisons as either positive or negative.[6]

Consistent with downward comparison theory (Wills, 1981), the present study found that cancer patients most frequently engaged in self-enhancing downward comparisons. We had proposed, however, that upward comparisons could be interpreted in a self-enhancing manner as well. This hypothesis was supported. In fact, a majority of the sample made self-enhancing upward comparisons, and these occurred nearly as often as self-enhancing downward ones. For example, one of our respondents said:

> When I was going through the worst period, you know; the acute time of therapy and stuff, it was gratifying to see people recovering, having their hair grow back, getting their strength, and so on. Yeah, that was very positive and very helpful.

Just as both directions of comparison may be interpreted positively, both may also lead to negative self-perceptions. Information that another person is doing worse than oneself can be depressing, as can information that someone is doing better than oneself. Interestingly, in the present study the former took place more often than did the latter: Downward comparisons more frequently led to negative affect than did upward comparisons. Respondents tended to be frightened by the experiences of patients who were not recovering from their cancer. For example, one respondent, a breast cancer patient who had been treated by lumpectomy, said:

> Well, my girl friend who had the second mastectomy, she has really been through the mill . . . it raises my anxiety terribly because she started off with a lumpectomy and radiation.

This ability to derive positive or negative affective consequences from social comparisons was, as evidenced by respondents' examples, not specific to comparisons of a particular aspect of one's cancer, such as prognosis or adjustment. There was, however, a tendency for upward comparisons on the dimension of coping to more often lead to positive affect than those made on other dimensions.

The second important set of findings for social comparison theory concerned the role of moderating factors in the affective consequences of social comparisons. The ability to avoid negative comparisons was more true of individuals high in self-esteem and (for downward comparisons) those who believed they could control the symptoms or course of the disease than of people low on these characteristics. With respect to self-esteem, we had hypothesized that high self-esteem individuals would be more likely to make self-enhancing comparisons in either direction, and less likely to experience comparisons as threatening, than would persons lower in self-esteem. Only the latter half of this hypothesis was supported. Whereas self-esteem did not affect the frequency with which

---

[5] One might conjecture that high self-esteem would be related to perceived control and, therefore, that the two sets of analyses would be redundant. However, this was not the case. Self-esteem was unrelated to either perceived control over daily symptoms ($r = .10$) or perceived control over the disease ($r = .13$).

[6] Rather than interpreting the same information differently, an alternative process of deriving particular effects from comparisons would entail the selection of either upward or downward comparison targets who are likely to reflect on oneself in a particular way (e.g., Tesser's, 1986, theory suggests the choice of similar or dissimilar targets). However, it is clear from the examples provided by subjects in the present study that many of them were interpreting exactly the same comparison information in different ways. Many referred to the same target in response to questions assessing both positive and negative reactions. In addition, when characteristics of the target were provided, they were often the same across positive and negative questions, even when the specific target was different.

comparisons were seen as positive, low self-esteem persons were significantly more likely to experience negative outcome comparisons than were persons of high self-esteem.

A similar effect was found with regard to psychological control. Those people who felt they could control their symptoms and the future course of the illness were less likely to feel threatened by exposure to very ill patients. They were not, however, any more likely to focus on the positive implications of another's successful recovery than were persons who felt their future health was uncontrollable.[7]

Third, the ability to avoid negative comparisons appears to depend more on the subjective than objective characteristics of the threatening event. We had predicted that prognosis would influence whether one derived hope from the knowledge that others were improving and despair at news of another's decline. However, the comparer's prognosis was not related to the frequency with which a comparison was seen as threatening or enhancing. The rating of prognosis was an objective measure, however, and many cancer patients retain the belief that they will recover in spite of indications to the contrary. Indeed, Wood and her colleagues (Wood *et al.*, 1985) also failed to find an effect of prognosis when using an objective measure to predict enhancing downward comparisons (see also Marks, Richardson, Graham, & Levine, 1986). Our positive findings concerning control suggest that a subjective measure of respondents' perceived prognosis might have been associated with the ability to derive benefit from comparisons.

Finally, self-serving social comparisons appear to mute the effect of negative information rather than enhance available positive information; that is, both self-esteem and control were associated with fewer negative affect comparisons, but were unrelated to positive comparisons.

Study 2

Although Study 1 demonstrated that comparisons in a given direction can produce divergent affective responses, it did so within a select population, cancer patients. Recovery is possible, but most patients are at least somewhat uncertain about their prognosis, and unexpected changes in physical states may take place. This factor may influence the data patterns obtained. Study 2 provided an opportunity to replicate the patterns of comparison responses obtained in Study 1 in a different population (Dutch married people) using a different comparison dimension, namely quality of one's marital relationship, with different but conceptually related moderating variables (namely uncertainty about the quality of one's marriage and marital dissatisfaction).

Specifically, by examining uncertainty about how things were going in one's marriage, we were able to assess the impact of uncertainty on social comparison processes. Festinger (1954) had suggested that the desire for social comparison is particularly strong in the case of uncertainty about one's opinions or abilities. Schachter (1959) maintained that the desire for self-evaluation (i.e., the desire to evaluate the appropriateness of one's reactions) is the primary motive underlying the tendency to affiliate under stress. Taken together and in conjunction with the data from Study 1, these points suggest that uncertainty may predispose people to be especially vigilant to comparison information generally and to negative information more specifically. We therefore predicted that those uncertain in their marriages would report making more social comparisons of all kinds and would be more likely to focus on the negative than the positive aspects of upward and downward comparisons.

In an effort to create a situational analogue to self-esteem, we also examined marital satisfaction as a determinant of the affect generated by upward

---

[7]Somewhat surprisingly, the perception that another agent controlled the course of the illness was unrelated to comparison effects. Previous research (Taylor, Lichtman, & Wood, 1984) found that both vicarious and personal control were associated with positive adjustment to cancer. Apparently, vicarious control does not have the same impact on self-serving social comparisons.

and downward comparisons. We predicted that, like the low-esteem individuals reacting to self-relevant comparison information in Study 1, individuals experiencing marital dissatisfaction might be more vigilant to the negative information suggested by comparisons of their own marriage to that of others. We therefore expected those high in marital dissatisfaction to make more negative affect comparisons and fewer positive affect comparisons than those higher in marital satisfaction.

Method

Subjects. The sample consisted of 632 married individuals, 304 men and 328 women. Of the sample, 432 subjects (69%) were recruited using an announcement placed in local newspapers, the remaining 200 (31%) by contacting a random sample of a middle-sized Dutch town. This last sample was provided by the city council. The average length of marriage was 16.4 years (range: less than 1 month to 55.3 years). The mean age was 40.6 years (range: 21 to 81), and 79% of the sample had children. Highest level of education achieved varied from elementary education (3.6%) to college education at the master's level or higher (10.9%). Of the sample, 83% of the men and 32% of the women were employed outside the home for 20 or more hours per week. A wide range of occupations were represented in the sample. The number of subjects in the following analyses varies because of occasional missing data.

Procedure. The data on the 434 subjects mentioned above were collected as part of the second measurement of a longitudinal study on social comparison processes in marriage (VanYperen & Buunk, 1990). The subjects were contacted by mail and were asked to complete, in privacy, an anonymous questionnaire about "marital relationships." They were not to discuss this questionnaire with their partner before completing it. After 2 weeks, nonrespondents received a reminder and after 4 weeks, a second reminder as well as a new questionnaire. The same procedure was followed for a randomly selected sample of 1,000 individuals from a middle-sized Dutch city. Of this sample, a total of 200

persons (20%) sent back the questionnaire, making up the remaining 31% of the total sample for this study. To obtain an indication of the reasons for nonparticipation, a brief questionnaire was sent to the nonsample. This questionnaire was sent back by 32% of these individuals. The reasons mentioned most often for nonparticipation were "My private life is my own business" (17%), followed by "I get annoyed when I receive a questionnaire without having asked for it" (13%), "I just don't feel like it" (6%), and "I am too old for these kinds of things" (5%).

Social comparison items. To assess the affect evoked by upward and downward comparisons, the subjects were presented with modified versions of the four questions from Study 1. To measure the frequency of positive affect evoked by downward comparisons, subjects were asked to answer the following question (translated from Dutch): "How often do you feel *happy* and *pleased* when you compare your own marital relationship with that of others who have a relationship that is *worse* than yours? A 5-point scale was used, with points labeled 1 (*never*), 2 (*seldom*), 3 (*sometimes*), 4 (*quite often*), and 5 (*very often*). To assess the frequency of negative affect evoked by downward comparisons, subjects were asked: "How often do you feel *unhappy* and *displeased* when you compare your own marital relationship with that of others who have a relationship that is *worse* than yours?" Similar questions were asked for negative and positive affect evoked by marriages that were better than one's own.

Uncertainty item. To assess the degree of uncertainty in marriage, the respondents were asked to indicate on a 5-point scale (1 = *not at all*, 2 = *hardly*, 3 = *somewhat*, 4 = *quite*, and 5 = *very much*) to what extent they felt uncertain about how things were going in their marriage.

Marital dissatisfaction. An 8-item scale (Buunk, 1990) was used to assess marital dissatisfaction. This scale has proven to have high reliability and stability and to relate meaningfully to other variables, including the stability of the relationship and self-rated coping with marital problems (e.g., Buunk, 1987; Buunk & Bosman, 1986). Respondents indicated how often an item applied to their marital relationship on the same 5-point scale that was used for the social comparison items, ranging from *never* (1) to *very often* (5). Five of the items referred to negative feelings and behaviors, such as "My partner irritates me" or "We have quarrels." Three items referred to positive experiences such as "Things are going well between us." Coefficient alpha of the scale was .85 in this sample. Marital dissatisfaction and uncertainty were correlated .50 in the sample.

Results

Frequency of comparisons. Table 7.2 makes clear that, as was the case in Study 1, positive affect comparisons were made more frequently than comparisons evoking negative affect. Downward comparisons generating positive affect were the most common. Nearly all subjects (95%) reported such comparisons, and 59% said they made this type of comparison quite or very often. Upward positive affect comparisons also occurred regularly among the subjects: 78% of subjects reported experiencing these at some time; 28% stated they made such comparisons quite or very often. Negative affect upward or downward comparisons were less frequent; 59% of the sample stated they made upward comparisons that made them unhappy sometimes, and only 3% made such comparisons quite or very often. About half of the sample (48%) reported downward comparisons evoking negative affect, and just 2% reported they made such comparisons

quite or very often. The only gender difference was that negative affect upward comparisons were reported more often by women ($M = 1.95$) than by men ($M = 1.79$), $t(614) = 2.30$, $p < .05$. That is, women more often than men felt bad when they learned about happier couples.

Marital dissatisfaction and comparisons. We had predicted that individuals with high marital dissatisfaction would make fewer positive and more negative comparisons in both directions, whereas the opposite pattern would be characteristic of individuals with satisfying marriages. In order to test this prediction, respondents were divided into three groups on the basis of their marital dissatisfaction scores. Because of ties in the scores on this scale, it was not possible to divide them into groups of equal size (for the high dissatisfaction group [scores 1.39 or lower], $n = 145$; for the medium dissatisfaction group [scores between 1.39 and 1.90], $n = 254$; and for the low dissatisfaction group [scores 1.90 or higher], $n = 198$).

Examining the effects of marital dissatisfaction on upward and downward comparisons, a MANOVA with three levels of marital dissatisfaction was conducted, using the four social comparison items as dependent measures. Analyses were conducted separately for each gender, inasmuch as previous literature suggests that men and women respond differently to sources of strain in relationships (Titus, 1980). The multivariate effect of relationship dissatisfaction on social comparisons was significant for men, $F(8, 556) = 7.33$, $p < .001$, as well as for women, $F(8, 582) = 9.94$, $p < .001$.

Univariate analyses showed that the level of marital dissatisfaction was significantly and strongly related to the frequency with which downward negative affect comparisons were reported: for men, $F(2, 280) = 10.96$, $p < .001$; for women, $F(2, 293) = 15.62$, $p < .001$. The frequency of upward negative effect comparisons was even more strongly related to level of marital satisfaction: for men, $F(2, 280) = 26.62$, $p < .001$; for women, $F(2, 293) = 33.23$, $p < .001$. As Figure 7.1 shows, the higher the level of marital dissatisfaction, the more often individuals felt unhappy and bad when they compared themselves with couples who had better

TABLE 7.2. Mean Frequency Ratings of Upward and Downward Comparisons Paired with Positive and Negative Affective Consequences among Married Individuals

Type of comparison	Affective consequence	
	Positive	Negative
Upward	2.70	1.87
Downward	3.59	1.62

Note: All differences among means are significant, $p \leq .001$. Scales ranged from 1 (*never*) to 5 (*very often*). N = 632.

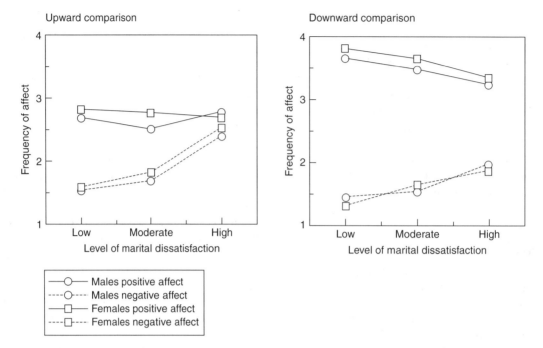

FIGURE 7.1 ■ Positive and negative affect generated by upward and downward comparisons for various levels of marital dissatisfaction.

marriages, and the more often marriages worse than their own also evoked negative affect.

In contrast, marital dissatisfaction had little influence on the frequency with which comparisons to other couples evoked positive affect (see Figure 7.l). There was no significant difference in the frequency with which positive affect upward comparisons were made. However, among women and marginally among men, there was an effect of marital dissatisfaction on the frequency of positive affect downward comparisons: for women, $F(2, 293) = 3.99, p < .05$; for men, $F(2, 280) = 2.64, p < .07$. People in less happy marriages felt less positively in response to downward comparisons than those whose marriages were more satisfying.

Marital uncertainty and comparisons. On the basis of responses to the uncertainty item, three groups were created, the first consisting of those who said they were not at all uncertain about how their marriage was going (score 1; $n = 199$), the second consisting of individuals who said they were hardly uncertain (scores 2; $n = 275$), and the third

consisting of those who indicated that they felt somewhat, quite, or very uncertain (scores 3, 4, and 5; $n = 157$).

We had predicted that uncertainty would increase comparisons of all types and that those high in marital uncertainty would make fewer positive and more negative comparisons than those low in uncertainty. Overall, those high in uncertainty made more social comparisons than those low in uncertainty. A MANOVA using three levels of uncertainty as the independent variable and the social comparison items as dependent variables yielded significant main effects for uncertainty, $F(8, 578) = 9.30, p < .001$, for men and $F(8, 618) = 9.55, p < .001$, for women. However, examination of Figure 7.2 suggests that this effect can be accounted for primarily by negative affect comparisons.

The univariate F tests confirm this suggestion. Uncertainty was clearly related to the frequency of negative affect downward comparisons: among men, $F(2, 291) = 11.33, p < .001$; among women, $F(2, 331) = 11.71, p < .001$. As Figure 7.2 shows, the more uncertain individuals felt about their own

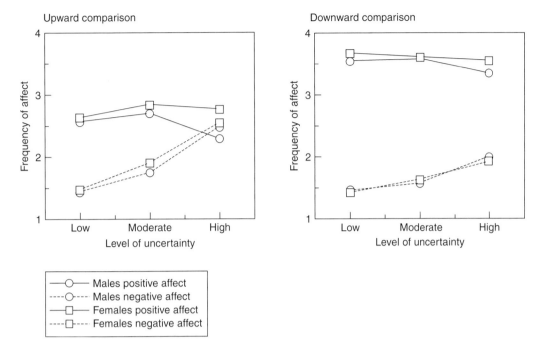

FIGURE 7.2 ■ Positive and negative affect generated by upward and downward comparisons for various levels of uncertainty.

marriages, the more they experienced negative affect when confronted with marriages that were worse. Comparisons with better marriages appear to generate negative affect even more often. The relationship between uncertainty and the frequency of negative affect upward comparisons was strong and significant among men, $F(2, 291) = 38.09$, $p < .001$, as well as among women, $F(2, 331) = 40.91$, $p < .001$. As is apparent from Figure 7.2, people who felt uncertain about how things were going in their marriages were unhappy and dissatisfied more often when they compared their own marriage with happier marriages. No significant effects of uncertainty were found with respect to the positive affect comparisons.

General Discussion

Taken together, the findings from two studies examining social comparison processes in different domains have important implications for social comparison theory. Both studies demonstrated that comparison direction (upward or downward) is not intrinsically linked to affect, as the previous literature has often assumed. Rather, both upward and downward social comparisons are capable of generating positive or negative affective responses, depending on which aspect of the comparison is focused on.

The results from the two studies also show some commonalities in the frequencies of different kinds of comparisons. Both studies found that positive affect comparisons were the most common comparisons reported, with positive downward comparisons more common than positive upward comparisons. There are some differences in frequency of types of comparisons between the two studies. Whereas in Study 1, upward comparisons evoked positive affect nearly as often as downward comparisons, in Study 2 upward comparisons were less potent in generating this effect than were downward comparisons. In the same vein, in Study 2, upward comparisons leading to negative affect were more frequent than downward comparisons leading to negative affect, whereas in Study 1 the reverse was true. Perhaps this difference depends on the two types of events, namely cancer and marriage. In normal situations (such as the evaluation of an ongoing marriage), upward comparisons may be relatively threatening because they remind people how poorly they are doing, whereas in stressful circumstances (such as undergoing cancer), seeing a positive example may be encouraging and inspiring. Further research is needed to determine whether individuals experiencing an unusual threat interpret comparison information differently from people in normal situations.

Another significant regularity in the data concerns the fact that the moderating variables of self-esteem and controllability (in Study 1) and uncertainty and marital satisfaction (in Study 2) largely affected the frequency of negative affect but not positive affect comparisons. Taken together, these results tie in with a larger body of literature in social cognition suggesting that there are cognitive filters of selective attention, representation, and recall that help people maintain positive beliefs (see Taylor & Brown, 1988, for a review). Consistent with that body of data, the results suggest that these filters operate more to keep the negative implications of information out of view than to enhance available positive information.

The results concerning self-esteem provide an interesting insight into a current issue in the comparison literature. Our findings are somewhat inconsistent with Wills's (1981) downward comparison theory, which predicts that low self-esteem individuals or individuals under threat should make a greater number of self-enhancing downward comparisons. Overall, individuals who evaluated themselves (Study 1) or their situation (Study 2)

negatively made substantial numbers of downward comparisons, but as just noted, they did not derive a greater amount of self-enhancing information as a result. This finding is more consistent with Crocker et al.'s (1987) results, which found that high self-esteem individuals were better able than low self-esteem individuals to make comparisons that are self-serving. Crocker et al.'s data had demonstrated that high self-esteem people make *downward* comparisons for this purpose. The present results suggest that high self-esteem individuals are better able to make use of *either* upward or downward comparisons for the purpose of self-enhancement than are low self-esteem individuals.

We had predicted that uncertainty would increase comparisons of all kinds, a prediction that was not upheld. Instead, in Study 2, uncertainty and dissatisfaction regarding one's marriage related to affective consequences of social comparisons the same way, namely in terms of more frequent negatively valenced comparisons. There are at least two possible explanations for this result. One is to argue that uncertainty and dissatisfaction are tapping the same construct. The two measures were highly correlated (.50). Arguing against this point is the fact that marital dissatisfaction also increased the frequency of positive affect downward comparisons, a finding that was not mirrored in the uncertainty data.[8] The other explanation maintains that these measures are tapping two separate dimensions, negativity and ambiguity, that have been previously identified in the stress literature as enhancing the perception of stress (e.g., Billings & Moos, 1984; Gal & Lazarus, 1975; Holahan & Moos, 1986; McFarlane, Norman, Streiner, Roy, & Scott, 1980; Myers, Lindenthal, & Pepper, 1972; Sarason, Johnson, & Siegel, 1978; Stokols, Ohlig, & Resnick, 1978; Vinokur & Selzer, 1975). Uncertainty and dissatisfaction may both increase the experience of strain, which in turn may increase vigilance to the negative information inherent in

[8] However, the single item measuring uncertainty may have been a less reliable indicator of a common underlying dimension than the multiple items assessing marital dissatisfaction. This could explain why marital dissatisfaction, as the more sensitive indicator, would be associated with positive affect downward comparisons, whereas uncertainty, as a relatively insensitive indicator, might not.

social comparisons. If uncertainty and dissatisfaction are indeed two separate dimensions of marital perceptions, dissatisfaction would seem to create a greater need for self-enhancing downward comparisons than uncertainty/ambiguity.

There are limitations to the studies. The direction of causality cannot be determined for the moderating variables. Those high in self-esteem, control, marital satisfaction, or certainty may make different comparisons than others, or, alternatively, the avoidance of threatening comparisons may result in a more positive self-image, elevated perceptions of control, greater certainty in one's perceptions, or greater satisfaction. As noted earlier, past research has demonstrated that the use of self-enhancing downward comparisons does improve self-esteem (Crocker & Gallo, 1985; Lemyre & Smith, 1985; Morse & Gergen, 1970). The avoidance of threatening comparisons may have the same effect: Avoiding negative comparisons may be one way in which people high in self-esteem, control, satisfaction, or certainty maintain these perceptions.[9]

The question arises as to whether the results from both studies can be interpreted as evidence of a positivity response bias. There is considerable evidence in the literature that people are biased toward perceiving events positively, a phenomenon that Matlin and Strang have termed the Pollyanna principle (Matlin & Strang, 1978). Several factors argue against a response bias interpretation. First, there is little evidence of a positivity bias in these data; rather, negativity is avoided. Second, subjects who reported particular affective consequences of particular comparisons generally had examples readily available to buttress their perceptions, a finding that suggests that more than an automatic response bias was involved. Third, reports of affective consequences of particular comparisons varied systematically with perceived control in Study 1 and with dissatisfaction and uncertainty in Study 2, which would not be expected from a simple response bias.

Moreover, the question of how to interpret positivity in psychological responses is itself under debate. Rather than representing a response bias, many psychologists have argued that mild positivity is how the majority of people experience a broad array of outcomes and that responses indicating such are not themselves a function of response set, but accurately reflect a mildly positive perception of the world (e.g., see Parducci, 1968; Taylor & Brown, 1988).

The present data have implications for certain long-standing issues in the social comparison and coping literatures, particularly how people respond to and cope with forced comparisons (Brickman & Bulman, 1977; Mettee & Smith, 1977). The comparison environment appears to be somewhat less malleable than was characterized by Festinger (1954; see Wood, 1989). As a result, comparison targets are sometimes forced on the comparer, as in the case of cancer patients exposed to other patients in the waiting room. The present analysis suggests that some people, particularly those who evaluate themselves or their situation positively or those with a sense of personal control, may respond to unwanted comparisons much as they respond to other negative information in their environments, filtering and distorting the data to fulfill their needs and expectations (see Taylor & Brown, 1988, for a review).

The results also have implications for the literature on coping and adaptation. Both Wills (1981) and Taylor and Lobel (1989) have assumed that the propensity to make downward comparisons under threat stems from an augmented need for self-enhancement induced by threat. Yet the results from Study 2 suggest that *negative* affect comparisons in both directions are especially augmented by marital dissatisfaction and that positive affect downward comparisons are slightly lower among those high in marital dissatisfaction relative to those low in marital dissatisfaction. Recall, too, that in

---

[9] In the case of the control results, it seems unlikely that the avoidance of negative information would lead to a stronger belief in personal control, except through the mediating variable of self-esteem. People who use comparisons to maintain the belief that they are capable may infer that they are also in control of their situations. However, self-esteem and control were unrelated in Study 1. It thus seems more likely that the belief in personal control enables one to avoid the negative impact of comparison information rather than the reverse.

Study 1 (in which all subjects were under some degree of threat), negative affect downward comparisons were relatively more prevalent than in Study 2. It appears that the effects of threat on social comparison may be more complex than has been previously assumed. Although threat may produce a propensity for self-enhancing downward comparisons, it may simultaneously increase all kinds of negative affect comparisons, an effect that may augment rather than diminish distress. Of relevance too is the finding that persons who feel relatively less control over their health may also be threatened by downward comparison information, rather than comforted by it, as previous theory and results have suggested (Wills, 1981; Wood *et al.*, 1985). Finally, the results of Study 2 suggest that those high in uncertainty, and therefore likely to seek comparison information, are also more likely to feel threatened by what they learn. The conditions that increase or decrease threatening interpretations of comparisons clearly merit additional study.

Finally, the finding that both upward and downward comparisons can be used for the purpose of self-enhancement addresses a long-standing question in the literature on social comparisons: How can people who are in need of self-enhancing feedback make use of better-off others to facilitate eventual change in their standing? If people are not capable of so doing, the preservation of self-esteem could have negative long-term consequences, leading people to ignore strategies of improvement. Our results address this concern, suggesting that people can make use of comparisons in either direction in order to simultaneously provide useful information and to maintain their positive self-perceptions (cf. Taylor & Lobel, 1989).

REFERENCES

Amoroso, D. M., & Walters, R. H. (1969). Effects of anxiety and socially mediated anxiety reduction on paired-associate learning. *Journal of Personality and Social Psychology, 11*, 388–396.

Billings, A. C., & Moos, R. H. (1984). Coping, stress, and social resources among adults with unipolar depression. *Journal of Personality and Social Psychology, 46*, 877–891.

Brickman, P., & Bulman, R. J (1977). Pleasure and pain in social comparison. In J. M. Suls & R. L. Miller (Eds.), *Social comparison processes: Theoretical and empirical perspectives* (pp. 149–186). Washington, DC: Hemisphere.

Buunk, B. (1987). Conditions that promote break-ups as a consequence of extradyadic involvements. *Journal of Social and Clinical Psychology, 5*, 237–250.

Buunk, B. (1990). Relationship interaction satisfaction scale. In J. Touliatos, B. F. Perlmutter, & M. A. Straus (Eds.), *Handbook of family measurement techniques* (pp. 106–107). Newbury Park, CA: Sage.

Buunk, B., & Bosnian, J. (1986). Attitude similarity and attraction in marital relationships. *Journal of Social Psychology, 126*, 133–134.

Crocker, J., & Gallo, L. (1985, August). *The self-enhancing effect of downward comparison.* Paper presented at the annual meeting of the American Psychological Association, Los Angeles.

Crocker, J., & Schwartz, I. (1985). Prejudice and ingroup favoritism in a minimal intergroup situation: Effects of self-esteem. *Personality and Social Psychology Bulletin, 11*, 379–386.

Crocker, J., Thompson, L. L., McGraw, K. M., & Ingerman, C. (1987). Downward comparison prejudice and evaluations of others: Effects of self-esteem and threat. *Journal of Personality and Social Psychology, 52*, 907–916.

Dakof, G. A. (1986). *Psychological and social adaptation to Parkinson's Disease.* Unpublished doctoral dissertation, University of California, Berkeley.

Diener, E. (1984). Subjective well-being. *Psychological Bulletin, 95*, 542–575.

Festinger, L. (1954). A theory of social comparison processes. *Human Relations, 7*, 117–140.

Fiske, S. T., & Taylor, S. E. (1984). *Social cognition.* Reading, MA: Addison-Wesley.

Friend, R. M., & Gilbert, J. (1973). Threat and fear of negative evaluation as determinants of locus of social comparison. *Journal of Personality, 41*, 328–340.

Gal, R., & Lazarus, R. S. (1975). The role of activity in anticipating and confronting stressful situations. *Journal of Human Stress, 1*, 4–20.

Gibbons, F. X. (1986). Social comparison and depression: Company's effect on misery. *Journal of Personality and Social Psychology, 51*, 140–148.

Goethals, G. R., & Darley, J. M. (1977). Social comparison theory: An attributional approach. In J. M. Suls & R. L. Miller (Eds.), *Social comparison processes: Theoretical and empirical perspectives* (pp. 259–278). Washington, DC: Hemisphere.

Gruder, C. L. (1971). Determinants of social comparison choices. *Journal of Experimental Social Psychology, 7*, 473–489.

Hakmiller, K. L. (1966). Threat as a determinant of downward comparison. *Journal of Experimental Social Psychology, Suppl. 1*, 32–39.

Holahan, C. J., & Moos, R. H. (1986). Personality, coping, and family resources in stress resistance: A longitudinal analysis. *Journal of Personality and Social Psychology*, *51*, 389–395.

Kiesler, S. B. (1966). Stress, affiliation and performance. *Journal of Experimental Research in Personality*, *1*, 227–235.

Latané, B. (1966). Studies in social comparison: Introduction and overview. *Journal of Experimental Social Psychology*, *Suppl. 1*, 1–5.

Lemyre, L., & Smith, P. M. (1985). Intergroup discrimination and self-esteem in the minimal intergroup paradigm. *Journal of Personality and Social Psychology*, *49*, 660–670.

Marks, G., Richardson, J. K., Graham, J. W., & Levine, A. (1986). Role of health locus of control beliefs and expectations of treatment efficacy in adjustment to cancer. *Journal of Personality and Social Psychology*, *51*, 443–450.

Marsh, H. W., & Parker, J. W (1984). Determinants of student self-concept: Is it better to be a relatively large fish in a small pond even if you don't learn to swim as well? *Journal of Personality and Social Psychology*, *47*, 213–231.

Matlin, M. W., & Strang, D. J. (1978). *The Pollyanna principle: Selectivity in language, memory, and thought*. Cambridge, MA: Schenkman.

McFarlane, A. H., Norman, G. R., Streiner, D. L., Roy, R., & Scott, D. J. (1980). A longitudinal study of the influence of the psychosocial environment on health status: A preliminary report. *Journal of Health and Social Behavior*, *21*, 124–133.

Mettee, D. R., & Smith, G. (1977). Social comparison and interpersonal attraction: The case for dissimilarity. In J. M. Suls & R. L. Miller (Eds.), *Social comparison processes: Theoretical and empirical perspectives* (pp. 69–101). Washington, DC: Hemisphere.

Morse, S., & Gergen, K. J. (1970). Social comparison, self-consistency, and the concept of self. *Journal of Personality and Social Psychology*, *16*, 148–156.

Myers, J. K., Lindenthal, J. J., & Pepper, M. P. (1972). Life events and mental status: A longitudinal study. *Journal of Health and Social Behavior*, *13*, 398–406.

Nosanchuk, T. A., & Erickson, B. H. (1985). How high is up? Calibrating social comparison in the real world. *Journal of Personality and Social Psychology*, *48*, 624–634.

Parducci, A. (1968). The relativism of absolute judgments. *Scientific American*, *219*, 84–90.

Rosenberg, M. (1965). *Society and the adolescent self image*. Princeton, NJ: Princeton University Press.

Salovey, P., & Rodin, J. (1984). Some antecedents and consequences of social-comparison jealousy. *Journal of Personality and Social Psychology*, *47*, 780–792.

Sarason, I. G., Johnson, J. H., & Siegel, J. M. (1978). Assessing the impact of life changes: Development of the Life Experiences Survey. *Journal of Consulting and Clinical Psychology*, *46*, 932–946.

Schachter, S. (1959). *The psychology of affiliation*. Stanford, CA: Stanford University Press.

Smith, R. H., & Insko, C. A. (1987). Social comparison choice during ability evaluation: The effects of comparison publicity, performance feedback, and self-esteem. *Personality and Social Psychology Bulletin*, *13*, 111–122.

Stokols, D., Ohlig, W., & Resnick, S. M. (1978). Perception of residential crowding, classroom experiences, and student health. *Human Ecology*, *6*, 33–57.

Taylor, S. E., & Brown, J. (1988). Illusion and well-being: A social psychological perspective on mental health. *Psychological Bulletin*, *103*, 193–210.

Taylor, S. E., Falke, R. L., Shoptaw, S. J., & Lichtman, R. R. (1986). Social support, support groups, and the cancer patient. *Journal of Consulting and Clinical Psychology*, *54*, 608–615.

Taylor, S. E., Lichtman, R. R., & Wood, J. V. (1984). Attributions, beliefs about control, and adjustment to breast cancer. *Journal of Personality and Social Psychology*, *46*, 489–502.

Taylor, S. E., & Lobel, M. (1989). Social comparison activity under threat: Downward evaluation and upward contacts. *Psychological Review*, *96*, 569–575.

Tesser, A. (1986). Some effects of self-evaluation maintenance on cognition and action. In R. M. Sorrentino & E. T. Higgins (Eds.), *Handbook of motivation and cognition: Foundations of social behavior* (pp. 435–464). New York: Guilford Press.

Tesser, A., Millar, M., & Moore, J. (1988). Some affective consequences of social comparison and reflection processes: The pain and pleasure of being close. *Journal of Personality and Social Psychology*, *54*, 49–61.

Testa, M., & Major, B. (April 1988). *Affective and behavioral consequences of social comparison*. Paper presented at the annual meetings of the Eastern Psychological Association, Buffalo, NY.

Thompson, S. G (1981). Will it hurt less if I can control it? A complex answer to a simple question. *Psychological Bulletin*, *90*, 89–101.

Titus, S. L. (1980). A function of friendship: Social comparisons as a frame of reference for marriage. *Human Relations*, *33*, 409–431.

VanYperen, N. W., & Buunk, B. (1990). A longitudinal study of equity in intimate relationships. *European Journal of Social Psychology*, *20*, 287–309.

Vinokur, A., & Selzer, M. (1975). Desirable versus undesirable life events: Their relationship to stress and mental distress. *Journal of Personality and Social Psychology*, *32*, 329–337.

Wheeler, L. (1966). Motivation as a determinant of upward comparison. *Journal of Experimental Social Psychology*, *Suppl. 1*, 27–31.

Wheeler, L., Shaver, K. G., Jones, R. A. Goethals, G. R., Cooper, J., Robinson, J. E., Gruder, C. L., & Butzine, K. W. (1969). Factors determining the choice of a comparison other. *Journal of Experimental Social Psychology*, *5*, 219–232.

Wheeler, L., & Zuckerman, M. (1977). Commentary. In J. M. Suls & R. L. Miller (Eds.), *Social comparison processes: Theoretical and empirical perspectives* (pp. 335–357). Washington, DC: Hemisphere.

Wills, T. A. (1981). Downward comparison principles in social psychology. *Psychological Bulletin*, *90*, 245–271.

Wills, T. A. (1987), Downward comparison as a coping mechanism. In C. R. Snyder & C. Ford (Eds.), *Coping with negative life events: Clinical and social-psychological perspectives* (pp. 243–268). San Diego, CA: Academic Press.

Wilson, S. R., & Benner, L. A. (1971). The effects of self-esteem and situation upon comparison choices during ability evaluation. *Sociometry*, *34*, 381–397.

Wood, J. V. (1984), *Social comparison in adjustment to breast cancer.* Unpublished doctoral dissertation, University of California, Los Angeles.

Wood, J. V. (1989). Contemporary social comparison theory. *Psychological Bulletin*, *106*, 231–248.

Wood, J. V., Taylor, S. E., & Lichtman, R. R. (1985). Social comparison in adjustment to breast cancer. *Journal of Personality and Social Psychology*, *49*, 1169–1183.

Received August 22, 1989
Revision received March 9, 1990
Accepted March 17, 1990 ■

Superstars and Me: Predicting the Impact of Role Models on the Self

Penelope Lockwood and Ziva Kunda

The authors propose that superstars are most likely to affect self-views when they are considered relevant. Relevant superstars provoke self-enhancement and inspiration when their success seems attainable but self-deflation when it seems unattainable. Participants' self-views were affected only when the star's domain of excellence was self-relevant. Relevant stars provoked self-enhancement and inspiration when their success seemed attainable in that participants either still had enough time to achieve comparable success or believed their own abilities could improve over time. Open-ended responses provided rich evidence of inspiration in these circumstances. Relevant stars provoked, if anything, self-deflation when their success seemed unattainable in that participants either had already missed the chance to achieve comparable success or viewed their abilities as fixed and so unlikely to improve.

It is a cultural cliché that superstars, that is, individuals of outstanding achievement, can serve as role models to others, inspiring and motivating them to do their utmost best. To promote such inspiration, prominent women scientists are often invited to address high school girls, eminent African Americans are introduced to African American children, and outstanding employees are profiled in corporate newsletters and bulletin boards. In the domain of public policy, affirmative action plans are often justified on the grounds that they will create role models who will inspire members of

Penelope Lockwood and Ziva Kunda, Department of Psychology, University of Waterloo, Waterloo, Ontario, Canada.

This research was supported by a grant from the Social Sciences and Humanities Research Council of Canada (SSHRC) and from the Natural Sciences and Engineering Research Council of Canada and by an SSHRC doctoral fellowship. Partial reports of these data were presented at the May 1996 conference of the Midwestern Psychological Association in Chicago and at the August 1996 conference of the American Psychological Association in Toronto. We are grateful to Lisa Sinclair and Joanne Wood for comments on an earlier version of this article and to Mike Busseri for his assistance with data collection.

Correspondence concerning this article should be addressed to Ziva Kunda, Department of Psychology, University of Waterloo, Waterloo, Ontario, Canada N2L 3G1. Electronic mail may be sent via the Internet to zkunda@watarts.uwaterloo.ca.

disadvantaged groups. In both the public and private sector, there are countless examples of programs showcasing the talents or successes of a superior individual that are designed to boost the aspirations and self-images of a particular target group.

However, our culture also holds the opposite cliché that superstars can demoralize and deflate less outstanding others. This notion was brilliantly captured in the movie *Amadeus* (Forman, 1984) in the image of Salieri, the accomplished musician whose self-view, indeed whose whole life, was shattered by exposure to Mozart's genius. More familiar everyday scripts include the image of the "superwoman" who makes other, less extraordinary women feel incompetent by comparison and the image of the perfectly competent child who is demoralized by a gifted sibling to the point of giving up on school. This notion, that outstanding others can be demoralizing, also gained support from the now classic "Mr. Clean and Mr. Dirty" study (Morse & Gergen, 1970), in which job applicants viewed themselves less positively when faced with a superior competitor than when faced with an inferior one.

It is assumed, then, that superstars can lead to self-enhancement and inspiration under some circumstances and to self-deflation and demoralization under others. In still other circumstances, superstars are expected to have no effect at all on people's self-views—one may watch the superb performance of Olympic medalists without experiencing any change in self-evaluation or motivation. Several theorists have struggled with the question of what determines whether and how people's self-views are affected by outstanding individuals (e.g., Brickman & Bulman, 1977; Collins, 1996; Taylor & Lobel, 1989; Tesser, 1991; Wood, 1989).

Despite these theoretical efforts, remarkably little research has examined the impact of outstanding others on people's self-perceptions (cf. Collins, 1996). Following Festinger's seminal (1954) article on social comparison, many studies have investigated the comparisons that people draw between themselves and others. However, most of this research has focused on identifying whom one will choose to compare oneself to under different circumstances (Wood, 1989). Much less attention

has been given to the consequences of comparisons that are thrust on one. A notable exception is the Self-Evaluation-Maintenance (SEM) model, developed by Tesser and his colleagues (e.g., Tesser, 1991; Tesser & Campbell, 1983), that examines the processes through which people maintain positive self-evaluations in the face of potentially threatening comparisons with others. However, in their research, Tesser and his colleagues have not actually assessed the impact of others on people's self-evaluations, focusing instead on uncovering evidence for cognitive and behavioral work aimed at maintaining and enhancing self-evaluations following social comparison. Their research did not address the question of what, if any, the remaining effects are on the self.

A small number of studies have examined the impact of upward comparisons, that is, comparisons to superior others, on self-evaluations. However, in most of these studies, participants were given only very impoverished information about the superior other in the form of a photograph revealing physical attractiveness (e.g., Brown, Novick, Lord, & Richards, 1992; Cash, Cash, & Butters, 1983) or a score on a single ability test (cf. Brewer & Weber, 1994). It is not obvious that reactions to such limited information will resemble reactions to a more realistically multidimensional person who has achieved more substantial and meaningful success. In particular, a richer portrayal may be crucial to the adoption of an outstanding other as a role model capable of clarifying one's goals and guiding one's aspirations. A handful of studies have included more detailed portraits of a high-achieving other. However, these studies examined the difference between upward comparisons to such a superior other and downward comparisons to an inferior other. They lack a crucial no-comparison control group (Brewer & Weber, 1994; Brickman & Bulman, 1977; Gastorf & Suls, 1978; Major, Sciacchitano, & Crocker, 1993; Morse & Gergen, 1970). It is therefore unclear from these studies whether differences in reactions to the superior and inferior individuals are due to the impact of the superior individual, the inferior individual, or both. An important line of work has investigated how people facing threats such as cancer or marital breakup are influenced by upward comparisons, that is, comparisons with others in similar circumstances who are doing better than they are (Buunk, Collins, Taylor, Van Yperen, & Dakof, 1990; Taylor & Lobel, 1989). However, this research typically involves self-reports of the effects of past comparisons, and these can be heavily influenced by participants' theories.

Methodological problems aside, the relevant studies do not paint a clear picture of the impact of outstanding others on the self because they have yielded mixed results. In some, comparisons to superior others appear to be self-enhancing, in some they appear to be self-deflating, and in some they seem to have no effect on self-views (for a review, see Collins, 1996). In this article, we aim to identify the circumstances under which each of these outcomes will occur. We examine what determines whether people compare themselves to superstars and, when they do, what determines the outcome of such comparison—when will it lead to self-enhancement and inspiration and when will it lead to self-deflation and discouragement?

We propose that superstars are most likely to affect self-views when they are considered relevant. The impact of relevant superstars depends on the perceived attainability of their success: Individuals will be enhanced and inspired by a superstar if they believe that they too can attain comparable success but will be demoralized and deflated if they believe that they cannot. Our thinking on these issues has been greatly influenced by the theoretical analysis of Major, Testa, and Bylsma (1991). These authors developed a similar model and also pointed to the lack of direct evidence for it. We turn next to a more detailed discussion of the two factors that we consider crucial in determining the impact of a superstar on others: the perceived relevance of the superstar to the self and the believed attainability of the star's success.

Relevance

A superstar will become a source of inspiration or discouragement only if one compares oneself to this person. One is most likely to draw such comparisons between oneself and an outstanding other when the other is viewed as relevant to the self (cf. Major *et al.*, 1991). What determines relevance? Our answer is informed by research on analogy, because social comparison may be viewed as drawing an analogy between the self and the other or, in other words, mapping the self onto the other (Thagard & Kunda, in press). People are most likely to draw analogies between two objects when the two resemble each other in features, structure, and purpose (Holyoak & Thagard, 1995; Markman & Gentner, 1993). These similarities are integrated and jointly affect the likelihood that one object, or, in the case of social comparison, one person, will be mapped onto the other (Holyoak & Thagard, 1989).

Research on social comparison confirms that similarity between self and other increases the likelihood of social comparison. People are particularly likely to seek comparisons with others who are similar to them in various ways (Goethals & Darley, 1977; Wood, 1989). When one is outperformed by another, one is especially likely to engage in defensive thoughts and actions if the other is similar to the self on dimensions such as age, race, gender, or personality (Tesser, 1986; Tesser & Campbell, 1983). Highly attractive others influence perceptions of one's own attractiveness only if they are of the same sex (Brown *et al.*, 1992). Also, comparisons with another who has performed better or worse than oneself are undermined on reflection when the other is known to have acted under circumstances that differ from one's own (Gilbert, Giesler, & Morris, 1995). All this suggests that as one's similarity in features or circumstances to an outstanding other decreases, the other is deemed less relevant for the purpose of social comparison and is therefore less likely to affect one's self-view.

The self-relevance of the superstar's domain of excellence can also contribute to the likelihood that one will compare oneself to the superstar (cf. Brewer & Gardner, 1996; Major *et al.*, 1993; Salovey & Rodin, 1984) inasmuch as it increases the correspondence between oneself and the star. The self-views of university professors seem more likely to be affected by academic superstars than by athletic ones, because an academic star can be more readily mapped onto a professor's self. Domain self-relevance is not an essential requirement for social comparison—if there are enough other similarities between the self and the superstar, the superstar may affect one's self-view even if he or she excels in an irrelevant domain (Tesser, 1986; Tesser & Campbell, 1983). This seems particularly likely if the superstar is a sibling or a close friend, because there are typically so many similarities in attributes and circumstances among siblings and friends that comparisons are all but inevitable. However, all other things being equal, domain self-relevance may determine whether or not one engages in comparison with more distant superstars in the first place.

Our view of the role that domain relevance plays in upward comparisons differs from that outlined in Tesser's SEM model (Tesser, 1988; Tesser & Campbell, 1983). In the SEM model, whether an outstanding other will have any impact on the self depends on the extent to which the other is psychologically close. Psychological closeness is assumed to increase with attribute similarity, physical proximity, family ties, similarity in place of origin, and so on. Tesser and his colleagues conceptualized domain self-relevance as a separate factor that determines only the direction of the target's impact on the self. In Tesser's model, the star is expected to have a negative impact when relevant (and therefore threatening) but a positive impact when irrelevant. In that model, relevance plays no role in determining whether the star will exert any impact on the self in the first place. In contrast, in our view, domain self-relevance, like psychological closeness, can serve to increase the correspondence between the self and the star. When a superstar excels at one's own domain of interest, this increases the similarity between oneself and the superstar and, thereby, the likelihood that one will draw an analogy between oneself and the star. Our studies focus on this role of relevance, which has thus far received little research attention. We assume that relevance and closeness can increase the likelihood of social comparison in a similar manner, but we do not examine whether these dimensions constitute a single construct or two orthogonal ones.

Attainability

When an outstanding individual seems relevant, one will compare oneself to this individual. The consequences of this comparison for the self will then depend on the perceived attainability of that individual's success. If the superstar's success seems attainable, one will be inspired. The superstar illustrates the wonderful heights of accomplishment one can hope to achieve, encourages and motivates one to strive for this now all the more palpable success, indicates particular goals to aim for along the way, points to the road one should follow to achieve them, and makes one feel more competent and capable of such achievement. On the other hand, if the superstar's success seems unattainable, one will be discouraged and demoralized. The superstar's success highlights one's own failures and shortcomings. One realizes that one can no longer hope for comparable stardom, one's own lesser achievement seems paltry by comparison, and one feels disheartened and inferior (cf. Major et al., 1991).

The notion of personal inspiration outlined above lies at the heart of the popular understanding of role models and their presumed positive impact. Yet this notion has received little attention in social psychological research. Researchers investigating cancer patients have noted that these patients gain hope and inspiration from better off cancer patients who can serve as a source of information on coping and survival (Taylor & Lobel, 1989). Reviewers of social comparison research have also noted that superior others can sometimes serve as inspirational role models (e.g., Collins, 1996; Wood, 1989). However, for the most part, these insights have not been incorporated into prevailing theories of how people are influenced by others who are superior to them in ability and achievement (e.g., Brewer & Weber, 1994; Tesser, 1991).

To be sure, several theorists have suggested that superior others can have positive consequences for the self; however, these benefits are typically conceptualized as resulting from a process that is quite different in nature from inspiration, Tesser's *reflection* process (1988) and Cialdini's *basking in reflected glory* (Cialdini et al., 1976) both describe mechanisms by which an individual is positively affected by the triumphs of a close other. However, such positive impact stems not from the opening up of possibilities for the self but, rather, from the pride of association with the other. One feels good about oneself not because "I can achieve wonderful heights" but because "I belong to a wonderful group." Indeed, such basking in the reflected glory of others has been shown to occur only when one's own central self-conceptions are not engaged: It occurs only when the other excels at a domain that is irrelevant to the self (Tesser, 1988); it occurs only when one holds one's own personal self at bay, highlighting instead one's social self (Brewer & Weber, 1994); and it occurs when one has no need to dwell on one's self-view because one is confident about it (Pelham & Wachsmuth, 1995). When these conditions are not met, the superior other is expected to have a negative rather than positive impact on the self. The implication is that when one's personal identity is salient, as is typically the case for North Americans (Markus & Kitayama, 1991), someone who is outstanding in a domain that one cares deeply about—the very definition of a role model—can only demoralize, never inspire one.

This emphasis on the negative consequences of comparisons to others who are superior on self-relevant dimensions is rooted in the original view of social comparison as providing a means of assessing one's current abilities (Festinger, 1954). Current abilities are inevitably inferior to those of a superior other, and if one were to focus only on that inferiority, demoralization would undoubtedly ensue. However, a different picture emerges if one recognizes that people's self-views incorporate more than their current abilities; possible future selves also play a central role in guiding aspirations and satisfaction and may sometimes be even more important to well-being than are current self-conceptions (Markus & Nurius, 1986). The realization that one is currently less successful than another may lose its sting if it is accompanied by the belief that one will attain comparable success in the future. Role models can enhance and inspire by making successful future selves appear more tangible and by illustrating how future achievements may be accomplished (Meichenbaum, 1971).

In focusing on such personal inspiration, we do not mean to challenge the reality or importance of the reflection process highlighted by other theorists, for which there is ample evidence (Brewer & Weber, 1994; Cialdini et al., 1976; Tesser, 1988). We do, however, wish to point out that outstanding others can also lead to a different kind of positive consequence—inspiration—that could arise under circumstances in which basking in reflected glory is unlikely. Moreover, we question a central supposition of Tesser's SEM model (Tesser, 1988; Tesser & Campbell, 1983), namely, that close others who excel at a self-relevant domain will invariably have negative consequences for the self. We believe that such negative consequences will occur only when the other's success seems unattainable. When it seems attainable, the consequences for the self will be positive.

Tesser and his colleagues may have overlooked the possibility that others who are superior on a self-relevant dimension can exert a positive impact on the self because, in their experiments, the other's elevated performance was typically unattainable and the other's superiority to the self irrevocable—precisely the conditions under which we too expect a negative impact on the self. In relevant SEM experiments, the other's superiority was established by informing participants that the other had outperformed them on a novel test that both had just taken. Participants were confronted either with a single score on a test that they did not expect to take again (Pleban & Tesser, 1981; Tesser & Cornell, 1991; Tesser & Paulhus, 1983) or with scores on several items given in rapid succession with no opportunity to practice and improve from one item to another (Tesser, Millar, & Moore, 1988). In such circumstances there can be no hope of improving one's standing relative to the other in the future; the other's superior level of success is unattainable and, therefore, threatening and demoralizing (cf. Major et al., 1991). This research leaves open the possibility that others who excel on a self-relevant domain can be inspiring when their excellence seems attainable.

There is some support for the prediction that relevant superstars lead to inspiration when their success seems attainable but to demoralization when it seems unattainable. Major *et al.*'s review (1991) concluded that the impact of a superior other was positive in studies in which participants most likely viewed their own performance as controllable (and so viewed future success as attainable; e.g., Meichenbaum, 1971; Seta, 1982), but the impact of superior others was negative in studies in which participants most likely viewed future success as unattainable (e.g., Salovey & Rodin, 1984; Tesser & Paulhus, 1983). However, the conclusion that the perceived attainability of success determines the impact of a superstar remains speculative because it is based mostly on post hoc comparison of studies that provided examples of attainable success to other studies that provided examples of unattainable success. One study that did vary the attainability of future success found that receiving lower test scores than others led to more negative consequence when participants believed their own performance could improve than when they believed it could not (Testa & Major, 1990). However, this study did not include a no-comparison baseline, so the absolute impact of comparisons in both these conditions remains unknown. Wood and VanderZee (in press), reviewing research on cancer patients' comparisons to better off others, concluded that such comparisons are pleasing and inspiring when similar outcomes seem attainable but demoralizing when they do not. However, that research involved patients' descriptions of their typical reactions to such comparisons rather than more rigorous experimental designs. Moreover, it is unclear whether the dynamics of upward comparisons in the domains of ability and achievement are the same as in the domains of health and survival. Thus, although there is reason to believe that the impact of superstars depends on the perceived attainability of their success, there is no direct and conclusive evidence for this hypothesis. We aimed to test it more directly.

In this article, we examine the impact of superstars on people's self-perceptions. In all our studies, we provided participants with detailed, richly portrayed descriptions of a person of outstanding accomplishment. We expected that the impact of such a superstar on the self would be greater when the superstar's domain of excellence was relevant to the self. Study 1 examined this hypothesis. We further expected that the direction of this impact would depend on the perceived attainability of the superstar's success. When a star's accomplishments appear attainable, people will be inspired and their self-views will be enhanced. In contrast, when the star's achievements seem out of reach, people will be threatened, and their self-views will be deflated. Studies 2 and 3 examined this hypothesis. We also attempted to document inspiration by analyzing participants' open-ended responses.

Study 1. Relevance: An Outstanding Teacher or Accountant Has Different Consequences for Future Teachers and Accountants

We hypothesized that superstars can be inspiring if they excel at a relevant domain and their success seems attainable. In our first study, we attempted to create a star whose success would seem attainable and focused on examining whether the star's impact would depend on the star's relevance. We expected that superstars would give rise to greater inspiration and self-enhancement when they were perceived as more self-relevant.

We manipulated the self-relevance of a superstar's domain of excellence by exposing students to someone who had excelled at their own intended profession or at a different profession. We focused on the professions of teaching and accounting because these were the most common intended professions in the available pool of participants. In addition, they seem sufficiently different from each other that a future teacher might consider an outstanding accountant to be completely irrelevant. We identified participants who planned to become teachers or accountants and exposed them to a description of either an outstanding teacher or an outstanding accountant. We reasoned that because the star had excelled at tasks that participants' themselves had not yet undertaken, participants would likely view similar levels of success to be within their own reach and so would be inspired by the star. We expected that participants would be more inspired by a superstar who excelled at their own intended profession than by one who excelled at a different profession.

Method

Participants. Participants were 50 female University of Waterloo undergraduates enrolled in Introductory Psychology who participated for course credit. At the beginning of the term, participants filled out a lengthy prescreening measure that included a questionnaire assessing career plans. The two most common future professions were teaching and accounting. We therefore focused on these and randomly selected participants from the lists of future teachers and future accountants. Because most of the future teachers were women, we included only women in the study. Altogether, 32 future teachers and 18 future accountants took part in the study.

Procedure. Three to ten weeks after completing the prescreening measure, participants were recruited for a study on the effects of journalistic styles on social perception. Experimental participants read a bogus newspaper article describing either a teacher or an accountant who had recently won an award for her outstanding career achievements; both targets were women. The high-achieving teacher was portrayed as having been highly successful in motivating her students at an inner city high school, meeting difficult challenges with enthusiasm. She was described by her school principal as "one of the most talented, creative, and innovative teachers" he had ever worked with. The high-achieving accountant was portrayed as having shown remarkable progress in her career, becoming one of the youngest employees ever to receive a partnership at her well-respected accounting firm. She was described by her supervisor as "one of the most extraordinarily talented and innovative individuals" that he had ever worked with.

Dependent measures. After reading the article, experimental participants read that before being asked about the article they would be asked some questions about themselves to determine whether their personality had any impact on their perceptions of the article. They then rated themselves on 40 adjectives among which were embedded 10 that related positively to general career success (e.g., bright, skillful) and 10 that related negatively to such success (e.g., incompetent, unintelligent).[1] All items were rated on an 11-point scale with endpoints labeled 1 (*not at all*) and 11 (*very*). Participants then rated the target on the same items.

Next, participants rated how relevant the target was to them for the purpose of comparison on an 11-point scale with endpoints labeled 1 (*completely irrelevant*) and 11 (*very relevant*). They then wrote an explanation of why they had answered this question as they had.

We also included a control group of future teachers who provided self-ratings without first reading about a target. We were unable to include a control group of future accountants because there were not enough of them in the available pool of participants. Control group participants read the same cover story but were asked to provide the self-ratings before they read the article.

In sum, the design was 2 (participants' future profession: teaching or accounting) $\times$ 2 (target's profession: teacher or accountant) with an additional no-target control group for future teachers. Participants in each future profession group were randomly assigned to conditions.

Results and Discussion

Ratings of target. We averaged success-related items into a single index of the target's success after first reversing the negative items (Cronbach's α = .79). A 2 (Participants' future profession) $\times$ 2 (Target's profession) analysis of variance (ANOVA) revealed that the accountant ($M = 10.09$) was rated higher than the teacher ($M = 9.56$), $F(1, 36) = 5.24$, $p < .05$. This effect poses no problems for the interpretation of participants' self-ratings because even the teacher was rated very highly, and, as we show below, the two targets provoked comparable effects. The high target ratings indicate

---

[1] One of these (inept) was removed from the index because several participants expressed uncertainty about its meaning.

that we were successful in portraying individuals of outstanding achievement. The main effect of participants' future profession and the interaction were not significant (both $ps > .20$).

Self-ratings. We recoded the variable reflecting the target's profession in terms of the target's relevance to participants. The target was coded as relevant when her profession was the same as participants' intended profession (i.e., the teacher was relevant to future teachers and the accountant to future accountants) and was coded as irrelevant when her profession differed from participants' intended profession (i.e., the teacher was irrelevant to future accountants and the accountant to future teachers). We used a 2 (participants' future profession) $\times$ 2 (relevance of target's occupation) factorial design with an additional non-orthogonal control group for future teachers. We first analyzed the data from the factorial design by using a 2×2 ANOVA. Next, we performed a one-way ANOVA on ratings made by future teachers with 3 levels of target (teacher, accountant, and control). This provided the error term used in planned comparisons among these conditions.

Self-ratings were averaged into an index of success as target ratings had been (Cronbach's $\alpha =$ .89). As can be seen in Table 8.1, both future teachers and future accountants who were exposed to a superstar evaluated themselves more positively when the superstar was relevant to them than when the superstar was irrelevant. This main effect was significant, $F(1, 36) = 5.39$, $p < .05$. The main effect for participants' future occupation and the interaction did not approach significance (both $Fs < 1$).

TABLE 8.1. Mean Self-Evaluations of Future Accountants and Future Teachers Exposed to a Relevant Target (Who Excelled at Their Own Intended Profession), an Irrelevant Target (Who Excelled at the Other Profession), or No Target

Future occupation	Target type		
	Relevant	Irrelevant	No target
Future accountants	8.24	7.68	—
Future teachers	8.64	7.66	7.67

Note: Higher numbers indicate more positive self-evaluations.

Examination of the control group included for future teachers suggests that the obtained differences in self-ratings following exposure to the relevant and irrelevant role models were due entirely to the self-enhancing impact of the relevant one; the irrelevant role model had no impact on self-ratings. The self-evaluations of future teachers exposed to the irrelevant accountant role model were almost identical to those of controls, as can be seen in Table 8.1. However, future teachers exposed to the relevant teacher role model rated themselves more positively than did controls or those exposed to the irrelevant role model. This difference was significant, as revealed by a planned contrast comparing future teachers exposed to the relevant target to the average of the irrelevant-target and control conditions, $F(1, 29) = 5.70$, $p < .05$. It appears, then, that the relevant role model had a positive influence on participants, but the irrelevant role model had no impact.

Ratings of target's relevance. As expected, participants rated the target who was outstanding in their own future profession as more relevant to them than the other target, $F(1, 36) = 13.32$, $p < .001$. The main effect for participants' future occupation and the interaction did not approach significance (both $Fs < 1$). Thus we had successfully manipulated the perceived relevance of the targets to participants.

Moreover, the differential impact of the two targets on the two groups of participants appears to have been due to these differences in the targets' perceived relevance. To test whether the target's perceived relevance mediated the impact of the target's future profession on self-ratings, we conducted a series of regression analyses (Baron & Kenny, 1986). First, we regressed relevance ratings on target's occupation (which was coded as relevant or irrelevant to participants as in the previous analysis) and obtained a significant effect ($\beta = .52$, $p < .001$). Second, we regressed self-ratings on target's occupation and obtained a significant effect ($\beta = .37, p < .02$). Third, we regressed self-ratings on both target's occupation and relevance ratings. Relevance ratings had a significant effect on self-ratings ($\beta = .40$, $p = .02$). The effects of target's occupation on self-ratings were substantially lower in the third than in the second regression equation and were no longer significant ($\beta = .16$, $p > .25$). Thus, controlling for the effects of relevance ratings eliminated the effects of target's occupation on self-ratings.

Explanations. We have suggested that the relevant superstars had a positive impact on participants because participants were inspired by these individuals. We examined participants' open-ended explanations of their ratings of the target's relevance for evidence of such inspiration. We expected that participants would articulate that they were inspired by the role model and that they would be more likely to do so when the role model was relevant to them.

Two raters unaware of the study's hypotheses coded participants' responses. Raters were also initially unaware of participants' condition, although participants' responses often revealed the target's profession and their own intended one. Participants were considered to show inspiration if they indicated that they had found the target motivating or inspiring (e.g., "This type of dedication and success in the teaching field is quite inspirational. It is amazing and motivating to see how just one teacher can affect so many individuals."), if they said the target had motivated them to work harder (e.g., "If I judge myself by her standards I will work harder to achieve my goals, so that I can have what she has [only better]."), if they indicated that exposure to the target had given them new or enhanced goals (e.g., "Moving up the ranks so quickly is something I can try to aim for figuring that an example has already been set."), if they said that they wanted to become like the target (e.g., "I want to see my name where hers is today."), or if they explicitly referred to the target as a role model. The raters agreed on 85% of the cases; discrepancies were resolved through discussion.

The relevant role model was considerably more likely than the irrelevant one to provoke inspiration. Of the participants exposed to the relevant role model, 45% indicated that the target had inspired them, whereas only 15% of participants exposed to the irrelevant target indicated any inspiration ($z = 2.07$, $p < 05$). Thus, the subjective experience of inspiration by an outstanding other is quite common and is particularly likely to be induced by relevant superstars.

Study 2. Attainability: An Outstanding Graduating Student Has Different Consequences for First- and Fourth-Year Students

Study 1 suggested that a star's perceived relevance can determine whether the star will have any impact on others. In Study 1, this impact was positive: The relevant star induced self-enhancement and inspiration. Other studies, however, have suggested that relevant stars can also exert a negative impact (Tesser, 1991). Study 2 examined what determines the direction of the impact exerted by relevant superstars. We predicted that this impact would be positive when the achievements of the star seemed attainable but negative when they seemed unattainable. As noted earlier, this prediction is consistent with prior research, although there is no direct evidence for it (Major *et al.*, 1991). It is also consistent with our everyday experience.

We have noticed that when an academic department is searching for a new professor, graduating doctoral students are often demoralized and deflated by job candidates whose credentials are superior to their own. But these same students seem inspired by outstanding visiting professors, even though these are typically far more accomplished than the job candidates that the students find so threatening. We believe that young job candidates are so much more threatening to graduate students because they are at the same stage in their careers. The students must realize that it is already too late for them to accomplish in graduate school what these stars have managed to achieve. The outstanding job candidate therefore seems far more competent than they are. Such invidious comparisons can lead to discouragement and self-deflation. In contrast, visiting professors are older and more advanced in their careers. As such, they illustrate possible future accomplishments that students can still hope and strive to obtain. Students may believe that if only they work hard enough from now on, they too can be as successful 10 years down the road. Such a model of seemingly attainable excellence can inspire students and lead them to view their own abilities and prospects more brightly.

This analysis suggests that the relevant star in Study 1 was inspiring because she was at a more advanced career stage than the participants. Participants had not yet undertaken the tasks that she had excelled at and could therefore still believe that they too could attain such excellence. A study by Brickman and Bulman (1977, Experiment 3) yielded results consistent with these ideas: Participants viewed themselves more negatively after exposure to an outstanding peer than after exposure to an outstanding older person. However, because that study had no control group, the absolute impact of either target remains unknown.

To examine these ideas, we presented participants with a superstar whose success would seem attainable or unattainable by virtue of each participant's own career stage. To this end, we created a description of a spectacular graduating student who had majored in accounting and presented this description to entering and graduating accounting students. We chose this major because accounting is a highly selective program at the University of Waterloo, drawing students who excelled in high school. We reasoned that the achievements of the graduating superstar would seem attainable to first-year accounting students whose university careers still lay ahead and for whom any level of accomplishment still seemed within reach given their history of academic excellence. Therefore these students should be inspired and self-enhanced by the star. In contrast, we expected that the achievements of the same superstar would seem unattainable to fourth-year accounting students, for whom it was already too late to achieve a similar level of success at university; they had already established a less stellar record and had no time left to improve upon it. Therefore these students should be discouraged and self-deflated by the star.

Method

Participants. Participants were 69 students of both genders enrolled in the School of Accountancy at the University of Waterloo. Students from first- and fourth-year accounting classes were recruited to participate, for pay, in a study on the effects of journalistic style on social perception. Four participants were excluded from the analyses, 2 because they did not list accounting as their intended occupation and 2 because their self-evaluation scores were more than three standard deviations from the mean, leaving a total of 65 participants. Participants' gender had no effects on any of the variables and therefore is not discussed further.

Procedure. Participants were randomly assigned to the experimental or control group. Experimental participants read a bogus newspaper article, ostensibly from a local campus newspaper, describing a stellar fourth-year accounting student. The target was said to have recently won an important award for outstanding academic achievement. This student had a "superb academic record" and was praised by the Chair of the Accounting program as "innovative and creative." Moreover, because we did not want participants to dismiss the target as a "geek," the article also described the target's involvement in student government groups, volunteer activities, and various sports teams. This graduating student was a bright, well-rounded high achiever who had "demonstrated a high level of leadership and community involvement." The article was the same for all participants, with the exception that women read about a female target (Jennifer Walker) and men read about a male target (Jeffrey Walker).

After reading the article, experimental participants rated first the target and then themselves on a set of 10 positive and 10 negative traits relevant to general career success. Ratings were made on an 11-point scale with endpoints labeled 1 (*not at all*) and 11 (*very*).

Next, experimental participants were asked to list their intended occupation. This enabled us to confirm that they were planning to become accountants and therefore likely to view the target as relevant. Participants then rated the extent to which the target was relevant to them for the purpose of comparison on an 11-point scale with endpoints ranging from 1 (*completely irrelevant*) to 11 (*very relevant*) and were also asked to write down explanations for their responses to this question.

Participants in the control group completed the self-ratings without first reading about the target. After completing the questionnaire, participants were probed for suspicion and debriefed.

Results and Discussion

Ratings of target. Success-related items were averaged into a single index of the target's success after first reversing the negative items (Cronbach's α = .83). Unexpectedly, fourth-year students (M = 9.72) rated the target somewhat less positively than did first-year students (M = 10.20), $F(1, 31) = 4.30, p = .05$. We suspect that this was due to a defensive reaction on the part of the fourth-year students; recognizing the target's achievements to be unattainable, they were perhaps attempting to cut the target down to size and thus minimize the negative impact on themselves (Tesser, 1988; Tesser & Campbell, 1983). As we show below, we have other evidence for defensiveness on the part of fourth-year students. Note that, if anything, this pattern acts against our hypothesis. A less extremely successful target should be less, not more, threatening. But we predicted that fourth-year students, who viewed this target as somewhat less extremely successful, would be far more threatened by the target than would first-year students, because only fourth-year students would view the target's accomplishments as unattainable. Note also that even fourth-year participants rated the target very highly, suggesting that we were successful in portraying an outstanding individual.

Self-ratings. Unlike in Study 1, the correlation between the positive and negative items on the self-evaluation scales was low ($r = -.31$).[2] Accordingly, we report the self-evaluation scores separately for the positive and negative items. The 10 positive items were averaged to form an index of positive self-evaluations (Cronbach's α = .86), and the 10 negative items were averaged to form an index of negative self-evaluations (Cronbach's α = .84).

Analyses of the positive self-evaluation index revealed that, as expected, the same outstanding graduating student exerted a different impact on first- and fourth-year students, as indicated by a significant interaction, $F(1, 61) = 4.98, p < .05$. As seen in Table 8.2, first-year students, for whom the target's achievements seemed attainable, were clearly enhanced by the target: First-year students exposed to the target rated themselves more positively than did first-year controls, $F(1, 61) = 4.37, p < .05$. In contrast, fourth-year students, for whom the target's accomplishments were unattainable, were, if anything, deflated by the target. Fourth-year students exposed to the target rated themselves less positively than did fourth-year controls, although this difference did not reach significance, $F(1, 61) = 1.23, p = .27$.

The target's impact on participants' self-views was restricted to the positive items. An analysis of the negative item index revealed no significant effects ($Fs < 1$). This may reflect a floor effect. Negative self-ratings may have been too low among these highly accomplished participants to permit any further lowering even when their self-views were enhanced.

Ratings of target's relevance. Participants' ratings of the target's relevance to them as a comparison other revealed that fourth-year students actually rated the target as less relevant to them (M = 6.81) than did the first-year students (M = 9.65), $F(1, 31) = 11.02, p < .01$. This pattern may seem surprising in that an objective observer might assume the opposite: students in the same class as the star (the fourth-year students) should view the star as more relevant than students in a different

TABLE 8.2. Mean Self-Evaluations of First- and Fourth-Year Students Who Were and Who Were Not Exposed to an Outstanding Graduating Student

Year in school	Target type	
	No target	Superstar
First	8.19	8.90
Fourth	8.29	7.88

Note: Higher numbers indicate more positive self-evaluations.

---

[2]The corresponding correlation in Study 1 was considerably stronger ($-.55$).

class (the first-year students). The obtained pattern is, however; consistent with research showing that people attempt to reduce their closeness to an outstanding other who threatens them (Pleban & Tesser, 1981; Tesser, 1986). The superstar was more threatening to the fourth-year students because only they viewed the star's accomplishments as unattainable.

As in Study 1, participants' relevance ratings were positively associated with their self-ratings ($r = .19$), but in this study, this effect was not significant ($p > .25$). Most likely, results in this study were weaker because it had a more restricted range of relevance ratings: In this study, we created the targets to be highly relevant to all participants, whereas in Study 1 we intentionally varied the target's relevance.

Explanations. Participants' open-ended explanations of their relevance ratings shed further light on their responses. Two judges unaware of the study's hypotheses and of participants' year in school coded these data for three types of responses: inspiration, denigration of the social comparison process, and similarity to the target. Agreement between the two coders was 94% for the inspiration category, 97% for the comparison denigration category, and 85% for the similarity category. Discrepancies were resolved through discussion.

The criteria for classifying a response as showing inspiration were the same as in Study 1. We found dramatic differences on this measure between first- and fourth-year students. Whereas a large majority of first-year students described themselves as inspired (82%), only a small minority of fourth-year students gave any indication of inspiration (6%). This difference in proportions was significant ($z = 4.41, p < .001$).

We have suggested that a superstar can inspire by helping one set up clearer goals to shoot for and by motivating one to work harder toward these goals. First-year students provided vivid accounts of such inspiration. As one of them commented,

> It is almost spooky how much alike Walker and I are: Firstly, I am in Arts Accounting Co-op and

am an overachiever just like she is. Therefore because we are both female, planning on becoming Accountants I almost now want to work super-hard so that I can get that award that she got....I just decided that I will go to the ASA [Accounting Students' Association] meeting tomorrow now because it is probably a good idea to get involved like Jennifer did.

This student clearly believed the achievements of the role model to be within her own grasp, had incorporated the award as a new goal to strive for, had learned how to go about obtaining it, and was determined to work, harder to achieve it.

Several of the first-year students indicated that the role model helped them delineate their achievement goals more clearly. As another first-year student noted,

> Jeffrey Walker is very relevant to me for the purpose of comparison because what he has done is what my goals are. My goal is to become a CA and more important, I want to be at the top of my class. I also want to be well-rounded and have a life outside academics. Jeffrey Walker has done this through his athletics and volunteer work, and I would like to do the same. After seeing what Jeffrey has accomplished, I know what I must strive for.

For this student, the role model's accomplishments have provided a template to guide his own aspirations. Thus, a role model whose achievements seem attainable can help individuals develop their goals in more practical, task-oriented ways.

As is clear from these representative responses, first-year students actively compared themselves to the superstar and were inspired by him or her. Fourth-year students, who provided little evidence of inspiration, reacted quite differently to the superstar. Analysis of the second class of responses that we coded for, denigrating the comparison process, shed light on their reactions. Participants were considered to have denigrated the comparison process if they stated that comparisons to another individual are pointless, that they preferred to judge themselves by their own standards rather than by referring to the achievements of others, or that they had too little information about the target to make a reasonable comparison. Below are representative examples of denigration of the comparison process, all voiced by fourth-year students:

> I try to improve myself, but using who I was yesterday as a model for that comparison. Jeffrey is unknown to me...I have a set of special circumstances unique only to me and so does everyone else. To think otherwise is absurd. You can't compare "success" between any 2 people on the planet because we are all different and successful in our own right.

> He is in the same program and has the same career plans. However, I do not know enough of his personal character for him to be relevant.

> JW is like a classmate to me. I'm usually influenced more by how I view myself than by how well I'm compared to my classmates. I'm more influenced by my own standards.

Such denigration of the comparison process was substantially more likely for fourth-year students (50%) than for first-year students (6%; $z = 2.80$, $p < .01$).

The third class of responses we coded for, similarity to the target, shed further light on participants' reactions to the target. For this measure, we counted only mentions of similarity on dimensions other than intended occupation (e.g., "She seems very similar to me. She aims to do well in school, like myself. She also participates in activities other than academic related like myself. Similarly, I like to help those in need," "[She has the] same interests in sports, and the other involvements are similar to those I would be interested in."). First-year students were considerably more likely to note such similarities between themselves and the target (53%) than were fourth-year students (19%; $z = 2.05$, $p < .05$). This difference may reflect motivated reactions on the part of both groups: First-year students may have exaggerated their similarity to the star so as to justify mapping themselves onto this outstanding person and inferring comparable future success for themselves, whereas fourth-year students may have played down any similarities between themselves and the star to justify viewing the star as irrelevant to them and as therefore nonthreatening.

In sum, it is apparent that first- and fourth-year students provided strikingly different accounts of their reactions to the target. Whereas first-year students focused on highlighting their similarity to the target and spelling out what they could learn from this outstanding person, fourth-year students concentrated on explaining why they could learn nothing about themselves from the target. Tesser and his colleagues (Tesser; 1986; Tesser & Campbell, 1983) have proposed that when one is threatened by a superior other, one may attempt to dispel the threat by reducing closeness to the other, minimizing the other's performance, or reducing the relevance of the other's domain of achievement to the self. We too found evidence for some of these processes. The lower target ratings given by fourth-year students may reflect an attempt to minimize the target's performance. Their lower relevance ratings and mentions of similarity may reflect, in part, an attempt to reduce closeness. In addition, fourth-year participants' explanations point to yet another mechanism that people can rely on to diffuse the threat of an upward comparison: They may attempt to denigrate the inherent value of any social comparison.

Together, these defensive reactions may have been effective in that they may have served to undermine the self-deflation induced by the threatening target in this study. That may be why the self-deflation obtained for fourth-year students was weaker than the self-enhancement obtained for first-year students.

Study 3. Attainability: An Outstanding Student Has Different Consequences for Students Holding Stable and Malleable Theories of Intelligence

We predicted that superstars would induce inspiration and self-enhancement when their accomplishments seemed attainable but demoralization and self-deflation when their accomplishments seemed unattainable. Study 2 provided partial support for these predictions. It is evident that the perceived attainability of a superstar's success can determine the star's consequences for the self and that a model of attainable success can be inspiring.

We found clear evidence that an outstanding graduating student could inspire and enhance the self-views of entering students, for whom comparable success seemed attainable. It also appears that a model of unattainable success can be threatening and can induce motivated reasoning aimed at dispelling the threat (Kunda, 1990; Tesser, 1988). It is less clear whether the end result in such cases will be self-deflation. We found that graduating students, for whom the target's level of success was no longer attainable, were somewhat deflated, as predicted, but not significantly so. It seems possible that the defenses that threatened individuals engage in can sometimes protect the self so effectively that self-views remain unchanged.

In Study 3, we further examined how the perceived attainability of a star's success contributes to the star's impact on others. This time, we varied perceived attainability in a very different manner, relying on ongoing individual differences rather than on external circumstances. People differ in their beliefs about the stability of academic abilities. Some view intelligence as fixed and unalterable, whereas others view it as malleable and increasable (Dweck & Leggett, 1988). We reasoned that people's beliefs about the stability of academic ability could influence the extent to which the achievements of an academic star would seem attainable to them. Those who view academic ability as stable and fixed should assume that they will be unable to improve or develop their own academic performance and so will never reach the star's level of excellence. These individuals should be discouraged by the star. In contrast, those who view academic ability as malleable and capable of improving over time may believe that they will be able to match the star's achievements in the future, as their own abilities develop. These individuals should be inspired and self-enhanced by the star.

Method

Participants. Participants were 58 University of Waterloo undergraduates of both genders enrolled in Introductory Psychology who participated for course credit. Participants' gender had no effect on any of the variables and therefore is not discussed further. We excluded fourth-year students because, on the basis of the results of Study 2, we believed that they would feel threatened by the target (again a graduating student) regardless of their theory of intelligence. One participant was removed from the analyses because she had changed her academic major since completing the prescreening questionnaire and consequently read about a target in a nonrelevant major. Altogether, 57 participants were included in the analyses.

Pretesting. At the beginning of the term, participants filled out a lengthy prescreening measure that included a questionnaire assessing their theories of intelligence. Participants rated a set of 20 items on an 11-point scale with endpoints labeled 1 (*not at all true*) and 11 (*very true*). Six items expressed a belief that intelligence is malleable (e.g., "People can become more intelligent over the course of their lifetime," "Intelligence is influenced by the environment a person lives in"). Six items expressed a belief that intelligence is fixed (e.g., "Intelligence is genetically pre-determined," "Extra schooling cannot make a person more intelligent"). The remaining 8 items addressed other aspects of academic skills (e.g., "People who excel at mathematics also tend to excel at languages") and were included to prevent participants from guessing the true purpose of the questionnaire.

We randomly selected participants from among those who had completed the theory of intelligence measure and subsequently used their scores on this measure to divide them into a malleable-theory group and a fixed-theory group, on the basis of a median split. We also assessed participants' academic major in this pretesting questionnaire.

Procedure. Two to 10 weeks after completing the pretesting questionnaire, participants were recruited for a study on the effect of journalistic styles on social perception and participated individually in a lab setting. The experimenter was unaware of their theory of intelligence score. Participants were randomly assigned to either the experimental or the control condition. Experimental participants read a bogus newspaper article about an outstanding student. The article was similar to the one used in Study 2: The target was academically gifted, a student leader, and involved in various sports and volunteer activities. To ensure relevance, the article was tailor-made for each participant, so that each student read about a target in his or her own academic program; for example, a computer science major read about a computer science student, and an English major read about an English student. The target was always of the same gender as the participant.

After reading the article, experimental participants rated the target and then themselves on the same success-related traits used in Study 2 and on the same perceived relevance measure. Control participants completed the self-ratings without first reading the article about the target.

Results and Discussion

Prior theory. The six items on the theory of intelligence scale that reflected fixed theories were reverse-scored and averaged with the six items that reflected malleable theories to form a single malleability of intelligence index (Cronbach's $\alpha = .69$). Participants scoring above the median on this measure were considered to have malleable theories of intelligence, whereas those scoring below the median were considered to have fixed theories. This resulted in sample sizes ranging from 11 to 17 in the four cells of the 2 (theory) $\times$ 2 (condition) design.

To ensure that experimental and control participants within each theory group did not differ in their prior theories of intelligence, we conducted a 2 $\times$ 2 ANOVA on the malleability index. There were no effects for condition or for the interaction (both $ps > .20$). Of course, malleable-theory participants ($M = 8.96$) had substantially higher malleability scores than did fixed-theory participants ($M = 6.98$), $F(1, 54) = 151.16, p < .001$.

Ratings of target. Success-related items were averaged into a single index of the target's success after first reversing the negative items (Cronbach's $\alpha = .85$). Experimental participants holding fixed and malleable theories did not differ in their ratings of the target ($Ms = 9.81$ and 9.98, respectively; $F < 1$), with both groups rating the target as highly successful.

Self-ratings. Self-ratings were averaged into an index of success as target ratings had been (Cronbach's $\alpha = .92$). As expected, the outstanding target exerted a different impact on fixed- and malleable-theory participants, as indicated by the significant Condition $\times$ Theory interaction, $F(1, 54) = 4.82, p < .05$. As can be seen in Table 8.3, malleable-theory participants, who were expected to view the target's accomplishments as attainable, were enhanced by the target. Malleable-theory participants exposed to the outstanding student rated themselves more positively than did malleable-theory controls, $F(1, 54) = 5.41, p = .02$. In contrast, fixed-theory participants, who were expected to view the target's achievements as unattainable, were, if anything, diminished by the target. Fixed-theory participants exposed to the target rated themselves less positively than did fixed-theory controls, although this difference was not significant ($F < 1$).

It is possible that fixed-theory participants failed to show stronger self-deflation in response to the target because they did not view intelligence as entirely fixed. The mean score of the fixed-theory participants on the malleability of intelligence measure was 6.98, above the midpoint of the 11-point scale. Thus, although these participants believed intelligence to be less alterable than did malleable-theory participants, they nevertheless viewed intelligence as at least somewhat alterable. That may be why the target's impact on them was not more severely negative. In addition, fixed-theory participants may have protected themselves from the negative impact of the upward social comparison through motivated reasoning.

TABLE 8.3. Mean Self-Evaluations of Students Holding Malleable and Fixed Theories of Intelligence Who Were and Who Were Not Exposed to an Outstanding Student

	Target type	
Theory of intelligence	No target	Superstar
Malleable	7.61	8.66
Fixed	7.82	7.52

Note: Higher numbers indicate more positive self-evaluations.

Relevance ratings. As in Study 2, participants who were expected to view the target's achievements as less attainable (i.e., the fixed-theory participants) rated the target as somewhat less relevant to them ($M = 7.21$) than did participants who were expected to view the target's achievements as attainable (i.e., the malleable-theory participants; $M = 8.06$). This difference, however, was not significant ($F < 1$).

For malleable-theory participants, relevance ratings were highly correlated with self-ratings ($r = .63$, $p < .01$). Although a correlation cannot point conclusively to causation, the finding that malleable-theory participants who viewed the target as more relevant rated themselves more highly is consistent with the findings of Study 1 that superstars exert greater impact on self-views the greater their perceived relevance. For fixed-theory participants, the correlation between relevance ratings and self-ratings was weaker and nonsignificant ($r = .22$, $p > .25$). Recall that the star exerted no significant impact on the self-ratings of these participants. It is therefore not surprising that the star's relevance was not associated with self-ratings for them.

Explanations. Participants also explained their responses to the relevance question. Two judges unaware of participants' condition and of the experimental hypotheses coded the explanations of experimental participants. As in Studies 1 and 2, responses were coded for inspiration due to the target on the basis of the same criteria used in those studies. Agreement between the two was 80%; discrepancies were resolved through discussion.

We expected greater inspiration for malleable-theory participants than for fixed-theory participants. However, mentions of inspiration were low for both groups, 25% and 28% respectively, and these proportions did not differ significantly from each other. Mentions of inspiration by malleable-theory participants in this study were substantially lower than by participants exposed to relevant models of attainable success in Study 1 (in which 45% of participants exposed to a star excelling at their own intended profession were inspired) and in Study 2 (in which 82% of first-year accounting

students were inspired by the stellar graduate of their program). Perhaps this was the case because, in this study, the target matched participants on their college majors rather than on their intended professions. Some majors, such as accounting or engineering, do reflect a clear choice of profession, but many others, such as English or psychology, do not. Therefore, even participants who were positively influenced by the star may have been less likely to view the star as a template embodying all that they were striving for.

We also coded responses for mentions of similarity to the target on dimensions other than major or future occupation, as we had in Study 2. Agreement between the coders was 94% on this measure. Results provided a conceptual replication of the findings of Study 2. Participants likely to view the target's success as attainable, that is, the malleable-theory participants (37%), were more likely to mention that they were similar to the target than were participants likely to view the target's success as unattainable, that is, the fixed-theory participants (7%; $z = 2.03$, $p < .05$). Once again, this finding may reflect motivated reasoning on the part of both groups: Malleable theory participants, for whom comparisons to the target could be self-enhancing, may have exaggerated their similarity to the target, whereas fixed-theory participants, for whom comparisons to the target could be self-deflating, may have played down their similarity to the target.

In sum, this study provided convergent evidence for the finding from Study 2 that the perceived attainability of a relevant star's success can determine the star's impact. The star led to self-enhancement among malleable-theory participants, who likely viewed the star's success as attainable, but not among fixed-theory participants, who likely viewed the star's success as unattainable. Fixed-theory participants showed a nonsignificant tendency in the opposite direction and were less likely to describe themselves as similar to the star. Thus, as in Study 2, we obtained strong evidence that a model of attainable success can have positive consequences for the self and weaker evidence that a model of unattainable success can have negative consequences for the self.

General Discussion

Superstars can sometimes be inspiring and self-enhancing, sometimes self-deflating, and sometimes have no consequences at all for the self. Whether superstars exert any impact on others depends on their perceived relevance. When they do, the direction of that impact depends on the believed attainability of their success: Models of attainable success can be inspiring and self-enhancing, whereas models of unattainable success can be threatening and deflating.

We found strong and consistent evidence that relevant superstars can exert a positive impact when their success seems attainable. Future teachers and accountants were inspired and self-enhanced by an outstanding member of their intended profession (Study 1), first-year accounting students were inspired and self-enhanced by an outstanding graduating accounting student (Study 2), and students who viewed intelligence as malleable and increasable were self-enhanced by a graduating student who had excelled at their own major (Study 3). In all these cases, the star's success seemed attainable in that it was based on excellence at tasks that participants themselves had not yet had the opportunity to tackle. Participants could therefore entertain the belief that their own futures would be as bright as the star's.

Perhaps the most important contribution of these studies is the demonstration that role models who excel at one's own domain of interest can be inspiring. Earlier theorists noted that outstanding individuals can have positive consequences for others' self-views through a process of reflection, that is, through basking in the reflected glory of close others (Brewer & Weber, 1994; Cialdini *et al.*, 1976; Tesser & Campbell, 1983; Tesser, 1988). We view inspiration as a different kind of positive reaction to a superstar. Consider, for example, the thoughts and feelings going through the minds of different U.S. viewers as they watch an American athlete receive a gold medal at the Olympics. Some budding athletes may be envisioning themselves standing on that same podium 4 years down the road and resolve to double their efforts to attain this goal. These people are inspired. Others, who

harbor no athletic aspirations, may simply feel proud to be American. These people are basking in the reflected glory of a fellow American.

Reflection and inspiration arise under different circumstances. Reflection engages one's collective identity, that is, that aspect of the self that is based on membership in a social group, be it one's family or one's nation (Brewer & Gardner, 1996; Brewer & Weber, 1994). It arises when a psychologically close other excels at a domain that is irrelevant to the self and so does not challenge cherished aspects of one's personal identity (Tesser, 1988). It can also arise when the domain of excellence is self-relevant, if one is led to focus on one's social rather than on one's personal self (Brewer & Weber, 1994). Self-enhancement associated with reflection results from an enhanced view of one's entire group, to which the self has been assimilated.

In contrast, to be inspired, one must engage one's personal identity, that is, one's sense of oneself as a unique individual striving to accomplish personal goals and ambitions (Brewer & Gardner, 1996; Markus & Kitayama, 1991). Unlike reflection, inspiration is most likely when the other's domain of excellence is self-relevant, because that is when one is most likely to model oneself on the other. To be inspired by another's outstanding accomplishments, one must believe oneself capable of comparable success. Self-enhancement stemming from inspiration results from strengthened belief in one's own capabilities.

Whereas reflection has played a central role in earlier models of upward social comparison, inspiration has been mostly overlooked. Theories about social comparisons under threats such as cancer have discussed inspiration (Taylor & Lobel, 1989), but, for the most part, the notion of inspiration has not been incorporated into theories about upward social comparisons in the domain of ability or achievement (for an exception, see Major et al., 1991). That is why earlier theorists have assumed that when one engages in comparison with a superior other who excelled at a relevant domain, the consequences of this comparison for the self are bound to be negative (Brewer & Weber, 1994; Tesser & Campbell, 1983; Tesser, 1988). Our studies suggest otherwise. We have found that comparisons to a superstar who excelled at one's own domain of interest can be self-enhancing and inspiring, if the star's achievements seem attainable.

One may question whether we have really demonstrated inspiration as we claim rather than providing yet another example of reflection. After all, in all our studies the superstars who provoked inspiration were members of participants' in-group—they were of the same gender and major or intended profession. Superior in-group members can provoke reflection if the in-group is a minority, because minority status highlights one's social rather than personal self (Brewer & Weber, 1994). Perhaps members of any college major or profession view themselves as minorities, and so our stars exerted their positive impact through reflection rather than inspiration. We have strong reasons to believe that this was not the case. Participants' self-reports clearly illustrate that they were inspired and were focusing on their personal selves, goals, and ambitions. Admittedly, these accounts were given in response to a question about the self-relevance of the star that may have increased the salience of personal selves. Nevertheless, these self-reports suggest, at the very least, that a relevant star's positive impact can survive the activation of personal selves. Moreover, if the stars provoked only reflection, the believed attainability of their success should not have affected their impact; attainability is crucial to one's own likelihood of achieving personal success, and so to inspiration, but is irrelevant to one's ability to bask in another's reflected glory. But attainability did determine the impact of superstars in our studies, suggesting that the self-enhancement resulted from inspiration rather than reflection.

Participants were self-enhanced and inspired by the star only when the star's success seemed attainable. However, we found little evidence for our prediction that participants would be self-deflated by a star whose success seemed unattainable. Such participants were somewhat self-deflated, as predicted, but not significantly so. We suspect that the self-deflation induced in these participants was relatively weak not because they did not find the unreachable superstars threatening, but because they had managed to defend themselves successfully against this threat. Gilbert, Giesler, and Morris (1995) suggested that people may compare themselves to others automatically but then mentally undo comparisons to irrelevant others. Our threatened participants may have also attempted to mentally undo the comparison, not because it was irrelevant, but because it was threatening. Tesser and his colleagues have shown that people engage in elaborate cognitive work to diffuse such threats (Tesser & Campbell, 1983; Tesser et al., 1988). We too found evidence for this. In Study 2, threatened fourth-year students appeared to try to minimize the magnitude of the star's performance and to reduce the star's relevance. We also uncovered a new strategy: Threatened participants denigrated the meaningfulness of any social comparison, insisting that people can learn nothing about themselves through comparisons to others. Thus, people may alter their theories about the social world so as to dispel the threat of upward comparison (Klein & Kunda, 1992; Kunda, 1990).

Our findings about how the self-relevance of a star's domain of excellence affects the star's impact on others contradict Tesser's SEM model (Tesser, 1988). We found that domain self-relevance can increase the likelihood that an outstanding other will have any impact on the self. We suggested that this was because domain self-relevance, like psychological closeness, can increase the correspondence between the self and other and, thereby, increase the likelihood of comparing oneself to the other. In contrast, in the SEM model, whether the outstanding other will affect the self depends only on the others' psychological closeness. Domain self-relevance plays a different role: It determines whether psychologically close superior others will have a positive or a negative impact on self-views. The SEM model assumes that the impact will be positive when the domain is irrelevant to the self but negative when it is relevant. This may be true when the other's success is unattainable. When the domain is relevant, one will compare oneself to the unreachable superior other and feel inferior. However, when the domain is irrelevant, one will not engage in comparison but may, instead, bask in reflected glory. But Tesser's predictions do not hold when the superior other's success seems attainable. We found that a superior other who has achieved attainable success at a self-relevant domain will exert a positive impact on the self, not, as Tesser predicted, a negative impact. Relevance may still determine the nature of the positive impact, though. We would expect inspiration when the domain is relevant but reflection when it is irrelevant. Reflection would only occur, however, if the other is sufficiently psychologically close, as predicted by Tesser (1988). Otherwise, we expect the star to have no impact, as was the case for future teachers and accountants exposed to a stranger who had excelled in a profession other than their intended one.

Note that we view domain relevance as but one of many factors that jointly determine whether one will compare oneself to another (Holyoak & Thagard, 1995; Thagard & Kunda, in press). It may be possible to increase the relevance of seemingly irrelevant superstars by stressing their similarity to the self on other dimensions or by pointing to similarity in the underlying structure and relations of one's life. Structural similarity, that is, similarity based on underlying patterns of relations among elements, can lead people to form analogies among objects that are superficially quite different from each other (Holyoak & Thagard, 1995). For example, one may draw an analogy between a woman and a squirrel if both are seen receiving food from another (Markman & Gentner, 1993). If one can compare a woman to a squirrel, surely one should be able to compare a professor to an athlete or a teacher to an accountant. Such comparisons may be facilitated if the star's accomplishments are described in general rather than specific terms. Whereas an Olympic medal may be irrelevant to a professor, achieving the top honor in one's field is undoubtedly a relevant goal. It would be of great theoretical and practical interest to determine whether it is possible to broaden the appeal of outstanding role models in this manner.

Our work has important practical implications for how to maximize the benefits of role models. We found that, consistent with lay intuitions, role models can be inspiring. But an inappropriate role model may fail to have any impact on others. This is the most likely outcome when the role model is a stranger whose domain of excellence seems irrelevant to the target audience. Worse, an inappropriate role model may lead to discouragement and self-deflation rather than the desired inspiration. This is likely to occur when the role model has achieved unattainable success at one's own domain of interest. A star's success can seem unattainable when the star is a peer and so already unreachable or when the star's success is so extreme as to appear beyond most people's grasp. It seems that the ideal role model is a person who is somewhat older and at a more advanced career stage than the target individuals and who has achieved what these individuals hope for—outstanding but not impossible success at an enterprise in which they too wish to excel.

REFERENCES

Baron, R. M., & Kenny, D. A. (1986). The moderator–mediator variable distinction in social psychological research: Conceptual, strategic, and statistical considerations. *Journal of Personality and Social Psychology, 51,* 1173–1182.

Brewer, M. B., & Gardner, W. (1996). Who is this "we"? Levels of collective identity and self representations. *Journal of Personality and Social Psychology, 71,* 83–93.

Brewer, M. B., & Weber, J. G. (1994). Self-evaluation effects on interpersonal versus intergroup social comparison. *Journal of Personality and Social Psychology, 66,* 268–275.

Brickman, P., & Bulman, R. J. (1977). Pleasure and pain in social comparison. In J. M. Suls & R. L. Miller (Eds.), *Social comparison processes: Theoretical and empirical perspectives* (pp. 149–186). Washington, DC: Hemisphere.

Brown, J. D., Novick, N. J., Lord, K. A., & Richards, J. M. (1992). When Gulliver travels: Social context, psychological closeness, and self-appraisals. *Journal of Personality and Social Psychology, 62,* 717–727.

Buunk, B. P., Collins, R. L., Taylor, S. E., VanYperen, N. W., & Dakof, G. A. (1990). The affective consequences of social comparison: Either direction has its ups and downs. *Journal of Personality and Social Psychology, 59,* 1238–1249.

Cash, T F., Cash, D. W., & Butters, J. W. (1983). "Mirror, mirror, on the wall…?": Contrast effects and self-evaluations of physical attractiveness. *Personality and Social Psychology Bulletin, 9,* 351–358.

Cialdini, R. B., Borden, R. J., Thorne, A., Walker, M. R., Freeman, S., & Sloan, L. R. (1976). Basking in reflected glory: Three (football) field studies. *Journal of Personality and Social Psychology, 34,* 366–375.

Collins, R. L. (1996). For better or worse: The impact of upward social comparisons on self-evaluations. *Psychological Bulletin, 119,* 51–69.

Dweck, C. S., & Leggett, E. L. (1988). A social–cognitive approach to motivation and personality. *Psychological Review, 95,* 256–273.

Festinger, L. (1954). A theory of social comparison processes. *Human Relations, 7,* 117–140.

Forman, M. (Director). (1984). *Amadeus* [film]. (Available from Republic Pictures, Los Angeles, California.)

Gastorf, J. W., & Suls, J. (1978). Performance evaluation via social comparison: Performance similarity versus related attribute similarity. *Social Psychology, 41,* 297–305.

Gilbert, D. T., Giesler, R. B., & Morris, K. A. (1995). When comparisons arise. *Journal of Personality and Social Psychology, 69,* 227–236.

Goethals, G. R., & Darley, J. M. (1977). Social comparison theory. In J. M. Suls & R. L. Miller (Eds.), *Social comparison processes: Theoretical and empirical perspectives* (pp. 259–278). Washington, DC: Hemisphere.

Holyoak, K. J., & Thagard, P. (1989). Analogical mapping by constraint satisfaction. *Cognitive Science, 13,* 295–355.

Holyoak, K. J., & Thagard, P. (1995). *Mental leaps: Analogy in creative thought.* Cambridge, MA: MIT Press/Bradford Books.

Klein, W. M., & Kunda, Z. (1992). Motivated person perception: Constructing justifications for desired beliefs. *Journal of Experimental Social Psychology, 28,* 145–168.

Kunda, Z. (1990). The case for motivated reasoning. *Psychological Bulletin, 108,* 480–498.

Major, B., Sciacchitano, A., & Crocker, J. (1993). In-group versus out-group comparisons and self-esteem. *Personality and Social Psychology Bulletin, 19,* 711–721.

Major, B., Testa, M., & Bylsma, W. H. (1991). Responses to upward and downward social comparisons: The impact of esteem-relevance and perceived control. In J. Suls & T. A. Wills (Eds.), *Social comparison: Contemporary theory and research* (pp. 237–260). Hillsdale, NJ: Erlbaum.

Markman, A. B., & Gentner, D. (1993). Structural alignment during similarity comparisons. *Cognitive Psychology, 25,* 431–467.

Markus, H., & Kitayama, S. (1991). Culture and the self: Implications for cognition, emotion, and motivation. *Psychological Review, 98,* 224–252.

Markus, H., & Nurius, P. (1986). Possible selves. *American Psychologist, 41,* 954–969.

Meichenbaum, D. H. (1971). Examination of model characteristics in reducing avoidance behavior. *Journal of Personality and Social Psychology, 17,* 298–307.

Morse, S., & Gergen, K. J. (1970). Social comparison, self-consistency, and the concept of self. *Journal of Personality and Social Psychology, 16,* 148–156.

Pelham, B. W., & Wachsmuth, J. O. (1995). The waxing and waning of the social self: Assimilation and contrast in social comparison. *Journal of Personality and Social Psychology, 69,* 825–838.

Pleban, R., & Tesser, A. (1981). The effects of relevance and quality of another's performance on interpersonal closeness. *Social Psychology Quarterly, 44,* 278–285.

Salovey, P., & Rodin, J. (1984). Some antecedents and consequences of social comparison jealousy. *Journal of Personality and Social Psychology, 47,* 780–792.

Seta, F. (1982). The impact of comparison processes on coactors' task performance. *Journal of Personality and Social Psychology, 42,* 281–291.

Taylor, S. E., & Lobel, M. (1989). Social comparison activity under threat: Downward evaluation and upward contacts. *Psychological Review, 96,* 569–575.

Tesser, A. (1986). Some effects of self-evaluation maintenance on cognition and action. In R. M. Sorrentino & E. T. Higgins (Eds.), *The handbook of motivation and cognition: Foundations of social behavior* (pp. 435–464). New York: Guilford Press.

Tesser, A. (1988). Toward a self-evaluation maintenance model of social behavior. In L. Berkowitz (Ed.), *Advances in experimental social psychology,* (pp. 181–227). New York: Academic Press.

Tesser, A. (1991). Emotion in social comparison and reflection processes. In J. Suls & T. A. Wills (Eds.), *Social comparison: Contemporary theory and research* (pp. 115–145). Hillsdale, NJ: Erlbaum.

Tesser, A., & Campbell, J. (1983). Self-definition and self-evaluation maintenance. In J. Suls & A. Greenwald (Eds.), *Social psychological perspectives on the self* (pp. 1–31). Hillsdale, NJ: Erlbaum.

Tesser, A., & Cornell, D. P. (1991). On the confluence of self processes. *Journal of Experimental Social Psychology, 27,* 501–526.

Tesser, A., Millar, M., & Moore, J. (1988). Some affective consequences of social comparison and reflective processes: The pain and pleasure of being close. *Journal of Personality and Social Psychology, 54,* 49–61.

Tesser, A., & Paulhus, D. (1983). Self-definition of self: Private and public self-evaluation strategies. *Journal of Personality and Social Psychology, 44,* 672–682.

Testa, M., & Major, B. (1990). The impact of social comparison after failure: The moderating effects of perceived control. *Basic and Applied Social Psychology, 11,* 205–218.

Thagard, P., & Kunda, Z. (in press). Making sense of people: Coherence mechanisms. In S. Read (Ed.), *Connectionist and PDP models of social reasoning and social behavior.* Hillsdale, NJ: Erlbaum.

Wood, J. V. (1989). Theory and research concerning social comparisons of personal attributes. *Psychological Bulletin, 106,* 231–248.

Wood, J. V., & VanderZee, K. (in press). Social comparisons among cancer patients: Under what conditions are comparisons upward and downward? In B. P. Buunk & F. X. Gibbons (Eds.), *Social comparison, health, and coping.* Hillsdale, NJ: Erlbaum.

Received November 13, 1996
Revision received February 28, 1997
Accepted March 3, 1997 ■

The Person Who Outperforms Me Is a Genius: Maintaining Perceived Competence in Upward Social Comparison

Mark D. Alicke, Frank M. LoSchiavo, Jennifer Zerbst, and Shaobo Zhang

People have many ways of protecting themselves against unfavorable social comparisons. Sometimes, however, the unfavorablenenss of a comparison is too unambiguous to deny. In such circumstances, people may indirectly protect their self-images by exaggerating the ability of those who outperform them. Aggrandizing the outperformer is conceived to be a construal mechanism that permits inferior performers to deflect the self-esteem threat of being outperformed while maintaining believability. The tendency to exaggerate an outperformer's ability was demonstrated in a context in which subjects learned they had been outperformed by a confederate on a perceptual intelligence test. Subjects' and observers' ratings of the confederate's intelligence showed that subjects consistently rated the confederate more favorably than did observers. Using a similar methodology in which subjects outperformed confederates, another study showed that subjects exaggerated the ability of the people they outperformed. The conditions in which these effects are most likely to be obtained are discussed.

From the time Festinger (1954) had the foresight to note what in hindsight appears obvious—that people define their social characteristics by comparing themselves with others—research in this area has emphasized the antecedents of social comparisons. The primary question has been whether people compare themselves with superior or inferior others. The most common methodology in this

Mark D. Alicke, Frank M. LoSchiavo, Jennifer Zerbst, and Shaobo Zhang, Department of Psychology, Ohio University. Shaobo Zhang is now at the Department of Psychology, Ohio State University.

Correspondence concerning this article should be addressed to Mark D. Alicke, Department of Psychology, Ohio University, Athens, Ohio 45701. Electronic mail may be sent via the Internet to alicke@oak.cats.ohiou.edu.

research has been to provide participants with absolute performance feedback and ask them to rank their preferences for viewing the scores of superior or inferior performers (Latané, 1966; Wheeler *et al.*, 1969; Wills, 1981).

This rank-order paradigm allows participants to select comparisons they feel will be most illuminating or self-enhancing. However, people are not always afforded the luxury of orchestrating their comparisons. Instead, comparisons are frequently foisted on people, such as when siblings are compared by their parents, students by their teachers, and employees by their employers (Wheeler & Miyake, 1992; Wood, 1989). Thus the antecedent side of the social comparison process—the selection of a comparison target—is often preempted by sources outside the comparer's control. When comparisons are predetermined, the focus of social comparison research shifts from the antecedents to the consequences of comparison process.

The present research focused on the consequences of receiving unfavorable social comparison feedback. Whereas most social comparison research has been interested in self-evaluation, in this research we examined people's perceptions of those who outperform them. Because being outperformed is potentially threatening to self-esteem, people may try to restore esteem by altering their perceptions of outperformers. Previously discussed mechanisms for maintaining esteem following unfavorable comparisons include downgrading the validity of the comparison and denigrating or distancing oneself from the outperformer (e.g., Hakmiller, 1966; Pyszcynski, Greenberg, & LaPrelle, 1985; Wills, 1981). In the present studies, we sought to demonstrate a diametrically opposite esteem-saving mechanism, namely exalting the comparison target. In particular, we explored conditions in which comparers exaggerate the ability of their outperformers, or what we call the "genius effect."

We assume exalting the outperformer is a strategy that is applied when a person is unambiguously outperformed and cannot easily distort the validity of the comparison. Mundane examples include a student who is consistently outperformed by a classmate, an academic whose publications are far exceeded by a colleague's, and a golfer who is trounced by a partner. By elevating the abilities of the person whose performance dwarfs their own, people can maintain their sense of competence while magnanimously acknowledging the superior attributes of the outperformer.

Although in the past researchers have assessed upward comparisons with superior performers, few have examined the consequences of actually being outperformed, and even fewer have examined perceptions of the outperformer. The consequences of being directly outperformed have been addressed most systematically in Tesser's self-evaluation maintenance model (Tesser, 1988, 1991). According to Tesser, unfavorable comparisons engender a reflection or comparison process. The reflection process occurs when the comparison target is close to the comparer and when the comparison is relatively unimportant for self-esteem. Under these conditions, comparers bask in upward comparisons and indirectly enhance their self-esteem. The comparison process occurs when comparers are outperformed on an important dimension by close others. When the comparison process is engaged, comparers can deemphasize their closeness to the target, downgrade the relevance of the comparison dimension, or hinder the target's performance.

The self-evaluation maintenance model assumes outperformers will be denigrated or avoided except when there is a close relationship with the superior performer and when the performance dimension is relatively trivial. These predictions accord with other perspectives on social comparison that assume upward social comparisons tend to evoke defensive attributional strategies, such as questioning the validity of the task or downgrading the importance of the comparison (e.g., Brickman & Bulman, 1977; Morse & Gergen, 1970). However, for defensive attributional strategies to be effective, they must be believable (Schlenker, 1985). In other words, people must have faith in their biased explanations. When people are directly and unambiguously outperformed, it may be difficult for them to deny, explain away, or ignore the comparison target's superiority.

In these conditions, exaggerating the outperformer's ability is a strategy that enables inferior performers to deflect the threat of unfavorable upward comparisons while satisfying the demands of believability. In a review of the upward social comparison literature, Collins (1996) argued that upward comparisons are preferable to downward comparisons when they can be construed to negate the implications of inferior performance. We propose that exaggerating the outperformer's ability is a construal mechanism that negates the potentially negative implications of unfavorable social comparisons by allowing inferior performers to discount the relevance of the comparison. Comparing unfavorably to a person with exceptionally high abilities, therefore, obviates the downward adjustments in one's perceived competence that would be likely to occur after being unambiguously outperformed by a lesser target (Mettee & Smith, 1977).

Exalting the outperformer also helps inferior performers resolve a perennial social comparison dilemma, namely, the dilemma of desiring informational clarity while fearing unpleasant hedonic consequences (Brickman & Bulman, 1977). Because elevating the outperformer's ability provides a buffer against diminutions in one's sense of competence, inferior performers acquire informational clarity by learning about the upper range of the ability distribution without suffering unpleasant hedonic consequences as a result. An anecdotal example would be a club tennis champion having the opportunity to play a match against Pete Sampras: Although the player would be resoundingly trounced, he would probably relish the opportunity to experience directly the highest level of tennis ability. Furthermore, his own status as club champion would be unthreatened by the comparison; thus, the club champion could enthusiastically declaim Sampras's ability without recalibrating his own ability level.

The hypothesis that people exaggerate the ability of superior performers requires comparison of the ability ratings of people who are and who are not outperformed. To effectuate this comparison, participants in the present studies completed a test of perceptual intelligence with a confederate and subsequently learned that the confederate's performance exceeded their own. An observer witnessed the performances of the subject and the confederate

and was made aware of each person's score. We directly tested the hypothesis that people exaggerate the ability of superior performers by comparing the ratings of the confederate's perceptual intelligence made by the outperformed subject and by the observer, who was simply aware of the scores. We predicted an interaction such that participants and observers would not differ in their ratings of the participant's perceptual intelligence but that participants would rate the confederate's perceptual intelligence more favorably than would observers.

Study 1

Method

Participants. Participants were 78 (37 male and 41 female) undergraduates who participated in partial fulfillment of a course requirement. No main effects or interactions were obtained for subject-gender in this or subsequent studies. Thus, the gender variable is not discussed further.

Materials and procedure. Participants enlisted for what they believed was a study of novel intellectual skills. There were three same-gender individuals in each session: one subject, one confederate, and one observer. Gender was held constant to avoid effects stemming from men's and women's different expectations for, or reactions to, each other's performance. For example, subjects might adhere to the stereo-type that men are better at spatial or perceptual tasks. Two male and two female confederates were used throughout these sessions.[1] Whichever subject arrived first was designated to be the observer and was brought to an adjoining room equipped with a one-way mirror. The purpose of watching from behind a one-way mirror was ostensibly to avoid making test takers anxious. Subjects, however, were actually unaware of being viewed by the observers. Observers were told their task was to observe carefully two students who were completing a novel test of perceptual intelligence and to rate their ability on the basis of their performance. Observers were then given the

---

[1] A different set of confederates was used for each study.

opportunity to see the items on the test and were asked to do two practice items. By giving observers experience with the test items before subjects began the test and allowing them to watch subjects answer each question, we sought to minimize problems arising from differences in familiarity with the test items.

A second experimenter led the subject and confederate into an adjacent room and seated them beside each other at a table. Subjects and confederates were told they would be completing a test measuring an important intellectual ability, perceptual intelligence. The test actually comprised 12 items from Raven's (1965) progressive matrices (2 practice items and 10 test items). This test presents a series of incomplete figures and requires the test taker to judge which of eight segments would accurately complete each figure. We selected 2 relatively easy items for the practice phase and 10 relatively difficult items for the test phase. Before beginning, participants read along while the experimenter read the following cover story.

> The psychology department has developed a test of perceptual intelligence that has been shown to be a highly reliable and valid instrument for assessing people's ability to process perceptual information. In this experiment, we are interested in seeing how well you can perform on this test.
>
> You will be given an answer sheet on which to mark all your answers, and one test booklet. All your answers will be made on your answer sheet. You will also notice that a subject number has been assigned to each of you. None of your scores will be paired with your name, only with your subject number.

The remaining instructions described the test and the participants' task in detail. Participants were given 10 min to complete all the problems. The confederate had been provided with the answers in advance. Pretesting established that the average student in the undergraduate population could answer approximately 3 of the 10 test items correctly. By prearrangement, the confederate always answered seven items correctly. The confederate was instructed to finish within 1 min after the subject.

Observers watched the subjects and confederates from behind a one-way mirror. The mirror was above subjects' heads so that they could not see themselves (thereby eliminating potential problems of objective self-awareness). The seats of subjects and confederates were angled so that observers could see their answers. At the end of the 10 min, the experimenter explained that he or she was not allowed to see how they performed and that, therefore, participants would score each other's tests. Subjects and confederates then exchanged tests. The experimenter read the answers and told subjects and confederates to cross out incorrect responses and write the correct answers underneath. A line was provided on the bottom of the answer sheet for indicating the number of correct items. After writing the number of problems answered correctly on the answer sheet, subjects and confederates returned each other's sheets and were given a chance to see their scores. The experimenter then brought both sheets to the observer to ensure the observer knew each person's score. Subjects and observers then made their ratings of the confederate and the subject.

Dependent variables. The dependent variables were subjects' and observers' ratings of the subjects' and confederates' perceptual intelligence. Ratings were made on a 10-point scale ranging from 0 (*extremely low*) to 9 (*extremely high*). To maintain the believability of our initial cover story, we asked subjects to also answer a variety of filler questions concerning their perceptions of the test.

Results and Discussion

Table 9.1 shows the means and standard deviations for ratings of subjects' and confederates' perceptual

TABLE 9.1. Means and Standard Deviations for Ratings of the Subject's and Confederate's Perceptual Intelligence (Study 1)

Rater	Target	
	Subject	Confederate
Subject		
M	4.28	7.51
SD	1.65	1.00
Observer		
M	4.33	6.44
SD	1.80	1.45

intelligence. The main statistical analysis included the within-subject variable of ratings of the subject versus the confederate and the between-subjects variable of the rater (subject or observer). Effect size calculations (Cohen's *d*) are included for each hypothesis test.

The within-subject variable yielded a significant effect, $F(1, 76) = 92.34, p < .0001, d = 2.20$, showing that ratings of the confederate's perceptual intelligence were generally higher than ratings of the subject's perceptual intelligence. More important, the predicted interaction was obtained between the rater (subject or observer) and the target being rated (subject or confederate), $F(1, 76) = 4.13, p < .05, d = 0.47$. Follow-up tests showed that there was no difference between subjects and observers in their judgments of the subjects' perceptual intelligence $(F < 1)$ but that subjects rated the confederate's perceptual intelligence more highly than did observers, $F(1, 76) = 14.65, p < .0003, d = 0.88$.

This interaction pattern eliminates a potential alternative interpretation of the findings. If subjects had rated their own perceptual intelligence more highly than observers, their higher ratings of the confederate could be an artifact of their elevated self-ratings. In other words, both subjects and observers might have had equally inflated perceptions of the confederate's perceptual ability, but the obtained differences could have been due to subjects' beginning at a different baseline because of their elevated self-ratings. The fact that subjects and observers did not differ in their ratings of subjects' perceptual intelligence effectively eliminates this interpretation.[2] These results, therefore, support

the hypothesis that people exaggerate the ability of those who outperform them. Even with perceptions of the subject's perceptual intelligence equated, subjects evaluated the confederate's ability more favorably than did observers.

Study 2

Study 2 was designed to enhance the privacy of subjects' responses to see whether self-presentational concerns are a necessary component of the genius effect. The potential importance of self-presentational concerns in upward comparisons was investigated by Gould, Brounstein, and Sigall (1977). Participants in this study first learned they had attained an average level of performance on a tactile perception task. In some conditions, participants expected to compete for money against a person who had previously competed successfully on this task. Participants then estimated the potential competitor's ability. Attributions were made either publicly (names and social security numbers were required on the questionnaires) or privately (responses were placed in a sealed envelope without names or social security numbers and taken to the department secretary). Results showed that higher ability was ascribed to the potential competitor when attributions were made publicly rather than privately.

Because Gould and his colleagues (1977) were concerned with the self-presentational aspect of ability attributions, their primary comparisons were between conditions of public and private responding. Thus, they included no controls (such as our

---

[2] We became aware of this potential problem after conducting an initial study that examined only general intelligence. Although subjects rated the confederate's general intelligence more favorably than did observers, they also rated their own general intelligence more favorably. Because subjects evaluated their own general intelligence more favorably than did observers, their elevated ratings of the confederate could have been an artifact of their elevated self-ratings. The same findings regarding general intelligence were obtained in the present study. As with ratings of perceptual intelligence, subjects rated the confederate's general intelligence more favorably than did observers, $F(1, 76) = 6.80, p < .02, d = 0.60$. In contrast to the results for perceptual intelligence, however, these results were

ambiguated by the aforementioned tendency for subjects to rate their own general intelligence more favorably than observers, $F(1, 76) = 10.54, p < .002, d = 0.74$, and by the lack of an interaction between the rater and the target $(F < 1)$. With the benefit of hindsight, it makes sense that subjects' assessments of their general intelligence would be undiminished by their poor performance on one aspect of intelligence, namely, perceptual intelligence. In fact, the argument that target aggrandizement buttresses subjects' sense of competence suggests that their evaluations of their general intelligence might actually improve as a result of exaggerating the target's ability. This issue is the primary focus of Study 3.

observer subjects) against which to compare subjects' attributions. For this reason, it is impossible to ascertain whether the tendency to exaggerate a potential outperformer's ability in their study was limited to public response conditions or was simply magnified in such conditions. Furthermore, Gould *et al.* assessed the consequences of anticipated rather than actual outperformance, whereas we were concerned with people's tendency to exaggerate the ability of others who actually outperform them. The relevance of Gould *et al.*'s findings for this purpose is limited by the fact that their subjects never interacted with the competitors and therefore did not know if the competitors were more competent at the task.

Nevertheless, Gould *et al.*'s (1977) findings raise the question of whether the tendency to exaggerate an outperformer's ability occurs in private conditions. Although neither names nor other forms of identification were attached to the questionnaires in Study 1, it is possible that participants were concerned that the experimenter or confederate would see their evaluations. If participants believed their responses would be scrutinized, they might be motivated to appear modest, polite, or magnanimous. Therefore, in addition to replicating the findings of Study 1, the purpose of Study 2 was to see whether the tendency to exaggerate the outperformer's ability would be obtained when responses were more carefully hidden from the experimenter and confederate.

Method

Participants. Students were 38 (18 male and 20 female) undergraduates participating in partial fulfillment of a course requirement.

Procedure. The procedure of Study 2 was similar to that of Study 1, with modifications added to increase the privacy of subjects' responses. As before, observers were brought to a room with a one-way mirror. By a bogus random drawing, the subject or confederate was brought either to an adjoining or a nonadjoining room. Bringing the subject to a separate room allowed for more private responding because there was no chance of the experimenter

or confederate seeing the subjects' ratings of the confederate. In addition, all questionnaires were placed in a sealed envelope. Placing the subject in a separate room also reduced the chances that observers would perceive the subject and confederate as an interacting unit. If observers saw subjects and confederates as partners, they might assimilate the confederate's ability to the subject's, thereby accounting for their tendency to evaluate the confederate less favorably.

After explaining the same procedural details as before, the experimenter told subjects they would take the test one at a time and that while one subject was completing the test, the other was free to work on homework or read the paper. After the first subject was finished, the subject and confederate switched rooms so that the observer could now see the second person complete the test. The order in which observers saw the subject and confederate was counterbalanced.

The experimenter again explained that test takers would score each other's tests. In Study 2, however, ability attributions were made in separate rooms and then placed in sealed envelopes. Thus, subjects could be more confident that neither experimenters nor confederates could see their responses. After the tests were scored, the experimenter returned to the observer's room and showed both score sheets to the observer.

Results and Discussion

Means and standard deviations of subjects' and observers' ratings of the confederate's perceptual intelligence are provided in Table 9.2. A significant

TABLE 9.2. Means and Standard Deviations for Ratings of the Subject's and Confederate's Perceptual Intelligence (Study 2)

	Target	
Rater	Subject	Confederate
Subject		
M	4.05	7.21
SD	2.01	1.22
Observer		
M	4.58	5.74
SD	2.14	1.23

main effect again showed that subjects and observers considered the confederate to be higher in perceptual intelligence than the subject, $F(1, 36) = 19.48, p < .0001, d = 1.47$. The critical interaction between the rater (subject or observer) and the person being rated (subject or confederate) was also significant, $F(1, 36) = 4.18, p < .05, d = 0.68$. Follow-up tests showed that the difference between subjects' and observers' ratings of the subject's perceptual intelligence was nonsignificant ($F < 1$). However, the comparison demonstrating subjects' tendency to exaggerate the confederate's ability relative to the observer was significant, $F(1, 36) = 9.92, p < .004, d = 1.05$.

Thus, the tendency to exaggerate the intelligence of a superior performer was again demonstrated in a context in which there were no differences between subjects' and observers' ratings of the subject's ability on the task. Furthermore, these findings were obtained in highly private response conditions, showing that the tendency to exaggerate an outperformer's ability cannot be adequately explained by concerns with self-presentation to a public audience.

Study 3

A fundamental assumption underlying the genius effect is that exaggerating the outperformer's ability protects or restores the inferior performer's threatened sense of competence. However, this assumption was tested only indirectly in the first two studies. To evaluate this interpretation more directly, in Study 3 we varied whether people who were outperformed had the opportunity to evaluate the outperformer. If exaggerating the outperformer's ability maintains the comparer's perceived competence, those given the chance to exaggerate the outperformer's ability should subsequently evaluate themselves more favorably than those who do not have this opportunity. In essence, exaggerating the outperformers ability serves to discount the relevance of the comparison for calibrating one's own ability level and provides a buffer against a loss in perceived competence. We expected, therefore, to obtain differences in subjects' perceptions of their own ability depending on whether they were given the chance to evaluate the outperformer.

As noted in the introduction, self-serving mechanisms must be believable to be effective. As many other social comparison studies have shown, people are more self-serving when the dimensions on which they evaluate their abilities and characteristics are ambiguous, thus allowing them some latitude for interpretation (Alicke, 1985; Dunning, Meyerowitz, & Holzberg, 1989; Messick, Bloom, Boldizar, & Samuelson, 1985). For people to restore their sense of competence as a result of aggrandizing the outperformer, therefore, the competence judgment must be somewhat ambiguous. For this reason, we did not expect participants who were unambiguously outperformed on a perceptual intelligence test to alter their evaluations of their perceptual intelligence. It would be unrealistic for participants to reassess their perceptual intelligence when they have just performed poorly on this dimension. In contrast, we did not expect aggrandizing the outperformer to influence self-assessments on extremely broad categories such as self-esteem or general competence. As a compromise between extremely specific and extremely broad response dimensions, therefore, we selected general intelligence as the dimension on which to assess the hypothesis that aggrandizing the outperformer protects people's threatened sense of competence.

Method

Participants. Students in Study 3 were 50 (27 male and 23 female) psychology undergraduates whose participation partially fulfilled a course requirement.

Procedure. The procedure for this study included only two conditions: one in which participants were outperformed and then given the opportunity (as in previous studies) to evaluate the outperformer and one in which participants who were outperformed were not given this opportunity. No observer subjects were used in Study 3. The experiment for subjects who did not evaluate the outperformer was completed after they rated their own general intelligence. Subjects who did have the opportunity to evaluate the outperformer evaluated their own and the outperformer's general intelligence on a 10-point scale ranging from 0 (*extremely low*) to 9 (*extremely high*).

Results and Discussion

If exaggerating the outperformer's ability helps maintain one's perceived competence on a task following upward comparisons, then subjects given the opportunity to rate the outperformer should subsequently evaluate their own general intelligence more favorably than subjects who were outperformed but not given this opportunity. This is precisely what happened, $F(1, 48) = 4.68$, $p < .04$, $d = 0.62$. As expected, aggrandizing the target led to increased ratings of general intelligence ($M = 6.40$, $SD = 1.19$) in comparison with subjects who were simply outperformed but did not rate the outperformer ($M = 5.60$, $SD = 1.41$).

The results of this study, therefore, fill a conceptual gap in our interpretation of the genius effect, which assumes that exaggerating the target's ability restores or enhances people's perceptions of their competence. One limitation of Study 3, however, is that we were unable to distinguish whether aggrandizing the outperformer actually restores a threatened sense of competence back to its baseline (i.e., preoutperformance) level or actually enhances perceived competence beyond baseline. The latter possibility suggests, counterintuitively, that being unambiguously outperformed can in some circumstances actually improve people's perceived competence. A person who lost an exhibition tennis match against Pete Sampras, for example, might be impressed by the one serve he returned or the accidental ace he hit and therefore might acquire new insight into his ability. This possibility seems more compelling, however, in direct competition rather than in the outperformance context of our studies.

Further research is also needed to establish the parameters within which restoration or enhancement of perceived competence takes place. We selected general intelligence as a compromise between perceptual intelligence, which is the dimension on which participants performed poorly, and self-esteem or general competence, which we thought were too broad. In the absence of previous research, however, it is difficult to predict which dimensions people will use to restore their threatened sense of competence. The most relevant literature for addressing this problem involves compensatory self-inflation following failure experiences. Our third study could plausibly be viewed as an instance of compensation in which people who have been outperformed on the dimension of perceptual intelligence and who have the opportunity to aggrandize the outperformer compensate by elevating their general intelligence ratings (relative to those who have no opportunity to aggrandize). There are a number of reasons, however, for doubting whether our results actually represent compensation effects. First, previous research has obtained compensation primarily on dimensions orthogonal to those on which the unfavorable feedback was provided. Brown and Smart (1991), for example, found that high-self-esteem subjects (but not low-self-esteem subjects) compensated for failure at an intellectual task by exaggerating the positivity of their social attributes. The same orthogonality exists in earlier compensation studies by Baumeister and Jones (1978) and Greenberg and Pyszczynski (1985). By contrast, the perceptual intelligence dimension on which our participants were outperformed is a component of general intelligence rather than an orthogonal dimension.

Another reason for doubting whether the results of Study 3 represent compensation as it has previously been defined is that compensation would seem more likely to occur in the group that has no opportunity to aggrandize. That is, one could argue that the only recourse for nonaggrandizing subjects is to compensate on other dimensions. As the results of Study 3 show, however, general intelligence ratings are higher in the group that does aggrandize the outperformer, a finding that is consistent with our interpretation that explicitly exaggerating the outperformer's ability restores a threatened sense of competence. Finally, compensation effects are not particularly robust; Baumeister and Jones (1978) obtained such effects only in highly public response conditions, and Brown and Smart (1991) found evidence of compensation only for high-self-esteem individuals.

Study 4

We have argued that exaggerating an outperformer's ability indirectly helps the comparer maintain a relatively favorable self-evaluation. The greater the ability of the vanquisher, the less negative are the implications for the vanquishee. Consider now the converse case, in which the subject is the outperformer. If relative ability comparisons are motivated by the need to maintain one's sense of competence, it stands to reason that people will also exaggerate the ability of the person they outperform. In general, the self-enhancing value of outperforming another person should increase commensurately with that person's ability. Just as there is no ignominy in a club champion losing a tennis match to Pete Sampras, there is no glory in defeating a novice. Thus, comparers should accord the highest ability level possible to the people they outperform. The possibility that people exaggerate the ability of those they outperform was examined in Study 4 with a methodology similar to those in the first two studies except that subjects outperformed rather than underperformed the confederate.

Method

Eighty (40 male and 40 female) undergraduate psychology students participated for partial course credit. The methodology of this study was similar to the first two studies except that we used test items that were easy to ensure that participants would outperform the confederate. By prearrangement, the confederate always received a score of three.

Results and Discussion

As expected, all subjects outperformed the confederate. Means and standard deviations for subjects' and observers' ratings of the subjects' and confederates' perceptual intelligence are provided in Table 9.3.

TABLE 9.3. Means and Standard Deviations for Ratings of the Subject's and Confederate's Perceptual Intelligence (Study 4)

Rater	Target	
	Subject	Confederate
Subject		
M	6.37	4.88
SD	1.37	1.34
Observer		
M	7.00	3.62
SD	1.36	1.31

The interaction between the rater (subject or observer) and the person being rated (subject or confederate) was again significant, $F(1, 78) = 20.21$, $p < .0001$, $d = 1.02$. Follow-up comparisons showed that observers actually rated subjects more favorably in perceptual intelligence than subjects rated themselves, $F(1, 78) = 4.19$, $p < .05$, $d = 0.46$. The critical finding showed that subjects rated the confederate who they outperformed to be higher in perceptual intelligence than did observers, $F(1, 78) = 17.70$, $p < .0001$, $d = 0.95$.

General Discussion

Sooner or later, we all meet our match. Even people with exceptional abilities or attributes will eventually encounter someone who is smarter, more attractive, happier, or wealthier than themselves. If the conditions in which upward comparisons occur are sufficiently ambiguous, the comparer has recourse to a variety of identity-repairing excuses. Consider the case of a college student who is outperformed by a roommate on a test. If she were unsure of how much each person studied, the student could perhaps convince herself her roommate had studied harder. Alternatively, she might claim the test was unfair, that she studied the wrong material, or that she had a bad day.

Unfortunately, good excuses can be hard to find. The aforementioned student might be well aware that she studied harder than her roommate, that the test was fair, and that she studied the right material. If she preferred excuses along these lines, she would have trouble maintaining believability to herself or others. We have argued that when people are unambiguously outperformed, they can salvage a favorable self-image by deploying a potent construal mechanism, namely, exaggerating the outperformer's ability. In the studies reported in this article, subjects who were outperformed by a confederate on a perceptual intelligence test rated the confederate's perceptual ability higher than did uninvolved observers. Specifically, significant interactions were obtained between rater and ratee showing that observers and subjects did not differ in their ratings of the subjects' perceptual intelligence but that subjects consistently rated the confederate more favorably than did observers. This interaction pattern eliminates the possibility that subjects' elevated ratings of the confederate were an artifact of their elevated self-ratings.

We increased the privacy of responding in Study 2 to show that the genius effect is not limited to conditions in which inferior performers want to appear modest or magnanimous. However, further research is needed to clarify the role of self-presentational concerns in upward social comparisons. Although Study 2 showed that self-presentational concerns are not a necessary component of the genius effect, they may nevertheless augment the effect's magnitude in some circumstances. The potential moderating effect of self-presentational concerns was not investigated in our studies because we did not attempt to create highly public response conditions. In the previously discussed research of Gould et al. (1977), publicity enhanced participants' tendencies to exaggerate the ability of a potential competitor. Research by Brown and Gallagher (1992) also suggests the tendency to exaggerate an outperformer's ability might be accentuated in public conditions. Participants in their studies received failure feedback on a novel intelligence test and then rated themselves and others on a series of trait adjectives. Half the participants made their responses with the experimenter watching whereas the other half made them privately. The most pertinent finding for present purposes was that participants who experienced public failure were relatively modest about their performance, that is, they rated themselves less favorably and

others more favorably when they failed than when they succeeded. In common with the Gould et al. research, however, participants in these studies were not actually outperformed by another person. Furthermore, the dependent variable involved generic ratings of others rather than ratings of specific outperformed. Thus, the question of whether self-presentational concerns influence the tendency to aggrandize specific outperformers awaits further research with the genius paradigm.

The assumption that exaggerating an outperformer's ability helps inferior performers maintain their sense of competence was assessed somewhat indirectly in Studies 1 and 2. In Study 3, we examined this assumption more directly by asking subjects to assess their general intelligence after being outperformed. Half of these subjects rated the outperformer's ability and the other half did not. Results showed that subjects given the chance to aggrandize the outperformer subsequently evaluated their own general intelligence more favorably than did subjects not given this opportunity. This study, therefore, provides more direct evidence that exaggerating the outperformer's ability is a construal mechanism that helps restore an inferior performer's threatened sense of competence.

However, Study 3 also raises a number of issues that must be addressed in future research. The first issue concerns the dimensions on which people recoup their perceived ability as a result of being outperformed. In our study, perceptual intelligence represented the dimension of outperformance, and general intelligence was the dimension used to assess whether ability maintenance occurred. We speculated that evidence of ability maintenance would not occur on more comprehensive dimensions, such as general competence or self-esteem. In other words, we did not think that people's sense of competence on all dimensions or overall sense of self-worth would be influenced by the opportunity to aggrandize the target. However, because we did not obtain ratings on these dimensions, it remains to be seen how far people's overall sense of competence or esteem will be affected by target aggrandizement.

Another limitation of Study 3 is that the absence of a baseline comparison makes it impossible to discern whether people who exaggerate the outperformer's ability actually enhance their perceptions of their general intelligence or simply maintain the status quo. This question could be answered with a within-subject design in which subjects' perceptions of their general intelligence (or some other appropriate competence measure) are assessed both before and after they are outperformed. One possibility is that the group given an opportunity to aggrandize the outperformer would actually show an increase in their perceived general intelligence, whereas the nonaggrandizing group would remain the same. This counterintuitive possibility would show that exaggerating the outperformer's competence actually improves one's own sense of competence in comparison to its pre-outperformance level. The possibility we have advocated is that the aggrandizing group's general intelligence ratings would remain constant whereas those of the nonaggrandizing group would decrease. This pattern would indicate that exaggerating an outperformer's ability serves to protect a threatened identity from further damage. Further research is needed to distinguish between these two interpretations of the genius effect.

Study 4 showed that in addition to exaggerating the ability of outperformers, people exaggerate the ability of those they outperform. These findings, along with the findings of the previous studies, can be parsimoniously explained if one assumes that perceived competence is generally best served by exaggerating the ability of both superior and inferior performers. Whereas the tendency to elevate an outperformer salvages a threatened identity image, aggrandizing an inferior performer advances an already favorable image. Thus, people not only believe the person who outperforms them is exceptional, they also believe the person they outperform is no slouch.

Although a preponderance of research on upward social comparisons emphasizes their threatening nature, recent work suggests that upward comparisons may be more prevalent and desirable than previously thought. A number of studies have shown, for example, that people experience improved mood after learning about others who are better-off than they (e.g., Buunk, Collins, Taylor, VanYperen, &

Dakof, 1990; Gibbons & Gerrard, 1989; Taylor, Aspinwall, Guiliano, Dakof, & Reardon, 1993). Other studies have shown favorable effects of upward comparisons on self-evaluations (e.g., Brewer & Weber, 1994) and on self-esteem (Brown, Novick, Lord, & Richards, 1992) in some circumstances. Although these studies did not incorporate ratings of the better-off individuals or superior performers, the genius effect provides a mechanism to help account for the beneficial effects of upward comparisons. This mechanism, as previously described, involves protecting inferior performers' sense of competence while maintaining believability.

Recent research on upward counterfactual reasoning is also relevant to the present research. Counterfactual reasoning refers to thoughts about how unexpected or unusual outcomes could have turned out differently (Kahneman & Miller, 1986; Roese & Olson, 1995). Upward counterfactuals refer specifically to thoughts of how unfavorable events could have turned out more favorably. Upward counterfactuals have an obvious analogue in upward comparison choices. People may reason, "I could perform as well as this person if only I had more practice or tried harder," and so on. Thus, people who have been outperformed may think that with a reasonable amount of effort, things may have turned out more favorably.

An important task for future research is to establish the parameters within which the genius effect occurs. The self-evaluation maintenance model assumes that the tendency to bask in a superior performer's glory occurs when the outperformer is close and the comparison dimension is unimportant. We assume that aggrandizing outperformers is consistent with basking in their superiority. In our research, however, the outperformer was not particularly close to the comparer. This suggests that the genius effect is not limited to comparisons with close others. Our divergence from the self-evaluation maintenance model in this regard hinges on the difference between basking in the outperformer's glory and aggrandizing the outperformer. We concur that basking without aggrandizing is unlikely to occur because of the threat posed by inferior performance. As we have argued previously, however, exaggerating the outperformer's ability is a powerful construal mechanism that deflects the threat to one's perceived competence without significantly distorting the outperformer's relative advantage. This mechanism can be successfully deployed, therefore, in comparisons with both close and distant others.

We further believe the tendency to exaggerate outperformers' abilities may be even stronger for dimensions that are central (versus peripheral) to the comparer's self-concept, because it is precisely in such circumstances that comparers must protect their sense of competence. In this regard, it will be important in future research to assess more central performance dimensions than perceptual intelligence. It would be useful, for example, to establish the importance of various dimensions to subjects in a pretesting session and then manipulate whether they are outperformed on dimensions that are most or least central to their self-concepts. However, an important logistical problem must be surmounted in varying the importance of the comparison dimension. If the comparison dimension is extremely important, comparers are likely to exaggerate their standing on the dimension, thus creating the previously discussed problem that comparers' elevated ratings of the outperformer could be a consequence of their higher self-evaluations. Because research has demonstrated that people are more self-serving on ambiguous than on unambiguous trait dimensions, this problem can potentially be circumvented if one defines the performance dimensions as unambiguously as possible.

As with other construal mechanisms, the tendency to exaggerate an outperformer's ability is limited by this tactic's plausibility. A healthy young adult who is bested in a weightlifting contest by a 90-year-old will have a hard time convincing himself or anyone else of the nonagenarian's prodigious strength. Inferior performers are also likely to forego the exaggeration tactic when extensive distributional information is available. The inferior performer is unlikely to aggrandize the outperformer, for example, when she knows that she and the outperformer both scored in the lower decile of the class distribution.

Because exaggerating the outperformer's ability entails acknowledging another's superiority, people may also refrain from using this construal mechanism when other self-serving mechanisms are readily available. As stated in the introduction, we believe the tendency to exaggerate another's ability is most likely to occur when other self-serving avenues are blocked by the unambiguous nature of the comparison. When social comparisons are relatively unambiguous, self-serving construal mechanisms must be especially subtle and convincing. We believe that exaggerating the partner's ability fulfills these requirements impeccably. The comparer appears not only truthful, by acknowledging the outperformer's ability, but also magnanimous, by extolling it.

A final word is in order about the criteria we used to establish the genius effect. The tendency to exaggerate an outperformer was defined in terms of differences between subjects' and observers' ratings of the outperformer. Few studies on upward comparison have included an external criterion against which to calibrate inferior performers' attributions. In our research, observers' attributions served as the criterion against which subjects' attributions were assessed. A different observer of the same gender was yoked to each subject who was outperformed. To minimize informational differences, these observers were given extensive exposure to the perceptual intelligence task, although they did not take the test themselves. Thus, it seems unlikely the results were tainted by differences in subjects' and observers' informational vantage. Nevertheless, it should be emphasized that the genius effect is defined in terms of relative differences between subjects and observers rather than with reference to an absolute standard of accuracy, and that the validity of the inferences drawn about subjects' attributions is related to the validity of the criterion against which their attributions are compared.

REFERENCES

Alicke, M. D. (1985). Global self-evaluations as determined by the desirability and controllability of trait adjectives. *Journal of Personality and Social Psychology, 49,* 1621–1630.

Baumeister, R. F., & Jones, E. E. (1978). When self-presentation is constrained by the target's knowledge: Consistency and compensation. *Journal of Personality and Social Psychology*, *36*, 608–618.

Brewer, M. B., & Weber, J. G. (1994). Self-evaluation effects of interpersonal versus intergroup social comparison. *Journal of Personality and Social Psychology*, *66*, 268–275.

Brickman, P., & Bulman, R. J. (1977). Pleasure and pain in social comparison. In J. M. Suls & R. L. Miller (Eds.), *Social comparison processes: Theoretical and empirical perspectives* (pp. 149–186). Washington, DC: Hemisphere.

Brown, J. D., & Gallagher, F. M. (1992). Coming to terms with failure: Private self-enhancement and public self-effacement. *Journal of Experimental Social Psychology*, *28*, 3–22.

Brown, J. D., Novick, N. J., Lord, K. A., & Richards, J. M. (1992). When Gulliver travels: Social context, psychological closeness, and self-appraisals. *Journal of Personality and Social Psychology*, *62*, 717–727.

Brown, J. D., & Smart, S. A. (1991). The self and social conduct: Linking self-representations to prosocial behavior. *Journal of Personality and Social Psychology*, *60*, 368–375.

Buunk, B. P., Collins, R. L., Taylor, S. E., VanYperen, N. W., & Dakof, G. A. (1990). The affective consequences of social comparison. Either direction has its ups and downs. *Journal of Personality and Social Psychology*, *59*, 1238–1249.

Collins, R. L. (1996). For better or worse: The impact of upward social comparison on self-evaluations. *Psychological Bulletin*, *119*, 51–69.

Dunning, D., Meyerowitz, J. A., & Holzberg, A. D. (1989). Ambiguity and self-evaluation: The role of idiosyncratic trait definitions in self-serving assessments of ability. *Journal of Personality and Social Psychology*, *57*, 1082–1090.

Festinger, L. (1954). A theory of social comparisons processes. *Human Relations*. *1*, 117–140.

Gibbons, F. X., & Gerrard, M. (1989). Effects of upward and downward social comparison on mood states. *Journal of Social and Clinical Psychology*, *8*, 14–31.

Gould, R., Brounstein, P. J., & Sigall, H. (1977). Attributing ability to an opponent: Public aggrandizement and private denigration. *Sociometry*, *40*, 254–261.

Greenberg, J., & Pyszczynski, T. (1985). Compensatory self-inflation: A response to the threat to self-regard of public failure. *Journal of Personality and Social Psychology*, *49*, 273–280.

Hakmiller, K. L. (1966). Threat as a determinant of downward comparison. *Journal of Experimental Social Psychology* (Suppl. 1), 32–39.

Kahneman, D., & Miller, D. T. (1986). Norm theory. Comparing reality to its alternatives. *Psychological Review*, *93*, 136–153.

Latané, B. (1966). Studies in social comparison—Introduction and overview. *Journal of Experimental Social Psychology*, 2 (Suppl. 1), 1–5.

Messick, D. M., Bloom, S., Boldizar, J. P., & Samuelson. C. D. (1985). Why we are fairer than others. *Journal of Experimental Social Psychology*, *21*, 480–500.

Mettee, D. R., & Smith, G. (1977). Social comparison and interpersonal attraction. The case for dissimilarity. In J. M. Suls & R. L. Miller (Eds.), *Social comparison processes. Theoretical and empirical perspectives*. Washington, DC: Hemisphere.

Morse, S., & Gergen, K. J. (1970). Social comparison, self-consistency, and the concept of self. *Journal of Personality and Social Psychology*, *16*, 148–156.

Pyszczynski, T., Greenberg, J., & LaPrelle, J. (1985). Social comparison after success and failure: Biased search for information consistent with a self-serving conclusion. *Journal of Experimental Social Psychology*, *21*, 195–211.

Raven, J. C. (1965). *Advanced progressive matrices, sets I and II*, London: Lewis.

Roese, N. J., & Olson, J. M. (Eds.). (1995). *What might have been: The social psychology of counterfactual thinking*. Mahwah, NJ: Erlbaum.

Schlenker, B. R. (1985). Identity and self-identification. In B. R. Schlenker (Ed.). *The self and social life* (pp. 65–99). New York: McGraw-Hill.

Taylor, S. E., Aspinwall, L. G., Gailiano, T. A., Dekof, G. A., & Reardon, K. A. (1993). Storytelling and coping with stressful events. *Journal of Applied Social Psychology*, *23*, 703–733.

Tesser, A. (1988). Toward a self-evaluation maintenance model of social behavior. In L. Berkowitz (Ed.), *Advances in experimental social psychology* (Vol. 21, pp. 181–227). New York: Academic Press.

Tesser, A. (1991). Emotion in social comparison and reflection processes. In J. Suls & T. A. Wills (Eds.), *Social comparison: Contemporary theory and research* (pp. 115–145), Hillsdale, NJ: Erlbaum.

Wheeler, L., & Miyake, K. (1992). Social comparison in everyday life. *Journal of Personality and Social Psychology*, *62*, 760–773.

Wheeler, L., Shaver, K. G., Jones, R. A., Goethals, G. R., Cooper, J., Robison, J. E., Gruder, C. L., & Butzine, K. W. (1969). Factors determining choice of a comparison other. *Journal of Experimental Social Psychology*, *5*, 219–232.

Wills, T. A. (1981). Downward comparison principles in social psychology. *Psychological Bulletin*, *90*, 245–271.

Wood, J. V. (1989). Theory and research concerning social comparisons of personal attributes. *Psychological Bulletin*, *106*, 231–248.

Received June 26, 1995
Revision received October 1, 1996
Accepted October 7, 1996 ■

READING 10

From Top Dog to Bottom Half: Social Comparison Strategies in Response to Poor Performance

Frederick X. Gibbons, Camilla Persson Benbow, and Meg Gerrard

Although the hypothesis that people will alter comparison behavior in response to threat is consistent with the formulation of social comparison theory, the empirical evidence for the natural occurrence of such shifts is weak. Two studies were conducted to examine this hypothesis. In the first study, adolescents' perceptions were assessed before, during, and 6 months after their participation in an academic program for gifted students. Male students who performed poorly, and also worse than they had expected in the program, demonstrated self-protective "strategies" by lowering the amount and level of academic comparison they reported engaging in and by lowering their perception of the importance of academics. Female students, who generally performed as well as expected, reported relatively little change. By follow-up, most of the male students' perceptions had returned to baseline. A second study found that both male and female college students who thought they had performed poorly academically also demonstrated these shifts in comparison. Motivations behind the strategies are discussed.

School children frequently find themselves in situations that can provide unfavorable information about themselves and especially about their performance. A number of theorists have discussed various "strategies" children can use to help them cope with this threatening information (e.g., Rosenberg, 1979). These strategies typically involve cognitive or behavioral reactions that either allow the

Frederick X. Gibbons, Camilla Persson Benbow, and Meg Gerrard, Department of Psychology, Iowa State University.

This research was supported by National Institute of Mental Health Grant 1 P50 MH48165-01 and National Science Foundation Grant MDR 8855625. We thank Lisa Aspinwall, Sue Boney McCoy, and Shelley Taylor for their helpful comments.

Correspondence concerning this article should be addressed to Frederick X. Gibbons, Department of Psychology, Iowa State University, Ames, Iowa 50011.

child to avoid the negative feedback or serve to reduce its impact. For example, Covington (1984) suggested that school children sometimes attempt to avoid failure by choosing easier tasks. When failure is unavoidable, they can obfuscate its attributional meaning by creating excuses or reducing effort (cf. Higgins, Snyder, & Berglas, 1991). At an interpersonal level, Rosenberg (1979) suggested that children, as well as adults, usually seek the company of others whom they believe think highly of them and avoid those who are likely to be critical. This type of "selectivity," as Rosenberg called it, reduces the likelihood that unfavorable information will be encountered.

We believe that children and adults demonstrate a similar kind of selectivity in social comparison behavior. In particular, they alter the amount and the level of their comparison in response to information suggesting that their performance has been relatively poor. This alteration process has both diagnostic and self-protective value. The current studies present longitudinal investigations of these social comparison "strategies," first among gifted adolescents and then among students entering college.

Interpersonal Strategies

Level of Social Comparison

The idea that people are selective in their social comparison choices was actually part of Festinger's (1954) original theory. Citing a study by Hoffman, Festinger, and Lawrence (1954), Festinger suggested that, in general, comparison with persons of ability levels different from one's own will be avoided. The Hoffman *et al.* study, in particular, demonstrated that people will cease comparing with an individual whose performance level is clearly superior to their own. The primary reason, according to Festinger, is because such comparisons are not very useful in terms of satisfying what he saw as the main goal of the social comparison process, which is self-evaluation. In this respect, comparison with others whose performance level is close to one's own is more likely to provide information that has diagnostic value and can be used to assess or evaluate one's own performance. Subsequent

theory and research in the area (e.g., Brickman & Bulman, 1977; see Suls & Miller, 1977) presented another reason people might avoid comparison with superior others, however. That reason is to protect self-esteem from the threat posed by such "upward comparisons."

One of the hypotheses tested in the current research is that a perception that one has not performed well on an important task will prompt a downward shift in preferred comparison level on that task. Although consistent with social comparison theory and its updates, this notion has received very little empirical attention. There are some studies that provide indirect support for the hypothesis, however. In one such study (Pyzsczynski, Greenberg, & LaPrelle, 1985; Experiment 2), college students were given a bogus social sensitivity test and then received false feedback indicating they had done either well or poorly on the test. They also were led to believe that most other subjects had performed at a level that was either worse than, the same, or better than their own level (i.e., a 2×3 between-subjects design). Results in the failure condition were strongest and most relevant to the current discussion: Among subjects who thought they had done poorly, those who believed others had done better than they had were less interested in social comparison (i.e., in obtaining information about others' performances) than were subjects who believed others had done either the same or worse than they had done. Smith and Insko (1987) also found that a belief that one has done poorly on a task was associated with less interest in upward comparison on that task.

Levine and Green (1984) gave elementary school children false feedback suggesting to some that their performance on a perceptual task (guessing how many letters had been flashed on a screen) was declining over time. Their results were similar to those of Pyzsczynski *et al.* (1985): The children who had been led to believe they were doing poorly showed increasing interest in the scores of other children who were thought to be doing worse. Finally, in a longitudinal study of comparison level preferences, Gibbons, Gerrard, Lando, and McGovern (1991) asked smokers who had joined smoking clinic cessation groups to indicate their preferences for other group members in terms of how much difficulty (relative to self) the potential member was having quitting. These preferences were strongly correlated with perceived problem seriousness: As their smoking problem became more severe, their interest in including others in the group who were having more difficulty (than the self) in quitting increased.

Taken together, these studies suggest that threat may alter comparison behavior in a downward direction. Only one of these studies used a longitudinal design, allowing for the assessment of change, however (Gibbons *et al.*, 1991), and that study did not concern performance. Thus, the very basic question of how threat affects performance comparison has not been answered definitively (Wheeler & Miyake, 1992).

Social Versus Temporal Comparison

In addition to lowering comparison level, another effective way of avoiding negative comparison information would be simply to reduce the amount of comparison in which one engages. In fact, others have demonstrated that comparisons with certain individuals may be avoided (usually others who are thought to be doing better than the self; Brickman & Bulman, 1977; Mettee & Smith, 1977); however, the general comparison-reduction hypothesis has never been tested directly. One reason for this may be that the hypothesis is not entirely consistent with Festinger's assumptions about the purpose of social comparison. To the extent that social comparison is useful for self-evaluative purposes, reducing the amount of comparison that one engages in is also likely to reduce the amount of diagnostic information that one has access to. In general, people do tend to seek out diagnostic information (Trope, 1986), much as they seek out social comparison, although, once again, that appears to be less true when that information is thought to be threatening (Trope, 1983; cf. Brickman & Bulman, 1977; Campbell, Fairey, & Fehr, 1986).

Diagnosticity

It is also possible that threatened individuals may actually be "trading" one type of diagnostic information for another. In this regard, Baumeister, Tice, and Hutton (1989) have suggested that "self-protectively oriented individuals" (they were talking about people with low self-esteem, in general, but the same logic should apply to anyone who has experienced a setback) may try to avoid social comparisons and, instead, prefer to "compare themselves primarily with their own past performances and internal standards" (p. 567). Baumeister *et al.* claimed that although these temporal or intrapersonal comparisons may be less diagnostic than social comparisons, they do allow threatened individuals to "monitor their progress at remedying possible deficiencies" (p. 567). Temporal comparisons also may be helpful because they can remind the individual of (performance) strategies that have been effective in the past. This leads to our second hypothesis, which is that when performance is poor or below expectations, social comparison activity on that dimension will decline, whereas temporal comparison will tend to increase.

Downward comparison versus downward shift

It should be pointed out that what we are examining in this research is downward shift in comparison level, which is not the same as downward comparison (Wills, 1981). As the term implies, *downward shift* refers to a decrease in comparison level over time. Whether that declines to a level that is actually lower than the self—what might be considered "true" downward comparison—is a different issue (that we do not consider in this research). One fundamental difference between the two processes has to do with the motives that prompt them. As Wills (1991) suggested, downward comparison reflects an attempt by an individual to alleviate the negative affect produced by a threat or failure of some kind. It has an ad hoc nature and it is typically short-lived. Downward shift and comparison reduction, on the other hand, both reflect (ongoing) attempts to reduce the likelihood that unfavorable comparisons will occur in the future. Thus, their impact on (negative) mood states is more preventive than ameliorative.

Self-Evaluation Maintenance

Tesser's self-evaluation maintenance model (Tesser, 1986, 1988) presents yet another strategy for mitigating the impact of poor performance. Tesser suggested that an unfavorable social comparison with a close other on a dimension of some importance to the individual will be threatening and will prompt an ego-protective response. Three such responses are postulated, the simplest of which is to lower the importance of the dimension to the self (the other two responses, which are not considered in the current research, involve changing one's own performance and psychologically distancing oneself from the other). In fact, the general hypothesis that people tend to "discount" those attributes or dimensions on which they perceive some existing deficiency is a simple and fairly intuitive one that has been offered by a number of theorists (Baumeister & Jones, 1978; Rosenberg, 1979; Taylor & Brown, 1988; Wood & Taylor, 1991) and has been applied to children as well as to adults (Harter, 1986; see Wigfield & Karpathian, 1991, for a review).

Tesser's (1986, 1988) model (and the current research) emphasizes change in perception, however. In fact, very few studies have looked at this kind of dynamic. Two studies by Tesser are most relevant. In one, Tesser and Paulhus (1983) told male subjects they had done either poorly or well, relative to a similar other, on a bogus "cognitive integration" task. Those who thought they had done poorly reported that the particular dimension was less relevant to them than did those who thought they had done well. Similar, but weaker, results were reported with female subjects in a second study by Tesser and Campbell (1980).

The Current Research

The current research examines three hypotheses, each of which reflects a different type of what we call *self-protective comparison strategies*. We have labeled them as such because we believe their primary goal is "damage control"—to protect the ego from the pain associated with unfavorable social comparisons. At least one of them (downward shift) also has diagnostic value, however. In particular, we are proposing that relative to those who think they have done well, people who perceive that their performance has been poor will report (a) a downward shift in preferred comparison level, (b) a reduction in amount of social comparison and an increase in amount of temporal comparison, and (c) a reduction in perceived importance of the dimension or activity on which the performance was based.

Each of these hypotheses is derived, either directly or indirectly, from social comparison theory, and there is some empirical support (although again mostly indirect) for the first and third hypotheses. The evidence that these shifts occur outside of the laboratory, however, is weak or, in the case of temporal comparison, nonexistent. Part of the reason for this is that longitudinal data on social comparison have not previously been available, which means change in comparison behavior has not been assessed. The purpose of the current research, then, is to determine whether naturally occurring threat prompts self-protective shifts in social comparison over time. In particular, the current studies use longitudinal data to assess shifts in social comparison among adolescents and college students who have experienced a natural and common disappointment (i.e., their academic performance did not match their expectations).

Study 1

Overview

The first study examined social comparison preferences and self-perceptions among 13- and 14-year-old adolescents before, during, and after their participation in a 3-week summer program for gifted children. They were asked to what extent and at what (target) level they engaged in social comparison, how often they engaged in temporal comparison, and how important academic and various nonacademic dimensions were to them. At the end of the session, they indicated how well they thought they had done in the program. Our primary focus was on those students who thought they had done poorly academically. We predicted that they would engage in the self-protective comparison strategies described earlier.

We also predicted that when these students returned to their regular classrooms, their comparison preferences and self-concepts would return to their preprogram levels. The reason for this hypothesis is that we are assuming that comparison preferences and self-concept are more responsive to current than to previous comparison activity (cf. Schlenker, Weigold, & Hallam, 1990). Academic comparisons with nongifted students—whether before or after the gifted program—should prove more favorable for the gifted students. And, the more favorable the comparison outcome, the higher the preferred comparison level (i.e., the less likely are downward shifts) and the higher the self-concept.

For several reasons, gifted adolescents in this setting are an interesting population for an examination of our hypotheses. One reason is that prior to participating in a program of this nature, most of them had had minimal experience with unfavorable academic comparisons. In fact, the scholastic aptitude of the current sample placed them above the 99th percentile of their age group. Nonetheless, half of them were "below average" in the program classes. A second reason is that the feedback that students receive in programs like this one is veridical and has a high impact on them (Benbow, 1983; Chan, 1988; Coleman & Fults, 1985). Thus, we should be able to assess their (comparison) reactions to initial experiences with "poor" academic performance and do so in a natural setting. Finally, the switch in comparison group (normal to gifted and then back to normal) provides a very good opportunity for assessing change in comparison behavior.

Method

Subjects

Two hundred 13- and 14-year-old adolescents who had been accepted into a university summer residential program for gifted students were sent materials for the study. From this group, 85 boys and 77 girls, who responded to both the presession and postsession measures, comprised the sample for the study. Acceptance into this program was highly competitive, requiring in the seventh grade a minimum Scholastic Aptitude Tests (SAT) total of 930 (SAT math >500, SAT verbal >430). The group mean was 995, which exceeds the average score earned by college-bound high school seniors.

Measures

A packet of information and preparatory materials was mailed to all summer program students at the end of their school year, at least 3 weeks prior to the start of the program (Time 1). These materials included the Self-Concept Scale (SCS) and the Self-Description Questionnaire (SDQ-II; Marsh, 1990).

The SCS. The SCS was designed specifically for this study and consisted of three primary sections. The first, the social comparison section, described what academic social comparison is—"When students get test scores back or receive grades on a project or paper, they often like to find out how other people did on that test or project (we call that social comparison)"—and then asked how often the subject did that (from *never* to *a lot*). All questions were answered by placing a slash mark on a 13-cm line. The next question pertained to level of preferred comparison target on academics: "Suppose you just got a test score back, with whom would you be most interested in comparing your score?" Subjects responded by placing a mark on a line with anchors labeled "Someone who *did poorly, got an average grade, got the highest grade* on the test." This was followed by the same question for a nonacademic dimension—athletics: "When it comes to things like athletic ability, with whom do you usually compare? Someone who is *very bad,* average, . . ." They were then asked how often they compared how well they were doing now in school with how well they were doing a year ago, which was the intrapersonal, or temporal, academic comparison question.

The performance assessment section asked students how well they expected to do in class at the upcoming summer session in both absolute and relative (to other students) terms. The third and final section of the SCS concerned dimension importance. It asked subjects to indicate how important each of the following dimensions was to them: academics ("doing well in school"); athletic ability, being popular, having friends, having many friends, having a boyfriend or girlfriend, helping others, and being attractive (each response item ranged from *not at all* to *very*).

The SDQ-II. The SDQ-II (Marsh, 1990) is a measure of 12 different aspects of self-concept (e.g., physical appearance and math ability). Only two subscales were used in this study: academic and general.[1]

Teacher ratings. At the end of the summer session (Time 2) instructors evaluated the academic performance of each gifted student relative to the other students in the class. This was done on a 3-point scale: *below average, average*, and *above average*.

Procedure

Summer session. Students participated in one of two consecutive 3-week summer sessions. Each student received approximately 6 hr of classroom instruction per day in the academic topic she or he had chosen. The rest of the time they interacted in social and athletic activities. Each session had five different course offerings. A majority of the students chose instruction in either a scientific or mathematical discipline (87% of the male students and 55% of the female students in computer science, math, biology, etc.). The next largest group was in writing classes (8% and 27% of male and female students, respectively), with the remaining students scattered among several alternatives (e.g.,

Latin).[2] The classes were geared at the college level and thus were extremely rigorous.

Postsession. At the end of the 3-week session, students completed the same scales as before, with the exception that the performance questions were worded in the past tense. In addition to comparative information that they were able to pick up from each other in class, all students received performance feedback on at least one exam, paper, or a project during the course of the session and thus were aware of their performance.

Follow-up. Follow-up questionnaires were mailed to subjects' homes about 6 months after the end of the summer session, when all of them were back in their regular classrooms. These T3 scales were identical to the T2 scales. Of the 162 subjects who responded at T1 and T2, 110 also returned the questionnaires at the T3 follow-up. There were 57 male and 53 female students in this latter group (67% and 69% of the T1 groups, respectively).

Plan of analyses

Our primary hypotheses involved comparisons of subjects who thought they had done well in their class with those who thought they had done less well. Separate indexes of expected (T1) and perceived (T2) performance were obtained by adding together the relative and absolute performance questions at each time (i.e., "How well will/did you do?" and "How well . . . relative to others;" alphas for the two indexes were .74 at T1 and .88 at T2). Subjects were then classified as "high" or "low" performers on the basis of a median split of their T2 perceived performance index. We present these academic performance data first. The primary results from the pre- and postsession analyses are

---

[1] These two generic subscales were chosen because it was thought that analysis of the other 10 specific subscales (e.g., honesty, verbal ability, and relations with parents) was beyond the scope of this article. Other materials in the packet included demographic and other types of background information as well as questionnaires for other research projects.

[2] All analyses reported here were repeated, including class choice as an additional independent variable (e.g., comparing male and female students in science and math with those in other areas). These analyses indicated that responses and results did not vary noticeably as a function of the academic discipline that students chose; this was true for both male and female students.

presented next, followed by those including the follow-up (i.e., T1, T2, and T3, data). Most analyses are presented in the form of 2 between-subjects (sex and perceived performance) × 2 within-subjects (dependent measure and time) repeated measures analyses of variance (ANOVAs), followed by specific comparisons and associated effect sizes for the primary comparisons.[3] Most of these comparisons are made across matched pairs of dependent measures. We did this on the social versus temporal comparison pair because we had opposite predictions for the two items. For the other pairs (e.g., academic vs. nonacademic importance), the second item was included as a comparison for the first. On these pairs we expected a specific change on the first item, but no change on the second, related item (e.g., decline on academic but not nonacademic importance).

Results

Academic performance

Self-perception. As might be expected, these gifted adolescents generally performed well, and for the most part they realized this. There was

some range on the perceived performance (T2) index, however (M for the two items = 8.3 on the 13-point scales; SD = 2.87), and so the high performance (HP) vs. low performance (LP) split is meaningful. Moreover, evidence of the validity of students' self-perceptions is provided by the correlation between their T2 self-ratings and the teacher evaluations (r = .46, p < .001). The correlation was somewhat higher for boys than for girls (r = .54 vs. .33), reflecting greater range in the boys' T2 performance perceptions.

Expected vs. perceived performance. The expected and perceived performance indexes were entered into a 2 (performance group) × 2 (gender) × 2 (time) repeated measures ANOVA. As can be seen in Table 10.1, T1 expectations varied somewhat as a function of eventual performance group, indicating that subjects had an idea before the session started of how well they might do. The correlation between expected and perceived performance was .38 for boys and .61 for girls (both ps < .002; these two correlations are significantly different from one another, p < .01). There was, of course, considerable variation at T2, which was reflected in a

TABLE 10.1. Mean Self-Perceived and Teacher-Evaluated Class Performance: Study 1

	LP				HP			
	Boys		Girls		Boys		Girls	
Performance type	*M*	*SD*	*M*	*SD*	*M*	*SD*	*M*	*SD*
Expected (Time 1)	7.03	1.7	6.65	1.9	8.64	2.0	8.86	2.0
Perceived[a] (Time 2)	5.32*	1.9	6.50	1.3	10.89*	1.5	10.35*	1.3
Evaluated[b] (Time 2)	0.74	0.70	1.12	0.64	1.58	0.55	1.41	0.67

*Note: n*s: LP boys = 43, LP girls = 35, HP boys = 42, and HP girls = 42. LP and HP = low and high performance groups, respectively.
[a] Mean of absolute plus relative performance assessed at Time 1 (expected) and Time 2 (perceived); scales ranged from 0–13, higher number reflects a more favorable perception.
[b] Teacher rating of performance; scale = 0–2, higher number indicates more favorable evaluation.
* Significant Time 1–Time 2 change (*p* < .05).

---

[3] Effect sizes for repeated measures were calculated using the standard deviation of the (T2–T1) change score for the particular variable as the denominator (cf. Hedges & Olkin, 1985). Also, regression analyses were performed on all of the dependent measures, regressing the T2 measures on the corresponding T1 responses and T2 perceived performance (which

was a continuous variable). Because the results of these analyses were quite comparable with those of the repeated measures ANOVA (see Footnote 6), and because the latter method provided (tabular) evidence of a clear and consistent pattern of means, those analyses are reported here.

TABLE 10.2. Mean Preferred Comparison Target Level on Academics and Athletics: Study 1

	Academics								Athletics							
	LP				HP				LP				HP			
	Boys		Girls		Boys		Girls		Boys		Girls		Boys		Girls	
Time period	M	SD	M	SD	M	SD	M	SD	M	SD	M	SD	M	SD	M	SD
Time 1	11.29	2.5	9.88	4.0	12.09	1.5	11.05	1.2	7.25	2.8	7.58	3.7	9.12	3.5	8.03	3.2
Time 2	10.49*	3.0	11.08*	2.4	12.38	1.4	11.45	1.8	8.14*	3.0	7.50	3.7	9.30	3.8	8.38	3.3
Time 3[a]	11.89	1.8	11.45	2.2	11.80	1.8	11.77	1.2	8.00	3.5	7.61	3.6	9.21	2.9	7.45	3.2

Note: n = 34 to 42 per cell for Time 1–Time 2; Time 3 ns = 28, 25, 29, and 27, respectively. The scales for both items ranged from 0–13; higher number reflects higher performing target preferred. LP and HP = low and high performance groups, respectively.
[a] Responses from subjects who answered at all three time periods (Time 1–Time 2 means are somewhat different for this subsample).
* Significant Time 1–Time 2 change ($p < .05$).

significant Performance × Time interaction ($p < .001$). This interaction, in turn, was qualified by an unexpected Performance × Sex × Time interaction, $F(1, 158) = 15.05, p < .001$. In general, the (T1−T2) difference between expected and perceived performance, especially among poor performers, was much greater for boys than for girls. In particular, HP boys and girls both did better than they had expected (for change in performance rating over time: both $ps < .001$), whereas LP boys did much worse than expected ($p < .001$), but LP girls did not ($p > .80$).

Teacher evaluation. An analysis of teachers' assessments of students' overall performance revealed a significant Sex × Performance interaction, $F(1, 158) = 7.43, p < .007$, as LP boys' performance was viewed more negatively than was LP girls' performance (simple effect $p < .004$; see Table 10.1).

Change in social comparison

To detect an overall pattern of change, a 2 (performance) × 2 (gender) × 2 (dimension) × 2 (time) repeated measures multivariate ANOVA (MANOVA) was performed on the three pairs of measures (i.e., social vs. temporal comparison, academic vs. nonacademic preferred comparison level, and academic vs. nonacademic dimension importance). This analysis revealed a significant four-way interaction, $F(3, 151) = 4.51, p < .005$. Repeated

measures ANOVAs were then performed separately on each of the three dimension pairs.

Social comparison: Level

T1 and T2. For the academic and athletic comparison level measures, we first conducted a repeated measures ANOVA on T1 responses. This analysis revealed a main effect of sex, as boys reported higher preferred comparison levels, $F(1, 155) = 4.97, p < .03$ (see Table 10.2). Interestingly, this gender difference was significant on the academic dimension ($F = 8.89, p < .004$, effect size $d = .46$), but not on the athletic dimension ($F < 1.0$). Our primary prediction on these measures was that those subjects who performed poorly would lower their preferred comparison level on the academic but not the athletic dimension. To test this, we performed a repeated measures ANOVA on the two variables over time. This analysis revealed main effects of performance and dimension, $Fs(1, 155) = 10.45$ and 113.80 (both $ps < .003$), as preferred comparison levels were higher among HP subjects and much higher on the academic dimension. These main effects were qualified, however, by the same four-way (Performance × Gender × Dimension × Time) interaction that had been detected on the MANOVA, $F(1, 155) = 9.75, p = .002$. As Table 10.2 indicates, the one group that showed "movement" on both dimensions was the LP boys. They lowered their preferred academic comparison level, as expected,

TABLE 10.3. Mean Frequency of Social and Temporal Comparison: Study 1

	Social								Temporal							
	LP				HP				LP				HP			
	Boys		Girls		Boys		Girls		Boys		Girls		Boys		Girls	
Time period	M	SD	M	SD	M	SD	M	SD	M	SD	M	SD	M	SD	M	SD
Time 1	9.55	3.1	9.61	3.2	9.25	4.1	8.90	3.1	6.07	3.6	4.99	3.6	5.62	4.1	5.87	4.0
Time 2	8.34*	3.8	9.29	3.3	9.00	3.9	9.08	3.0	6.55	3.8	5.41	3.4	6.16	4.3	6.20*	3.7
Time 3	9.42	3.3	10.06	2.6	9.65	3.96	8.44	3.4	6.10	3.0	5.09	3.52	4.73	4.2	6.07	3.9

Note: ns = 34–42 for Time 1–Time 2 and 25–29 for Time 3. LP and HP = low and high performance groups, respectively. Scales range from 0–13; higher number means more frequent comparison.
* Significant Time 1–Time 2 change (p < .05).

whereas (unexpectedly) they raised their athletic comparison level, simple effect $ts(155) = 2.31$ and 2.32, both $ps < .03$ ($ds = .35$ and .36). No other group showed significant change in athletic level (all $ts < 1.1$). On the academic comparison level, LP girls increased, $t(155) = 3.15, p < .003,$[4] but neither HP group changed significantly.

T3 analyses: Comparison level. T2 perceived performance was again used as the basis for the LP-HP split for the T1, T2, and T3 analyses (the LP and HP groups also differed in their T3 recollections of program performance; $p < .001$). The primary four-way interaction on the comparison level variables remained significant when T3 responses were included, $F(2, 200) = 5.60, p < .005$. This is largely attributable to the LP male subjects who, again, showed the most movement, this time returning, at T3, to a level of response comparable with their presession levels (slightly higher on the academic preference item). Their T2–T3 increase was statistically significant, $t(200) = 3.52, p < .001$ ($d = .73$), whereas their decline in athletic preference was not.

Social comparison: Type and amount

T1 and T2. The second primary hypothesis concerned alteration of frequency and type of academic comparison. Analysis of T1 responses on these measures (see Table 10.3) indicated that subjects reported engaging in much more social than temporal comparison, $F(1, 155) = 95.74, p < .001$; the same was true at T2 ($p < .001$). There were no other significant effects at T1. The repeated measures analysis revealed a Type × Time interaction, $(F1, 155) = 4.91, p < .03$, as the tendency to engage in social comparison declined slightly, whereas reports of temporal comparison increased. There was no evidence that LP subjects switched frequency or type of comparison more than did HP subjects. It is worth noting, however, that LP boys did lower the amount of social comparison they engaged in from T1 to T2, $t(155) = 2.66, p < .01$ ($d = .41$), and they were the only group to do that (all other $ts < .8$).

T3. As with the T1–T2 data, the four-way interaction with the T1, T2, and T3 data was not significant ($p = .36$). However, LP boys once again

[4]This unexpected increase in LP girls' preferred academic comparison level is largely attributable to the unusually low level they reported on this measure at T1. That low T1 level in turn, is due, in part, to three subjects in this condition whose T1 scores were well below the mean of the cell (M = 0.3 vs.

overall M = 11.3). One of these subjects clearly had misread the scales and so her data were discarded. In short, there is some question about the reliability of the LP girls' T1 academic comparison level mean and, therefore, the change (increase) in this measure.

TABLE 10.4. Mean Importance of Academic and Nonacademic Dimensions: Study 1

	Academic[a]								Nonacademic[a]							
	LP				HP				LP				HP			
	Boys		Girls		Boys		Girls		Boys		Girls		Boys		Girls	
Time period	M	SD	M	SD	M	SD	M	SD	M	SD	M	SD	M	SD	M	SD
Time 1	10.42	2.3	11.04	2.1	11.39	1.7	11.42	2.3	7.29	2.6	7.97	2.6	7.86	2.6	7.43	2.2
Time 2	9.75*	2.6	10.92	1.8	11.58	2.1	11.51	2.0	7.97*	2.7	8.06	2.4	8.15	2.7	7.86	2.4
Time 3	9.39	3.0	11.03	1.9	11.66	2.0	11.54	1.8	7.78	1.9	7.63	2.5	7.87	2.9	7.06	2.2

Note: n = 35–42 for Time 1–Time 2 and 25–29 for Time 3. LP and HP = low and high performance groups, respectively.
[a] Mean of academic and six nonacademic dimensions. Scale ranged from 0–13; higher number indicates dimension is more important.
* Significant Time 1–Time 2 change ($p < .05$).

altered their responses back in the direction of their presession levels. Their increase in social comparison from T2 to T3 was significant ($t = 2.48$, $p < .02$, $d = .46$), whereas the decline in temporal comparison was not.[5]

Dimension importance

T1 and T2. The final section of the SCS concerned perceived importance of academic and nonacademic dimensions. The seven nonacademic items were first submitted to a principal-components factor analysis with varimax rotation. This revealed one factor, comprising all but the "helpful" item, which explained 47% of the variance (eigenvalue = 3.29; all loadings > .50; helpful loading = −.06). Consequently, the helpful item was dropped, and nonacademic indexes for T1 and T2 were created by averaging the remaining six items (mean T1 and T2 alpha = .84). This nonacademic index was then included with the academic importance item in a repeated measures ANOVA to determine if the hypothesized change

on the latter also appeared on the former. An initial analysis of just the T1 responses indicated that all subjects thought academics were more important than nonacademic activities ($p < .001$; see Table 10.4); there were no other significant differences (including gender). The repeated measures ANOVA yielded a Dimension × Time interaction, $F(1, 155) = 8.56$, $p < .004$, as subjects raised their perceived importance of the nonacademic dimension ($p < .004$) but did not alter academic importance, which was and remained quite high. In addition, this interaction was qualified by the familiar four-way interaction, $F(1, 155) = 4.08$, $p < .05$, which, again, was mostly due to a change among LP boys. They were the only group who significantly altered the importance of either dimension. In particular, they lowered the importance of academics, as anticipated, $t(155) = 2.38$, $p < .02$, d = .36 (*t*s for all other groups < .2), and they raised the importance of nonacademics, which was not expected, $t(155) = 2.82, p < .006, d = .44$ (other *t*s < 1.85, *n*s).

---

[5] Subjects were also asked directly how they compared with the "typical gifted student" academically and in nonacademic dimensions (e.g., athletically and socially). Repeated measures analyses of these two dimensions also revealed a four-way interaction, $F(1, 158) = 4.56$, $p < .04$, following the same pattern as the other measures: LP male subjects started off with fairly high perceptions of their academic ability relative to the typical gifted student (in fact, LP and HP male students were quite comparable at T1), but that perception declined significantly over time ($p < .005$); their nonacademic comparison

perceptions increased slightly. No other group reported significant change. Moreover, correlational analyses indicated that change in academic comparison was predicted by subjects' performance and the typical amount of social comparison they reported engaging in at T1. Among LP students, the more academic comparison they engaged in initially, the more negative their academic self-perception became vis-à-vis the typical gifted student ($r = −.24, p < .04$; cf. Ruble & Frey, 1991); the opposite was true among the HP students ($r = .30, p < .007$); these correlations differ significantly ($p < .001$).

TABLE 10.5. Mean Academic and General Self-Concept: Study 1

	Academic[a]								General[a]							
	LP				HP				LP				HP			
	Boys		Girls		Boys		Girls		Boys		Girls		Boys		Girls	
Time period	M	SD	M	SD	M	SD	M	SD	M	SD	M	SD	M	SD	M	SD
Time 1	5.41	0.5	5.56	0.5	5.70	0.4	5.77	0.2	5.06	0.8	5.19	0.7	5.41	0.6	5.41	0.6
Time 2	5.14*	0.8	5.45	0.8	5.64	0.6	5.73	0.3	4.77*	0.9	5.15	0.6	5.51	0.5	5.45	0.6
Time 3	5.48	0.5	5.48	0.4	5.79	0.3	5.75	0.2	5.17	0.7	5.21	0.8	5.57	0.4	5.38	0.7

Note: ns = 35–40 for Time 1–Time 2 and 25–27 for Time 3. LP and HP = low and high performance groups, respectively.
[a] Academic and general Self-Concept subscales from the SDQ-II. Scale ranged from 1–6.
* Significant T1–T2 change ($p < .05$).

T3. The T1–T2 change on dimension importance persisted it T3. Specifically, the decline in academic importance reported by LP boys from T1 to T2 continued at T3, and the four-way interaction was not significant ($p = .17$).

Self-concept

Repeated measures analyses of the academic and general self-concept subscales of the SDQ-II revealed a Performance × Time interaction ($p < .02$), indicating that LP subjects' self-concepts declined somewhat at T2, whereas HP subjects did not change over time (see Table 10.5). Nonetheless, the self-concepts, especially academic, of all students were very high at T1 and remained so at T2. In fact, even LP boys at T2 had very high academic self-concepts in comparison with the norm on that subscale (5.14 vs. 4.50; cf. Marsh, 1990). This ceiling effect needs to be considered when interpreting the results on the self-concept measure. Looking at all three time periods, a Gender × Time interaction on the self-concept measure ($p < .04$) reflected the fact that girls' self-concepts stayed relatively constant, whereas boys' dropped at T2, but then improved considerably at T3, when they returned to their regular classrooms (both the drop and the increase in academic self-concept were reliable for boys; $ps < .02$, $ds = .42$ and .57). Perhaps most significant about these data, however, is the fact that at T3, self-concepts were as high as they had been at T1 for virtually all subjects, including the LP boys.

T3 conclusion

In general, the subset of 110 subjects who responded to the T3 follow-up appeared to be representative of the entire group, on the basis of a comparison of their T1 and T2 responses with those of the T3 "nonresponders" on most measures (actual performance, academic and nonacademic importance, and preferred comparison level; all $ps > .10$). Those who did respond at T3 thought they had done better in the program, however, and they reported engaging in less social comparison at T2 ($ps < .01$ and .05). Keeping these differences in mind, the pattern of responses at T3 does appear to be consistent: With a few exceptions, subjects' T3 responses were quite similar to those they had provided at T1. In particular, the comparison responses of the LP boys (i.e., amount of temporal, and level and amount of academic, comparison), and their self-concepts had returned to their T1 levels by the time of the follow-up.

Expected versus actual performance

Performance discrepancy. The fact that LP boys' perceived performance was much worse than their expectations suggests this discrepancy may be related to their comparison strategy. To examine this possibility, correlations were calculated between change in each of the academic measures (i.e., comparison level and frequency and dimension importance) and a performance discrepancy index (perceived-expected, or T2–T1, performance). These correlations, presented in Table 10.6 by group,

TABLE 10.6. Correlations Between Change in Perceived Performance[a] and Academic Comparison Strategies: Study 1

Group	Target level[b]	SC frequency[c]	Dimension importance[d]	Strategy index[e]
All subjects	.20**	.18*	.26***	.30***
Boys	.25*	.20*	.28**	.35***
Girls	.14	.10	.20*	.16

Note: n = 85 boys and 76 girls.
[a] Time 2–Time 1 performance discrepancy (high number means an increase in perceived performance).
[b] Time 2–Time 1 change in level of preferred academic social comparison (SC).
[c] Change in frequency of academic social comparison.
[d] Change in perceived importance of academics.
[e] Strategy index = sum of z scores for all four comparison changes; higher number reflects less self-protective change.
*p < .05. **p < .01. ***p < .001 (one-tailed).

indicate that the academic change–discrepancy index relations were positive for all three measures for the entire sample and for the boys. Put another way, the worse subjects thought they did, relative to their expectations, the more they altered their comparison strategy in the expected directions. The relations were similar for the girls, but tended to be weaker, due partly to their restricted range on the perceived versus expected performance discrepancy index. (The magnitude of all of these correlations is attenuated somewhat given that they all include a fair amount of measurement error associated with multiple assessments.)[6]

"Shift" index. To get an overall picture of self-protective comparison change, a summary index was then calculated. T2–T1 change scores for each of the four comparison strategy measures (i.e., social and temporal comparison frequency, comparison level, and academic importance) were standardized and then added together. The correlation between this total change index and the performance discrepancy index (see Table 10.6) indicated that performance discrepancy was related to overall comparison strategy, $r(159) = .30, p < .001$. In sum, it appears

that a perception of performance that is below expectations, in addition to poor perceived performance, is a factor contributing to the changes in comparison strategy reported here.

Comparison strategy and self-concept change

Finally, to examine the relation between comparison strategy and change in self-concept, subjects were divided at the median on the shift index described above and then a Performance × Gender × Shift (i.e., high *vs.* low amount) × Time repeated measures ANOVA was performed on their T1 and T2 general self-concept scores. This analysis revealed a significant four-way interaction, $F(1, 140) = 4.01, p < .05$, which, once again, was due largely to the LP boys. Specifically, the LP boys who engaged in relatively little comparison alteration (i.e., were below the median on the shift index; n = 11) reported a substantial decline in self-concept ($M = -.62$), $t(140) = 4.03, p < .001$. In fact, although comprising only 30% of the LP male group, they were responsible for the significant decline of that entire group ($M = -.27$).

---

[6] All analyses were repeated using a series of hierarchical multiple regressions in which all T1 measures of interest (academic comparison level, dimension importance, etc.) were entered as predictors of their corresponding T2 measures, along with the performance discrepancy index (a continuous variable). In essence, this uses performance discrepancy to predict change in the various dependent measures. These analyses were performed separately for male and female students. Results indicated that performance discrepancy added significantly to the

predictive power of the T1 measure (i.e., it predicted change in the measure) for each of the following variables, but only for the male students: academic dimension importance, academic comparison level, academic comparison with typical gifted student, and general self-concept (all *p*s for increase in $R^2 < .02$). Moreover, stepwise regressions indicated that the performance discrepancy index was a (slightly) better predictor than just T2 perceived performance for each of the criterion variables.

None of the other groups of subjects, including the LP boys who did engage in comparison alteration, reported a significant decline (for the LP boys high-strategy group, $n = 26$; M decline $= -.17, t = 1.70, p = .10$; all other ts $< .5, n$s). Moreover, the self-concept decline among the LP low-strategy boys was significantly greater than that of any other group, including the LP high-strategy boys (all ps $< .05$). Although only suggestive, this finding is consistent with the hypothesis that the comparison strategy does serve a self-protective function for those who engage in it.

Comparison with a nongifted sample

To put the responses of the gifted subjects in some perspective, we compared their T1 responses with those of a comparison sample of 271 nongifted students. They were also seventh and eighth graders from local school districts who completed the scales in return for $7 payment. Comparison analyses indicated that the gifted students tended to engage in less social comparison, although all students reported a substantial amount ($M = 9.3$ vs. 9.9), $F(1, 422) = 3.85$, $p < .06$. The gifted group also reported less temporal comparison ($M = 5.6$ vs. 7.1, $p < .001$), a much higher academic comparison level ($M = 11.0$ vs. 8.2, $p < .001$), and a lower athletic comparison level ($M = 8.0$ vs. 8.9, $p < .01$). Surprisingly, there was no difference on perceived academic importance (gifted $M = 11.1$ vs. nongifted $M = 10.7$, $p > .16$), although the gifted sample did think non-academic activities were less important ($M = 7.7$ vs. 9.5, $p < .001$). In sum, these gifted students compared at a higher level academically, and lower athletically, and valued nonacademic pursuits less than did the nongifted students; otherwise, the two samples were comparable.

Discussion

Evidence of a self-protective comparison strategy can be seen in virtually all pairs of measures, but only among the male subjects. In particular, male subjects who thought they had done poorly lowered their preferred level of academic social comparison and the importance of academics. They also

decreased their social and increased their temporal comparisons. The same pattern was not seen in the responses of the LP girls, however.

We did not anticipate the gender differences on these measures, primarily because previous work in the area, with one possible exception, has not provided clear evidence of social comparison differences between male and female subjects (Chafel, 1988; Wills, 1987). The exception is a tendency, reported in some studies, for male subjects to prefer comparison at a higher level (Veroff, 1969; Wilson & Benner, 1971), perhaps due to their greater competitiveness (especially in academic matters; cf. Ahlgren, 1983). There is also some evidence that females tend to have lower performance expectations than do males on important, intelligence-related tasks (see Roberts, 1991, for a review). The gifted classes would certainly qualify on this characteristic, and in fact, we did find some evidence of lower performance expectations among LP girls (undoubtedly attenuated somewhat by their gifted status). At any rate, the combination of marginally higher expectations and lower performance resulted in a significant expectation–performance difference for LP boys but not for LP girls. Our assumption, then, is that the change in comparison behavior is a function of this difference and not an indication of a gender difference. To check this assumption and also replicate the comparison strategy effects, a second study was conducted, this time using a sample that, we assumed, would not be characterized by gender differences in expected or perceived performance.

Study 2

The sample for the second study consisted of college freshmen who were matriculating at a large university. Their comparison preferences and self-perceptions were assessed at the beginning of their freshmen year and then again 6 months later. Because the majority of freshmen at the university had high school GPAs that placed them in the top 25% of their graduating class, the situation for these students was comparable with that of the gifted students, although the change in reference group was not nearly as pronounced. Similarly, the academic and overall involvement for the college students was longer term, but certainly not as intense. In addition, the fact that there were no gender differences in the sample, in terms of ACT scores or high school GPA, led us to assume there would be no such differences in actual or perceived college academic performance. With this in mind, our predictions were essentially the same as in the first study: More so than high performing students, those who thought they had performed poorly, regardless of gender, would engage in the comparison strategies identified earlier.

Method

Subjects and procedure

Participants were incoming freshmen who had responded to letters mailed to a random sample of university acceptees soliciting participation in a longitudinal study of cognitions and health behavior. The sample included about 15% of the total number of incoming freshmen, and it was representative of that entire group. The first wave of data collection took place during the period from 2 weeks before until 2 weeks after the start of classes; for most subjects, this was done through the mail, before arriving on campus. The second wave occurred 6 months later. Of the 679 subjects who completed the first questionnaire, 278 male and 348 female subjects (92%) also completed the second wave; they comprised the sample. All subjects completed the second wave in our laboratory, individually, with a graduate student interviewer supervising the process. Subjects were paid $20 each time they completed the scales.

Measures

Participants completed a questionnaire that included a variety of scales pertaining to health-related behaviors (e.g., drinking and smoking). In addition, they were asked the same social comparison and importance questions as in Study 1 (frequency of social and temporal comparison, level of academic and athletic comparison, and importance of academics and nonacademics; the latter included the items athletic ability, having friends, and being attractive; T1 and T2 alphas = .57). At T2 they were

also asked four questions about their performance: "In your opinion how well did you do academically last semester?"; "Compared to the typical freshmen, how well . . . ?"; "What was your GPA?"; and "How does this GPA compare with how well you thought you would do?" All but the GPA question were answered on 7-point scales (e.g., ranging from *much worse* to *much better* than expected). Written permission was obtained to verify the GPAs (although we did not actually do that). A median split performed on the first question (how well did you do?) allowed a comparison of high and low performers (results were essentially the same when each of the other two perceived performance measures was used to categorize subjects).

Results

Perceived performance

An ANOVA performed on the T2 perceived performance measure indicated that male and female subjects had almost identical perceptions of their performance the previous semester (see Table 10.7). Using this item as the basis for the performance split, a Gender × Performance ANOVA on the performance relative to expectations item indicated that the LP male and female subjects had both done (equally) worse than they had expected. They also had very comparable GPAs, as did the HP male and female subjects. Thus, the HP–LP split again appeared to be appropriate. Moreover, there were no significant gender differences this time on any of the perceived performance items (all $Fs < 1.1$).

TABLE 10.7. Mean Performance in Study 2

Performance[a]	LP		HP	
	Males	Females	Males	Females
GPA	2.06	2.18	3.10	3.07
Perceived	2.05	1.93	5.09	5.09
Relative to expectations	2.07	1.94	4.22	4.62

Note: n = 278 for the low performance (LP) group and 349 for the high performance (HP) group. GPA = grade point average.
[a] Scales for perceived performance and performance relative to expectations ranged from 1–7; GPA scale ranged from 1–4.

Social comparison and dimension importance

Overall. Our prediction was that LP subjects would lower their self-reported amount and level of academic social comparison and importance of academics, while raising their amount of temporal comparison. No change was expected on nonacademic importance or level of athletic comparison. As in Study 1, to examine the overall pattern, a MANOVA was performed on the paired items at T1 and T2 (i.e., amount of temporal vs. social comparison, level of academic vs. athletic comparison, and importance of academics vs. nonacademics). This MANOVA revealed a significant Performance × Dimension × Time interaction, which was consistent with the self-protective strategy pattern, $F(3, 618) = 5.18, p < .002$. This time, however, the pattern was the same for male and female subjects, as indicated by the lack of a four-way interaction involving gender ($F = .82$, ns). All social comparison and dimension importance means, collapsed across gender, are presented in Table 10.8.

Type and amount of comparison. Again, subjects reported much less temporal than social comparison at T1 ($p < .001$). This tendency had disappeared by T2, however, as reflected in a Type of Comparison × Time interaction, $F(1, 622) = 74.83, p < .001$. All subjects lowered the amount of social

comparison they reported engaging in and raised the amount of temporal comparison, $ts(622) = 3.73$ and 6.88, $ps < .001$. Consistent with expectations, this tendency was much stronger among the LP subjects, as reflected in a Performance × Type × Time interaction, $F(1, 622) = 8.19, p < .004$ (effect sizes: for decrease in social comparison, LP $d = .26$ and HP $d = .14$; for increase in temporal comparison, LP $d = .35$ and HP $= .17$). Gender was not a factor in this analysis (four-way interaction $F = .70$). As in Study 1, however, the drop in amount of social comparison was significant only among LP males ($p < .002$; all other $ps > .06$), and that drop was significantly larger than it was among each of the other three groups (all $ps < .05$).

Level of academic versus nonacademic comparison. A separate analysis performed on just the T1 responses revealed that the male subjects, once again, had a higher preferred level of academic comparison, prior to entering college, $F(1, 623) = 6.63, p < .01$. In addition, a Dimension × Time interaction indicated that all subjects lowered their preferred level of academic comparison, whereas their preferred level of athletic comparison changed only slightly, $F(1, 623) = 31.07, p < .001$. This tendency was again stronger among LP subjects, as reflected in a significant Performance × Dimension × Time interaction, $F(1, 623) = 5.27, p = .02$ (for decline in academic comparison; LP $d = .49$ and HP $d = .31$). In spite of the initial difference on preferred academic comparison level, the pattern of change was again quite similar for the male and female subjects (four-way interaction $F = .34$).

Dimension importance. A Dimension × Time interaction on the dimension importance pair indicated that subjects slightly raised their perceived importance of nonacademics, whereas they significantly lowed the importance of academics, $F(1, 621) = 20.99, p < .001$. The latter tendency was significant only among LP subjects, however ($d = .27$), and the Performance × Dimension × Time interaction was again significant, $F(1, 621) = .79, p = .05$.

TABLE 10.8. Comparison Frequency, Comparison Level, and Dimension Importance in Study 2

Measure	LP		HP	
	Time 1	Time 2	Time 1	Time 2
Comparison frequency				
Social	9.04	8.33	9.31	8.91
Temporal	8.08	9.46	7.78	8.43
Comparison level				
Academic	9.73	8.31	9.99	9.08
Athletic	8.52	8.24	8.38	7.95
Dimension importance				
Academic	11.40	10.99	11.41	11.25
Nonacademic	9.52	9.59	9.38	9.42

Note: $n = 278$ for the low performance (LP) group and 349 for the high performance (HP) group. Scales ranged from 1–13.

Summary

As predicted, the amount of comparison and perception change (i.e., "comparison strategy") reported by LP subjects was significantly greater than that reported by HP subjects on all four measures (see Figure 10.1), that is, decline in social comparison amount and level ($ps < .05$ and $.003$), decline in academic importance ($p < .008$), and increase in temporal comparison ($p < .002$). Moreover, a calculated shift index (once again comprising the sum of the standardized changes in the four strategies) correlated with both T2 perceived performance and performance relative to expectations, $rs(625) = .19$ and $.15$, $ps < .001$.

Discussion

There were some differences between the gifted adolescent and the college samples in absolute terms. For example, even HP college students tended to lower their preferred academic comparison levels, whereas only LP boys did that in Study 1. On the other hand, there were a number of similarities between the two samples, including two gender differences in Study 2 that were consistent with results from the gifted sample. First, male college students reported higher initial comparison levels than did female college students. Although we did not assess performance expectations, this effect seems to be consistent with the general tendency for males to exceed females on this latter dimension. Second, LP male subjects decreased their amount of social comparison more than did LP female subjects, as was the case in Study 1. These LP male college students did not differ from their LP female counterparts on any of the other comparison shifts reported by LP male subjects in Study 1, however. Moreover, the general pattern of responses among LP subjects relative to HP subjects in the college sample was the same as that of LP male students relative to all other subjects in the adolescent sample. This is consistent with the fact that the absolute and perceived performance of the male and female subjects in the college sample, whether they were

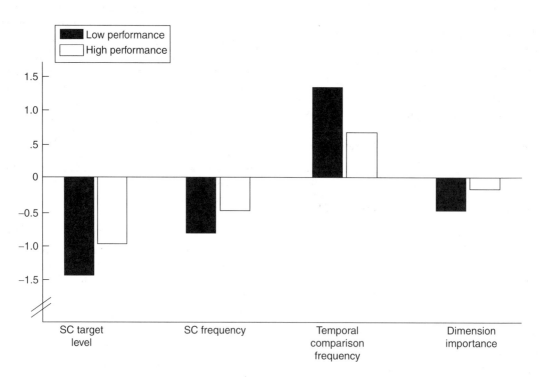

FIGURE 10.1 ■ Change in academic comparisons and perceptions (Study 2). SC = social comparison.

above or below the median, were quite comparable. In short, the results support our assumption that the differences in comparison strategy between LP boys and girls in Study 1 were due to differences in their perceived performances and are not an indication of a gender effect.

General Discussion

Comparison Strategies

Students in both samples made a transition from one academic environment to another, much more competitive environment. In so doing, they altered their social comparison preferences and perceptions in a manner that reflected a self-protective motive. We discuss each of the strategies these students used individually and then discuss the motives behind them.

Academic comparison level

Both samples entered their new academic environments with fairly high preferred levels of academic comparison. As expected, the much higher level of academic competition they faced in those new environments led students who had done relatively poorly to lower their academic, but not their athletic, comparison levels. In fact, the "stiffer" competition prompted most of the college sample, regardless of their actual performance, to lower their preferred levels somewhat. In contrast, the HP adolescents actually raised their reported comparison levels slightly. We suspect one reason for this latter effect is that the only comparison targets available to these gifted students at that time (T2) were other exceptional students. Because the question was asked in the present tense, and at the time these gifted students were, in fact, comparing at a very high level, their reports were probably an accurate reflection of reality for them. More generally, however, two conclusions can be drawn from these results: (a) Changes in reference group lead to changes in preferred comparison level, and (b) poor performance does prompt a downward shift in that preference.

Amount and type

In addition to lowering their level of comparison, poor performance students also lowered the amount of social comparison in which they reported engaging, while increasing their reported amount of temporal comparison. Once again, we suspect that the former change was a reaction to the fact that their comparisons with members of the current, more competent, reference group were generally less favorable for them (cf. Brickman & Bulman, 1977). The latter change was actually reported by some HP as well as LP college subjects. One likely reason for this is that by spring semester, all of them had an "academic past" on which to reflect. The fact that the shift was more pronounced among the LP students, however, is in line with our hypothesis. It also should be pointed out that we are basing our conclusions on subjects' self-reports of their comparison behavior. Although we can think of no reason why these reports might be systematically distorted as a function of performance, it is possible that participants may have underestimated the amount of comparison they actually engaged in (cf. Wheeler & Miyake, 1992).

Dimension importance

The decline in perceived academic importance among the LP subjects (primarily the boys in the adolescent sample) is consistent with the reasoning of a number of theorists who have suggested that dimension importance varies as a function of perceived competence (e.g., Harter, 1986; Wigfield & Karpathian, 1991; cf. Tesser, 1988). The current studies extend the previous research in this area by including impactful and veridical performance feedback that was delivered in a natural setting and by using a longitudinal design that allowed assessment of changes in perceptions over time.

Expectations

Additional internal analyses indicated that those LP male students in Study 1 and LP students in Study 2 whose self-reports of performance relative to expectations were above the median (i.e., those few LP subjects who had actually expected to do poorly) demonstrated much less of the comparison change than did the majority of LP subjects, who reported doing worse than expected. Moreover, the correlation between change in comparison and difference in (expected vs. perceived) performance in both studies also attests to the importance of subjects' performance expectations. More generally, it would appear that it is poor performance that prompts the comparison alteration process. If poor performance is anticipated, however, then less alteration or decline in comparison will occur. One reason for this is that levels of comparison should already be relatively low, prior to the new comparison opportunities, among people who expect to do poorly. An experimental study in which changes in comparison behavior are examined in response to poor performance feedback that follows manipulation of performance expectations would most likely provide a more conclusive answer to this question.

Strategy Motives

Wills (1981) has suggested that people who are experiencing threat will seek out comparisons with others who are thought to be doing worse than they are. The primary motive for this behavior is believed to be self-enhancement or improvement of subjective well-being; in fact, such comparisons have been shown to produce an amelioration of negative mood (Gibbons, 1986; see Gibbons & Gerrard, 1991, for a review). We did not measure subjects' moods in these studies, and our comparison level items assessed preferences in absolute rather than relative (to self) terms, so we cannot determine for sure if what they are reporting fits the "true" definition of downward comparison. It does seem unlikely that the primary motive behind the strategies was self-enhancement, however. For one thing, what we were examining was a change in general academic comparison level preference over time. We do not believe that even threatened individuals engage in downward comparison on a regular basis (cf. Wills, 1987); that is especially true when considering ongoing performance, such as would be the case with academics. Rather, downward comparisons are more often isolated (or occasional) attempts to

garner information that pertains to one's current situation. They can produce short-term mprovements in mood, but they are not likely to have long-lasting effects on subjective well-being. Thus, like many other forms of "emotion-focused" coping (Lazarus & Folkman, 1984), they do not occur on a continuing basis (Gibbons & Gerrard, 1994).

Instead, what these students appeared to be doing was altering their comparison behavior in such a way that it would reduce the possibility that they would be exposed to unfavorable comparative information. Lowering the amount of social comparison and the level at which it occurs would both serve this self-protective function. In this regard, earlier work has demonstrated that selective downward comparisons can boost a damaged or threatened ego; the current results, on the other hand, suggest that certain instrumental steps can be taken that will reduce the likelihood either that damage will occur in the first place or that more damage will occur in the future. In short, whereas downward comparisons are often self-enhancing, downward shifts are self-protective.

Temporal comparisons

There are several reasons why these subjects may have increased their temporal comparison. First, as suggested earlier, thinking about one's previous performance may prove helpful, either in assessing one's progress over time (cf. Baumeister et al., 1989) or in recalling previous behaviors that may have been more performance effective. Second, it is also possible that these students may have shown some internal "selective focus" (Taylor, Wood, & Lichtman, 1983) by choosing times in their past when they were having even more difficulty, thereby making their current performance look better (Affleck & Tennen, 1991). For most of these students, however, we can assume that past performance, relative to others, was probably superior to current, which makes this hypothesis somewhat less likely. Yet a third possibility, which seems more likely than the selective focus explanation, is that the LP students were trying to reassure themselves by reminiscing about times when they had done well, a form of "basking in retrospective glory." Future longitudinal research may determine what these temporal comparisons tend to focus on and, therefore, what their goal actually is.

Diagnosticity

By the same token, there is clearly some diagnostic value associated with at least one of these comparison strategies. For those who have done relatively poorly, continued comparison at a high level would not only be painful (Brickman & Bulman, 1977), it also would not be very informative (Trope, 1983). In this sense, comparison at a level that is lower, and therefore closer to one's own performance, serves a diagnostic function by providing information that is more useful from a self-evaluation perspective. The same may also be true for temporal comparison. That is, one's own previous performance may provide information that is useful in terms of assessing current performance. We believe, however, that the general pattern across all of the strategies is more consistent with a self-protective than a diagnostic motive. In particular, reducing the amount of comparison in which one engages is not likely to prove of much diagnostic value. Similarly, reducing the importance of academic performance, especially when it occurs among students who have just entered college or a program for academic enhancement, is probably more protective than informative. Of course, determining which motive is primary is not possible with these data. Once again, an experimental study, in this case one that looked at the impact of perceived performance on change in preference for social comparison information that was clearly diagnostic but also threatening, might help tease apart these motives.

Education Implications

Although the drop in academic importance was anticipated, the magnitude of the decline and the lack of a rebound in perceived importance at T3 by the gifted LP boys in Study 1 was surprising. It is somewhat ironic that these young people responded to their new, more intense and certainly richer, academic environments by lowering their perceived importance of academic performance. It should be

kept in mind, however, that it was perceptions of academic performance and not academics per se that declined in value. And even that lower value was still quite high for the LP subjects in both studies (LP $Ms = 9.4$ and 11.0 on the 13-point scales). Perhaps a decline or de-emphasis is appropriate in highly competitive environments such as these (cf. Richardson & Benbow, 1990). That is especially true given that there is some evidence that the decline may be accompanied by an increase in perceived importance of other dimensions (e.g., social behavior), suggesting that a compensation process may be occurring (cf. Wood, 1989).

More generally, there is no evidence that the comparison strategies adopted by students in either sample in any way adversely affected their performance. Perhaps the primary concern, however, is what impact the program experience and comparison strategies had on the gifted students' perceptions in the long-term. In this respect, the data from the T3 follow-up are encouraging. To begin with, the decline in comparison amount and type reported by the LP boys at T2 was no longer evident at T3. In addition, the academic comparison levels of the LP boys at T3 appeared to have returned to their presession levels. Presumably, this degree of flexibility in comparison behavior can facilitate learning by providing comparative information that is useful but not so threatening as to discourage competition and effort. The LP boys' experiences in the summer session apparently did alter their impressions of how important academic performance was, as they lowered their ratings to a level that was still well above the midpoint of the scale, but below where they were before the start of the session. For the gifted sample at least, this level may actually have been more appropriate. On the other hand, the impact that this decline might have on college students' academic motivation is an empirical question worthy of further investigation.

Finally, the general and academic self-concepts of the LP boys did decline at T2. That decline is typical for this type of program, however. As would be expected, this initial experience with less than superior performance can be difficult for these high achievers (Coleman & Fults, 1985; Richardson &

Benbow, 1990). We suspect that those self-concepts would have declined even more were it not for the changes in social comparison they initiated. In fact, analysis of change in self-concept among the gifted adolescents did indicate significantly greater decline among LP boys who did not engage in the comparison strategy (relative to those who did). Perhaps most encouraging is the fact that their self-concepts returned to a very high level by T3.

Conclusion

In sum, the self-protective strategies and relative "failure experience" at the summer session had no apparent lasting harmful impact on the gifted students. Presumably, the more favorable comparisons they engaged in when back in their regular classrooms served to offset the more negative comparisons they had experienced in the session. In the process, their social comparison behavior and self-concepts returned to their more typical levels. Among the college students, comparison activity and preferences were shifted downward to a degree that was more appropriate given the higher level of competition they were facing in their new schools. Once again, this shift appears to be self-diagnostic as well as self-protective. Finally, the comparability of results across the two studies suggests that these comparison strategies are not related to level of intelligence or (initial) level of comparison. Rather, they are a common and functional reaction to a changing environment.

REFERENCES

Affleck, G., & Tennen, H. (1991). Social comparison and coping with major medical problems. In J. Suls & T. A. Wills (Eds.), *Social comparison: Contemporary theory and research* (pp. 369–393). Hillsdale, NJ: Erlbaum.

Ahlgren, A. (1983). Sex differences in the correlates of cooperative and competitive school attitudes. *Developmental Psychology, 19*, 881–888.

Baumeister, R., & Jones, E. (1978). When self-presentation is constrained by the target's knowledge: Consistency and compensation. *Journal of Personality and Social Psychology, 36*, 608–618.

Baumeister, R. F., Tice, D. M., & Hutton, D. G. (1989). Self-presentational motivations and personality differences in self-esteem. *Journal of Personality, 57*, 547–577.

Benbow, C. P. (1983). Adolescence of the mathematically precocious: A five-year longitudinal study. In C. P. Benbow & J. C. Stanley (Eds.), *Academic precocity: Aspects of its development* (pp. 9–37). Baltimore: Johns Hopkins University Press.

Brickman, P., & Bulman, R. J. (1977). Pleasure and pain in social comparison. In J. M. Suls & R. L. Miller (Eds.), *Social comparison processes: Theoretical and empirical perspectives* (pp. 149–186). Washington, DC: Hemisphere.

Campbell, J. D., Fairey, P. J., & Fehr, B. (1986). Better than me or better than thee? Reactions to intrapersonal and interpersonal performance feedback. *Journal of Personality, 54*, 479–493.

Chafel, J. A. (1988). Social comparisons by children: An analysis of research on sex differences. *Sex Roles, 18*, 461–487.

Chan, L. K. (1988). The perceived competence of intellectually talented students. *Gifted Child Quarterly, 32*, 310–314.

Coleman, J. M., & Fults, B. A. (1985). Special-class placement, level of intelligence, and the self-concepts of gifted children: A social comparison perspective. *Remedial and Special Education, 6*, 7–12.

Covington, M. (1984). The motive for self-worth. In R. Ames & C. Ames (Eds.), *Research on motivation in education: Student motivation* (Vol. 1, pp. 77–112). San Diego, CA: Academic Press.

Festinger, L. (1954). A theory of social comparison processes. *Human Relations, 7*, 117–140.

Gibbons, F. X. (1986). Social comparison and depression: Company's effect on misery. *Journal of Personality and Social Psychology, 51*, 140–148.

Gibbons, F. X., & Gerrard, M. (1991). Downward comparison and coping with threat. In J. Suls & T. A. Wills (Eds.), *Social comparison: Contemporary theory and research* (pp. 317–346). Hillsdale, NJ: Erlbaum.

Gibbons, F. X., & Gerrard, M. (1994). *Social comparison over time: The interactive effects of threat and comparison direction.* Manuscript in preparation, Iowa State University.

Gibbons, F. X., Gerrard, M., Lando, H., & McGovern, P. (1991). Smoking cessation and social comparison: The role of the "typical smoker." *Journal of Experimental Social Psychology, 27*, 239–258.

Harter, S. (1986). Processes underlying the construction, maintenance, and enhancement of the self-concept in children. In J. Suls & A. Greenwald (Eds.), *Psychological perspectives on the self* (Vol. 3, pp. 137–181). Hillsdale, NJ: Erlbaum.

Hedges, L. V., & Olkin, I. (1985). *Statistical methods for meta-analysis.* San Diego, CA: Academic Press.

Higgins, R. L., Snyder, C. R., & Berglas, S. (1991). *Self-handicapping: The paradox that isn't.* New York: Plenum Press.

Hoffman, P. J., Festinger, L., & Lawrence, D. H. (1954). Tendencies toward group comparability in competitive bargaining. *Human Relations, 7*, 141–159.

Lazarus, R. S., & Folkman, S. (1984). *Stress, appraisal, and coping.* New York: Springer.

Levine, J. M., & Green, S. M. (1984). Acquisition of relative performance information: The roles of intrapersonal and interpersonal comparison. *Personality and Social Psychology Bulletin, 10,* 385–393.

Marsh, H. W. (1990). *Self-Description Questionnaire—II: Manual and research monograph.* New York: Harcourt Brace Jovanovich.

Mettee, D., & Smith, G. (1977). Social comparison and interpersonal attraction: The case for dissimilarity. In J. Suls & R. Miller (Eds.), *Social comparison processes* (pp. 69–101). New York: Wiley.

Pyzsczynski, T., Greenberg, J., & LaPrelle, J. (1985). Social comparison after success and failure: Biased search for information consistent with a self-serving conclusion. *Journal of Experimental Social Psychology, 21,* 195–211.

Richardson, T. M., & Benbow, C. P. (1990). Long-term effects of acceleration on social and emotional adjustment of mathematically precocious youth. *Journal of Educational Psychology, 82,* 464–470.

Roberts, T. (1991). Gender and the influence of evaluations on self-assessments in achievement settings. *Psychological Bulletin, 109,* 297–308.

Rosenberg, M. (1979). *Conceiving the self.* New York: Basic Books.

Ruble, D. N., & Frey, K. S. (1991). Changing patterns of comparative behavior as skills are acquired: A functional model of self-evaluation. In J. Suls & T. Wills (Eds.), *Social comparison: Contemporary theory and research.* Hillsdale, NJ: Erlbaum.

Schlenker, B., Weigold, M., & Hallam, J. (1990). Self-serving attributions in social context: Effects of self-esteem and social pressure. *Journal of Personality and Social Psychology, 58,* 855–863.

Smith, R. H., & Insko, C. A. (1987). Social comparison choice during ability evaluation: The effects of comparison publicity, performance feedback, and self-esteem. *Personality and Social Psychology Bulletin, 13,* 111–122.

Suls, J., & Miller, R. (1977). *Social comparison processes: Theoretical and empirical perspectives.* Washington, DC: Hemisphere.

Taylor, S. E., & Brown, J. D. (1988). Illusion and well-being: A social-psychological perspective on mental health. *Psychological Bulletin, 103,* 193–210.

Taylor, S. E., Wood, J. V., & Lichtman, N. N. (1983). It could be worse: Selective evaluation as a response to victimization. *Journal of Social Issues, 29,* 19–40.

Tesser, A. (1986). Some effects of self-evaluation maintenance on cognition and action. In R. M. Sorrentino & E. T. Higgins (Eds.), *The handbook of motivation and cognition: Foundations of social behavior* (pp. 435–464). New York: Guilford/Academic Press.

Tesser, A. (1988). Toward a self-evaluation maintenance model of social behavior. In L. Berkowitz (Ed.), *Advances in experimental social psychology* (Vol. 21, pp. 181–227). San Diego, CA: Academic Press.

Tesser, A., & Campbell, J. (1980). Self-definition: The impact of the relative performance and similarity of others. *Social Psychology Quarterly, 43*(3), 341–347.

Tesser, A., & Paulhus, D. (1983). The definition of self: Private and public self-evaluation management strategies. *Journal of Personality and Social Psychology, 44,* 672–682.

Trope, Y. (1983). Self-assessment in achievement behavior. In J. M. Suls & A. G. Greenwald (Eds.), *Psychological perspectives on the self* (Vol. 2, pp. 93–121). Hillsdale, NJ: Erlbaum.

Trope, Y. (1986). Self-enhancement and self-assessment in achievement behavior. In R. M. Sorrentino & E. T. Higgins (Eds), *Handbook of motivation and cognition: Foundations of social behavior* (pp. 350–378). New York: Guilford Press.

Veroff, J. (1969). Social comparison and the development of achievement motivation. In C. P. Smith (Ed.), *Achievement-related motives in children.* New York: Sage.

Wheeler, L., & Miyake, K. (1992). Social comparison in everyday life. *Journal of Personality and Social Psychology, 62,* 760–773.

Wigfield, A., & Karpathian, M. (1991). Who am I and what can I do? Children's self-concepts and motivation in achievement situations. *Educational Psychologist, 26*(3–4), 233–261.

Wills, T. A. (1981). Downward comparison principles in social psychology. *Psychological Bulletin, 90,* 245–271.

Wills, T. A. (1987). Downward comparison as a coping mechanism. In C. R. Snyder & C. Ford (Eds.), *Coping with negative life events: Clinical and social-psychological perspectives* (pp. 243–267). New York: Plenum Press.

Wills, T. A. (1991). Similarity and self-esteem in downward comparison. In J. Suls & T. A. Wills (Eds.), *Social comparison: Contemporary theory and research* (pp. 51–78). Hillsdale, NJ: Erlbaum.

Wilson, S. R., & Benner, L. A. (1971). The effects of self-esteem and situation on comparison choices during ability evaluation. *Sociometry, 34,* 381–397.

Wood, J. V. (1989). Theory and research concerning social comparisons of personal attributes. *Psychological Bulletin, 106,* 231–248.

Wood, J. V., & Taylor, K. L. (1991). Serving self-relevant goals through social comparison. In J. Suls & T. A. Wills (Eds.), *Social comparison: Contemporary theory and research* (pp. 23–50). Hillsdale, NJ: Erlbaum.

Received May 27, 1992
Revision received November 16, 1993
Accepted February 18, 1994 ■

PART 4

Breakdowns in Comparison

Implicit in many of the articles to this point is the view that people seek comparisons because they are functional. Social comparisons can serve to reduce uncertainty about the social world, defend against threats to self-esteem, and assist in efforts to improve. But comparisons do not always "work" as one might like. The articles in this section highlight some of the ways in which social comparisons can go awry. Each of them suggests ways that social comparison tendencies drive people to focus on a limited set of information when a more expansive or inclusive view might be in one's best interest or lead people to make more sound decisions.

The study by Neil Weinstein documents what has since become one of the most widely (and easily) replicated effects in the social comparison literature. Specifically, when people think of themselves in comparative terms, they tend to be unrealistically optimistic about their futures. Weinstein and others have shown that, across a wide range of situations, people on average rate their chances of experiencing positive events as being above average and their chances of experiencing negative events as being below average. Of course it is a statistical impossibility for the average person to differ from the average, and so Weinstein appears to have uncovered an error in how we think about ourselves in relation to others. Weinstein's study also reveals a number of cognitive and motivational factors that lead to this effect, but it is the applied implications of this work that have caused unrealistic optimism to be of great interest to many social psychologists.

Investigators who have followed up on Weinstein's research have expressed concern that the tendency to be unrealistically optimistic might drive people to act in ways that are not in their self-interest. Not only does it appear that unrealistic optimism is a determinant of health-risk behaviors (Gerrard, Gibbons, Reis-Bergan, & Russell, 2000), but even individuals who engage in unusually risky behaviors (e.g., unprotected sex with multiple partners) seem to be able to retain the belief that they are less likely than others to experience the misfortunes that can result from these actions (e.g., pregnancy; see Gerrard, Gibbons, & Warner, 1991). Unfortunately, attempts to reduce unrealistic optimism have met with limited success (Weinstein & Klein, 1995). As Weinstein notes, a range of cognitive and motivational forces drives people to feel unique, and so it is perhaps not surprising that it is hard to shake this belief.

Unrealistic optimism is also of interest to psychologists, because it tells them something about the degree of interest people have in social comparison. Recall that Festinger (1954) thought that objective comparison should dominate social comparisons, in the sense that people should only turn to social standards when more objective standards are not available. But the fact that people cling to inaccurate comparative beliefs in the face of disconfirming evidence suggests that social comparisons at times dominate objective comparisons. This theme is reinforced in the article in this section by Klein. He shows situations in which people attend to social comparison information, even when more useful objective information is made readily available to them. His work suggests, for instance, that people will worry about misfortunes that are unlikely in an absolute sense if they are likely in a relative sense. The bias Klein reveals can be maladaptive, as it might lead people not to prepare for risks that are

likely, or lead them to wager on outcomes that have a low probability of occurring.

Despite the tendency for people to put too much weight on social comparison information when they make judgments, people do not seem particularly skilled at accurately comparing themselves to others. This point was made in the article by Weinstein and it is also underscored in the article by Moore and Kim. These authors argue that people's tendency to focus too much attention on the self during comparisons can cause them to draw faulty inferences about their chances of succeeding in competitive tasks (see Dunning & Hayes, 1996). Moore and Kim show that when competing with others, people fail to consider that their own performances will be affected by the same factors that influence their opponents' performances. Consider as examples two opposing army generals who confidently predict victory because they will meet one another on (the same) easy terrain, or two gamblers who place large bets on different horses because the nice weather favors a fast race. It thus appears that, although people rely heavily on social comparisons when they make decisions, these perceptions are systematically distorted in ways that can result in suboptimal decision making.

A clear example of suboptimal decision making can be found in the article by Schroeder and Prentice. Their study considered the negative health consequences of a very simple fact: It is easier to see what a person does than what a person thinks. This basic truth is one reason why people often draw faulty inferences about their hidden internal states from comparing observable behaviors. Schroeder and Prentice illustrate this point in an analysis of the determinants of high alcohol consumption rates at

American colleges and universities. They note that there often are quite liberal norms at college campuses that encourage unhealthy drinking. At the same time, however, many college students report private misgivings about conforming to excessive drinking norms. Because it is easier for students to observe their classmates' heavy drinking behaviors than it is for them to observe their classmates' private misgivings, students at times conclude that they are alone in their concerns about alcohol. The result is that they decide to conform to the behavioral norms, lest they be viewed negatively by other students.

Shroeder and Prentice thus argue that *pluralistic ignorance* leads college students to drink more than they would like to drink. Pluralistic ignorance occurs when individuals incorrectly attribute unique (internal) causes for their own (observable) actions. Fortunately for the health of college students, however, Schroeder and Prentice find that this type of error is easier to eliminate than the type of error that Weinstein studied. Because pluralistic ignorance occurs when people fail to compare their opinions with those of others, these researchers were able to reduce pluralistic ignorance (and bring down heavy drinking rates at an American university) by simply having students discuss the private reservations they had about heavy drinking.

To summarize, and as these four articles clearly demonstrate, there are many ways in which our social comparisons can break down, but this does not mean that social comparison tendencies are broken. Many of the shortcomings we highlight in this section can and will be adaptive in other social contexts, and this is perhaps why people exhibit the types of errors and biases to the extent that they

do: They have been rewarded for them in the past. Consider Klein's discovery that people pay attention to social comparison information when they should not. It seems reasonable that people have this bias in part because, across a wide range of situations, it is adaptive to be focused more on relative standing than absolute standing. Klein simply studied a situation in which it was not adaptive.

In this regard, we are reminded of a joke that we have modified slightly for our purposes here. In our version of the joke, a social comparison researcher and his friend encounter a grizzly bear while walking through the woods. The social comparison researcher sees the bear and immediately leans down to tie his running shoes, so that he will not trip as he flees. His friend observes the comparison researcher for doing this and chides him for bothering to run. "Why try to get away?" he asks. "We're as good as dead, because no man can outrun a grizzly bear." The social comparison researcher ignores this advice and begins running as fast as he can. As he leaps across a boulder in his path, the social comparison researcher turns back and yells to his friend. He yells that he's not trying to outrun the bear—he is trying to outrun his friend.

If the social comparison literature at times highlights the shortcomings in how people compare with others, it is important to remember that these same "maladaptive" tendencies may have saved any number of our ancestors from any number of bears.

REFERENCES

(Asterisks indicate Key Readings in this section.)

Dunning, D., & Hayes, A. F. (1996). Evidence for egocentric comparison in social judgment. *Journal of Personality and Social Psychology, 71*(2), 213–229.

Festinger, L. (1954). A theory of social comparison processes. *Human Relations*, *7*, 117–140.

Gerrard, M., Gibbons, F. X., Reis-Bergan, M., & Russell, D. W. (2000). Self-esteem, self-serving cognitions, and health risk behavior. *Journal of Personality*, *68*(6), 1177–1201.

Gerrard, M., Gibbons, F. X., & Warner, T. D. (1991). Effects of reviewing risk-relevant behavior on perceived vulnerability among women marines, *Health Psychology*, *10*(3), 173–179.

* Klein, W. M. (1997). Objective standards are not enough: Affective, self-evaluative, and behavioral responses to social comparison information. *Journal of Personality and Social Psychology*, *72*(4), 763–774.

* Moore, D., & Kim, T. (2003). Myopic social prediction and the solo comparison effect. *Journal of Personality and Social Psychology*, *85*, 1121–1135.

* Schroeder, C. M., & Prentice, D. A. (1998). Exposing pluralistic ignorance to reduce alcohol use among college students. *Journal of Applied Social Psychology*, *28*, 2150–2180.

* Weinstein, N. D. (1980). Unrealistic optimism about future life events. *Journal of Personality and Social Psychology*, *39*, 806–820.

Weinstein, N. D., & Klein, W. M. (1995). Resistance of personal risk perceptions to debiasing interventions. *Health Psychology*, *14*(2), 132–140.

Discussion Questions

1. Discuss the relation between unrealistic optimism and rationality. Can the two live together?
2. If people are such bad predictors at social comparison (as some of these readings suggest), how is it that people rely on it so much?
3. It might seem that this tendency would get people in trouble more often than not. If you do not agree with this statement, what are some of the traps that cause people to draw maladaptive inferences from social comparisons?
4. Of the "mistakes" that people appear to make, which do you believe would be amenable to interventions to reduce their occurrence?
5. What shape would these interventions take and which groups would be most affected by them?

Suggested Readings

Dawes, R. M. (1998). Statistical criteria for a truly false consensus effect. *Journal of Experimental Social Psychology*, *25*, 1–17.

Dunning, D., & Hayes, A. F. (1996). Evidence for egocentric comparison in social judgment. *Journal of Personality and Social Psychology*, *71*, 213–229.

Gerrard, M., & Warner, T. D. (1991). Comparison of Marine and college women's HIV/AIDS-relevant sexual behaviors. *Journal of Applied Social Psychology*, *24*, 959–980.

Kruger, J. (1999). Lake Wobegon be gone! The "below-average effect" and the egocentric nature of comparative ability judgments. *Journal of Personality and Social Psychology*, *77*, 221–232.

Miller, D. T., & McFarland, C. (1991). When social comparison goes awry: The case of pluralistic ignorance. In J. Suls & T. A. Wills (Eds.), *Social comparison: Contemporary theory and research* (pp. 287–313). Hillsdale, NJ: Lawrence Erlbaum Associates Inc.

Unrealistic Optimism About Future Life Events

Neil D. Weinstein

Two studies investigated the tendency of people to be unrealistically optimistic about future life events. In Study 1, 258 college students estimated how much their own chances of experiencing 42 events differed from the chances of their classmates. Overall, they rated their own chances to be above average for positive events and below average for negative events, $ps < .001$. Cognitive and motivational considerations led to predictions that degree of desirability, perceived probability, personal experience, perceived controllability, and stereotype salience would influence the amount of optimistic bias evoked by different events. All predictions were supported, although the pattern of effects differed for positive and negative events. Study 2 tested the idea that people are unrealistically optimistic because they focus on factors that improve their own chances of achieving desirable outcomes and fail to realize that others may have just as many factors in their favor. Students listed the factors that they thought influenced their own chances of experiencing eight future events. When such lists were read by a second group of students, the amount of unrealistic optimism shown by this second group for the same eight events decreased significantly, although it was not eliminated.

According to popular belief, people tend to think they are invulnerable. They expect others to be victims of misfortune, not themselves. Such ideas imply not merely a hopeful outlook on life, but an error in judgment that can be labeled *unrealistic optimism.*

It is usually impossible to demonstrate that an individual's optimistic expectations about the future are unrealistic. An individual might be quite correct in asserting that his or her chances of experiencing a negative event are less than average. On a group basis, however, it is relatively easy to test for an

The author is indebted to Dorothy Schmidt for her valuable assistance in conducting this research and to Claudia Cohen, David Wilder, Carol Weinstein, Ilene Gochman, and Richard Ashmore for helpful suggestions during the preparation of this manuscript.

Requests for reprints should be sent to Neil D. Weinstein, Department of Human Ecology and Social Sciences, Cook College, Rutgers—The State University, P.O. Box 231, New Brunswick, New Jersey 08903.

optimistic bias. If all people claim their changes of experiencing a negative event are less than average, they are clearly making a systematic error, thus demonstrating unrealistic optimism.

Various data suggest that people do tend to be unrealistically optimistic about the future. Surveys concerning automobile accidents (Robertson, 1977), crime (Weinstein, Note 1), and disease (Harris & Guten, 1979; Kirscht, Haefner, Kegeles, & Rosenstock, 1966; American Cancer Society, Note 2) find many people who say their risk is less than average but few who say their risk is greater than average. When people are asked to predict the outcomes of social and political issues, their predictions tend to coincide with their preferences (Cantril, 1938; Lund, 1925; McGregor, 1938; McGuire, 1960). Even for purely chance events (picking a card out of a deck, for example), people sometimes show optimistic biases (Irwin, 1953; Langer & Roth, 1975; Marks, 1951). None of these studies, however, has examined a range of positive and negative events to determine the extent of optimistic biases and the conditions under which they occur.

The principal goal of the present research was to test the following hypothesis:

1. People believe that negative events are less likely to happen to them than to others, and they believe that positive events are more likely to happen to them than to others.

In addition, the two studies described here tested several specific hypotheses about the factors that influence the amount of optimistic bias evoked by different events and about the mechanisms that produce this bias.

Event Characteristics Affecting Unrealistic Optimism

In past research, optimistic biases were generally regarded as evidence of defensiveness or wishful thinking. People were said to exaggerate the likelihood of events the anticipation of which produces positive affect and underestimate the likelihood of events the anticipation of which produces negative affect. Presumably, the stronger the affect, the

stronger the distortion of reality. This motivational analysis of expectations about future life events suggests the second hypothesis:

2. Among negative events, the more undesirable the event, the stronger the tendency to believe that one's own chances are less than average; among positive events, the more desirable the event, the stronger the tendency to believe that one's own chances are greater than average.

Supporting this degree of desirability/undesirability prediction, Kirscht *et al.* (1966) reported that judgments of disease susceptibility were correlated with perceptions of disease severity. The people who regarded a disease as very serious were the ones most likely to believe that their own chances were less than average. No data or significance levels were given, however.

In recent years, explanations that emphasize flaws in the information handling capabilities of human beings have been advanced for phenomena once explained in motivational terms (e.g., Miller & Ross, 1975; Ross, Greene, & House, 1977; Slovic, Kunreuther, & White, 1974). According to this perspective, people may be unrealistically optimistic because they lack certain information needed to make accurate risk assessments or use procedures to judge future probabilities that introduce systematic errors.

In making comparative risk assessments, errors may arise because people have difficulty in adopting the perspective of others (cf. Jones & Nisbett, 1971; Ross *et al.*, 1977; Ross & Sicoly, 1979). Many of the factors that make us feel that an event is likely or unlikely to happen to us may also make other people feel that it is likely or unlikely to happen to them. If people focus only on their own circumstances, they may conclude incorrectly that their chances differ from those of other people. Through this mechanism, any factor that influences people's beliefs about their own chances could influence comparative judgments. One factor that will affect these beliefs is the perceived probability of the event for the general population. The preceding reasoning then suggests the hypothesis:

3. The greater the perceived probability of an event, the stronger the tendency for people to believe that their own chances are greater than average.

Another factor that should influence people's beliefs about their chances of experiencing an event is past personal experience (Lichtenstein, Slovic, Fischhoff, Layman, & Combs, 1978; Hoffman & Brewer, Note 3). Personal experience should make it easier to recall past occurrences of the event and to imagine situations in which the event could occur, leading to greater perceived probability through the mechanism of "availability" (Tversky & Kahneman, 1973, 1974). Furthermore, for many events causal sequences can be constructed which imply that past experience increases the probability of future experience. Someone who has had a heart attack or has close relatives with heart disease is more likely to have a heart attack in the future than someone who has had no contact with heart ailments. Consequently, we predict:

4. *Previous personal experience with an event increases the likelihood that people will believe their own chances are greater than average.*

Hypotheses 3 and 4 concern two event characteristics that may lead people to make systematic errors when comparing their own chances with those of other people, but they do not explain the phenomenon of unrealistic optimism. The direction of the errors produced by these characteristics depends on the probability of the event and the frequency of personal experience, not on the type of event. To explain why people would say that their chances are greater than average for positive events but less than average for negative events by using these hypotheses would require that positive events always be associated with high probability or high personal experience and that negative events always be associated with low probability or low personal experience.

There is a way, however, in which egocentric tendencies can produce an optimistic bias for both positive and negative events. If an event is perceived to be controllable, it signifies that people believe there are steps one can take to increase the likelihood of a desirable outcome. Because they can more easily bring to mind their own actions than the actions of others, people are likely to conclude

that desired outcomes are more likely to happen to them than to other people. Even for events that are far in the future and have not yet been associated with any overt behavior, people may still be aware of their intentions to act in ways that will help them achieve the desired outcomes.

The preceding argument assumes that people generally bring to mind actions that facilitate rather than impede goal achievement. They might do this because facilitating actions really are more plentiful, because they find reassurance in selectively recalling facilitating actions or in exaggerating their importance (a motivational explanation), or because actions taken to produce desired outcomes are, for various reasons, actually easier to remember (a cognitive viewpoint).

Since the process just outlined would not apply to uncontrollable events, we are led to the prediction:

5. *The greater the perceived controllability of a negative event, the greater the tendency for people to believe that their own chances are less than average; the greater the perceived controllability of a positive event, the greater the tendency for people to believe that their own chances are greater than average.*

The final event characteristic to be examined was suggested by the "representativeness" heuristic (Kahneman & Tversky, 1972; Tversky & Kahneman, 1977). Representativeness denotes the process of judging the probability that an individual fits into a particular category by examining the degree to which the individual displays a few salient features of category members but ignoring base rates for the categories. For many events—contracting lung cancer and becoming an alcoholic, for example—people may have a stereotyped conception of the kind of person to whom this event happens. If they do not see themselves as fitting the stereotype, the representativeness heuristic suggests that people will conclude that the event will not happen to them, overlooking the possibility that few of the people who experience the event may actually fit the stereotype.

If stereotypes of the victim tend to serve an ego-defensive function, people would seldom see themselves as representing the type of person who falls prey to misfortune. Furthermore, if stereotypes are defensive, an individual's image of the people who experience positive events would overemphasize his or her own characteristics. These tendencies would exaggerate optimistic biases for any event associated with a stereotype.

A different line of reasoning does not assume any motivational bias in the construction or use of stereotypes. It suggests that people may be struck by the superficial differences between themselves and the stereotype (differences such as sex, age, or appearance) and fail to see more fundamental similarities between themselves and the people to whom the event occurs. This would lead people to conclude that the event will not happen to them, producing optimism for negative events but pessimism for positive events.

The final hypothesis states:

6. *When a stereotype exists of a particular type of person to whom a negative event is likely to happen, people will tend to believe that their own chances are less than average.* (No clear prediction can be made from the preceding discussion about the effects of stereotype salience on expectations for positive events.)

The preceding hypotheses can each be reached by several lines of reasoning, often involving both motivational and cognitive considerations. Personal experience, for example, might decrease optimism about negative events by making images of the events more available or by undercutting defensive denial. Consequently, these hypotheses are not offered as a test of motivational versus cognitive points of view or as an examination of the importance of availability and representativeness in generating unrealistic optimism.

Study 1 was designed to test the hypotheses themselves. Its goal was to determine the amount of unrealistic optimism associated with different events and to relate this optimism to the characteristics of the events.

Study 1

In this study college students estimated how much their own chances of experiencing future life events differed from the average chances of their classmates. If all students claimed that their chances of experiencing a negative event were less than average (or that their chances of experiencing a positive event were greater than average), this would clearly indicate unrealistic optimism. However, a simple comparison of the numbers of optimistic and pessimistic responses is not sufficient to demonstrate a systematic bias. Unless the median and the mean of the actual probability distribution happen to coincide, there is no reason why the number of people whose chances are below the average (below the mean) should equal the number whose chances are above the average. If the probability distribution is positively skewed, for example, most people's chances will be below the average.

To determine the presence of a systematic bias we have to consider the degree of optimism or pessimism expressed. The comparative judgments students were asked to make in the present studies concern the difference between their own individual chances and the population average. (The population, as defined here, included all the other students at the same college.) Mathematically, this difference is $(P_i - \bar{P})$, where P_i is the probability that the event will happen to a particular individual and $\bar{P}$ is the population mean of P_i[1]. Because $\bar{P}$, is defined as the average of P_i over the population, the mean value of this difference score ought to be zero. In other words, if the judgments students generate are unbiased and the students form a representative sample of the population, the mean value of their comparative judgments should be zero. If the mean of their judgments is significantly different from zero, it indicates that their judgments have a systematic bias. Whenever the mean value of students' comparative judgments departs significantly from zero in an optimistic direction, this will be interpreted as unrealistic optimism, and the size of the mean will be taken as a measure of the magnitude of the optimistic bias.

---

[1] Actually subjects expressed this difference as a percentage of the average chances—$100 \times (P_i - \bar{P})/\bar{P}$. Estimating the percentage difference is easier and more natural for students and does not alter the interpretation of their responses.

Method

Subjects

One group of students made comparative judgments about the likelihood that specific events would take place in their lives (comparative rating group). These subjects were enrolled in two interdisciplinary courses at Cook College, Rutgers University, that attract an extremely diverse group of students.

Event characteristics were rated by a group of 120 female students (event rating group) from an introductory psychology course at the same university These students also served as the subjects in Study 2.

Materials

Events. The 18 positive and 24 negative life events used in the study are listed in Table 11.1. The intention was to assemble a diverse group of events that satisfied two criteria. First, each event had to be clearly positive or negative. Second, there could be no obvious precondition that would make any event relevant to only a limited number of people. For example, the event "being injured while skiing" would be inappropriate because it only applies to people who choose to ski.

Comparative rating forms. The 42 events were divided randomly between two rating forms. Positive and negative events were intermixed. Instructions on the forms stated *"Compared to other Cook students*—same sex as you—what do you think are the chances that the following events will happen to you? The choices range from much less than average, through average, to much more than average"* (italics in original). Beneath the description of each event were the following choices: "100% less (no chance), 80% less, 60% less, 40% less, 20% less, 10% less, average, 10% more, 20% more, 40% more, 60% more, 80% more, 100% more, 3 times average, and 5 times average." The lowest choice possible was 100% less than average, since this indicated a probability of zero. At the other extreme, no probability could exceed 100%, but this upper limit could be many times the average probability. The task of comparing one's

own chances with the average chances of other students was readily accepted by students and carried out without any apparent confusion.

To calculate the mean comparative judgment, the 15 response choices were given the values -100%, -80%, -60%, -40%, -20%, -10%, 0%, 10%, 20%, 40%, 60%, 80%, 100%, 200%, and 400% to reflect their deviation from a response of "average."

Event ratings. For the rating of event characteristics, events were divided into the same sets as on the comparative rating forms. Written instructions asked subjects to evaluate first the *probability* of each event. Students were required to estimate the percentage of students at the university to whom the event would occur. Several examples were presented to illustrate the relationship between percentage ratings and odds ratios. Next, events were rated for *controllability* (1 = there is nothing one can do that will change the likelihood that the event will take place; 2 = things one can do have a small effect on the chances that the event will occur; 3 = things one can do have a moderate effect; 4 = things one can do have a large effect; 5 = completely controllable) and *desirability* (1 = extremely undesirable; 3 = undesirable; 5 = neutral; 7 = desirable; 9 = extremely desirable). Finally, events were rated for *personal experience* (1 = has not happened to anyone I know; 2 = has happened to acquaintances; 3 = has happened to friends or close relatives; 4 = has happened to me once; 5 = has happened to me more than once) and *salience of a high chance group* (1 = no type of person with a particularly high chance comes to mind; 2 = when I think about the event a type of person comes to mind to whom it is likely to happen, but this image is not very clear; 3 = when I think about the event a clear picture comes to mind of a particular type of person to whom it is likely to happen).

Procedure

The experimenter visited the classes selected for the comparative rating measure and explained that the project concerned college students' expectations about the future. Task instructions emphasized

TABLE 11.1. Unrealistic Optimism for Future Life Events

Abbreviated event description	Measures of optimism	
	Mean comparative judgment of own chances vs. others' chances (%)[a,b]	No. of optimistic responses divided by no. of pessimistic responses[b,c]
Positive events		
1. Like postgraduation job	50.2***	5.93***
2. Owning your own home	44.3***	6.22***
3. Starting salary > $10,000	41.5***	4.17***
4. Traveling to Europe	35.3***	2.25***
5. Starting salary > $15,000	21.2**	1.56*
6. Good job offer before graduation	15.3**	1.42
7. Graduating in top third of class	14.2	1.02
8. Home doubles in value in 5 years	13.3*	1.78*
9. Your work recognized with award	12.6*	1.72*
10. Living past 80	12.5**	2.00**
11. Your achievements in newspaper	11.3	1.66*
12. No night in hospital for 5 years	8.5	1.23
13. Having a mentally gifted child	6.2*	2.26**
14. Statewide recognition in your profession	2.1	1.00
15. Weight constant for 10 years	2.0	.82
16. In 10 years, earning > $40,000 a year	−.7	.64*
17. Not ill all winter	−.7	.89
18. Marrying someone wealthy	− 9.l	.36*
Negative events		
19. Having a drinking problem	−58.3***	7.23***
20. Attempting suicide	−55.9***	8.56***
21. Divorced a few years after married	−48.7***	9.50***
22. Heart attack before age 40	−38.4***	5.11***
23. Contracting venereal disease	−37.4***	7.56***
24. Being fired from a job	−31.6***	7.56***
25. Getting lung cancer	−31.5***	4.58***
26. Being sterile	−31.2***	5.94***
27. Dropping out of college	−30.8***	3.49***
28. Having a heart attack	−23.3***	3.18***
29. Not finding a job for 6 months	−14.4***	2.36***
30. Decayed tooth extracted	−12.8	2.22***
31. Having gum problems	−12.4**	1.39
32. Having to take unattractive job	−11.6	1.84**
33. Car turns out to be a lemon	−10.0*	2.12**
34. Deciding you chose wrong career	−8.8	1.43
35. Tripping and breaking bone	−8.3*	1.66*
36. Being sued by someone	−7.9	2.38***
37. Having your car stolen	−7.3	2.94***
38. Victim of mugging	−5.8	3.17***
39. Developing cancer	−4.4	1.28
40. In bed ill two or more days	−3.2	1.75*
41. Victim of burglary	2.8	1.21
42. Injured in auto accident	12.9*	.80

[a] In making a comparative judgment, students estimated the difference in percent between the chances that an event would happen to them and the average chances for other same-sex students at their college. $N = 123$ to 130, depending on rating form and missing data. Student's t was used to test whether the mean is significantly different from zero.

[b] For positive events, the response that one's own chances are greater than average is considered optimistic, and the response that one's own chances are less than average is considered pessimistic. For negative events, the definitions of optimistic and pessimistic responses are reversed.

[c] Significance levels refer to a chi-square test of the hypothesis that frequencies of optimistic and pessimistic responses are equal.

* $p < .05$. ** $p < .01$. *** $p < .001$.

that subjects should compare themselves with other students and not merely rate each event in terms of how likely or unlikely it seemed. The different versions of the comparative rating form, each listing 21 events, were handed to alternate students.

The ratings of the event characteristics were completed separately by members of the event rating group after their participation in Study 2.

Results

The ratings of event characteristics showed that a clear differentiation between positive and negative events was achieved. The least undesirable of all the negative events was still perceived to be relatively undesirable ($M = 3.92$), and the least desirable of all the positive events was still perceived to be relatively desirable ($M = 6.37$). Both values are significantly different from the neutral rating of 5 ($ps < .001$).[2]

Unrealistic optimism: Hypothesis 1

Both positive and negative events in Table 11.1 are arranged in order of decreasing optimism as indicated by the mean comparative judgment. A positive value in Column 1 indicates that subjects tend to believe that their own chances are greater than average; a negative value indicates that students believe their chances are less than average. These values strongly support Hypothesis 1; the means in Column 1 are in the predicted direction for 37 of the 42 events ($p < .001$ by the binomial test). Averaged over all positive events, the comparative judgments of individuals were significantly greater than zero, $M = 15.4\%, t(255) = 6.8, p < .001$; averaged over negative events, individuals' judgments were significantly less than zero, $M = -20.4\%, t(255) = 13.9, p < .001$.

Column 2 shows the ratio of the number of optimistic to pessimistic responses. Although the significance levels derived from the statistics in Columns 1 and 2 differ for a few events, the existence of strong optimistic tendencies is clear in both. The correlation between the ratio in Column 2 and the values in Column 1 was .90 for both positive and negative events.[3]

An additional calculation tested whether differences in comparative judgments for positive and negative events might have been caused by unintended differences in the perceived probability, personal experience, perceived controllability, or stereotype salience of the two types of events. To control for the possible effects of such differences, the partial correlation was calculated between the mean comparative judgments (Column 1) and event type (a dummy variable differentiating between positive and negative events; -1 = negative event; 1 = positive event) controlling for these four other variables. The significant result ($r = .74, p < .001$) demonstrates that event type has a powerful effect independent of the effects of the other event characteristics.

Event characteristics influencing unrealistic optimism: Hypotheses 2–6

It is clear from Table 11.1 that the amount of unrealistic optimism evoked by different events varied greatly. In many cases the mean comparative judgment was not significantly different from zero, indicating the absence of a significant optimistic bias. Hypotheses 2 through 6 attempt to explain these variations. They were each tested separately by means of a linear model that included the terms event type (positive or negative), event characteristic (the mean rating for the characteristic cited in the

---

[2] All statistical tests reported in this article are two-tailed.
[3] The possibility that artifacts might have been introduced by the use of a response scale with unequal intervals was tested by ignoring the response labels and simply treating the choices as a 15-point, equal-interval scale. The insensitivity of the results to such changes is indicated by the correlation of .98 between event means from this new scale and the mean values from Column 1. In addition, a pilot study examined a simple scale

labeled: "1—below average, 2—slightly below average, 3—average, 4—slightly above average, and 5—above average." This scale was completed by 98 members of an introductory psychology class for 15 of the events included in the present study. A correlation of .91 was found between the mean rating of the events on this 5-point scale and the values in the first column of Table 11.1.

hypothesis; median probability ratings were used because of the large variability of these estimates), and Type × Characteristic interaction. (Hypothesis 6 makes a specific prediction only for negative events and was tested by a separate correlation coefficient for each type of event.)[4]

The event characteristic term in the models tests whether the pooled within-type regression coefficient for that characteristic is significantly different from zero. The Type × Characteristic interaction tests whether the regression lines for positive and negative events have the same slope.[5] The data for these analyses consisted of the mean comparative judgments for the 42 events, the mean characteristic ratings, and the type designations. Consequently, significance tests refer to the null hypothesis that the effects are zero in the larger population of events from which the present sample was drawn.[6]

The significance levels for the event characteristic terms and the magnitudes of the corresponding pooled within-type correlation coefficients are shown in the first column of Table 11.2. Separate correlations for positive and negative events are presented in Columns 2 and 3. The figures show that all of the correlations predicted by Hypotheses 2–6 were in the predicted direction and that all of the event

characteristic terms were statistically significant. Columns 2 and 3, however, reveal different patterns of associations for positive and negative events. (Differences in the sizes of the positive event and negative event correlation coefficients were statistically significant only for perceived probability, $p < .06$, and stereotype salience, $p < .05$.) For positive events, perceived probability and degree of desirability were significantly correlated with the amount of optimistic bias; for negative events, the correlations with stereotype salience, perceived controllability, and personal experience were significant.

Multiple regression analyses

Further calculations revealed significant correlations between two pairs of event characteristics: between stereotype salience and perceived controllability, .69 and .78 for positive and negative events, respectively, and between perceived probability and personal experience, .53 and .57 for positive and negative events, respectively (cf. Lichtenstein et al., 1978). Since these event characteristics are interrelated, the significant correlations in Table 11.2 do not necessarily identify independent

---

[4] The dependent variable in the models that tested the contributions of degree of desirability, perceived probability, and personal experience was the mean comparative judgment from Column 1 of Table 11.1. Hypothesis 5, however, was phrased differently, predicting a positive association between perceived controllability and optimism. Therefore, the dependent variable in the test of this hypothesis was the degree of optimism produced. For positive events, the mean comparative judgment indicates the size of the optimistic bias, but for negative events, the measure of optimistic bias was obtained by reversing the sign of the mean comparative judgment.

[5] If the analysis found no appreciable Type × Characteristic interaction ($p < .2$), the event characteristic effect was estimated after first removing the event type sum of squares from the total sum of squares. If a Type × Characteristic effect did appear to be present ($p < .2$), both event type and Type × Characteristic sums of squares were removed before estimating the event characteristic effect. The latter procedure was needed only for degree of desirability, interaction $F(1, 38) = 1.91$, $p = .18$, and perceived controllability, interaction $F(1, 38) = 3.23$, $p < .08$.

[6] Because the data were analyzed on an event basis, with variables averaged over all subjects, it was not necessary for the

same individuals to rate both the event characteristics and their own chances of experiencing the events. What was necessary was that the perceptions of the event characteristics and the amount of personal experience with these events be essentially the same for the comparative rating group and the event rating group. In addition to the fact that all subjects were students at the same university, there are several specific indications that this condition was satisfied. In a pilot study, a mixed-sex group of students from another of the special interdisciplinary courses from which subjects in Study 1 were drawn rated 21 of the events in Table 11.1 on three of the dimensions used here. Correlations between the pilot ratings and those utilized in Study 1 were: controllability, .78; desirability, .98; and probability, .50 (.54 among positive events and .80 among negative events). Thus, ratings seem unlikely to change greatly from one group to another, although probability ratings do seem to be somewhat variable. It was also found that the relationships between event characteristics (rated by females) and comparative judgments were the same when the judgments of male and female members of the comparative rating group were examined separately. Apparently the event characteristic ratings were equally relevant to males and females.

TABLE 11.2. Correlations Between Mean Comparative Judgments[a] and Mean Ratings of Event Characteristics[b]

Event characteristic and hypothesis number	All events ($n = 42$)[c]	Positive events ($n = 18$)	Negative events ($n = 24$)
Degree of desirability (2)	.30*	.45*	.14
Perceived probability (3)	.49**	.74***	.29
Personal experience (4)	.39*	.35	.42*
Perceived controllability (5)	.52***[d]	.32	−.67***
Stereotype salience (6)	—[e]	.26	−.76***

[a] Means over subjects in comparative rating group.
[b] Mean over subjects in event rating group. (The median estimate was used for perceived probability.)
[c] Pooled within-type correlation coefficient, with positive and negative events as separate types. Significance levels refer to the magnitude of the corresponding pooled within-type regression coefficient, the parameter directly tested by the statistical analysis.
[d] Correlation between event characteristic and optimism. For positive events, own chances greater than others' implies optimism. For negative events, own chances less than others' implies optimism.
[e] For Hypothesis 6, positive and negative events were examined separately.
* $p < .06$. ** $p < .01$. *** $p < .001$.

predictors or unrealistic optimism. To examine this issue further, multiple regression analyses were carried out for positive and negative events to predict the size of the optimistic bias from event characteristics. Since the number of degrees of freedom in these calculations was quite small, however, the statistical power was necessarily low, and conclusions reached from these multivariate analyses must remain tentative.

In a stepwise regression for positive events, perceived probability ($p < .001$) and degree of desirability ($p < .1$) entered the prediction equation, $R = .79$, $F(2,15) = 12.55$, $p < .001$. With all five variables entered, however, only the contribution of perceived probability was still statistically significant ($p < .02$). For negative events, stereotype salience ($p < .001$) and personal experience ($p < .02$) entered the stepwise prediction equation, $R = .82$, $F(2, 21) = 22.74$, $p < .001$. With all five variables, only stereotype salience was still significant ($p < .005$). The failure of perceived controllability to appear in the negative event equation was clearly due to its very high correlation with stereotype salience.

Discussion

The present data provide evidence of unrealistic optimism for both positive and negative life events. As expected, the magnitude of this optimistic bias varied from event to event, but most of the variability could be explained by reference to a few dimensions on which the events differed.

Although all six hypotheses posed in the introduction were supported, different factors appeared to govern responses to positive and negative events. For negative events, optimism, perceived controllability, and stereotype salience were all strongly intercorrelated. When an event was judged to be controllable, a stereotype existed in subjects' minds of the kind of person to whom the event generally occurred. Presumably, this person was believed to be at risk because he or she failed to take any action to control the risk. Subjects seemed to compare themselves with the stereotypic victim, leading them to conclude that their own risks were less than average. For events perceived to be uncontrollable, there was no stereotype of the victim, and subjects did not show any systematic bias.

In retrospect, some of the different correlations for positive events are not surprising. It seems likely that everyone would want to avoid the negative events in this study; yet just because the result of an event is desirable does not mean that everyone is committed to achieving that result. For example, an award for community service may be very attractive, but it may be a goal for very few people. The finding that optimism was not greater among the positive events judged to be controllable or found to be associated with a stereotypic, high-chance group may simply reflect the fact that many subjects were not attempting to control (i.e., influence) these events.

This same explanation may account for the strong correlation for positive events between perceived probability and comparative judgments. Examination of the positive events in Table 11.1 suggests that the high probability events are the only ones likely to be widely accepted as personal goals. Subjects are presumably working toward these goals, and because their efforts should increase the likelihood that they will succeed, they mistakenly conclude that their prospects are better than average. Of course, one can only work toward a goal if the outcome is somewhat controllable, and in fact, the high probability positive events in the study were also relatively high in controllability.[7] There is no obvious reason why personal experience and degree of desirability were significant for one type of event but not the other.

Thus, for both positive and negative events, an optimistic bias appears to result when two conditions are satisfied. First, the event is perceived to be controllable, so that there are things one can do or contemplate doing to influence the event. Second, people have some degree of commitment or emotional investment in the outcome. Under these conditions, optimism arises because people compare themselves with an inappropriate standard: a person who does little or nothing to improve his or her prospects.

Contrary to expectations based on a motivational interpretation of optimism, degree of desirability had no appreciable effect on the size of the optimistic bias for negative events. In fact, optimism was not appreciably greater for the seven life threatening events in the sample—numbers 20, 22, 25, 28, 38, 39, and 42 ($M = -20.4\%$)—than for the other negative events ($M = -19.5\%$).

Study 2

Previously it was suggested that people may be optimistically biased because their image of other people is inaccurate or incomplete. Aware of the factors that improve their own chances of achieving desirable outcomes, they may not realize that others may have just as many factors in their favor. The different conditions created in Study 2 were designed to manipulate subjects' awareness of the factors that other people consider when estimating their chances of experiencing various events.

Subjects in Study 2 made written lists of the factors that increase or decrease the likelihood that specific events would happen to them. (It was hypothesized that people normally prepare similar mental lists when making comparative judgments, so requiring subjects to prepare such lists was not expected to influence their optimism.) Some subjects were then given copies of the lists generated by others and asked to make comparative judgments of their chances of experiencing these events as in Study 1. It was predicted that exposure to others' lists would decrease and perhaps eliminate subjects' optimistic biases. Furthermore, since participants in this experiment both made comparative judgments and listed the event-influencing reasons, it was possible to examine the relationship between these two variables at the individual level.

One other variable was added to the experiment to examine the possibility that subjects in Study 1 were incorrectly reporting the perceived likelihood that events would happen to them rather than the

---

[7] The proposed difference in commitment between the positive and negative events in this study was subjected to a preliminary test. A mixed-sex group of students from Cook College ($n = 64$) rated all events on a scale that ranged from 1 (not at all important to me whether or not the event occurs) to 4 (quite important to me whether or not the event occurs). It was expected that: (a) negative events would be rated higher in importance than positive events; (b) importance would be positively correlated with optimism for both positive and negative events; and (c) for positive events, importance would be strongly related to event probability. The results strongly supported all three predictions. Mean ratings of importance for negative and positive events were 3.22 and 2.58, respectively, $t(40) = 4.05$, $p < .001$. The correlation of importance with optimism was .62 ($p < .01$) for positive events, and .46 ($p < .025$) for negative events. Finally, importance and probability were strongly correlated for positive events, .63 ($p < .01$), but uncorrelated for negative events ($-.22$, ns).

relative likelihood using their peers as a comparison group. Half of the subjects in each condition of Study 2 were explicitly warned about making this mistake and received suggestions designed to help them remember to make comparative judgments.

Method

Subjects

Students in this experiment were 120 female members of an introductory psychology class at Rutgers University who participated to fulfill a course requirement.

Materials

Comparative rating booklets. A booklet was prepared containing many of the events that had evoked unrealistic optimism in Study 1. The booklet was divided into three parts (pretreatment events, treatment events and posttreatment events) that were similar in the numbers of positive and negative events and the amount of optimistic bias that had been produced by these events. The exact sequence of events (using identification numbers from Table 11.1) was: 8, 24, 40, 13, 23, 30, 1, 22, and 27 (pretreatment events); 31, 2, 19, 25, 32, 3, 21, and 26 (treatment events); and 10, 34, 38, 11, 28, 36, 4, 20, and 29 (posttreatment events). The response format was unchanged from Study 1.

A cover sheet on half of the booklets was entitled *Warning.* It stated: "It's easy to forget the directions and start to respond to events in terms of how likely they are INSTEAD of how likely they are for you compared to other students. . . . Don't do that." A specific example was then given. The warning concluded: "To help you keep this in mind, when you see the choice '40% more,' think of it as 'my chances are 40% more than other students'."

Own reasons lists. Subjects generated lists of the factors that tend to increase or decrease the chances that the eight treatment events would happen to them. A detailed instruction sheet requested subjects to "think of things you do now and things you might do in the future" and to think of any personal characteristics—"including your personality, abilities, physical characteristics, attitudes, etc."—

that would influence the chance of this event happening to them.

Others' reasons packets. During the first day of the experiment only control groups were tested. Multiple copies of the lists of personal reasons prepared by these groups were prepared. The packets of others' reasons given to subjects in the experimental group were then made up. Each packet contained five lists chosen at random from among the 19 lists that had been reproduced. Twenty-five different packets were prepared in this way. This random-selection procedure assured that, on the average, the reasons read by subjects in the experimental group were just as numerous and as optimistic as the reasons they listed themselves.

Procedure

Three different conditions were created, one experimental condition and two controls. During every session, two of the three conditions were conducted simultaneously in adjacent rooms by different experimenters. Subjects arriving for the study were assigned randomly to one of these conditions. All subjects worked independently.

The experimenters' introductory instructions were essentially the same as those in Study 1. Subjects in all conditions then made comparative judgments for the pretreatment events. Next, members of the experimental group ($n = 39$) were told, "We want to get your thoughts about the factors that increase or decrease the chances that certain events will happen to you," and they were given a blank form on which to list their own reasons concerning the treatment events. Then experimental group subjects received one of the packets of others' reasons for these same events along with the explanation: "These forms were taken at random from people who were in our study in the past. Each set is different. Their ideas may be helpful to you in estimating how your chances compare to others', but keep in mind that you're supposed to compare yourself with all Rutgers females, not just these five." Finally, experimental group subjects made comparative judgments for the treatment events and for the posttreatment events.

Control Group 1 ($n = 41$) was employed to test whether just listing one's own reasons might influence the degree of optimism expressed on treatment events. Their procedure differed from the experimental group only in that they did not receive the packet of others' reasons. Members of Control Group 2 ($n = 40$) made comparative judgments without either generating their own lists of reasons or seeing lists produced by other students. Subjects in Control Group 2 did, however, list their own reasons for the treatment events after they finished the comparative rating booklet.

Half of the subjects in each group received a comparative rating booklet with the cover sheet warning them to make comparative judgments. To conclude the sessions, participants in all conditions rated the characteristics of 21 events as described in Study 1.

Results and Discussion

Effects of experimental treatments

Mean comparative judgments are presented in Table 11.3 for each of the three groups in the study. Figures are given for each set of events, and values for positive and negative events are presented separately.

TABLE 11.3. Optimism of Experimental Groups on Different Sets of Events

Events	% difference between own chances and others' chances		
	Experimental group[a]	Control Group 1[b]	Control Group 2[c]
Positive events			
Pretreatment	11.0	18.0	14.4
Treatment	17.3	24.0	40.1
Posttreatment	18.3	27.2	21.4
Negative events			
Pretreatment	−24.2	−25.6	−31.5
Treatment	−17.4	−31.7	−35.7
Posttreatment	−13.2	−12.2	−15.5

Note: Entries are group means over all events of the type specified. All means are significantly different from zero, $p < .001$.
[a] Own and others' reasons group, $n = 39$.
[b] Own reasons group, $n = 41$.
[c] No reasons group, $n = 40$.

The data were first examined by an analysis of variance that included the variables group, warning, and event set. Event set was a within-subject variable, whereas group and warning were between-subjects variables. Positive and negative events were tested separately. The calculations revealed that the warning manipulation main effects and interactions were not significant, $ps > .2$. Apparently, even without the extra reminder, subjects understood the comparative nature of the task and tried to compare their own chances with those of other students.

In contrast, Group × Event Set interactions for both negative and positive events were statistically significant, $F(4, 227) = 2.80$, $p < .05$, and $F(4, 227) = 2.48$, $p < .05$, respectively. These interactions show that the experimental treatments did change the responses of the experimental groups. These changes were studied in additional analyses that treated pretreatment event responses as covariates and tested for group differences on treatment and posttreatment events (Huck & McLean, 1975). These calculations showed that the manipulations produced group differences on negative and positive treatment events, $F(2, 116) = 6.20$, $p < .005$, and $F(2, 116) = 5.06$, $p < .01$, respectively. Comparisons among the covariance adjusted negative events means (SAS Institute, 1979) indicated that the experimental group was significantly less optimistic than the two control groups ($ps < .005$), and that the control groups did not differ from one another ($p < .2$). For positive events, both the experimental group and Control Group 1 were significantly less optimistic than Control Group 2 ($p < .01$), but they did not differ from one another.

The negative event results provide support for the proposition that people tend to use an inaccurate image of others when making comparative judgments. In the case of positive events, however, just asking subjects to list the factors that influence their own chances decreased their optimism, and providing information about others had no additional effect. This second finding suggests that people's first thoughts about their future may be more optimistic than their later, more reflective conclusions. Further research is needed to clarify these apparent differences between positive and negative events.

The analyses of covariance found no significant group differences on posttreatment events ($Fs < 1$). The experimental interventions were only able to reduce optimistic biases temporarily.

The preceding analyses suggest that optimistic biases arise because people tend not to think carefully about their own and others' circumstances or because they lack significant information about others. Yet there also appear to be more persistent sources of optimism, ones that cannot be eliminated just by encouraging people to think more carefully about their comparative judgments or by providing them with information about others. The treatment event data in Table 11.3 reveal that the experimental manipulations reduced but did not eliminate optimistic biases. Comparative judgments were still unrealistically optimistic ($p < .001$) for both positive and negative events. A detailed examination of the judgments for negative events showed that experimental group subjects gave fewer strongly optimistic responses and more mildly optimistic responses and responses of "average" than subjects

in the control groups. Exposure to others' reasons did not, however, increase the frequency of pessimistic responses.

Relationships between reasons and optimism

When the reasons listed by subjects were examined (Columns 2 and 3 of Table 11.4),[8] it was found that favorable reasons—those increasing the likelihood of a positive event or decreasing the likelihood of a negative event—outnumbered unfavorable reasons. (Recall, however, that this was not a random sample of events. They were included in the comparative rating booklet expressly because they had evoked unrealistic optimism in Study 1.) The size of the t statistics in Column 4 demonstrates that the preponderance of favorable reasons was very consistent across subjects.

Further calculations revealed that there was greater excess of favorable reasons for the two negative treatment events that had produced the greatest

TABLE 11.4. Relationships Between Optimism and Reasons Influencing Event Likelihood

Event	% difference between own chances and others' chances[b]	Number of reasons listed[c]			Reasons—optimism r[d]
		Increasing chances	Decreasing chances	t	
Positive events					
Owning your own home (2)[a]	42.3	3.22	.98	11.1	.38**
Starting salary > $10,000 (3)	21.6	2.53	.83	8.5	.48**
Negative events					
Having a drinking problem (19)	−53.8	1.05	3.46	11.4	.49**
Divorced a few years after married (21)	−52.0	.84	3.58	11.9	.25*
Getting lung cancer (25)	−29.0	1.32	2.19	4.2	.57**
Having gum problems (31)	−23.7	1.41	2.66	6.2	.57**
Having to take unattractive job (32)	−16.4	1.83	1.88	.2	.54**

[a] Number of event as it appears in Table 11.1.
[b] Mean rating for subject in Control Groups 1 and 2. All entries significantly different from zero, $p < .001$.
[c] Mean for subjects in all groups. Student's $t(df = 119)$ tests the hypothesis that the number of reasons listed that increase chances equals the number listed that decrease chances. All ts significant beyond the .001 level except the last, *ns*.
[d] Correlations based on individual responses of control group subjects between the degree of optimism and the difference between the number of goal facilitating and goal inhibiting reasons, $df = 79$.
* $p < .05$. ** $p < .001$.

---

[8] Event 26, "not being able to have a child because you're sterile," was not included in Table 11.4 because a substantial number of the reasons listed did not conform to the instructions (e.g., "I may never marry," or "I don't want to have

children"). None of the conclusions about group differences in comparative judgments would be changed if Event 26 were excluded from the statistical analysis of treatment effects.

optimism (Events 19 and 21) than for the two nega-tive events that evoked the least optimism (Events 31 and 32), $t(119) = 8.71$, $p < .001$. Similarly, the excess of favorable reasons over unfavorable reasons was greater for positive Event 2, which elicited strong optimism, than for positive Event 3, which evoked less optimism, $t(119) = 2.16$, $p < .05$.

The last column in Table 11.4 shows that this relationship between the kinds of reasons listed and the degree of optimism persists between subjects. When individual students in Control Groups 1 and 2 made their comparative judgments,[9] the responses they gave for each event correlated strongly with the difference between the number of likelihood-increasing and likelihood-decreasing reasons they had listed for those events. The magnitudes of these correlations were the same whether they were based only on Control Group 1 subjects, who listed their reasons before estimating their chances, or Control Group 2 subjects, who listed their reasons only after completing the comparative rating booklet. This close correspondence between the degree of opti-mism reported and the number of favorable and unfavorable reasons listed—both across events and between subjects within events—reinforces the sug-gestion that the generation of similar mental lists forms an important stage in the process of deciding whether one's own chances differ from average.

Relationship of desirability to optimism between subjects

A final set of calculations looked for an association between an individual's rating of the desirability of an event and the degree of optimism shown by that individual. Correlation coefficients based on data from Groups 2 and 3 between desirability rat-ings and optimism were greater than zero for seven of the eight positive events, but the coefficients were quite small (median $r = .14$). For negative events, the correlations tended to be negative and small (13 negative, 5 positive, median $r = .13$). That is, individual students who regarded a negative event

---

[9] Data from subjects in the experimental group were excluded from these calculations and from Column 1 of Table 4 because their comparative judgments had been affected by the lists of others' reasons.

as particularly undesirable were slightly more optimistic about avoiding it than students who did not think that the event was so undesirable, a find-ing similar to that reported by Kirscht *et al.* (1966). Thus, 20 of 26 correlation coefficients were in the direction predicted by a motivational interpretation of optimistic biases ($p < .01$ by the binomial test).

General Discussion

In the past, unrealistic optimism about the future was regarded as a defensive phenomenon, a distortion of reality motivated to reduce anxiety (e.g., Kirscht *et al.*, 1966; Lund, 1925). The present article has described several ways in which purely cognitive errors might be responsible for optimistic biases. Two studies were carried out to test hypotheses about the conditions under which unrealistic opti-mism would appear, hypotheses derived from both cognitive and motivational considerations. Although the results provide some support for both points of view, the studies were not designed to pit one against the other, nor is there any reason why optimism can-not have both cognitive and motivational sources.

What these investigations have demonstrated is the existence of an optimistic bias concerning many future life events. As predicted in Hypothesis 1, stu-dents tend to believe that they are more likely than their peers to experience positive events and less likely to experience negative events. Cognitive and motivational considerations led to the identification of five event characteristics—degree of desirability, perceived probability, personal experience, per-ceived controllability, and stereotype salience (Hypotheses 2–6)—that were shown in Study 1 to determine the amount of optimistic bias evoked by different events. It was also demonstrated in Study 2 that providing information about the attributes and actions of others reduced the optimistic bias for neg-ative events but did not eliminate it.

The results suggest a mechanism that may partly explain these optimistically biased expectations. In comparing their chances with those of their classmates, it appears that students brought to mind any personal actions, plans, or attributes that might affect their chances of experiencing the events. If an event was one they perceived to be controllable and if they were committed to a particular outcome, the majority of factors they brought to mind were ones that increased the likelihood that it would turn out the way they would like. Comparing themselves to an unrealistic stereotype of a person who does nothing to improve his or her chances or even engages in counterproductive activity, students concluded that their own prospects were better than average.

Yet there seems to be more to unrealistic optimism than just an inappropriate comparison group or a possible bias in the recall of relevant actions, plans, and attributes. When experimental group subjects in Study 2 received the packet of event-influencing factors listed by other students, they should have concluded that their chances were about the same as those of their classmates. Their classmates had listed the same types of reasons and just as many optimistic reasons as they had. Instead, subjects continued to claim that they were more likely to experience positive events and less likely to experience negative events. Unfortunately, we do not know how they justified this conclusion.

Further research is obviously needed to test the event characteristics and mechanisms proposed here, with other populations of subjects, with a wider sample of events, and with other methods of assessing optimism. Optimistic biases may be much less prevalent among older people, for example. Studies must also examine the relationship between unrealistic optimism and self-protective behavior. People who believe, falsely, that their personal attributes exempt them from risk or that their present actions reduce their risks below those of other people may be inclined to engage in risky behaviors and to ignore precautions. To discover whether unrealistic optimism about the future increases individual and societal vulnerability to disease, accidents, criminal victimization, and hazard loss is thus a central goal for future research.

REFERENCE NOTES

1. Weinstein, N. D. *Coping with environmental hazards: Reactions to the threat of crime.* Paper presented at the meeting of the American Psychological Association, San Francisco, September 1977.
2. American Cancer Society. *A study of motivational and environmental deterrents to the taking of physical examinations that include cancer tests.* Unpublished report, 1966. (Available on loan from Medical Library, American Cancer Society, 219 East 42nd Street, New York, New York 10017.)
3. Hoffman, D. M., and Brewer, M. B. *Perception of rape: A subjective probability analysis.* Paper presented at the meeting of the American Psychological Association, Toronto, Canada, September 1978.

REFERENCES

Cantril, H. The prediction of social events. *Journal of Abnormal and Social Psychology*, 1938, *33*, 364–389.

Harris, D. M., & Guten, S. Health protective behavior: An exploratory study. *Journal of Health and Social Behavior,* 1979, *20*, 17–29.

Huck, S. W., & McLean, R. A. Using a repeated measures ANOVA to analyze the data from a pretest–posttest design: A potentially confusing task. *Psychological Bulletin*, 1975, *82*, 511–518.

Irwin, F. W. Stated expectations as functions of probability & desirability of outcomes. *Journal of Personality*, 1953, *21*, 329–335.

Jones, E. E., & Nisbett, R. E. The actor and the observer: Divergent perceptions of the causes of behavior. In E. E. Jones *et al.* (Eds.), *Attribution: Perceiving the causes of behavior.* Morristown, N.J.: General Learning Press, 1971.

Kahneman, D., & Tversky, A. Subjective probability: A judgment of representativeness. *Cognitive Psychology*, 1972, *3*, 430–454.

Kirscht, J. P., Haefner, D. P., Kegeles, S. S., & Rosenstock, I. M. A national study of health beliefs. *Journal of Health and Human Behavior*, 1966, *7*, 248–254.

Langer, E. J., & Roth, J. Heads I win, tails it's chance: The illusion of control as a function of the sequence of outcomes in a purely chance task. *Journal of Personality and Social Psychology*, 1975, *32*, 951–955.

Lichtenstein, S., Slovic, P., Fischhoff, B., Layman, M., & Combs, B. Judged frequency of lethal events. *Journal of Experimental Psychology: Human Learning and Memory*, 1978, *4*, 551–578.

Lund, F. H. The psychology of belief. *Journal of Abnormal and Social Psychology*, 1925, *20*, 63–81; 174–196.

Marks, R. W. The effect of probability, desirability, and privilege on the stated expectations of children. *Journal of Personality*, 1951, *19*, 431–465.

McGregor, D. The major determinants of the prediction of social events. *Journal of Abnormal and Social Psychology*, 1938, *33*, 179–204.

McGuire, W. J. A syllogistic analysis of cognitive relationships. In M. J. Rosenberg, C. I. Hovland, W. J. McGuire, R. P. Abelson, & J. W. Brehm (Eds.), *Attitude organization and change.* New Haven: Yale University Press, 1960.

Miller, D. T., & Ross, M. Self-serving biases in the attribution of causality: Fact or fiction? *Psychological Bulletin*, 1975, *82*, 213–225.

Robertson, L. S. Car crashes: Perceived vulnerability and willingness to pay for crash protection. *Journal of Community Health*, 1977, *3*, 136–141.

Ross, L., Greene, D., & House, P. The "false consensus effect": An egocentric bias in social perception and attribution processes. *Journal of Experimental Social Psychology*, 1977, *13*, 279–301.

Ross, M., & Sicoly, F. Egocentric biases in availability and attribution. *Journal of Personality and Social Psychology*, 1979, *37*, 322–337.

SAS Institute. *User's guide to SAS* (1979 ed.), Raleigh, North Carolina: Author, 1979.

Slovic, P., Kunreuther, H., & White, G. F. Decision processes, rationality, and adjustment to natural hazards. In G. F. White (Ed.), *Natural Hazards: Local, national, global*. New York: Oxford University Press, 1974.

Tversky, A., & Kahneman, D. Availability: A heuristic for judging frequency and probability. *Cognitive Psychology*, 1973, *5*, 207–232.

Tversky, A., & Kahneman, D. Causal schemata in judgments under uncertainty. In M. Fishbein (Ed.), *Progress in social psychology*. Hillsdale, N.J.: Erlbaum, 1977.

Tversky, A., & Kahneman, D. Judgment under uncertainty: Heuristics and biases. *Science*, 1974, *185*, 1124–1131.

Received August 27, 1979 ■

Objective Standards Are Not Enough: Affective, Self-Evaluative, and Behavioral Responses to Social Comparison Information

William M. Klein

Three studies examined affective, self-evaluative, and behavioral responses to objective and social comparison information. In the first study, 437 male and female college undergraduates imagined they had a 30% or 60% risk of experiencing a negative event and that the average person's risk was higher or lower. All types of responses were sensitive to relative but not absolute risk. In the second study, 60 male and female college undergraduates learned that they scored 40% or 60% on a task and that this score was above or below average. Subsequent behaviors whose outcomes depended largely on objective ability still reflected attention to relative standing. This effect of comparative feedback was shown to be mediated by changes in self-evaluation. A third, follow-up study demonstrated that attention to comparative feedback (in the context of objective information) hinges on its desirability. Implications for social comparison theory are discussed.

Without the freedom to draw comparisons, many of the judgments we make would be difficult if not impossible. Accordingly, many psychological phenomena are influenced by comparative processes. For example, prospect theory (Kahneman & Tversky, 1979) holds that people are more attuned to changes in risk than they are to absolute levels of risk. Moreover, the emotions evoked by

This research was supported by Colby College Social Science Grants 01-2207, 01-2230, and 01-2242. I thank Luke Blanchford, Colleen Burnham, Ann Faranetta, Heather Regan, and Susan Sarno for their assistance in data collection, and Michelle Buck, George Goethals, Ziva Kunda, and Neil Weinstein for their helpful comments on drafts of the article.

Correspondence concerning this article should be addressed to William M. Klein, Department of Psychology, Colby College, Waterville, Maine 04901. Electronic mail may be sent via the Internet to wmklein@colby.edu.

certain outcomes are dependent on comparisons with easily imagined alternative outcomes (e.g., Miller & Turnbull, 1990), and people often judge their health and skills by comparing their past condition with their present condition (Albert, 1977; Conway & Ross, 1984; Suls, Marco, & Tobin, 1991).

Perhaps the most well known example of using comparative or relative information is *social comparison* (Wood, 1989). Unless we perceive that doing so will be unfavorable (Brickman & Bulman, 1977), we compare ourselves with others on a wide variety of dimensions, including academic skills (Gibbons, Benbow, & Gerrard, 1994), attractiveness (Richins, 1991), current living situation (Bernstein & Crosby, 1980), coping abilities (Wood, Taylor, & Lichtman, 1985), health risk (Klein & Weinstein, in press), illness symptoms (Sanders, 1982), and behavior cessation efforts (Gibbons, Gerrard, Lando, & McGovern, 1991). Other people's performances and self-appraisals are sometimes highly predictive of our own self-appraisals (Felson & Reed, 1986), and when we judge our risk of negative outcomes, we might compare ourselves with prototypes of individuals who experience these outcomes (Gibbons, Gerrard, & Boney McCoy, 1995; Weinstein, 1980).

In many situations, social comparison information is the only standard by which to judge ourselves. How does one evaluate attractiveness, ability at an unusual task, or the success with which one is coping, without looking at how others fare on these attributes? However, there are domains in which clear objective standards may be used as a benchmark. An emergency medical technician whose skills are superior to those of her classmates but who cannot administer cardiopulmonary resuscitation quickly will still not be able to save a heart attack victim. In negotiation, one's absolute outcome should be more important than how this outcome compares with the negotiating partner's outcome (assuming the goal is to maximize winnings). A biology student whose academic performance does not match that of other students may still become a highly competent biologist. And a retiring couple whose savings exceed those of their friends may still struggle if their investments have not kept up with inflation. In short, there are many examples where meeting an objective criterion is necessary to achieve a desired outcome (cf. Frank, 1985).

Festinger's (1954) theory of social comparison provided for the availability of objective standards in self-evaluation. Hypothesis II states that "to the extent that objective, non-social means are not available, people evaluate their opinions and abilities by comparison respectively with the opinions and abilities of others" (Festinger, 1954, p. 118). Taking this one step further, Corollary IIB suggests that "when an objective non-social basis for the evaluation of one's ability or opinion is readily available persons will not evaluate their opinions or abilities by comparison with others" (Festinger, 1954, p. 120). According to Festinger, then, people who are given objective standards with which to evaluate their standing on a dimension should be much less interested in social comparison.[1]

But are they? Intuitive as this may seem, there are reasons to believe otherwise. Festinger (1954) himself noted that even when objective criteria are available, they may not be used: "The belief, for example, that tomatoes are poisonous to humans . . . is unlikely to be tested" (p. 119). It seems more likely that people will instead seek out social confirmation of this opinion. In a study by Sanders (1981), participants who were asked to imagine that they tested negative on an objective test for a medical disorder still believed they would see a doctor if their friends and family urged them to do so. The well-known effects of peer pressure on the decision to engage in a variety of objectively harmful behaviors testify to the facility with which objective information may be dismissed.

Recent evidence also suggests that social comparison information, even when it is nondiagnostic,

---

[1] In this article, *social comparison information* is defined as information about how one's standing on a dimension compares with that of other individuals. Other sources of social information (such as peer pressure) might also be identified as social comparison information but are not part of the conceptual basis of this investigation.

may be processed beyond conscious awareness and may subsequently modify self-evaluations. In a study by Gilbert, Giesler, and Morris (1995), participants who were or were not cognitively busy completed a judgment task after watching on videotape the good or poor performance of another participant at the same task. In all conditions, the videotaped individual's performance was said to have been influenced by outside factors not relevant to the participants themselves (thereby making this person's performance a nondiagnostic source of social comparison information). After performing the task themselves, participants rated their own ability. When not cognitively busy, participants' observations of the person in the videotape did not affect their own self-assessments. Thus, they appeared to acknowledge the nondiagnosticity of the other individual's performance. However, when cognitively busy, participants' ratings were sensitive to the performance of the other individual. Gilbert *et al.* reasoned that busy participants did not possess the cognitive resources to notice the nondiagnosticity of this social comparison information. In a follow-up study, Gilbert et al. showed that even when people do not believe they have used nondiagnostic social comparison information, they show subtle affective responses to the information.

In addition to processing social comparison information effortlessly, individuals place enormous stock in such information. People engage in social comparison every day (Wheeler & Miyake, 1992) and do so to serve a variety of goals, such as self-improvement, self-assessment, self-enhancement, and self-verification (Taylor, Neter, & Wayment, 1995). Additional research shows that relative standing is sometimes a better predictor of life satisfaction than are objective criteria. For example, Emmons and Diener (1985) found that comparisons with others were more predictive than objective criteria of participants' satisfaction with their friends, love life, family, recreational activities, standard of living, grades, and future career prospects. People have also been found to define themselves by those attributes on which they are relatively better than those on which they are objectively better (Campbell, Fairey, & Fehr, 1986; Levine & Green, 1984; Tesser & Campbell, 1980; Tesser, Millar, & Moore,

1988). Additionally, people are more intrinsically motivated to engage in tasks at which they are relatively better (Boggiano & Ruble, 1979; Koestner, Zuckerman, & Olsson, 1990). Overall, then, research in a variety of traditions illustrates the grave importance of social comparison to self-evaluation. This research also suggests that social comparisons may be more influential than objective criteria. Thus, it is conceivable that when diagnostic, objective criteria are available, people may still pay more attention to social comparison information even if it is nondiagnostic.

One might argue that comparison information will be used to the exclusion of objective information only for certain kinds of responses. In particular, objective information may play a more important role when people are making consequential decisions (e.g., whether to adopt a health precaution or to withdraw funds from a risky investment) whose outcomes depend primarily on objective criteria. Although social comparison may provide an important source of self-evaluative information and comfort, it does not necessarily follow that decisions to engage in subsequent behaviors that are dependent on objective standing will be equally sensitive to comparison information. In a study by Raats and Sparks (1995), for example, participants' intentions to change their diets were more sensitive to their absolute fat-intake levels than to their relative fat-intake levels. On the other hand, research in negotiation has shown that negotiators tend to compare their negotiation outcomes with those of their opponents and may choose an objectively undesirable outcome that is equitable over an objectively desirable outcome that is inequitable (Loewenstein, Thompson, & Bazerman, 1989). People are even willing to walk away with nothing to avoid the prospect of winning less than someone else (Guth, Schmittberger, & Schwarze, 1982). On balance, past research suggests that people may show greater behavioral responsivity to social comparison information than to objective information, although a likely possibility is that the effects of objective information will be more apparent on behavior than on affect or self-evaluation.

Before drawing any conclusion about the importance of comparison information, however, it is important to consider that the processing of such information depends a great deal on its contents (Kruglanski & Mayseless, 1990). One factor that may be important in this regard is the comparison information's desirability. A vast literature demonstrates that people harbor esteem-bolstering biases about how they compare with others on a variety of dimensions (Taylor & Brown, 1988). People tend to overestimate the number of people who share their undesirable characteristics and underestimate those who share their desirable characteristics (Campbell, 1986; Goethals, Messick, & Allison, 1991; Marks & Miller, 1987), and as noted earlier, people prefer relative superiority to objective success (Tesser & Campbell, 1980). Indeed, students would often rather be a "big fish in a small pond" than just another good student at a top-notch school (Marsh & Parker, 1984). Finally, research on downward comparison shows that people who are threatened tend to compare themselves with others owning worse fates (Wills, 1987; Wood et al., 1985), and research on relative deprivation shows that people are not happy unless they are "keeping up with the Joneses" (e.g., Bernstein & Crosby, 1980).

Owing to this preference for desirable feedback, use of nondiagnostic comparison feedback might be more apparent when the feedback is positive. When receiving feedback that one is worse than one's peers, people may not experience negative affect or reduce their perceived standing on the dimension because of the variety of strategies they use to buffer themselves against undesirable feedback (Taylor, Collins, Skokan, & Aspinwall, 1989). For example, when challenged with information suggesting they engage in risky behaviors no less often than their peers, individuals may reduce estimates of how often they engage in these behaviors or come to see the behaviors as less dangerous (Klein, 1996; Klein & Kunda, 1993). On the other hand, in the Gilbert et al. (1995) study, attention to nondiagnostic feedback under cognitive load was high whether the comparison target performed very well or very poorly. Moreover, Collins (1996) finds a surprisingly large number of studies showing that people seek out and derive many benefits from upward comparisons. Thus, it is unclear whether

desirability will qualify attention to nondiagnostic social comparison feedback.

One possible outcome is that desirability plays a role only in affective and self-evaluative responses to social comparison feedback. Behavioral responses may be more sensitive to negative comparison feedback because people might be all too aware of the correlation between their comparative standing and the outcome of their behavior. Although a woman might convince herself erroneously that her musical skills are comparable to those of professional musicians, she will not necessarily attempt to become one.

In summary, contrary to Festinger's (1954) original proposition, objective information may be passed over in favor of social comparison information, even when the former is more diagnostic. This is reasoned to be true of not only affective and self-evaluative responses but also behavioral responses. The desirability of feedback may play an important role; affective and self-evaluative responses may reveal attention to only desirable comparison feedback, whereas behavioral responses may reveal attention to comparison feedback regardless of desirability. Objective standards may also exert a greater influence on behavior than on affect or self-evaluation, regardless of desirability.

On the basis of the above, there were four goals in this investigation. The first was to show that affective and self-evaluative responses are sensitive to social comparison information even when unambiguous objective information is available. This hypothesis is consistent with several studies reviewed above, but methodological features of those studies make this conclusion problematic. In studies of life satisfaction, people may infer their relative standing from their global satisfaction rather than vice versa. This may be particularly true in domains where social comparison information is scarce (Fox & Kahneman, 1992). The more experimental studies generally involve performance on novel tasks such as social sensitivity (Tesser & Campbell, 1980) and thus are not associated with clear, objective standards. Furthermore, comparative and objective information are rarely presented orthogonally. For example, participants in Campbell et al. (1986) performed two tasks and were then told that they and the comparison target had both scored a 6 on Task A but that on Task B, the participants had scored an 8, whereas the target had scored an 11. Thus, there were not conditions in which, in Task B, (a) participants performed objectively higher than in Task A and higher than the target, (b) participants performed objectively lower than in Task A and lower than the target, or (c) participants performed objectively lower than in Task A but higher than the target. In some studies, objective feedback is given in terms of one's score relative to the average score, itself a comparative source of feedback (e.g., Boggiano & Ruble, 1979). In the current studies, objective and comparative sources of information are presented in orthogonal designs where clear, diagnostic objective information is available. In Study 1, for example, participants complete several hypothetical scenarios in which they are given objective and comparative information about their risk for a health or safety problem and must report how they might respond.

The second purpose of this investigation was to show that behaviors whose outcomes are dependent on objective standards will still be sensitive to comparison information. Studies 2 and 3 investigate this hypothesis in a situation in which participants are given absolute and relative feedback about their performance on a laboratory task and must then make a subsequent decision whose outcome is dependent on objective standing but independent of relative standing. Note that the first two hypotheses do not imply that people will not attend to absolute information. People may attend to both sources but more so to comparative information, a pattern that would still be consistent with the hypothesis. And, as argued above, objective information may turn out to be more influential on behavior than on other, less consequential, responses.

A third goal was to determine whether attention to nondiagnostic social comparison information may be greater when the information is self-enhancing than when it is not. Undesirable comparison information might be found to influence behavior more than it does affect and cognition, due to the greater consequences of behavior and to the variety of buffering mechanisms that people may use to cope with the affective consequences of undesirable

social comparison information. To test this idea, Study 3 includes a no-comparison control group with which desirable and undesirable feedback groups may be contrasted.

If comparative standards exert influence over behaviors whose outcomes are independent of those standards, it is helpful to determine the way in which this influence operates. The fourth goal was to show that this effect results in part from changes in how people judge their standing on the comparison dimension. Suppose Fred, a 50-year-old man, is told by his physician that he must reduce his dietary cholesterol to bring his heart attack risk to acceptable levels. Should Fred learn that many other men his age consume even more cholesterol than he, Fred might elect to ignore his physician's recommendations. Thus, his behavior would be most sensitive to comparative information (when his objective diet and physician's recommendations are more important). Why might this happen? The social comparison information probably increases Fred's perception of personal invulnerability. This inference could be erroneous because Fred's diet, however superior to others' diets, may still be health threatening. Festinger's (1954) discussion of how people evaluate their opinions suggests a similar model (although opinions do not often have an objective standard). When people learn that others do not share their opinion (a form of relative feedback), they become less confident in the validity of that opinion (self-perception), which may be followed by attitude and behavior change. In general, people may infer that their objective standing on an attribute is desirable if their relative standing on the attribute is desirable. The role of self-assessment in mediating the effect of comparison information on behavior was explored in Studies 2 and 3.

Study 1

This study consisted of three hypothetical scenarios in which participants were asked to imagine that they had a specified risk of enduring a negative event and that this risk was above or below the average risk of their peers. In all cases, participants' reactions to these scenarios were measured, with the prediction that such reactions would be more sensitive to their relative than to their absolute level of risk.

Problem 1

Respondents to Problem 1 were 193 Princeton University undergraduates (57% women and 43% men),[2] participating in a mass-testing session. They were asked to imagine that they had either a 30% chance or a 60% chance of causing an automobile accident sometime during their life and that this probability was 20% higher or 20% lower than that of the average, same-age, same-sex person. For example, participants in the 30%–below average condition read the following problem:

> Suppose that we are able to determine, based on your driving record, vision, personality, and other factors, that your risk of causing a car accident sometime during your life is 30%. Similar tests show that the average person of your age and sex has a 50% chance of causing a car accident. Upon hearing this information, how safe a driver would you consider yourself?

Participants made their safety ratings on a 10-point scale ranging from *not at all safe* (1) to *extremely safe* (10). These ratings were then analyzed by means of a 2×2 analysis of variance (ANOVA), with absolute risk (30% or 60%) and relative risk (20% higher or lower than average) as between-subjects variables. There emerged a main effect of relative risk, $F(1, 189) = 27.09, p < .0001$; participants whose risk was said to be lower than average considered themselves to be safer drivers ($M = 5.99$) than those who learned that their risk was higher than average ($M = 4.47$). Remarkably, participants who were said to have a 60% chance of causing an accident when the average was 80% believed they would characterize themselves as safer drivers ($M = 5.82$) than participants who

were said to have a 30% chance of causing an accident when the average was 10% ($M = 4.41$), $t(189) = 3.41, p < .001$. There was no effect of absolute risk nor an interaction.[3]

In this problem, it would seem that comparative standing played a more prominent role than absolute standing in participants' judgments of their driving safety. One possible criticism of this problem is that judgments of driving safety can only be made with reference to relative standards. Of course, driving safety can be entirely objective if it is measured in terms of how often one causes automobile accidents. Nevertheless, a more convincing demonstration of the role of relative standing might be one that shows relative risk to influence an affective response. A vast literature illustrates the effect of social comparison on affect (e.g., Collins, 1996), yet it is unclear what influence comparison will exert in the context of objective information.

Problem 2

In the second problem, respondents (138 Princeton University undergraduates, 51% female and 49% male, again participating in a mass-testing session) were asked to imagine that they had tested positive on a salivary litmus test of a genetic marker for pancreatic disease. One group of participants imagined that they had a 30% chance of developing this health disorder, and the other group of participants imagined that they had a 60% chance of developing the disorder. Orthogonal to this variable, participants were told that their chances were either above or below average (relative to the average person of their age and sex) by 20%. For example, participants in the 30%–above average condition were told that the risk of the average person was 10%. Participants then rated how disturbed they would be with this diagnosis, on a 10-point scale ranging from *not at all disturbed* (1) to *very disturbed* (10).

---

[2] Sex did not qualify any of the effects in the studies reported in this article, so all analyses were collapsed across this variable.

[3] One interesting tendency in all three of the problems in Study 1 was for relative risk to play a seemingly greater role

among participants imagining themselves to have a 30% risk than those imagining themselves to have a 60% risk. However, because the interaction between absolute and relative risk was never significant, it is unclear whether this is a reliable finding.

Disturbance ratings were submitted to a 2×2 ANOVA, with absolute risk (30% or 60%) and relative risk (20% higher or 20% lower than average) as between-subjects variables. There was a main effect of relative risk, $F(1, 134) = 28.41$, $p < .0001$, such that participants whose risk was said to be below average were less disturbed by their diagnosis ($M = 4.79$) than those whose risk was said to be above average ($M = 6.89$). No other effects were significant. Paralleling Problem 1, participants whose risk of 60% was said to be below average indicated they would be less disturbed ($M = 5.28$) than participants whose risk of 30% was said to be above average ($M = 7.11$), $t(136) = 3.33$, $p < .01$.

It would appear, then, that participants' relative standing on this attribute was considerably more influential than their absolute standing. There were no overall differences in level of estimated negative affect between participants said to have a 30% chance and those said to have a 60% chance of the disorder. On the other hand, participants whose risk was said to be below average indicated they would be considerably less disturbed than those whose risk was said to be above average.

Problem 3

The results of the first two problems show that self-evaluative and affective responses to feedback may depend in large part on relative standing. However, the first dependent measure was a self-evaluation that may be inherently comparative. The second was an emotional reaction, a judgment for which it is not fruitful to argue that relative information was not important. Whether or not it is relevant to a judgment or decision, social comparison is very often a source of comfort. One could also argue that social comparison information is inherently more affective than objective information, making the dominance of relative information over absolute information in Problem 2 less surprising. It is thus unclear whether relative risk may have effects above and beyond those on self-judgment and emotional response. In particular, does learning that one has below average risk lead to lower interest

in adopting precautions, even if the objective level of risk is high? This question served as the impetus for Problem 3.

Respondents were 106 Colby College undergraduates (56% women and 44% men), approached at the campus library. As in Problem 1, participants imagined that they had a 30% or 60% chance of causing an automobile accident and that their risk was 20% lower or 20% higher than average. In addition to rating their driving safety, participants also indicated how disturbed they would be by this information and how concerned they would be (all on 10-point scales ranging from *not at all* [1] to *extremely* [10]) and how likely they would be to enroll in a driver's education program, buy an inexpensive booklet on driver safety tips, drive slower on the highway, drive slower on residential streets, walk more often, have their vehicle inspected more often, take public transit more often, and wear their seat belt more often (all on 7-point scales anchored with the end-points *not at all likely* [1] and *extremely likely* [7]).

Responses on these items were standardized and submitted to a 2×2 between-subjects multivariate analysis of variance (MANOVA), with absolute and relative risk as independent variables. This analysis revealed a significant main effect of relative risk, $F(11, 91) = 2.04$, $p < .05$,[4] and no other effects. Univariate ANOVAs revealed a significant effect of relative risk on ratings of driving safety, $F(1, 101) = 4.20$, $p < .05$, and intentions to drive slower on the highway, $F(1, 101) = 4.55$, $p < .05$, take public transit more often, $F(1, 101) = 3.97$, $p < .05$, and wear a seat belt more often, $F(1, 101) = 10.71$, $p < .001$. In contrast to participants imagining their risk to be above average, those imagining their risk to be below average felt that they would rate themselves as safer drivers and that they would be less likely to take these precautions after receiving the risk information. Means for all other variables (with the exception of enrolling in a driver education program) followed a similar pattern but did not achieve acceptable levels of significance (see Table 12.1).

---

[4] All multivariate tests in this article were based on Wilks's lambda.

TABLE 12.1. Study 1: Mean Responses on All Dependent Variables in Problem 3, by Absolute and Relative Risk of Causing Automobile Accident

Dependent variable	20% higher risk than average		20% lower risk than average	
	30% risk	60% risk	30% risk	60% risk
Driving safety[a]	6.04	5.68	5.12	4.89
Disturbance	6.19	5.88	5.16	5.79
Concern	6.33	5.96	5.60	6.00
Take driver's education	1.70	1.72	1.92	2.04
Buy booklet on tips	2.41	2.16	2.20	2.32
Drive slower on highway	4.00	3.80	2.80	3.46
Drive slower on streets	4.30	4.52	3.28	4.14
Walk more often	2.22	2.52	1.80	2.07
Vehicle inspected more often	3.00	3.12	2.20	2.96
Public transit more often	2.52	2.96	2.28	1.92
Wear seat belt more often	6.78	6.16	4.88	5.89

[a] Safety ratings were reverse coded, so that higher ratings signified less safety.

Discussion

In all three problems, participants' responses were sensitive to relative but not absolute risk. Participants who were told that their risk of 60% was below average were actually less disturbed, more self-congratulatory about their ability, and less likely to intend changes in their behavior than those whose risk of 30% was above average. These findings support the strongest form of the first hypothesis (that responses would be dependent on comparative information), because there was no effect of absolute risk.

A limitation of this study was that participants were answering hypothetical scenarios and thus had very little at stake. What might have happened if participants were asked to make a consequential decision that depended on their absolute standing on a dimension? For example, if participants needed to attain a particular score on a task to win a prize, their ability to meet this objective criterion would be more diagnostic of their chances of winning the prize than would their comparative standing on this ability. In this case, would they ignore comparative information in favor of the objective criterion?

Although comparative information may produce impressive effects on people's emotions, self-assessments, and behavioral intentions, it does not necessarily follow that people would prefer comparative to absolute information when making choices with tangible consequences. Moreover, the absolute information in these problems may have been too uninvolving or abstract, thereby reducing attention to it. The aim of the next study was to determine how the provision of absolute and comparative information would impinge on actual behavior.

Study 2

In this study, participants were given false feedback about their own score and other participants' scores on an ability task about which they had no a priori beliefs. Participants then learned that they needed to achieve a certain score on the next run of this task to receive a prize, regardless of how their first trial performance compared with that of other participants. Subsequently, they were given a choice of whether to try winning the prize by completing the next run of the task or by engaging in a chance-determined task. The key dependent variable was this choice. As in Study 1, absolute and relative feedback appeared in a fully crossed design.

If people rely solely on objective information when making this decision, then those who exceed the criterion the first time should be the most likely group to choose the ability task again, whereas those who did not exceed the criterion should be the most likely group to choose the chance task, regardless of relative standing. However, the implication of Study 1 is that people might take their relative performance information into account as well, so that those learning their score was above average (whether it was above or below the objective criterion) would be more likely to choose another attempt at the task. If behaviors are sensitive to both sources of information, main effects of both relative and absolute score should be observed. This study also explored whether this effect of comparative feedback on behavior was mediated by changes in self-assessment.

Method

Participants. Participants were 60 Colby College undergraduates (55% women and 45% men), who participated for pay. They were tested individually and were randomly assigned to one of the four conditions.

Materials and procedure. The experimenter greeted the participant and explained that she was studying individual preferences for various types of cognitive tasks. Participants learned that they would first be presented several pairs of pictures and, for each pair, they would have to determine which picture was esthetically superior. The experimenter explained that in each case there was a right answer—a panel of professional artists had allegedly viewed each pair and selected the more esthetically pleasing one.[5] Each pair was presented for 20 s, after which the experimenter recorded the participant's answer. Once 20 trials had been completed, the experimenter left the room and returned 3 min later with performance feedback. All participants received a computer printout detailing the participants' ostensible number of correct responses on the picture-judging task, as well as the supposed average score achieved by 47 other participants in the study.

At this point, the two manipulations were administered. Participants were told that they had chosen the correct response either 40% or 60% of the time and that the average participant in the study had achieved a score that was 20% higher or 20% lower than the participant's score. Participants were given these scores in terms of the number of items correct; for example, participants in the 60%–below average condition were told that they scored a 12 and that the average participant had scored a 16. To reinforce the comparison manipulation, the experimenter voiced informally ("for their own information") that participants had scored above

or below the average (depending on condition). After viewing the feedback sheet, participants were given a questionnaire containing all of the dependent measures. Participants kept their feedback sheet while completing the questionnaire.

On the first page of the questionnaire, participants began by completing four measures of satisfaction: how good they were at esthetic judgment, how good they thought they were at this particular task (both on 7-point scales ranging from *very poor* [1] to *excellent* [7]), how happy they were with their performance, and how confident they were in their ability (both on 7-point scales ranging from *not at all* [1] to *extremely* [7]). Participants then indicated whether performance on the esthetic judgment task was a matter of luck or of ability, on a 7-point scale ranging from *determined only by luck* (1) through *determined equally by luck and ability* (4) to *determined only by ability* (7). This was followed by ratings of how personally important it was to do well at this task and how related this task was to esthetic judgment, both on 7-point scales ranging from *not at all* (1) to *extremely* (7). Finally, participants were asked to estimate how much out of $50 they thought they might bet on another 20 trials of the esthetic judgment task (with the provision that if they answered 10 out of 20 correctly they would double their money).

On the second page, participants were presented with a choice between two tasks for which they could win a $10 prize. One option was to complete 20 new trials of the esthetic judgment task. It was explained that if participants amassed 10 or more correct responses on the task (in other words, 50% of the items), they would win the prize. The other option was to spin a roulette wheel 20 times, and if the ball landed on a red space on half the trials, the participant would win the prize.[6] All participants seemed to understand that the probability of

---

[5] The picture pairs were taken from the Meier Art Judgment Test (Meier, 1940). I thank John Achee, Susan Sarno, Abe Tesser, and Jennifer Waters for their help in locating an original copy of the test.

[6] At the conclusion of the study, participants were asked to indicate which of these tasks they would enjoy more and

which afforded them a greater probability of winning, on 7-point scales ranging from *roulette task* (1) to *esthetic judgment task* (7). The means of these two variables across all conditions were 4.43 and 4.38, respectively, neither of which was significantly different from the midpoint of the scale (4). Thus, differences in preferences between the two tasks cannot be landing on red in any trial was 50%. After reading the description of the two choices, participants reported their preference and then indicated how confident they were in their choice, on a 7-point scale ranging from *not at all confident* (1) to *extremely confident* (7). Participants were also asked to guess which task they thought the average Colby student would choose.

After completion of the dependent measures, participants were debriefed and dismissed. Because they did not have the opportunity to win a prize, their names were entered into a lottery whose winners were awarded $10.

Results

Task choice. Participants were assigned a 0 for task choice if they chose to play the roulette wheel (the chance task) and a 1 if they chose to engage in the esthetic judgment task again. Thus, higher means on this variable signify a greater tendency to choose the esthetic judgment task again (and the mean in any one group is equal to the proportion of participants choosing the esthetic judgment task in that group). Task choice was then analyzed by a 2 × 2 between-subjects ANOVA, with absolute score (40% or 60%) and relative score (20% below average or 20% above average) as independent variables.[7] Cell means are reported in Table 12.2. This analysis revealed a main effect of absolute score, $F(1, 56) = 6.52$, $p < .02$; as seen in Table 12.2, participants were more likely to choose the esthetic judgment task again when they scored 60% the first time ($M = 0.77$) than when they scored 40% the first time ($M = 0.47$). Participants evidently did consider their score on the first task when making their choice. As predicted, there was also a main effect of relative score, $F(1, 56) = 3.94$, $p \leq .05$. Those participants who learned that their

TABLE 12.2. Study 2: Mean Responses on All Dependent Variables by Absolute and Relative Score

Dependent variable	20% higher than average score		20% lower than average score	
	40% score	60% score	40% score	60% score
Task choice[a]	0.67	0.80	0.27	0.73
Confidence in choice	3.20	3.60	3.20	3.40
Estimate of average student's choice[a]	0.36	0.27	0.60	0.47
Skill at esthetic judgment	4.13	4.47	3.13	3.80
Skill at picture-judging task	3.80	4.27	2.87	3.27
Happiness with performance	3.20	4.33	2.80	2.86
Confidence in ability	2.86	3.53	2.60	3.00
Importance of doing well	3.20	2.87	2.33	2.53
Task related to esthetic judgment	4.07	4.07	3.13	3.67
Role of luck and ability[b]	4.60	4.47	4.20	4.86
Amount bet on future trials	$20.40	$37.13	$21.53	$36.00

[a] Higher numbers on this variable signify greater preference for the esthetic judgment task. [b] Higher numbers on this variable signify greater attributions to ability than to luck.

score was above average were more likely to choose the esthetic judgment task ($M = 0.73$) than were those whose score was said to be below average ($M = 0.50$). There was no interaction. Participants' confidence in these choices was equivalent across the four groups; an ANOVA on this variable revealed no significant effects.

Guesses of what the average Colby student would choose were assessed by a similar 2 × 2 ANOVA. No significant effects emerged. Thus, although participants said to be above average were more likely

---

attributed to perceptions that one task was more attractive or afforded a greater chance of winning than the other. A pair of 2 × 2 ANOVAs on these variables revealed no effects for enjoyment and an unusual interaction on estimated likelihood of winning, such that estimates were highest in the 60%–above average condition, lowest in the 30%–above average condition, and moderate in the other two conditions.

[7] The effects of relative and absolute score on task choice were also assessed by means of z tests for proportions, a nonparametric alternative for dichotomous dependent variables. These analyses revealed identical results. F tests on dichotomous variables are generally good approximations of nonparametric tests (Winer, Brown, & Michels. 1991, p. 1028).

to choose the esthetic judgment than those said to be below average, they did not project this decision onto other participants. This finding suggests that the personalized feedback was not taken to be generally informative about the esthetic judgment task.

Satisfaction with performance. The four measures of satisfaction were submitted to a 2 (relative score: above average vs. below average) × 2 (absolute score: 40% vs. 60%) MANOVA, which revealed a significant main effect of relative score, $F(4, 51) = 6.76, p < .0001$, and no main effect of absolute score or an interaction. As seen in Table 12.2, univariate ANOVAs showed that below average participants rated themselves less highly than did above average participants on general esthetic judgment ability ($Ms = 3.50$ and 4.30, respectively), $F(1, 56) = 9.47, p < .01$, and picture-judging ability ($Ms = 3.07$ and 4.03, respectively), $F(1, 56) = 13.53, p < .001$, and were not as happy with their performance ($Ms = 2.83$ and 3.77, respectively), $F(1, 55) = 7.94, p < .01$. There was no effect of relative score on confidence in esthetic judgment ability.

Additional measures. Participants' ratings of how important it was to do well at the esthetic judgment task and how relevant the task was to esthetic judgment ability were also submitted to a 2 × 2 MANOVA. As seen in Table 12.2, it seemed that above average participants rated the importance of doing well at this task and the relevance of the task to esthetic judgment ability more highly than did below average participants. However, the MANOVA yielded only a marginal effect of relative score, $F(2, 55) = 2.88, p < .10$. There were no other significant effects.

Judgments of the relevance of luck and ability to performance at the task were submitted to a separate 2 × 2 ANOVA, which yielded no effects. It does not appear that participants made differential attributions about performance at the task as a consequence of the feedback they received.

Finally, a 2 × 2 ANOVA conducted on participants' estimates of how much money they would bet on future trials of the esthetic judgment task did

reveal a main effect of absolute score; participants scoring 60% indicated they would bet more ($M = \$36.55$) than those scoring 40% ($M = \$20.97$), $F(1, 55) = 20.11, p < .0001$. There were no other significant effects.

Mediational analyses. How did relative score influence participants' task choices? Social comparison feedback (regardless of its diagnosticity) was hypothesized to influence subsequent behavior through changes in people's self-evaluations. This hypothesis was tested by means of Baron and Kenny's (1986) procedure for determining mediation. To establish that self-assessment mediates the effect of comparative feedback on task choice, it is necessary to show that (a) when self-assessment is regressed on comparison feedback alone, the coefficient of comparison feedback is significant, (b) when task choice is regressed alone on comparison feedback, the coefficient of comparison feedback is significant, (c) when task choice is regressed alone on self-assessment, the coefficient of self-assessment is significant, and, finally, (d) when task choice is regressed on both self-assessment and comparison feedback, the coefficient of comparison feedback is reduced. In these analyses, comparison feedback was represented by relative score condition, and self-assessment was defined as the sum of the two items measuring perceived esthetic judgment ability ($r = .77, p < .0001$), both of which were shown earlier to be affected by the relative score manipulation. Owing to the dichotomous nature of the dependent variable (task choice), it was necessary to use logistic regressions whenever task choice was regressed on any other variables.

These analyses adhered to all four of Baron and Kenny's (1986) criteria. Steps a and b were shown earlier, and Step c was confirmed by a significant coefficient associated with self-assessment when task choice was regressed on it ($B = .74, p < .02$). Step d showed that the aforementioned effect of comparative feedback on task choice was reduced to nonsignificance ($B = .25, p = .41$) when controlling for self-assessment. Thus, changes in self-assessment seem to have mediated the effects of relative feedback on task choice.

Discussion

Paralleling Study 1, participants in this study attended to comparative information when judging their ability at this task. Relative to participants whose score was below average, those whose score was above average were more laudatory about their ability at this task and at esthetic judgment in general and were happier with their performance, regardless of what their absolute score was on the task. Given that participants had just received a score on an unusual test about which they had no prior beliefs, their use of comparative information in assessing performance seems understandable. However, in the next stage of the study, participants were forced to make a choice between two risky options, and in neither option was the probability of success tied to participants' comparative ability. Nevertheless, comparative standing still played a role in participants' choices. When they learned that their score on the first task was below average, they were less likely to choose this task again over the chance option than when their score was said to be above average.

Although the current data are consistent with the hypothesis that participants would use nondiagnostic social comparison information when making a decision, these data should not be interpreted to suggest that the use of such information was illogical. Participants who earned below average scores (whether the scores were above or below the 50% criterion) may have anticipated feeling exceptionally incompetent were they to nominate the esthetic judgment task and fail to achieve the criterion. Alternatively, participants may simply have chosen the task at which they felt most comfortable, and the data show that they were happiest with their performance on the first task when their score was above average. Several additional motives may have been present in this experimental situation. The idea that motives associated with the processing of social comparison information may enhance the effects of such information on behavior is an interesting one and deserves further attention.

It is also plausible that relative feedback provided subtle information about the general ease and enjoyability of the task, leading participants to make choices for themselves that they would expect anyone to make. However, when participants were asked to guess what the average student would choose, there were no effects of relative feedback, suggesting that participants' task choices were not projected onto their peers (and, as indicated in footnote 6, there were no effects on ratings of the enjoyability of the task). A similar argument holds that someone whose score of 40% was below average has learned that others have been able to achieve the criterion, suggesting that he or she may be able to do so; the person whose score of 40% was above average might have learned that a score of 50% was unattainable by anyone. If this was true, however, below average participants would have been more, rather than less, likely to choose the ability task than would above average participants, a pattern opposite to that found.

Finally, it is conceivable that relative feedback provided attributional information about the task; for example, participants whose score of 40% was said to be above average might have inferred that the task was highly ability driven (and might be more likely to infer that their experience on the first task would help them to improve on the next set of trials), whereas those whose score of 60% was below average might have inferred that they were lucky the first time and that they may not be able to sustain their good performance. Yet, when participants were asked to rate the extent to which luck and ability determined performance at the task, there were no effects of condition, reducing the viability of this account (although participants need not alter attributions about general performance at the task to attribute their own performance to luck, a possibility to which the data do not speak).[8]

As predicted, task choices also reflected sensitivity to objective standing. Consequential behaviors would appear to be more sensitive than affective or self-evaluative responses (or behavioral intentions) to objective information. Although people may ignore their absolute standing when judging their ability and their emotions, they may find it

---

[8] I thank two anonymous reviewers for their suggestions regarding these various alternative accounts.

more difficult to ignore this information when it bears on a decision with self-relevant implications. This account is underlined by the observation that participants' monetary bets on a hypothetical future esthetic judgment task were sensitive only to their absolute score on the first task.

How does relative standing influence risky decision making, even when the outcome of the decision is independent of relative standing? Mediational analyses showed that relative feedback affected behavior through changes in self-evaluation. Learning that one was below or above average seemed to lead to the inference that one was incapable or capable of achieving the experimenter's criterion in another round of the esthetic judgment task.

In Studies 1 and 2, relative feedback influenced a variety of different psychological variables. However, these main effects do not identify what particular type of relative feedback was influential. As noted in the introduction, people prefer desirable comparison feedback. Thus, participants in the below average condition of Study 2 may not have altered their self-perceptions of ability; instead, the main effect of relative score may have emerged because participants in the above average condition increased their self-perceptions of ability. Similarly, the difference in task choice between above and below average participants may have been due to heightened self-perceptions of ability among above average participants. To address these possibilities, the next study included a control group that did not receive any relative feedback. The below and above average groups were then compared with this control group, to determine which group (or groups) was responsible for the main effects of relative feedback in Study 2. Study 3 also provided an opportunity to replicate the mediational findings of Study 2.

Study 3

Method

Participants. Participants were 60 Colby College undergraduates (82% women and 18% men), who participated for pay. They were tested individually

and were randomly assigned to one of the three conditions.

Materials and procedure. The materials and procedure were identical to those in Study 2, with two exceptions. First, because none of the predictions of Study 3 involved effects of absolute feedback, all participants were told they answered 40% correctly on the esthetic judgment task. Second, in addition to the above and below average conditions, a control condition was included, in which participants were given no information about their relative standing.

Results

Task choice. As in the previous study, participants were assigned a 0 if they chose the roulette wheel and a 1 if they chose the esthetic judgment task. Task choice was then submitted to a one-way ANOVA, with condition (below average, control, or above average) as a between-subjects independent variable. As seen in Table 12.3, this analysis

TABLE 12.3. Study 3: Mean Responses on All Dependent Variables, by Condition

	Condition		
Dependent variable	Below average	Control	Above average
Task choice[a]	0.35_x	0.55_{xy}	0.75_y
Confidence in choice	3.40	3.21	3.65
Estimate of average student's choice[a]	0.60	0.32	0.30
Skill at esthetic judgment	3.60	3.95	4.50
Skill at picture-judging task	2.95_x	3.25_x	4.30_y
Happiness with performance	2.35_x	2.89_x	3.90_y
Confidence in ability	2.80	2.95	3.45
Importance of doing well	2.10_x	2.00_x	3.00_y
Task related to esthetic judgment	3.05	3.40	4.10
Role of luck and ability[b]	3.50	4.10	4.00
Amount bet on future trials	$\$26.15_x$	$\$17.11_y$	$\$28.25_x$

Note: Means in the same row having different superscripts differ significantly at $p < .05$ in the Tukey honestly significant difference comparison.
[a] Higher numbers on this variable signify greater preference for the esthetic judgment task. [b] Higher numbers on this variable signify greater attributions to ability than to luck.

revealed a main effect of condition, $F(2, 57) = 3.44$, $p < .05$. Participants in the above average condition were most likely ($M = 0.75$) and participants in the below average condition least likely ($M = 0.35$) to choose the esthetic judgment task again. These means were similar to those found in the 40% conditions of Study 2 ($Ms = 0.67$ and 0.27, respectively). The control group mean fell directly in between those of the above and below average groups ($M = 0.55$). Tukey honestly significant difference (HSD) comparisons showed that the difference between the feedback groups was significant ($p < .05$) but that the differences between each feedback group and the control group fell short of significance ($p > .10$). Although the percentage of participants in the control group choosing esthetic judgment was no greater than chance (or 50%), the two feedback groups yielded percentages that were significantly above and below 50%, $ts(19) = 3.85$, $ps < .01$. There was no effect of condition on participants' confidence in these choices, showing that participants in the three conditions were equally confident in the choices they made.

A one-way ANOVA conducted on estimates of what the average student would choose did not reveal a significant main effect of condition. As in Study 1, then, participants did not project their task preferences to other people, suggesting that the feedback was not informative with regard to the general ease or desirability of the esthetic judgment task.

Satisfaction with performance. The four satisfaction measures were included in a one-way MANOVA, with condition as a between-subjects independent variable. This analysis yielded the predicted main effect of condition, $F(8, 106) = 3.24$, $p < .002$. Univariate ANOVAs yielded a main effect of condition on how good participants believed they were at the picture task, $F(2, 56) = 10.23$, $p < .0001$, and how happy they were with their performance, $F(2, 56) = 8.63$, $p < .001$. As seen in Table 12.3, the above average group was significantly higher on these measures than the below average and control groups, which did not differ among themselves (based on Tukey HSD comparisons). Although

significant main effects did not emerge for ratings of happiness with performance and confidence in ability, the means for these items followed the same pattern as above. On the basis of these findings, it would appear that participants increased their self-evaluations of ability when receiving feedback that they were above average but were unaffected when receiving feedback that they were below average.

Additional measures. Ratings of personal importance to do well at the task and perceived relevance of the task to esthetic judgment ability were also submitted to a one-way MANOVA, which, unlike Study 1, yielded a main effect of condition, $F(4, 112) = 2.63$, $p < .05$. Univariate tests showed a significant main effect of condition on ratings of personal importance, $F(2, 57) = 4.23$, $p < .02$; Tukey's HSD comparisons showed that above average participants considered it more important to do well at this task than did the below average and control groups, which did not differ among themselves (see Table 12.3). Ratings of relevance to esthetic judgment followed the same pattern but did not reveal acceptable levels of significance.

No main effect of condition emerged in a one-way ANOVA conducted on ratings of whether performance on the esthetic judgment task was related more to luck or ability. Thus, participants did not modify their attributional beliefs about the task after the receipt of feedback.

Finally, there was a main effect of condition on the amount of money participants were willing to bet in hypothetical future trials of the task, $F(2, 56) = 3.41$, $p < .05$, with participants in the two feedback groups indicating they would bet more money than those in the control group (see Table 12.3). Because there were no differences between the feedback groups, these findings will not be discussed further.

Mediational analyses. In Study 2, it was found that the effect of comparative feedback on task choice was mediated by self-assessment. To determine the replicability of these findings, it was necessary to once again submit the data to Baron and Kenny's (1986) procedure for determining mediation. Once again, self-assessment was defined as the sum of the two items measuring esthetic judgment ability ($r = .64, p < .0001$).[9]

As in Study 1, this procedure required independent effects of comparison feedback on self-assessment and task choice; these effects are reported above. It was also necessary for self-assessment to reveal a significant effect when task choice was regressed on it. Such an effect was observed, although it was marginal ($B = .46, p = .08$). Finally, when controlling for self-assessment, the effect of comparison feedback on task choice became nonsignificant ($p = .15$). These findings mirror those of Study 1, with the exception of the marginal relationship between self-assessment and task choice.[10]

Discussion

As in Study 2, participants in this study were faced with a choice between another 20 trials of the esthetic judgment task, in which they needed to answer 50% correctly to win a prize, and a chance-determined task affording the participant a 50% probability of winning. Although all participants were told that they answered 40% of the items correctly in the first task, those who believed this score to be above average were significantly more likely than those believing it to be below average to choose the esthetic judgment task. Once again, then, participants made task choices that were sensitive to social comparison information, and as before, this effect seemed to be mediated by changes in self-evaluation of ability.

The inclusion of a control group permitted an assessment of how the desirability of comparison feedback qualifies reactions to this feedback. Although above average feedback elevated participants' ratings of ability and of the personal importance of doing well at the task, below average feedback did not have the opposite effect. It is likely that the below average feedback evoked coping mechanisms designed to reduce its thrust. The effects on task choice, however, seemed to show a different pattern. Compared with the control group, the above average group seemed more likely, and the below average group less likely, to choose the esthetic judgment task again, suggesting that participants' behaviors were sensitive to relative standing regardless of its valence. Unfortunately, this conclusion is only tentative because the differences between the feedback and control groups were not significant. The percentages of participants in the feedback groups choosing esthetic judgment did turn out to be significantly different than what one might expect by chance, whereas the percentage in the control group was not. On balance, the study provided very tentative evidence that negative comparison feedback may exert different effects on behavior than on affect or self-evaluation.

General Discussion

When people attempt to evaluate themselves, objective criteria are often elusive, necessitating the use of social comparison information. Someone who receives a score on an intelligence test cannot be sure what this score suggests without some knowledge about how others have performed. In other situations, objective standards are more accessible, and in such cases, one might expect attention to social comparison information to be minimal and attention to objective standards to be maximal. The findings of the current investigation tell a different story. In Study 1, individuals indicated that they would be less disturbed, would be less likely to change their behaviors, and would consider their

---

[9]Because relative score did not exert a significant effect on the general measure of perceived esthetic judgment ability (as it did in Study 2), the analyses that follow were also conducted on just the item measuring perceived ability at the specific experimental task. The results were identical.

[10]Because relative score was also shown to influence participants' reported importance of doing well at the task, similar analyses were conducted with this item as a mediator. Again,

all four criteria of Baron and Kenny's (1986) procedure were achieved. In the last step, when controlling for self-rated importance, the effect of relative score on task choice was reduced to nonsignificance. However, because the effect of relative score on importance was only marginal in Study 2 (and in follow-up analyses was shown not to mediate the effect of relative score on task choice), these findings may not be reliable.

abilities in more glowing terms, were they to learn that they possessed a lower level of risk than that of their peers, even if this risk level was objectively high. In Studies 2 and 3, when participants weighed the choice of whether to engage in a task at which they were required to meet an objective criterion to succeed, their decision was influenced by whether their score on their first attempt at the task was above or below average. These results point to the power of social comparison information and also question Festinger's (1954) hypothesis that people will only attend to social comparison standards when objective standards are unavailable.

Why did participants assign such importance to their relative standing? Attention to such information may reflect any number of possible motives. In Studies 2 and 3, for example, participants might have anticipated feeling greater regret from failing at the second task after achieving a below rather than above average score. Moreover, in the context of highly diagnostic objective information, seemingly irrelevant social comparison information may still prove useful. If individuals rely on the (potentially accurate) heuristic that they are more likely to improve on dimensions for which they already show relative superiority, comparative feedback may be singularly helpful. At the same time, people might also dismiss health precautions or make inadvisable career decisions due to an overuse of comparison information vis-à-vis objective information. Thus, although attention to social comparisons in the context of objective criteria is not necessarily illogical or detrimental, it seems essential to explore in future work the conditions under which it might be so.

One could argue that participants in these studies used the relative information only because they inferred that they should do so, thinking that investigators would not have provided it if it did not serve a purpose (cf. Bless, Strack, & Schwarz, 1993). Although this is possible, objective information in these studies was not portrayed by the experimenters as any less useful and attention to the relative feedback depended in part on the desirability of the feedback, a result that could not be predicted by demand characteristics alone. Moreover, in the latter two studies, the experimenters gave participants the social comparison information informally

and implied that it was provided only for their own interest. Finally, and most important, people often receive absolute and relative information about a dimension in much the same way as in these studies, adding to the external validity of the approach taken here. For example, patients receiving a health risk appraisal are told their own risk and the risk of the average person in their peer group (e.g., Shoenbach, 1987), and students receive both their own score and the average student's score on exams. Despite these observations, however, it will be important in future research to investigate people's spontaneous use of social comparison information when objective criteria are available.

Naturally, objective information will not always be ignored when social comparison information is accessible: A constellation of personal and situational factors is likely to determine the use of each. The current findings suggest that objective information may play a more substantial role in the decision to engage in a behavior than in one's affect or self-evaluation, as suggested indirectly by the emergence of a main effect of absolute standing in Study 2 (where participants made a decision with immediate consequences) but not Study 1 (where participants estimated reactions to hypothetical scenarios). Such a conclusion is also supported by the finding in Study 2 that participants' willingness to bet money on future trials of the esthetic judgment task was determined by their absolute scores but not their relative scores. Attention to comparative feedback may also be dampened when it is undesirable. In Study 3, comparison feedback affected participants' self-perceptions only when the feedback was desirable (see also Weinstein & Klein, 1995). However, Study 3 offers the tentative possibility that comparison feedback may influence behavior regardless of its desirability.

Objective information might also be more influential when it is consistent with a desired conclusion, particularly when social comparison information is inconsistent with this conclusion. For example, a skier whose prowess pales in comparison with that of her friends may nevertheless conclude that her skiing ability is outstanding on the basis of the objective facts that she can negotiate black diamond trails and successfully teach others to ski. Furthermore, social comparisons may be influential before an objective criterion is achieved and less so once that criterion is surpassed. Would-be ballet dancers might consider comparisons with other dancers more important before auditioning for a role in a dancing troupe than they would after getting the role. It is also likely that the cost, ambiguity, and availability of objective information may determine one's interest in obtaining it. For example, Raats and Sparks (1995) may have observed greater attention to absolute than relative fat intake because such information was disambiguated by contextualizing it within recommendations given by health professionals. In general, further research is needed on how people use comparative and objective information, particularly given that a large proportion of social comparison research has focused on the processes characterizing such comparisons rather than the way in which social comparison information is used once it is secured.

How does the processing of nondiagnostic comparison feedback influence behavior? Mediational analyses in Studies 2 and 3 begin to provide an answer. In both studies, the effects of relative feedback on behavior seemed to occur through changes in participants' self-evaluations of their ability. On the surface, the inference that one possesses high absolute standing after learning that one is better than others seems reasonable. Indeed, many judgments of ability are based on where one stands relative to others: The best student in a class graded on a normal distribution gets the A, the salesperson with the smallest remaining inventory gets the promotion, and the shortstop with the highest fielding percentage gets the Gold Glove Award. However, as noted throughout this article, such an inference is often not warranted. Nevertheless, even when relative standing is independent of absolute standing, relative standing may affect behavior through this process of modifying self-evaluations.

Our comparisons with others clearly play an important role in the way we see ourselves. In many ways, Western culture encourages a comparative ideology by promoting competition for scarce resources. Sometimes people are said to have

succeeded because they are better than others and not because they have achieved a particular criterion, such as when the fastest runner gets the medal. Nevertheless, in some cases, particularly when making judgments of ability and personal risk and decisions under uncertainty, how we compare with others may not be as important as how we stand up to an objective criterion. It is this realization that would help people to acknowledge that having below average risk is not necessarily equivalent to having low risk, without the need to take precautions. Likewise, it would help investors who expect comfortable retirements because their incomes are above average to recognize that their savings may still fall short of what they need. A better understanding of when and how people use objective and relative standards would be an important theoretical step, as well as a boon to those in health and other professions whose goal it is to change consequential behavior.

REFERENCES

Albert, S. (1977). Temporal comparison theory. *Psychological Review, 84*, 485–503.

Baron, R. M., & Kenny, D. A. (1986). The moderator–mediator variable distinction in social psychological research: Conceptual, strategic, and statistical considerations. *Journal of Personality and Social Psychology, 51*, 1173–1182.

Bernstein, M., & Crosby, F. (1980). An empirical examination of relative deprivation theory. *Journal of Experimental Social Psychology, 16*, 442–456.

Bless, H., Strack, F., & Schwarz, N. (1993). The informative functions of research procedures: Bias and the logic of conversation. *British Journal of Social Psychology, 23*, 149–165.

Boggiano, A. K., & Ruble, D. N. (1979). Competence and the overjustification effect: A developmental study. *Journal of Personality and Social Psychology, 37*, 1462–1468.

Brickman, P., & Bulman, R. J. (1977). Pleasure and pain in social comparison. In J. M. Suls & R. L. Miller (Eds.), *Social comparison processes: Theoretical and empirical perspectives* (pp. 149–186). Washington, DC: Hemisphere.

Campbell, J. D. (1986). Similarity and uniqueness: The effects of attribute type, relevance, and individual differences in self-esteem and depression. *Journal of Personality and Social Psychology, 50*, 281–294.

Campbell, J. D., Fairey, P. J., & Fehr, B. (1986). Better than me or better than thee? Reactions to intrapersonal and interpersonal feedback. *Journal of Personality, 54*, 479–493.

Collins, R. L. (1996). For better or worse: The impact of upward social comparison on self-evaluations. *Psychological Bulletin, 119*, 51–69.

Conway, M., & Ross, M. (1984). Getting what you want by revising what you had. *Journal of Personality and Social Psychology, 47*, 738–748.

Emmons, R. A., & Diener, E. (1985). Factors predicting satisfaction judgments: A comparative examination. *Social Indicators Research, 16*, 157–167.

Felson, R. B., & Reed, M. D. (1986). Reference groups and self-appraisals of academic ability and performance. *Social Psychology Quarterly, 49*, 103–109.

Festinger, L. A. (1954). A theory of social comparison processes. *Human Relations, 7*, 117–140.

Fox, C. R., & Kahneman, D. (1992). Correlations, causes, and heuristics in surveys of life satisfaction. *Social Indicators Research, 27*, 221–234.

Frank, R. H. (1985). *Choosing the right pond: Human behavior and the quest for status.* New York: Oxford University Press.

Gibbons, F. X., Benbow, C. P., & Gerrard, M. (1994). From top dog to bottom half: Social comparison strategies in response to poor performance. *Journal of Personality and Social Psychology, 67*, 638–652.

Gibbons, F. X., Gerrard, M., & Boney McCoy, S. (1995). Prototype perception predicts (lack of) pregnancy prevention. *Personality and Social Psychology Bulletin, 21*, 85–93.

Gibbons, F. X., Gerrard, M., Lando, H. A., & McGovern, P. G. (1991). Social comparison and smoking cessation: The role of the "typical smoker." *Journal of Experimental Social Psychology, 27*, 239–258.

Gilbert, D. T., Giesler, R. B., & Morris, K. A. (1995). When comparisons arise. *Journal of Personality and Social Psychology, 69*, 227–236.

Goethals, G. R., Messick, D. M., & Allison, S. T. (1991). The uniqueness bias: Studies of constructive social comparison. In J. Suls & T. A. Wills (Eds.), *Social comparison research: Contemporary theory and research* (pp. 149–176). Hillsdale, NJ: Erlbaum.

Guth, W., Schmittberger, R., & Schwarze, B. (1982). An experimental analysis of ultimatum bargaining. *Journal of Economic Behavior and Organization, 3*, 367–388.

Kahneman, D., & Tversky, A. (1979). Prospect theory: An analysis of decision under risk. *Econometrika, 47*, 263–291.

Klein, W. M. (1996). Maintaining self-serving social comparisons: Attenuating the perceived significance of risk-increasing behaviors. *Journal of Social and Clinical Psychology, 15*, 120–142.

Klein, W. M., & Kunda, Z. (1993). Maintaining self-serving social comparisons: Biased reconstruction of one's past behaviors. *Personality and Social Psychology Bulletin, 19*, 732–739.

Klein, W. M., & Weinstein, N. D. (in press). Social comparison and unrealistic optimism about personal risk. In B. P. Buunk & F. X. Gibbons (Eds.), *Health, coping, and well-being: Perspectives from social comparison theory.* Hillsdale, NJ: Erlbaum.

Koestner, R., Zuckerman, M., & Olsson, J. (1990). Attributional style, comparison focus of praise, and intrinsic motivation. *Journal of Research in Personality, 24*, 87–100.

Kruglanski, A. W., & Mayseless, O. (1990). Classic and current social comparison research: Expanding the perspective. *Psychological Bulletin, 108*, 195–208.

Levine, J. M., & Green, S. M. (1984). Acquisition of relative performance information: The roles of intrapersonal and interpersonal comparison. *Personality and Social Psychology Bulletin, 10*, 385–393.

Loewenstein, G. F., Thompson, L., & Bazerman, M. H. (1989). Social utility and decision making in interpersonal contexts. *Journal of Personality and Social Psychology, 57*, 426–441.

Marks, G., & Miller, N. (1987). Ten years of research on the false-consensus effect: An empirical and theoretical review. *Psychological Bulletin, 102*, 72–90.

Marsh, H. W., & Parker, J. W. (1984), Determinants of student self-concept: Is it better to be a relatively large fish in a small pond even if you don't learn to swim as well? *Journal of Personality and Social Psychology, 47*, 213–231.

Meier, N. C. (1940). *The Meier art tests: Art judgment.* Iowa City: University of Iowa, Bureau of Educational Research and Service.

Miller, D. T., & Turnbull, W. (1990). The counterfactual fallacy: Confusing what might have been with what ought to have been. *Social Justice Research, 4*, 1–19.

Raats, M. M., & Sparks, P. (1995, July). *Evidence for unrealistic optimism about diet-related risks: Practical and theoretical implications.* Paper presented at the meetings of the European Congress of Psychology, Athens, Greece.

Richins, M. L. (1991). Social comparison and the idealized images of advertising. *Journal of Consumer Research, 18*, 71–83.

Sanders, G. S. (1981). The interactive effect of social comparison and objective information on the decision to see a doctor. *Journal of Applied Social Psychology, 11*, 390–400.

Sanders, G. S. (1982). Social comparison and perceptions of health and illness. In G. S. Sanders & J. Suls (Eds.), *Social psychology of health and illness* (pp. 129–157). Hillsdale, NJ: Erlbaum.

Schoenbach, V. J. (1987). Appraising the Health Risk Appraisal. *American Journal of Public Health, 77*, 347–352.

Suls, J., Marco, C. A., & Tobin, S. (1991). The role of temporal comparison, social comparison, and direct appraisal in the elderly's self-evaluations of health. *Journal of Applied Social Psychology, 21*, 1125–1144.

Taylor, S. E., & Brown, J. D. (1988). Illusion and well-being: A social psychological perspective on mental health. *Psychological Bulletin, 103*, 193–210.

Taylor, S. E., Collins, R. L., Skokan, L. A., & Aspinwall, L. G. (1989). Maintaining positive illusions in the face of negative information: Getting the facts without letting them get to you. *Journal of Social and Clinical Psychology, 8*, 114–129.

Taylor, S. E., Neter, E., & Wayment, H. A. (1995). Self-evaluation processes. *Personality and Social Psychology Bulletin, 12*, 1278–1287.

Tesser, A., & Campbell, J. (1980). Self-definition: The impact of relative performance and similarity of others. *Social Psychology Quarterly, 43*, 341–347.

Tesser, A., Millar, M., & Moore, J. (1988). Some affective consequences of social comparison and reflection processes: The pain and pleasure of being close. *Journal of Personality and Social Psychology, 54*, 49–61.

Weinstein, N. D. (1980). Unrealistic optimism about future life events. *Journal of Personality and Social Psychology, 39*, 806–820.

Weinstein, N. D., & Klein, W. M. (1995). Resistance of personal risk perceptions to debiasing interventions. *Health Psychology, 14*, 132–140.

Wheeler, L., & Miyake, K. (1992). Social comparison in everyday life. *Journal of Personality and Social Psychology, 62*, 760–773.

Wills, T. A. (1987). Downward comparison as a coping mechanism. In C. R. Snyder & C. Ford (Eds.), *Coping with negative life events: Clinical and social-psychological perspectives* (pp. 243–268). New York: Plenum.

Winer, B. J., Brown, D. R., & Michels, K. M. (1991). *Statistical principles in experimental design.* New York: McGraw-Hill.

Wood, J. V. (1989). Theory and research concerning social comparisons of personal attributes. *Psychological Bulletin, 106*, 231–248.

Wood, J. V., Taylor, S. E., & Lichtman, R. R. (1985). Social comparison in adjustment to breast cancer. *Journal of Personality and Social Psychology, 49*, 1169–1183.

Received February 7, 1996
Revision received August, 1996
Accepted August 19, 1996 ■

Myopic Social Prediction and the Solo Comparison Effect

Don A. Moore and Tai Gyu Kim

Four experiments explored the psychological processes by which people make comparative social judgments. Each participant chose how much money to wager on beating an opponent on either a difficult or a simple trivia quiz. Quiz difficulty did not influence the average person's probability of winning, yet participants bet more on a simple quiz than on a difficult quiz in the first 3 experiments. The results suggest that this effect results from a tendency to attend more closely to a focal actor than to others. Experiment 4 directly manipulated focusing; when participants were led to focus on the opponent instead of themselves, the effect was reversed. The discussion relates the results to other literatures including overly optimistic self-evaluation, false consensus, overconfidence, and social comparison.

Would you be more likely to win a race in excellent conditions, on a dry track and at comfortable temperatures, or in the pouring rain at frigid temperatures? Certainly it is easier to imagine that you would perform well under ideal conditions, but what about your opponents? Comparative social judgments are an important aspect of psychological theories such as those on social comparison, intergroup perception, and social identity (Clement & Krueger, 2002; Messick & Mackie, 1989; Suls & Wheeler, 2000; Turner, 1987). They are also central to research findings on the false consensus effect,

Don A. Moore, Graduate School of Industrial Administration, Carnegie Mellon University, and Australian Graduate School of Management, University of New South Wales, Sydney, Australia; Tai Gyu Kim, Graduate School of Industrial Administration, Carnegie Mellon University.

This research was funded by a Berkman junior faculty development grant at Carnegie Mellon University. Thanks go to Max Bazerman, Daylian Cain, Corey Fallon, Adam Galinsky, George Loewenstein, Denise Rousseau, Kavita Shah, Sapna Shah, Sam Swift, Georg Weiszäcker, and Paul Windschitl for their comments on a previous version of this article. We also appreciate Laurie Weingart, Seungwoo Kwon, Wemi Peters, Erin Morgan, and Jeff Crilley for their help with data collection.

Correspondence concerning this article should be addressed to Don A. Moore, Graduate School of Industrial Administration, Carnegie Mellon University, 5000 Forbes Avenue, Pittsburgh, Pennsylvania 15213. E-mail: don.moore@alumni.carleton.edu the false uniqueness effect, the spotlight effect, and the above-average effect (Epley & Dunning, 2000; Gilovich, Medvec, & Savitsky, 2000; Goethals, Messick, & Allison, 1991; Krueger & Clement, 1994; Ross, Greene, & House, 1977). In addition to their theoretical importance, comparative social judgments also have tremendous practical implications. Anticipating how one will perform relative to competitors is fundamental to a variety of decisions, such as whether to open a new business, apply for a job, ask someone out on a date, or bet on a contest. This article advances theory and research by illuminating the processes by which people make comparative interpersonal judgments and argues that such judgments tend to be overly focused on a single causal agent. In other words, even ostensibly comparative social judgments are often myopic solo judgments of a single actor.

Recent work (Klar & Giladi, 1999; Kruger, 1999) has shown that relative judgments ("How happy are you compared with the average person?") are more strongly correlated with self-judgments ("How happy are you?") than with judgments of others ("How happy is the average person?"; see also Eiser, Pahl, & Prins, 2001; Epley & Dunning, 2000). It follows that if most people see themselves as happy, then when asked "How happy are you compared with the average person?" people will, on average, rate themselves above average. Kruger (1999) replicates the *above-average* effect by demonstrating that people rate themselves above average in domains for which the average person feels capable, such as driving a car or operating a computer mouse. These same people, however, rate themselves *below average* in more challenging domains such as juggling and computer programming.

Explanations

One possible explanation for these above- and below-average effects is egocentrism: When people are asked to compare themselves with others, they focus primarily on themselves and use self-ratings as a basis for relative ratings. The logic for this explanation lies in the privileged status necessarily held by the self in awareness. There will always be special interest and attention devoted to self-relevant activities, outcomes, and judgments (Markus, 1977; Mussweiler, Gabriel, & Bodenhausen, 2000; Ross & Sicoly, 1979). People know more about themselves, think more about themselves, and care more about themselves than about any other single individual. In addition, people are more sensitive to situational influences on their own behavior than on the behavior of others (Jones & Nisbett, 1972; Ross, 1977). It makes sense, then, that people might tend to focus egocentrically on the self when predicting joint social outcomes.

The second possible explanation for these myopic errors in social judgment is a more general one based on focusing: People focus their attention too much on one actor, which may or may not be the self, at the expense of considering other relevant people. There are many domains in which people give undue weight, undue thought, and undue attention to a focal cause, actor, or hypothesis, and neglect the consideration of other causes, actors, or hypotheses (Kahneman & Tversky, 1973, 1982; Legrenzi, Girotto, & Johnson-Laird, 1993; Schkade & Kahneman, 1998; Wilson, Wheatley, Meyers, Gilbert, & Axsom, 2000). For example, research shows that people routinely give special consideration to a focal hypothesis, evaluating evidence in its light, and failing to give adequate attention to alternative hypotheses or disconfirming evidence (Brenner, Koehler, & Tversky, 1996; Gilovich, 1991; Klayman & Ha, 1987; Tversky & Koehler, 1994). Tversky (1977) identified focusing as a natural result of making comparative judgments, especially when the comparison is directional. For example, Tversky and Gati (1978) reported that 98.6% of their Israeli participants preferred the phrase "Canada is similar to the U.S.A." over "The U.S.A. is similar to Canada." The more prominent or salient object takes on a special position as the referent due to the directional nature of this comparative judgment.

The notion that egocentrism is merely a subset of focusing is not a new one in social psychology. Some important phenomena that were first documented as exclusively egocentric effects later came to be viewed as the product of focusing on the self.

Evidence for focusing has come from manipulations that change "egocentric" effects by leading people to focus on others rather than themselves. For example, the actor–observer difference describes the egocentric tendency for people to explain their own behavior using more situational attributions than do observers, whose explanations tend to be more dispositional (Jones & Nisbett, 1972). Storms (1973) was able to show that actors could be made into observers simply by changing the perspective from which they viewed the interaction: People who watched a videotape of themselves made more situational attributions for their own behavior. Such simple perspective-taking manipulations can be sufficient to get people to take on others' points of view and make decisions that focus on others as they normally would focus on themselves (Galinsky & Moskowitz, 2000; Taylor & Fiske, 1975; Thompson, 1995).

The Present Research

Both the egocentrism and the focusing explanations have an intriguing and previously unexplored implication for the psychological processes at work in predicting competitive social outcomes. If people focus on themselves, they will myopically predict that they will benefit more from favorable circumstances than others will, and that they will also suffer more from situational constraints. As a result, people will predict themselves likely to win competitions based on simple tasks (on which all competitors perform well) and likely to lose competitions based on difficult tasks (on which all competitors perform poorly).

There are two distinct reasons to expect such myopic comparisons: differential weighting and differential error. Differential weighting describes the tendency to attend more closely to one's own performance than that of others. Evidence for differential weighting appears in the weight that people give their own performances relative to those of their opponents in predicting relative performance (see Kruger, 1999). The second reason to expect myopic comparisons is differential error. People's predictions of others are likely to be made with more error than their predictions of themselves simply because they have less information about others. On simple problems, error is likely to result in underestimation of performance because of ceiling effects. If nearly everyone gets the problem right, then any error in assessing performance will underestimate it. On difficult problems, by contrast, error is likely to result in overestimation of performance because of floor effects (see Erev, Wallsten, & Budescu, 1994). If people estimate others' behavior with more error than they estimate their own behavior, their predictions of others will be more regressive than their predictions of themselves. As a result, people will predict that others will perform worse than themselves on simple tasks, and that others will perform better than themselves on difficult tasks.

In this article, we present a series of experiments that investigate the influence of task difficulty on comparative social judgment and test the psychological processes involved. This research makes at least three unique contributions. First, although prior work has documented above- and below-average effects when individuals are comparing themselves with the group average (Klar & Giladi, 1997; Kruger, 1999), the experiments presented here also obtain comparative judgments in which people compare two individuals with each other: We examine above- and below-average effects both when individuals compare themselves with a randomly selected group member and when they compare two randomly selected individuals with each other. This is important because some explanations for this type of effect have been based on the difficulties associated with comparing one with many (Giladi & Klar, 2002; Klar & Giladi, 1997; Koehler, Brenner, & Tversky, 1997).

Second, the present experiments take place in a competitive context. This contrasts with prior research on egocentric social comparison conducted in nonstrategic situations (Klar & Giladi, 1999; Klein & Kunda, 1994; Kruger, 1999). The participants in the experiments presented here were all betting on contests. We manipulated the difficulty of the quiz on which the contest was based. Although quiz difficulty does not influence the average competitor's probability of winning (because everyone is competing with others taking the same quiz), we expected it to influence participants' predictions regarding their probability of winning. If there is a familiar social situation in which people should have both the motivation and the experience to think strategically about others, it would be in competitions. Therefore, it would be somewhat ironic if people made myopic judgments in competitions, given the importance of accurate interpersonal comparison in competitive contexts, and given prior research showing that people attend closely, even obsessively, to comparative social information in other domains (Blount & Bazerman, 1996; Gilbert, Giesler, & Morris, 1995; Loewenstein, Thompson, & Bazerman, 1989).

Third, the present research presents the strongest evidence to date identifying the causes at work behind myopic social comparison effects. The studies presented here are able to distinguish the focusing explanation from pure egocentrism and explore the two underlying mechanisms of differential weighting and differential error.

Experiment 1 demonstrates self-focused social judgment in a competitive context. Experiment 2 highlights its robustness by replicating the effect of quiz difficulty in a situation that should minimize its impact. The results of Experiment 3 replicate Experiments 1 and 2, and find that they hold even when participants compare two randomly selected individuals. In addition, the results from Experiment 3 help rule out several of the most likely alternative explanations for Experiments 1 and 2. Finally, Experiment 4 directly manipulates attentional focus. Experiment 4 replicates the results of Experiments 1–3 among participants focusing on themselves. However, outcome is reversed for participants focusing on the opponent.

Experiment 1: The Trivia Game

In Experiment 1, participants were invited to bet on a competition. Because winning depended on relative scores, the amount that people bet should have depended on predictions of relative standing. However, consistent with the logic of myopic prediction, we expected that participants would correctly anticipate that they would get better scores on a

simple quiz than on a difficult quiz, but would not fully appreciate that others would also perform better on a simple quiz. We hypothesized that participants would be more likely to predict success— and to bet more—when the quiz was simple than when it was difficult. This logic also predicts that manipulations that influence the probability of winning should not have a strong effect on betting if they do not directly influence the individual's absolute score. We therefore also manipulated the hurdle: Participants had to beat either one other person or five other people in order to win. We expected that the manipulation that should not affect bets—quiz difficulty—would; and the manipulation that should influence bets—the hurdle— would not. Both predictions are consistent with a myopic prediction process in which people focus on their own absolute performances and over-simplify, ignore, or underweight the behavior of others.

Method

Participants. We recruited 78 undergraduate students at Carnegie Mellon University by offering them money to participate in an experiment.[1] All participants participated at the same time in a large auditorium in which they could see everyone else and knew they were all completing the same exercise. Participants began the experiment with a promise to be paid $4. They were given the choice of keeping all $4 or wagering any portion of it on their performance in a trivia competition. Participants who won their bets would have any amount they wagered doubled and added to the portion of the $4 not wagered. Participants who lost would only receive the unwagered portion of the $4. This exercise took roughly 5 min to complete and could yield a maximum payoff of $8, a substantial sum for students whose maximum wage for on-campus work was $10 per hour.

Design. The experiment had a 2 (hurdle: beat one vs. five opponents) × 2 (quiz difficulty: easy vs. difficult) between-subjects factorial design. All participants were told their scores would be compared with those of five others, all of whom would

---

[1] Participants also took part in two other experiments in the same experimental session.

be taking the same quiz. Participants in the high-hurdle condition had to beat the highest score of the five to win. Participants in the low-hurdle condition only had to beat the lowest score of the five to win.

Participants in the simple quiz condition were told they would be taking a simple trivia quiz and shown the following example question:

> What is the common name for the star inside our own solar system?
> Answer: the sun

Participants in the difficult quiz condition were told they would be taking a difficult trivia quiz and shown the following example question:

> What is the name of the closest star outside our solar system?
> Answer: Proxima Centauri

Participants were told that they would be competing against others taking the same quiz.

After making and submitting their bets, participants took their trivia quizzes, which included six questions and a seventh tiebreaker question (on which scores were a function of the distance from the correct answer) that virtually eliminated the possibility of a tied score.

Results

Participants wagered an average of $2.35 ($SD$ = $1.62). Wagers were subject to a 2 (quiz difficulty) $\times$ 2 (hurdle) factorial analysis of variance (ANOVA). The results are consistent with our predictions in demonstrating a highly significant effect of quiz difficulty, $F(1, 74) = 29.81$, $p < .001$. As Figure 13.1 shows, participants taking a simple quiz wagered significantly more (M = $2.95, SD = $1.43) than did participants taking a difficult quiz (M = $1.74, SD = $1.59). Notably, neither the main effect of hurdle, $F(1, 74) = 2.03$, ns, nor its interaction with quiz difficulty, $F(1, 74) = 1.31$, ns, is significant.

In actuality, the difficulty of the quiz had no bearing on the average likelihood of winning. Mean scores on the simple quiz (M = 4.03, SD = 1.35) were higher than on the difficult quiz (M = 1.84, SD = 1.46), $t(76) = 6.86$, $p < .001$, and individual ability may interact with quiz difficulty. Nevertheless, because each participant was competing

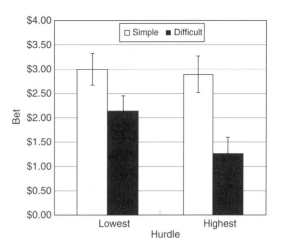

FIGURE 13.1 ■ Bets (Experiment 1). Bars indicate standard errors.

with others who had taken the same quiz, the odds of winning were equal on the two quizzes. However, the hurdle manipulation had dramatic consequences on the average participant's chance of winning. When participants had to beat five others, the probability of winning was roughly 16%, whereas when participants had to beat one of five others, the probability of winning was 84%. This was the case for both the simple and the difficult quizzes.

Discussion

In a competitive game with real money on the line, participants' bets were influenced by quiz difficulty, which impinged on their absolute scores but not on their relative scores. There is evidence that financial incentives lead people to behave differently, and sometimes more rationally, in strategic contexts (Parco, Rapoport, & Stein, 2002; Smith & Walker, 1993). The fact that the manipulation of difficulty influenced bets despite monetary incentives for more accuracy attests to the robustness of the effect. More importantly, it suggests that the effect is not attributable to simple lack of motivation.

Participants appear to have focused on absolute self-assessment and not on relative interpersonal assessment. Quiz difficulty did not influence participants' average probability of winning, but it had a powerful influence on participants' predictions of winning. Remarkably, the hurdle manipulation did not have a significant influence on participants' bets despite its powerful effect on their chances of winning. In this experiment, we found that the manipulation that should not have affected bets did, and the manipulation that should have influenced bets did not. Both results can be explained by self-focus.

Participants' myopic predictions appear to focus on the self at the expense of considering others. When people make mistakes because they ignore relevant data, it is often possible to correct that error by drawing their attention to the omitted information (Brenner *et al.*, 1996; Croson, 1999). If the failure to consider others is a simple error of omission, it may be possible to eliminate it or reduce it by drawing participants' attention to their competitors' performance. If the results observed in Experiment 1 are due to an excessive focus on self while failing to think about others, forcing participants to think about others should reduce the effect. Experiment 2 tests this hypothesis: Before betting, some participants predicted their own and their opponent's percentile rankings.

Experiment 2 also addresses two potential concerns regarding the generalizability of Experiment 1's results. First, the difficulty of thinking about others increases with the number of others to think about. It is possible that participants in Experiment 1 had particular trouble thinking systematically about competition with five opponents. Experiment 2 simplified the competition so that each participant was only competing with one opponent. Second, Experiment 2 had all participants bet on and compete in both a simple and a difficult trivia quiz competition. We implemented this repeated measures design in the hope that if people saw both the simple and the difficult quizzes, it would lead them to think more systematically about the task and would lead to a decrease in the difference between bets on the simple and the difficult quizzes.

Experiment 2: Multiple Bets

Method

Participants. Participants were 88 undergraduates at Carnegie Mellon University and the University of Pittsburgh who signed up for a series of experiments in which they could make money. Each of the experiments offered a cash reward. In this experiment, participants were then given a choice of wagering up to $4 of their earnings on a trivia competition. Any amount participants wagered would be doubled if they won and taken from them if they lost.

Design. This experiment had two major dependent variables: bets and predicted percentile rankings. Each participant bet on whether his or her score on a trivia quiz would exceed that of one randomly chosen opponent. In addition to betting on the contest's outcome, each participant was also asked to predict percentile rankings on the trivia quiz for both self and opponent, relative to all other participants who had already taken the same quiz. In the interests of providing a motivation for accuracy, participants were promised an extra $0.50 in payment if their predicted rankings were accurate within 5%.[2]

The experiment had a 2 (quiz difficulty: easy vs. difficult) $\times$ 2 (order: easy first vs. difficult first) $\times$ 2 (prediction: bet before predicting rank vs. predict rank before betting) mixed design, with quiz difficulty manipulated within subject. All participants in Experiment 2 made bets on both the difficult and the simple quizzes. For each quiz, the experimental instructions emphasized that the competition would only compare participants' scores with others' scores on the same quiz. The manipulation of quiz difficulty, as in Experiment 1, varied the expected difficulty of the trivia competition using the same simple and difficult sample questions. The order manipulation varied (between subjects) the order in which the two quizzes were presented.

The prediction manipulation varied (between subjects) whether participants made their bets before or after predicting percentile rankings for self and opponent. By asking participants in the rank-before-bet condition to predict both their own and their opponents' performances before betting, we

---

[2] Participants' actual percentile ranks were measured relative to all those who had previously taken the quizzes. It was possible to compute percentile rankings even for the first participants in Experiment 2 because the set of scores included data from pretesting of the simple and difficult quizzes.

intended to prompt more reflection regarding the opponent and relative standing. Participants in the bet-before-rank condition, however, bet first and then made percentile rank predictions. Participants in this condition, like participants in Experiment 1, were not asked to do any extra thinking about themselves or their opponent before betting.

Results

Five individuals were dropped from the analysis for not following instructions. Instead of making their predictions in percentile rankings, as instructed, they made them in terms of raw scores (number of answers correct), making their responses difficult to compare with those of the other participants.

Bets. In a 2 (difficulty) × 2 (order) × 2 (prediction) mixed ANOVA on bets with repeated measures on quiz difficulty (simple vs. difficult), the results show a powerful within-subject effect of quiz difficulty. Participants bet more on the simple quiz (M = \$2.82, SD = \$1.16) than they did on the difficult quiz (M = \$1.88, SD = \$1.31), $F(1, 79)$ = 47.44, $p < .001$. None of the other main or interaction effects are significant. In particular, the hypothesized interaction between quiz difficulty and prediction condition was not significant, $F(1, 79) < 1$, ns.

We expected that the difference between bets on the simple and difficult quizzes would be smaller within subject than it would be between subjects, because seeing both contests would highlight their similarity. The difference on first bets between those who bet on the difficult quiz first and those who bet on the simple quiz first was \$0.69, $t(81)$ = 2.60, $p < .05$, replicating the primary result of Experiment 1. The average within-subject difference between bets on simple and difficult quizzes is \$0.94. Seeing both problems back-to-back clearly did not help reduce the tendency to bet more on the simple than on the difficult quiz.

Predicted percentile rankings. To test whether participants' predictions of percentile rankings were consistent with their bets, we conducted a 2 (difficulty) × 2 (target) repeated measures ANOVA. The results show that participants predicted higher percentile rankings for both self and opponent on the simple (M = 67.20, SD = 23.63) than on the difficult (M = 57.34, SD = 17.87) quizzes, $F(1, 82)$ = 44.84, $p < .001$. In other words, they predicted that, on average, everyone would do better than everyone else on a simple quiz, and these delusions of grandeur are somewhat moderated for the difficult quiz.

This within-subjects effect of quiz difficulty is qualified by a marginally significant within-subjects interaction between quiz difficulty and target (self vs. other), $F(1, 82)$ = 3.74, $p = .057$. This interaction is a result of the fact that average predicted percentile rank for self (M = 72.94, SD = 19.04) is higher than for other (M = 68.56, SD = 19.26), $t(82)$ = 2.44, $p < .05$, on the simple quiz, but this is not true on the difficult quiz, $t(82)$ = 0.06, ns. On the difficult quiz, participants predicted similar scores for themselves (M = 57.41, SD = 21.24) and their opponents (M = 56.80, SD = 14.31).

If participants were betting rationally, they should have bet more when they believed that their scores would exceed those of their opponents. Because this was a purely competitive game, it was only the relative score that mattered for winning. However, the differential weighting hypothesis would predict that one's own score would be weighted more heavily when deciding how much to bet. To test how participants were betting, we conducted two regression analyses on bets. For bets on both simple and difficult quizzes, we regressed them on predicted percentile rank for both self and opponent. Both regressions produced similar results. Participants' predicted rankings for self were highly predictive of betting, but opponents' were not (see Table 13.1).

TABLE 13.1. Bets Regressed on Predicted Performance in Experiment 2

Independent variable	Simple bet	Difficult bet
Own predicted percentile rank	0.41**	0.50***
Opponent's predicted percentile rank	−0.03	−0.04
Adjusted R^2	0.13**	0.21***

Note: Table shows standardized beta weights for independent variables. ** $p < .01$. *** $p < .001$.

Discussion

Several results of Experiment 2 offer insight into the mechanisms at work in myopic prediction. First, the strong within-subject effect of quiz difficulty attests to the robustness of the effect. Second, the regression results support the differential weighting hypothesis that myopic judgments in this competitive game occur because individuals focus too much on their own outcomes and too little on others or on relative standing. Finally, whereas Kruger (1999) and Klar and Giladi (1999) examined comparative judgments among individuals comparing themselves with a group average, our results come from individuals comparing themselves with other individuals, which should reduce the size of the effect (Alicke, Klotz, Breitenbecher, Yurak, & Vredenburg, 1995). Indeed, Klar and Giladi (1997) explained their results with the singular-target-focusing model of comparative judgment in which they theorize that people have particular trouble comparing individuals with groups. The present results demonstrate myopic social comparisons even when individuals are comparing themselves with just one other person.

Participants' behavior in Experiments 1 and 2 appears to be profoundly egocentric: Comparative social judgments are based primarily on the self. Kruger (1999) and Klar and Giladi (1999) showed, consistent with the regression results of Experiment 2, that rankings of the self relative to others correlate strongly with self-ratings but not at all with ratings of others. However, these findings may have underestimated the predictive value of both ratings of self and ratings of others because of the way these constructs were measured. In Experiment 2, people evaluated self and other on percentile scales, which depend on performance relative to the group. Likewise, evaluations of self and other obtained by Klar and Giladi (1999) and Kruger (1999) were made on verbally anchored Likert scales. For example, participants in Kruger's (1999) first study evaluated themselves and their classmates on scales running from 1 (*very unskilled*) to 10 (*very skilled*). Judgments on verbally anchored scales tend to be influenced by the implicit comparison group, suggesting they

are not pure measures of absolute evaluation (Biernat, Manis, & Kobrynowicz, 1997; Heine, Lehman, Peng, & Greenholtz, 2002). A more stringent test of the differential weighting hypothesis would be possible using pure assessments of absolute performance (such as number of questions answered correctly)—such measures were collected in Experiment 3. These measures of absolute performance also allow us to test the differential error explanation for myopic social comparisons. The differential error explanation holds that people's expectations of others are systematically more regressive than their predictions of themselves.

A potential problem with Experiments 1 and 2 is that participants only saw an example question and did not take the quiz before they bet on its outcome. It is possible that the effect of quiz difficulty on bets in Experiments 1 and 2 was a result of participants' inaccurate assumptions about the content of the quizzes they were about to take. For example, participants could have imagined that the difficult quiz would be so challenging that it would practically be a guessing game of chance. Another potential problem with Experiments 1 and 2 is that along with the sample question, participants were told explicitly to expect either a simple or a difficult quiz. It is possible that this instruction could have acted as a demand effect, telling participants that they should expect to succeed on the competition they were told was easy and that they should expect to fail on the competition that they were told was difficult. Giving participants the quiz first and asking them to bet afterward allows us to test both these alternative explanations. Participants in Experiment 3 were not given any preview of the quiz or its difficulty—they simply took the quiz before they bet.

Experiment 3: Betting on the Self Versus a Randomly Selected Person

Experiment 3 tests the possibility that the solo comparison effect observed in Experiments 1 and 2, in which ostensibly comparative judgments are really solo judgments, is not a purely egocentric error but a more general focusing error. If the effect is primarily a result of focusing, then it should operate similarly for others as well as for self. That is, if participants bet on the performance of some other person, they should bet more on that person when competing on a simple quiz than on a difficult one. However, if the focusing bias demonstrated in Experiments 1 and 2 is the result of the "inside view," in which people tend to ignore relevant contextual variables such as base rates when they are thinking about themselves (Kahneman & Lovallo, 1993), then betting on someone else should highlight the "outside view" and reduce or eliminate the effect. Some participants in Experiment 3 were given exactly this opportunity.

Method

Participants. Participants were 144 students at Carnegie Mellon University, 48% of whom were master's students and 52% of whom were undergraduates. At the end of six different classes, we invited students to remain and participate in exchange for the opportunity to earn money. Participants were given $3 and invited to bet as much or as little as they wanted on a trivia competition.

Winning participants would have the amount they bet doubled; those who lost would be left with only the unwagered portion of the $3.

Design. The experiment had a 2 (quiz difficulty: easy vs. difficult) × 2 (protagonist: self vs. random person) between-subjects design. The protagonist manipulation varied the person on whom participants were betting: Half of the participants were betting on whether they themselves would beat a randomly selected opponent; the other half was betting on a randomly selected "Person A" beating a randomly selected opponent, "Person B."

Procedure. Participants in Experiment 3 took the quiz first. The trivia questions from the difficult and simple quizzes are listed in Table 13.2. After they had bet, participants were given a questionnaire that asked them to estimate: (a) the probability that they would win; (b) how well the protagonist would do, both in relative terms (percentile rank) and in absolute terms (number of questions correct on the quiz); (c) a 90% confidence interval around their estimate of the protagonist's absolute score; (d) how well the opponent would do in absolute

TABLE 13.2. Trivia Questions Used in Experiment 3

Simple	Difficult
1. How many inches are there in a foot?	Which creature has the largest eyes in the world?
2. What is the name of Pittsburgh's professional hockey team?	How many verses are there in the Greek national anthem?
3. Which species of whale grows the largest?	What company produced the first color television sold to the public?
4. Who is the president of the United States?	How many bathrooms are there in the White House (the residence of the U.S. President)?
5. Harrisburg is the capital of what U.S. state?	Which monarch ruled Great Britain the longest?
6. What was the first name of the Carnegie who founded the Carnegie Institute of Technology?	The word "planet" comes from the Greek word meaning what?
7. How many states are there in the United States?	What is the name of the traditional currency of Italy (before the Euro)?
8. What continent is Afghanistan in?	What is Avogadro's number?
9. What country occupies an entire continent?	Who played Dorothy in "The Wizard of Oz"?
10. Paris is the capital of what country?	Who wrote the musical "The Yeoman of the Guard"?
Tiebreaker question: How many people live in Pennsylvania?	

Note: Answers—Simple: (1) 12, (2) Penguins, (3) Blue, (4) George W. Bush, (5) Pennsylvania, (6) Andrew, (7) 50, (8) Asia, (9) Australia, (10) France; Difficult: (1) Giant squid, (2) 158, (3) RCA, (4) 32, (5) Queen Victoria, (6) wanderer, (7) Lira, (8) 6.02×10^{23}, (9) Judy Garland, (10) Gilbert & Sullivan; Tiebreaker: 12,281,054.

terms; and (e) a 90% confidence interval around their estimate of the opponent's absolute score.

Results and Discussion

Manipulation check. The manipulation of quiz difficulty was successful. Scores on the simple quiz were significantly higher ($M = 8.71$, $SD = 1.10$) than on the difficult quiz ($M = 1.47$, $SD = 1.01$), $t(142) = 40.98$, $p < .001$. Indeed, only 1 of the 75 participants who took the simple quiz got as few as 5 out of the 10 questions correct, and 1 of the 69 participants who took the difficult quiz got as many as 5 out of 10 correct.

Bets. To test for the effects of the independent variables, we first conducted a 2 (difficulty) $\times$ 2 (protagonist) between-subjects ANOVA on bets. This test reveals that participants who were betting on the simple trivia quiz bet significantly more ($M = 1.95, $SD = 1.10) than did those who were betting on the difficult trivia quiz ($M = 1.29, $SD = 1.17), $F(1, 140) = 11.82$, $p < .01$ (see Figure 13.2). Notably, the Difficulty $\times$ Protagonist interaction is not significant. When people were betting on some randomly selected "Person A," they made predictions about the relative performance of that person in much the same way they made relative performance predictions about themselves.

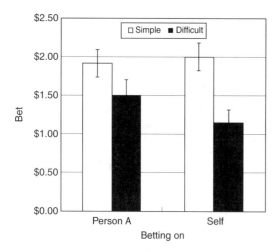

FIGURE 13.2 ■ Bets (Experiment 3). Bars indicate standard errors.

The correlation between participants' bets and their estimation of the probability of winning is substantial ($r = .54$, $p < .001$). The results of Experiment 3 would not change appreciably if participants' estimated probability of winning replaced their bets in all statistical analyses. This rules out the alternative hypothesis that participants bet more on the simple than on the difficult quiz because of some reason unrelated to their estimated probability of winning.

Participants' predictions regarding variance allow us to test another alternative explanation for their bets. In particular, low variance on the difficult quiz could reflect a fear that the test would be so difficult that it would overwhelm individual skill in determining performance and that outcomes would be primarily a product of chance rather than ability. In fact, when asked to specify a range of scores such that they were 90% confident their opponent's score would fall within it, participants in the difficult quiz condition actually estimated a wider range ($M = 3.56$, $SD = 1.89$) than did those who took the simple quiz ($M = 2.64$, $SD = 1.43$), $F(1, 125) = 26.51$, $p < .001$. This renders implausible the alternative explanation for low bets in the difficult condition based on expectations of tie scores.

Differential weighting. We conducted three regression analyses on participants' predictions of performance (see Table 13.3). In Experiment 3, the absolute predicted scores for protagonist and

TABLE 13.3. Results of Regressions on Participants' Predictions of Relative Standing Using Predictions of Absolute Performance of Protagonist and Opponent as Independent Variables (Experiment 3)

Independent variable	Relative standing (1–7 Likert scale)	Bet ($0–$3)	Probability of winning (0%–100%)
Protagonist's score (0–10)	1.21***	0.88***	1.01***
Opponent's score (0–10)	−0.68***	−0.61***	−0.64***
Adjusted R^2	0.43***	0.17***	0.26***

Note: Table shows standardized beta weights for independent variables. *** $p < .001$.

opponent were both significant predictors of (a) bets, (b) estimated likelihood of winning, and (c) estimates of relative performance. In each of these analyses, participants' predictions of the absolute performance (number of questions answered correctly) of protagonist and opponent were used as independent variables. In all three cases, the score of the protagonist was weighted more heavily than that of the opponent for predicting relative standing ($ps < .05$), consistent with the differential weighting hypothesis. However, the results do not replicate those of Klar and Giladi (1999), of Kruger (1999), or of Experiment 2 in the present article, that judgments of relative standing were uncorrelated with evaluations of others.

The explanation for this apparent inconsistency in the significance of the opponent's performance probably lies in the exact technique used to measure it. In these regression equations, absolute performance of self and other was measured on an easily interpretable scale that was a relatively pure measure of individual performance: scores on the trivia quiz. This objective measure is less subject to influence by the reference group. This result highlights the importance of specifying how evaluations are measured and raises the question of how exactly participants were thinking about others.

Differential error. To test the differential error hypothesis that people would predict their opponents more regressively than the protagonist, predictions of absolute performance were subject to a 2 (difficulty) × 2 (target: protagonist vs. opponent) mixed ANOVA with repeated measures on target. The results reveal the predicted Target × Difficulty interaction effect, $F(1, 141) = 13.0$, $p < .001$. Participants betting on the difficult quiz predicted that the protagonist ($M = 2.93$, $SD = 1.48$) would score worse than the opponent ($M = 3.36$, $SD = 1.45$), $t(67) = -2.48$, $p < .05$, whereas those betting on the simple quiz predicted that the protagonist ($M = 8.22$, $SD = 1.32$) would score better than the opponent ($M = 7.88$, $SD = 1.39$), $t(74) = 2.63$, $p < .05$.

Participants estimated their own scores with some error. As Figure 13.3 shows, those who obtained low scores tended to overestimate their

performance—a natural consequence of error in their estimates and the effect of the floor at a score of zero. If participants accurately estimated their own scores, then their estimates would have fallen along the diagonal. On very difficult problems (that everyone gets wrong) error will tend to result in an overestimation of one's performance, leading to apparent overconfidence. On very simple problems, error will tend to lead to underestimation of one's performance, or underconfidence (Erev *et al.*, 1994). If they assumed that others would perform as they themselves did, predictions of others would likewise fall along this consensus diagonal.

Participants' predictions of their opponents' scores are highly correlated with predictions of protagonists' scores ($r = .90$, $p < .001$), even after controlling for quiz difficulty ($pr = .60$, $p < .001$),[3] but are more regressive. On the difficult quiz, despite the fact that they had just overestimated their own performances, participants predicted that their opponents would perform even better. Figure 13.3 illustrates this pattern. These results are entirely consistent with the differential error hypothesis. The result is that for self-reports

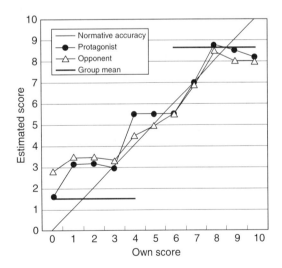

FIGURE 13.3 ■ Estimated scores for protagonist and opponent, conditional on participants' actual scores on the trivia quiz (Experiment 3).

---

[3] These results are similar for those betting on self and betting on Person A.

of relative standing, persistent overconfidence prevailed on the simple quiz, with persistent underconfidence on the difficult quiz. Participants taking the simple quiz on average overestimated the percentage of their peers that they would beat by 18% ($SD = 30\%$); by contrast, participants taking the difficult quiz underestimated the percentage of their peers that they would beat by 14% ($SD = 31\%$), $t(72) = 4.44$, $p < .001$.

Focusing. Like those betting on themselves, those betting on Person A predicted that the protagonist would do better than others on the easy task but worse than others on the difficult task. This result highlights the role of focusing errors in myopic social comparison, and is attributable to the fact that participants made predictions differently for those who were in focus and those who were out of focus. Those out of focus are predicted more regressively than those in focus.

Is this error of myopic social comparison inevitable? If the results of Experiments 1–3 are attributable to attentional focus, then we should be able to influence it by manipulating focus. People who focused less on themselves and more on the opponent should be less likely to commit the error. Experiment 4 introduced such a debiasing manipulation, in which some participants were led to focus on the opponent.

Although the results of Experiments 1–3 are consistent with a focalism explanation for myopic social comparison, an alternative explanation remains. The results of all three experiments show people betting more on simple than on difficult competitions. It may simply be that people enjoy betting more on simple than on difficult competitions. Heath and Tversky (1991) have shown that people prefer to bet in areas where they feel confident and have more knowledge of the uncertainties involved. This is true even holding the expected value of the bets constant (Goodie, 2003). If focusing is indeed the cause, then it should be possible to reduce the effect or even reverse it by manipulating focusing. Experiment 4 tests the focusing explanation by manipulating focusing. Its design replicates that of Experiment 3, but with an additional focusing manipulation.

Experiment 4: Focusing Manipulated

Method

Participants. Participants were 113 individuals recruited by flyers posted around campus and by announcement in classes at Carnegie Mellon University and the University of Pittsburgh. Prospective participants were offered the chance to earn money for experimental participation. Each person who participated was given $4 and the opportunity to bet any portion of the $4 on winning a trivia competition. If the participant won, the wagered portion of the $4 was doubled.

Design. The experiment had a 2 (quiz difficulty: simple vs. difficult) × 2 (protagonist: self vs. random person) × 2 (focus: protagonist vs. opponent) between-subjects design. The focus manipulation varied whether participants' attention was focused on the protagonist (the person on whom they were betting) or the opponent when they made their bets. Given the failure of the subtle prediction manipulation in Experiment 2, we designed a more powerful focusing manipulation for this experiment. The manipulation contained three parts. First, participants were given perspective-taking instructions that asked them to put themselves in the shoes of the person on whom they were to focus. For example, participants who were betting on themselves but focusing on the opponent received the following instructions:

> Before you bet, it may be valuable to spend some time thinking about Person B, against whom you will be competing. Please put yourself in the perspective of Person B. Person B was asked to write a page or less on the topic of "What makes me unique." Please turn the page and read Person B's essay. Think about how they are likely to have done on the trivia quiz. Then turn the page, and as you answer the questions there, imagine how Person B might answer those same questions. Try to visualize Person B as you give your answers.

For the second part of the focusing manipulation, participants reviewed an essay by the person on whom they were focusing, on the topic "What makes me unique." Participants who were focusing on themselves wrote the essay after getting the following instructions:

> Please take a few minutes to write a page or less about yourself on the topic of "What makes me unique." As a starting point, please begin the essay by talking about who you are: your gender, your age, your race, your family background, your home, and your major field of study at the university. You may also want to mention your interests, your skills, and your abilities.

Participants in the other conditions—those who were focusing on the opponent or on Person A—were given an essay written by another participant and were told that it had been written by the person on whom they were focusing. For the third part of the focusing manipulation, participants answered questions about the performance of the in-focus person. The questions asked them to predict absolute performance, predict relative performance, and estimate the probability of that individual winning the competition. All participants then made their bets. After betting, participants were asked the same set of questions about the out-of-focus competitor. Participants were then paid on the basis of the outcomes of their bets.

Results and Discussion

Manipulation check. The manipulation of quiz difficulty was successful. Scores on the simple quiz were significantly higher ($M = 9.47$, $SD = 1.02$) than on the difficult quiz ($M = 1.70$, $SD = 1.25$), $t(111) = 36.29$, $p < .001$. Again, the distributions were nearly nonoverlapping. Only 1 of the 57 participants who took the simple quiz got fewer than 7 out of the 10 questions correct, and none of the 56 participants who took the difficult quiz got more than 5 out of 10 correct.

Bets. We first conducted a 2 (simple vs. difficult) × 2 (betting on self vs. Person A) × 2 (focus on protagonist vs. opponent) ANOVA on bets. The results show a significant main effect of difficulty, $F(1, 105) = 7.67$, $p < .01$. This main effect is qualified by a significant Difficulty × Focus interaction, $F(1, 105) = 84.97$, $p < .001$ (see Figure 13.4). Planned contrasts reveal that people focusing on the

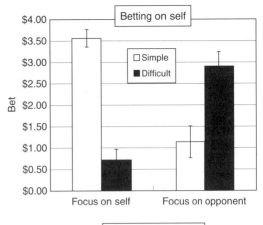

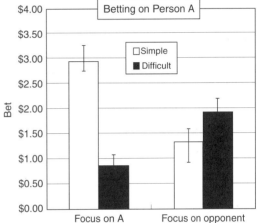

FIGURE 13.4 ■ Bets by those betting on self and Person A (Experiment 4). Bars indicate standard errors.

protagonist demonstrated the usual tendency to bet more on the simple ($M = \$3.24$, $SD = \$1.09$) than the difficult ($M = \$.79$, $SD = \$.90$) quiz, $t(1, 109) = 8.44$, $p < .001$. However, people focusing on the opponent bet significantly more on the difficult ($M = \$2.52$, $SD = \$1.19$) than the simple ($M = \$1.18$, $SD = \$1.22$) quiz, $t(1, 109) = 4.50$, $p < .001$. This two-way interaction is qualified by a significant three-way interaction, $F(1, 105) = 4.35$, $p < .05$. This three-way interaction reflects the fact that the Difficulty × Focus effects are stronger for those betting on themselves than for those betting on Person A, as shown in Figure 13.4. No other main effects or interactions are significant.

It is worth noting that the effect size associated with the difficulty manipulation (in the standard condition in which people were betting on themselves and focusing on themselves) is substantially larger ($\eta^2 = .74$) than it was in Experiment 1 ($\eta^2 = .15$), Experiment 2 ($\eta^2 = .11$), or Experiment 3 ($\eta^2 = .12$). This difference is likely the result of the fact that although participants tended to focus on themselves in Experiments 1–3, Experiment 4's focusing manipulation reinforced that natural tendency. The significant Difficulty × Focus interaction effect stands in contrast to the weak focusing manipulation used in Experiment 2. The results of the present experiment demonstrate that focusing can be manipulated, but it also took a heavy-handed manipulation to do so. This powerful manipulation appears to have succeeded in leading participants to focus on the opponent, so much so that the results of Experiments 1–3 were reversed, and participants focusing on the opponent bet more on winning competitions based on a difficult quiz than on a simple one. The Difficulty × Focus interaction does not reflect debiasing of the participants focused on the opponent.

Differential weighting. We conducted separate regression analyses on bets for those focusing on the protagonist and those focusing on the opponent. The results appear in Table 13.4. Experiment 4 replicates the differential weighting effects of Experiments 2 and 3 among those focusing on the protagonist, who weighted the protagonist's score more heavily than the opponent's score in determining their bets. However, this tendency was

reversed among those focusing on the opponent, who weighted the opponent's score more heavily than the protagonist's in determining their bets. This last finding seems particularly difficult to account for using an explanation based on egocentrism, and implicates focusing as the cause for differential weighting.

Differential error. Experiment 4 replicated the differential error effects from Experiment 3. Those focusing on the protagonist, like participants in Experiment 3, tended to predict that the protagonist's performance would be more extreme (higher on the simple quiz and lower on the difficult quiz) than would the opponent's performance. But this pattern was reversed among those focusing on the opponent. In a 2 (difficulty) × 2 (focus) × 2 (protagonist: self vs. Person A) × 2 (target: protagonist vs. opponent) mixed ANOVA on predicted scores with repeated measures on target, the predicted Difficulty × Focus × Target interaction is significant, $F(1, 105) = 22.43$, $p < .001$. Figure 13.5a shows that those focusing on the protagonist replicate the pattern shown in Experiment 3, in which participants' predictions of the opponent are more regressive than are their predictions of the protagonist; this pattern holds both for those betting on self and on Person A. However, as shown in Figure 13.5b, this difference reverses itself for those focusing on opponent, whose score predictions are more regressive for protagonist than for opponent.[4]

Subadditivity. All participants were asked to report both the probability that the protagonist would beat the opponent and the probability that the opponent would beat the protagonist. Naturally, these should sum to 100%. However, for those taking the simple quiz, these two probabilities summed, on average, to 110% ($SD = 28.3\%$), which is significantly greater than 100%, $t(56) = 2.79, p < .05$. For those taking the difficult quiz, these two probabilities summed to 95% ($SD = 16.5\%$), which is significantly less than 100%, $t(55) = -2.21, p < .05$ (see Table 13.5).

TABLE 13.4. Results of Regressions on Participants' Bets Using Predictions of Absolute Performance of Protagonist and Opponent as Independent Variables, Comparing Those Focused on Protagonist and Those Focused on Opponent (Experiment 4)

	Bets	
Independent variable	Focusing on protagonist	Focusing on opponent
Protagonist's score (0–10)	1.51***	0.53*
Opponent's score (0–10)	−0.76**	−0.97**
Adjusted R^2	0.70***	0.26***

Note: Table shows standardized beta weights for independent variables. * $p < .10$. ** $p < .01$. *** $p < .001$.

---

[4] These results are similar for those betting on self and betting on Person A.

General Discussion

Participants in the present experiments stood to benefit from accurate predictions of their performance relative to others in general, and their competitors

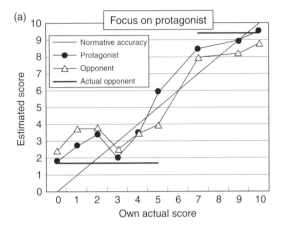

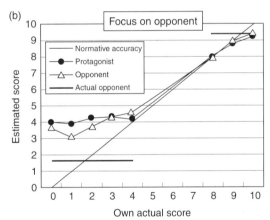

FIGURE 13.5 ■ Estimated scores for protagonist and opponent, conditional on participants' actual scores on the trivia quiz (Experiment 4), comparing those focused on the protagonist and those focused on the opponent.

in particular, by betting wisely. However, participants based their predictions on absolute performance of a focal actor even though winning depended exclusively on relative performance. Experiments 1 and 2 showed that people made this error when they were focusing on themselves. Experiment 3 showed that they also made the error when focusing on a randomly selected, unfamiliar protagonist. Experiment 4 showed that they made the error even when they were focusing on their own opponent in the competition. The present results were obtained in a competitive social context in which participants compared individuals against each other, not individuals against group means, and in which they were making predictions of future outcomes, not just retrospective evaluations of evidence.

When making strategic social comparisons, participants focused on the absolute performance of one actor despite the importance of other people and other features of the situation. Participants' bets were relatively insensitive to factors that were out of focus, including the performance of out-of-focus competitors and the hurdle manipulation in Experiment 1, despite their important effects on the probability of winning. The results show that focusing had its effect through two underlying causes: differential error and differential weighting. Differential error tended to increase the regressiveness of predictions regarding those who were out of focus. At the same time, regression analyses show that participants tended to overweight the performance of the focal person in predicting outcomes. In fact, it is possible that differential error may have led to differential weighting. Variance in participants' estimations of the opponent's score was lower than the variance in the estimation of their own scores. This is consistent with the greater regressiveness of

TABLE 13.5. Predicted Probabilities of Winning for Protagonist and Opponent (Experiment 4)

Dependent measure	Focus on protagonist		Focus on opponent	
	Difficult	Simple	Difficult	Simple
Probability that protagonist beats opponent	39.9 (19.6)	65.9 (18.8)	51.3 (16.3)	54.9 (19.2)
Probability that opponent beats protagonist	54.2 (17.7)	40.2 (20.5)	44.9 (19.9)	60.1 (23.2)
Summed probability	94.1 (15.6)	106.1 (24.2)	96.2 (17.7)	115.0 (29.1)

Note: Standard deviations are shown in parentheses.

estimates of others. It is also consistent with a rational estimate of the opponent's score, given that all participants were facing opponents drawn from the same group. The lower variance in estimates of others' scores would naturally lead it to have a lower regression weight than estimates of their own scores.

Egocentrism Versus Focalism

The results of Experiments 1 and 2 are consistent with errors of both egocentrism and focalism. However, the tendency for participants betting on a randomly selected protagonist in Experiment 3 to bet more on a simple than on a difficult quiz cannot easily be explained by pure egocentrism, and highlights the role of more general focusing errors. Furthermore, when participants focused on their opponents in Experiment 4, patterns in bets as well as in the predicted probability of winning reversed themselves. The power of the focusing manipulation to reverse the effect suggests strongly that focusing is a key driver of the effect.

Other researchers have manipulated focusing by changing the subject of comparison (Eiser *et al.*, 2001; Weinstein & Lachendro, 1982; Windschitl, Kruger, & Simms, 2003). For example, Eiser *et al.* (2001) asked people to consider performance on a future exam. Some participants were asked how they would perform relative to others. These participants showed more excessive optimism (a stronger above-average effect) than did those who were asked to rate others relative to themselves. Similarly, Windschitl *et al.* (2003) asked the participants in their fourth experiment to estimate the probability of winning a trivia contest against a fellow student. Half the participants estimated the probability that they would beat the other student. The other half estimated the probability that the other student would beat them. They replicated the solo comparison effect shown here among those predicting their own chances of winning: On average, participants predicted that they had only a 17% chance of winning a trivia contest on "indigenous vegetation of the Amazon," but a 61% chance of winning a contest on "fast food chains." However, participants predicted that the other side had a 57% chance of winning a trivia contest on "indigenous

vegetation of the Amazon" and a 47% chance of winning a contest on "fast food chains." Because changing the subject of the comparison did not reverse the effect but only weakened it, Windschitl *et al.* concluded that both egocentrism and focalism were at work.

These manipulations are likely to have had their effect because they induced people to focus on others. But they are relatively subtle manipulations, and their effects tended to be weaker than that of the focusing manipulation in Experiment 4. Although not denying the natural tendency to focus on the self, the results of our Experiment 4 demonstrate that the failure of these other subtle focusing manipulations to reverse the solo comparison effect is not because such reversal is impossible. Instead, the implication is that these earlier manipulations were too subtle to adequately test the hypothesis that the effect is an egocentric one.

Biases in the Assessment of Support for Focal Hypotheses

Support theory (Tversky & Koehler, 1994) addresses the way in which people use descriptions of events to assess their probabilities. Assume that there are two mutually exclusive outcomes, A and B. Imagine that outcome A is the protagonist wins the competition and outcome B is the protagonist loses the competition. Tversky and Koehler (1994) proposed that the judged probability of event A occurring, $P(A, B)$, will depend on the perceived support for the focal hypothesis, $s(A)$, and the perceived support for the alternative, or residual hypothesis, $s(B)$:

$$P(A, B) = \frac{s(A)}{s(A) + s(B)}$$

So, for example, the probability of winning the competition depends on how well one has done on the quiz and how well one's opponent has done. If support for the focal hypothesis and the residual hypothesis are assessed similarly, then this formula yields sensible probability estimates.

However, Tversky and his colleagues (Brenner, Koehler, & Rottenstreich, 2002; Koehler *et al.*,

1997; Rottenstreich & Tversky, 1997) have documented systematic biases in the way people assess support for hypotheses that include multiple subsidiary hypotheses. Their general finding is that the judged probability of an event depends on the explicitness of its description. Focusing on and elaborating a specific hypothesis can increase its perceived likelihood. When implicit disjunctions are unpacked into their components, the perceived support for them goes up. So, for example, people estimate the probability of death by natural causes at 58%, but estimate the probability of death because of heart disease, cancer, or other natural causes at 73% (Tversky & Koehler, 1994, p. 552).

Our data are consistent with an extension of support theory that Koehler *et al.* (1997) called the "enhancement effect": the tendency for the total judged probability of a set of mutually exclusive and exhaustive probabilities to increase with the degree to which the evidence is compatible with the hypotheses. High performance on the quiz is compatible with winning, and participants in Experiment 4 judged the summed probability that protagonist and opponent would win as more probable in the simple competition (110%) than in the difficult competition (95%). However, support theory as it was originally articulated would not predict solo comparison effects in binary outcomes. Koehler *et al.* (1997) explained the enhancement effect on the basis of the packing and unpacking of the residual hypothesis. In Experiments 2–4, each participant was competing against another individual. The residual hypothesis cannot be unpacked in a one-on-one competition. We must turn to other reasons for the observed effects, such as biases in the evaluation of support for nonfocal hypotheses. The present data suggest specifically what these biases might be: differential weighting and differential error.

Overconfidence, Underconfidence, and Differential Error

The present results show participants to be more confident of winning competitions based on simple tests than they are of winning competitions based on difficult tests. This result would seem to conflict with over 25 years of research on overconfidence showing that people are more overconfident of their performance on difficult than on simple problems (Lichtenstein & Fischhoff, 1977; Soll, 1996; see also Gigerenzer, Hoffrage, & Kleinboelting, 1991). The reconciliation of our results with the so-called hard/easy effect in overconfidence comes from distinguishing between absolute overconfidence (e.g., I believe I got six correct when in fact I got three correct) and relative overconfidence (e.g., I believe I beat 70% of my peers, when in fact I beat 50% of them). As Figures 13.3 and 13.5 show, our results replicate the standard hard/easy effect in absolute measures of confidence: People tend to overestimate how many questions they answered correctly on the difficult quiz, but tend, if anything, to underestimate the number of questions they got right on the simple quiz. If participants accurately estimate their own scores, then their estimates would fall along the diagonal. However, people estimate their own scores with some error. On very difficult problems (that everyone gets wrong), error will tend to result in an overestimation of one's performance, or apparent overconfidence. On very simple problems, error will tend to lead to underestimation of one's performance, and to apparent underconfidence.

For self-reports of relative standing, persistent overconfidence prevailed on the simple quiz, with persistent underconfidence on the difficult quiz. Participants taking the simple quiz tended to overestimate the percentage of their peers that they would beat and their performance relative to their opponents. By contrast, participants taking the difficult quiz tended to underestimate the percentage of their peers that they would beat as well as their own performance relative to their opponents. It makes sense that people would estimate the performance of others with more error than they would their own performance, and that this accounts for their regressiveness. However, what is striking about the results of the focusing manipulation in Experiment 4 is that those who were focusing on the opponent actually estimated their own performances more regressively than those of their opponents.

As the present results show, despite the fact that competition with others establishes clear incentives to anticipate their behavior correctly, people have trouble doing so. Even in economic contexts in which consideration of others' perspectives is fundamental to determining the rational strategy, people routinely ignore, oversimplify, or disregard others (Ball, Bazerman, & Carroll, 1991; Camerer & Lovallo, 1999; Messick, Moore, & Bazerman, 1997). People seem to assume that the behavior of others is fundamentally unpredictable, even in situations in which their behavior is highly predictable (Beard & Beil, 1994). Essentially, people appear to make predictions of others that assume others will behave more randomly and less predictably than they actually do (Huck & Weizsacker, 2002). Future research will have to explore the question of exactly how it is people think about (or fail to think about) others in these contexts. Is it that people see others' behavior as unknown, and so begin with the simplistic assumption of equal probabilities across all possible outcomes (Bruine de Bruin, Fischhoff, Millstein, & Halpern-Felsher, 2000; Fox & Rottenstreich, 2003)? Or is it simply that others' behavior is predicted with less certainty than one's own? These questions cannot be answered using the data presented here, and answers will depend on the future study of people's beliefs about the behavior of others.

False Consensus and False Uniqueness

The present results contrast with work on false consensus or projection effects (Ross *et al.*, 1977), which shows that people assume others are more similar to themselves than they actually are (Krueger & Clement, 1994). Indeed, false consensus findings are so robust that Krueger and Clement (1994) argued that "the idea that 'most people are like me' may be spontaneous" (p. 609). By contrast, participants in the present experiments made mistakes that suggested they thought others were less like them than they actually were. Reconciling our findings with research on false consensus depends on a clarification of the experimental paradigms used in each. Classic experiments on false consensus held the situation constant and exploited differences between individuals to show that people

expected others would see the world as they did. In contrast, our experiments varied the situation and show that people's beliefs about others are insufficiently sensitive to situational influences. The results show that both effects are present simultaneously: People's beliefs about others are correlated with their own behavior, and there are mean differences between their own behavior and their assumptions about the behavior of others.

Clearly, it is not the case that our participants were focusing only on one person and ignoring others completely. Participants were able to specify predictions of performance for both protagonist and opponent, and they appear to have been using that information sensibly: Higher predicted performance by the protagonist was associated with higher bets, and higher predicted performance by opponent was associated with lower bets. However, estimates of the performance of the out-of-focus individual err in two systematic ways. First, participants' predictions of their scores are highly correlated with predictions of the scores of the individual in focus. This assumed similarity is consistent with false consensus and the supposition that others will perform similarly to oneself (Krueger & Clement, 1994; Ross *et al.*, 1977). Second, as described by the differential error effect, participants' predictions of the scores of the person out of focus were regressive. Put another way, they predicted that the performance of the individual in focus would be more extreme (higher scores on the simple quiz and lower scores on the difficult quiz) than would the performance of the person out of focus. This result is consistent with the research on false uniqueness (Perloff & Brickman, 1982), showing that people believe their own personal outcomes, experiences, and abilities to be more exceptional and unique than they actually are.

There are three noteworthy features of these results. The first is that the results display both false consensus and false uniqueness: Participants expected that "others will behave like me, only less so." Although both McFarland and Miller (1990) and Biernat et al. (1997) have shown that simultaneous false consensus and false uniqueness can be displayed by the same individuals, they did so on two different measures. The present results, by contrast, demonstrate false consensus and false uniqueness on the same dependent measure. The second noteworthy feature is that they highlight cognitive, nonmotivational causes. It is easy to imagine why people might want to believe themselves to be happier (Andrews & Withey, 1976), more intelligent (Wylie, 1979), and better drivers (Slovic, Fischhoff, & Lichtenstein, 1977) than average. Although participants' overestimation of relative standing on the simple quiz could serve a self-enhancing function, self-enhancement does not constitute a good explanation for their underestimation of their standing on the difficult quiz. The third noteworthy feature of the results is that they suggest that both false consensus and false uniqueness effects may be moderated by attentional focus. In Experiment 4, the false uniqueness effects shown by those focusing on themselves were reversed among those focusing on the opponent: They reported that the opponent's outcomes would be more extreme than their own. This last implication is particularly noteworthy, because so much of the theorizing regarding both the false consensus effect and false uniqueness effect have centered on their egocentric origins.

Social Comparison Versus Solo Comparison

The results presented here fly in the face of a great deal of research on social comparison. Whereas we show people making solo judgments when comparative judgments are explicitly called for, other research suggests that explicitly solo judgments inevitably elicit comparative social information that compares the person being judged with other people. Research dating back to Festinger (1954) has shown that self-evaluation is fundamentally social and comparative in nature. Asking people to rate themselves on some attribute ("How tall are you?") predictably invites social comparison with others ("Am I taller or shorter than other people?") to construct such a judgment (Mussweiler & Strack, 2000). An American woman who measures 5 feet 9 in. (1.75 m) might see herself as tall, but an American man of the same height would not. In this case, as in innumerable others, social

judgment depends crucially on the context of relevant comparison with others. People also rely on comparative social information even when doing so leads them to make apparently dysfunctional choices. For example, when they learn that they would be earning less than others, people reject money-making opportunities that they would otherwise happily accept (Blount, 1995; Blount & Bazerman, 1996; Güth & Tietz, 1990). Blount and Bazerman (1996) offered students $7 for participating in a study, and 72% accepted the invitation. However, when students were offered $8, participation dropped to 54%. Why? Those offered $8 were also informed that some people were being paid $10 for participating in the same study.

By contrast, the present experiments show people focusing on themselves and discounting the social context when asked to make judgments that are fundamentally and inextricably comparative in nature. One possible reconciliation to this discrepancy might address the readiness of the data at one's disposal: When people have clear and immediate information, such as height, they tend to rely on systematic social comparison. However, when people only have ready information about either themselves or others, it is likely that the immediately available information will be put to use and other information will be ignored or underweighted in comparative judgments. There is some support for this view in research showing that the more familiar and individuated the comparison individual is, the less myopic the social comparison (Windschitl et al., 2003). Future research should specify the circumstances under which people rely on comparative social information for judging target individuals and when such information is discounted.

Conclusion

Prior research on social comparison has often assumed that when people are asked to rate themselves relative to others, they do just that. Yet the results presented here show that explicitly comparative judgments are often focused solo judgments. The fact that people make this focusing error in decisions on which they are betting their money suggests that the effect is not easily attributable to lack of motivation. This effect is general and robust enough that it would appear to result from a more profound process: the tendency to focus myopically on a single causal agent and to oversimplify the behavior of others when making comparisons.

REFERENCES

Alicke, M. D., Klotz, M. L., Breitenbecher, D. L., Yurak, T. J., & Vredenburg, D. S. (1995). Personal contact, individuation, and the better-than-average effect. *Journal of Personality and Social Psychology, 68*, 804–825.

Andrews, F. M., & Withey, S. B. (1976). *Social indicators of well-being.* New York: Plenum Press.

Ball, S. B., Bazerman, M. H., & Carroll, J. S. (1991). An evaluation of learning in the bilateral winner's curse. *Organizational Behavior and Human Decision Processes, 48*, 1–22.

Beard, R., & Beil, R. (1994). Do people rely on the self-interested maximization of others? An experimental test. *Management Science, 40*, 252–262.

Biernat, M., Manis, M., & Kobrynowicz, D. (1997). Simultaneous assimilation and contrast effects in judgments of self and others. *Journal of Personality and Social Psychology, 73*, 254–269.

Blount, S. (1995). When social outcomes aren't fair: The effect of causal attributions on preferences. *Organizational Behavior and Human Decision Processes, 63*, 131–144.

Blount, S., & Bazerman, M. H. (1996). The inconsistent evaluation of absolute versus comparative payoffs in labor supply and bargaining. *Journal of Economic Behavior and Organization, 30*, 227–240.

Brenner, L. A., Koehler, D. J., & Rottenstreich, Y. (2002). Remarks on support theory: Recent advances and future directions. In T. Gilovich, D. Griffin, & D. Kahneman (Eds.), *Heuristics and biases: The psychology of intuitive judgment* (pp. 489–509). Cambridge, England: Cambridge University Press.

Brenner, L. A., Koehler, D. J., & Tversky, A. (1996). On the evaluation of one-sided evidence. *Journal of Behavioral Decision Making, 9*, 59–70.

Bruine de Bruin, W., Fischhoff, B., Millstein, S. G., & Halpern-Felsher, B. L. (2000). Verbal and numerical expressions of probability: "It's a fifty-fifty chance." *Organizational Behavior and Human Decision Processes, 81*, 115–131.

Camerer, C., & Lovallo, D. (1999). Overconfidence and excess entry: An experimental approach. *American Economic Review, 89*, 306–318.

Clement, R. W., & Krueger, J. (2002). Social categorization moderates social projection. *Journal of Experimental Social Psychology, 38*, 219–231.

Croson, R. T. A. (1999). The disjunction effect and reason-based choice in games. *Organizational Behavior and Human Decision Processes, 80*, 118–133.

Eiser, J. R., Pahl, S., & Prins, Y. R. A. (2001). Optimism, pessimism, and the direction of self-other comparisons. *Journal of Experimental Social Psychology, 37*, 77–84.

Epley, N., & Dunning, D. (2000). Feeling "holier than thou": Are self-serving assessments produced by errors in self- or social prediction? *Journal of Personality and Social Psychology, 79*, 861–875.

Erev, I., Wallsten, T. S., & Budescu, D. V. (1994). Simultaneous over- and underconfidence: The role of error in judgment processes. *Psychological Review, 101*, 519–527.

Festinger, L. (1954). A theory of social comparison processes. *Human Relations, 7*, 117–140.

Fox, C. R., & Rottenstreich, Y. (2003). Partition priming in judgment under uncertainty. *Psychological Science, 14*, 195–200.

Galinsky, A. D., & Moskowitz, G. B. (2000). Perspective-taking: Decreasing stereotype expression, stereotype accessibility, and in-group favoritism. *Journal of Personality and Social Psychology, 78*, 708–724.

Gigerenzer, G., Hoffrage, U., & Kleinboelting, H. (1991). Probabilistic mental models: A Brunswikian theory of confidence. *Psychological Review, 98*, 506–528.

Giladi, E. E., & Klar, Y. (2002). When standards are wide of the mark: Nonselective superiority and inferiority biases in comparative judgments of objects and concepts. *Journal of Experimental Psychology: General, 131*, 538–551.

Gilbert, D. T., Giesler, R. B., & Morris, K. A. (1995). When comparisons arise. *Journal of Personality and Social Psychology, 69*, 227–236.

Gilovich, T. (1991). *How we know what isn't so: The fallibility of human reason in everyday life.* New York: Free Press.

Gilovich, T., Medvec, V. H., & Savitsky, K. (2000). The spotlight effect in social judgment: An egocentric bias in estimates of the salience of one's own actions and appearance. *Journal of Personality and Social Psychology, 78*, 211–222.

Goethals, G. R., Messick, D. M., & Allison, S. T. (1991). The uniqueness bias: Studies of constructive social comparison. In J. Suls & T. A. Wills (Eds.), *Social comparison: Contemporary theory and research* (pp. 149–176). Hillsdale, NJ: Erlbaum.

Goodie, A. S. (2003). The effects of control on betting: Paradoxical betting on items of high confidence with low value. *Journal of Experimental Psychology: Learning, Memory, and Cognition, 29*, 598–610.

Güth, W., & Tietz, R. (1990). Ultimatum bargaining behavior: A survey and comparison of experimental results. *Journal of Economic Psychology, 11*, 417–449.

Heath, C., & Tversky, A. (1991). Preference and belief: Ambiguity and competence in choice under uncertainty. *Journal of Risk and Uncertainty, 4*, 5–28.

Heine, S. J., Lehman, D. R., Peng, K., & Greenholtz, J. (2002). What's wrong with cross-cultural comparisons of subjective Likert scales?: The reference-group effect. *Journal of Personality and Social Psychology, 82*, 903–918.

Huck, S., & Weizsacker, G. (2002). Do players correctly estimate what others do? Evidence of conservatism in beliefs. *Journal of Economic Behavior and Organization, 47*, 71–85.

Jones, E. E., & Nisbett, R. E. (1972). The actor and the observer: Divergent perceptions of the causes of behavior.

In E. E. Jones, D. E. Kanouse, H. H. Kelley, R. E. Nisbett, S. Valins, & B. Weiner (Eds.), *Attribution: Perceiving the causes of behavior* (pp. 79–94). Morristown, NJ: General Learning Press.

Kahneman, D., & Lovallo, D. (1993). Timid choices and bold forecasts: A cognitive perspective on risk and risk taking. *Management Science, 39,* 17–31.

Kahneman, D., & Tversky, A. (1973). On the psychology of prediction. *Psychological Review, 80,* 237–251.

Kahneman, D., & Tversky, A. (1982). The simulation heuristic. In D. Kahneman, P. Slovic, & A. Tversky (Eds.), *Judgment under uncertainty: Heuristics and biases* (pp. 201–208). New York: Cambridge University Press.

Klar, Y., & Giladi, E. E. (1997). No one in my group can be below the group's average: A robust positivity bias in favor of anonymous peers. *Journal of Personality and Social Psychology, 73,* 885–901.

Klar, Y., & Giladi, E. E. (1999). Are most people happier than their peers, or are they just happy? *Personality and Social Psychology Bulletin, 25,* 585–594.

Klayman, J., & Ha, Y.-W. (1987). Confirmation, disconfirmation, and information in hypothesis testing. *Psychological Review, 94,* 211–228.

Klein, W. M., & Kunda, Z. (1994). Exaggerated self-assessments and the preference for controllable risks. *Organizational Behavior and Human Decision Processes, 59,* 410–427.

Koehler, D. J., Brenner, L. A., & Tversky, A. (1997). The enhancement effect in probability judgment. *Journal of Behavioral Decision Making, 10,* 293–313.

Krueger, J., & Clement, R. W. (1994). The truly false consensus effect: An ineradicable and egocentric bias in social perception. *Journal of Personality and Social Psychology, 67,* 596–610.

Kruger, J. (1999). Lake Wobegon be gone! The "below-average effect" and the egocentric nature of comparative ability judgments. *Journal of Personality and Social Psychology, 77,* 221–232.

Legrenzi, P., Girotto, V., & Johnson-Laird, P. N. (1993). Focusing in reasoning and decision making. *Cognition, 49,* 37–66.

Lichtenstein, S., & Fischhoff, B. (1977). Do those who know more also know more about how much they know? *Organizational Behavior and Human Decision Processes, 20,* 159–183.

Loewenstein, G., Thompson, L., & Bazerman, M. H. (1989). Social utility and decision making in interpersonal contexts. *Journal of Personality and Social Psychology, 57,* 426–441.

Markus, H. (1977). Self-schemata and processing information about the self. *Journal of Personality and Social Psychology, 35,* 63–78.

McFarland, C., & Miller, D. T. (1990). Judgments of self-other similarity: Just like other people, only more so. *Personality and Social Psychology Bulletin, 16,* 475–484.

Messick, D. M., & Mackie, D. M. (1989). Intergroup relations. *Annual Review of Psychology, 40,* 45–81.

Messick, D. M., Moore, D. A., & Bazerman, M. H. (1997). Ultimatum bargaining with a group: Underestimating the importance of the decision rule. *Organizational Behavior and Human Decision Processes, 69,* 87–101.

Mussweiler, T., Gabriel, S., & Bodenhausen, G. V. (2000). Shifting social identities as a strategy for deflecting threatening social comparisons. *Journal of Personality and Social Psychology, 79,* 398–409.

Mussweiler, T., & Strack, F. (2000). The "relative self": Informational and judgmental consequences of comparative self-evaluation. *Journal of Personality and Social Psychology, 79,* 23–38.

Parco, J. E., Rapoport, A., & Stein, W. E. (2002). Effects of financial incentives on the breakdown of mutual trust. *Psychological Science, 13,* 292–297.

Perloff, L. S., & Brickman, P. (1982). False consensus and false uniqueness: Biases in perceptions of similarity. *Academic Psychology Bulletin, 4,* 475–494.

Ross, L. (1977). The intuitive psychologist and his shortcomings: Distortions in the attribution process. In L. Berkowitz (Ed.), *Advances in experimental social psychology* (Vol. 10, pp. 173–220). New York: Academic Press.

Ross, L., Greene, D., & House, P. (1977). The false consensus effect: An egocentric bias in social perception and attribution processes. *Journal of Experimental Social Psychology, 13,* 279–301.

Ross, M., & Sicoly, F. (1979). Egocentric biases in availability and attribution. *Journal of Personality and Social Psychology, 37,* 322–336.

Rottenstreich, Y., & Tversky, A. (1997). Unpacking, repacking, and anchoring: Advances in support theory. *Psychological Review, 104,* 406–415.

Schkade, D. A., & Kahneman, D. (1998). Does living in California make people happy? A focusing illusion in judgments of life satisfaction. *Psychological Science, 9,* 340–346.

Slovic, P., Fischhoff, B., & Lichtenstein, S. (1977). Accident probabilities and seatbelt usage: A psychological perspective. *Accident Analysis and Prevention, 10,* 281–295.

Soll, J. B. (1996). Determinants of overconfidence and miscalibration: The roles of random error and ecological structure. *Organizational Behavior and Human Decision Processes, 65,* 117–137.

Smith, V. L., & Walker, J. M. (1993). Monetary rewards and decision cost in experimental economics. *Economic Inquiry, 31,* 245–261.

Storms, M. D. (1973). Videotape and the attribution process: Reversing actors' and observers' points of view. *Journal of Personality and Social Psychology, 27,* 165–175.

Suls, J. M., & Wheeler, L. (Eds.). (2000). *Handbook of social comparison: Theory and research.* New York: Kluwer Academic/Plenum Publishers.

Taylor, S. E., & Fiske, S. T. (1975). Point of view and perceptions of causality. *Journal of Personality and Social Psychology, 32,* 439–445.

Thompson, L. (1995). "They saw a negotiation": Partisanship and involvement. *Journal of Personality and Social Psychology, 68,* 839–853.

Turner, J. C. (1987). *Rediscovering the social group: A self-categorization theory.* Oxford, England: Basil Blackwell.

Tversky, A. (1977). Features of similarity. *Psychological Review, 84,* 327–352.

Tversky, A., & Gati, I. (1978). Studies of similarity. In E. Rosch & B. B. Lloyd (Eds.), *Cognition and categorization* (pp. 78–98). Hillsdale, NJ: Erlbaum.

Tversky, A., & Koehler, D. J. (1994). Support theory: A nonextensional representation of subjective probability. *Psychological Review, 101,* 547–567.

Weinstein, N. D., & Lachendro, E. (1982). Egocentrism as a source of unrealistic optimism. *Personality and Social Psychology Bulletin, 8,* 195–200.

Wilson, T. D., Wheatley, T., Meyers, J. M., Gilbert, D. T., & Axsom, D. (2000). Focalism: A source of durability bias in affective forecasting. *Journal of Personality and Social Psychology, 78,* 821–836.

Windschitl, P. D., Kruger, J., & Simms, E. (2003). The influence of egocentrism and focalism on people's optimism in competitions: When what affects us equally affects me more. *Journal of Personality and Social Psychology, 85,* 389–408.

Wylie, R. C. (1979). *The self-concept: Theory and research on selected topics.* Lincoln: University of Nebraska Press.

Received June 7, 2002
Revision received July 15, 2003
Accepted July 30, 2003 ■

Exposing Pluralistic Ignorance to Reduce Alcohol Use Among College Students

Christine M. Schroeder * and Deborah A. Prentice

Research has shown that students' beliefs about alcohol use are characterized by pluralistic ignorance: The majority of students believe that their peers are uniformly more comfortable with campus alcohol practices than they are. The present study examines effects of educating students about pluralistic ignorance on their drinking behavior. Entering students (freshmen) participated in either a peer-oriented discussion, which focused on pluralistic ignorance, or an individual-oriented discussion, which focused on decision making in a drinking situation. Four to 6 months later, students in the peer-oriented condition reported drinking significantly less than did students in the individual-oriented condition. Additional results suggest that the peer-oriented discussion reduced the prescriptive strength of the drinking norm. The implications of these results for models of social influence and for the representation of peer opinion are discussed.

* University of Medicine & Dentistry of New Jersey.

This article is based on a dissertation submitted by Christine M. Schroeder to Princeton University Graduate School in partial fulfillment of the requirements for the doctoral degree. This research was supported by Grant P-183A 1015-01/02 from the United States Department of Education's Fund for the Improvement of Post-Secondary Education, Grant MH44069 from the National Institute of Mental Health, and a Grant-In-Aid from the Society for the Psychological Study of Social Issues. Thanks are extended to Jessica Haile, who assisted in the preparation of materials and in the collection of follow-up data, Diane Cook, Jonathan Folkers, Diane Hood, Jen Kates, Betty Langan, and June Nehrod, who helped to coordinate and conduct the discussion sessions, and especially Susan Packer and Karen Gordon, who helped to plan and implement the entire project. In addition, the research benefited from the helpful comments of Gregory Clark and Barry Jacobs, who served on Christine Schroeder's dissertation committee, and John Darley and Dale Miller who both served on the dissertation committee and provided comments on earlier drafts of this article.

Correspondence concerning this article should be addressed to Deborah Prentice. Department of Psychology, Princeton University, Green Hall, Princeton, NJ 08544-1010, e-mail: predebb@princeton.edu

Alcohol use by college undergraduates is a major concern of university administrators and public-health officials across the country. Surveys of college students estimate that over 90% have tried alcohol, and approximately 20 to 25% exhibit symptoms of problem drinking (cf. Engs, Diebold, & Hanson, 1996; Haberman, 1994; Meilman, Stone, Gaylor, & Turco, 1990; Perkins & Berkowitz, 1989; see Berkowitz & Perkins, 1986; and Prendergast, 1994, for reviews). Alcohol and alcohol-related events are cited as the number-one cause of death among young people in the United States, primarily because of alcohol-related car accidents and the role that alcohol plays in suicide (Thorner, 1986). In addition, heavy drinking among college students is associated with lower academic performance, a higher rate of getting into trouble with authorities, disruptions in personal relationships, and, for male students, an increased risk of fighting or of damaging property (Berkowitz & Perkins, 1986).

Social Influence and Alcohol Use

There is now considerable evidence to suggest that social processes play a powerful role in promoting drinking among college students. In particular, numerous studies have shown that one of the most consistent predictors of an adolescent's alcohol use is perceived alcohol use by his or her peers (e.g., Ellickson & Bell, 1990; Kandel, 1980; Marks, Graham, & Hansen, 1992; Perkins, 1985; Stein, Newcomb, & Bentler, 1987). For example, in a review of the literature on alcohol and other drug use, Kandel found that the extent of perceived drug use in the peer group, self-reported drug use by peers, and perceived tolerance for use were all strong predictors of an adolescent's own drug use (Orford, 1985). More recently, Mooney and Corcoran (1991) found that perceived peer alcohol consumption and attitude predicted variance in alcohol consumption beyond that attributable to personal characteristics. Similarly, Werner, Walker, and Greene (1996) found that students' impressions of their friends' drinking correlated with concurrent and future risk for problem drinking. These

and many similar findings have been taken as evidence that perceptions of peers exert a considerable influence on adolescents' drinking behavior, even though few of the studies have directly addressed the question of causality (Kandel, 1980).

Peer influence in and of itself is not sufficient to explain why college students tend toward high levels of alcohol consumption. Presumably, peers could as easily encourage moderation as excess. However, on most college campuses, peer influence is directed by injunctive norms that promote heavy alcohol use (Perkins & Berkowitz, 1986; Prentice & Miller, 1993). Indeed, drinking, sometimes to excess, is central to the social identity of many college students and is an important part of social life on most campuses. Thus, it is not surprising that the move to college produces an increase in alcohol consumption, especially among students with little previous experience with alcohol (Friend & Koushki, 1984; Hill & Bugen, 1979; Perkins, 1985; Wechsler & McFadden, 1979). Further evidence suggests that a normative frequency of binge drinking (neither too often nor too seldom) is associated with greater intimacy and higher levels of disclosure in peer relations (Nezlek, Pilkington, & Bilbro, 1994). These findings are precisely what one would expect if students' alcohol use was driven by social influence processes. They reflect pressures toward increasingly uniform and norm-consistent behaviors over time (for similar examples in other domains, see Crandall, 1988; Festinger, Schachter, & Back, 1950; Newcomb, 1943).

Pluralistic Ignorance

This emerging picture of the ways in which social influence processes promote alcohol use among college undergraduates would not be complete without one additional fact about the norm for drinking on campus: It does not map well onto the private sentiments of individual students. Indeed, even though students acknowledge the liberal drinking norm and often conform to it in their outward behavior, they still harbor considerable misgivings about the safety, wisdom, and desirability of drinking. The norm that guides their public behavior does not enjoy their private support. If students were aware of this disjunction between the behavioral norm and private attitudes, presumably the norm would lose its prescriptive force. However, students are aware of this disjunction only in their own cases: They assume that their peers hold private views that are much more consistent with the drinking norm than are their own.

In short, students' beliefs about alcohol use on campus are characterized by pluralistic ignorance: They assume that their own private attitudes are more conservative than are those of other students, even though their public behavior is identical (Miller & McFarland, 1991). Numerous studies have documented this systematic divergence of students' own attitudes about alcohol practices from their assumptions about the attitudes of their peers. For example, Prentice and Miller (1993) found that a cross-section of students sampled from all four college classes (i.e., freshman through senior years) rated themselves as less comfortable than the average student and as less comfortable than their friends with drinking on campus. In addition, students' estimates of others' attitudes were characterized by an illusion of universality (Allport, 1924): Not only did they overestimate their peers' support for the drinking norm, they overestimated the uniformity of that support (Prentice & Miller, 1993). Perkins and Berkowitz (1986) also found a sizable disparity between students' own attitudes toward alcohol use and their assessments of the general campus attitude. These researchers asked students to select from among five statements the one that best represented their own feelings about drinking and the one that best represented "the general campus attitude toward drinking alcoholic beverages" (p. 964). Almost two thirds of their sample endorsed the moderate statement, "An occasional 'drunk' is okay as long as it doesn't interfere with grades or responsibilities," and less than 20% endorsed the two more permissive statements. By contrast, over 60% selected one of those two more permissive statements as representing the campus attitude toward drinking.

These findings reveal that students' perceptions of their peers' attitudes are in error. They exaggerate the extent to which other students are comfortable with excessive drinking. Ironically, it appears that this misperception may play a role in maintaining the pro-alcohol norm on campus. Prentice and Miller (1993), for example, found evidence for attitudinal conformity among male students, who modified their private attitudes over time in the direction of the position they mistakenly assumed to be held by the average student. In a separate study, Prentice and Miller also found that both male and female students showed signs of alienation from the university and from their peers when they (mistakenly) believed their attitudes to be discrepant from those of the average student. And as we noted earlier, previous research on substance use has shown that the perceived level of tolerance for alcohol and drug use among peers is a strong predictor of one's own use (Kandel, 1980). It is clear that perceptions of peer opinion, even if erroneous, have significant consequences.

Changing Drinking Behavior

Thus, considerable evidence suggests that pluralistic ignorance plays a very negative role in campus social life, perpetuating dysfunctional drinking norms and engendering alienation within the campus community. At the same time, pluralistic ignorance has one positive feature: It offers a clear route to behavior change. If students' drinking practices are fostered, or at least maintained, by the erroneous perception that other students feel more positively toward these practices than they do, then correcting this misperception should lower their alcohol consumption. Most attempts to promote responsible drinking on college campuses have taken the form of informational programs, designed to convey legal and pharmacological information about the effects of alcohol (Berkowitz & Perkins, 1987). More sophisticated programs have sought to teach individual students to make responsible decisions about alcohol and alcohol consumption in drinking situations (e.g., Meacci, 1990). Yet, until recently, attempts at alcohol intervention have focused on changing individual students' beliefs and attitudes about alcohol and have ignored the social context in which most drinking on college campuses takes place (see Donaldson, Graham, Piccinin, & Hansen, 1995; Ellickson, Bell, & McGuigan, 1993; and MacKinnon *et al.*, 1991, for some notable exceptions using pre-college-age populations).

We wish to argue that a more effective way to change students' drinking behavior would focus instead on revealing their erroneous assumptions about the attitudes of their peers. Previous studies have shown that the majority of students already hold the moderate attitudes toward drinking that informational campaigns and individual counseling sessions seek to foster (Perkins & Berkowitz, 1986; Prentice & Miller, 1993). What students need, in addition, is to understand that those attitudes are shared. We contend that if students were made aware that their estimates of other students' attitudes were too liberal—that is, if they were exposed to the concept of pluralistic ignorance in a group setting—then they should experience much less social pressure to consume alcohol. As a result, they should drink less and should feel more comfortable with their drinking behavior.

Exposing pluralistic ignorance could change drinking behavior in at least two ways. First, it could change the level of drinking that students perceive to be condoned by their peers. Given the news that their peers are not as comfortable with current drinking practices as they had thought, students might construct a new, more conservative norm for drinking; one that corresponds to true campus sentiment. This change in the level of drinking prescribed by the norm would produce changes in drinking behavior. Students would still experience social pressure to drink, but the level of drinking they felt pressured to achieve would be lower, more in line with their private sentiments, and would have much less deleterious consequences.

Alternatively, exposing pluralistic ignorance could change drinking behavior by changing the prescriptive strength of the norm. Social norms derive much of their prescriptive power from the perception that they have universal support (Turner, 1991). Indeed, the presence of even one alternative viewpoint in a group sharply reduces the power of the group norm to induce conformity (e.g., Asch, 1951). Providing students with evidence that their

peers are not entirely comfortable with current drinking practices would certainly indicate to them that support for the drinking norm is less universal than they may have supposed, and thus should weaken the norm's prescriptive power. This change in the strength of the norm would produce changes in drinking behavior. Students would no longer feel the same degree of social pressure to bring their own alcohol use into line with the campus standard.

It is important to note that the drinking norm to which we refer in this analysis is an injunctive norm, not a descriptive norm (Cialdini, Kallgren, & Reno, 1991). Descriptive norms are defined by what individuals do; injunctive norms are defined by what they approve (or disapprove) of doing. The drinking norms that drive pluralistic ignorance are defined by what college students think is appropriate and good behavior, rather than what they think is common behavior. The discrepancy that we find between students' own comfort with campus alcohol practices and their perceptions of the average student's comfort represents a misperception of how other students feel about drinking (the injunctive norm), rather than of how much they drink (the descriptive norm). Interestingly, researchers have documented a similar misperception of the descriptive drinking norm (Baer & Carney, 1993; Baer, Stacy, & Larimer, 1991), but that finding is not directly relevant to this investigation.

Present Study

The research reported in this article was designed to explore the behavioral and psychological consequences of correcting students' misperceptions of their peers' attitudes toward drinking. Entering students were randomly assigned to participate in one of two types of discussions about alcohol use during their first week on campus. In the peer-oriented condition, students were introduced to the data showing systematic misperception of other students' comfort with campus drinking practices, and were encouraged to talk about this phenomenon and the social dynamics surrounding drinking more generally. In the individual-oriented condition, students participated in a discussion of how to make responsible personal decisions in a drinking situation. This latter condition served as a control, from which to evaluate the effects of the peer-oriented discussion;[1] it was chosen as the comparison because it was representative of many existing programs designed to change drinking behavior. Four to 6 months after the discussions, all students completed self-report measures of their alcohol consumption. We expected to find lower levels of reported alcohol consumption among students in the peer-oriented condition than among students in the individual-oriented condition.

In addition to demonstrating the effects of dispelling pluralistic ignorance, we were also interested in understanding the psychological mechanisms underlying these effects. Thus, we included several additional measures designed to shed some light on why exposure to evidence of pluralistic ignorance might reduce students' alcohol consumption. First, we asked all participants to rate their own comfort with alcohol use and the comfort of the average student, both directly before the discussion sessions and at the time of the follow-up. If dispelling pluralistic ignorance reduces drinking by changing the level of drinking prescribed by the norm, then we would expect the condition difference in drinking to be mirrored by a condition difference in the comfort attributed to the average student, and significant, uniform correlations between these two measures across conditions. Second, immediately following the discussion sessions, we asked all participants to complete the short form of Watson and Friend's (1969) Fear of Negative Evaluation Scale (Leary, 1983). This scale assesses the extent to which people are characteristically anxious about others' evaluations of them and fearful of a loss of social approval. We intended it to serve as a measure of the extent to which students were sensitive to normative social influence. If dispelling pluralistic ignorance reduces

drinking by reducing the strength of the norm, then the effects of this manipulation should be greatest for those students who are most sensitive to, and thus most influenced by, social pressure. We expected that fear of negative evaluation might moderate differences between the individual-oriented and peer-oriented conditions.

Method
Overview

First-year students participated in one of two types of discussion groups about alcohol use during their second week on campus. Brief questionnaires administered immediately before and after the discussions tapped students' demographic characteristics, attitudes and beliefs about alcohol use on campus, and fear of negative evaluation. Four to 6 months later, a subsample of the participants completed a third questionnaire that again assessed their attitudes and beliefs about alcohol use on campus and also included questions about their own drinking behavior.

Participants and design

Princeton University has five residential colleges that provide housing for virtually all first- and second-year students. Within each residential college, first-year students are divided into residential advisor (RA) groups that range in size from 12 to 20 students. The RA groups in four of the five residential colleges were invited to participate in this study as one of a series of activities designed to orient them to campus life.[2] A total of 452 first-year students attended one of the September discussion sessions with their RA group. This sample included approximately half of the students who were eligible to attend the discussions; it was representative of the first-year class in terms of all demographic categories for which class statistics were available (gender, ethnicity, and varsity athlete status). The discussions took place during the first week of classes on 3 successive nights in the

---

[1] For research purposes, we would have liked to include a no-treatment control group in the design. However, ethical considerations argued against a no-treatment control. In particular, university officials felt very strongly that it was not appropriate to offer some students an opportunity to participate in a discussion group with potential benefits without offering something comparable (and also potentially beneficial) to other students.

[2] The failure of one residential college to participate in the study was due to administrative and staffing difficulties that do not bear in any way on the interpretation of the results.

residential colleges. Each college had two 1-hr discussions each evening, and each discussion was attended by the members of two RA groups.

We chose to conduct this study with entering students for two reasons. First, they did not already have well-established drinking patterns within the local environment. Having just arrived on campus, they did not yet know who their friends would be, how they would spend their evenings and weekends, or what role alcohol use would play in their social lives. We anticipated that it would be easier to affect the formation of their drinking habits than to change the already-established habits of more advanced students. Second, the perceptions that entering students had of the campus and their peers were not yet as well entrenched as those of older students. Although they certainly were not without some beliefs and preconceptions about what college life would be like, they had little direct experience with which to back those up. Again, we anticipated that it would be easier to affect their beliefs in the formative stages than to change their way of thinking later on.

There were two types of discussions: a peer-oriented discussion and an individual-oriented discussion. RA groups were systematically assigned to discussion type so that both types were represented on all 3 nights and in all residential colleges. This procedure was designed to minimize possible confounds due to scheduling or to different characteristics of the residential colleges. In all, 235 students participated in peer-oriented discussions and 217 in individual-oriented discussions.

Four to 6 months after the discussions, 143 of the students completed the follow-up questionnaire. The representativeness of this subsample was assessed by comparing students who returned for the follow-up to those who did not, on a number of measures. Likelihood of returning for the follow-up did not vary with gender, ethnicity (ethnic groups considered were African American, Asian American, Caucasian, and Hispanic), or varsity athlete status (all $\chi^2 < 1$). In addition, follow-up participants did not differ from dropout participants in their self-reported comfort with alcohol use on campus or in their fear of negative evaluation; separate logistic regressions predicting

return for the follow-up from comfort with alcohol and fear of negative evaluation showed no association (both $\chi^2 < 1$). Finally, and most importantly, likelihood of returning for the follow-up did not vary with discussion condition, $\chi^2(1, N = 143) = 1.93$, $p > .10$. Thus, we could be reasonably certain that the follow-up sample was representative of the population of interest and that students were not electing to return for the follow-up based on their comfort with alcohol, their social anxiety, or the type of discussion they had attended in September. The final sample included 66 students (35 males, 31 females) in the peer-oriented condition, and 77 students (44 males, 33 females) in the individual-oriented condition. The analyses reported in this article include data from only those students who participated in all phases of the study.

Measures

Prediscussion questionnaire. At the beginning of the discussion sessions, participants completed a brief questionnaire that assessed their membership in various demographic groups, their own comfort with alcohol use on campus, and their estimates of the average student's comfort with alcohol.

Students were first asked to indicate their gender, ethnicity, religious background, home state, whether they attended a public or private high school, whether they were members of a varsity sports team, and the last four digits of their Social Security numbers. For purposes of the current research, only gender was of interest. Other demographic data were used to match the initial questionnaires with the follow-up questionnaire for each participant and to assess the representativeness of the sample.

In addition, students were asked to indicate their own comfort with alcohol use on campus and to estimate the comfort of the average student, as in Prentice and Miller (1993). The two questions were as follows:

1. How comfortable are you with students' drinking habits?
2. Given what you know about Princeton students, how comfortable do you think the average Princeton student is with students' drinking habits?

Students responded to each question by circling a number on the corresponding 11-point scale, ranging from 1 (*not at all comfortable*) to 11 (*very comfortable*).[3]

Postdiscussion questionnaire. Following the discussions, participants completed a second questionnaire that included questions about their plans for their first year at college, their reactions to the discussion groups, and, of particular relevance to the present investigation, their fear of negative evaluation (FNE).

FNE was assessed with the short form of Watson and Friend's (1969) Fear of Negative Evaluation Scale (Leary, 1983). This 12-item index measures the extent to which an individual is characteristically anxious about the evaluations of others. Items include: "I worry about what people will think of me even when I know it doesn't make any difference"; "I am afraid that others will not approve of me"; "Other people's opinions of me do not bother me" (reverse scored). Students indicated their agreement with each statement using a 5-point scale ranging from 1 (*not at all like me*) to 5 (*extremely like me*). Each student's ratings of the 12 items were summed to create a single index of fear of negative evaluation ($\alpha = .90$). Possible scores on the index ranged from 12 to 60, with higher scores indicating higher levels of fear.

Follow-up questionnaire. Approximately 4 to 6 months after the discussions, follow-up participants completed a final questionnaire. They were asked to indicate their gender and the last four digits of their Social Security numbers on the questionnaire so that each student's responses could be matched with his or her earlier questionnaires.

In the follow-up questionnaire, students were again asked to indicate their own comfort with students' drinking habits and the comfort of the average student on 11-point scales, as in the prediscussion questionnaire. In addition, they were asked a series of standard questions about their own alcohol consumption. The first two items assessed whether they drank alcohol:

1. Have you ever tried alcohol at all?
2. Have you consumed alcohol for recreational or social reasons in the past semester?

Students responded to each of these questions by circling *Yes* or *No*. The next two items assessed how much alcohol they drank, using an open-ended format:

3. How many alcoholic drinks have you had in the past week?
4. How many alcoholic drinks do you have in a typical week during the semester?

Students estimated their weekly alcohol intake.[4]

---

[3] We did not include a measure of students' drinking behavior in this initial assessment because it would not have provided a valid baseline to which to compare later drinking. The discussion sessions were conducted with first-year students in their first week on campus; neither the number of drinks they had had in the last week nor the number of drinks they had in a typical week would serve as a relevant comparison for their drinking behavior during the upcoming semester. Thus, we relied on the between-subjects comparison across conditions, rather than the within-subjects comparison across time, to assess the effects of the discussion sessions. It is worth noting that the effectiveness of alcohol interventions has been shown to vary with baseline levels of consumption (e.g., Ellickson et al., 1993). However, because we randomly assigned participants to conditions, we had no reason to expect baseline drinking to have a differential effect across the two types of discussion groups.

[4] Although the self-report measure of alcohol consumption that we used in this study is similar to those used in virtually all

studies of drinking among adolescents and college students, its validity is still dependent on participants' willingness and ability to accurately report on their own drinking behavior. Encouraging evidence for the validity of these self-reports comes from consistent findings of sensible relations between self-reported alcohol consumption and a variety of factors known to influence drinking behavior (e.g., gender, ethnicity, religiosity, fraternity, and sorority membership) across many previous investigations (see Berkowitz & Perkins, 1986; Prendergast, 1994, for reviews). The present study replicated these findings. In addition, it showed no evidence of a systematic relation between self-reported alcohol consumption and scores on the Fear of Negative Evaluation scale, an individual difference measure of sensitivity to others' views of the self. Thus, it appears that social desirability did not have a strong influence on students' reports of their drinking behavior.

Procedure

The discussion groups were conducted as part of the orientation program for first-year students. They were led by peer facilitators who were second-, third-, and fourth-year students at the university. The facilitators were recruited from several existing peer-education programs on campus. Peer facilitators participated in a 3-hr workshop several days before the discussion groups began, in which they were trained to lead one of the two types of discussions. Each facilitator led only peer-oriented or individual-oriented discussion groups.

The discussions took place in the residential colleges in closed-off lounge areas with TV and VCR equipment. When students arrived, they were introduced to the project by the peer facilitator and were asked to sign an informed consent sheet. They then completed the prediscussion questionnaire.

Next, students saw a video presentation that lasted approximately 7 min. The video portrayed several alcohol-related social scenes in a university setting. The video clips were meant to be descriptive, rather than prescriptive; their primary purpose was to provide a basis for the following discussion.

After the video, students took part in a 20-min discussion about drinking on campus. The format was the same for all discussions, but the specific topic varied by condition. In the individual-oriented condition, the discussion centered on the individual and how he or she makes responsible decisions about alcohol consumption. Students were encouraged to reflect on the types of situations in which they might encounter alcohol at the university, to explore their options in those situations, and to consider the personal and social consequences of various courses of action. They also talked about the effects of alcohol and how it might interfere with their decision-making abilities. In the peer-oriented condition, the discussion centered on pluralistic ignorance and its implications. The facilitator began by describing to students the finding of a self–other discrepancy in comfort with drinking on campus and briefly explaining the phenomenon of pluralistic ignorance. Students were encouraged to talk about how and why these misperceptions of peer opinion might have developed. They were also asked to reflect on how misperceiving each other's

attitudes toward drinking might affect social life on campus. An outline of the discussion questions used in each condition appears in the Appendix.

The length and format of the two types of discussion sessions were identical. In both, the peer facilitator introduced the topic of the discussion and interjected occasional questions to keep the discussion on track. Students were encouraged to speak openly about their opinions and experiences with alcohol. After the discussions, students completed the postdiscussion questionnaire. No mention was made of any follow-up assessment at this time.

Follow-up participants were contacted 4 to 6 months after the discussion sessions and were asked to complete an attitude survey for first-year students. No mention was made of the alcohol discussion groups until after they had completed the questionnaire, and none of the students reported making the connection themselves. Students were contacted on an individual basis, via campus mailings, posters, and telephone; they received $3 for completing the follow-up questionnaire. It is important to note that very few of the students who were contacted for the follow-up refused to participate. Instead, data collection had to be terminated when an article describing the project and related research appeared in the student newspaper. Again, we have no reason to believe that the follow-up participants were a biased subset of the original sample.

Results

The primary goal of this investigation was to assess the effects of educating students about pluralistic ignorance on their drinking behavior. We expected that students who had learned about pluralistic ignorance in the peer-oriented discussion would report drinking less than students who had participated in an individual-oriented discussion. In addition, we sought evidence regarding the mechanism underlying the effect. The data allowed us to test two possibilities. One, the peer-oriented discussion could reduce drinking behavior by changing the level of drinking prescribed by the norm, moving it in a more conservative direction. In this case, we would expect to find condition differences in drinking mirrored by differences in pluralistic ignorance and a significant and consistent relation between estimates of the average student's comfort and drinking behavior across conditions. Two, the peer-oriented discussion could reduce drinking by reducing the level of perceived support for the norm, thereby weakening social pressure to conform to it. In this case, we might or might not find a difference in pluralistic ignorance across conditions, but we would expect to find moderating effects of condition and fear of negative evaluation on the relation between estimates of the average student's comfort and drinking behavior.

Students answered four questions about their drinking behavior: (a) whether they had ever tried alcohol, (b) whether they had used alcohol for social or recreational purposes in the past semester, (c) how many alcoholic drinks they had in the past week, and (d) how many alcoholic drinks they had in a typical week. Their responses to the latter two questions were highly correlated, $r(141) = .70$, $p < .0001$, and thus were averaged to form a single index of alcohol consumption. Descriptive statistics on this index are shown in Table 14.1.[5] To evaluate the representativeness of these data, we compared students' reports of their drinking to data gathered on the same campus in the 1992 Core Alcohol and Drug Survey.[6] The 1992 survey indicated that 10% of students had never tried alcohol, whereas 21% had not used it in the past 30 days. In the current sample, 10% of the students indicated having never tried alcohol, and 20% indicated that they had not used it for social or recreational purposes in the past semester. On the 1992 survey, male students reported consuming 5.4 drinks per week on average, and female students reported consuming 3.0 drinks per week. In the current sample, at the time of the follow-up, the figures were 5.0 drinks for male students and 3.2 drinks for female students. In addition. Prentice and Miller (1993) found comparable levels of drinking in their research on the same campus. Thus, the current

TABLE 14.1 Average Number of Drinks Per Week Reported by Condition

	Condition	
	Peer-oriented	Individual-oriented
Women		
M	2.29	4.02
SD	2.88	5.99
Interquartile range	0–3.5	0–5.5
Men		
M	3.81	5.81
SD	4.95	7.15
Interquartile range	0–6.5	0–10.0
Total		
M	3.10	5.05
SD	4.15	6.70
Interquartile range	0–5.0	0–6.5

data on drinking behavior were in line with recent campus samples.

The primary hypothesis of this study was that students in the peer-oriented condition, who had been educated about pluralistic ignorance, would drink less than would students in the individual-oriented condition. A 2×2 (Student Gender $\times$ Condition) ANOVA on students' scores on the drinking index revealed the predicted effect of condition, $F(1, 137) = 3.80$, $p = .05$. As shown in Table 14.1, students in the peer-oriented condition consumed significantly fewer drinks each week than did students in the individual-oriented condition. This difference was not attributable to differences in rates of abstinence, as there was no effect of condition on the percentage of participants who did not drink during the semester (21.2% in the peer-oriented condition and 19.5% in the individual-oriented condition), $z = 0.25$, $p > .50$. Thus, it appears that the peer-oriented condition reduced alcohol consumption relative to the individual-oriented condition among students who actually drank alcohol.

---

[5] An initial exploration of scores on the drinking measure (separately for men and women in each condition) revealed no outliers, so all data were included in the analyses.

[6] The Core Alcohol and Drug Survey is a standardized questionnaire that was developed in 1988 with the funding of the United States Department of Education. It is administered yearly to

samples of students at a number of American universities, and the data are tabulated and made available by the Department of Education. Because the data are aggregated across all 4 years of college, they do not provide an ideal standard of comparison for the data in the present study. Nevertheless, they do provide a useful context in which our data can be evaluated.

The analysis also revealed a marginally significant gender difference, $F(1, 137) = 3.02, p < .10$. Male students drank more than did female students across both conditions.

Mechanism: A Change in the Level of Drinking Prescribed by the Norm?

We next sought to determine the mechanism underlying the condition difference in drinking. We first considered the possibility that students in the peer-oriented condition drank less because they used the information on peer (dis)comfort to construct a new, more conservative norm. In this case, at the follow-up assessment, students in the peer-oriented condition should rate the average student as less comfortable with campus drinking practices than do students in the individual-oriented condition, and than they themselves did before participating in the discussion sessions. Moreover, this condition difference in average-student comfort ratings should account for the difference in drinking behavior. As a first step in testing this hypothesis, we examined the patterns of own and average-student comfort ratings in the prediscussion and follow-up questionnaires. These data were analyzed using a $2 \times 2 \times 2 \times 2$ (Student Gender $\times$ Condition $\times$ Target: Self or Average Student $\times$ Time) ANOVA, with gender and condition as between-subjects factors, and target and time as within-subjects factors. The analysis revealed a significant main effect of target, $F(1, 137) = 6.54, p < .05$, which was qualified by an interaction of target with time, $F(1, 137) = 8.73, p < .01$. Incoming students showed evidence of pluralistic ignorance, as manifested in a discrepancy between their own comfort with drinking habits and their perceptions of the average student's comfort (in September, $Ms = 6.98$ for own comfort and 7.76 for average student's comfort); this discrepancy was reduced by the end of the semester (at the follow-up, $Ms = 7.06$ for own comfort and 7.31 for average student's comfort). There was no evidence that the reduction in pluralistic ignorance varied by condition, as the Target $\times$ Condition, Time $\times$ Condition, and Target $\times$ Time $\times$ Condition interactions were all nonsignificant (all $Fs < 1$). Thus, students' own comfort and their perceptions

of the average student's comfort with alcohol did converge over time, but this convergence did not depend on their being exposed to the concept of pluralistic ignorance.

However, the reduction in pluralistic ignorance did vary by gender. Means for the two comfort questions are shown in Table 14.2, calculated separately for male and female students at the initial and follow-up assessments. The analysis revealed a significant Time $\times$ Gender interaction, $F(1, 137) = 4.60, p < .05$, which reflected a greater change in comfort ratings by male students than by female students. As the means in Table 14.2 indicate, this differential change occurred primarily in perceptions of the average student. For male students, a simple effects analysis revealed a main effect of time, $F(1, 137) = 6.26, p < .02$, and an interaction of time with target, $F(1, 137) = 7.32, p < .01$, indicating that the initial discrepancy between own and average-student comfort with drinking was significantly reduced at the follow-up assessment. For female students, a simple effects analysis revealed only a main effect of target, $F(1, 137) = 4.50, p < .05$ (for the Target $\times$ Time interaction, $F[1, 137] = 2.18, p > .10$), reflecting the persistence of pluralistic ignorance over time.

We wish to highlight two aspects of these results. First, the absence of any significant effect of condition on the pattern of comfort ratings suggests that the behavioral effects of educating students about pluralistic ignorance did not result from a reconstruction of the drinking norm. Although students in the peer-oriented condition did show a reduction in the level of comfort attributed to the

TABLE 14.2. Rating of Own Comfort and the Average Student's Comfort With Alcohol Drinking

	September		Follow-up	
	Self	Average student	Self	Average student
Women				
M	6.76	7.63	7.08	7.54
SD	2.55	1.68	2.15	1.54
Men				
M	7.15	7.87	7.05	7.12
SD	2.80	1.51	2.77	1.66

average student, so did students in the individual-oriented condition. Therefore, this reduction cannot account for the condition difference in drinking. Second, consistent with Prentice and Miller (1993), male students showed a greater tendency than female students to reduce the discrepancy between own and average-student comfort over time. But whereas Prentice and Miller's second-year students reduced pluralistic ignorance by shifting their own comfort in the direction of the average student's comfort, the first-year students in this study tended to do the reverse. We will consider possible reasons for this difference in the Discussion section.

Mechanism: A Change in the Prescriptive Strength of the Norm?

Next, we considered the possibility that the discussion of pluralistic ignorance in the peer-oriented condition reduced the level of perceived support for the norm and thus its prescriptive strength. We reasoned as follows: In a situation with strong, consensual social norms, individuals will be guided in their behavior both by what they believe those norms to prescribe and by how fearful they are of the negative evaluations of their peers. Individuals who are highly fearful of negative evaluation should show a stronger relation between their estimates of the norm and their behavior than individuals who are less fearful. In a situation with weak social norms, there should be no relation between fear of negative evaluation and behavioral conformity. In the absence of strong, uniform support for the norms, one has no reason to fear social censure for violating them. Therefore, if educating students about pluralistic ignorance reduced the prescriptive

strength of the drinking norm, we should find a difference across conditions in the relations among FNE estimates of the average student's comfort, and drinking behavior.[7]

To test these predictions, we conducted a regression analysis in which we predicted students' scores on the drinking index from condition (1 = peer oriented, 0 = individual oriented), FNE, and estimates of the average student's comfort with alcohol. We expected to find a three-way interaction of these variables: Students should drink in accordance with their perceptions of the norm to the extent that they are fearful of negative evaluation, but only if they are in the individual-oriented condition. Students in the peer-oriented condition, who were informed about pluralistic ignorance, should show no such pattern of results. In addition, we included own comfort level and gender (1 = males, 0 = females) in the analysis because of their strong associations with alcohol consumption. Thus, the final equation regressed drinking behavior on gender, own comfort, average-student comfort, condition, and FNE; the two-way interactions between average-student comfort and condition, average-student comfort and FNE, and condition and FNE; and the three-way interaction between condition, FNE, and average-student comfort. The regression was simultaneous, and all continuous variables were standardized before they were entered into the equation.[8] The overall regression equation accounted for 39% of the variance in reported drinking behavior and is shown in Table 14.3.

The results of this analysis yielded support for our proposed mechanism. In particular, there was a significant interaction between FNE and average-student comfort ($\beta = 0.27$), $t(129) = 2.12, p < .05$, which was qualified by the predicted three-way

---

[7] One potential concern about this use of FNE as an individual-differences variable is that the measure was collected after the condition manipulation. We decided not to include the FNE scale in the prediscussion questionnaire because we feared that it would prime social-evaluative concerns, and thus might inhibit students from being completely open and honest during the group discussions. Instead, we included the measure in the postdiscussion questionnaire. The major concern raised by this

procedure is that the condition manipulation might have affected students' scores. Fortunately, the data provided no evidence of such an effect; a 2 × 2 (Gender × Condition) ANOVA showed the main effect of condition to be nonsignificant, $F(1, 140) - 2.60, p > .10$.

[8] Standardizing has the effect of centering the variables, as recommended by Aiken and West (1991).

TABLE 14.3. Regression Predicting Drinking Behavior

Predictor	Standardized β
Gender	0.13
Own comfort	0.60**
Average-student comfort	−0.25*
Fear of negative evaluation	0.06
Condition	−0.17*
FNE × Average-Student Comfort	0.27*
Condition × Average-Student Comfort	−0.02
FNE × Condition	−0.08
FNE × Condition × Average-Student Comfort	−0.25*

Note: The peer-oriented conditions was coded as 1 and individual-oriented condition as 0; males were coded as 1 and females as 0. *$p < .05$. **$p < .01$.

interaction with condition ($\beta = -0.25$), $t(129) = -1.98$, $p < .05$.[9] To determine the form of this three-way interaction, we used the regression equation to predict drinking index scores for a hypothetical student in each cell of the $2 \times 2 \times 2$ matrix representing the crossing of the three interaction factors: average-student comfort (high and low), FNE (high and low), and intervention condition (individual oriented or peer oriented; Aiken & West, 1991). High and low values for average-student comfort and FNE were defined as 1 standard deviation above and 1 standard deviation below the mean.[10] The results are shown in Figure 14.1.

Two details of this procedure should be noted. First, because own comfort was included in the regression equation, average-student comfort is calibrated in relative terms. High average-student comfort means rating the average student as relatively comfortable, holding constant one's own rating of oneself; low average-student comfort means rating the average student as relatively uncomfortable, holding constant one's rating of oneself. This accounts for the inverse relation between

average-student comfort and drinking. Second, because high and low scores on the continuous variables were defined in a conservative manner (i.e., as only 1 standard deviation above and below the mean), all predicted values are within 1 standard deviation of the mean for drinking behavior.

With these points in mind, inspection of Figure 14.1 reveals support for our proposed mechanism. In the individual-oriented condition, students low in FNE drank less, to the extent that they perceived the average student to be more comfortable than they were themselves. By contrast, students high in FNE did not show this pattern; they uniformly drank at an above-average level. In the peer-oriented condition, students low in FNE again drank less, to the extent that they perceived the average student to be more comfortable. But in this condition, students high in FNE showed the identical pattern: They also drank less as the self–other discrepancy increased.

These results support the hypothesis that the observed differences in drinking across conditions were due, at least in part, to differences in the prescriptive strength of the drinking norm. Students who were not informed about pluralistic ignorance showed strong evidence of social influences on their alcohol use: The extent to which their perceptions of the average student's comfort with drinking related to their own drinking behavior depended on how sensitive they were to social pressure. Students who were informed about pluralistic ignorance showed no such pattern: Their sensitivity to social pressure did not moderate the relation between perceptions of the average student and drinking behavior.

Discussion

Investigations of alcohol use among college undergraduates have time and again cited the importance of social influence, or peer pressure, in promoting heavy drinking on campus. Although the

---

[9] In order to investigate the possibility that these results were driven primarily by the non-drinking students, the regression was also carried out using only students who reported drinking in the past semester. The results for this subset of the data were identical to those reported for the full data set, although the significance of the findings was, of course, affected by the reduction in the sample size.

[10] Since FNE and average-student comfort were standardized, the values entered into the prediction equation were simply −1 for the low-score prediction and +1 for the high-score prediction. Drinking behavior was also standardized, which is why some of the predicted drinking scores are below 0.

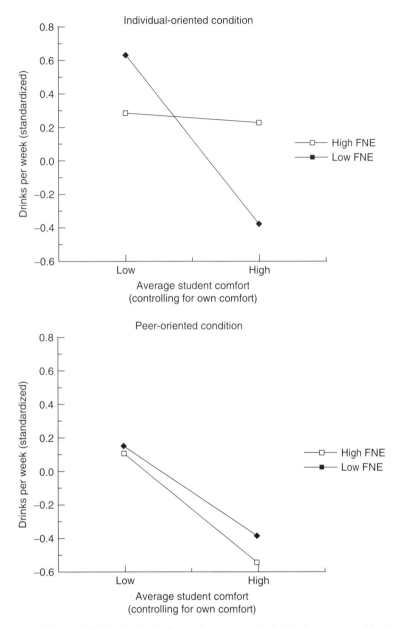

FIGURE 14.1 ■ Predicted level of drinking behavior for students 1 standard deviation above and below the mean on FNE and perceptions of average-student comfort by condition.

consistency of this finding has been satisfying for researchers who were interested in explaining students' drinking behavior, it has been quite disconcerting for those who wished to change it. How can one change a behavior that has the force of social influence behind it? The present study sought to answer this question by taking advantage of a well-documented disjunction between students' private attitudes about excessive alcohol consumption and their estimates of the attitudes of their peers.

Specifically, we exposed some students to evidence suggesting that their beliefs about alcohol use on campus were characterized by pluralistic ignorance. These students reported drinking less 4 to 6 months later, relative to a comparable control group. Given the modest success of most programs designed to reduce drinking among college students (Perkins & Berkowitz, 1986), the fact that a 1-hr discussion, held during the first week of the semester, could produce this effect is quite impressive.

Reducing social influence by exposing pluralistic ignorance

We were able to gain some insight into how educating students about pluralistic ignorance changed the social dynamics of alcohol use by examining the relations among their estimates of the average student's attitude toward drinking, their own drinking behavior, and their fear of negative evaluation. For students who had not learned about pluralistic ignorance but who instead had participated in an individual-oriented discussion, these relations reflected the workings of social influence: Those high in fear of negative evaluation drank more than did those low in fear of negative evaluation the more comfortable they perceived the average student to be with drinking on campus. For students who had participated in a peer-oriented discussion where they learned about pluralistic ignorance, this moderating effect of fear of negative evaluation on the relation between peer opinion and behavior was eliminated. We interpret these results as evidence that educating students about pluralistic ignorance reduced the prescriptive strength of the norm.[11] Students who learned that their peers were no more comfortable with alcohol than they were did not behave as if they were under normative pressure.

From a more general perspective, these results illustrate the utility of a social influence model for understanding students' alcohol use. Our analysis of drinking on campus shares much in common with earlier models of social influence processes and, in particular, with Crandall's (1988) model of the acquisition of binge eating within college sororities. Like Crandall, we begin with the assumption that a student's drinking behavior is a function of both the social pressures present in the campus environment and his or her vulnerability to those pressures. When injunctive norms are strong, as they typically are regarding alcohol use, students who are vulnerable will be influenced. In this study, we assessed students' vulnerability with the Fear of Negative Evaluation Scale (Leary, 1983; Watson & Friend, 1969). Although this scale has rarely been used in studies of social influence, it appears ideally suited for identifying individuals who are likely to be susceptible to social pressures (Leary, 1983). And indeed, the moderating effects of fear of negative evaluation found in this study lend credence to this claim.

When we educated students about pluralistic ignorance, the social pressures associated with alcohol use were presumably reduced. What does a social influence model predict about drinking behavior under these conditions? It simply predicts that students will no longer be driven by fear of negative evaluation to drink. No doubt some students who are knowledgeable about pluralistic ignorance will still consume excessive amounts of alcohol, but this behavior will not be motivated by a desire to gain the approval (or to avoid the censure) of their peers.

One remaining question that we were unable to address in the present study is how the drinking patterns of students in the individual-oriented and peer-oriented conditions differed. Although we know that educating students about pluralistic ignorance led them to drink less than students who had not been exposed to it, we do not know how this

---

[11] Of course, the pattern of results is equally consistent with the claim that something about the individual-oriented condition heightened concern with drinking. Without a no-treatment control condition, we cannot evaluate the validity of this claim empirically. However, our own and others' previous research has provided considerable evidence for the presence of strong injunctive norms governing alcohol use—evidence that is quite consistent with the results of the individual-oriented condition. Therefore, we believe that it is reasonable to interpret the results of this study as reflecting the effects of a reduction of social-evaluative concern in the peer-oriented condition.

difference in drinking was manifested in their day-to-day behavior. It is possible, for example, that students in the peer-oriented condition were less likely to binge drink (i.e., drink five or more drinks in a row), drank slightly less alcohol at each party, or attended fewer events each week at which alcohol was available, relative to students in the individual-oriented condition. A more precise understanding of how educating students about pluralistic ignorance changes their patterns of drinking might provide further insight into the ways in which social pressures influence alcohol use.

Representations of peer opinion

The present research has some important implications for our understanding of how individuals represent the opinions of their peers. In this regard, two findings deserve closer analysis. First, why did male students in both conditions estimate the average student to be less comfortable with alcohol at the end of the semester than at the beginning? And second, given that there was no apparent difference in the way students in the two conditions represented peer opinion, why did those representations relate so differently to their drinking behavior?

Consider first the change by male students in their estimates of the average student's attitude over the course of the semester. It is interesting to compare the results of this study to those of Prentice and Miller (1993). Both studies showed a reduction in the discrepancy between own and average-student comfort over time for male but not for female students. However, the two studies differed in the form that that reduction took: Prentice and Miller's subjects moved their own attitudes in the direction of the average student's, whereas our subjects moved the average student's attitude in the direction of their own. What accounts for this difference? We assume that the psychological processes underlying discrepancy reduction were similar in the two cases. That is, we assume that students in both studies were motivated by a desire to reduce the discomfort of finding themselves at odds with their group. Moreover, we assume that students' choice of how to reduce the discrepancy followed a least-effort principle analogous to that proposed by

cognitive consistency theorists (Abelson, 1968). Thus, we are left with the task of explaining why it was easier for our subjects to change their estimates of the average student's attitude, whereas it was easier for Prentice and Miller's subjects to change their own attitudes.

We offer two speculative lines of reasoning to account for this difference. First, it is possible that the first-year students who participated in our study were much less certain of their estimates of peer opinion than were Prentice and Miller's (1993) second-year students. Because they had just arrived on campus, our subjects' estimates were necessarily based on very little direct experience. What they did know was probably gleaned from orientation week, recruitment visits, and especially stories from alumni parents and friends about Princeton in the pre-coeducation days, all of which would exaggerate the already pro-alcohol sentiment on campus. Thus, their revision of their estimates over time may simply have reflected a more realistic assessment of peer opinion, based on a semester's worth of experience. Alternatively, it is possible that there was more evidence for a change in students' sentiments about drinking during our study than during Prentice and Miller's earlier investigation. Several years of concerted efforts by the university to raise consciousness about the dangers of alcohol use may have finally been paying off. Thus, our subjects may have found it easier to construct a case for a change in peer opinion than did students several years earlier.

Whatever the reason for the difference between the two studies, their general patterns of results are quite similar. Both studies show clear differences in the ways male and female students respond to pluralistic ignorance: Men resolved the discrepancy, and women retained it over time. Like Prentice and Miller (1993), we suspect that the resolution achieved by male students was only temporary. Numerous demonstrations of pluralistic ignorance on this campus and others (e.g., Perkins & Berkowitz, 1986), with older as well as younger students, suggest that it is not so easily resolved. Nevertheless, the gender difference in response to perceived deviance is clearly a real phenomenon that warrants investigation (see Prentice & Miller,

1993, for a more thorough discussion of the literature relevant to gender differences in response to peer pressure).

A second finding that deserves further analysis is the absence of a condition difference in estimates of the average student's attitude at the time of the follow-up assessment. On the face of it, this result would seem to suggest that students in both conditions held similar representations of how their peers felt about alcohol use on campus. But if this were the case, why did peer opinion matter so much more to one group than to the other?

We again offer two speculative lines of reasoning to account for this pattern of results. First, it may be that students in the two conditions did hold similar representations of peer opinion by the time of the follow-up assessment, but that the processes through which they acquired these representations differed in ways that impacted on their drinking behavior. Students in the peer-oriented condition learned very early on that other students were not as comfortable with campus drinking practices as they thought. When they saw their peers looking relaxed with, and even amused by, excessive alcohol consumption, they knew enough to discount their perceptions. They knew that public acquiescence did not necessarily signal private acceptance. Thus, from the outset, these students probably experienced little social pressure to conform to local drinking practices. By contrast, students in the individual-oriented condition arrived at their representations of peer opinion on their own. The change in their perceptions of the average student's comfort almost certainly occurred more gradually, over the course of their first semester on campus. It is likely that these students experienced considerable social pressure to adopt campus drinking practices during their first few weeks at the university, and only later came to realize that their peers' private sentiments were not as pro-alcohol as they had thought. This difference in the early experiences of students in the two groups could account for why the norm had more prescriptive power for those in the individual-oriented condition.

A second possibility is that students in the two conditions did not hold similar representations of peer opinion, even though they rated the average student's opinion the same. Their representations may have differed instead in their variability. Through the discussion of their own and others' opinions about drinking, students in the peer-oriented condition learned not only that their peers were not as comfortable with alcohol as they had thought, but also that different people feel differently. The information on pluralistic ignorance, combined with the sharing of views within the group, served to dispel the illusion of universality (Allport, 1924) that gives peer opinion its prescriptive force. Students in the individual-oriented condition had no evidence to counter this illusion. They almost certainly represented the distribution of opinions as clustered much more tightly around the position of the average student.

This explanation serves as a reminder that pluralistic ignorance is manifested in not just one, but two errors in the estimation of peer opinion (Miller & McFarland, 1991). Earlier research highlighted the importance of the self–other discrepancy (Prentice & Miller, 1993). The implication was that victims of pluralistic ignorance err primarily in where they locate the central tendency of the group. But the present study suggests that their more consequential error may be the underestimation of the variability of the group. Students experience pressure to drink and feelings of alienation not because they believe that they are in the bottom half of the distribution of comfort with drinking, but because they believe that they are outliers, that they are deviant in their level of discomfort. Once they appreciate that there is no consensus of opinion on drinking, their position relative to the average student's becomes inconsequential.

Concluding remarks

The present investigation occupies a curious place in a discipline that marks the distinction between basic and applied research. It is, in fact, a little of both: It seeks to advance our understanding of basic psychological processes by examining how they operate in a particular setting. The processes explored in this study are those that underlie social influence—specifically, how individuals represent the opinions of their peers, how those representations are affected by consensus information, and how they ultimately influence behavior. We have shown that behavioral norms depend for their prescriptive power on the perception that they have private support, and that individuals overestimate the uniformity of that support, even when they themselves feel otherwise. We have also shown that revealing that support for the norm is illusory does not lead to a revision of what the norm prescribes, but simply reduces its power to induce conformity. We contend that none of these findings is restricted to the issue of alcohol use on campus; it simply serves as an excellent vehicle to illustrate them.

Of course, from an applied perspective, alcohol use is of interest in its own right. The findings of this research suggest that educating students about pluralistic ignorance may be one component of an effective intervention strategy for reducing drinking on college campuses.[12] Although previous alcohol-intervention programs have recognized the importance of social influence, most have attempted to combat it by strengthening the resolve of the individual student. Our results suggest that it may be more effective to weaken the prescriptive power of the norm (see also Hansen & Graham, 1991). This strategy does not eliminate alcohol consumption altogether, but it frees students to act in accordance with their own, typically more conservative attitudes. Indeed, we believe that this approach may have widespread applicability. Most of the deleterious behaviors that put young people at risk (e.g., smoking, drinking, binge eating, unprotected sexual activity) are driven, at least in part, by peer pressure. Revealing to adolescents and young adults that many of their peers share their concerns about these activities may prove to be a very powerful message.

---

[12]Note that we are in no way claiming that the alleviation of pluralistic ignorance serves as a magic-bullet solution to the problem of excessive drinking among college students. For an intervention strategy to be maximally effective, it should include multiple approaches, and be sustained over time.

REFERENCES

Abelson, R. P. (1968). Psychological implication. In R. P. Abelson, E. Aronson, W. J. McGuire, T. M. Newcomb, M. J. Rosenberg, & P. H. Tannenbaum (Eds.), *Theories of cognitive consistency: A sourcebook* (pp. 112–139). Chicago, IL: Rand McNally.

Aiken, L. S., & West, S. G. (1991). *Multiple regression: Testing and interpreting interactions.* Beverly Hills, CA: Sage.

Allport, F. H. (1924). *Social psychology.* Boston, MA: Houghton-Mifflin.

Asch, S. E. (1951). Effects of group pressure upon the modification and distortion of judgments. In H. Guetzkow (Ed.), *Group leadership and men* (pp. 177–190). Pittsburgh, PA: Carnegie.

Baer, J. S., & Carney, M. M. (1993). Biases in the perceptions of the consequences of alcohol use among college students. *Journal of Studies on Alcohol, 54,* 54–60.

Baer, J. S., Stacy, A., & Larimer, M. (1991). Biases in the perception of drinking norms among college students. *Journal of Studies on Alcohol, 52,* 580–586.

Berkowitz, A. D., & Perkins, H. W. (1986). Problem drinking among college students: A review of recent research. *Journal of American College Health, 35,* 21–28.

Berkowitz, A. D., & Perkins, H. W. (1987). Current issues in effective alcohol education programming. In J. S. Sherwood (Ed.), *Alcohol policies and practices on college and university campuses* (NASPA monograph series, Vol. 7, pp. 69–85). Washington, DC: National Association of Student Personnel Administrators.

Cialdini, R. B., Kallgren, C. A., & Reno, R. R. (1991). A focus theory of normative conduct: A theoretical refinement and reevaluation of the role of norms in human behavior. In M. Zanna (Ed.), *Advances in experimental social psychology* (Vol. 24, pp. 201–234). San Diego, CA: Academic.

Crandall, C. S. (1988). Social contagion of binge eating. *Journal of Personality and Social Psychology, 55,* 588–598.

Donaldson, S. I., Graham, J. W., Piccinin, A. M., & Hansen, W. B. (1995). Resistance-skills training and onset of alcohol use: Evidence for beneficial and potentially harmful effects in public schools and in private Catholic schools. *Health Psychology, 14,* 291–300.

Ellickson, P. L., & Bell, R. M. (1990). Drug prevention in junior high: A multi-site longitudinal test. *Science, 247,* 1299–1305.

Ellickson, P. L., Bell, R. M., & McGuigan, K. (1993). Preventing adolescent drug use: Long-term results of a junior high program. *American Journal of Public Health, 83,* 856–861.

Engs, R. C., Diebold, B. A., & Hanson, D. J. (1996). The drinking patterns and problems of a national sample of college students, 1994. *Journal of Alcohol and Drug Education, 41,* 13–33.

Festinger, L., Schachter, S., & Back, K. (1950). *Social pressures in informal groups.* New York, NY: Harper & Row.

Friend, K. E., & Koushki, P. A. (1984). Student substance abuse: Stability and change across college years. *International Journal of the Addictions, 19,* 571–575.

Haberman, S. E. (1994). A survey of alcohol and other drug use practices among college students. *Journal of Alcohol and Drug Education, 39*, 85–100.

Hansen, W. B., & Graham, J. W. (1991). Preventing alcohol, marijuana, and cigarette use among adolescents: Peer pressure resistance training versus establishing conservative norms. *Preventive Medicine, 20*, 414–430.

Hill, F. E., & Bugen, L. A. (1979). A survey of drinking behavior among college students. *Journal of College Student Personnel, 20*, 236–243.

Kandel, D. B. (1980). Drug and drinking behavior among youth. *Annual Review of Sociology, 6*, 235–285.

Leary, M. R. (1983). A brief version of the Fear of Negative Evaluation Scale. *Personality and Social Psychology Bulletin, 9*, 371–375.

MacKinnon, D. P., Johnson, C. A., Pentz, M. A., Dwyer, J. H., Hansen, W. B., Flay, B. R., & Wang, E. Y. (1991). Mediating mechanisms in a school-based drug prevention program: First year effects of the Midwestern Prevention Project. *Health Psychology, 10*, 164–172.

Marks, G., Graham, J. W., & Hansen, W. B. (1992). Social projection and social conformity in adolescent alcohol use: A longitudinal analysis. *Personality and Social Psychology Bulletin, 18*, 96–101.

Meacci, W. G. (1990). An evaluation of the effects of college alcohol education on the prevention of negative consequences. *Journal of Alcohol and Drug Education, 35*, 66–72.

Meilman, P. W., Stone, J. E., Gaylor, M. S., & Turco, J. H. (1990). Alcohol consumption by college undergraduates: Current use and 10-year trends. *Journal of Studies on Alcohol, 51*, 389–395.

Miller, D. T., & McFarland, C. (1991). When social comparison goes awry: The case of pluralistic ignorance. In J. Suls & T. Wills (Eds.), *Social comparison: Contemporary theory and research* (pp. 287–313). Hillsdale, NJ: Lawrence Erlbaum.

Mooney, D. K., & Corcoran, K. J. (1991). Personal and perceived peer alcohol expectancies: Their influences on alcohol consumption. *Psychology of Addictive Behaviors, 5*, 85–92.

Newcomb, T. M. (1943). *Personality and social change.* New York, NY: Holt, Rinehart, & Winston.

Nezlek, J. B., Pilkington, C. J., & Bilbro, K. G. (1994). Moderation in excess: Binge drinking and social interaction among college students. *Journal of Studies on Alcohol, 55*, 342–351.

Orford, J. (1985). *Excessive appetites: A psychological view of addictions.* Chichester, UK: John Wiley & Sons.

Perkins, H. W. (1985). Religious traditions, parents, and peers as determinants of alcohol and drug use among college students. *Review of Religious Research, 27*, 15–31.

Perkins, H. W., & Berkowitz, A. D. (1986). Perceiving the community norms of alcohol use among students: Some research implications for campus alcohol education programming. *International Journal of the Addictions, 21*, 961–976.

Perkins, H. W., & Berkowitz, A. D. (1989). Stability and contradiction in college students' drinking following a drinking-age law change. *Journal of Alcohol and Drug Education, 35*, 60–77.

Prendergast, M. L. (1994). Substance use and abuse among college students: A review of recent literature. *Journal of American College Health, 43*, 99–113.

Prentice, D. A., & Miller, D. T. (1993). Pluralistic ignorance and alcohol use on campus: Some consequences of misperceiving the social norm. *Journal of Personality and Social Psychology, 64*, 243–256.

Stein, J. A., Newcomb, M. D., & Bentler, P. M. (1987). An 8-year study of multiple influences on drug use and drug use consequences. *Journal of Personality and Social Psychology, 53*, 1094–1105.

Thorner, G. (1986). A review of the literature on alcohol abuse, and college students and the alcohol awareness program at SUNYAB. *Journal of Alcohol and Drug Education, 31*, 41–53.

Turner, J. C. (1991). *Social influence.* Pacific Grove, CA: Brooks/Cole.

Watson, D., & Friend, R. (1969). Measurement of social-evaluative anxiety. *Journal of Consulting and Clinical Psychology, 33*, 448–457.

Wechsler, H., & McFadden, M. (1979). Drinking among college students in New England. *Journal of Studies on Alcohol, 40*, 969–996.

Werner, M. J., Walker, L. S., & Greene, J. W. (1996). Concurrent and prospective screening for problem drinking among college students. *Journal of Adolescent Health, 18*, 276–285.

APPENDIX

Discussion Questions Used in the Individual-Oriented and Peer-Oriented Conditions

(*Note*: The video that students saw before the discussions included a party scene and a drinking-game scene. The discussions were structured around these typical college drinking situations.)

Individual-Oriented Condition

Alcohol use at parties:

- Why do people drink at parties?
- What are some of the positive results of drinking at a party? What are some of the negative results of drinking at a party? Do you think that males and females have similar concerns in party situations?

- Why might people decide not to drink at a party? Do you think it is possible to have a good time socially without drinking? How are things different if you do not drink?
- How does your drinking behavior affect how other people see you? How you see yourself?

Drinking games:

- Why do drinking games develop? Have you already experienced them?
- What are the negative effects of drinking games? Physical effects? Social effects?
- What would happen if you refused to play a drinking game? If you criticized a drinking game? On what grounds might you refuse to take part in and/or criticize a drinking game? What do you think other students would say if you refused to participate?

Effects of alcohol use on relationships:

- How does alcohol affect your ability to meet friends and potential dates?
- What are the long-term effects that drinking may have on your social and dating relationships?

Peer-Oriented Condition

(*Note*: As a prelude to the discussion, the facilitators told students about the results of our earlier research demonstrating pluralistic ignorance regarding alcohol use on campus. They began the discussions by asking students to speculate on the reasons why students hold erroneous beliefs about the opinions of their peers.)

Alcohol use at parties:

- How might party situations lead one to believe that everybody is comfortable with heavy drinking?
- Do you think that there is an advantage to drinking or appearing that you are drinking in party situations? Other situations? Do you think that these considerations are the same for males and females?
- Do you think that it is possible to have a good time socially without drinking? How are things different if you do not drink?

Drinking games:

- Given the research we discussed earlier, why would people take part in a drinking game?
- What would happen if you refused to play a drinking game? If you criticized a drinking game? On what grounds might you refuse to take part in and/or criticize a drinking game? What do you think other students would say if you refused to participate? Suppose that some of them agreed with you. Do you think that they would support you? Why or why not? What factors do you think would make them more or less likely to support your decision not to participate? Have you ever been in this kind of situation?

PART 5

Implications in Everyday Life

It goes without saying that most social psychologists love the field they study, but many are less than charmed with specific fads and trends within the field. One very broad concern that many social psychologists express pertains to the laboratory methods that are used to examine psychological processes and the relationship these methods have to everyday life. Modern social psychology places a high importance on theoretical precision and experimental control, and this has caused many to researchers to live their entire research lives in the psychological laboratory. In this artificial environment, it is possible to employ clean experimental designs, random assignment to condition, and the very latest in measurement technology (e.g., response latencies, event-related potentials).

Although these trends have placed social psychology on firmer footing when it tries to comment on the truth value of psychological theories, they have also moved the field away from the "real world" that is of interest to most non-social psychologists. At times, concerns about the lack of "mundane realism" in our studies have found their voice in informal conversations among social psychologists, and they have even bubbled up in conference presentations and book chapters with titles such as "Fads and fashions in social psychology," "The crisis in social psychology," "Where is the social in social psychology?," and "Why not study real people?" (see e.g., Stapel, 2000).

In contrast to these trends, the search for scientific rigor and the quest for basic principles within the social comparison literature has largely been carried out in a way that is mindful of real experiences in the lives of individuals. As many of the papers in this collection of readings attest, some of the best research on social comparison has been carried out in applied settings. In fact, social comparison is rare within social psychology, in that basic theory has been advanced primarily in the service of answering tangible questions and finding solutions to applied problems. An example of both the theoretical and applied nature of social psychology can be found in Buunk *et al.'s* (1991) reading in Part 3. They identified the conditions under which upward versus downward comparisons will result in enhanced versus diminished self-esteem. Their work is heavily grounded in applied work that considers how we deal with major life stressors (see Taylor & Lobel, 1989, in Part 2), but the basic theory they advanced tells us a great deal about how people perceive the self in the context of other individuals.

The current section brings together articles that provide insights into the shapes and forms that social comparisons take in everyday interactions. At the same time, they also reveal theoretical advancements in our understanding of social comparison process more generally. These studies rely heavily on high-impact research methods that engage participants in "life-like" psychological states, and they examine social phenomena that would likely occur even when people are not under the microscope of experimental social psychologists. These articles also investigate aspects of social comparison processes that are not systematically covered in the other sections, such as "What deter-mines the extremity of the upward comparison standards people choose?" or "Is it better to be good but surrounded by people who are better, or

to be ok but surrounded by people who perform worse?". However, although the content of the issues these articles address is important, we have put them together in this particular section because each elegantly shows why social comparison processes matter in people's everyday lives.

The first article in this section illustrates how deeply enmeshed social comparisons can be in a person's strategies to win at competitive games. Specifically, Nosanchuk and Erickson (1985) study the comparison behavior of competitive bridge players engaging in a so-called "you hold" game, a common activity in the world of bridge players. Nosanchuk and Erickson are especially interested in the question of how particular social comparison motives (evaluation, improvement, enhancement) determine the extremity of the selected comparison standard. As they put it, their research focuses on the question "How high is up?" Their findings help to reveal which motivational states generate slight, moderate, or extreme upward comparisons and the effects these comparisons have on performance.

Marsh and Hau (1984) present a correlational study on the big-fish–little-pond effect (BFLPE) in a study of high-school students' self-concept. This effect suggests that, when it comes to academic self-concept, it is better to be a "big fish" in a small pond (an ok student in a moderate-quality school) than a "small fish" in a large pond (a good student in an excellent school). This research supports the provocative conclusion that there are advantages for some students if they attend less selective schools, because these less challenging environments can foster greater self-confidence and thus higher aspiration levels. On the more technical side, these researchers also show that whether or not the BFLPE will be found in a data set will depend on the measures used and the type of analysis conducted.

Hagerty (2000) studies a phenomenon that is much like the BFLPE, but instead focuses on a "frog pond" that can determine what level of salary will be associated with a high level of life satisfaction. He shows evidence from several large survey studies that social comparison of income affects people's happiness or subjective well-being. What people earn and how this compares to others in their surroundings (their nation or their community) is an important determinant of how happy they are. Interestingly, Hagerty uses his findings to argue that national governments can do something to elevate the happiness of their citizens. He argues that by decreasing the inequality of income distributions, governments can increase their people's subjective well-being. This is an impressive example of how knowledge about social comparison processes and effects can lend new insights into people's daily lives and inform social policies that might influence them further.

In the final article of this section, Tiedens and Fragale (2003) show that people engage in automatic, nonconscious social comparisons with people when they come into brief contact with them. Tiedens and Fragale exposed participants to a confederate who demonstrated either dominant or submissive behavior. They then examined how these behaviors affected the participants' behaviors and found that most people responded to such power moves with complementary responses. They also found that

when complementarity occurred, people felt more comfortable. These results are especially interesting because they show social comparison effects on nonverbal behavior (posture) rather than only or simply on self-evaluation measures ("I feel dominant") or performance measures ("I can do this"). As Tiedens and Fragale discuss in their paper, their complementarity effects also have important implications for modern social cognit on research. The main theme in this literature is that imitation, rather than complementarity, is what people automatically do, what smoothes interactions, and what makes people feel socia comfortable (see Chartrand & Bargh, 1999). Apparently, there is something to the power, dominance–submission dimension that makes complementarity a more natural response than is the case in other situations (see also Stapel & Van der Zee, 2006).

REFERENCES

Buunk, B., Collins, R., Taylor, S., Dakof, G., & Van Yperen, N. (1990). The affective consequences of social comparisons: Either direction has its ups and downs. *Journal of Personality and Social Psychology, 59,* 1238–1249.

Chartrand, T. L., & Bargh, J. A. (1999). The chameleon effect: The perception-behavior link in social interaction. *Journal of Personality and Social Psychology, 76,* 893–910.

Hagerty, M. R. (2000). Social comparisons of income in one's own community: Evidence from national surveys of income and happiness. *Journal of Personality and Social Psychology, 78*(4), 764–771.

Marsh, H. W., & Hau, K.-T. (2003). Big-fish–little-pond effect on academic self-concept. *American Psychologist, 58*(5), 364–376.

Nosanchuk, T. A., & Erickson, B. H. (1985). How high is up? Calibrating social comparison in the real world. *Journal of Personality and Social Psychology, 48*(3), 624–634.

Stapel, D. A. (2000). Moving from fads and fashions to integration: Illustrations from knowledge accessibility research. *European Bulletin of Social Psychology, 12,* 4–27.

Stapel, D. A., & Van der Zee, K. I. (2006). The Self Salience Model of other-to-self effects: Integrating principles of self-enhancement, complementarity, and imitation. *Journal of Personality and Social Psychology, 90,* 258–271.

Taylor, S. T., & Lobel, M. (1989). Social comparison activity under threat: Downward evaluation and upward contacts. *Psychological Review, 96,* 569–575.

Tiedens, L. Z., & Fragale, A. R. (2003). Power moves: Complementarity in dominant and submissive nonverbal behavior. *Journal of Personality and Social Psychology, 84*(3), 558–568.

Discussion Questions

1. Is social comparison a ubiquitous phenomenon?
2. Can social comparison research help in understanding real-life phenomena? Why?
3. Can people gain self-knowledge without engaging in at least some type of social comparison?

Suggested Readings

Van der Zee, K. I., Buunk, B. P., & Sanderman, R. (1998). Neuroticism and reactions to social comparison information among cancer patients. *Journal of Personality, 66,* 801–810.

Wheeler, L., & Miyake, K. (1992). Social comparisons in everyday life. *Journal of Personality and Social Psychology, 62,* 760–773.

Wood, J. V., Micheal, J. L., & Giordano, C. (2000). Downward comparison in everyday life: Reconciling self-enhancement models with the mood-cognition priming model. *Journal of Personality and Social Psychology, 79,* 563–579.

Wood, J. V., & Wilson, J. V. (2003). How important is social comparison? In M. Leary & J. Tangney (Eds.), *Handbook of self and identity* (pp. 344–366). New York: Guilford Press.

How High Is Up? Calibrating Social Comparison in the Real World

T. A. Nosanchuk and Bonnie H. Erickson*

Research generated by social comparison theory has been criticized for its deficiencies in conceptual clarity and mundane realism. In the present study, the respondents are competitive bridge players engaging in a form of the "you-hold" game, a social comparison activity common to this subculture. Because this game is played seriously, with real and meaningful comparators, mundane realism should be heightened. Clarification of some key concepts, notably "comparison upward", is anticipated because the setting makes possible valid assessments of the abilities of the various players. The method makes use of nominational responses to scenarios in which comparison motive is varied with outcome valence and locus of control. Ability scores of nominations are regressed against those of the choosers with the lines constrained to pass through the origin to simplify comparison. A similar strategy was employed using various sociometric nominations both to validate the method and provide a baseline for comparison. The results suggest that information seeking induces the greatest degree of upward comparison, ego enhancement was found to be lower, and ego defense lowest; though even here comparison was found to be reliably upward. Items describing "fixes" where ability was not implicated were found, surprisingly, to give results very similar to those for ego enhancement. Events with negative outcomes were unexpectedly found to generate greater comparison upward than ones with positive outcomes. Finally, locus of control provided little differences.

*Department of Sociology, University of Toronto.

We gratefully acknowledge support from the Centre for Urban and Community Studies, University of Toronto, the Office of the Dean of Graduate Studies, Carleton University, and the Social Sciences and Humanities Research Council of Canada. Peter Carrington and Alexandra Radkewycz assisted with the data analysis.

The authors would like to thank the editors and anonymous referees for their helpful criticism. An earlier version of this article was read at the CASA meetings in June 1984 in Guelph, Ontario.

Requests for reprints should be sent to T. A. Nosanchuk, Department of Sociology, Carleton University, Ottawa, Ontario, K1S 5B6.

Arrowood (1978) describes social comparison as everybody's second favorite theory but almost nobody's first, perhaps owing to the "lack of clarity surrounding certain key concepts" (p. 491). One pivotal lack of clarity centers on the measurement of the degree of upward or downward comparison of ability. Not only is a meaningful metric for degree of comparison lacking, so are precise predictions and tests. We do not know how the degree to which comparison is upward may vary with the motive, nor can we tell whether a given motive generates "slight", "moderate", or "extreme" upward comparison on the average.

Social comparison theory also suffers from research of questionable validity and little mundane realism. The dominant experimental format, the ranking paradigm, uses fictive groups, false feedback, and nonconsequential problems. Such procedures omit many components of natural comparison such as "interpersonal attraction, the cohesiveness of groups, level of aspiration, and a host of other motives, drives and aspirations" (Singer 1980, p. 177).

We argue that both problem areas can be addressed by research in a strategically chosen natural setting, using a novel method. To improve validity, the setting should be one in which ability comparisons occur often on matters highly consequential for participants. The setting for the present study is a local unit of the American Contract Bridge League (ACBL), a group geared to the organization and fostering of competitive bridge in North America. Social comparison behavior is a frequent and important feature of competitive bridge. Often referred to as "you-hold," this analysis game is commonly played during lulls between rounds, after sessions, the day after an important game (often on the phone) or whenever the addicted meet. In its usual form, P presents O with a bridge hand; "you hold (the hand is described), the bidding has been…, these events follow; what would you do now?" The you-hold game is not only common among competitive bridge players, its a meaningful, highly consequential activity, associated with high arousal, where ego, reputation, partnerships (and occasionally marriages) can be at stake. Some sense of the intensity that may be associated with this activity is evidenced in the following excerpt from a column by the late bridge player and columnist M. Harrison-Gray (1972):

> Imagine, if you can, that you are an exhausted expert at the end of the Masters' Pairs. Along comes a delegation headed by a competitor in the grip of some strong emotion. Warned by anticipatory grins, you recognise a situation that calls for caution and tact.

Details of a hand follow.

> You plead brain fatigue; you say: "This sounds like a very close decision; I can't give an opinion without a knowledge of the exact cards held by West, the personnel at the table and sundry other details." (This attempted evasion yields more detail and renewed demands for a judgment).
> "Yes," you murmur warily, "if East held such a hand…" But the delegation made an about turn at the word "Yes," searching for the next victim. You sigh, and brace yourself for the second wave of the attack.
> "You say that West should lead a spade!", says a wild-eyed character (East, you presume), ignoring your protestations. "And why, may I ask, is East barred from doubling on a hand like this?" etc. (p. 25).

Although the author may have exaggerated somewhat for effect, tournament players regularly report witnessing comparable encounters. Further, every bridge magazine has at least one readers' corner, where problem hands are discussed and blame for disasters allocated.

Although the foregoing indicates that bridge players are motivated to discuss hands, one might ask whether it is legitimate to view this as social comparison of ability. We would answer this question, "yes", on two grounds. First, that with few exceptions, players do not have a clear, stable impression of their bridge ability; and second, that the scenarios top a major component of such an ability—judgment.

One might expect that experienced bridge players would have had enough success and failure experiences over time to have generated an accurate assessment of their bridge abilities. But for several reasons such experiences are correctly perceived to be fallible measures of ability. Chiefly, the game involves an almost continuous exercise of decision making under uncertainty. Thus, in the short run, players can make consistently good judgments while obtaining poor results, and vice versa. Further, players can make poor judgments while convinced that they are good, irrespective of the outcome. Sometimes, such delusory evaluations can be effected by the experience of moving to a tougher level of competition. Alan Sontag, a professional bridge player, describes his first international competition:

> I had hoped Gladys and I would charge for the lead right at the start. Instead we were left at the post: …I learned from my first international tournament, (that) I was not the great player I had thought" (1977, pp. 45–46; see also Davis, 1966).

Sontag, perhaps because he was unusually adept at thinking objectively about his game, rather than rationalizing his loss, subsequently became a great player.

We would argue further that among expert players judgment would generally be viewed as a major component of overall bridge ability—bridge books broadly concerned with the game abound with the phrases "keen judgements", "needle decisions", "expert judgement", and so forth. And as indicated earlier such judgments cannot be adequately evaluated by outcome, the only objective measure available. So, lacking meaningful objective measures on an aspect of the self, which is highly salient for many players, we expect them to be motivated to compare socially. Consequently, we see the you-hold game as useful natural setting to research such behavior.

To improve clarity, the setting should permit measurement of degree and direction of comparison under various conditions and comparison motives. Extensive observation suggests that the theoretically important motives are common in discussions of hands. Players may present hands in which they have done exceptionally well (ego-enhancement); in which they took action they believe to be but do not know to be reasonable (validation); in which something undesirable happened but the where causal locus is unclear (information seeking); or in which they are clearly at fault (ego defense).

The you-hold game is also played with "fixes" or outcomes (whether positive or negative) beyond the player's control. Because the player's ability or performance is irrelevant to such events, the comparison motive (if any) is not clear, yet the discussion of the fix is common and can be as intense as other sorts of comparison. (If such discussions resemble acknowledged comparison behavior in detail, perhaps the theory should make room for comparison of such predicaments—which surely occur in many things besides duplicate bridge.)

We also explore the role of outcome valence (positive or negative) and locus of causality (partnership, opponents or chance) in the degree of upward comparison. Degree of upward comparison is accurately measurable here because the ACBL awards and keeps track of master points, a performance measure known by and meaningful to participants; below we describe our method of taking advantage of this measure.

Theory

The consensus interpretation of Festinger's (1954) theory of ability comparison is: People compare to those slightly better than themselves (e.g., Goethals & Darley, 1977, p. 264). Although this may be broadly true, common experience suggests that some comparisons are higher than others. The weekend golfer may compare his short game to Sam Snead or to his regular opponent who won $5 from him the previous week. The theory as presently constituted gives us little guidance as to the variables that might effect the degree of upward (or indeed, downward) comparison.

The literature on motives provide some guidance on direction of comparison. Comparison may be made downward, to those of less ability, when the actor's performance has been poor. Gruder (1977) comments that "…when self-esteem is clearly and specifically threatened, subjects respond by attempting to protect their self-esteem rather than by trying to evaluate" (p. 26). This contrasts with more favorable situations in which the actor compares upward for motives such as ego enhancement, validation, or information seeking. However, the literature does not address the question of the degree of upward-ness of comparison each of the various motives is expected to generate.

As noted earlier, we also propose to explore at least preliminarily, the effects of locus of control and outcome valence on upward comparison. The locus of control may lie with the actor, or partner(s), with opponents or rivals, or with none of these but with chance (One may "get fixed" because one's opponent does something exceptionally good, but this too is attributed to luck, e.g., "why couldn't we get easy hands against these guys"). We conjecture that events, at least partly controlled by the actor and partner, should result in increased upward-ness of comparison because discussing such events is likely to be more ego-enhancing. This is consistent with Goode's (1978) argument that equal sharing among partners is likely "...where it is difficult to divide, but all contribute to the cost of the good" (p. 354).

Further, the outcome valence may be positive or negative. Valence should be distinguished from performance: in bridge and elsewhere, an actor may perform brilliantly yet have very poor results. Nevertheless good outcomes are enjoyable and easily confused with performance, hence likely to be more ego-enhancing than bad outcomes, so we conjecture that the degree of upward comparison will be greater for positive outcomes.

The consensus prediction raises another conceptual problem: How can we decide whether real-world comparisons are indeed made to those slightly better? Just what is slight? In natural settings people select comparators, not from a list of fictive persons and an abstract continuum of ability but from the actual people known to them in terms of abilities as perceived by them. The perceived ability of available comparators defines the real range of possible comparisons, and calibrates comparisons indirectly. We examine other kinds of choices (sociometric ones of various kinds), which we feel confident are made to those equal, moderately higher or much higher in ability. We then place social comparison choices on this scale jointly defined by respondent social networks and their perceptions of them.

Given the lack of clarity in existing theory, this study is necessarily exploratory. Yet it is also paradigmatic, in that we will be attempting to estimate parameters (the degree of upward comparison) for key theoretical components (especially comparison motives) for the first time.

Method

Respondents

The respondents are 544 current members of the ACBL, 82% of the potential respondents in the Ottawa-Hull area of the local unit. See Erickson and Nosanchuk (1983) for details.

Instrument

The items relevant to the present inquiry make up two parts of a lengthy, wide ranging interview schedule. Of principal interest here is a set of eight scenarios. Each scenario describes a plausible occurrence at the bridge table, varying with respect to valence of outcome, positive or negative, causal locus, and anticipated comparison motive. Illustrative of these is the following (DBL), which is characterized by a positive outcome, partnership locus, and ego-enhancement motive:

> Now suppose that by aggressive and resourceful bidding you force your opponents into 5 Hearts (everyone's favorite contract!) You and your partner then co-operate in a double-dummy defence that gets you one of the very few plus scores.
>
> Suppose that you did in fact want to discuss this situation with a fellow player. Who would you most prefer to talk to:
>
> ___ a) a player you consider to be somewhat weaker than you
> ___ b) someone you regard as being very similar to you in their bridge ability
> ___ c) someone you regard as being a better player than you
>
> NAMES: _____

Table 15.1 contains the complete set of scenarios.

Note that the respondent has the option to compare categorically (similar to the responses elicited in the ranking paradigm), or to make nominational

TABLE 15.1. Set of Scenarios Together With Valence, Locus of Control, and Motive

	Scenarios
EAS	For example, suppose that you are playing against a very timid and inexperienced pair. To your delight one of their auctions stops at two spades. They have an easy play for eleven tricks and make only ten. However, the traveling score shows that every other pair has bid to 6S and you have the only minus score (negative outcome; chance locus; motive unclear).
RAR	Now suppose your partner gets excited during an auction and lands you in a near to impossible slam contract. After studying the hand at length, you conclude that there is only one way the hand might be made—and that is with a rare play that you have read about, but never actually tried. You play for that holding, and to your delight you bring it off (positive outcome; partnership locus; ego-enhancement motive).
BID	Again, imagine the auction is a very competitive one, and the opponents reach a contract you dearly would like to double. However, your partner doesn't give you the chance, bidding once more (when you feel that s/he's already said her/his piece)—and landing you in a poor contract. To make matters worse, you are so annoyed that you lose one more trick than you might have, going down two for a very poor score (negative outcome; partnership locus; ego-defense motive).
BLA	Imagine that you and your partner had a bidding misunderstanding, got to the wrong contract for a poor score, and then disagreed about who was to blame (negative outcome; partnership locus; information-seeking motive).
TEN	Next, suppose you are the declarer in four spades, get what appears to be a standard lead and standard defense, and make ten tricks. To your surprise you find that everyone else in four spades made eleven tricks (negative outcome; unclear locus; information seeking motive).
THR	This time, the opponents have bid to a standard 3 no trumps. While you are thinking of what to lead, a card you weren't even considering leading falls out of your hand face up and becomes your lead. When the smoke clears, you have beaten the contract and were the only pair to do so (positive outcome; chance locus; motive unclear).
BAD	Finally, you have a very competitive auction and thinking the opponents are overboard you double. Your defense is nearly perfect and would ordinarily defeat the contract. However, declarer plays this difficult hand perfectly to score his contract and give you a bottom (negative outcome; opposition locus; ego-enhancement motive).

Note: EAS = EASY; RAR = RARE; BID = BID; BLA = BLAME; TEN = TEN; THR = THREE; BAD = BAD.

comparisons by giving names of players with whom he or she is acquainted, or to make no comparison.

The second relevant part of the schedule is a set of eight sociometric style relational items.

Typical of this set is the item *local partner*:

> Now I would like to turn to some questions _____ about the ways players know each other, because this is a very important part of any activity. First, we would like to know about _____ your partners. In local club games, who do you play with most often. (PROBE FOR THREE NAMES, AND ORDER OF _____ FREQUENCY.)

Finally, we have information on recorded master points for each player in the unit, both at the start of the study and at its conclusion. These master points, available from ACBL records provide an objective measure of each player's skill because most players want to have them recorded, and the ACBL does so scrupulously. Master points index more than skill, chiefly frequency of (mainly) tournament play and number of years played. We have examined various ways of controlling for years played, but none appears to give an appreciably better index than master points without such controls.

Validation and Calibration

Scenarios. We ask first whether the scenario approach addresses the same phenomenon as the standard ranking paradigm, that is, whether the scenarios give the same sort of results where directly comparable to the more usual method. Table 15.2 reports the percent of respondents making various categorical comparison choices, by scenario.

TABLE 15.2. Categorical Comparisons by Scenario

Scenario	Locus	Motive	% Comparing				% Other comparisons	% No comparisons	Total
			Outcome	Downward	Similar	Upward			
EAS	chance	unclear	−	1	40	28	5	26	100
RAR	partnership	ego enhancement	+	−	43	36	7	14	100
BID	partnership	ego defense	−	1	47	21	7	24	100
DBL	partnership	ego enhancement information	+	−	46	30	7	17	100
BLA	partnership	seeking information	−	−	23	53	3	21	100
TEN	unclear	seeking	−	−	28	47	7	18	100
THR	chance	unclear	+	1	38	19	16	26	100
BAD	opponents	ego enhancement	−	−	38	33	7	22	100

Note: EAS = EASY; RAR = RARE; BID = BID; DBL = DOUBLE; BLA = BLAME; TEN = TEN; THR = THREE; BAD = BAD.

Results are generally consistent with previous research and theoretical predictions. First, the great majority of respondents make a comparison of some sort, with only about one fifth choosing not to compare. Second, only a negligible number of comparisons are downward, even for BID—the scenario viewed as most likely to generate ego defence. Comparisons are made at the same level or upward, consistent with results from studies using the ranking paradigm (see, e.g., Wheeler, Koestner, & Driver, 1982). Third, excepting the two scenarios that involve information seeking, the model comparator is similar. The scenarios involving informational comparison show a substantial shift toward upward choosing. The one exception to previous predictions is BID, which although it implicates ego defense does not lead to downward comparison (although this scenario does have nearly the lowest rate of upward comparison). Respondents here appear to preserve their self-esteem not by downward comparison but by comparison with equals, avoiding upward comparison more typical of other motives.

Nominations and master points. The most novel and powerful innovation here involves the use of master points of nominated comparators as a measure of exact comparison level. Again, does this approach produce data consistent with and of comparable quality to those used previously? One way of obtaining such a validation is by examining data from persons who provide both categorical and nominational responses. Nearly 40% of our subjects responded nominationally, by providing from one to three names for the scenarios, and most of these, from 138 to 217 depending on the scenario, provided categorical responses as well. These data have been used to construct a two-way table in which the columns are the categorical nominations, *better player*, *similar player*, and *weaker player*, the rows are nominators divided into high, medium, and low thirds on ability as measured by master-point levels, and the entries are the master point holdings of the players nominated (where the respondent nominated more than one player, we have taken the mean number of master points). The master point measure used here and throughout the article is the lifetime master point accumulation as of the start of our research.

There is one such table for each of the eight scenarios, but the tables are all so similar that we present only a single summary table, Table 15.3 in which each cell is the mean of the corresponding cells in the eight scenario tables. The ordering of master point levels among the cells of Table 15.3 reproduces almost exactly the ordering in the eight scenario tables being summarized. The scenario THR is the only exception with the ordering of cells 1, 2 and 2, 1 being inverted. The table entries are clearly consistent with reasonable expectations about choice patterns. For each level of nominator, respondents choosing to compare with a better player

TABLE 15.3. Summary Table of Master Point Scores of Nominees by Master Point Levels of Nominators and Category of Comparators

Nominator level	Category of comparator		
	Better player	Similar player	Weaker player
High master points	1247	606	a
Medium master points	792	109	a
Low master points	465	54	a

[a] n is less than 5 in this cell.

also named specific comparators with substantially higher master-point scores than respondents choosing a similar player. The better means are also higher than the master point levels of the nominators themselves (the median master point level for our population is less than 200). We conclude that our use of master points and nominational data appears valid.

Regression approach. Next we turn to the sociometric items to validate two aspects of our approach: the use of master points as a performance measure, already partially validated above, and the use of a particular regression approach in the data analysis. For these items, we begin with a reasonably clear idea of the degree of upward choice each of the eight items is likely to generate. Should our analysis produce results consistent in detail with these expectations, it would provide strong evidence of validity.

Several of the sociometric items are expected to yield nominations that are, on average, at the nominators' level of bridge ability. Miller and Suls (1977) found that Rs preferred partners of similar or higher abilities to their own. As both partners are likely to share this preference, the resultant of these tendencies will be a partnership pool that is, on average, at about the player's own level of ability. Therefore, we expect *local partner*; frequent partners at club games, the least important form of competition, to result in nominations of similars.

In the same study, the authors also found strong preferences for ability homophily in opponents. It is reasonable to expect such preferences at the table to carry over into extra-game interaction in which

case we would anticipate ability homophily for the items, *sees socially*, the players seen most often; *friend*, the players felt closest to as people or as friends in general, and *best liked*, the players named as most pleasant and likeable to play with. Two items were expected to yield names of players viewed as of slightly higher ability than R; *tournament partner*, or persons preferred as tournament partners and *talks bridge*, players with whom R can discuss bridge. We expected respondents to draw such others from much the same pool as that tapped for partnerships in club games, less the (presumably) small number of players of much lower ability. Lastly, two items were expected to result in distinct upward choosing; the most skilled players (*top skill*) and those preferred as partners for a major tournament (*important partner*). All of these items are restricted to players in the respondent's social network. Even *top skill* and *important partner* were so limited: the first to people R had played with, the second to local players R knows.

The method used here is linear, OLS regression using choosers' master points as X and master points of chosen as Y. Where P selected more than one other, the mean of their points was used. For these and subsequent regressions, we have chosen to transform points by taking square roots to maximize homogeneity. Furthermore, the regression lines have been constrained to pass through the origin, the reason for this being that the single parameter slope now conveys all the linear information, greatly simplifying comparison. Thus, slopes lower than 1.0 are indicative of downward choice, slopes greater than 1.0 indicate upward choice and slopes in the near neighborhood of 1.0 indicate choice of similars. Table 15.4 gives slopes and standard errors for the eight sociometric items.

The plots were examined for violations of the assumptions of regression. In none of the plots is there any serious departure from linearity. However, because lifetime master-prints are highly skewed with density decreasing as master points increase, the plots are slightly wedgelike in appearance, but this does not appear to constitute an appreciable departure from homogeneity.

With the exception of *best liked*, the slopes are consistent with predictions; the first three are each

TABLE 15.4. Regressions of Sociometric Items, Slopes, and Standard Errors

Item	Slope	Standard error	n
Local partner	.994	.025	446
Sees socially	.978	.033	314
Friend	1.017	.032	345
Best liked	1.219	.055	332
Tournament partner	1.078	.027	366
Talks bridge	1.111	.037	370
Top skill	1.921	.091	421
Important partner	1.515	.063	399

within one standard error of 1.0; *tournament partner* and *talks bridge* slightly but significantly higher, more than two standard errors greater than 1.0; and top skill and *important partner* each substantially greater than 1.0, by about 10 standard errors. The slope for *best liked*, however, is substantially in excess of that predicted. But this should probably be viewed less as an exception and more as a poor prediction, because there exists abundant evidence that sociometric items tapping the general referent *liking* tend to generate choices of higher status others (see, e.g., Laumann & Senter, 1976). There is one minor peculiarity; the coefficient for *top skill* is substantially higher than that for *important partner*, where we had anticipated that the two items would yield similar nominations. But the wording of the latter item includes a compatibility component absent in the former: *important partner* asks not only for the name of an excellent player, but also one whose style will be compatible with R's. Thus the results suggest that regression analysis of master points provides a valid and internally consistent measure of the direction and degree of choice.

Calibration. The preceding section provides a subjectively and sociometrically meaningful scale for choices. For this ability measure in this population, a regression slope of about 1.0 indicates that the typical choice is a similar, whereas slopes less than one would typify downward choice. At the other extreme, a slope near 2.0 would suggest an extraordinary degree of upward choosing as relatively few advanced players can play or interact

with others holding four times as many master points, for demographic reasons. "Slight" upward choosing is then a slope around 1.1 or 1.2 perhaps like *tournament partner* and *talks bridge*. In short, then, the evidence supports the view that the use of (a function of) master points as an indicator of player's skill gives valid and internally consistent results.

Results

Social Comparison

The analysis of the nominational responses to the eight scenarios was conducted in precisely the same way as that reported for the sociometric items. Square-rooted master point scores of choosers were regressed against the square-rooted mean points of chosens, with the line constrained to pass through the origin. The plots were examined for violations of regression assumptions and were found, as before, to be essentially linear and generally homogeneous, with some tendency to wedge-shapedness.

Examination of the slopes in Table 15.5 is very suggestive. First, all of the slopes are reliably greater than 1.0, the slope produced by choice of similars, in the analysis of the sociometric items. Moreover, they are all reliably greater than the two sociometric items, *tournament partner* and *talks bridge*, which generated moderately upward choice. In fact, if we take the mean slope from *local partner*, *sees socially* and *friend,* the items associated with choice of similars (b = .992) and the mean slope from the high skill items *top skill* and *important partner* (b = 1.718), we find the mean social comparison slope to be almost exactly half way between these points (b = 1.339).

The variable expected to account for the largest proportion of the variance among slopes was comparison motive. Examination of Table 15.5 by motive implies the findings in Table 15.6.

We see in Table 15.6 that the information-seeking items generate slopes reliably greater than those from any other motive. At the other extreme, the slope from the ego defense item is reliably lower

TABLE 15.5. Regressions of Scenario Items; Slopes and Standard Errors

Scenario	Slope	Standard error	n	Characteristics
EAS	1.335	.081	184	negative chance unclear
RAR	1.343	.062	226	positive partnership ego enhancement
BID	1.210	.069	175	negative partnership ego defense
DBL	1.281	.065	203	positive partnership ego enhancement
BLA	1.558	.082	220	negative partnership information seeking
TEN	1.558	.083	195	negative unclear information seeking
THR	1.309	.082	142	positive chance unclear
BAD	1.449	.082	177	negative opposition ego enhancement

TABLE 15.6. Mean Slopes for the Various Comparison Motives

Motive	Scenario	Slope	Slope
Information seeking	BLA	1.558	
	TEN	1.558	1.558
Ego enhancement	RAR	1.343	
	DBL	1.283	1.334
	BAD	1.449	
Chance (fix)	EAS	1.335	1.322
	THR	1.309	
Ego defense	BID	1.210	1.210
Grand M	–	–	1.381

Note: BLA = BLAME; TEN = TEN; RAR = RARE; DBL = DOUBLE; BAD = BAD; EAS = EASE; THR = THREE; BID = BID.

than any of the others (but still more than three standard errors above 1.0). Just as we found in Table 15.2, ego defense leads not to downward choices but rather to a lesser degree of upward choice. The items *RAR*, *DBL*, and *BAD* are classified as ego enhancement, despite the fact that the outcomes are not uniformly positive, because they all involve bridge of very high quality and are the sorts of events that please serious players. The mean slope, b = 1.334 suggests substantial upward comparison and in fact is nearly identical to the grand mean of the social comparison slopes.

We began with no clear predictions for the fix items, and their theoretical status remains uncertain. On the one hand, their slopes are characteristic social comparison slopes with a mean only slightly lower than that for ego enhancement. Perhaps R wishes to be reassured that the fix was a fix, not an "oversight" and hence no reflection on ability. Or, the lack of opportunity to use ability may create arousal best relieved by discussing the event with players good enough to understand the reaction and to be experienced in handling it. Composure in the face of frustrating events is a valuable competitive ability in its own right and perhaps associated with bridge performance (with many notorious exceptions). On the other hand, the motive for discussion of a fix may be something other than social comparison. One item, THR, stands out in two ways: by far the smallest number of Rs (142) chose to make nominations and by far the largest proportion (13%) said they would tell "anyone they spoke to." Such a diffuse response suggests that the motive may be anecdotal rather than reflecting a need for social comparison. We note that fix slopes most nearly resemble the best liked slope from the sociometric items: perhaps both reflect an attraction to, and desire to have an entree to, higher status others.

We had hypothesized that locus of control would be an important determinant of degree of upward comparison because the perception of being in control would be more ego enhancing than that of being controlled, either by opponents or by chance. The results for this variable are not easily interpretable, however, because of problems in scenario construction. It turned out to be difficult to write believable opponent-control scenarios that respondents did not react to as fixes. Hence only two of the possible loci, chance (CH) and partnership (PA), are represented by more than one item, and the mean slopes for these loci;

$$b_{CH} = 1.322$$

$$b_{PA} = 1.368$$

are not interestingly different. Perhaps looking at self-locus rather than partnership locus would yield clearer results.

The results for outcome valence are, on the other hand, quite suggestive. Our initial expectation had been that positive outcomes would be more enhancing than negative ones and would subsequently lead to more comparing upward. This is clearly not what we found. Perhaps the least ambiguous way of looking at this is to make comparisons within motive. If we examine the three ego-enhancement items, the items RAR and DBL both have positive outcomes and their mean slope is b = 1.312, whereas BAD, with a negative outcome has a slope, b = 1.449, reliably higher. Similarly, the two fix items *EAS* and *THR* differ in outcome with the slope of the negative item $b_{EAS} = 1.335$ greater than that of the positive item $b_{THR} = 1.309$ though the difference here is not reliable. Possibly, events with negative outcomes may have an element of information seeking, for example, "was I right to take this action?" or "was there anything I could have done?", for BAD and EAS, respectively.

Discussion

Several issues have been raised in the present study. The first concerns the possibility of examining social comparison behavior arising out of an activity that is highly consequential for the actors and has a real and important set of potential comparators. By so situating the study we expected to substantially increase mundane realism with little or no loss in validity. The evidence is consistent with this view. Where the data are comparable to those from the traditional ranking paradigm, the results are consistent. Moreover, a fine grained analysis indicates strong internal consistency. In addition, respondents appeared highly motivated to compare, and even many of the "no-answers" involved, according to the interviewers, a deliberate and thoughtful decision not to mention the event to anyone.

A second important theme in this study involves the use of nominational rather than rank responses. These nominations, together with an objective and fairly valid measure of ability, makes possible the use of regression analysis between choosers and chosens. This approach was validated on a set of sociometric items with both gross and fine grained

comparisons appearing sensible. One great advantage of the regression approach is that the slopes may be directly and easily compared, giving information on the degree of upwardness in comparison as a function of comparison motive, locus of control and outcome valence. Such information has not previously been available.

Overall, the findings regarding the direction of comparison are consistent with the general literature, that is, somewhat upward. In fact, the social comparison slopes fit almost exactly half way between the median slope for sociometric nomination of similars and that for high skill others.

Comparison motive was expected to be one of the strongest predictors of degree of upward comparison. So it turned out, with degree of upwardness generally following the order predicted in the literature, for example, ego defense lower than ego enhancement and information seeking. However, ego defense comparisons were not downward as predicted (Hakmiller, 1966) but only less upward. Perhaps the substantial and uniform upward direction to comparison here may derive from the very high motivation invested by the participants in this activity (see Wheeler, 1966).

We had conjectured that positive outcomes would be more ego-enhancing and so perhaps lead to more upward choosing. One of the most suggestive of the unanticipated findings was that for both ego enhancement and fix scenarios, unfavorable outcomes were associated with more upward comparison than where the outcome was favorable. One possibility suggested earlier is that events with negative outcomes may contain an information seeking component. That is, many of these players are highly committed to the game and so may be strongly motivated to improve, even at the cost of exposing a weakness. This would be analogous to touring pros in golf turning to other pros for lessons when their game goes off a bit. Alternatively it may be more acceptable to complain about how doing the right thing turned out badly than to gloat about how doing the right thing turned out well; a "we wuz robbed" statement may be perceived as less self-aggrandizing than "ain't we great".

Predictions about the locus of control on comparison behavior were based on rather vaguely founded expectations, and the results turned out to be inconclusive. It was suggested that looking at self rather than partnership, perhaps in combination with valence, might give clearer results.

Finally, we note the anomalous role of the fix. The nature of these events in which chance rather than ability dictates outcome would not lead one to expect social comparison behavior. Yet respondents do compare and compare upward, nearly to the extent generated by ego enhancement. We suggested the possibilities that either the players sought reassurance that it was a fix and not an oversight, or that chance elements in a skill activity may generate arousal. Additional research on valence, locus of control, and fixes might well be productive.

As noted at several points, the availability of nominational data as well as quality, objective information on task ability had been expected to make possible stronger inferences from social comparison settings and the results support this expectancy. But the potentially strongest payoffs are expected to accrue from this study being embedded in a study of networks of bridge players. As Castore and DeNinno (1977) note, "... there has been little attention devoted to the possible extent of overlap of a person's associates in the various reference groups. There is also no clear understanding to date of the conditions under which a particular reference group might become salient in a particular situation." (p. 127). With our fairly complete and intensive information on a working set of networks, we may be in a position to begin to address the question of how actors decide which of several competing cohesive groups provide the most appropriate comparators on a given issue. This, at least, is our long-range goal.

REFERENCES

Arrowood, A. J. (1978). Social comparison theory: Retrieved from neglect. [Review of *Social Comparison Processes*]. *Contemporary Psychology*, 23, 490–491.

Castore, C. H., & DeNinno, J. A. (1977). Investigations in the social comparison of attitudes. In J. M. Suls &. R. L. Miller (Eds.), *Social comparison processes* (pp. 125–148). Washington DC: Hemisphere.

Davis, J. A. (1966). The campus as a frog pond, *American Journal of Sociology*, 72, 17–32.

Erickson, B. H., & Nosanchuk, T. A. (1983). Applied Network Sampling. *Social Neiworks*, 5, 367–382.

Festinger, L. (1954). A theory of social comparison processes. *Human Relations*, 7, 117–140.

Goethals, G. R., &. Darley, J. M. Social comparison theory: An attributional approach. In J. M. Suls & R. L. Miller (Eds.), *Social comparison processes* (pp. 259–278). Washington DC: Hemisphere.

Goode, W. J. (1978). *The celebration of heroes.* Berkeley: University of California Press.

Gruder, C. (1977). Choice of comparison persons in evaluating oneself. In J. M. Suls & R. M Miller (Ed.), *Social comparison processes* (pp. 21–41). Washington DC: Hemisphere.

Hakmiller, K. (1966). Threat as a determinant of downward comparison, *Journal of Experimental Social Psychology*, Suppl. 1, 32–39.

Harrison-Gray, M. (1972). *Country life book of bridge*, London: Hamlyn.

Laumann, E., & Senter, R. (1976). Subjective social distance, occupational stratification, and forms of status and class consciousness. *American Journal of Sociology*, 81, 1304–1338.

Miller, R. L., & Suls, J. M. (1977). Affiliation preferences as a function of attitude and ability similarity. In J. M. Suls & R. L. Miller (Eds.), *Social comparison processes* (pp. 103–124). Washington DC: Hemisphere.

Singer, J. E. (1980). Social comparison: The processes of self evaluation. In L. Festinger (Ed.). *Retrospections on social psychology* (pp. 158–179). New York: Oxford University Press.

Sontag, A. (1977). *The bridge bum,* New York: William Morrow.

Wheeler, L. (1966). Motivation as a determinant of upward comparison. *Journal of Experimental Social Psychology,* Suppl. 1, 27–31.

Wheeler, L., Koestner, R., & Driver, R. E. (1982). Related attributes in the choice of comparison others: It's there, but it isn't all there is, *Journal of Experimental Social Psychology, 18,* 489–500.

Received December 12, 1983
Revision received April 17, 1983 ■

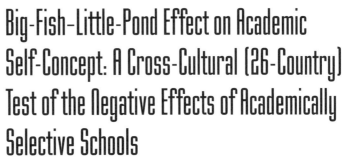

Big-Fish-Little-Pond Effect on Academic Self-Concept: A Cross-Cultural (26-Country) Test of the Negative Effects of Academically Selective Schools

Herbert W. Marsh and Kit-Tai Hau

Academically selective schools are intended to affect academic self-concept positively, but theoretical and empirical research demonstrates that the effects are negative. The big-fish–little-pond effect (BFLPE), an application of social comparison theory to educational settings, posits that a student will have a lower academic self-concept in an academically selective school than in a nonselective school. This study, the largest cross-cultural study of the BFLPE ever undertaken, tested theoretical predictions for nationally representative samples of approximately 4,000 15-year-olds from each of 26 countries ($N = 103,558$) who completed the same self-concept instrument and achievement tests. Consistent with the BFLPE, the effects of school-average achievement were negative in all 26 countries (M beta $= -.20$, $SD = .08$), demonstrating the BFLPE's cross-cultural generalizability.

Editor's note. Wayne Camara served as action editor for this article.

Author's note. Herbert W. Marsh, SELF Research Centre, University of Western Sydney, Penrith, New South Wales, Australia; Kit-Tai Hau, Department of Educational Psychology, The Chinese University of Hong Kong, Shatin, New Territories, Hong Kong, China.

Kit-Tai Hau pursued this research while a visiting scholar at the SELF Research Centre at the University of Western Sydney.

The research was funded in part by grants from the Australian Research Council. We thank Wolfram Schulz and Ken Rowe for comments on an earlier version of the article.

Correspondence concerning this article should be addressed to Herbert W. Marsh, SELF Research Centre, University of Western Sydney, Bankstown Campus, Penrith, New South Wales 1797, Australia. E-mail: h.marsh@uws.edu.au

At the heart of our research is the universal importance and multidisciplinary appeal of self-concept as one of the most important constructs in the social sciences. This importance of self-concept and related constructs is highlighted by the regularity and consistency with which self-concept enhancement is identified as a major focus of concern in diverse settings, including education, child development, mental and physical health, social services, organizations, industry, and sport (e.g., Branden, 1994; Marsh & Craven, 1997). Thus, educational policy statements throughout the world list self-concept enhancement as a central goal of education and an important vehicle for addressing social inequities experienced by disadvantaged groups. For example, in their model of effective schools, Brookover and Lezotte (1979) proposed academic self-concept, self-reliance, and academic achievement as the major outcome variables for schools to foster in their students.

In addition to being an important outcome variable, self-concept is an important mediating construct that facilitates the attainment of other desirable psychological and behavioral outcomes. From a social-cognition perspective, self-concept is a "hot" variable that makes things happen. The need to think and feel positively about oneself and the profound benefits of these positive cognitions on choice, planning, and subsequent accomplishments transcend traditional disciplinary barriers and are central to goals in many social policy areas. More generally, individuals in all walks of life are likely to accomplish more if they feel competent in what they do, are self-confident, and feel positively about themselves. Programs or societal changes that undermine self-concepts are also likely to also have negative effects on accomplishments. These basic ideas can easily be translated into many different disciplines. Thus, for example, Marsh (2002) reported that physical self-concept contributed to the prediction of the performances of elite swimmers at international events beyond what could be explained in terms of their previous performances (personal bests and international rankings). In an organizational setting, Parker (1998) summarized research showing that employees who feel more able to perform particular tasks will actually perform better on these tasks, will persist in the face

of adversity, and will cope more effectively with change. Judge and Bono (2001) presented a meta-analysis showing that components of a positive self-concept construct were among the best predictors of job performance and job satisfaction. Marsh, Byrne, and Yeung (1999) reviewed educational research showing that prior academic self-concept had a positive effect on subsequent academic achievement (school grades and standardized test scores) beyond what could be explained by prior levels of academic achievement.

Recent self-concept research has emphasized the importance of a multidimensional perspective to self-concept and the significance of frames of reference. Historically, self-concept research has focused on a relatively unidimensional global component of self. More recently, however, researchers have emphasized the multidimensionality of self-concept and the specific components of self-concept most appropriate to a particular setting. Because the same person can have a positive self-concept in one domain (e.g., social) and a negative self-concept in another domain (e.g., academic), global measures cannot adequately describe self-concepts in different domains. Particularly if researchers are concerned with outcomes in a particular domain, measures of global self-concept and self-concepts in other domains may be of limited relevance. Thus, for example, academic self-concept is particularly important in educational settings and educational psychology research that is the focus of the present investigation.

Self-concept research continues to emphasize that self-concept cannot be adequately understood if the role of frames of reference is ignored. The same objective characteristics and accomplishments can lead to disparate self-concepts depending on the frames of reference or standards of comparison that individuals use to evaluate themselves. Whereas this phenomenon is evident in many different domains, the focus of the present investigation is academic self-concept in educational settings. According to the big-fish–little-pond effect (BFLPE), an individual student's academic self-concept is based partly on the academic achievement levels of the individual student and partly on the average of achievement levels of other students in the same school that the student attends. In the present investigation we begin by demonstrating the importance of academic self-concept and providing considerable support for these predictions based on the BFLPE as well as the theoretical and policy implications of these findings. This support, however, is based largely on responses by students from Western countries—particularly English-speaking students in the United States, Australia, and Canada—and almost entirely on studies conducted in a single country. In pursuing this limitation of existing research, we evaluated the cross-cultural generalizability of these BFLPE predictions based on large representative samples of 15-year-olds from 26 countries.

Importance of Academic Self-Concept in Educational Settings

The emphasis on the multidimensionality of self-concept is particularly important in educational settings. Whereas academic achievement, persistence, coursework selection, and long-term educational aspirations are systematically related to academic self-concept, they are nearly uncorrelated (or even negatively related) to nonacademic (social and physical) self-concept responses (e.g., Byrne, 1996a; Hattie, 1992; Marsh, 1990, 1993; Marsh & Craven, 1997; Marsh & Yeung, 1997a, 1997b, 1998).

Theoretical models of the relations among self-cognitions, behavior, and subsequent attainment suggest that such changes in academic self-perceptions may affect academic choices, academic effort, and subsequent achievement (Bandura, 1986; Marsh & Craven, 1997). In particular, important research has focused on disentangling the causal ordering of academic self-concept and academic achievement (see Marsh & Craven, 1997; Marsh et al., 1999). Whereas researchers recognize academic self-concept as an important outcome variable in its own right, much of the interest in the self-concept and achievement relation stems from the belief that academic self-concept has motivational properties such that changes in academic self-concept will lead to changes in subsequent academic achievement. According to the self-enhancement model, self-concept is a primary determinant of academic achievement, thus

supporting self-concept enhancement interventions explicit or implicit in many educational programs. Because self-concept and academic achievement are not readily amenable to experimental manipulations, most research relies on longitudinal panel data in which both self-concept and achievement are measured on multiple occasions. Hence, the theoretical question is, What comes first: academic self-concept (how I think and feel about myself academically) or academic achievement (how well I perform in academic settings)? Not surprisingly, either-or answers to this question are too simplistic, and a growing body of research supports a reciprocal effects model in which academic self-concept both affects and is affected by academic achievement (Byrne, 1996a; Marsh et al., 1999; Marsh & Yeung, 1997a). Importantly, this research shows that prior academic self-concept has an effect on subsequent academic achievement beyond what can be explained in terms of prior achievement.

Marsh and Yeung (1997b) also evaluated the impact of academic self-concept on future coursework selection. In a longitudinal study, they related students' prior school grades and academic self-concepts in specific school subjects with subsequent decisions about what school subjects were pursued by these same students. Although academic self-concept and school grades in specific school subjects were substantially correlated, academic self-concepts were better predictors of the school subjects that students subsequently pursued. In related research, Marsh (1991) used the nationally representative U.S. High School and Beyond database to demonstrate that academic self-concept information collected in high school was an important determinant of a student's subsequent decision about whether to attend university.

In summary, previous research in educational settings has demonstrated the importance of considering the multi-dimensionality of self-concept and the critical relationship between academic self-concept and desirable educational outcomes. This research demonstrated that self-concept has an important influence on students—how they feel about themselves, their accomplishments, persistence, and educational decisions. This research is important in that it has established that increases in academic self-concept lead to increases in subsequent academic achievement and other desirable educational outcomes. Hence, not only is self-concept an important outcome variable in itself, but it also plays a central role in mediating the effects of other desirable educational outcomes. These findings have significant implications for international educational policy and practice.

Frame-of-Reference Effects in the Formation of Academic Self-Concept: The BFLPE

Psychologists from the time of William James (1890/1963) have recognized that objective accomplishments are evaluated in relation to frames of reference. Thus James indicated, "we have the paradox of a man shamed to death because he is only the second pugilist or the second oarsman in the world" (p. 310). Social comparison theory (Festinger, 1954) is one approach for studying frame-of-reference effects that has a long history in social psychology and provides the theoretical underpinning for the present investigation. In an educational context, Marsh (1984; Marsh & Parker, 1984) proposed the BFLPE to encapsulate frame-of-reference effects posited in social comparison theory, and this is the focus of the present investigation.

The BFLPE hypothesizes that students compare their own academic achievements with the academic achievements of their peers and use this social comparison impression as one basis for forming their own academic self-concept. Consider a capable student who has been evaluated as a top student throughout primary school. If the student is accepted into an academically selective high school, the student may be average or below average in relation to other students in this school rather than at the top of the class. This can have detrimental effects on the student's academic self-concept as the student is no longer a big fish in a small pond (top of the class) but is in a large pond full of even larger fish (other students who are even brighter), so that this student is average or below average in relation to the achievement levels in this new, academically selective high school.

Case study evidence also supports the underlying processes of the BFLPE (Marsh, 1991). A student named Jane was attending an academically selective Australian high school, but she was doing poorly and not attending school regularly. A change in employment forced her parents to move, and Jane changed to a new high school that was not a selective school. Because of her poor progress at the last school, Jane was initially placed in a class with low-achieving students in the new school. It quickly became evident, however, that she was a high-achieving student, and she soon worked her way into the most advanced classes in the new school. Her parents found that she was taking school more seriously and spending more time on her homework. Jane indicated that at the old (selective) school she had to work really hard to get just average marks that was not worth the effort. However, if she worked hard in her new school, she could be one of the best, which was apparently worth the effort.

The BFLPE is very specific to academic self-concept. Marsh and Parker (1984) and Marsh (1987) showed that there were large negative BFLPEs for academic self-concept but little or no BFLPEs on general self-concept or self-esteem. Marsh, Chessor, Craven, and Roche (1995) reported two studies of the effects of participation in gifted and talented programs on different components of self-concept over time and in relation to a matched comparison group. There was clear evidence for negative BFLPEs in that academic self-concept in the gifted and talented programs declined over time and in relation to the comparison group. These BFLPEs were consistently large for Math, Verbal, and Academic self-concepts but were small and largely nonsignificant for four nonacademic self-concepts and for general esteem.

Theoretical Basis and Implications of the BFLPE

The historical and theoretical underpinnings of this research (see Marsh, 1974, 1984, 1991, 1993; Marsh & Parker, 1984) were derived from research in psychophysical judgment (e.g., Helson, 1964;

Marsh, 1974; Parducci, 1995), social judgment (e.g., Morse & Gergen, 1970; Sherif & Sherif, 1969; Upshaw, 1969), sociology (e.g., Alwin & Otto, 1977; Hyman, 1942; Meyer, 1970), social comparison theory (e.g., Festinger, 1954; Suls, 1977), and the theory of relative deprivation (e.g., Davis, 1966; Stouffer, Suchman, DeVinney, Star, & Williams, 1949). In the theoretical model underlying the BFLPE (Marsh, 1984), it is hypothesized that students compare their own academic achievement with the academic achievements of their peers and use this social comparison impression as one basis for forming their own academic self-concept. For example, if students with average levels of achievement attend a high-achievement school (i.e., a school in which the average achievement level of other students is high) such that their academic achievements are below the average of other students in the school, it is predicted that this educational context will foster social comparison processes that will lead to academic self-concepts that are lower than if the same students attended an average-achievement school. Thus, academic self-concepts depend not only on one's academic accomplishments but also on the accomplishments of those in the school that a student attends. According to this model, academic self-concept will be affected positively with individual achievement (higher achieving children will have higher academic self-concepts). However, academic self-concept should be affected negatively by school-average achievement (equally able students will have lower academic self-concepts in a school in which the average achievement is high and will have higher academic self-concepts in a school in which the average achievement is low). Empirical support for this negative effect of school-average achievement on academic self-concept (the BFLPE) comes from numerous studies based on a variety of different experimental/analytical approaches (see review by Marsh & Craven, 2001).

Davis (1966) previously proposed a theoretical model similar to the BFLPE in a study of career decisions of American college men. He sought support for a theoretical explanation of why the academic quality of a college had so little effect on career choice. Expanding the educational policy implications of his research, Davis (1966) concluded,

> Counselors and parents might well consider the drawbacks as well as the advantages of sending a boy to a "fine" college, if, when doing so, it is fairly certain that he will end up in the bottom ranks of his graduating class. The aphorism "It is better to be a big frog in a small pond than a small frog in a big pond" is not perfect advice but it is not trivial. (p. 31)

A theoretically important issue with profound educational implications is the extent to which the BFLPEs vary across different individual student achievement levels. In particular, is the BFLPE limited primarily to the lowest achieving students in academically selective settings (i.e., settings in which the average level of achievement is high), or do the BFLPEs generalize across the achievement continuum? There is some theoretical and empirical disagreement about this issue. Coleman and Fults (1985), for example, predicted and found that students in the top half of academically selective classes experienced little or no decline in self-concepts. In contrast, Marsh (1984, 1987, 1991, 1993; Marsh et al., 1995; Marsh & Rowe, 1996) argued that attending selective schools should lead to reduced academic self-concepts for students of all achievement levels based on several different theoretical perspectives. For a large, nationally representative (United States) database, Marsh and Rowe (1996) found that the BFLPE was clearly evident for students of all achievement levels and that the size of the BFLPE varied only slightly with individual student achievement. In two studies demonstrating BFLPEs in students attending gifted and talented programs, Marsh et al. (1995) found no significant interaction between the size of the BFLPE and achievement level of individual students. However, Marsh, Köller, and Baumert (2001) found small interaction effects in their large German study based on three waves of data. Whereas the size of the BFLPE—the negative effect of class-average achievement—did not vary with individual student achievement at any of the three times considered separately, or for self-concept changes between Time 1 and Time 2, the size of this negative effect diminished slightly for the most able students over the three occasions.

Diener and Fujita (1997) related BFLPE research to the broader social comparison literature in which the focus of research is typically not academic self-concept per se. They emphasized that Marsh's BFLPE provided the clearest support for predictions based on social comparison theory in an imposed social comparison paradigm. They also emphasized that the frame of reference, based on classmates within the same school, is more clearly defined than in most other research settings. It is clear that the importance of the school setting and the relevance of the social comparisons in school settings are much more ecologically valid than manipulations in the typical social psychology experiments involving introductory psychology students in contrived settings. Indeed, except for opting out altogether, it is difficult for students to avoid the relevance of achievement as a reference point within a school setting or the social comparisons provided by the academic accomplishments of their classmates. Following from Diener and Fujita's review, Marsh and Craven (2001) highlighted strong links between social comparison theory and BFLPE research, emphasizing that the BFLPE in educational settings provides an ideal opportunity to evaluate social comparison theory predictions that have broad theoretical implications for many psychology disciplines.

Broader Policy Implications of the BFLPE

The results of the BFLPE are important for understanding the formation of academic self-concept, testing theoretical models based on social comparison theory, and evaluating the effects of frames of reference. However, classroom teachers, policymakers, and parents might ask, "So what?" What are the consequences of attending high-achievement schools on other academic outcomes other than academic self-concept? Educators and particularly parents often assume that there are academic benefits associated with attending higher achievement schools. After all, academic achievement,

aspirations, and subsequent attainment are typically higher in these schools. This naive analysis, however, fails to account for the initially higher achievement levels and other preexisting differences of students who attend academically selective high schools. A better test would be to compare academic outcomes after controlling the preexisting differences.

Marsh (1991) considered the influence of school-average achievement on a much wider array of outcomes in a very large, nationally representative, longitudinal study of U.S. high school students. In this High School and Beyond Study, 36 students each from 1,000 high schools were surveyed in Year 10 (Time 1), Year 12 (Time 2), and again two years after graduation from high school (Time 3). The outcomes in this study included most of the important outcomes of education. After background and initial achievement were controlled for, the effects of school-average achievement were negative for almost all of the Year 10, Year 12, and postsecondary outcomes: 15 of the 17 effects were significantly negative and 2 were nonsignificant. School-average achievement most negatively affected academic self-concept (the BFLPE) and educational aspirations, but school-average achievement also negatively affected general self-concept, selection of advanced coursework, school grades, standardized test scores, occupational aspirations, and subsequent college attendance. Even after controlling for all Year 10 outcomes, school-average achievement negatively affected many subsequent outcomes. This implies that school-average achievement continued to negatively affect Year 12 and postsecondary outcomes beyond the negative effects experienced at Year 10. Consistent with the proposal that these negative effects were substantially mediated by academic self-concept, controlling for the negative effects of school-average achievement on academic self-concept substantially reduced the size of negative effects on other outcomes.

The focus of BFLPE research has been on the negative effects achievement segregation has on academically gifted students, but the theoretical basis of the BFLPE has important policy implications for the placement of learning-disadvantaged students as well (also see Robinson, Zigler, &

Gallagher, 2000). Tracey and Marsh (2000) extended this research to focus on BFLPE predictions for special classes for academically disadvantaged students (also see Chapman, 1988; Marsh & Johnston, 1993). They studied 211 special education students in Grades 2–6 who had learning difficulties (IQ of 56 to 75). These students were either in regular classroom settings or in full-time special education classes with other students who had learning difficulties. Consistent with BFLPE predictions, students in full-time special education classes had significantly higher self-concepts for all three academic scales (Reading, Math, School) but did not differ significantly from other special education students in regular classes for Parents, Physical Ability, and Physical Appearance self-concepts. Somewhat unexpectedly, students in the special education classes also had significantly higher Peer self-concepts.

Cross-Cultural Support for the BFLPE

Cross-cultural comparisons provide researchers with a valuable, heuristic basis to test the external validity and generalizability of their measures, theories, and models. Matsumoto (2001) argued, "Cultural differences challenge mainstream theoretical notions about the nature of people and force us to rethink basic theories of personality, perception, cognition, emotion, development, social psychology, and the like in fundamental and profound ways" (p. 9). In their influential overview of cross-cultural research, Segall, Lonner, and Berry (1998) emphasized that cross-cultural research's three complementary goals were

> to transport and test our current psychological knowledge and perspectives by using them in other cultures; to explore and discover new aspects of the phenomenon being studied in local cultural terms; and to integrate what has been learned from these first two approaches in order to generate more nearly universal psychology, one that has pan-human validity. (p. 1102)

Similarly, Sue (1999) argued that researchers have not taken sufficient advantage of cross-cultural

comparisons that allow them to test the external validity of their interpretations and to gain insights about the applicability of their theories and models. From this perspective, it is important to note that there is clear support for the BFLPE outside of Australia and the United States, countries that have been the basis for most of this research.

Jerusalem (1984) examined the self-concepts of West German students who moved from nonselective, primary schools to secondary schools in which selection was based on academic achievement. At the transition point, students who were selected to enter the high-achievement schools had substantially higher academic self-concepts than did those entering the low-achievement schools. However, by the end of the first year in the new schools, no differences in academic self-concepts were present for the two groups. Path analyses indicated that the direct influence of school type on academic self-concept was negative. The most able students in the low-achievement schools were less able, but had much higher academic self-concepts, than the least able children in the high-achievement schools.

In 1991, former East and West German students experienced a remarkable social experiment—the reunification of very different school systems after the fall of the Berlin Wall. Self-concepts were collected at the start, middle, and end of the first school year after reunification (Marsh *et al.*, 2001). East German students had *not* previously been grouped according to achievement. For them, the BFLPE was initially small, then moderate, and then substantial by the end of the year. West German students had attended schools based on achievement grouping for the two years prior to the reunification. For them, the BFLPE was substantial at all three times. A large East–West difference in the size of the BFLPE at the start of the year disappeared completely by the end of the year. The evolvement of the BFLPE in the East and West German settings supported the social comparison process posited to underlie the BFLPE and its cross-cultural generalizability.

In Hong Kong, schools are more highly segregated in relation to achievement than anywhere else in the world. However, collectivist cultural values prevail that are posited to counter social comparison processes (compared with more individualistic values in most Western countries). Marsh, Kong, and Hau (2000) followed a large, nationally representative sample of Grade 7 students through high school (7,997 students in 44 high schools followed for four years) based on a Chinese translation of the Self-Description Questionnaire II (SDQII). Consistent with the BFLPE, school-average achievement (based on measures collected in Grade 6, prior to the start of high school) had negative effects on academic self-concept in Grade 8 and Grade 9. The sizes of these effects ($bs = -.22$ to $-.24$) were similar to those found in U.S. studies based on nationally representative samples. Even after controlling for the negative effect in Grade 8, there was an additional negative effect in Grade 9 (beyond those already experienced in Grade 8).

Zeidner and Schleyer (1999) tested the BFLPE in a large-scale study based on a nationally representative sample ($N = 1,020$) of Israeli gifted students participating in either special homogeneous classes for the gifted or mixed-achievement classes. Path analyses indicated that gifted students in mixed-achievement classes evidenced markedly higher academic self-concepts, lower anxiety, and higher school grades than did gifted students in specialized classes.

Replication of the BFLPE in different countries provides strong support for its cross-cultural generalizability. Each of these studies, however, has been conducted in a single country using self-concept assessments, achievement tests, and, to some extent, analytical procedures that were idiosyncratic to each particular study. It is clear that stronger cross-cultural studies would explicitly compare the results from at least two countries—and preferably as many as possible—based on comparable samples from each country, the same academic self-concept instrument, and the same measures of achievement. Because of the difficulty in achieving these criteria, apparent cross-cultural differences are typically confounded with potential differences in the composition of samples being compared and, perhaps, the appropriateness of materials. One purpose of the present investigation is to address these limitations in previous tests of the cross-cultural generalization of the BFLPE.

The Present Investigation

Thus far, we have demonstrated the importance of academic self-concept in educational settings as both a valued outcome and a means to facilitate other desired educational outcomes such as academic achievement, coursework selection, academic effect, educational aspirations, and subsequent university attendance. We then provided an extensive theoretical rationale, empirical support, and implications for the BFLPE that is the focus of the present investigation. According to the BFLPE (see Figure 16.1), the predicted effect of a student's own individual achievement is positive and substantial (+ + symbol in Figure 16.1),

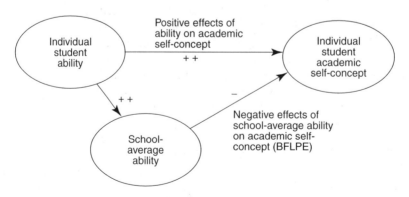

FIGURE 16.1 ■ The Big-Fish–Little-Pond Effect (BFLPE): theoretical predictions.

whereas the effect of school-average achievement is negative and smaller (− symbol in Figure 16.1). In the present investigation we consider the largest cross-cultural test of the BFLPE ever undertaken, consisting of nationally representative samples of approximately 4,000 15-year-olds from each of 26 countries attending a total of 3,851 different high schools (total $N = 103,558$ students) who completed the same self-concept instrument and achievement tests. On the basis of previous research and the assumption of the cross-cultural generalizability of the BFLPE, we offer the following predictions:

1. The effect of individual student achievement on academic self-concept is predicted to be positive. Whereas there is likely to be some country-to-country variation in the size of this effect, the direction of the effect is predicted to be consistently positive and substantial across all 26 countries.
2. The effect of school-average achievement on academic self-concept (the BFLPE) is predicted to be negative. Whereas there will be some country-to-country variation in the size of this effect, the direction of the effect is predicted to be consistently negative across all 26 countries.
3. As shown in Figure 16.1, the absolute size of this negative effect of school-average achievement (– symbol in Figure 16.l) is predicted to be smaller than the absolute size of the positive effect of individual achievement (+ + symbol in Figure 16.l). This pattern of results is predicted to occur across all 26 countries.
4. The size of the BFLPE (the negative effect of school-average achievement) is predicted to be reasonably consistent across different levels of individual student achievement (i.e., the interaction between individual student achievement and school-average achievement is predicted to be small or nonsignificant). In particular, higher achieving students as well as lower achieving students are predicted to suffer BFLPEs.

In pursuing tests of these predictions, we applied multilevel modeling, state-of-the-art statistical methodology specifically designed to evaluate multilevel data. This allowed us to partition variance associated with different effects into components associated with the individual student (Level 1), the school (Level 2), and the country (Level 3). More specifically, it provided appropriate tests of the extent to which the effects of individual student achievement and school-average achievement vary from country to country.

Method

Data Source and Sample

The study was based on the Program of Student Assessment (PISA) database compiled by the Organisation for Economic Cooperation and Development that consists of nationally representative responses by 15-year-olds collected in 32 countries in the year 2000 (see Organisation for Economic Cooperation and Development, 2001a, 2001b, for a description of the database and variables). The PISA database was collected in response to the need for internationally comparable evidence of student performance and related competencies within a common framework that was internationally agreed on. Selection of the measures was made on the basis of advice from substantive and statistical expert panels and results from extensive pilot studies. Substantial efforts and resources were devoted to achieving cultural and linguistic breadth in the assessment materials, stringent quality-assurance mechanisms were applied in the translation of materials into different languages, and data were collected under independently supervised test conditions. Paper-and-pencil assessments consisted of a combination of multiple-choice items and written responses. Whereas all students completed some reading assessment items (which were the focus of the 2000 data collection), only random samples of students completed mathematics or science assessments. In addition, countries were given the option of collecting materials on a Cross Curriculum Competencies questionnaire that included the academic self-concept items that are the focus of the present investigation; 26 of 32 countries in the PISA project administered this additional survey (see Table 16.l for a list of the 26 countries

TABLE 16.1. Summary of Effects from Multilevel Models Applied Separately to Each of 26 Countries

Country	Background descriptions			Effects (predicting academic self-concept)		
	No. of students	No. of schools	Reliability of academic self-concept	Individual student achievement— linear	Individual student achievement— quadratic	School average achievement (BFLPE)
1. Australia	4,916	223	.74	.28*	.05*	−.23*
2. Austria	4,444	163	.77	.40*	.08*	−.23*
3. Belgium	3,715	119	.70	.14*	.04*	−.12*
4. Brazil	4,015	258	.73	.35*	.06*	−.26*
5. Czech Republic	4,785	189	.77	.40*	.03*	−.24*
6. Denmark	3,973	199	.80	.48*	.07*	−.17*
7. Finland	4,768	153	.84	.52*	.11*	−.14*
8. Germany	4,815	208	.78	.38*	.06*	−.30*
9. Hungary	4,526	147	.72	.27*	.09*	−.05
10. Iceland	2,991	83	.81	.63*	.08*	−.18*
11. Ireland	3,785	136	.77	.39*	.03*	−.24*
12. Italy	4,931	163	.74	.43*	.04*	−.36*
13. Korea	4,913	134	.78	.41*	.13*	−.02
14. Latvia	3,552	128	.66	.33*	.04*	−.06*
15. Liechtenstein	297	9	.76	.27*	.03	−.20*
16. Luxembourg	3,009	24	.74	.32*	.06*	−.17*
17. Mexico	4,231	158	.70	.32*	.07*	−.08*
18. Netherlands	2,480	100	.76	.26*	.05*	−.26*
19. New Zealand	3,473	152	.79	.39	.11	−.26*
20. Norway	3,863	162	.84	.62*	.09*	−.18*
21. Portugal	4,528	147	.73	.42	.08	−.18*
22. Russia	6,316	217	.72	.46*	.05*	−.21*
23. Sweden	4,325	149	.81	.42*	.07*	−.33*
24. Switzerland	5,522	213	.74	.26*	.06*	−.17*
25. United Kingdom	2,264	89	.74	.28*	.07*	−.23*
26. United States	3,121	126	.78	.45*	.04*	−.26*
M	3,983	148	.76	.38	.07	−.20
Mdn	4,123	150	.76	.39	.06	−.20
SD	1,190	57	.04	.11	.03	.08

Note: A separate multilevel analysis was done for each country in which academic self-concept was predicted on the basis of individual student achievement (linear and quadratic components) and school-average achievement. Consistent with a priori predictions, the effects of individual student achievement are consistently positive, whereas the effects of school-average achievement (the big-fish–little-pond effect [BFLPE], presented in bold) are consistently negative. $N = 103,558$ students, 3,849 schools, 26 countries.
*$p < .05$.

and the number of students and high schools in each country).

Our study is based on students who completed the academic self-concept items on the Cross Curriculum Competencies questionnaire and standardized academic achievement tests that were developed specifically for the PISA. The self-concept items were from the highly regarded SDQII (Byrne, 1996b; also see Marsh, 1990, 1993; Marsh & Craven, 1997). However, because of limitations on the length of the total instrument, only the 3 best items from the 10-item academic

self-concept scale on the SDQII questionnaire were used to represent academic self-concept in the PISA database. Nevertheless, the reliability for this scale was consistently reasonable across all 26 countries (mean coefficient $\alpha = .76$, $SD = .04$; see Table 16.l), particularly given the brevity of the scale. It is interesting to note that the reliability of responses in Australia (.74), the country in which the SDQII was developed, did not differ systematically from the mean reliability across all countries.

Because of the nature of the PISA project, nine versions of the achievement tests were administered that contained different combinations of verbal, mathematics, and science test items. Owing to the focus of the PISA study, all students completed at least some verbal test items, whereas only about half of the students completed math and science tests. Using test-equating procedures based on item response theory, scores based on each version of the various achievement tests were put onto a comparable scale. For present purposes, a total achievement test score was obtained by taking an average score for all the achievement test scores available for each student. As recommended in the database documentation (Organisation for Economic Cooperation and Development, 2001a, 2001b), analyses were conducted using sample weights to obtain unbiased estimates of population parameters. For purposes of the present investigation, the effective sample size for each country was set equal to the number of cases for that country, prior to weighting, so that the weighted sample size was the same as the unweighted sample size (i.e., the average weight across all cases was 1.0). Although 104,186 students completed Cross Curriculum Competencies questionnaire, only 103,558 had complete data for the variables considered here (i.e., the sample size after listwise deletion for missing data, the basis of the present investigation).

Statistical Analysis

In the present investigation, individual student achievement (linear and quadratic components) and school-average achievement are related to academic self-concept. To evaluate the size, nature, and statistical significance of the interaction between individual achievement (linear and quadratic components) and school-average achievement, we also included cross-product terms reflecting these variables in the analyses. As noted by Marsh and Rowe (1996), the inclusion of the quadratic component of individual student achievement and the interaction terms allowed us to pursue additional research questions about whether the size of the BFLPE varied with the level of individual student achievement (i.e., whether the effect of school-average achievement effect was larger for students achieving at the highest levels, the lowest levels, or some intermediate

levels). Hence, individual student self-concept is the main outcome (dependent) variable, whereas predictor variables were individual student achievement (linear and quadratic terms), school-average achievement, and the interaction between school-average and individual achievement.

We began by standardizing (z scoring) all measures of academic self-concept and individual student achievement to have $M = 0$, $SD = 1$, across the entire sample (see Marsh & Rowe, 1996; also see Aiken & West, 1991; Raudenbush & Bryk, 2002). School-average measures of achievement were determined by taking the average of achievement scores for students in each school (but not restandardizing these scores so that individual student and school-average achievement scores were in the same metric). Product terms were used to test interaction and quadratic effects. In constructing these product variables, we used the product of individual (z score) standardized variables (and the product terms were not restandardized).

Consistent with the design of the PISA data, we considered a three-level multilevel model in which students (Level 1) were nested within schools (Level 2) and schools were nested within countries (Level 3). In general, it is inappropriate to pool responses of individual students without regard to school or country unless it can be shown that schools and countries do not differ significantly from each other. If, for example, there are systematic differences between schools, then the typical single-level analyses that ignore this clustering of students into schools are likely to be invalid (violate statistical assumptions in a way that increases the likelihood of finding a significant effect when there is none). Furthermore, characteristics associated with individual students are likely to be confounded with those based on schools.

From a practical perspective, a systematic multilevel approach allows researchers to pursue new questions about how effects vary from school to school and from country to country and the characteristics of schools and countries that are associated with this variation. This is particularly important in studies such as the present investigation in which critical variables are associated with both the individual student level (academic self-concept and achievement) and the school level (school-average achievement). In the present investigation, for example, the use of a multilevel approach allows us to determine the extent to which the observed pattern of relations between academic self-concept and achievement generalizes from school to school and from country to country. Hence, the multilevel approach provides a much richer and more appropriate approach to test our theoretical predictions than would be possible with traditional single-level approaches that ignore the fact that students are clustered within schools and that schools are clustered within countries (Goldstein, 1995; Raudenbush & Bryk, 2002).

For purposes of this investigation, we posited a three-level model to estimate fixed and random effects associated with the variables of interest (see Table 16.2). The fixed effects consisted of (a) the main effects of individual student achievement (linear and quadratic components) and school-average achievement, (b) the interaction effects of individual student achievement (linear and quadratic components) by school-average achievement, and (c) a constant term (that is approximately zero because of the use of standardized variables and, thus, is of little practical interest). Random effects consisted of intercept terms associated with each level of the model, indicating the extent to which intercepts of the regression equation varied from country to country (Level 3), from school to school (Level 2), and from student to student (Level 1). These terms reflect the amount of unexplained variance at each of the three levels. In addition, the effects of individual achievement were allowed to be random at both the school and the country level, providing an indication of how much the effect of individual achievement on academic self-concept varied from country to country and from school to school. Finally, the effects of school-average achievement were allowed to be random at the country level, providing an indication of how much the effect of school-average achievement on academic self-concept varies from country to country. In preliminary, unreported analyses we considered models in which the interaction terms were not included. Because the effects of individual student achievement and school-average achievement were nearly unaffected by

TABLE 16.2. Academic Self-Concept: The Effects of Individual Student Achievement and School-Average Achievement

Effect	β	SE
Fixed effects		
Main effects		
Individual student achievement—linear (IAch-L)	.378	.023
Individual student achievement—quadratic (IAch-Q)	.069	.003
School-average achievement (SAAch)	−.206	.019
Interaction effects		
IAch-L × SAAch	.011	.008
IAch-Q × SAAch	.008	.003
Constant	−.034	.060
Random effects		
Level 3 country intercept	.091	.026
Level 3 individual student achievement	.013	.004
Level 3 school average achievement	.007	.002
Level 2 school intercept	.019	.001
Level 2 individual student achievement	.006	.001
Level 1 student intercept	.779	.004

Note: Individual student achievement and academic self-concept (the dependent variable) were standardized ($M = 0$, $SD = 1$). All beta weights are statistically significant when they differ from zero by more than two standard errors (SEs). Analyses are based on responses from 26 countries, 3,851 schools, and 103,558 students.

the inclusion of interaction effects, these preliminary models were not considered further. Particularly relevant for the present investigation are the fixed effects (individual student achievement, school-average achievement, and their interaction) and the random effects representing country-to-country variation in the effects of individual and school-average achievement.

Results and Discussion

Results of the three-level model (see Table 16.2) indicate the extent to which academic self-concept can be explained in terms of the fixed and random effects posited in the present investigation. Particularly relevant are the fixed effects (individual student achievement, school-average achievement, and their interaction) and the random effects representing country-to-country variation in the effects of individual and school-average achievement. Consistent with a priori predictions, the effects of individual student achievement are substantial and positive (.378), whereas the effects of school-average achievement are less substantial and negative (−.206). The linear component of the Individual Student Achievement × School-Average Achievement interaction is small and not even statistically significant. The random effects associated with country-to-country variation in the individual student achievement effect (.013) are small but statistically significant (due in part to the large sample size), as are the random effects associated with country-to-country variation in school-average achievement effect (.007). We now offer interpretations of these results in terms of the substantive questions underpinning the present investigation.

Is there support for the BFLPE for the cross-national data? Yes. Results of multilevel model of the BFLPE (see Table 16.2) indicated that the effects of individual achievement were positive (linear term = .384, quadratic term = .069), whereas the effects of school-average achievement were negative (−.206). Thus, students with achievement levels one standard deviation above the mean had academic self-concepts that were .384

standard deviations above the mean academic self-concept score, whereas students in schools in which the school-average level of achievement was one standard deviation above the mean (in the metric of individual student achievement) had academic self-concepts that were −.206 standard deviations below the mean. These effects were statistically significant (all estimates were at least 10 times the corresponding standard error) and provide a strong replication of the BFLPE.

Does the size of the BFLPE vary with individual student achievement? No. The interaction between the linear effect of individual student achievement and school-average achievement was not statistically significant. Although there was a statistically significant interaction between the quadratic component of individual student achievement and school-average achievement, the size of this effect (.008) was small. The nature of this interaction suggested that the negative effects of school-average achievement were slightly smaller for students of intermediate achievement levels. Particularly given the extremely large sample size, these results indicated that the negative effect of school-average achievement was consistent across the range of student achievement levels. There was no support for the suggestion that the BFLPE is linearly related to individual student achievement (i.e., that it is larger for less-able students and smaller for high-achievement students).

How much does the BFLPE vary from country to country? Because this question is so central to the present investigation, we evaluated it from several different perspectives. In Table 16.2 the random effect associated with country for the school-average achievement effect (.007) is small but statistically significant. This indicated that there was statistically significant variation from country to country in the size of the BFLPE.

To clarify the extent of this country-to-country variation in the BFLPE, we conducted separate models of the BFLPE for each of the 26 countries. In these country-specific analyses, we included individual student (linear and quadratic components) and school-average achievement as predictors of (individual student) academic self-concept. Across the 26 countries, the BFLPE varied from

−.02 to −.36 (Table 16.1). The effect of school-average achievement was significantly negative in 24 of 26 countries and nonsignificantly negative in the remaining 2 countries. The effect of school-average achievement was not positive in any of the 26 countries. The mean of school-average achievement effects across the 26 countries (−.20) was approximately equal to the effect of school-average achievement in the three-level model (−.206 in Table 16.2). Similarly, the standard deviation of the school-average achievement effects across the 26 countries (−.08) was approximately equal to the square root of the variance component for the random effect of school-average achievement in the three-level model ($.007^{1/2}$ = .084 in Table 16.2).

In each of the 26 countries, the effect of individual achievement on academic self-concept was statistically significant and varied from .14 to .63 (M = .38, SD = .11 in Table 16.1). Again, the average effect in analyses of the individual countries (.38 in Table 16.2) was approximately equal to the effect of individual student achievement in the three-level model (.378 in Table 16.2), and the standard deviation (.11 in Table 16.2) was approximately equal to the square root of the variance component for the random effect of individual achievement at the school level ($.013^{1/2}$ = .114 in Table 16.2). Also consistent with a priori predictions, the absolute value of the positive effect of individual school achievement was consistently higher than the absolute value of the negative effect of school-average achievement (for 25 of 26 countries, all but the Netherlands in Table 16.1).

Summary, Conclusions, and Implications

International interest in the BFLPE and its relevance to educational settings throughout the world provide exciting new opportunities to evaluate the cross-national and cross-cultural generalizability of our theory and empirical findings. This internationally collaborative research project provided a unique opportunity to evaluate the cross-cultural generalizability of the BFLPE in a large number of different countries, using the same self-concept items, the same achievements tests, and a nationally representative sample from each country. Hence, the remarkably strong support for the generalizability of the BFLPE is particularly important. These results suggest that the social comparison processes leading to the BFLPE may approach what Segall *et al.* (1998, p. 1102) referred to as a "nearly universal psychology, one that has pan-human validity"—one of the goals of cross-cultural research.

Potential Limitations

In the present investigation we discuss the *effects* of school-average achievement, which is the typical term used to describe the results of statistical analyses such as regression, path analysis, and structural equation models. Whereas predictions based on the BFLPE are clearly causal, it is important to emphasize that the results in the present investigation are based on correlational data collected at a single point in time. Although true random assignment is a desirable design strategy, it is not a feasible alternative for research into school effectiveness such as that considered here. Hence, it is likely that researchers will continue to struggle with interpretation complications that are inherent in research designs with nonequivalent groups. In this regard, the present investigation needs to be viewed in the context of a larger body of research reviewed earlier. The negative effects of school-average achievement represent complicated combinations of the social comparison processes emphasized here, the quality of the education (e.g., resources, curriculum, expertise of the teachers) and, perhaps, family background factors. Furthermore, these effects are likely to be confounded (see Gamoran, Nystrand, Berends, & LePore, 1995). In BFLPE studies based on true longitudinal data in which the first wave was collected before the start of high school (e.g., Marsh, 1994; Marsh *et al.*, 2000), it is possible to unconfound characteristics of the students from subsequent school effects. These results show that it is the initial school-average level of achievement levels that drives the BFLPE rather than subsequent school effects (although Marsh and Craven, 2001, argued that school policies in academically selective schools can exacerbate the

BFLPE). Even in true longitudinal studies, however, the effects of school-average achievement are likely to be confounded with family background variables and school characteristics such as school resources. However, because features associated with academically selective schools other than the achievement grouping per se are likely to have a positive effect on subsequent outcomes, potential biases are likely to be conservative in relation to the negative BFLPE. Thus, for example, schools in which the school-average achievement is higher are likely to have students from more advantaged backgrounds who attend schools that have higher levels of resource support. Because of the direction of this potential bias, interpretations of the negative effects of school-average achievement on academic self-concept are likely to underestimate the true BFLPE. Offsetting these limitations of the present investigation is the fact that the study is the largest and strongest cross-cultural study of the BFLPE ever undertaken and provides a unique and valuable perspective on the phenomena.

Another feature of the present investigation is that the achievement tests were specifically designed to reflect generic skills rather than the curriculum in any particular school or country. Furthermore, students had no opportunity to study for any of these examinations, they were given no feedback on the examination, and they knew that it would have no consequences for them. Marsh (1987, 1990, 1993; Marsh & Yeung, 1998) argued that relations between academic self-concept and academic achievement were likely to be stronger when achievement was based on (a) classroom performance measures such as school grades that are more easily influenced by characteristics such as quality and amount of student effort, (b) high-stakes achievement tests that have important implications for students' future education and career path, and (c) tests that closely match the school curriculum in a particular school. Following from this reasoning, the BFLPE is likely to be smaller when based on "low-stakes" tests that do not specifically match the school curriculum like those used in the present investigation. This consideration is, however, a double-edged sword in that achievement tests that did match the curriculum of each school

and country would not have provided a common basis of comparison.

Implications and Directions for Further Research

BFLPE research provides an alternative, contradictory perspective to educational policy on the placement of students in special education settings that is being enacted throughout the world. Remarkably, despite the very different issues, this clash between our research and much existing policy exists at both ends of the achievement continuum (also see Robinson *et al.*, 2000). In gifted education research and policy, there is an increasing trend toward the provision of highly selective educational settings—special gifted and talented classes and academically selective schools for very bright students. This policy direction is based in part on a labeling theory perspective, suggesting that bright students will have higher self-concepts and will experience other psychological benefits from being educated in the company of other academically gifted students. Yet, our BFLPE and empirical evaluation of the effects of academically selective settings show exactly the opposite effects. Placement of gifted students in academically selective settings results in lower academic self-concepts, not higher academic self-concepts. In recent research and policy for academically disadvantaged students, there is a worldwide inclusion movement to integrate these students into mainstream, regular classroom settings. Although economic rationalist perspectives appear to be the underlying motive for such decisions, the espoused rhetoric is based on a direct application of labeling theory. According to labeling theory, academically disadvantaged children are likely to be stigmatized and suffer lower self-concepts as a consequence of being placed in special education classes with other academically disadvantaged students. Yet, theory underpinning our BFLPE and empirical evaluation of the effects of including academically disadvantaged students in regular mainstream classrooms show exactly the opposite effects. Placement of academically disadvantaged children into regular classrooms results in lower academic self-concepts, not higher academic self-concepts. Furthermore, the negative effects of inclusion on peer self-concept reported by Tracey and Marsh (2000) suggested that academically disadvantaged children in regular classrooms actually felt socially excluded, not included. We do not claim that all gifted and talented students will suffer lower academic self-concepts when attending academically selective high schools, but many will. Similarly, we do not claim that all academically disadvantaged students will suffer lower academic self-concepts when attending regular, mixed-achievement classes, but many will. Rather, our research provides an important alternative perspective to existing policy directions that have not been adequately evaluated in relation to current educational and psychological research. The present investigation is particularly important in demonstrating the cross-cultural generalizability of the theoretical and empirical basis of our claims.

The BFLPE is posited to be a function of frame-of-reference effects associated with school-average ability that are in addition to specific practices that are idiosyncratic to particular schools. Hence, support for the BFLPE does not negate the potentially positive effects claimed, for example, by advocates of academically selective schools (e.g., accelerated learning, provision of more challenging materials). Rather, the results show that the net effect of school-average academic achievement—the combined effects of potential benefits and the negative effects of the BFLPE—is negative. Indeed, to the extent that positive effects associated with other characteristics of selective schools are controlled, then the size of the BFLPE would be even larger (see related discussion by Marsh *et al.*, 2000). It is also important to emphasize that the negative effects of school-average achievement in the present investigation represented an average, across responses by 103,558 students attending 3,851 schools in 26 countries. Hence, there are some academically selective schools that produce academic outcomes commensurate with the high achievement levels of their students and some students who are advantaged by attending such schools. Whereas it is unjustified to assume that high achievement level schools necessarily advantage students, some parents apparently choose to send their children to academically selective schools on the basis of the assumption that such schools are necessarily good for all students. Are there individual student or school characteristics that offset or negate the BFLPEs? Individual student achievement is an obvious suggestion, a characteristic that is the main selection criterion for many academically selective schools with explicit entry criteria. However, the results of the present investigation and previous research suggest that the size of the BFLPE does not vary much with individual students achievement. Hence, an important direction for further research is to identify individual student characteristics that will predict students who may benefit from academically selective schools and to evaluate school policies that maximize benefits.

A major focus of BFLPE research has been on the substantively important and surprising implications of this research, undermining the assumed advantages of attending academically selective schools and mainstreaming academically disadvantaged students. Although obviously supportive of these well-established concerns, the present investigation also provides stronger links between BFLPE and broader areas of social comparison theory (e.g., Diener & Fujita, 1997; Lazarus & Folkman, 1984; Taylor & Lobel, 1989; Tessor, 1988; Wills, 1981) that have relevance to a variety of psychology disciplines.

REFERENCES

Aiken, L. S., & West, S. G. (1991). *Multiple regression: Testing and interpreting interactions.* Newbury Park, CA: Sage.

Alwin, D. F., & Otto, L. B. (1977). High school context effects on aspirations. *Sociology of Education, 50,* 259–273.

Bandura, A. (1986). *Social foundations of thought and action: A social cognitive theory.* Englewood Cliffs, NJ: Prentice-Hall.

Branden, N. (1994). *Six pillars of self-esteem.* New York: Bantam.

Brookover, W. B., & Lezotte, L. W. (1979). *Changes in schools characteristics coincident with changes in student achievement.* East Lansing: Michigan State University, Institute for Research on Teaching. (ERIC Document Reproduction Service No. ED 181 005).

Byrne, B. M. (1996a). Academic self-concept: Its structure, measurement, and relation to academic achievement. In B. A. Bracken (Ed.), *Handbook of self-concept* (pp. 287–316). New York: Wiley.

Byrne, B. M. (1996b). *Measuring self-concept across the lifespan: Issues and instrumentation.* Washington, DC: American Psychological Association.

Chapman, J. W. (1988). Learning disabled children's self-concepts. *Review of Educational Research, 58,* 347–371.

Coleman, J. M., & Fults, B. A. (1985). Special class placement, level of intelligence, and the self-concept of gifted children: A social comparison perspective. *Remedial and Special Education, 6,* 7–11.

Davis, J. A. (1966). The campus as a frog pond: An application of theory of relative deprivation to career decisions for college men. *American Journal of Sociology, 72,* 17–31.

Diener, E., & Fujita, F. (1997). Social comparison and subjective well-being. In B. P. Buunk & F. X. Gibbons (Eds.), *Health, coping, and well-being: Perspectives from social comparison theory* (pp. 329–358). Mahwah, NJ: Erlbaum.

Festinger, L. (1954) A theory of social comparison processes. *Human Relations, 7,* 117–140.

Gamoran, A., Nystrand, M., Berends, M., & LePore, P. C. (1995). An organizational analysis of the effects of ability grouping. *American Educational Research Journal, 32,* 687–715.

Goldstein, H. (1995). *Multilevel statistical models.* London: Arnold.

Hattie, J. A. (1992). *Self-concept.* Hillsdale, NJ: Erlbaum.

Helson, H. (1964). *Adaptation-level theory.* New York: Harper & Row.

Hyman, H. (1942). The psychology of subjective status. *Psychological Bulletin, 39,* 473–474.

James, W. (1963). *The principles of psychology.* New York: Holt, Rinehart & Winston. (Original work published 1890)

Jerusalem, M. (1984). Reference group, learning environment and self-evaluations: A dynamic multi-level analysis with latent variables. In R. Schwarzer (Ed.), *The self in anxiety, stress and depression* (pp. 61–73). Amsterdam: Elsevier Science.

Judge, T. A., & Bono, J. E. (2001). Relationship of core self-evaluations traits: Self-esteem, generalized self-efficacy, locus of control, and emotional stability—with job satisfaction and job performance: A meta-analysis. *Journal of Applied Psychology, 86,* 80–92.

Lazarus, R. S., & Folkman, S, (1984). *Stress, appraisal and coping.* New York: Springer-Verlag.

Marsh, H. W. (1974). *Judgmental anchoring: Stimulus and response variables.* Unpublished doctoral dissertation, University of California, Los Angeles.

Marsh, H. W. (1984). Self-concept: The application of a frame of reference model to explain paradoxical results. *Australian Journal of Education, 28,* 165–181.

Marsh, H. W. (1987). The big-fish–little-pond effect on academic self-concept. *Journal of Educational Psychology, 79,* 280–295.

Marsh, H. W. (1990). A multidimensional, hierarchical self-concept: Theoretical and empirical justification. *Educational Psychology Review, 2,* 77–172.

Marsh, H. W. (1991). The failure of high ability high schools to deliver academic benefits: The importance of academic self-concept and educational aspirations. *American Educational Research Journal, 28,* 445–480.

Marsh, H. W. (1993). Academic self-concept: Theory, measurement and research. In J. Suls (Ed.), *Psychological perspectives on the self* (Vol. 4, pp. 59–98). Hillsdale, NJ: Erlbaum.

Marsh, H. W. (1994). Using the National Educational Longitudinal Study of 1988 to evaluate theoretical models of self-concept: The Self-Description Questionnaire. *Journal of Educational Psychology, 86,* 439–456.

Marsh, H. W. (2002). A multidimensional physical self-concept: A construct validity approach to theory, measurement, and research. *Psychology, The Journal of the Hellenic Psychological Society, 9,* 459–493.

Marsh, H. W., Byrne, B. M., & Yeung, A. S. (1999). Causal ordering of academic self-concept and achievement: Reanalysis of a pioneering study and revised recommendations. *Educational Psychologist, 34,* 155–167.

Marsh, H. W., Chessor, D., Craven, R. G., & Roche, L. (1995). The effects of gifted and talented programs on academic self-concept: The big fish strikes again. *American Educational Research Journal, 32,* 285–319.

Marsh, H. W., & Craven, R. (1997). Academic self-concept: Beyond the dustbowl. In G. Phye (Ed.), *Handbook of classroom assessment: Learning, achievement, and adjustment* (pp. 131–198). Orlando, FL: Academic Press.

Marsh, H. W., & Craven, R. (2001). The pivotal role of frames of reference in academic self-concept formation: The big fish little pond effect. In F. Pajares & T. Urdan (Eds.), *Adolescence and education* (Vol. II, pp. 83–123). Greenwich, CT: Information Age.

Marsh, H. W., & Johnston, C. F. (1993). Multidimensional self-concepts and frames of reference: Relevance to the exceptional learner. In F. E. Obiakor & S. Stile (Eds.), *Self-concept of exceptional learners: Current perspectives for educators* (pp. 72–112). Dubuque, IA: Kendall/Hunt.

Marsh, H. W., Köller, O., & Baumert, J. (2001). Reunification of East and West German school systems: Longitudinal multilevel modeling study of the big fish little pond effect on academic self-concept. *American Educational Research Journal, 38,* 321–350.

Marsh, H. W., Kong, C.-K., & Hau, K.-T (2000). Longitudinal multilevel modeling of the big fish little pond effect on academic self-concept: Counterbalancing social comparison and reflected glory effects in Hong Kong high schools. *Journal of Personality and Social Psychology, 78,* 337–349.

Marsh, H. W., & Parker, J. (1984). Determinants of student self-concept: Is it better to be a relatively large fish in a small pond even if you don't learn to swim as well? *Journal of Personality and Social Psychology, 47,* 213–231.

Marsh, H. W., & Rowe, K. J. (1996). The negative effects of school-average ability on academic self-concept: An application of multilevel modeling. *Australian Journal of Education, 40,* 65–87.

Marsh, H. W., & Yeung, A. S. (1997a). The causal effects of academic self-concept on academic achievement: Structural equation models of longitudinal data. *Journal of Educational Psychology, 89*, 41–54.

Marsh, H. W., & Yeung, A. S. (1997b). Coursework selection: The effects of academic self-concept and achievement. *American Educational Research Journal, 34*, 691–720.

Marsh, H. W., & Yeung, A. S. (1998). Longitudinal structural equation models of academic self-concept and achievement: Gender differences in the development of math and English constructs. *American Educational Research Journal, 35*, 705–738.

Matsumoto, D. (2001). Cross-cultural psychology in the 21st century. In J. S. Halonen & S. F. Davis (Eds.), *The many faces of psychological research in the 21st century* (chap. 5). Retrieved 18 December, 2001 from http://teachpsych. lemoyne.edu/teachpsych/faces/script/ch05.htm

Meyer, J. W. (1970). High school effects on college intentions. *American Journal of Sociology, 76*, 59–70.

Morse, S., & Gergen, K. J. (1970). Social comparison, self-consistency, and the concept of self. *Journal of Personality and Social Psychology, 16*, 148–156.

Organisation of Economic Cooperation and Development. (2001a). *Knowledge and skills for life: Results from the first OECD programme for international student assessment (PISA) 2000.* Paris: Author.

Organisation of Economic Cooperation and Development. (2001b). *PISA international data base* (Technical Report). Paris: Author.

Parducci, A. (1995). *Happiness, pleasure, and judgment: The contextual theory and its applications.* Mahwah, NJ: Erlbaum.

Parker, S. K. (1998). Enhancing role breadth self-efficacy: The roles of job enrichment and other organizational interventions. *Journal of Applied Psychology, 83*, 835–852.

Raudenbush, S. W., & Bryk, A. S. (2002). *Hierarchical linear models: Applications and data analysis methods* (2nd ed.). Thousand Oaks, CA: Sage.

Robinson, N. M., Zigler, E., & Gallagher, J. J. (2000). Two tails of the normal curve: Similarities and differences in the study of mental retardation and giftedness. *American Psychologist, 55*, 1413–1424.

Segall, M. H., Lonner, W. J., & Berry, J. W. (1998). Cross-cultural psychology as a scholarly discipline: On the flowering of culture in behavioral research. *American Psychologist, 53*, 1101–1110.

Sherif, M., & Sherif, C. W. (1969). *Social psychology.* New York. Harper & Row.

Stouffer, S. A., Suchman, E. A., DeVinney, L. C., Star, S. A., & Williams, R. M. (1949). *The American soldier: Adjustments during army life* (Vol. 1). Princeton, NJ: Princeton University Press.

Sue, S. (1999). Science, ethnicity and bias: Where have we gone wrong? *American Psychologist, 54*, 1070–1077.

Suls, J. M. (1977). Social comparison theory and research: An overview from 1954. In J. M. Suls & R. L. Miller (Eds.), *Social comparison processes: Theoretical and empirical perspectives* (pp. 1–20). Washington, DC: Hemisphere.

Taylor, S. E., & Lobel, M. (1989). Social comparison activity under threat: Downward evaluation and upward contacts. *Psychological Review, 96*, 569–575.

Tessor, A. (1988). Toward a self-evaluation maintenance model of social behavior. In L. Berkowitz (Ed.), *Advance in experimental social psychology* (Vol. 21, pp. 181–227). San Diego, CA: Academic Press.

Tracey, D., & Marsh, H. W. (2000). Self-concepts of primary students with mild intellectual disabilities: Issues of measurement and educational placement. In *Conference proceedings of the 2000 SELF Research Centre conference.* Sydney, Australia: University of Western Sydney, SELF Centre.

Upshaw, H. S. (1969). The personal reference scale: An approach to social judgment. *Advances in Experimental Social Psychology, 4*, 315–370.

Wills, T. A. (1981). Downward comparison principals in social psychology. *Psychological Bulletin, 90*, 245–271.

Zeidner M., & Schleyer, E. J. (1999). The big-fish–little-pond effect for academic self-concept, test anxiety and school grades in gifted children. *Contemporary Educational Psychology, 24*, 305–329.

Social Comparisons of Income in One's Community: Evidence From National Surveys of Income and Happiness

Michael R. Hagerty

Two studies provide evidence for social comparison effects of income on subjective well-being (SWB). The 1st study of 7,023 persons from nationally representative samples in the United States shows that the range and skew of the income distribution in a community affects a person's happiness, as predicted by range–frequency theory. The 2nd study of 8 nations over a period of 25 years shows that decreasing the skew (inequality) of the income distribution in a country increases average national SWB. Both studies strongly support social comparison effects of income within a community, and both results are predicted by range–frequency theory. These studies are the first to successfully extend earlier results of R. H. Smith, E. Diener, and D. H. Wedell (1989) from the laboratory into naturalistic situations. The magnitude of the social comparison effects is smaller than the main effect of income, which implies that nations can avoid creating a "hedonic treadmill."

"**K**eeping up with the Joneses" describes a common belief that people make social comparisons with others in their community and that their happiness declines when others' income or possessions increase. Measuring the existence and size of this "social comparison" effect is important in researching the determinants of human happiness. It has been measured and modeled precisely in laboratory experiments (Smith, Diener, & Wedell, 1989). However, a surprising result of research until

I thank Prasad Naik, Scott Davis, Eitan Gerstner, Eyal Biyalogorsky, and Barbara Atkinson for many helpful comments on earlier versions of this article. I also thank the seminar participants at the Survey Research Center, University of California, Berkeley. The Institute for Governmental Affairs, University of California, Davis, provided data retrieval.

Correspondence concerning this article should be addressed to Michael R. Hagerty, Graduate School of Management, University of California, One Shields Avenue, Davis, California 95616. Electronic mail may be sent to mrhagerty@ucdavis.edu.

317

now is that social comparison on subjective well-being (SWB) has not received support in natural settings. A review by Diener, Sun, Lucas, and Smith (1999) states, "… the influence of one's immediate social environment appears *not* [italics added] to produce long-term effects on people's SWB via social comparison" (p. 283). Similarly, Diener and Fujita (1997) summarized current research as the following:

> Comparisons that are induced in the laboratory seem sometimes to influence satisfaction judgments that are made immediately in that setting.… When natural situations have been examined where the level of surrounding people's social circumstances differed, it was found that long-term subjective well-being judgments were not affected by the social environment. (p. 345)

In this article I show that income of others in a natural setting does affect SWB, in the ways predicted by laboratory experiments. I first show how previous studies have used measures of income that can confound the distribution of income with other factors. I then describe two studies, conducted in natural settings, that show that improved measures of income distribution affect SWB, as predicted by social comparison theory.

Social Comparison and Subjective Well-Being

Many theorists have suggested that all judgments are relative and that satisfaction is not determined by the absolute value of an event but rather by its value in relation to other people (Helson, 1964; Parducci, 1968). In these theories, the same event can be judged as positive or negative, depending on what other people (their social comparisons) attain. However, the theories differ depending on exactly how people compare themselves with others. For example, do they compare themselves only to the richest person and the poorest person, ignoring all others? Do they instead rank themselves in the distribution of all people? Parducci (1968, 1995) conducted laboratory experiments on this question, and

found that participants used both of these strategies. His range–frequency theory predicts that a person i with a given income forms a judgment that is a weighted average of a range principle (R) and a frequency principle (F) applied to the distribution of all people's income:

$$SWB_i = wR_i + (1 - w)F_i,$$

where SWB_i is the subjective well-being experienced by person i. In turn, the range principle is written as:

$$R_i = (I_i - min)/(max - min),$$

where R_i is the range principle for person i; I_i is the person's own income, independent of context; min is the value of the smallest income in the distribution; and max, the value of the largest. R_i is called the range principle because the stimulus is compared with only the largest and smallest stimuli (range) of the distribution. In this article, range will be determined primarily by the maximum income because the variation in minimum income is very small—almost every community has some people that declare zero income.

In contrast to the range principle, the frequency principle compares one person's income with the income of all people in the distribution:

$$F_i = Rank_i/N,$$

where $Rank_i$ is the rank of person i's own income in the entire distribution of people (where rank is 1 for the lowest income and is N for the highest income), and N is the size of the distribution. Thus, F may be thought of as the percentile rating of stimulus i.

Helson's (1964) adaptation theory is a special case of range–frequency theory where the frequency distribution is the simplest possible: a uniform distribution. Parducci (1995) develops several predictions from range–frequency theory, which will be tested here.

1. Increasing the maximum of the distribution should decrease a person's SWB when all else is held constant because the maximum appears

in the divisor of the equation for the range principle.

2. Increasing the skew[1] of the distribution (reducing the mass of the upper tail) should increase an individual's SWB because more people will be ranked below any given income i. Hence a higher score on the frequency principle results. This effect is demonstrated in Figure 17.1, where two hypothetical income distributions are plotted. Both income distributions have the same range, and both are positively skewed, but the bottom distribution has higher skew than the top. This is because its upper tail is "thinner" than the top distribution. This implies that fewer people are near the top of the distribution and that more are near the bottom. Hence a person with a fixed income (e.g., $20,000) is predicted to feel happier in the bottom distribution because more people are ranked below that person's income ($20,000) in the bottom distribution.

3. The above predictions concern an individual's happiness. When the concern is predicting *aggregate* happiness for all people in the community, Parducci shows that increasing the skew of the distribution should decrease the average SWB.

Prediction 3 differs from Prediction 2 because of the inherent conflict between the individual and

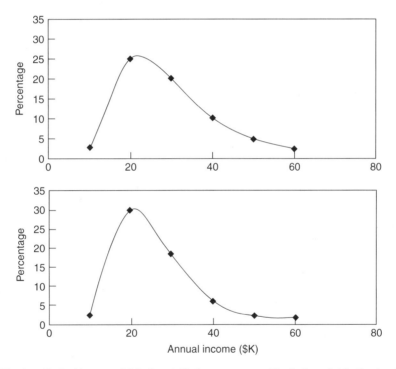

FIGURE 17.1 ▪ Two hypothetical income distributions with the same range. The bottom distribution has higher skew (thinner upper tail), so that range–frequency theory predicts that an individual will feel happier in the bottom distribution because more people are ranked below any given income level.

---

[1] *Skew* is defined as the third moment around the mean, and is defined as $n\Sigma z^3/(n-1)(n-2)$, where z are standardized scores. It measures the asymmetry of a distribution. Distributions with a positive skew have a thinner tail at their upper end, whereas distributions with a negative skew have a thinner tail at their lower end. Parducci (1995) worked with both negatively and positively skewed distributions. However, in this article, all distributions are positively skewed because real distributions of income are all positively skewed. Hence, I write in terms of "more skewed," meaning one distribution is more positively skewed than another.

the group in social comparison models. An increasing skew will make an individual's own income look better because more people are ranked below him or her. But the group average loses more happiness than the individual gains with positively skewed distributions.

4. Happiness is affected by both "upward" and "downward" comparisons. That is, the frequency principle predicts that people compare themselves with all other people in the distribution, not just to people above them or people below them. In contrast, some theories of social comparison (see, e.g., McFarland & Miller, 1994; Wood, 1996) predict that people will compare themselves with only people below them (to feel better) or with only people above them (to motivate themselves to do better).

Laboratory studies have already shown a good deal of support for these social comparison predictions. In an elegant experiment, Smith, Diener, and Wedell (1989) showed that Parducci's (1995) range–frequency theory predicted the effect of social comparison on SWB quite well. For example, participants were asked to rate their satisfaction with gratuities they earned at a hypothetical job. For each rating, they were shown their own gratuities as well as the gratuities earned by others at the job. The distribution of gratuities was manipulated to be either positively or negatively skewed. The subjects' satisfaction rating with a given amount of money varied with what others received (evidence of social comparison). Ratings were found to depend not only on the range of the distribution, but also on the frequency distribution (skew). Ratings of individuals were highest (holding own income constant) with positively skewed distributions (distributions where many people receive tips near the bottom of the range). But aggregate ratings over the entire distribution were highest with negatively skewed distributions, consistent with the above predictions. The numerical ratings closely fit the predictions of range–frequency theory.

Given such clear results in the laboratory, researchers might have expected to find clear confirmation

in the field. Instead, no evidence of social comparison has been found in the field. Diener, Sandvik, Seidlitz, and Diener (1993) examined a survey of 4,942 American adults for evidence of social comparisons but found none. However, their method for testing the effects of social comparisons did not compute the range or skew of the distribution for each community. Instead, they simply compared communities on their mean income (p. 210). It is important to note that measuring only the mean income can confound the range and frequency effects predicted by theory.

This confounding can be demonstrated by reviewing actual income distributions in the United States. Income data from the U.S. Census show that as the mean income has increased over 20 years, the maximum has increased and the skew has become more positive (Wolfson & Murphy, 1998). Prediction 1 of range–frequency theory implies that the increasing maximum will decrease happiness, but Prediction 2 implies that the increasing skew will increase individuals' happiness, for a given level of income. Hence these effects would tend to cancel each other out when only mean income is measured. This may be the reason social comparison effects have not been detected in previous studies. I tested social comparison effects in the data by controlling directly for skew and for range of the income distribution in each community.

Another major field study was done by Diener, Diener, and Diener (1995). They examined the effect of income at the national level and its relation to national SWB for 55 countries. Once again, their primary measure of social comparison was the mean income of neighboring countries. Once again, they found no significant relationship after controlling for effects of development region. But they included additional measures suggested by range–frequency theory that were supportive of the theory. They measured the amount of positive skew for income within each nation, as well as the Gini coefficient (a measure of equality of income such that 0 denotes perfect equality of all citizens' incomes and 1 denotes maximal inequality). The effect of positive skew was negative (correctly predicted by Prediction 3) for four of the five samples, but did not reach significance in their sample of 55. The effect of the Gini coefficient for income was negative for all five samples and was significant for two. In summary, the two measures recommended by range–frequency theory showed 9 of 10 correlation coefficients in the predicted direction, with two of them significantly so. In the present study, I searched for similar national-level effects using a more powerful within-subjects design.

The studies reported next measure people's happiness in a naturalistic setting, using national surveys of income and happiness. In the first, I examined data from more than 7,000 people in the United States in more than 300 community settings to search for social comparison effects within community. In the second, I examined data from eight nations over 25 years to search for social comparison effects within nation.

Study 1: National Happiness Surveys in the United States

Method

The General Social Survey (GSS; Davis & Smith, 1996) is a continuing survey that has monitored attitudes and behavior of adults in the United States since 1972. Each wave, using multistage, stratified national probability sampling, surveys a different sample of people older than 18 years who reside in the United States. A new wave is executed every 1 or 2 years and consists of between 1,500 and 3,000 persons. In each wave, between 84 and 100 primary sampling units (PSUs) are selected by random stratified sampling. The PSUs correspond to standard metropolitan statistical areas (SMSAs). For each SMSA, I obtained U.S. Census Bureau measures of household income distribution. In this way, the mean, range, and skew of household income in each community was determined for each year of the GSS survey.

Detailed U.S. Census Bureau identification of SMSAs began in 1989. Therefore I selected all 1989–1996 GSS respondents who lived in SMSAs. This totaled 8,362 persons in 311 different communities across these years. Of these, 8% refused to answer the income question or had some missing data, leaving a total of 7,023 respondents analyzed. The breakdown of respondents by year was 923 (1989); 786 (1990); 884 (1991); 1,018 (1993); 1,749 (1994); and 1,659 (1996). No surveys were fielded in 1992 or 1995.

The GSS item that taps overall happiness is phrased identically for each year: "Taken all together, how would you say things are these days—would you say that you are very happy, pretty happy, or not too happy?" I reversed the original coding of the GSS so that *very happy* = 3, *pretty happy* = 2, and *not too happy* = 1. Veenhoven (1993) showed that this scale is equal-interval. However, I tested this assumption by using only the ordinal properties of the scale.

The GSS item that measures household income was collected at the same time using a categorical scale, with the wording "In which of these groups did your total family income, from all sources, fall last year before taxes?" Categories ranged from *under $1,000* (1) to *$75,000 or over* (21). (For the earlier years 1989–1990, only 20 categories were used, with the highest category being *$60,000 or over*.) The actual income of a respondent was transformed to the midpoint of the dollar value of the category marked and was deflated to 1984 dollar value using the Consumer Price Index. The midpoint of the lowest category was estimated at $500, and the midpoint of the highest category was estimated at $75,000 ($60,000 for 1989–90). Later tests showed that these estimates for lowest and highest income did not affect results.

To get reliable estimates of a community's income distribution, the Census Bureau (see Moffitt, 1998) provides the Current Population Survey (March supplement), which surveys a representative sample of households in SMSAs on their exact household income. More than 50,000 households are interviewed each year, so that a community's mean income, skew, and minimum and maximum income can be computed for the exact SMSA for the exact year that the GSS was fielded. The mean sample size for computing the income distribution for each SMSA for each year was 365. In this way, respondent's income, happiness, and SMSAs' income distribution were all collected for the same year.

Results

The distribution of each community's income was measured in five different ways, including the maximum income, minimum income, skewness, income of the household at the 20th percentile (I20), and income of the household at the 80th percentile (I80).

Table 17.1 shows the means, standard deviations, and simple correlations among the variables. The first row shows that the correlation between happiness and respondent's real household income is positive and significant ($r = .18, p < .001$). It also shows that the correlation between happiness and mean community income is not significant. Both of these replicate the results of Diener et al. (1993), The third row shows the simple correlations among mean income, maximum of income, and skew of income for the community. Note that mean income increases significantly with maximum ($r = .11$, $p < .001$), but decreases significantly with skew ($r = -.13, p < .001$). This is consistent with the conjecture that the effects of range and skew tend to cancel each other when only the mean community income is examined. This would explain why Diener et al. (1993) found no effect of mean community income. Note further that maximum and skew are substantially correlated in these communities. To control simultaneously for the several variables that are intercorrelated, multiple regression was applied next.

Table 17.2 shows the multiple regressions predicting an individual's happiness from that person's own income and their community's income distribution. The first set of columns replicates the analysis of Diener et al. (1993), where the person's own income and the mean of the community's income were used as predictors. The top row shows that the person's own income positively and significantly increases their happiness. The second row shows that the mean income of the community did not even approach significance. This successfully replicates the results of Diener et al., and explains why they concluded that the community's income does not affect a person's happiness. (The analysis of variance test which they used similarly showed no effect for mean income, $F(2, 7022) = 0.19$, and no interaction with own income, $F(4, 7022) = 1.10$.) The last rows of each column control for various demographics and show that, on average, married people and more educated people are somewhat happier. This updates and replicates Davis's (1984) findings on the demographic correlates of happiness.

The second set of columns shows the regression when all variables from range–frequency theory are included. Again, the first row shows that the person's own income very significantly affects their happiness. The next rows show that both the maximum and the skew were significant and in the predicted direction. As the maximum increases, happiness declines for a given level of income. Also, as the skew becomes more positive, an individual's happiness increases for a given level of income. Hence the first two of the range–frequency predictions are supported.

TABLE 17.1. Simple Correlations, Means, and Standard Deviations Among Variables (N = 7,023)

Variable	1	2	3	4	5	6	7	8
1. Happiness	—	.18**	.02	−.03*	−.01	.03*	.05**	−.02
2. Household income		—	.13**	.10**	.02	−.04**	.04**	.16**
3. Community mean income			—	−.11**	−.13**	−.02*	.75**	.75**
4. Community maximum income				—	.83**	−.23**	−.33**	.61**
5. Community skew income					—	−.02	−.41**	.36**
6. Community minimum income						—	.09**	−.14**
7. 20th percentile mean income (I20)							—	.20**
8. 80th percentile mean income (I80)								—
M	2.22	26,793	26,870	173,422	1.89	−1,434	3,618	63,170
SD	0.61	15,325	5,481	85,813	0.95	3,592	3,625	10,542

*p < .05. **p < .01.

TABLE 17.2. Coefficients and *t* Statistics From Three Multiple Regressions Predicting a Person's Happiness as a Function of Person's Income (in $K) and Community's Income Distribution

Variable	Equation 1			Equation 2			Equation 3		
	B	*t*(7018)	*β*	*B*	*t*(7016)	*β*	*B*	*t*(7016)	*β*
Household income	.004	7.47	.102**	.004	8.15	.112**	.004	7.92	.109**
Community mean income	−.001	0.40	.005						
Community income maximum				−.001	−3.88	−.077**			
Community income skew				.034	2.40	.053*	.025	2.62	.038**
Community income minimum				.002	1.12	.014			
80th percentile mean income							−.004	−4.37	.060**
20th percentile mean income							.012	4.98	.069**
Marital status[a]	.210	13.40	.169**	.201	13.0	.163**	.204	13.10	.165**
Years of education	.009	3.47	.044**	.010	3.62**	.046	.010	3.85	.049**
Sex[b]	−.025	−1.75	−.020	−.027	−1.86	−.022	.026	−1.82	−.021
R²			.058			.060			.062

[a] 1 = *married*, 0 = *other*. [b] 1 = *male*, 2 = *female*.
* *p* < .05. ** *p* < .01.

The minimum income was not significant in this regression. One interpretation of these effects is that people make upward comparisons (comparing themselves with the highest income households) but not downward comparisons (comparing themselves with lowest income households). However, another interpretation is that the minimum income was not significant simply because of its low variation in the sample—note that its standard deviation in Table 17.1 is less than 1/20 of the variance of the maximum income. To investigate further whether people use upward or downward comparisons, the third regression uses alternative measures of upper (I80) and lower (I20) points of the income distribution. The third set of columns shows again that own income and skew are significant as before. Similarly, the higher the community's I80, the less happy is an individual with a given income. However, the new measure of the lower limit, I20, is now significant such that the lower the community's income near the bottom, the happier an individual is, holding own income constant. The standardized beta for these effects are about equal and opposite in sign, suggesting that people do make downward comparisons and weight them about equally with upward comparisons. This provides support for Prediction 4.

The robustness of these results was checked in several ways. First, the equal-interval assumption of the happiness scale was relaxed. All three equations were reestimated using the ordered probit model, which uses only the ordinal properties of the happiness scale. The coefficients for all three equations retained the same sign and significance levels, supporting Veenhoven's (1993) conclusion that the scale is indeed equal-interval. Second, those responding with the lower (<$1,000) and upper income categories (>$75,000 after 1990; >$60,000 before 1990) were removed from the data because these categories were open ended. Hence the estimates for the respondent's income in these categories may have contained considerable bias. Nevertheless, after removal of these respondents, coefficients for the three regressions retained the same signs and significance levels. In summary, this marks the strongest evidence to date supporting the range–frequency model in natural settings.

Discussion

The results show that the mean of the community's income distribution is insufficient to predict social judgment effects correctly. Instead, both range and frequency information is necessary. Using these measures, Predictions 1, 2, and 4 of range–frequency theory for individual happiness are confirmed. Prediction 3 requires data on aggregate happiness of entire populations. Therefore, in Study 2, I examine aggregate happiness in eight countries over 25 years.

These aggregate data have the advantage that they cover more people in more countries, but the disadvantage (similar to the data of Diener *et al.*, 1995) that they lack the detail available in Study 1. In particular, the aggregate data lack measures on individuals' happiness and income, and the data rely on means computed for each country. In addition, they lack information on the range of incomes in each country. Nevertheless, we can usefully examine the effect of income mean and distribution for evidence of social comparison.

Study 2: Extension to Aggregate Measures in Eight Countries

Method

Mean real income for each nation was measured as gross domestic product (GDP) per capita, published annually by the World Bank (1996). Data on distribution of income are collected by the World Bank (1996) and tabulated by the International Labour Office (Tabatabai, 1996). For each country, they report the Gini coefficient. In addition they report Ql (the percentage of national income received by households in the lowest quintile) and Q5 (the percentage of national income received by the households in the highest quintile). Skew of income is not reported, but was estimated from the five quintiles of the income distribution. Income ranges are not reported and could not be estimated. Mean income is available for every year since 1960, but data on income distributions are collected infrequently by most nations because of the expense of household-level surveys.

Data on average national happiness are collected by Veenhoven (1993) and updated data are available on his web site. In the United States, data on national happiness were collected using the item described above in the GSS. In the other countries, life satisfaction was assessed by the following item (suitably interpreted): "On the whole, are you very satisfied, fairly satisfied, not very satisfied, or not at all satisfied with the life you lead?" A total of eight nations have reported more than three surveys of income distribution, for a total of 61 observations. The

TABLE 17.3. Number of Observations Contributed by Each Country to Study 2

Country	No. of observations	Years
United States	19	1972–1994
United Kingdom	5	1973–1991
Netherlands	5	1977–1991
France	3	1975–1989
Germany	4	1973–1988
Italy	4	1977–1991
Denmark	4	1976–1992
Japan	17	1972–1989
Total	61	

Note: Japan does not report quintile data, so it was excluded from regressions containing quintiles.

countries are shown in Table 17.3, together with the number of observations and years spanned for each.

Results

Table 17.4 shows the multiple regressions predicting national happiness from mean income per person and distribution of income. All regressions included mean national income (GDP per capita), with different measures for income distribution. In addition, all regressions included dummy variables for each country to control for well-documented differences between nations in average happiness (Easterlin, 1995). These dummy variables explain the variance between nations, allowing the remaining variables to be estimated with more precision as within-subjects factors.

The first columns of Table 17.4 show the regression that used skew as the measure of income distribution. The top rows display the dummy variables for each nation. For example, the United States has a (standardized) value of .899, indicating that its average happiness is significantly above the base case of France. The R^2 using these dummy variables alone is .914, indicating that the total variance can be fairly well explained by between-country factors modeled by the dummy variables. However, the bottom rows show that additional variance can be explained by the within-country variables of mean income and distribution of income. The bottom rows of the first column show that the effect of mean income is positive and

TABLE 17.4. Multiple Regressions Predicting Mean National Happiness as a Function of Mean Income and Four Alternative Measures of Income Distribution in Each Nation

Variable	Skew			Gini coefficient			Q5			Q1		
	B	t(37)	β	B	t(52)	β	B	t(36)	β	B	t(36)	β
United States	1.190	10.30	.899**	1.190	10.80	.824**	1.200	11.30	1.120**	1.120	8.90	.956**
United Kingdom	0.760	5.30	.462**	0.770	6.00	.381**	1.000	8.70	.422**	1.000	7.67	.540**
Netherlands	1.360	10.30	.768**	1.360	10.90	.530**	1.200	10.50	.802**	1.320	9.37	.770**
France	0.000		.000	0.000		.000	0.000		.000	0.000		.00
Germany	0.540	3.75	.345**	0.540	4.00	.207**	0.650	5.70	.263**	0.590	4.44	.290**
Italy	−0.087	−0.61	.030	−0.087	−0.65	−.007**	−0.010	0.08	−.043	−0.034	−0.26	−.020
Denmark	1.920	13.50	.749**	1.920	14.20	.602**	1.600	11.50	.947**	1.700	12.50	.840**
Japan				−0.110	−1.03	−.117						
R^2 (first regression)			.914			.944			.913			.913
Mean income	0.061	4.49	.305**	0.051	4.47	.210**	0.071	4.96	.359**	0.059	3.82	.299**
Income distribution[a]	−0.778	−2.89	−.170**	−2.530	−2.15	−.165*	−0.041	−2.92	−.246**	0.043	0.95	.115
R^2 (Second regression)			.949			.960			.949			.939
R^2, within-nation[b]			.407			.286			.414			.300

Note: Q5 = percentage of national income received by households in the highest quintile; Q1 = percentage of national income received by households in the lowest quintile. $n = 61$ for regression using Gini; $n = 44$ for other regressions.
[a] Income distribution measure in the first set of columns was skew, in the second set was Gini, Q5, and Q1.
[b] Within-nation variance accounted for was computed as (R^2, second regression ~R^2, first regression)/(1 − R^2, first regression).
* $p < .05$.   ** $p < .01$.

significant, with the standardized coefficient of .305. In addition, the effect for skew is significant and negative, such that thinner upper tails cause a decline in happiness. This confirms Prediction 3 of range–frequency theory.

The variance accounted for when these two additional variables were added was .949. Although the increment in the multiple correlation squared appears small compared with between-nation variance explained, it accounts for almost half of the total within-nation variance (computed as [.949 − .914]/[1 − .914] = .407).

The second set of columns of Table 17.3 reports the regression when using the Gini coefficient as the measure of income distribution. As in the first column, mean income significantly increases national happiness, and higher inequality significantly decreases happiness.

The last two columns show the existence of upward versus downward comparisons. Similar to the results in Study 1, a thinner upper tail (higher Q5) significantly reduces national happiness. However, a thinner lower tail (higher Ql) does not significantly affect national happiness, contrary to Prediction 4.

Because these data are a time series, several tests were made to check the robustness of the above results. First, a Durbin–Watson test assessed whether residuals were random or whether they were "serially correlated" (which would indicate the presence of some omitted variable; see Judge, Griffiths, Hill, Lutkerpohl, & Lee, 1985). All tests were nonsignificant, suggesting that the residuals were random. Second, a test for "contemporaneous correlation" of residuals measured in the same year was performed (which would indicate an omitted variable such as the occurrence of an oil crisis that was affecting all countries' estimates during a given year; see Judge *et al.,* 1985), by adding dummy variables for each year. Hence if an oil crisis, for example, were contaminating satisfaction for all countries in that year, its effect could be successfully partialed out. Results again showed that coefficients for all four income distribution measures remained significant.

In summary, aggregate happiness of these nations across time shows significant effects of income distribution, supporting the hypothesis that people compare their own household income with the national distribution, as predicted by range–frequency theory.

General Discussion

Evidence for Social Comparison

Two studies showed how the distribution of income in natural communities and nations affects happiness, as predicted by social comparison theory. In the first study, more than 7,000 U.S. adults were analyzed in more than 300 communities. Results showed that a person's own absolute income has the largest effect on happiness, consistent with previous research. In addition, the range (particularly the upper limit) and skew of the income distribution in the community had an effect predicted by range–frequency theory (Parducci, 1995)—for individuals with a given income, communities with higher maximum income and lower skew (more massive upper tails) result in decreasing happiness, in contrast, the mean of the community's income did not affect happiness, because higher mean income was confounded in these communities with higher maximum income and higher skew. This explains why previous studies that measured mean community income did not find the expected social comparison effects.

In the second study, aggregate national happiness was examined in eight nations over a period of 25 years. Once again, the skew of the income distribution within a nation was found to affect national happiness in the predicted direction. For aggregate happiness, higher skew (less mass in the upper tail) was associated with lower happiness, consistent with predictions of range–frequency theory. The only deviation from the theory was that the lower tail of the distribution did not affect national happiness. Instead, only the upper tail appeared to be the relevant comparison group in these data.

An important caveat in these interpretations is that neither survey directly measured people's comparison group. Therefore social comparison is simply inferred by the effects that a community's income distribution has on happiness (similar to the inferences by Diener *et al.*, 1993, 1995). Better evidence would be obtained by eliciting respondents' reports of which groups they actually compare themselves with and then by using these reports as a mediating variable.

A related problem is that range–frequency theory is silent on the appropriate comparison group. Do individuals compare their own income with other individuals in their household or with other households on their block, in their city, or in their country? In the present study, I assumed that people compare their own household income with others' household income, where "others" are defined as the surrounding SMSA (in Study 1) or as the surrounding country (in Study 2). Future work could profitably test alternative definitions of comparison group by using the methods above.

The variance accounted for in Study 1 was rather small, though is larger than the R^2 of 1.7% reported by Diener *et al.* (1993). This small multiple regression coefficient squared is common in cross-sectional studies of individuals in natural settings. In contrast, aggregate studies of entire nations tend to show much higher variance accounted for. More than 40% of within-nation variance in Study 2 was explained by mean income and skew. These results also agree with findings on the relationship between happiness and unemployment. Clark and Oswald (1994) reported that British workers' happiness declined less when unemployed in a community where many people were unemployed; these results are supportive of social comparison effects.

Are We Doomed to the Hedonic Treadmill Because of Social Comparison Effects?

Brickman and Campbell (1971) and Easterlin (1995) point out that if people judge happiness through purely relative comparisons, then society may be doomed to the "hedonic treadmill." The treadmill results when each person attempts to increase their own happiness (e.g., by working for more income), but when all others do the same, everyone's happiness returns to its starting value, and the cycle begins all over again. Such an outcome

would be disheartening for social planners who wish to increase overall SWB.

Although the results here confirm the existence of social comparison effects, the magnitude of their effects is always smaller than the magnitude of the effect of absolute income. The standardized beta coefficient for absolute income in Study 1 was about as large as the sum of all betas for social comparison effects. Similarly, Study 2 showed that the beta coefficient for absolute mean income was always significant (contrary to a pure social comparison model), and it was always larger than that for income distribution. Hence, although social comparison does play a role in judgments of SWB, its role is not so large that we are doomed to the hedonic treadmill. On the contrary, the results here open three possible paths to increase national happiness: (a) by increasing average national income, (b) by reducing the range or skew of income distribution, or (c) by changing the reference group with which people compare themselves.

The most direct route to increasing national happiness would be to increase average income in the country. This is the traditional path followed by proponents of economic development. But my results show that the distribution of income matters, too.

As an example of this, researchers have long been puzzled about why national happiness in the United States has not increased much since 1972, even though average real income has increased by over 40% (Easterlin, 1995). The results above supply an answer: range and skew of income in the United States have been increasing at the same time (in my data, skew increased from .68 to .92), thus canceling out some of the gains due to increased average income. In contrast, several European countries (where skew has not increased so much) have successfully increased average happiness (Hagerty & Veenhoven, 1999).

However, far more research is needed on the long-term effects of income distribution before policy recommendations can be made. For example, social comparison theory does not take into account a possible feedback loop that economists propose. If skew is reduced by limiting maximum incomes (as European socialist governments propose), then overall happiness may be improved in the current period, but future periods may be impacted because the rewards to scientists and entrepreneurs to innovate are reduced. Under this argument, average income in future periods is reduced, which in turn reduces happiness. Future studies could examine this feedback hypothesis.

Although reducing skew or range may reduce innovation, there is a third way of increasing aggregate happiness through social comparison: by changing the reference group with which people compare themselves. Currently, people compare themselves with others in their community and nation that are currently alive (and in Study 2, to the richest people alive). Parducci (1995) recommended that the perceived reference group could be modified by increasing the salience of a new reference group. For example, people could choose to compare themselves with (and media could feature stories about) others who are much worse off, extending the range downward. This would be a conscious selection of the coping variant (Wood, 1996) of social comparison to increase happiness.

I propose another reference group, that people compare themselves with their own ancestors and ask themselves, "Am I better off or worse off than they were?" Such a historical comparison has the advantage that aggregate human happiness can increase even though no living persons are kept miserable, in contrast to most social comparison solutions. It also has the benefit that it focuses attention on whether the person (and the nation) is making progress over time.

Finally, moral philosophers may be disappointed that the existence of poverty (the lower tail of the income distribution) does not detract from the happiness of the rest of the nation through altruistic empathy. On the contrary, both studies confirm the social comparison prediction that the existence of the lower income tails actually increases average happiness (though not significantly in Study 2). Even though altruism is a well-documented effect in small groups of animals or in family groups, it does not appear to operate in the larger communities studied here (SMSAs in Study 1, and nations in Study 2). This result might seem to reduce the motivation of the majority to relieve the suffering of a minority. However, concern over equity issues may act at a later point in the causal chain. For example, Klandermans (1989) found that people who have already achieved higher income or success are more likely to initiate political action and protest. These are challenging issues for future research. I invite others to join in mapping the determinants of human happiness.

REFERENCES

Brickman, P., &. Campbell, D. T. (1971). Hedonic relativism and planning the good society. In M. H. Appley (Ed.), *Adaptation level theory: A symposium* (pp. 287–302). New York: Academic Press.

Clark, A. E., & Oswald, A. J. (1994, May). Unhappiness and unemployment. *The Economic Journal, 104,* 648–659.

Davis, J. A. (1984). New money, an old man/lady and "two's company": Subjective welfare in the NORC General Social Surveys, 1972–1982. *Social Indicators Research, 15,* 319–350.

Davis, J. A., & Smith, T. W. (1996). *General Social Surveys, 1972–1996* [Electronic data file]. Chicago: National Opinion Research Center [Producer]. Ann Arbor, MI: Inter-University Consortium for Political and Social Research [Distributor].

Diener, E., Diener, M., & Diener, C. (1995). Factors predicting the subjective well-being of nations. *Journal of Personality and Social Psychology, 69,* 851–864.

Diener, E., & Fujita, F. (1997). Social comparisons and subjective well-being. In B. P. Buunk & F. X. Gibbons (Eds.), *Health, coping, and well-being* (pp. 329–357). Mahwah, NJ: Erlbaum.

Diener, E., Sandvik, E., Seidlitz, L., & Diener, M. (1993). The relationship between income and subjective well-being: Relative or absolute? *Social Indicators Research, 28,* 195–223.

Diener, E., Sun, E. M., Lucas, R. E, & Smith, H. L. (1999). Subjective well-being: Three decades of progress. *Psychological Bulletin, 125,* 276–302.

Easterlin, R. A. (1995). Will raising the incomes of all increase the happiness of all? *Journal of Economic Behavior and Organization, 27,* 35–47.

Hagerty, M. R., & Veenhoven, R. (1999). *Wealth and happiness revisited: Growing wealth of nations does go with greater happiness.* Manuscript in preparation, University of California, Davis.

Helson, H. (1964). *Adaptation-level theory.* New York: Harper & Row.

Judge, G. G., Griffiths, W. E, Hill. C. R., Lutkerpohl, H., & Lee, T. S. (1985). *The theory and practice of econometrics* (2nd ed.). New York: Wiley.

Klandermans, B. (1989). Does happiness soothe political protest? In R. Veenhoven (Ed.), *How harmful is happiness?* (pp. 61–78). Rotterdam, the Netherlands: University of Rotterdam.

McFarland, C., & Miller, D. T. (1994). The farming of relative performance feedback: Seeing the glass as half empty or half full. *Journal of Personality and Social Psychology, 66,* 1061–1073.

Moffitt, R. (1998). *Current population surveys: March individual-level extracts, 1968–1992* (2nd ICPSR version) [Electronic data file]. Madison, WI: University of Wisconsin, Institute for Research on Poverty [Producer]. Ann Arbor, MI: Inter-University Consortium for Political and Social Research [Distributor].

Parducci, A. (1968, April). The relativism of absolute judgments. *Scientific American, 219,* 84–90.

Parducci, A. (1995). *Happiness, pleasure, and judgment: The contextual theory and its applications.* Mahwah, NJ: Erlbaum.

Smith, R. H., Diener, E., & Wedell, D. H. (1989). Intrapersonal and social comparison determinants of happiness: A range–frequency analysis. *Journal of Personality and Social Psychology, 56,* 317–325.

Tabatabai, H. (1996). *Statistics on poverty and income distribution: An ILO compendium of data.* International Labour Office, Geneva, Switzerland.

Veenhoven, R. (1993). *Happiness in nations.* Rotterdam, the Netherlands: Risbo. Data available from web site: *http://www.eur.nl/fsw/research/happiness.*

Wolfson, M. C., & Murphy, B. B. (1998, April). New views on inequality trends in Canada and the United States. *Monthly Labor Review, 121,* 3–23.

Wood, J. V. (1996). What is social comparison and how should we study it? *Personality and Social Psychology Bulletin, 22,* 520–537.

World Bank (1996). *World Development Report.* New York: Oxford University Press.

Received May 4, 1999
Revision received September 13, 1999
Accepted September 16, 1999 ■

Power Moves: Complementarity in Dominant and Submissive Nonverbal Behavior

Larissa Z. Tiedens and Alison R. Fragale

Two studies examine complementarity (vs. mimicry) of dominant and submissive nonverbal behaviors. In the first study, participants interacted with a confederate who displayed either dominance (through postural expansion) or submission (through postural constriction). On average, participants exposed to a dominant confederate decreased their postural stance, whereas participants exposed to a submissive confederate increased their stance. Further, participants with complementing responses (dominance in response to submission and submission in response to dominance) liked their partner more and were more comfortable than those who mimicked. In the second study, complementarity and mimicry were manipulated, and complementarity resulted in more liking and comfort than mimicry. The findings speak to the likelihood of hierarchical differentiation.

Social interactions are filled with subtle behaviors that communicate much about the nature of the relationship (Argyle, 1988; Giles & Powesland, 1975; Goffman, 1959; Mehrabian, 1972; Patterson, 1983). Research has shown that even slight movements of the arm or of a facial muscle affect people's views of their interaction partners (for reviews, see Argyle, 1988; DePaulo & Friedman, 1998).

One aspect of interpersonal impression that appears to be affected by subtle and nonintrusive nonverbal behavior is the dominant–submissive dimension of interpersonal perception (Argyle,

Larissa Z. Tiedens and Alison R. Fragale, Graduate School of Business, Stanford University.

We thank Colin W. Leach and Eileen Zurbriggen for many conversations about this work and detailed comments on earlier versions of this article. We are also grateful to Chris Folkman, Christina Fong, Cristina Jimenez, Arthur Lauer, Joanna Leavitt, Susan Linton, Oliver Sheldon, and Ranjini Vijayaragghavan for their work as experimenters and confederates and to Pam Hinds for allowing us to recruit participants from her classes.

Correspondence concerning this article should be addressed to Larissa Z. Tiedens, Graduate School of Business, Stanford University, 518 Memorial Way, Stanford, California 94305-5015. E-mail: ltiedens@stanford.edu

1988; Ellyson & Dovidio, 1985; Exline, Ellyson, & Long, 1975; Gifford, 1991; Henley, 1977; Keating, 1985; Knutson, 1996). Simple changes in posture are accompanied by differences in perceived dominance. When people expand themselves and take up a lot of space, they are perceived as dominant, whereas when they constrict themselves and take up little space, they are perceived as submissive (Argyle, 1988; Aries, Gold, & Weigel, 1983; Eibl-Eibesfeldt, 1989; Gifford, 1991; Mehrabian, 1972; Spiegel & Machotka, 1974; Weisfeld & Beresford, 1982). Postural expansion can be achieved by moving one's limbs out from oneself (as in arms or legs akimbo), and constriction is achieved by drawing the limbs in or crossing them over one's body and curving the torso inwards. At the very least, these "power moves" communicate the actor's likely status position to observers, probably because postural expansion occurs more frequently among people who are high status and constriction more frequently among people who are low status (Eibl-Eibesfeldt, 1975). Although research has established the effects these movements have on impressions of an actor's status, far less is known about how these behaviors influence behavioral responses of others and whether they affect the nature of relationships with onlookers.

There are at least two forms of systematic effects of these displays on the behaviors of others. First, it is possible that observers respond to these behaviors with assimilative behaviors. People may respond to others who display dominance with dominant displays of their own and respond to submissive behaviors with mutual submission, a pattern we will refer to as *postural mimicry*. Second, it is possible that an observer could respond to dominant and submissive behaviors with contrasting behaviors. Dominant displays could invite submissive responses and submissive displays could invite dominant behavior, a pattern we will refer to as

postural complementarity. The first goal of this article is to determine which of these responses is most likely.[1]

Establishing the typical pattern of responses will elucidate processes involved in defining the relationship between two individuals, and could provide insight into the ways in which status positions are negotiated in relationships. If, in a given relationship, people tend to complement, it suggests that they are prone to differentiate along the dominant–submissive dimension and that this relationship will likely become hierarchical. If instead they mimic, it suggests that they strive toward similarity on the hierarchy dimension and that the relationship can be defined as oriented toward either mutual submission or domination.

The second goal of this article is to examine how these behavioral responses affect the relationship between the two actors. In general, people within a dyad can display behavior that is either similar or different in terms of dominance and submission. We will examine whether this affects the relationship. Specifically, we will test whether postural mimicry or postural complementarity leads to greater affection between people and more comfort in the relationship.

Research in social psychology on the attractiveness of similarity, nonverbal mimicry, and automatic behavior suggests that postural mimicry is the most likely response and will result in the greatest comfort and liking in the relationship. However, research on nonhuman animal behavior suggests that postural complementarity is the norm in many other species, including some of our closest evolutionary relatives. In addition, interpersonal circumplex theories also have suggested that postural complementarity is more likely and creates more warmth in the relationship than mimicry of dominant and submissive behaviors. Each of these approaches is described below.

---

[1] One can imagine a number of additional possible responses. For example, people might accommodate, that is, mimic high-status behaviors but not low-status behaviors (Giles & Powesland, 1975; Gregory & Webster, 1996). Or, people might consistently express dominance with the hopes of always being in a dominant position in the relationship. Finally, people's dominant and submissive behavior might be a reflection of their personality rather than a function of what interaction partners do (Gifford, 1991). Our data will speak to these possibilities as well as to mimicry and complementarity.

The Likelihood and Benefits of Mimicry

People's tendency toward, and preference for, similarity is at the cornerstone of social psychology. Classic studies showed that people change their behavior and conform to others (Asch, 1955, 1956; Sherif, 1936), and, in both romantic relationships and friendships, people are attracted to and like similar others more than dissimilar others (Byrne, 1971; Byrne & Griffitt, 1969; Clore & Byrne, 1974; Duck & Craig, 1978; Hendrick & Page, 1970). Further, they become more similar to their friends and romantic partners over time (Zajonc, Adelmann, Murphy, & Niedenthal, 1987), and relationships with similar others are more satisfying (Antill, 1983; Eysenck & Wakefield, 1981).

One way in which people create similarity is to engage in motor mimicry. The production of a behavior in one person that has just been exhibited by an interaction partner has been demonstrated in a number of contexts and with a number of behaviors (Cappella, 1997; Hatfield, Cacioppo, & Rapson, 1993; Hess, Philippot, & Blairy, 1999). Mimicry is heightened when people perceive themselves as similar (Cappella & Palmer, 1990; Gump & Kulik, 1997), have aligned goals (Lanzetta & Englis, 1989), share attitudes (McHugo, Lanzetta, & Bush, 1991), like the target (Bernieri & Rosenthal, 1991; Noller, 1984), want the actor to have positive perceptions and like them (Bavelas, Black, Lemery, & Mullett, 1986), or have the desire to empathize with the actor (Hoffman, 1984) or with people in general (Chartrand & Bargh, 1999), but these attributes are not necessary (Chartrand & Bargh, 1999; Hatfield et al., 1993). In fact, people seem to mimic without intending to and without realizing that they have done so, a phenomenon that Chartrand and Bargh (1999) called "the chameleon effect."

Like other findings having to do with the benefits of similarity, mimicry seems to result in greater liking, rapport, and comfort with the interaction partner (Bates, 1975; Bernieri, 1988; Bernieri, Gilles, Davis, & Grahe, 1996; Charney, 1966; Chartrand & Bargh, 1999; Hess et al., 1999; LaFrance, 1979; LaFrance & Broadbent, 1976; Manusov, 1993; Trout & Rosenfeld, 1980; for an exception see LaFrance & Ickes, 1981). Indeed, these positive

outcomes of mimicry may be the reason that people are so likely to engage in this behavior (Argyle, 1990). In short, motor mimicry is functional. It serves to create greater warmth and affiliation among interactional partners.

Chartrand and Bargh (1999) provided a methodologically sound test of the tendency for mimicry and its interpersonal consequences, and they suggested a new explanation for the mechanism underlying this phenomenon. They argued that mimicry is a form of automatic behavior. It occurs because the original behavior functions as a prime. They reason that because unconsciously primed constructs appear to create behaviors that reflect the concept (Bargh, Chen, & Burrows, 1996; Dijksterhuis & van Knippenberg, 1998), so too might unconsciously processed behavior of one person create similar behavior in another person. In other words, Person A's behavior primes that behavior in Person B, and thus produces that behavior in Person B. They further suggested that the automaticity of mimicry is particularly functional because it allows people to create interpersonal warmth with little effort.

Research on mimicry is clear, however, that even if it is functional, it does not always occur. Because mimicry is particularly effective at increasing affiliation, it is most likely in those contexts in which affiliation goals are primary (Bavelas et al., 1986; Bernieri & Rosenthal, 1991; Hoffman, 1984; Lanzetta & Englis, 1989; Noller, 1984). For example, Lanzetta and Englis (1989) found that when individuals are in competition, they do not mimic. Similarly, the display of dominance and submissive behavior might implicitly define the context as a competitive one, or at least one in which affiliation is not the most important goal. In addition, Giles and Powesland (1975) suggested that mimicry depends on the status of the actor and argued that people mimic high status people, a pattern they call "accommodation" (also see Gregory & Webster, 1996). Research on accommodation also suggests that mimicry might take a different form for dominance and submissive behaviors. Specifically, because dominance behaviors suggest high status (Ellyson & Dovidio, 1985), it might be that only those behaviors are mimicked, whereas submissive behaviors are not. Thus, although research on nonverbal mimicry suggests that mimicry is widespread, it also provides reason to think that it may not generalize to dominant and submissive nonverbal behavior.

The Likelihood and Benefits of Complementarity

Another possible response to dominant and submissive behavior is complementarity. That is, people might not only avoid mimicking these behaviors, they may in fact engage in the opposite type of behavior. Research in animal behavior and in interpersonal circumplex theories suggests this possibility.

Some researchers have argued that human postural expansion and constriction is reminiscent of the dominance displays in other species. Just as is the case with humans, in at least some species of nonhuman primates such as chimpanzees, dominant group members regularly adopt postures that make them appear as large as possible (de Waal, 1982). Their hair stands on end and they hold their arms and legs extended out from their body. Important for our questions, de Waal (1982) noted that in the chimpanzee colony he studied, these dominance displays were typically responded to with submissive displays. Chimps observing a dominant display constricted themselves and made themselves appear as small as possible. They bowed low to the ground with their limbs pulled in. In other words, the normal pattern of behavior in that chimpanzee colony was a complementary one where dominance was met with submissiveness (also see Goodall, 1986). de Waal's description of the chimpanzees' relationships with each other also suggests that postural complementarity leads to more peaceful relations. On the occasions where dominant displays were responded to with dominant displays, it usually marked the beginning of a long period of sometimes quite violent conflict. Observations of other animals suggest the same kind of pattern (Tinbergen, 1953; Wilson, 1975). However, even though these researchers who work in the context of evolutionary theory suggest that the same patterns characterize

human relations, it is not clear that they must. First of all, human group members may be more conscious and strategic about dominant and submissive behavior, leading them to notice these behaviors and question their legitimacy to a greater degree than other animals. Second, some researchers have suggested that humans have evolved to be more egalitarian in their relationships (Ehrlich, 2000), perhaps making complementarity both less common and less comfortable.

Research in the area of interpersonal circumplex theories also provides some predictions about the dominance–submission dimension of human behavior in social interactions. Interpersonal circumplex theories organize interpersonal behavior along two dimensions (Carson, 1969; Kiesler, 1983; Leary, 1957; Wiggins, 1979, 1982): the affiliation dimension (anchored by *agreeableness* and *quarrelsomeness*) and the control dimension (anchored by *dominance* and *submission*).[2] Circumplex theorists predict that people's behaviors will be similar to interactional partners along the affiliation dimension and opposite along the control dimension, and that when this complementary response occurs, the partners will like each other more and will be more comfortable (Carson, 1969; Horowitz *et al.*, 1991; Kiesler, 1983).

Research testing the predictions of interpersonal circumplex models has provided mixed results. Some studies are supportive (Dryer & Horowitz, 1997; Estroff & Nowicki, 1992; Horowitz *et al.*, 1991; Strong *et al.*, 1988) whereas others are not (Nowicki & Manheim, 1991; Orford, 1986). However, methodological problems abound in this literature (Orford, 1986; Tracey, 1994). For example, these studies often videotape participants, but when the videotapes are coded, the reliability of coders for the control dimension is frequently below acceptable levels. This lack of agreement among coders is probably due to the coding schemes used, which rarely focus on specific behaviors and instead ask for general impressions (Gifford & O'Connor, 1987; Tracey, 1994). Additionally, many

---

[2] Interpersonal circumplex theories suggest that these dimensions are equally applicable to goals and personalities as well as to behaviors.

studies examine complementarity in personalities rather than in specific behaviors. Similarly, confederates are often given general directions about how to act dominantly rather than instructed to engage in specific behaviors resulting in difficulties in knowing how dominance or submission was actually expressed or the timing of the confederates' and participants' behaviors. Further, the interactional partners in these studies sometimes have unequal status roles (such as supervisor and supervisee or therapist and client), which may moderate or interfere with the basic patterns by producing role-consistent expectations and behavior (Orford, 1986; Tracey & Sherry, 1993). Finally, investigators often have not considered baseline behavior rates (Tracey, 1994). Thus, some believe that complementarity hypotheses deserve more careful and precise testing (Estroff & Nowicki, 1992; Nowicki & Manheim, 1991; Tracey, 1994). In the studies presented in this article, we examine complementarity in equal status dyads by looking at a specific behavior (postural expansion vs. constriction), and we examine change over time, which controls for baseline behavior.

All three of the approaches we have discussed (motor mimicry, animal behavior, and circumplex theories) predict that people will behave in the way that will ultimately create the most comfortable relationships. But, they differ in their predictions about what response will lead to the greatest liking and comfort. Mimicry approaches suggest that postural mimicry will have the most positive effects, whereas circumplex theories and the animal research suggest that postural complementarity will have the most positive effects. Therefore, whereas circumplex theories and animal research suggest that dominant behaviors will invite submissive behaviors, motor mimicry research suggests that dominant behavior will evoke the same dominant behavior in another person.

The behavioral responses to submissive and dominant behavior and the psychological outcomes of these responses are important to understand for several reasons. First, these patterns can help us understand the processes underlying the emergence and stability of hierarchies in human groups. Behavioral postural complementarity and comfort with postural complementarity could be two mechanisms that support the spontaneous and unintentional emergence of hierarchical relationships. Second, they allow for an examination of the degree of similarity or difference between humans and some of their animal relatives. Third, they provide an important test of interpersonal circumplex theories. Finally, the existence of dominance complementary behavior would have important implications for recent theorizing about automatic behavior. If postural complementarity occurs, it suggests that there are domains in which a primed construct leads to contrasting rather than assimilative behaviors (also see Dijksterhuis et al., 1998; Park, Yoon, Choi, Kim, & Wyer, 2001; Spears et al., 2001; Stapel & Koomen, 2000).

The Current Research

Our studies examine postural expansion and constriction. These behaviors are ideal because they signal opposite ends of the control dimension and they are also at the opposite ends of a physical continuum (i.e. body span), allowing us to pit a postural complementarity hypothesis against a postural mimicry hypothesis in a precise manner. In the first experiment we tested whether people mimic or complement another's posture, and whether these responses are related to the participants' liking of their partner and their comfort with the interaction. In the second experiment, participants were posed to either mimic or complement a confederate and again we examined how these poses affected comfort in the interaction and liking for the confederate.

The studies presented in this article were designed to be comparable with those of Chartrand and Bargh's (1999). In their first study, participants engaged in a picture description task with a confederate. The confederate then engaged in a nonverbal behavior (a foot movement or a rub on the face). The participants were videotaped and these tapes were later coded for indications of whether the participant engaged in the same behavior as the confederate (i.e. whether they mimicked). The results showed that participants mimicked; they rubbed their face more when interacting with the face-rubbing confederate and they tapped their feet more when interacting with the foot-tapping confederate. In the second study, confederates either mimicked or did not mimic participants while they engaged in the same picture description task. Those who were mimicked liked the confederate more and thought the interaction was smoother than those who were not mimicked.

Our two studies followed roughly the same procedures. However, we examined nonverbal behaviors that communicate dominance or submission. The dominant behavior was postural expansion and the submissive behavior was postural constriction. In the first study, participants engaged in a picture description task with a confederate who was either posed in an expansive (dominant) posture or in a constricted (submissive) posture, and we examined whether the participants expanded or constricted in response. A mimicry approach predicts expansion in the participants exposed to an expanded confederate, whereas a complementary approach predicts expansion in response to the constricted confederate. In the second study both the confederate and the participant were posed in either dominant or submissive postures. We examined whether mimicry or complementarity in posture resulted in the greatest comfort in the interaction and the greatest liking of the confederate.

Experiment 1

Method

Participants

Ninety-eight people (59 male and 39 female), who were on average 22 years old, participated in this experiment. When asked to indicate their ethnicity, 47 described themselves as having European roots, 28 as Asian, 11 as Latino/Hispanic, 8 as African, 1 as Middle Eastern, 1 as Native American, and 2 did not provide any information about their ethnic heritage. Some of the participants ($N = 50$) were paid $15 for their participation. They were recruited from an electronic mailing list maintained by the Stanford Graduate School of Business that

advertises behavioral studies to people who have indicated that they are interested in participating in them. Other participants ($N = 48$) participated in exchange for course credit for an organizational behavior class. Participants from both sources and of both genders were assigned to all conditions and the proportions across conditions were roughly equal. Initial analyses showed that there were no main or interaction effects due to the different sources of participants, so this variable is not discussed further. All participants were run individually with a same-gender confederate.

The data from 3 participants were excluded because during debriefing they said they suspected that their partner was actually a confederate.[3] In addition, 1 participant refused to be videotaped, and equipment malfunction resulted in our losing the video data for another. Therefore, the analyses are based on the remaining 93 cases (56 males and 37 females).

Procedure

Upon arrival at the laboratory, the experimenter led the participant and confederate to the testing room. After the confederate and participant were seated, the experimenter provided a brief description of the study and then both filled out consent forms. The experimenter then provided more detailed directions about how to complete the picture description task. Specifically, the experimenter said that the point of the study was to investigate what features of unique information were important to share. Each participant would see a series of three pictures projected onto the wall behind their partner's head. They were not allowed to turn and look at the pictures displayed behind them and thus would only see the pictures displayed behind their partner. Their task was to provide informative descriptions of the six pictures. The experimenter indicated that the confederate would describe the first picture, which the participant should listen to, and that the participant would describe the second. The two would alternate describing and listening until all

---

[3] Two of these were in the confederate constricted condition and one was in the confederate expanded condition. All three were recruited from the electronic mailing list.

six pictures had been described. The participants were told that after the description component of the task they would be given a stack of similar pictures from which they would have to identify those that had been described to them. In actuality, this picture identification task did not occur. When the picture task began the confederate adopted the required postural position.

Once they were done with the picture descriptions, the experimenter told the participant and confederate that they needed to be separated for the remaining portion of the session. The experimenter led the confederate out, ostensibly to another room. The experimenter returned and handed the participant a questionnaire that contained the questions about the interaction. Once the participant finished the questionnaire, the experimenter told the participant that the experiment was over. Following the methods described in Chartrand and Bargh (1999), the experimenter queried the participants in a "funneled sequence" starting with quite general questions and moving toward more specific questions. In this debriefing session, experimenters noted whether the participants suspected that their partner was actually a confederate, the participants' belief about the hypotheses, their awareness of the posture of the confederate, and their beliefs about how the confederate's posture affected them and the interaction (Chartrand & Bargh, 1999; Neumann & Strack, 2000). Finally, participants were thanked and paid or given course credit.

Materials

The room. The study was run in an approximately 17-ft × 9-ft room that was set up with two chairs side by side against one wall facing a couch against the opposite wall. The confederate always walked in the room first and sat in one of the chairs and the participant was always directed to sit in the couch, across from the confederate. The participants had ample room to move regardless of the confederates' posture. There was a video camera in the corner of the room recording the participant.

Stimuli. Six slides of Kandinsky paintings were used. Three of them ("Black Lines," "Between the

Light," and "Composition in Red") were always shown to the confederate and three of them ("Composition VII," "No. 58," and "Composition No. 2") were always shown to the participant. All of the slides were modern, abstract paintings. These slides were projected using two Kodak Etagraphic slide projectors. One projector displayed the image on the wall behind the confederate and the other displayed the image on the wall behind the participant.

Confederates. There were six confederates; three males and three females. The confederates were undergraduate students and young graduate students. All of them were normally sized for their gender. All were directed to present themselves as a typical undergraduate would and to take care not to wear or do anything that would stand out as unusual or odd to the participants. Participants were always paired with a same-gender confederate. All confederates memorized scripts for each painting they described. There were three conditions in this study: expansion ($N = 36$), constriction ($N = 40$), and neutral ($N = 17$). All confederates were in all three conditions. In the expansion condition, the confederates draped their left arm over the back of the empty chair that was on their left side and they crossed their right leg such that the right ankle rested on the left thigh and the right knee protruded out to the right beyond the edge of the chair they sat in. In the constricted position, the confederates sat with their legs together and their hands in their lap and they slouched slightly. In the neutral condition, the confederates sat straight up with their legs slightly parted and their arms resting on the armrests of their chair. The confederates adopted the required position when the picture description task began and held it throughout the task. The confederates were obviously aware of the conditions, but they were not aware of the hypotheses.

Dependent variables. The most important dependent variable was the posture of the participants, which was coded from the videotapes of the sessions. However, after the picture description task, the participants also filled out a questionnaire on which they indicated the degree to which they felt comfortable with the interaction, the degree to which they liked their partner (the confederate), and the degree to which they considered their partner to be dominant. Four items were averaged to create a composite measure of comfort. These items were ratings of (a) how comfortable the participant was describing the pictures, (b) how comfortable the participant found the interaction, (c) the degree to which the participant felt relaxed during the task, and (d) the reverse of the degree to which the participant felt anxious during the task. All of these ratings were made on 7-point scales, anchored by *not at all* and *very*. The liking composite consisted of ratings of how much the participant liked the partner and how popular the participant thought the partner was. Again, these ratings were made on 7-point scales anchored with *not at all* and *very*. The perceived dominance measure was the average of two trait ratings (self-confident and unself-conscious) made by the participants about their partner on 7-point scales anchored with *not at all* and *very*. Self-confident and unself-conscious are indicators of dominance in Wiggins's (1979) taxonomy interpersonal traits. This measure was used as a manipulation check to determine whether the confederates' postures communicated the desired dominance level.

Posture coding

The videotapes were coded to measure the postural expansion versus constriction of the participants. Coders measured the amount of space that the participant filled by holding a ruler up on the screen and counting the inches from the farthest out points of the body. They took the first posture measure once the confederate started the picture description task and stopped the tape every minute and measured the posture at each of these stopping points. The length of the videos varied, depending on how long the participant spoke, thus the number of measures for a participant ranged from 7 to 16. One coder coded all participants and then another coder coded 48 of the participants to check whether the measure was reliable. The two coders' ratings were highly correlated ($r = .88$), suggesting that this

kind of coding is quite objective. Therefore, the original coder's measures were used in the analyses.

We were interested in how the participants' posture changed over time, and specifically whether they responded to the confederates' positions by becoming larger over time (expanding) or becoming smaller (constricting) over time. Thus, for each participant, we examined the relationship between the body span measure and the time interval at which the measure was taken. Specifically, for each participant, we regressed the body span measure on the time measure. These analyses provided two data points for each participant: a beta score and an intercept. The beta indicates whether the participant tended to expand over time (a positive beta from the regression of body span on time) or whether their posture constricts over time (a negative beta). The betas ranged from −.94 to .89. Using the beta as an indicator of expansion and constriction is ideal because it takes into account and controls for the participants' natural body size and positioning (Tracey, 1994). The intercept is the body span at the first reading (i.e. time = 0). This measure is an estimate of the participants' posture at the beginning of the session and provides the context for the betas. Essentially, it allows us to determine whether people in the different conditions began with a similar or different body span, and thus allows us to better interpret the meaning of the betas.

Results

Manipulation checks

The perceived dominance measure was subjected to a one-way (confederate position: expanded vs. constricted vs. neutral) analysis of variance (ANOVA) in which the three-level confederate position factor was used as a predictor. This analysis showed a main effect for confederate position, $F(2, 90) = 4.42$, $p < .05$, reflecting the predicted pattern that expanded confederates were perceived as most dominant ($M = 4.85$, $SD = 0.81$), then neutral ($M = 4.35$, $SD = 1.53$), and then constricted confederates ($M = 4.16$, $SD = 0.92$); and a linear contrast of these levels was also significant, $F(2, 90) = 8.53$, $p < .01$, providing a replication of the finding that the more expanded an individual is the more dominant that individual appears.[4]

Participants' posture

Initial posture (the intercepts). First, we analyzed the intercepts to determine whether there was consistency across conditions in the participants' initial body span. These intercepts were analyzed by a 3 (confederate posture: expanded vs. constricted vs. neutral) $\times$ 2 (gender: male vs. female) ANOVA. There was a main effect of gender, $F(1, 87) = 7.46$, $p < .01$, because men tended to have a larger initial body span ($M = 11.92$, $SD = 2.80$) than women ($M = 10.58$, $SD = 2.83$). There was no main effect for confederate posture nor an interaction between confederate posture and gender (both $Fs < 0.5$). These null results indicate that there were no differences in the initial postures of participants across conditions (confederate constricted: $M = 11.44$; confederate expanded: $M = 11.42$; confederate neutral: $M = 11.11$).

Posture over time (the betas). The betas derived from the regressions of body span on time indicate the degree to which people expanded or constricted from their original starting point. We performed a Fisher's Z transformation on these betas following the recommendations of Judd and McClelland (1989). We then analyzed this transformed variable with an ANOVA in which the confederates' posture (constricted, expanded, or neutral) and gender were the independent variables. In this analysis, the only significant effect was a main effect of confederate's position, $F(2, 87) = 3.64$, $p < .05$. The pattern supported the complementarity hypothesis. The mean in the expanded condition was negative, indicating constriction ($M = -0.26$, $SD = 0.64$); the mean in the constricted condition was positive, indicating expansion ($M = 0.20$, $SD = 0.68$); and the mean correlation in the neutral condition was close to zero ($M = 0.10$, $SD = 0.72$). A linear contrast

---

[4]Contrast weights here and the subsequent analysis on the beta weights were –1 for constriction, 0 for neutral, and 1 for expansion.

provided evidence that the body span of the participants was linearly negatively related to the body span of the confederates, $F(2, 87) = 7.23$, $p < .01$.

The interaction of participants' and confederates' postural position on impressions

To examine whether participants experienced the greatest liking of the confederate and comfort with the interaction when they mimicked or when they complemented, we transformed the beta measure into a three-level variable (constricting vs. expanding vs. neither constricting nor expanding) by creating three equal sized groups. The range of betas for the constricting group was –.94 to –.33, and the range for the expanding group was .35 to .89. The middle third were considered to be neither constricting nor expanding. Near-zero betas of time and body span can indicate either that the participant's body span was constant over time, or that their movement was random.[5] When this variable is crossed with the confederates' position variable, nine cells are produced, two of which represent mimicry (both participants and confederates expanded and both participants and confederates constricted), two cells represent complementarity (participants expanded while confederate constricted and participants constricted while confederate expanded), and five cells for which there were no predictions either because the confederate was posed in a neutral fashion or because the participant was neither clearly expanding nor clearly constricting. The means, standard deviations, and cell sizes for the liking and comfort variables are displayed in Table 18.1. Because our hypotheses were about the differences between complementary cells and mimicry cells, and because the cell sizes for some of the neutral cells were so small, we collapsed

---

[5]Although it can be problematic to create categorical versions of continuous variables, we thought that the test of the categorical variable better represented our conceptual framework. We were not concerned with the relative rate of expansion or constriction, but rather whether people complemented *or* mimicked. However, the results for regression analyses in which this variable was kept continuous are reported in Footnote 7.

TABLE 18.1. Mean Impression Ratings (and Standard Deviations) as a Function of Confederates' and Participants' Postures in Experiment 1

Relationship impressions and participant's posture	Confederate's posture		
	Expanded	Neutral	Constricted
Liking			
Participant expanding	4.17 (1.20)	4.50 (1.48)	4.44 (1.08)
Cell size	9	6	16
Neither expanding nor constricting	4.62 (.74)	3.70 (2.20)	4.50 (0.85)
Cell size	12	5	14
Participant constricting	5.17 (1.30)	4.50 (0.71)	3.65 (1.08)
Cell size	15	6	10
Comfort			
Participant expanding	4.27 (1.50)	4.99 (1.71)	5.07 (0.91)
Cell size	9	6	16
Neither expanding nor constricting	4.70 (0.97)	4.73 (2.71)	5.45 (0.96)
Cell size	12	5	14
Participant constricting	5.00 (1.24)	4.35 (0.78)	3.98 (0.94)
Cell size	15	6	10

these nine cells into the three most relevant conditions (complementarity, mimicry, and neither complementary nor mimicry) and performed two one-way ANOVAs using this three-level variable as a predictor for the composite liking and comfort variables.[6]

The ANOVA on the liking variable was significant, $F(2, 90) = 3.54, p < .05$,[7] and the complementarity hypothesis was supported over the mimicry hypothesis. Mimicry was associated with less liking ($M = 3.89, SD = 1.14$) than the neither mimicry nor complementary group ($M = 4.44, SD = 1.11$), $t(90) = 1.72, p < .10$, or the complementary group ($M = 4.79, SD = 1.23$), $t(90) = 2.66, p < .01$. The difference between mimicry and complementarity was significant, $F(2, 90) = 7.07, p < .01$.

The ANOVA on the comfort variable was also significant, $F(2, 90) = 3.80, p < .05$, and again provided more support for the complementarity

hypothesis than for the mimicry hypothesis because mimicry ($M = 4.11, SD = 1.21$) was associated with less comfort than neither mimicry nor complementarity ($M = 4.94, SD = 1.35$), $t(90) = 2.43, p < .05$, or complementarity ($M = 5.04, SD = 1.07$), $t(90) = 2.57, p < .05$. Once again, the difference between mimicry and complementarity was significant, $F(2, 90) = 5.63, p < .05$.

Participants' awareness of their responses

We examined the role of conscious cognition about complementarity in two ways; first by looking at the relationship between the manipulation check and the behavioral response, and second by considering the participants' responses to the debriefing. A correlational analysis on the perceptions of dominance and the degree of expanding showed no relationship between these two variables ($r < .1$). Further, during the funnel debriefing, participants

---

[6] Initial analyses showed that the only effect involving gender was a main effect on the liking variable, due to male participants liking the confederates they interacted with more than females. However, because gender did not interact with the postural variable, we present the simpler analyses here.

[7] We also examined the interaction term for the full 3×3 ANOVA. The interaction was marginally significant for both

variables—liking: $F(4, 84) = 2.44, p = .053$; comfort: $F(4, 84) = 2.27, p = .07$. We examined this interaction with regression, keeping the beta variable in its continuous form and examining the interaction between it and the confederates' position. For both liking and comfort, the interaction was significant—liking: $\beta = -.26, t(89) = 2.60, p < .05$; comfort: $\beta = -.22, t(89) = 2.10, p < .05$.

were asked if there was anything that particularly stood out to them about the way in which their partner was seated during the interaction. Only 5 people responded with answers that described something unique about the condition they were in. In addition, none of the participants suggested either the complementarity or mimicry hypothesis when questioned.

Discussion

Overall, this study provides more support for the postural complementarity hypothesis than the postural mimicry hypothesis. Indeed, we found no evidence for generalized mimicry or a more specified mimicry of only certain behavior (i.e. accommodation). Yet, that does not mean that people were insensitive to others' behavior. When the confederate displayed a dominant or submissive posture, participants were likely to respond with the opposite kind of display. Dominance appears to invite submissiveness and submissiveness appears to invite dominance. Dominant and submissive behaviors do not just affect perceptions of the actor, as has been shown in previous research, but also the behavior of people around that actor. These behaviors seem to function as influence techniques that communicate the appropriate positions of each party. But, people seem to be unaware of these effects. Nonetheless, we observed that quickly and automatically people become situated in such a way as to suggest a hierarchically differentiated relationship.

This study also provides some information about the consequences of complementary versus mimicked responses. The results suggest that when people respond to dominance with submissiveness and submissiveness with dominance there is greater comfort and liking. However, when dominance is met with dominance or submissiveness with submissiveness, there is less liking between the interaction partners and the interaction is less comfortable. These patterns suggest that in the short

term, going along with a hierarchical configuration can be more comfortable than fighting it. Indeed, the discomfort that can be a consequence of two people having the same posture may be one reason that people are likely to complement rather than mimic dominant and submissive postural stances.

This study does not establish the causal or sequential nature of the comfort and liking effects. In fact, the design of this study cannot distinguish between the explanation that complementary behavior leads to liking and comfort and the explanation that people complemented when they felt comfortable and liked the confederate and mimicked when they didn't. Thus, in the second study, we used a similar paradigm, but randomly assigned people to either complementary or mimicking conditions. This design allowed us to test whether dominance complementary behavior causes comfort and liking.

Experiment 2

Method

Participants

Eighty participants (34 men and 46 women), who were on average 20 years old,[8] were recruited from two sources. Thirty-seven were recruited from the Stanford Graduate School of Business electronic mailing list described in Experiment 1 and were paid $10 for their participation. Another 43 were recruited from an undergraduate course in organizational behavior, and received course credit for their participation. All of the analyses were originally conducted using participant source as a predictor variable, but because no significant main effects or interaction effects were found, we collapsed this variable and it is not discussed further. The data from 2 participants were excluded because of confederate and experimenter error and from 4 others who suspected that their partner was a confederate.[9]

---

[8] We did not query the participants about their ethnicity in this study, but because the recruitment methods were so similar as the previous study, we expect that the ethnic composition would be similar.

[9] Two of the suspicious participants were recruited from the class and two were recruited from the electronic mailing list. One was in the mimic constricted condition, and the other 3 were in the participant expanded, confederate constricted condition.

Materials and procedure

The picture description task. The picture description task was essentially the same as in Experiment 1. Participants once again sat across from a confederate, who assumed either the constricted or expanded posture. Participants and confederates took turns describing the same six pictures used in the previous experiment. After the picture description task, the participant and the confederate were separated, the participants filled out a short questionnaire, and then the participant was debriefed in the same way as in Experiment 1.

The cover story. The cover story was altered from the previous study. We told the participants that not only were we interested in what features of unique information were shared, but also how physiological arousal is involved in the sharing of unique information. The experimenter explained that we only had sufficient equipment to measure one person's physiological state. The experimenter showed a small skin conductor measurement device (Advanced Technology AT_{64} Portable SCR, Autogenic Systems, Wood Dale, IL) and said that this machine would be used to monitor one person's physiological responses. The experimenter paused and looked back and forth between the participant and confederate, as if choosing between them, and finally asked the participant whether he or she would be willing to have his or her physiological state monitored. All participants agreed. The experimenter then placed small sensors, attached by Velcro, to the fingers of the participants.

Independent variables. The change in the cover story provided justification for the additional randomly assigned variable that was part of this study: the participants' postural pose, which had two levels. The participants were either posed in an expanded or constricted fashion. In the expanded condition, the participants were told that in order for the physiological monitoring to be accurate, the participants needed to keep their hands at heart level. Thus, the participants were

directed to place their arms up on the backs of the empty chairs next to them. In the constricted condition, the participants were told that in order for the physiological monitoring to be accurate, they needed to keep their hands below heart level and thus we requested that they hold their legs together and place their hands on their thighs. Participants in both of these conditions were asked to hold these positions and keep as still as possible through the duration of the information exchange.

Participants were paired with one of six same-gender confederates. The confederates were posed in either an expanded or constricted fashion. As in Experiment 1, the confederates posed once the picture description task began and acted as though it was spontaneous behavior. Thus, the design of the study was a 2 (participant position: expanded vs. constricted) × 2 (confederate position: expanded vs. constricted) factorial, resulting in two mimicry conditions (both expanded and both constricted) and two complementarity conditions (participant expanded and confederate constricted, and participant constricted and confederate expanded).

Dependent variables. The same questionnaire items that were used in Experiment 1 were used in this study to measure liking for the confederate and comfort with the interaction.

Results

Liking the confederate

A 2 (confederate position: expanded or constricted) × 2 (participant position: expanded or constricted) ANOVA was used to analyze the participants' ratings of their liking of the confederate. There were no significant main effects, but the interaction between confederate posture position and participant posture position was significant, $F(1, 70) = 4.89$, $p < .05$. The means involved in this interaction can be found in Table 18.2. The predicted mimicry versus complementarity contrast was significant, $t(70) = 2.21$, $p < .05$, and indicated that participants liked the confederates more in complementary conditions ($M = 5.01$,

TABLE 18.2. Mean Impression Ratings (and Standard Deviations) as a Function of Confederates' and Participants' Postures in Experiment 2

Relationship impressions and participant's posture	Confederate's posture	
	Expanded	Constricted
Liking		
Participant expanded	4.06 (1.08)	4.37 (0.72)
Cell size	20	16
Participant constricted	4.64 (0.97)	4.10 (0.70)
Cell size	19	19
Comfort		
Participant expanded	4.46 (0.98)	5.01 (0.66)
Cell size	20	16
Participant constricted	5.08 (0.95)	4.63 (1.09)
Cell size	19	19

$SD = 0.80$) than in mimicry conditions ($M = 4.56$, $SD = 0.95$).[10]

Comfort with the interaction

A 2 (confederate position: expanded vs. constricted) × 2 (participant position: expanded vs. constricted) ANOVA was also used to analyze the participants' ratings of their comfort with the interaction. There were no main effects, but the predicted interaction between participant and confederate posture position was significant, $F(1, 70) = 4.31$, $p < .05$. The means involved in this interaction are also presented in Table 18.2. Again, the predicted mimicry versus complementarity planned contrast was significant, $t(70) = 2.08, p < .05$, and indicated that participants were more comfortable in complementary conditions ($M = 5.04$, $SD = 0.79$) than in mimicry conditions ($M = 4.59$, $SD = 1.03$).[11]

Participants' awareness of effects

In the funnel debriefing, when asked about what they noticed about how their partner was sitting,

only 5 people in the mimicry conditions noticed that their interaction partner was either "mirroring" their posture or "sitting in the same way" as they were. These people were approximately evenly distributed across the expanded mimicry condition ($N = 3$) and the constricted mimicry condition ($N = 2$). However, none of these participants believed this similarity affected their feelings about the interaction. Three people in the complementarity conditions noticed the way their partner was sitting. None of these participants thought their feelings about the interaction were affected by their partner's posture. None of the participants guessed either the mimicry or complementarity hypothesis. So, once again, most participants were simply unaware of the manipulation, and even those who were aware, did not notice the effects of it.

General Discussion

In the two experiments in this article, participants were exposed to a confederate who displayed dominant or submissive behavior. We examined how these behaviors affected the participants' behavior and their impressions of the interaction. In the first study, we observed that most people respond to another's power moves with complementary responses, and in both studies, we observed that when complementarity occurs, people feel more comfortable. People did not seem aware of their tendency to respond to dominant behaviors with submissive behaviors and submissive behaviors with dominant behaviors, nor did they seem aware of the ways in which interpersonal configurations of dominant and submissive behaviors affected their feelings about their partner and the interaction.

These patterns might help us understand the formation and maintenance of status hierarchies. They show just how easily people can slip into status-differentiated behavior and the feelings that support and reinforce status differentiation. These findings also have implications for recent theorizing on automatic behavior and for interpersonal circumplex theories.

---

[10] This analysis was also run with gender as a predictor. This analysis showed a main effect for gender with women liking the confederate they interacted with more than men. There were no interactions involving gender.

[11] A similar analysis including gender showed no main or interaction effects due to gender.

Implications

These studies provide insight into the negotiation of status positions in relationships in which no prior hierarchy exists. People face such situations continuously through their lives. We meet new people, or work on a new project with an old acquaintance; in these situations people quickly determine who is dominant and who is submissive. These decisions impact future access to resources, power to influence outcomes, and patterns of who will evaluate whom. In initially egalitarian groups and relationships, the first dominant or submissive display provided by an individual may be the result of random movement or may be tactical strategy, but whatever its cause, its result can be a hierarchical relationship if an observer responds in a complementary fashion. The comfort and liking that individuals experience when in complementary situations would further support the emergence of the hierarchical relationship. If people feel better when there are signals that one person is dominant and one person is submissive than when people are displaying similar signals, then people are likely to promote that differentiation. Thus, nonverbal complementarity and the comfort and liking associated with it may encourage hierarchical relationships and help maintain them. Automatic nonverbal complementarity may be one reason that hierarchies are so common and widespread.

Chartrand and Bargh (1999) argued that the combination of the participants' lack of awareness of the confederates' effects on their own nonverbal behavior and the functional interpersonal consequences of this behavior suggest that these behavioral patterns are automatic. Our studies show the same characteristics. The participants were largely unaware of the nonverbal patterns that occurred. Nonetheless, these behaviors affected their comfort and liking, even though they were unaware of this functional aspect of their behavior. Thus, according to Chartrand and Bargh's logic, complementary behavior could also be considered automatic (also see Darwin, 1872/1998, about the habitual nature of many expressive displays; Leary, 1957, who likened complementary behavior to a reflex; and Wright, 1994, who argued that complementarity in animals probably occurs without consciousness).

This means that mimicry may not be the only form of automatic behavior response to others' nonverbal behavior.

Further evidence about whether postural complementarity is automatic is needed, but if indeed it is, then a number of other questions need attention. First, research should investigate whether the automaticity of postural complementarity is an evolved characteristic or, like so many other automatic behaviors, learned through repetition and experience. If it is learned rather than evolved, complementarity should be heightened in people with more experience in hierarchical group settings than in people with less experience in hierarchies. Second, future research should be directed toward understanding the mechanisms involved in this effect. Several possibilities have been suggested to explain automatic unconscious behavior (see Wheeler & Petty, 2001), and of these, two seem the most likely. In his work on the automatic behavior, Bargh has argued that behavior can be created automatically through exposure to semantically similar stimuli (Bargh *et al.*, 1996; Chen & Bargh, 1999; also see Dijksterhuis & van Knippenberg, 1998). However, here we found a contrasting response. This finding allows for the possibility that, in this case, there are stronger associates between opposing constructs (i.e. dominance–submission) than between similar constructs (i.e. dominance–big, submissive–little). Another possibility is that the confederates provided a social comparison target from which the participants contrasted themselves (Dijksterhuis *et al.*, 1998). The confederates' behaviors may have created an extreme exemplar of dominance or submission, from which the participants contrasted in their own self-views. Their behavior may have then reflected those contrasted self-construals (also see Wheeler & Petty, 2001).

Regardless of the exact mechanism involved in producing the behavior, the tendency of people to respond to dominant behavior with submissive behavior and submissive behavior with dominant behavior is consistent with the propositions made by interpersonal circumplex theorists (Carson, 1969; Kiesler, 1983; Leary, 1957). The effects that complementarity had on comfort and liking also support the predictions of interpersonal circumplex theories (Carson, 1969). Thus, these results suggest that interpersonal circumplex theories can help predict and understand interpersonal patterns of nonverbal behavior. Indeed interpersonal circumplex theories could likely be used to understand a host of nonverbal interchanges (Gifford, 1991; Gifford & O'Connor, 1987).

Interpersonal circumplex theorists have been primarily interested in whether personalities can be described along the control and affiliation dimension, whether specific behaviors are affected by proximal relational surroundings, and how the interaction of people's personalities affect relationship satisfaction and quality. Yet, postural complementarity in behavior also has profound implications for topics such as likely group structures. In these studies we showed that people are likely to respond to dominance with submission and submission with dominance and that people are most comfortable when they are in an interaction in which nonverbal behaviors are opposite along the control dimension. Other research has shown that when people display dominant nonverbal behavior, not only do others think they are stronger and more competent (Keating, 1985), but also that they deserve to hold higher status positions (Tiedens, 2001). Thus, these complementing nonverbal behaviors might start a cycle in which people accrue status simply by displaying these behaviors.

Possible Boundary Conditions

Of course, there are probably a number of important boundary conditions to complementary behavior and the interpersonal consequences associated with it. For example, animals are unlikely to display dominance signals unless they are dominant in the group; and, when animals of a lower rank or new to the group or territory display dominance, others express dominance in return (de Waal, 1982). This suggests that complementarity will be strongest when it coincides with formal roles or positions, and may not occur when it contradicts those positions. The kinds of spontaneous reactions we found may be limited to contexts in which there is no prior hierarchy. However, because many relationships, groups, and organizations begin without a formal hierarchy in place, these nonverbal patterns have the potential for powerful effects in many contexts.

Complementary behavior may also be more likely in some kinds of situations than in others. For example, if people are more focused on creating an affiliative and friendly relationship, they may be less likely to engage in hierarchically differentiated behavior than when they are in a task setting. Alternatively, when there are greater rewards associated with being in a dominant position, people may be less willing to adopt a submissive stance.

In addition, complementary behavior in human egalitarian relationships may depend on it remaining unconscious. If people consciously thought about their interaction partner engaging in "a power move," their response might be quite different. They would likely consider whether there is evidence that their partner has the right to behave dominantly and deserves a submissive response. Indeed, consciousness of the expression of dominant and submissive nonverbal behaviors and their effects may empower individuals to purposefully decide on the structure of their relationships, rather than simply falling into a complementary pattern of behavior.

These two studies showed that people's level of comfort with the interaction and the degree to which they liked their partner depended on the interaction of their display and their partner's display. These results suggest that there are some benefits associated with complementary nonverbal behavior. Yet, it is important to be clear about the nature of these benefits. It is likely that in the short term it is easiest and most comfortable not to rock the boat, but that should not be confused with long-term psychological consequences of hierarchically differentiated relationships. In fact, quite a lot of research has shown the severely damaging effects chronic low status can have on mental and physical health (Gilbert, 1992; Stansfield & Marmot, 1992). It is also likely that people who find themselves in domineering positions without the skills or attributes necessary for that position are unhappy and uncomfortable in the long term. Complementary behavior then simply avoids conflict in the short term. Noncomplementary behavior, or dominance-mimicking behavior, may increase conflict immediately, but such conflict may have benefits for the parties in the long term.

Many researchers have noted that hierarchical group structures are omnipresent in both human and nonhuman primate groups (de Waal, 1982, Eibl-Ebbesfeldt, 1989; Goodall, 1971; Lonner, 1980; Murdock, 1945; Wright, 1994), yet, particularly for human groups, there is little information about how group members end up in different status positions and how the negotiation of the positions is achieved. These studies suggest that automatic and unconscious nonverbal postural complementarity may be one crucial step in the little understood process of hierarchy emergence and stability.

REFERENCES

Antill, J. K. (1983). Sex role complementarity versus similarity in married couples. *Journal of Personality and Social Psychology, 45,* 145–155.

Argyle, M. (1988). *Bodily communication* (2nd ed.). London: Methuen.

Argyle, M. (1990). The biological basis of rapport. *Psychological Inquiry, 1,* 297–300.

Aries, E., Gold, C., & Weigel, R. (1983). Dispositional and situational influences on dominance behavior in small groups. *Journal of Personality and Social Psychology, 44,* 779–786.

Asch, S. E. (1955). Opinions and social pressure. *Scientific American, 11,* 31–35.

Asch, S. E. (1956). Studies of independence and conformity: A minority of one against a unanimous majority. *Psychological Monographs, 70* (9, Whole No. 416).

Bargh, J. A., Chen, M., & Burrows, L. (1996). Automaticity of social behavior: Direct effects of trait construct and stereotype activation on action. *Journal of Personality and Social Psychology, 71,* 230–244.

Bates, J. E. (1975). Effects of a child's imitation versus non-imitation on adults' verbal and nonverbal positivity. *Journal of Personality and Social Psychology, 31,* 840–851.

Bavelas, J. B., Black, A., Lemery, C. R., & Mullett, J. (1986). "I show how you feel": Motor mimicry as a communicative act. *Journal of Personality and Social Psychology, 50,* 322–329.

Bernieri, F. J. (1988). Coordinate movement and rapport in teacher-student interactions. *Journal of Nonverbal Behavior, 12,* 120–138.

Bernieri, F. J., Gilles, J. S., Davis, J. M., & Grahe, J. E. (1996). Dyad rapport and the accuracy of its judgment across situations: A lens model analysis. *Journal of Personality and Social Psychology, 71,* 110–129.

Bernieri, F. J., & Rosenthal, R. (1991). Interpersonal coordination: Behavior matching and interactional synchrony. In R. S. Feldman & B. Rime (Eds.), *Fundamentals of nonverbal behavior* (pp. 401–432). Cambridge, England: Cambridge University Press.

Byrne, D. (1971). *The attraction paradigm.* New York: Academic Press.

Byrne, D., & Griffitt, W. (1969). Similarity and awareness of similarity of personality characteristic determinants of attraction. *Journal of Experimental Research in Personality, 3,* 179–186.

Cappella, J. N. (1997). Behavioral and judged coordination in adult informal social interactions: Vocal and kinesic indicators. *Journal of Personality and Social Psychology, 72,* 119–131.

Cappella, J. N., & Palmer, M. T. (1990). Attitude similarity, relational history, and attraction: The mediating effects of kinesic and vocal behaviors. *Communication Monographs, 57,* 161–183.

Carson, R. C. (1969). *Interaction concepts of personality.* Chicago: Aldine de Gruyter.

Charney, J. E. (1966). Psychosomatic manifestations of rapport in psychotherapy. *Psychosomatic Medicine, 28,* 305–315.

Chartrand, T. L., & Bargh, J. A. (1999). The chameleon effect: The perception behavior link and social interaction. *Journal of Personality and Social Psychology, 76,* 893–910.

Chen, M., & Bargh, J. A. (1999). Consequences of automatic evaluation: Immediate behavioral predispositions to approach or avoid the stimulus. *Personality and Social Psychology Bulletin, 25,* 215–224.

Clore, G. L., & Byrne, D. (1974). A reinforcement-affect model of attraction. In T. L. Huston (Ed.), *Foundations of interpersonal attraction* (pp. 143–170). New York: Academic Press.

Darwin, C. (1998). *The expression of the emotions in man and animals* (P. Ekman, Ed.). New York: Cambridge University Press. (Original work published 1872)

DePaulo, B. M., & Friedman, H. S. (1998). Nonverbal communication. In S. T. Fiske, D. Gilbert, & G. Lindzey (Eds.), *The handbook of social psychology* (3rd ed., Vol. 2, pp. 3–40). Boston: McGraw-Hill.

de Waal, F. (1982). *Chimpanzee politics: Sex and power among apes.* Baltimore: Johns Hopkins University Press.

Dijksterhuis, A., Spears, R., Postmes, T., Stapel, D., van Knippenberg, A., & Scheepers, D. (1998). Seeing one thing and doing another: Contrast effects in automatic behavior. *Journal of Personality and Social Psychology, 75,* 862–871.

Dijksterhuis, A., & van Knippenberg, A. (1998). The relation between perception and behavior, or how to win a game of trivial pursuit. *Journal of Personality and Social Psychology, 74,* 865–877.

Dryer, D. C., & Horowitz, L. M. (1997). When do opposites attract? Interpersonal complementarity versus similarity. *Journal of Personality and Social Psychology, 72,* 592–603.

Duck, S. W., & Craig, G. (1978). Personality similarity and the development of friendship. *British Journal of Social and Clinical Psychology, 17,* 237–242.

Ehrlich, P. R. (2000). *Human natures: Genes, cultures and the human prospect*. Washington, DC: Island Press/Shearwater Books.

Eibl-Eibesfeldt, I. (1975). *Ethology: The biology of human behavior*. New York: Holt, Rinehart & Winston.

Eibl-Eibesfeldt, I. (1989). *Human ethology*. New York: Aldine de Gruyter.

Ellyson, S. L., & Dovidio, J. F. (Eds.). (1985). *Power, dominance, and nonverbal behavior*. New York: Springer-Verlag.

Estroff, S. D., & Nowicki, S. (1992). Interpersonal complementarity, gender of interactants, and performance on word puzzles. *Personality and Social Psychology Bulletin, 18,* 351–356.

Exline, R. V., Ellyson, S. L., & Long, B. (1975). Visual behavior as an aspect of power role relationships. In P. Pliner, L. Krames, & T. Alloway (Eds.), *Nonverbal communication of aggression* (pp. 21–52). New York: Plenum Press.

Eysenck, H. J., & Wakefield, J. A. (1981). Psychological factors as predictors of marital satisfaction. *Advances in Behavior Research and Therapy, 3,* 151–192.

Gifford, R. (1991). Mapping non-verbal behavior on the interpersonal circle. *Journal of Personality and Social Psychology, 61,* 279–288.

Gifford, R., & O'Connor, B. (1987). The interpersonal circumplex as a behavior map. *Journal of Personality and Social Psychology, 52,* 1019–1026.

Gilbert, P. (1992). *Depression: The evolution of powerlessness*. New York: Guilford Press.

Giles, H., & Powesland, P. F. (1975). *Speech style and social evaluation*. London: Academic Press.

Goffman, E. (1959). *The presentation of self in everyday life*. New York: Anchor Books.

Goodall, J. (1971). *In the shadow of man*. Boston: Houghton Mifflin.

Goodall, J. (1986). *The chimpanzees of Gombe: Patterns of behavior*. Cambridge, MA: Harvard University Press.

Gregory, S. W., & Webster, S. (1996). A nonverbal signal in voices of interview partners effectively predicts communication accommodation and social status perceptions. *Journal of Personality and Social Psychology, 70,* 1231–1240.

Gump, B. B., & Kulik, J. A. (1997). Stress, affiliation, and emotional contagion. *Journal of Personality and Social Psychology, 72,* 305–319.

Hatfield, E., Cacioppo, J. T., & Rapson, R. L. (1993). *Emotional contagion*. Madison, WI: C. W. Brown.

Hendrick, C., & Page, H. (1970). Self-esteem, attitude similarity, and attraction. *Journal of Personality and Social Psychology, 38,* 588–601.

Henley, N. (1977). *Body politics: Power, sex, and nonverbal communication*. Englewood Cliffs, NJ: Prentice Hall.

Hess, U., Philippot, P., & Blairy, S. (1999). Mimicry: Facts and fiction. In P. Philippot, R. S. Feldman, & E. J. Coats (Eds.), *The social context of nonverbal behavior* (pp. 213–241). Cambridge, England: Cambridge University Press.

Hoffman, M. L. (1984). Interaction of affect and cognition on empathy. In C. E. Izard, J. Kagan, & R. B. Zajonc (Eds.), *Emotion, cognition, and behavior* (pp. 103–131). Cambridge, England: Cambridge University Press.

Horowitz, L. M., Locke, K. D., Morse, M. B., Waikar, S. V., Dryer, D. C., Tarnow, E., & Ghannam, J. (1991). Self-derogations and the interpersonal theory. *Journal of Personality and Social Psychology, 61,* 68–79.

Judd, C. M., & McClelland, G. H. (1989). *Data analysis: A model-comparison approach*. San Diego, CA: Harcourt Brace Jovanovich.

Keating, C. (1985). Human dominance signals: The primate in us. In S. L. Ellyson & J. F. Dovidio (Eds.), *Power, dominance, and nonverbal behavior* (pp. 89–108). New York: Springer-Verlag.

Kiesler, D. J. (1983). The 1982 interpersonal circle: A taxonomy for complementarity in human transactions. *Psychological Review, 90,* 185–214.

Knutson, B. (1996). Facial expressions of emotion influence interpersonal trait inferences. *Journal of Nonverbal Behavior, 20,* 165–182.

LaFrance, M. (1979). Nonverbal synchrony and rapport: Analysis by the cross-lag panel technique. *Social Psychology Quarterly, 42,* 66–70.

LaFrance, M., & Broadbent, M. (1976). Group rapport: Posture sharing as a nonverbal indicator. *Group and Organizational Studies, 1,* 328–333.

LaFrance, M., & Ickes, W. (1981). Posture mirroring and interactional involvement: Sex and sex typing effects. *Journal of Nonverbal Behavior, 5,* 139–154.

Lanzetta, J. T., & Englis, B. G. (1989). Expectations of cooperation and competition and their effects on observers' vicarious emotional responses. *Journal of Personality and Social Psychology, 33,* 354–370.

Leary, T. (1957). *Interpersonal diagnosis of personality*. New York: Ronald Press.

Lonner, W. J. (1980). The search for psychological universals. In H. C. Triandis & W. W. Lambert (Eds.), *Handbook of cross-cultural psychology* (Vol. 1, pp. 143–204). Boston: Allyn & Bacon.

Manusov, V. (1993). "It depends on your perspective": Effects of stance and beliefs about intent on person perception. *Western Journal of Speech Communication, 57,* 27–41.

McHugo, G., Lanzetta, J. T., & Bush, L. K. (1991). The effect of attitudes on emotional reaction to expressive displays of political leaders. *Journal of Nonverbal Behavior, 15,* 19–41.

Mehrabian, A. (1972). *Nonverbal communication*. Chicago: Aldine-Atherton.

Murdock, G. P. (1945). The common denominator of culture. In R. Linton (Ed.), *American Ethological Society monographs* (pp. 123–142). Locust Valley, NJ: J. J. Augustin.

Neumann, R., & Strack, F. (2000). "Mood contagion": The automatic transfer of mood between persons. *Journal of Personality and Social Psychology, 79,* 211–223.

Noller, P. (1984). *Nonverbal communication and marital interaction*. Oxford, England: Pergamon Press.

Nowicki, S., & Manheim, S. (1991). Interpersonal complementarity and time of interaction in female relationships. *Journal of Personality, 25*, 322–333.

Orford, J. (1986). The rules of interpersonal complementarity: Does hostility beget hostility and dominance, submission. *Psychological Review, 93*, 365–377.

Park, J., Yoon, S., Choi, S. J., Kim, K., & Wyer, R. S. (2001). Effects of priming a bipolar attribute concept on dimension versus concept-specific accessibility of semantic memory. *Journal of Personality and Social Psychology, 81*, 405–420.

Patterson, M. L. (1983). *Nonverbal behavior: A functional approach.* New York: Springer-Verlag.

Sherif, M. (1936). *The psychology of social norms.* New York: Harper & Row.

Spears, R., Grodijn, E., Dijksterhuis, A., van Aarst, F., Berg, M., van Dillen, L., *et al.* (2001). *Reaction in action: Intergroup contrast in automatic behavior.* Manuscript submitted for publication.

Spiegel, J., & Machotka, P. (1974). *Messages of the body.* New York: Free Press.

Stansfield, S. A., & Marmot, M. G. (1992). Social class and minor psychiatric disorder in British civil servants: A validated screening survey using the General Health Questionnaire. *Psychological Medicine, 22*, 739–749.

Stapel, D. A., & Koomen, W. (2000). The impact of opposites: Implications of trait inferences and their antonyms for person judgment. *Journal of Experimental Social Psychology, 36*, 439–464.

Strong, S. R., Hills, H. I., Kilmartin, C. T., DeVries, H., Lanier, K., Nelson, B. N., *et al.* (1988). The dynamic relations among interpersonal behaviors: A test of complementarity and anticomplementarity. *Journal of Personality and Social Psychology, 54*, 798–810.

Tiedens, L. Z. (2001). Anger and advancement versus sadness and subjugation: The effects of negative emotion expressions on status conferral. *Journal of Personality and Social Psychology, 80*, 86–94.

Tinbergen, N. (1953). *Social behavior in animals.* New York: Wiley.

Tracey, T. J. (1994). An examination of the complementarity of interpersonal behavior. *Journal of Personality and Social Psychology, 67*, 864–878.

Tracey, T. J., & Sherry, P. (1993). Complementary interaction over time in successful and less successful supervision. *Professional Psychology: Research and Practice, 24*, 304–311.

Trout, D. L., & Rosenfeld, H. M. (1980). The effect of postural lean and body congruence on the judgment of psychotherapeutic rapport. *Journal of Nonverbal Behavior, 4*, 176–190.

Weisfeld, G. E., & Beresford, J. M. (1982). Erectness of posture as an indicator of dominance or success in humans. *Motivation and Emotion, 6*, 113–129.

Wheeler, S. C. & Petty R. (2001). The effects of stereotype activation on behavior: A review of possible mechanisms. *Psychological Bulletin, 127*, 797–826.

Wiggins, J. S. (1979). A psychological taxonomy of trait-descriptive terms: The interpersonal domain. *Journal of Personality and Social Psychology, 37*, 395–412.

Wiggins, J. S. (1982). Circumplex models of interpersonal behavior in clinical psychology. In P. C. Kendall & J. N. Butcher (Eds.), *Handbook of research methods in clinical psychology* (pp. 183–221). New York: Wiley.

Wilson, E. O. (1975). *Sociobiology: The new synthesis.* Cambridge, MA: Harvard University Press.

Wright, R. (1994). *The moral animal: Evolutionary psychology and everyday life.* New York: Vintage Books.

Zajonc, R. B., Adelmann, P. K., Murphy, S. T., & Niedenthal, P. M. (1987). Convergence in the physical appearance of spouses. *Motivation and Emotion, 11*, 335–346.

Received December 7, 2001
Revision received May 28, 2002
Accepted June 7, 2002 ■

PART 6

Social Identity and Reference Group Comparisons

Early research on social comparisons focused on the freedom people have to choose with whom they compare (Hackmiller, 1966; Thornton & Arrowood, 1966; Wheeler *et al.*, 1969), whereas more recent work has focused on the ways in which people respond to comparisons that they encounter (Blanton, 2001; Collins, 1996; Stapel & Koomen, 2001; Tesser, 1988). Both perspectives are of value, but they can each draw attention away from the simple fact that social comparisons are often not about how individuals decide or react. They are often about how group members cannot help but see the implications of their comparisons with others. People frequently cannot help but notice intergroup comparisons, because this information can speak to the value of different groups in society. They also at times cannot help but notice intragroup comparisons, because this information can speak to their own standing within important groups. Fleeing these comparisons would mean leaving the groups that lend a sense of purpose and meaning to an individual's life.

The articles in this section focus attention on two distinct ways in which the group has come alive in the social comparison literature. The first conception of the social group is the *social identity*. A social identity is a self-conception that is derived from membership in a valued group. This type of identification leads group members to "behave the part" of their in-group by adopting stereotypic group attitudes and values. The type of social comparisons that should promote self-esteem would thus be ones that create positive distinctions between the in-group and other out-groups. People should thus seek intergroup comparisons that suggest high in-group status and low out-group status. When individuals compare within their own social groups, this should be in a manner that is characteristic of Tesser's (1988) reflection process. They should seek upward comparisons with in-group members who exemplify the positive qualities of the group, and avoid downward comparisons with in-group members who exemplify the negative qualities of the group.

We refer to the second conception of the group as the *reference frame* view. A reference frame view of a group differs from a social identity view in that in-groups are not seen as identities that are incorporated into the self-concept. Rather, in-groups are treated as social contexts, within which comparisons are made and identities formed. From a reference frame perspective, people do not derive a sense of self-worth from knowing that their groups are high in status. Rather, they gain a sense of self-worth from knowing that they personally are high in status, within the in-group. This view of the group builds on Festinger's (1954) notion that people are most interested in comparing with similar others, and it highlights the importance we often place on comparisons with people who are similar to us via their shared group membership. From a reference frame perspective, the type of comparisons that occur within the group should thus be consistent with Tesser's (1988) comparison process: They should seek downward and avoid upward comparisons with in-group members (and see Brewer & Weber, 1994).

These two distinct views of the group, the social identity view and the reference frame view, can be found in the first two articles in this section. The article by Tajfel and Turner (1986) suggests that

many acts of intergroup discrimination do not simply reflect negative attitudes towards out-groups or actual conflicts that occur when groups compete for limited resources. Rather, discrimination can stem simply from individuals' desire to achieve and maintain self-esteem. By diminishing the status of out-groups (through acts of discrimination), group members raise the status of the in-group, which should promote in-group status and esteem.

In contrast, Miller, Turnbull, and McFarland (1988) point to status conflicts that can occur within a group. Consistent with Festinger's (1954) similarity hypothesis, they argue that people often want to know that they will perform well compared to similar others. However, Miller *et al.*'s conceptualization of "similarity" differs from Festinger's (1954) in that it is based on a shared in-group identity. Recall from the earlier sections that Festinger at times seemed to argue that people want to compare with others on the dimension being compared (e.g., comparing tennis ability with those who are similar in tennis ability). Later, researchers like Goethals and Darley (1977) argued that we seek comparisons with people who are similar on related attributes (e.g., comparing tennis ability with individuals who are the same age, gender, and level of experience). Miller *et al.* suggest another sense in which similarity can matter. They argue that at times we want to know how we stack up relative to people with whom we share important group identities, regardless of whether these others share related attributes or not.

Although the first two articles differ in their description of the group, they resemble one another in their chosen method. They both show that assignment to a "minimal group" can alter the way people act in the laboratory. Specifically, a minimal group assignment can orient people to seek intergroup status (when the group acts as a social identity) or intragroup status (when the group acts as a reference frame). Although these articles focus on minimal groups at the methodological level, they still draw conclusions about real-world group phenomena. The authors consider how their results shed light on problems of class inequality, intergroup conflict, and intergroup discrimination.

The gap between the minimalism of the groups that are studied in the first two articles and the reality of the concerns that the authors wish to consider speaks to a fundamental criticism that many have levelled against social psychology. Many have argued that contrived laboratory methods cannot tell us much about meaningful behaviors that occur in the "real" world. With minimal groups, for instance, it seems doubtful that the experience of being given a label by a psychologist is as meaningful as being born into a racial group or having a lifelong association with a particular ethnicity. It might then seem that a psychological literature that is based on minimal groups cannot speak to the very important everyday groups that structure our lives. Psychologists have responded to this criticism by turning it on its head and arguing that it is *because* many of the groups they study are minimal (and not *despite* this fact) that the social-psychological literature has so much to tell us about group behavior (see Prentice & Miller, 1992). Evidence that something as a seemingly inconsequential as an arbitrary group assignment will alter the way people feel or act towards one another, suggests that people do take their groups very seriously. The first two articles employ groups that are minimal in method, but they hint at two distinct group psychologies that

may be quite rich in meaning: the social identity and the reference frame.

But still, there is value in studying real groups. It is only by studying actual groups that one can understand the specific ways in which groups take hold on individuals. The three remaining articles thus investigate real-world groups. The study by Crandall (1988) was conducted in the reference frame tradition, and it shows that the groups people join exert influence on them, not just because they identify with them, but also because group members work hard to extract conformity from members. Recall that Festinger (1950) argued for exactly this in his paper on social communication. He noted that group members have a shared investment in conformity of opinion and so they actively accept or reject members based on their degree of conformity to group norms. The individual who does not try to live by the rules risks social isolation, diminished self-esteem, and depression. It is for this reason that people often strive to gain status and acceptance in their groups, even when doing so comes at great personal costs. Crandall provides a powerful illustration of this. He shows the destructive influence that groups can have on the health of group members. His study reveals some of the informal social pressures that can promote eating disorders in college sororities. The sad conclusion from his work is that there are times when one must choose between health and status.

The article by Major and Forcey (1985) shows that gender can also create an important frame of reference. Recall that Hagerty (2000) showed in Part 5 that national borders prevent people from comparing their pay with those of people living in other countries. The results of Major and Forcey suggest that our own gender can act as a small nation and define the borders of our comparisons. Because gender is an important identity to many of us, and because we often prefer comparisons with similar others, there is a robust tendency for individuals to compare with others of the same sex. Although there is nothing inherently "wrong" with this tendency, it can be maladaptive if it blinds and pacifies individual to gender-based discrepancies. In their study, Major and Forcey show that the preference to compare with only same-sex others might cause women not to see pay discrimination against women. The use of gender as a reference frame may thus lead women to feel content, even when they are systematically disadvantaged.

But can gender also form a social identity? The article by Blanton, Christie, and Dye suggests that it can. They looked at the effects of math performance comparisons on self-esteem. They hypothesized that whether gender would be treated in this instance as a frame of reference or as a social identity would depend on women's belief in gender stereotypes. Consistent with Goethals and Darley's (1977) concept of related attributes, a woman should be more interested in comparing with other women if she believes that women typically perform worse than men on math tasks. She should therefore feel better when she outperforms other women but not care so much about how she stacks up relative to men. However, if a woman does not buy into gender stereotypes, then the presence of this common stereotype could threaten the value of an important social identity, her gender. She should thus feel encouraged when she sees a woman to do well in math. Women who excel at math challenge a negative gender stereotype and thereby raise the status of a shared social identity. Consistent with this analysis, Blanton et al. found that stereotype endorsement was a crucial moderator of whether women treated their gender as a frame of reference or as a social identity. Sterotype endorsement thus appears to be one factor that can influence how people construe intragroup comparisons, but no doubt there are other variables that lead to dynamic shifts in whether people engage in social identity or reference frame comparisons.

REFERENCES

(Asterisks indicate Key Readings in this section.)

Blanton, H. (2001). Evaluating the self in the context of another: The three-selves model of social comparison assimilation and contrast. In G. B. Moskowitz (Ed.), *Cognitive Social Psychology: The Princeton Symposium on the Legacy and Future of Social Cognition* (pp. 75–87). Mahwah, NJ: Lawrence Erlbaum Associates Inc.

* Blanton, H., Christie, C., & Dye, M. (2002). Social identity versus reference frame comparisons: The moderating role of stereotype endorsement. *Journal of Experimental Social Psychology, 38,* 253–267.

Brewer, M. B., & Weber, J. G. (1994). Self-evaluation effects of interpersonal versus intergroup social comparison. *Journal of Personality and Social Psychology, 66,* 268–275.

Collins, R. L. (1996). For better or worse: The impact of upward social comparison on self-evaluations. *Psychological Bulletin, 119,* 51–69.

* Crandall, C. S. (1988). Social contagion of binge eating, *Journal of Personality and Social Psychology, 55,* 588–598.

Festinger, L. (1950). Informal social communication. *Psychological Review, 57,* 271–282.

Festinger, L. (1954). A theory of social comparison processes. *Human Relations, 7,* 117–140.

Goethals, G. R., & Darley, J. M. (1977). Social comparison theory: An attributional approach. In J. M. Suls & R. L. Miller (Eds.), *Social comparison processes: Theoretical and empiical perspectives* (pp. 259–278). Washington, DC: Hemisphere.

Hackmiller, K. L. (1966). Threat as a determinant of downward comparison. *Journal of Experimental Social Psychology,* (Suppl. 1), 32–39.

Hagerty, M. R. (2000). Social comparisons of income in one's community: Evidence from national surveys of income happiness. *Journal of Personality and Social Psychology, 78,* 746–771.

* Major, B., & Forcey, B. (1985). Social comparisons and pay evaluations: Preferences for same-sex and same-job wage comparisons. *Journal of Experimental Social Psychology, 21,* 393–405.

∗ Miller, D. T., Turnbull, W., & McFarland, C. (1988). Particularistic and universalistic evaluation in the social comparison process. *Journal of Personality and Social Psychology*, *55*, 908–917.

Prentice, D. A., & Miller, D. T. (1992). When small effects are impressive. *Psychological Bulletin*, *112*, 160–164.

Stapel, D. A., & Koomen, W. (2001). I, we, and the effects of others on me: How self-construal moderates social comparison effects. *Journal of Personality and Social Psychology*, *80*, 766–781.

∗ Tajfel, H., & Turner, J. C. (1986). The social identity theory of intergroup behavior. In S. Worchel & G. A. Williams (Eds.), *Psychology of intergroup relations* (pp. 7–24). Chicago: Nelson-Hall.

Tesser, A. (1988). Toward a self-evaluation maintenance model of social behavior. In L. Berkowitz (Ed.), *Advances in experimental social psychology* (*Vol. 21*), (pp. 181–227). New York: Academic Press.

Thornton, D. A., & Arrowood, A. J. (1966). Self-evaluation, self-enhancement, and the locus of social comparison. *Journal of Experimental Social Psychology*, (*Suppl. 1*), 40–48.

Wheeler, L., Shaver, K., Jones, R., Goethals, G. R., Cooper, J., Robinson, J. E. *et al.* (1969). Factors determining choice of a comparison other. *Journal of Experimental Social Psychology*, 5, 219–232.

Discussion Questions

1. Compare and contrast the reference frame and social identity views of social comparisons.
2. What predictions are made from each, and under what conditions are they likely to occur?
3. Festinger (1954) pointed out that people like to compare with others who are similar to them. In what ways can these tendencies in disadvantaged groups lead to the reinforcement of their condition?
4. In what situations might comparisons with similar others help to break the norms that hold their groups down?
5. Both Tajfel and Turner (1986) and Miller, Turnbull, and McFarland (1988) used minimal groups to study group-based comparisons. In what ways do their interpretations of minimal group effects differ?
6. How might these authors use their results to explain such phenomena as: (a) ethnic hatred, (b) the presence of stereotypes, (c) the formation of social cliques in grad schools?

Suggested Readings

Brewer, M. B., & Weber, J. G. (1994). Self-evaluation effects of interpersonal versus intergroup social comparison. *Journal of Personality and Social Psychology*, *66*, 268–275.

Forsyth, D. R. (2000). Social comparison and influence in groups. In J. Suls, & L. Wheeler (Eds.), *Handbook of social comparison: Theory and research* (pp. 81–103). New York: Kluwer Academic/Plenum Publishers.

Hogg, M. A. (2000). Social identity and social comparison. In J. Suls, & L. Wheeler (Eds.), *Handbook of social comparison: Theory and research* (pp. 401–422). New York: Kluwer Academic/Plenum Publishers.

Mullen, B. (1991). Group composition, salience, and cognitive representations: The phenomenology of being in a group. *Journal of Experimental Social Psychology*, *27*, 297–323.

Schachter, S. (1951). Deviation, rejection and communication. *Journal of Abnormal and Social Psychology*, *46*, 190–207.

The Social Identity Theory of Intergroup Behavior

Henri Tajfel* and John C. Turner**

The aim of this chapter is to present an outline of a theory of intergroup conflict and some preliminary data relating to the theory. First, however, this approach to intergroup behavior and intergroup conflict must be set in context, in relation to other approaches to the same problem.

Much of the work on the social psychology of intergroup relations has focused on patterns of individual prejudices and discrimination and on the motivational sequences of interpersonal interaction. Outstanding examples of these approaches can be found, respectively, in the theory of authoritarian personality (Adorno *et al.*, 1950) and in the various versions and modifications of the theory of frustration, aggression, and displacement (such as Berkowitz, 1962, 1969, 1974). The common denominator of most of this work has been the stress on the intraindividual or interpersonal psychological processes leading to prejudiced attitudes or discriminatory behavior. The complex interweaving of individual or interpersonal behavior with the contextual social processes of intergroup conflict and their psychological effects has not been in the focus of the social psychologist's preoccupations (see

* Formerly of the University of Bristol, UK.
** Macquarie University, Australia.

Tajfel, 1981, pp. 13–56, and Turner & Giles, 1981, for more detailed discussions).

The alternative to these approaches has been represented by the work of Muzafer Sherif and his associates and has been referred to by D. T. Campbell (1965) as the "realistic group conflict theory" (RCT). Its point of departure for the explanation of intergroup behavior is in what Sherif (1967) has called the functional relations between social groups. Its central hypothesis—"real conflict of group interests causes intergroup conflict"—is deceptively simple, intuitively convincing, and has received strong empirical support (including Avigdor, 1953; Bass & Dunteman, 1963; Blake & Mouton, 1961, 1962; Diab, 1970; Harvey, 1956; Johnson, 1967; Sherif *et al.*, 1961; Sherif & Sherif, 1953).

RCT was pioneered in social psychology by the Sherifs, who provided both an etiology of intergroup hostility and a theory of competition as realistic and instrumental in character, motivated by rewards which, in principle, are extrinsic to the intergroup situation (see Deutsch, 1949; Julian, 1968). Opposed group interests in obtaining scarce resources promote competition, and positively interdependent (superordinate) goals facilitate cooperation. Conflicting interests develop, through competition, into overt social conflict. It appears, too, that intergroup competition enhances intra-group morale, cohesiveness, and cooperation (Fiedler, 1967; Kalin & Marlowe, 1968; Vinacke, 1964). Thus, real conflicts of group interests not only create antagonistic intergroup relations but also heighten identification with, and positive attachment to, the in-group.

This identification with the in-group, however, has been given relatively little prominence in RCT as a theoretical problem in its own right. The development of in-group identifications is seen in RCT almost as an epiphenomenon of intergroup conflict. As treated by RCT, these identifications are associated with certain patterns of intergroup relations, but the theory does not focus either upon the processes underlying the development and maintenance of group identity nor upon the possibly autonomous effects upon the in-group and intergroup behavior of these "subjective" aspects of group membership. It is our contention that the relative neglect of these processes in RCT is responsible for some inconsistencies between the empirical data and the theory in its "classical" form. In this sense, the theoretical orientation to be outlined here is intended not to replace RCT, but to supplement it in some respects that seem to us essential for an adequate social psychology of intergroup conflict—particularly as the understanding of the psychological aspects of social change cannot be achieved without an appropriate analysis of the social psychology of social conflict.

The Social Context of Intergroup Behavior

Our point of departure for the discussion to follow will be an a priori distinction between two extremes of social behavior, corresponding to what we shall call interpersonal versus intergroup behavior. At one extreme (which most probably is found in its pure form only rarely in real life) is the interaction between two or more individuals that is fully determined by their interpersonal relationships and individual characteristics, and not at all affected by various social groups or categories to which they respectively belong. The other extreme consists of interactions between two or more individuals (or groups of individuals) that are fully determined by their respective memberships in various social groups or categories, and not at all affected by the interindividual personal relationships between the people involved. Here again, it is probable that pure forms of this extreme are found only infrequently in real social situations. Examples that might normally tend to be near the interpersonal extreme would be the relations between wife and husband or between old friends. Examples that would normally approach the intergroup extreme are the behavior of soldiers from opposing armies during a battle, or the behavior at a negotiating table of members representing two parties in an intense intergroup conflict.

Some of the theoretical issues concerning this continuum are discussed by Turner (1982, 1984), Brown and Turner (1981), and Stephenson (1981); the main empirical questions concern the conditions that determine the adoption of forms of social behavior nearing one or the other extreme. The first—and obvious—answer concerns intergroup conflict. It can be assumed, in accordance with our common experience, that the more intense is an intergroup conflict, the more likely it is that the individuals who are members of the opposite groups will behave toward each other as a function of their respective group memberships, rather than in terms of their individual characteristics or interindividual relationships. This was precisely why Sherif (1967, for example) was able to abolish so easily the interindividual friendships formed in the preliminary stages of some of his field studies when, subsequently, the individuals who had become friends were assigned to opposing groups.

An institutionalized or explicit conflict of objective interests between groups, however, does not provide a fully adequate basis, either theoretically or empirically, to account for many situations in which the social behavior of individuals belonging to distinct groups can be observed to approach the "group" extreme of our continuum. The conflict in Sherif's studies was "institutionalized" in that it was officially arranged by the holiday camp authorities; it was "explicit" in that it dominated the life of the groups; and it was "objective" in the sense that, given the terms of the competition, one of the groups had to be the winner and the other group the loser. And yet, there is evidence from Sherif's own studies and from other research that the institutionalization, explicitness, and objectivity of an intergroup conflict are not necessary conditions for behavior in terms of the "group" extreme, although they will often prove to be sufficient conditions. One clear example is provided by our earlier experiments (Tajfel, 1970; Tajfel *et al.*, 1971), which we shall discuss briefly below, in which it was found that intergroup discrimination existed in conditions of minimal in group affiliation, anonymity of group membership, absence of conflicts of interest, and absence of previous hostility between the groups.

Other social and behavioral continua are associated with the interpersonal–intergroup continuum. One of them may serve to summarize a quasiideological dimension of attitudes, values, and beliefs that may be plausibly hypothesized to play a causal role in relation to it. This dimension will also be characterized by its two extremes, which we shall refer to as "social mobility" and "social change." These terms are not used here in their sociological sense. They refer instead to individuals' belief systems about the nature and the structure of the relations between social groups in their society. The belief system of "social mobility" is based on the general assumption that the society in which the individuals live is a flexible and permeable one, so that if they are not satisfied, for whatever reason, with the conditions imposed upon their lives by membership in social groups or social categories to which they belong, it is possible for them (be it through talent, hard work, good luck, or whatever other means) to move individually into another group that suits them better. A good example of this system of beliefs, built into the explicit cultural and ideological traditions of a society, is provided in the following passage from Hirschman (1970):

> The traditional American idea of success confirms the hold which exit has had on the national imagination. Success—or, what amounts to the same thing, upward social mobility—has long been conceived in terms of evolutionary individualism. The successful individual who starts out at a low rung of the social ladder, necessarily leaves his own group as

he rises; he "passes" into, or is "accepted" by, the next higher group. He takes his immediate family along, but hardly anyone else. (pp. 108–109)

At the other extreme, the belief system of "social change" implies that the nature and structure of the relations between social groups in the society is characterized by marked stratification, making it impossible or very difficult for individuals, as individuals, to divest themselves of an unsatisfactory, underprivileged, or stigmatized group membership. The economic or social realities of a society may be such (as, for example, in the case of the millions of unemployed during the Depression of the 1930s) that the impossibility of "getting out" on one's own, as an individual, becomes an everyday reality that determines many forms of intergroup social behavior. But even this example is still relatively extreme. Many social intergroup situations that contain, for whatever reasons, strong elements of stratification perceived as such may tend to move social behavior away from the pole of interpersonal patterns toward the pole of intergroup patterns. This is as true of groups that are "superior" in a social system as of those that are "inferior" in it. The major characteristic of social behavior related to this belief is that, in the relevant intergroup situations, individuals will not interact *as* individuals, on the basis of their individual characteristics or interpersonal relationships, but as members of their groups standing in certain defined relationships to members of other groups.

Obviously, one must expect a marked correlation between the degree of objective stratification in a social system (however measured) and the social diffusion and intensity of the belief system of "social change." This, however, cannot be a one-to-one relationship for a number of reasons, some, of which will be discussed below, although we cannot in this chapter go into the details of the many social-psychological conditions that may determine the transition in certain social groups from an acceptance of stratification to behavior characteristic of the intergroup pole of our first continuum—that is, to the creation of social movements aiming to change (or to preserve) the status quo (see Tajfel, 1978a; Giles & Johnson, 1981, provide a thorough discussion of this issue in the context of seeking to predict the conditions under which ethnic groups will accentuate their distinctive languages, dialects, or accents).

It may be interesting, however, to point to the close relationship that exists between an explicit intergroup conflict of interests, on the one hand and the "social change" system of beliefs on the other. One of the main features of this belief system is the perception by the individuals concerned that it is impossible or extremely difficult to move individually from their own group to another group. This is precisely the situation in an intense conflict of interests, in which it is extremely difficult for an individual to conceive of the possibility of "betraying" his or her own group by moving to the opposing group. Although this does happen on occasion, sanctions for such a move are, on the whole, powerful, and the value systems (at least in our cultures) are in flagrant opposition to it. To usean example from social-psychological research, it seems hardly possible that one of the boys in Sherif's holiday camps would decide to change sides, even though some of his previously contracted friendships overlapped group boundaries.

The intensity of explicit intergroup conflicts of interests is closely related in our cultures to the degree of opprobrium attached to the notion of "renegade" or "traitor." This is why the belief systems corresponding to the "social change" extreme of our continuum are associated with intense intergroup conflicts. These conflicts can be conceived, therefore, as creating a subclass or a subcategory of the subjective intergroup dichotomization characteristic of that extreme of the belief continuum. They share the basic feature of the "social change" system of beliefs, in the sense that the multigroup structure is perceived as characterized by the extreme difficulty or impossibility of an individual's moving from one group to another.

The continuum of systems of beliefs discussed so far represents one conjecture as to one important set of subjective conditions that may shift social behavior toward members of out-groups between the poles of "interpersonal" and "intergroup" behavior within particular situations and societies. To conclude this part of our preliminary discussion, we must characterize briefly two further and overlapping

continua, which can be considered as encompassing the major consequences of social behavior that approaches one or the other end of the interpersonal–intergroup continuum. They both have to do with the variability or uniformity within a group of behavior and attitudes concerning the relevant out-groups. The first may be described as follows: The nearer members of a group are to the "social change" extreme of the belief-systems continuum and the intergroup extreme of the behavioral continuum, the more uniformity they will show in their behavior toward members of the relevant out-group; an approach toward the opposite extremes of both these continua will be correspondingly associated with greater in-group variability of behavior toward members of the out-group. The second statement is closely related to the first: the nearer members of a group are to the "social change" and the "intergroup" extremes, the more they will tend to treat members of the out-group as undifferentiated items in a unified social category, rather than in terms of their individual characteristics. The vast literature in social psychology on the functioning of group stereotypes in situations of intense intergroup tensions is no more than an example of this general statement.

Thus, this preliminary conceptualization represents an approach to the social psychology of intergroup relations that takes into account social realities as well as their reflection in social behavior through the mediation of socially shared systems of beliefs. This convergence occurs at both ends of the sequence just discussed; at the beginning, because it can be assumed without much difficulty that the "social change" belief system is likely to reflect either an existing and marked social stratification or an intense intergroup conflict of interests, or both; at the end, because the consequences of the systems of beliefs arising from the social situations just mentioned are likely to appear in the form of unified group actions—that is, in the form of social movements aiming either to create social change or to preserve the status quo. We shall return later to an elaboration of the kinds of hypotheses that can be put forward concerning the creation of change versus the preservation of status quo. But before this is done, the realistic group conflict theory must be considered against this general background.

The implications of this conceptualization for intergroup relations in stratified societies and institutions are both evident and direct. Whenever social stratification is based upon an unequal division of scarce resources—such as power, prestige, or wealth—and hence there is a real conflict of interests between social groups, the social situation should be characterized by pervasive ethnocentrism and out-group antagonism between the over- and underprivileged groups (Oberschall, 1973, p. 33). However, decades of research into ethnic-group relations suggest that ethnocentrism among stratified groups is, or at least it has been, very much a one-way street. Milner (1975, 1981) and Giles and Powesland (1975) summarize a great deal of evidence that minority or subordinate group members—such as the American Blacks, the French Canadians, the New Zealand Maoris, or the South African Bantus—have frequently tended to derogate the in-group and display positive attitudes toward the dominant out-group. In other words, deprived groups are not always ethnocentric in the simple meaning of the term; they may, in fact, be positively oriented toward the depriving out-group. Data of this kind are not consistent with a simple application of RCT. (Recent detailed reviews of other field and laboratory data relevant to assessing the validity of the theory are provided by Brewer, 1979, Stephenson, 1981, and Turner, 1981.)

Some writers (including Gregor & McPherson, 1966; Milner, 1975, 1981; Morland, 1969) have argued that the status relations between dominant and subordinate groups determine the latter's identity problems. (By social status we mean a ranking or hierarchy of perceived prestige.) Subordinate groups often seem to internalize a wider social evaluation of themselves as "inferior" or "second class," and this consensual inferiority is reproduced as relative self-derogation on a number of indices that have been used in the various studies. Consensual status itself—where subjective and accorded prestige are identical—is problematic for RCT, which conceptualizes prestige as a scarce resource, like wealth or power. Status differences between groups, like other inequalities, should tend to accentuate the intergroup conflict of interests. Therefore, according to RCT, the impact of low status upon a subordinate group should be to intensify its antagonism toward the high-status group (Thibaut, 1950). Yet, under some conditions at least, low social status seems to be correlated with an enhancement, rather than a lessening, of positive out-group attitudes.

It could be argued that only conflicts of interest perceived as such create hostility. This requires that groups must compare their respective situations. And, according to some views, it is only relatively similar groups that engage in mutual comparisons; therefore, many forms of status differences will reduce perceived similarity (see Festinger, 1954; Kidder & Stewart, 1975). It follows that status systems may reduce social conflict by restricting the range of meaningful comparisons available to any given group. This hypothesis may be a useful tool to account for some of the determinants of social stability; but if it is taken to its logical conclusion, it can account for no more than that. It fails to account for social change (in the sense of changes in the mutual relations, behavior, and attitudes of large-scale human groups that have been distinctly different in status in the past), particularly when the processes of change become very rapid. Status differences between groups often do not remain unilaterally associated with low levels of intergroup conflict. For example, the generalization made above—that certain forms of political, economic, and social subordination of a social group tend to eliminate or even reverse its ethnocentrism—is already dated. Research conducted over the last two decades reveals a changing pattern in intergroup relations. American Blacks (Brigham, 1971; Friedman, 1969; Harris & Braun, 1971; Hraba & Grant, 1970), French Canadians (Berry, Kalin, & Taylor, 1977), New Zealand Maoris (Vaughan, 1978), and the Welsh (Bourhis, Giles, & Tajfel, 1973; Giles & Powesland, 1975), for instance, now seem to be rejecting (or have already rejected) their previously negative in-group evaluations and developing a positive ethnocentric group identity. (Milner, 1981 & Tajfel, 1982b, argue that these new data are likely to be a genuine reflection of social change.) This construction of positive in-group attitudes has often been accompanied by a new militancy over political and economic objectives (see Tomlinson, 1970).

But these developments do not rescue RCT in its original form. The very suddenness with which the scene has changed effectively rules out objective deprivation and therefore *new* conflicting group interests as sufficient conditions for the "subordinate" group ethnocentrism. On the contrary, there has often been less objective deprivation than there was in the past. An active and new search for a positive group identity seems to have been one of the critical factors responsible for the reawakening of these groups' claims to scarce resources (Dizard, 1970).

In summary, RCT states that opposing claims to scarce resources, such as power, prestige, or wealth, generate ethnocentrism and antagonism between groups. Therefore, low status should tend to intensify out-group hostility in groups that are politically, economically, or socially subordinate. The evidence suggests, however, that where social-structural differences in the distribution of resources have been institutionalized, legitimized, and justified through a consensually accepted status system (or at least a status system that is sufficiently firm and pervasive to prevent the creation of cognitive alternatives to it), the result has been less and not more ethnocentrism in the different status groups. The price of this has often been the subordinate group's self-esteem. On the other hand, whenever a subordinate group begins, for whatever reasons, to question or deny its presumed characteristics associated with its low status, this seems to facilitate the reawakening of a previously dormant conflict over objective resources. At the same time, it is likely that one of the counter-reactions from the dominant groups in such situations will be to work for the preservation of the previously existing "subjective" and "objective" differentiations.

A tentative hypothesis about intergroup conflict in stratified societies can now be offered: An unequal distribution of objective resources promotes antagonism between dominant and subordinate groups, provided that the latter group rejects its previously accepted and consensually negative self-image, and with it the status quo, and starts working toward the development of a positive group

identity. The dominant group may react to these developments either by doing everything possible to maintain and justify the status quo or by attempting to find and create new differentiations in its own favor, or both. A more detailed specification of some of the strategies and "solutions" that can be adopted in this situation can be found in Tajfel (1978a); we shall return later to a discussion of some of them. For the present, it will be sufficient to state that, whether valid or not, the hypothesis raises some important theoretical problems that need to be considered. The first question is: What social-psychological processes are involved in the development of positive group identity? The second question concerns the conditions under which the status differences between social groups are likely to enhance or to reduce intergroup conflict. In order to continue the discussion of these questions, we must now abandon speculation and consider some relevant data.

Social Categorization and Intergroup Discrimination

The initial stimulus for the theorizing presented here was provided by certain experimental investigations of intergroup behavior. The laboratory analogue of real-world ethnocentrism is in-group bias—that is, the tendency to favor the in-group over the out-group in evaluations and behavior. Not only are incompatible group interests not always sufficient to generate conflict (as concluded in the last section), but there is a good deal of experimental evidence that these conditions are not always necessary for the development of competition and discrimination between groups (Brewer, 1979; Turner, 1981), although this does not mean, of course, that in-group bias is not influenced by the goal relations between the groups.

All this evidence implies that in-group bias is a remarkably omnipresent feature of intergroup relations. The phenomenon in its extreme form has been investigated by Tajfel and his associates. There have now been in addition to the original studies (Tajfel, 1970; Tajfel *et al.*, 1971) a large number of other experiments employing a similar procedure (methodological and conceptual issues concerning the experimental paradigm are discussed by Aschenbrenner & Schaefer, 1980; Bornstein *et al.*, 1983a; Bornstein *et al.*, 1983b; Branthwaite, Doyle, & Lightbown, 1979; Brown, Tajfel, & Turner, 1980; Turner, 1980, 1983a, 1983b; and the results of the relevant studies are summarized most recently by Turner, 1983a, and in a wider theoretical and empirical context by Brewer, 1979; Brown & Turner, 1981; Turner, 1981, 1982), all showing that the mere perception of belonging to two distinct groups—that is, social categorization per se—is sufficient to trigger intergroup discrimination favoring the in-group. In other words, the mere awareness of the presence of an out-group is sufficient to provoke intergroup competitive or discriminatory responses on the part of the in-group.

In the basic paradigm the subjects (both children and adults have acted as subjects in the various studies) are randomly classified as members of two nonoverlapping groups—ostensibly on the basis of some trivial performance criterion. They then make "decisions," awarding amounts of money to pairs of other subjects (excluding self) in specially designed booklets. The recipients are anonymous, except for their individual code numbers and their group membership (for example, member number 51 of the X group and member number 33 of the Y group). The subjects, who know their own group membership, award the amounts individually and anonymously. The response format of the booklets does not force the subjects to act in terms of group membership.

In this situation, there is neither a conflict of interests nor previously existing hostility between the "groups." No social interaction takes place between the subjects, nor is there any rational link between economic self-interest and the strategy of in-group favoritism. Thus, these groups are purely cognitive and can be referred to as "minimal."

The basic and highly reliable finding is that the trivial, ad hoc intergroup categorization leads to in-group favoritism and discrimination against the out-group. Fairness is also an influential strategy. There is also a good deal of evidence that, within the pattern of responding in terms of in-group

favoritism, maximum difference (MD) is more important to the subjects than maximum in-group profit (MIP). Thus, they seem to be competing with the out-group, rather than following a strategy of simple economic gain for members of the in-group. Other data from several experiments also show that the subjects' decisions were significantly nearer to the maximum joint payoff (MJP) point when these decisions applied to the division of money between two anonymous members of the in-group than when they applied to two members of the out-group; that is, relatively less was given to the out-group, even when giving more would not have affected the amounts for the in-group. Billig and Tajfel (1973) have found the same results even when the assignment to groups was made explicitly random. This eliminated the similarity on the performance criterion within the in-group as an alternative explanation of the results. An explicitly random classification into groups proved in this study to be a more potent determinant of discrimination than perceived interpersonal similarities and dissimilarities not associated with categorization into groups. Billig (1973), Brewer and Silver (1978), Locksley, Ortiz, and Hepburn (1980), and Turner, Sachder, and Hogg (1983) have all replicated this finding that even explicitly arbitrary social categorizations are sufficient for discrimination, and Allen and Wilder (1975) have provided additional evidence for the importance of group classification compared to similarities between people without such classification.

The question that arises is whether in-group bias in these minimal situations is produced by some form of the experimenter effect or of the demand characteristics of the experimental situation—in other words, whether explicit references to group membership communicate to the subjects that they are expected to, or ought to, discriminate. The first point to be made about this interpretation of the results is that explicit references to group membership are logically necessary for operationalizing in these minimal situations the major independent variable—that is, social categorization per se. This requires not merely that the subjects perceive themselves as similar to or different from others as individuals, but that they are members of discrete and discontinuous categories—that is, "groups." Second, a detailed analysis of the subjects' post-session reports (Billig, 1972; Turner, 1975a) shows that they do not share any common conception of the "appropriate" or "obvious" way to behave, that only a tiny minority have some idea of the hypothesis, and that this minority does not always conform to it. Thirdly, the relevant experimental data do not support this interpretation. St. Claire and Turner (1982) exposed observer-subjects to exactly the same experimental cues as normal categorized subjects; the former were required to predict the responses of the latter in the standard decision booklets. The categorized subjects did discriminate significantly, but the observers failed to predict it and in fact expected significantly more fairness than was actually displayed.

The more general theoretical problem has been referred to elsewhere by one of us as follows:

Simply and briefly stated, the argument (e.g., Gerard and Hoyt, 1974) amounts to the following: the subjects acted in terms of the intergroup categorization provided or imposed by the experimenters, not necessarily because this has been successful in inducing any genuine awareness of membership in separate and distinct groups, but probably because they felt that this kind of behavior was expected of them by the experimenters, and therefore they conformed to this expectation. The first question to ask is why should the subjects be expecting the experimenters to expect of them this kind of behavior? The Gerard and Hoyt answer to this is that the experimental situation was rigged to cause this kind of expectation in the subjects. This answer retains its plausibility only if we assume that what was no more than a hint from the experimenters about the notion of "groups" being relevant to the subjects' behavior had been sufficient to determine, powerfully and consistently, *a particular form* of intergroup behavior. In turn, if we assume this—and the assumption is by no means unreasonable—we must also assume that this particular form of intergroup behavior is one which is capable of being induced by the experimenters much more easily than other forms (such as cooperation between the groups in extorting the maximum total amount of money from the experimenters, or a fair division of the spoils between the groups, or simply random responding). And this last assumption

must be backed up in its turn by another presupposition: namely, that for some reasons (whatever they may be) competitive behavior between groups, at least in our culture, is extraordinarily easy to trigger off—at which point we are back where we started from. The problem then must be restated in terms of the need to specify why a certain *kind* of intergroup behavior can be elicited so much more easily than other kinds; and this specification is certainly not made if we rest content with the explanation that the behavior occurred because it was very easy for the experimenters to make it occur. (Tajfel, 1978a, pp. 35–36)

Two points stand out: first, minimal intergroup discrimination is not based on incompatible group interests; second, the baseline conditions for intergroup competition seem indeed so minimal as to cause the suspicion that we are dealing here with some factor or process inherent in the intergroup situation itself. Our theoretical orientation was developed initially in response to these clues from our earlier experiments. We shall not trace the history of its development, however, but shall describe its present form.

Social Identity and Social Comparison

Many orthodox definitions of "social groups" are unduly restrictive when applied to the context of intergroup relations. For example, when members of two national or ethnic categories interact on the basis of their reciprocal beliefs about their respective categories and of the general relations between them, this is clearly intergroup behavior in the everyday sense of the term. The "groups" to which the interactants belong need not depend upon the frequency of intermember interaction, systems of role relationships, or interdependent goals. From the social-psychological perspective, the essential criteria for group membership, as they apply to large-scale social categories, are that the individuals concerned define themselves and are defined by others as members of a group.

We can conceptualize a group, in this sense, as a collection of individuals who perceive themselves to be members of the same social category, share some emotional involvement in this common definition of themselves, and achieve some degree of social consensus about the evaluation of their group and of their membership in it. Following from this, our definition of intergroup behavior is basically identical to that of Sherif (1967, p. 62): any behavior displayed by one or more actors toward one or more others that is based on the actors' identification of themselves and the others as belonging to different social categories.

Social categorizations are conceived here as cognitive tools that segment, classify, and order the social environment, and thus enable the individual to undertake many forms of social action. But they do not merely systematize the social world; they also provide a system of orientation for *self-reference*: they create and define the individual's place in society. Social groups, understood in this sense, provide their members with an identification of themselves in social terms. These identifications are to a very large extent relational and comparative: they define the individual as similar to or different from, as "better" or "worse" than, members of other groups. It is in a strictly limited sense, arising from these considerations, that we use the term *social identity*. It consists, for the purposes of the present discussion, of those aspects of an individual's self-image that derive from the social categories to which he perceives himself as belonging. With this limited concept of social identity in mind, our argument is based on the following general assumptions:

1. Individuals strive to maintain or enhance their self-esteem: they strive for a positive self-concept.
2. Social groups or categories and the membership of them are associated with positive or negative value connotations. Hence, social identity may be positive or negative according to the evaluations (which tend to be socially consensual, either within or across groups) of those groups that contribute to an individual's social identity.
3. The evaluation of one's own group is determined with reference to specific other groups through social comparisons in terms of value-laden attributes and characteristics. Positively discrepant comparisons between in-group and out-group

produce high prestige; negatively discrepant comparisons between in-group and out-group result in low prestige.

From these assumptions, some related theoretical principles can be derived:

1. Individuals strive to achieve or to maintain positive social identity.
2. Positive social identity is based to a large extent on favorable comparisons that can be made between the in-group and some relevant out-groups: the in-group must be perceived as positively differentiated or distinct from the relevant out-groups.
3. When social identity is unsatisfactory, individuals will strive either to leave their existing group and join some more positively distinct group and/ or to make their existing group more positively distinct.

The basic hypothesis, then, is that pressures to evaluate one's own group positively through in-group/out-group comparisons lead social groups to attempt to differentiate themselves from each other (Tajfel, 1978a; Turner, 1975b). There are at least three classes of variables that should influence intergroup differentiation in concrete social situations. First, individuals must have internalized their group membership as an aspect of their self-concept: they must be subjectively identified with the relevant in-group. It is not enough that the others define them as a group, although consensual definitions by others can become, in the long run, one of the most powerful causal factors determining a group's self-definition. Second, the social situation must be such as to allow for intergroup comparisons that enable the selection and evaluation of the relevant relational attributes. Not all between-group differences have evaluative significance (Tajfel, 1959), and those that do vary from group to group. Skin color, for instance, is apparently a more salient attribute in the United States than in Hong Kong (Morland, 1969); whereas language seems to be an especially salient dimension of separate identity in French Canada, Wales, and Belgium (Giles & Johnson, 1981; Giles & Powesland, 1975).

Third, in-groups do not compare themselves with every cognitively available out-group: the out-group must be perceived as a relevant comparison group. Similarity, proximity, and situational salience are among the variables that determine out-group comparability, and pressures toward in-group distinctiveness should increase as a function of this comparability. It is important to state at this point that, in many social situations, comparability reaches a much wider range than a simply conceived "similarity" between the groups.

The aim of differentiation is to maintain or achieve superiority over an out-group on some dimensions. Any such act, therefore, is essentially competitive. Fully reciprocal competition between groups requires a situation of mutual comparison and differentiation on a shared value dimension. In these conditions, intergroup competition, which may be unrelated to the objective goal relations between the groups, can be predicted to occur. Turner (1975b) has distinguished between social and instrumental or "realistic" competition. The former is motivated by self-evaluation and takes place through social comparison, whereas the latter is based on "realistic" self-interest and represents embryonic conflict. Incompatible group goals are necessary for realistic competition, but mutual intergroup comparisons are necessary and often sufficient, for social competition. The latter point is consistent with the data from the minimal group experiments that mere awareness of an out-group is sufficient to stimulate in-group favoritism, and the observations (Doise & Weinberger, 1973; Ferguson & Kelley, 1964; Rabbie & Wilkens, 1971) that the possibility of social comparison generates "spontaneous" intergroup competition.

Social and realistic competition also differ in the predictions that can be made about the consequences for subsequent intergroup behavior of winning or losing. After realistic competition, the losing groups should be hostile to the out-groups victors, both because they have been deprived of a reward and because their interaction has been exclusively conflictual. However, when winning and losing establish shared group evaluations concerning comparative superiority and inferiority, then so long as the terms of the competition are perceived

as legitimate and the competition itself as fair according to these terms, the losing group may acquiesce in the superiority of the winning out-group. This acquiescence by a group considering itself as legitimately "inferior" has been shown in studies by Caddick (1980, 1982), Commins and Lockwood, (1979) and Turner and Brown (1978). Several other studies report findings that are in line with this interpretation: losing in-groups do not always derogate, but sometimes upgrade, their evaluations of the winning out-groups (for example, Bass & Dunteman, 1963; Wilson & Miller, 1961).

Retrospectively, at least, the social-identity/social-comparison theory is consistent with many of the studies mentioned in the preceding section of this chapter. In particular, in the paradigm of the minimal group experiments, the intergroup discrimination can be conceived as being due not to conflict over monetary gains, but to differentiations based on comparisons made in terms of monetary rewards. Money functioned as a dimension of comparison (the only one available within the experimental design), and the data suggest that larger absolute gains that did not establish a difference in favor of the in-group were sacrificed for smaller comparative gains, when the two kinds of gains were made to conflict.

There is further evidence (Turner, 1978a) that the social-competitive pattern of intergroup behavior holds even when it conflicts with obvious self-interest. In this study, the distribution of either monetary rewards or "points" was made, within the minimal intergroup paradigm, between self and an anonymous other, who was either in the in-group or in the out-group. As long as minimal conditions existed for in-group identification, the subjects were prepared to give relatively less to themselves when the award (either in points or in money) was to be divided between self and an anonymous member of the in-group, as compared with dividing with an anonymous member of the out-group. These results seem particularly important, since the category of "self," which is by no means minimal or ad hoc, was set here against a truly minimal in-group category, identical to those used in the earlier experiments. Despite this stark asymmetry, the minimal group affiliation affected the responses.

The theoretical predictions were taken outside of the minimal categorization paradigm in a further by Turner (1978b). He used face-to-face groups working on a discussion task. In each session, two three-person groups discussed an identical issue, supposedly to gain an assessment of their verbal intelligence, and then briefly compared their respective performance. The subjects were 144 male undergraduates. The criterion for intergroup differentiation was the magnitude of in-group bias shown in the ratings of the groups' work. Half the triads, composed of Arts students, believed that verbal intelligence was important for them (High Importance); half, composed of Science students, did not (Low Importance). Half the sessions involved two Arts or two Science groups (Similar Out-group), and half involved one Arts and one Science group (Dissimilar Out-group). Finally, in the Stable Difference condition, subjects were instructed that Arts students were definitely superior and Science students definitely inferior in verbal intelligence; in the Unstable Difference condition, there was no explicit statement that one category was better than the other. These variables were manipulated in a $2 \times 2 \times 2$ factorial design.

The results showed that the Arts (High Importance) groups were more biased than the Science (Low Importance) groups, that similar groups differentiated more than dissimilar groups in the Stable condition, but that they were no more biased (and sometimes even less so) in the Unstable condition; and that, on some of the measures, there was a significant main effect for out-group similarity: in-group bias increased against a similar out-group. Although these data are relatively complex, they do support some of our theoretical expectations and provide an illustration that variations in in-group bias can be systematically predicted from the social-identity/social-comparison theory.

We have argued that social and realistic competition are conceptually distinct, although most often they are empirically associated in "real life." In an experiment by Turner, Brown, and Tajfel (1979) an attempt was made to isolate the effects on intergroup behavior of the postulated autonomous processes attributed to a search for positive social identity. Children were used as subjects, and the manipulations involved decisions by the subjects about the distribution of payments for participation in the experiment, to be shared equally by the in-group, between the in-group and the out-groups that were made relevant or irrelevant to comparisons with the in-group's performance. Monetary self-interest (of a magnitude previously ascertained to be of genuine significance to the subjects) would have produced no difference in the distribution decisions involving the two kinds of out-group; it would also have led to decisions tending toward maximum in-group profit (MIP) rather than toward maximum difference (MD).

MD was the most influential strategy in the choices. Furthermore, when the subjects could choose in-group favoritism (MD + MIP) and/or a fairness strategy, they were both more discriminatory and less fair toward the relevant than the irrelevant comparison group. Other measures of in-group favoritism produced an interaction between reward level and type of out-group: more discrimination against the relevant than the irrelevant group with high rewards, and less with low rewards. Whatever may be other explanations for this interaction, we can at least conclude that when reward levels are more meaningful, in-group favoritism is enhanced against a more comparable out-group, independently of the group members' economic interests. Indeed, insofar as the subjects used the MD strategy, they sacrificed "objective" personal and group gain for the sake of positive in-group distinctiveness.

A study by Oakes and Turner (1982) also deserves mention here since it seems to provide some direct evidence for the social competition interpretation of the minimal group experiments. They simply compared the self-esteem of subjects categorized as in Tajfel *et al.* (1971) but who were not asked to complete the decision booklets with subjects who were categorized and also discriminated in the normal manner. The latter subjects were found to have higher self-esteem than the former—in line with the idea that discrimination serves to achieve a positive social identity. Needless to say, work is progressing to replicate and explore this finding.

On the whole, the above studies provide some confirmation for the basic social-identity/social-comparison hypothesis. Further studies testing the theory in both field and laboratory settings and discussions of its application to the analysis of specific social contexts (e.g., male–female relations, linguistic conflict, Protestant–Catholic conflict in Northern Ireland, prejudice and black identity, etc.) are to be found or are reviewed in Tajfel (1978b, 1982a, 1982b) and Turner and Giles (1981). We shall now attempt to outline in general terms the analysis of inter-group behavior in stratified societies implied by the theory when it is applied to some of the problems raised in the second section.

Status Hierarchies and Social Change

The reconceptualization of social status attempted earlier needs now to be made more explicit. Status is not considered here as a scarce resource or commodity, such as power or wealth; it is the *outcome* of intergroup comparison. It reflects a group's relative position on some evaluative dimensions of comparison. Low subjective status does not promote intergroup competition directly; its effects on intergroup behavior are mediated by social identity processes. The lower is a group's subjective status position in relation to relevant comparison groups, the less is the contribution it can make to positive social identity. The variety of reactions to negative or threatened social identity to be discussed below are an elaboration of the principles outlined earlier in this chapter.

1. Individual Mobility

Individuals may try to leave, or dissociate themselves from, their erstwhile group. This is probably more likely the more they approach the "social mobility" pole of the continuum of belief-systems described previously. This strategy usually implies attempts, on an individual basis, to achieve upward social mobility, to pass from a lower- to a higher-status group. In a four-group hierarchy, Ross (1979) found a direct linear relationship between low status and the desire to pass upward into another group. Many earlier studies report the existence of strong forces for upward social movement in status hierarchies. Tendencies to dissociate oneself

psychologically from fellow members of low-prestige categories are known to many of us from everyday experience: they have been noted more systematically by Jahoda (1961) and Klineberg and Zavalloni (1969), among others, and indiectly by the whole literature on racial identification and preference. The most important feature of individual mobility is that the low status of one's own group is not thereby changed: it is an individualist approach designed, at least in the short run, to achieve a personal, not a group, solution. Thus, individual mobility implies a disidentification with the erstwhile in-group.

2. Social Creativity

The group members may seek positive distinctiveness for the in-group by redefining or altering the elements of the comparative situation. This need not involve any change in the group's actual social position or access to objective resources in relation to the out-group. It is a group rather than an individualistic strategy that may focus upon:

(a) Comparing the in-group to the out-group on some new dimension. Lemaine (1966) found, for example, that children's groups that could not compare themselves favorably with others in terms of constructing a hut—because they had been assigned poorer building materials than the out-group—tended to seek out other dimensions of comparison involving new constructions in the hut's surroundings. The problems that obviously arise here are those of legitimizing the value assigned to the new social products—first in the in-group and then in the other groups involved. To the extent that this legitimization may threaten the out-group's superior distinctiveness, an increase in intergroup tension can be predicted.

(b) Changing the values assigned to the attributes of the group, so that comparisons which were previously negative are now perceived as positive. The classic example is "black is beautiful." The salient dimension—skin color—remains the same, but the prevailing value system concerning it is rejected and reversed. The same process may underlie Peabody's (1968) finding that even when various groups agree about their respective characteristics, the trait is evaluated more positively by the group that possesses it.

(c) Changing the out-group (or selecting the out-group) with which the in-group is compared—in particular, ceasing or avoiding to use the high-status out-group as a comparative frame of reference. Where comparisons are not made with the high-status out-group, the relevant inferiority should decrease in salience, and self-esteem should recover. Hyman's (1942) classic paper on the psychology of status suggested that discontent among low-status-group members is lessened to the degree that intraclass rather than intergroup comparisons are made. More recently, Rosenberg and Simmons (1972) found that self-esteem was higher among blacks who made self-comparisons with other blacks rather than whites. Other work also suggests (see Katz, 1964; Lefcourt & Ladwig, 1965) that, in certain circumstances, black performance was adversely affected by the low self-esteem induced by the presence of the members of the dominant out-group. It follows that self-esteem can be enhanced by comparing with other lower-status groups rather than with those of higher status. This is consistent with the fact that competition between subordinate groups is sometimes more intense than between subordinate and dominant groups—hence, for example, lower-class or "poor white" racism.

3. Social Competition

The group members may seek positive distinctiveness through direct competition with the out-group. They may try to reverse the relative positions of the in-group and the out-group on salient dimensions. To the degree that this may involve comparisons related to the social structure, it implies changes in the groups' objective social locations. We can hypothesize, therefore, following RCT, that this strategy will generate conflict and antagonism between subordinate and dominant groups insofar as it focuses on the distribution of scarce resources. Data relevant to this strategy have been referred to earlier in this chapter.

Let us assume as an ideal case some stratification of social groups in which the social hierarchy is reasonably correlated with an unequal division of objective resources and a corresponding status system (based on the outcomes of comparisons in terms of those resources). Under what conditions will this *not* lead to intergroup conflict—or, more precisely, to the development of competitive ethnocentrism on the part of the subordinate group?

First, to the extent that the objective and the subjective prohibitions to "passing" are weak (see our earlier discussion of the "social mobility" system of beliefs), low status may tend, in conditions of unsatisfactory social identity, to promote the widespread adoption of individual mobility strategies, or at least initial attempts to make use of these strategies. Insofar as individual mobility implies disidentification, it will tend to loosen the cohesiveness of the subordinate group. This weakening of subjective attachment to the in-group among its members will tend: (a) to blur the perception of distinct group interests corresponding to the distinct group identity; and (b) to create obstacles to mobilizing group members for collective action over their common interests. Thus, the low morale that follows from negative social identity can set in motion disintegrative processes that, in the long run, may hinder a change in the group status.

Second, assuming that the barriers (objective, moral, and ideological prohibitions) to leaving one's group are strong, unsatisfactory social identity may stimulate social creativity that tends to reduce the salience of the subordinate/dominant group conflict of interest. Strategy 2(c) mentioned above is likely to be crucial here since, in general, access to resources such as housing, jobs, income, or education is sufficiently central to the fate of any group that the relevant comparisons are not easily changed or devalued. Few underprivileged groups would accept poverty as a virtue, but it may appear more tolerable to the degree that comparisons are made with even poorer groups rather than with those that are better off (see Runciman, 1966).

As noted above, some writers (Festinger, 1954; Kidder & Stewart, 1975) imply that strategy 2(c) is a dominant response to status differences between groups. The assumption is that intergroup comparability decreases as a direct function of perceived dissimilarity. If this were the whole story, then, somewhat paradoxically, the creation of a consensual status system would protect social identity from invidious comparisons. The causal sequence would be as follows: similar groups compare with each other; the outcome determines their relative prestige; the perceived status difference reduces their similarity and hence comparability; intergroup comparisons cease to be made; subjective superiority and inferiority decrease in salience; correspondingly, the groups' respective self-esteems return to their original point. There may be occasions when this social-psychological recipe for the maintenance of the status quo can be observed in something like its pure form. However, we shall argue presently that there are many status differences that do not reduce comparability.

For the moment, we can note that both individual mobility and some forms of social creativity can work to reduce intergroup conflict over scarce resources—though with different implications. The former is destructive of subordinate-group solidarity and provides no antidote to negative social identity at a group level. The latter may restore or create a positive self-image but, it can be surmised, at the price either of a collective repression of objective deprivation or, perhaps, of spurious rivalry with some other deprived group. It is interesting in this context that the French Canadians, having recently gained a more assertive identity, are now apparently more disparaging of other minority groups than are the English Canadians (Berry *et al.*, 1977).

By reversing the conditions under which social stratification does not produce intergroup conflict, we can hypothesize that negative social identity promotes subordinate-group competitiveness toward the dominant group to the degree that: (a) subjective identification with the subordinate group is maintained; and (b) the dominant group continues or begins to be perceived as a relevant comparison group. As a great deal of work has been done in social psychology on the determinants of cohesiveness and loyalty within groups—Hogg (1983), Turner *et al.* (1983), and Turner, Sachdev, and Hogg (1983) have recently looked in particular at the problem of how groups that are associated with

costs and deprivations (such as subordinate ones) are able to maintain their cohesiveness—we shall concentrate on the second condition.

Our hypothesis is that a status difference between groups does not reduce the meaningfulness of comparison between them providing that there is a perception that *it can be changed.* For example, consider two football (or any other) teams that at the end of their season may have come first and second in their league respectively. There is no argument about which has the higher status, but alternative comparative outcomes were and, in the future, still will be possible. When the new season begins, the teams will be as comparable and competitive as they had been before. This example illustrates Tajfel's (1978a) distinction between *secure* and *insecure* intergroup comparisons. The crucial factor in this distinction is whether *cognitive alternatives* to the actual outcome are available—whether other outcomes are conceivable. Status differences between social groups in social systems showing various degrees of stratification can be distinguished in the same way. Where status relations are perceived as immutable, a part of the fixed order of things, then social identity is secure. It becomes insecure when the existing state of affairs begins to be questioned. An important corollary to this argument is that the dominant or high-status groups, too, can experience insecure social identity. Any threat to the distinctively superior position of a group implies a potential loss of positive comparisons and possible negative comparisons, which must be guarded against. Such a threat may derive from the activity of the low-status group or from a conflict between the high-status group's own value system (for example, the sociopolitical morality) and the actual foundations of its superiority. Like low-status groups, the high-status groups will react to insecure social identity by searching for enhanced group distinctiveness.

In brief, then, it is true that clear-cut status differences may lead to a quiescent social system in which neither the "inferior" nor the "superior" groups will show much ethnocentrism. But this "ideal type" situation must be considered in relation to the perceived stability and legitimacy of the system. Perceived illegitimacy and/or instability provide new dimensions of comparability that are directly relevant to the attitudes and behavior of the social groups involved, whatever their position in the system. This is the social-psychological counterpart to what is widely known today as "the revolution of rising expectations." Providing that individual mobility is unavailable or undesirable, consensual inferiority will be rejected most rapidly when the situation is perceived as both unstable and illegitimate. This is (or was) probably the set of conditions underlying the development of ethnocentrism among black Americans, French Canadians, and New Zealand Maoris, for instance. Vaughan (1978) reports that the perceived feasibility of social change (probably including, in this instance, the perceived illegitimacy of the present situation) is an important predictor of the developing Maori ethnocentrism; Friedman (1969) argues that what we may term the "cognitive alternative" of black nationalism in the developing countries was influential in enhancing black American social identity.

On the other hand, when the dominant group or sections of it perceive their superiority as legitimate, they will probably react in an intensely discriminatory fashion to any attempt by the subordinate group to change the intergroup situation. Such perhaps was the postbellum situation in the southern United States: the whites, threatened by those who had been their slaves, rapidly abandoned their paternalistic stereotypes of the blacks as "child-like" in favor of openly hostile and derogatory ones (Van Der Berghe, 1967). The reactions of illegitimately superior groups are more complex (Turner & Brown, 1978). It seems that conflicts of values are reduced by greater discrimination when superiority is assured, but by less discrimination when it is unstable. This calls to mind some Prisoner Dilemma studies in which white discrimination against black opponents increased the more cooperative was the opponent, but decreased the more competitive he was (Baxter, 1973; Cederblom & Diers, 1970). Baxter suggested in the title of his article ("Prejudiced Liberals?") that a conflict of values may underlie his data. Research on the different effects of secure and insecure status differences is reported in Tajfel (1978b, 1982a, 1982b; see also Caddick, 1980; Skevington, 1980).

Many of the points and hypotheses we have advanced in this chapter are not, in themselves, new (see, for instance, Sherif, 1967; Runciman, 1966; Milner, 1975; Billig, 1976). What is new, we think, is the integration of the three processes of social categorization, self-evaluation through social identity, and intergroup social comparison, into a coherent and testable framework for contributing to the explanation of various forms of intergroup behavior, social conflict, and social change. This framework contains possibilities of further development, and to this extent, we hope that it may stimulate theoretically directed research in areas that have not been considered here.

But some cautionary points should be made. The equation of social competition and intergroup conflict made above rests on the assumptions concerning an "ideal type" of social stratification in which the salient dimensions of intergroup differentiation are those involving scarce resources. In this respect, we have simply borrowed the central tenet of RCT. There is no reason, in fact, to assume that intergroup differentiation is inherently conflictual. Some experimental work already points clearly to the conclusion that evaluative derogation of an out-group is conceptually and empirically distinct from out-group hostility (Turner *et al.*, 1979). On the other hand, social identity processes may provide a source of inter-group conflict (in addition to the cases outlined above) to the degree that the groups develop conflicting interests with respect to the maintenance of the comparative situation as a whole. It seems plausible to hypothesize that, when a group's action for positive distinctiveness is frustrated, impeded, or in any way actively prevented by an out-group, this will promote overt conflict and hostility between the groups. This prediction, like many others, still remains to be tested.

"Objective" and "Subjective" Conflicts

None of the arguments outlined in this chapter must be understood as implying that the social-psychological or "subjective" type of conflict is being considered here as having priority or a more important causal function in social reality than the "objective" determinants of social conflict of which the basic analysis must be sought in the social, economic, political, and historical structures of a society. The major aim of the present discussion has been to determine what are the points of insertion of social-psychological variables into the causal spiral; and its argument has been that, just as the effects of these variables are powerfully determined by the previous social, economic, and political processes, so they may also acquire, in turn, an *autonomous* function that enables them to deflect in one direction or another the subsequent functioning of these processes.

It is nearly impossible in most natural social situations to distinguish between discriminatory intergroup behavior based on real or perceived conflict of objective interests between the groups and discrimination based on attempts to establish a positively valued distinctiveness for one's own group. However, as we have argued, the two can be distinguished theoretically, since the goals of actions aimed at the achievement of positively valued ingroup distinctiveness often retain no value outside of the context of intergroup comparisons. An example would be a group that does not necessarily wish to increase the level of its own salaries but acts to prevent other groups from getting nearer to this level so that differentials are not eroded. But the difficulty with this example—as with many other similar examples—is that, in this case, the preservation of salary differentials is probably associated with all kinds of objective advantages that cannot be defined in terms of money alone. In turn, some of these advantages will again make sense only in the comparative framework of intergroup competition. Despite this confusing network of mutual feedbacks and interactions, the distinctions made here are important because they help us to understand some aspects of intergroup behavior that have often been neglected in the past.

A further distinction must be made between explicit and implicit conflicts—a distinction that has to do with conflicts that are "objective" in a different sense. A conflict may be "objective" despite the fact that the goals the groups are aiming for have no value outside of the context of inter-group comparison in that it may be institutionalized and

legitimized by rules and norms (of whatever origin) accepted by the groups themselves. This was the case in Sherif's studies in their phase of competition between the groups; and it also is the case in any football match and in countless other social activities. The behavior toward out-groups in this kind of explicit conflict can be classified, in turn, into two categories, one of which can be referred to as *instrumental* and the other as *noninstrumental*. The instrumental category consists of all those actions that can be directly related to causing the group to win the competition. The noninstrumental category, which could be referred to as "gratuitous" discrimination against the out-group, includes the creation of negative stereotypes and all other aspects of the "irrelevant" in-group/out-group differentiations so well described, for example, in Sherif's studies. The first category of actions is both commonsensically and theoretically accounted for by assuming nothing more than the group's desire to win the competition—although this poses all the theoretical "comparison" problems discussed in this chapter; the second category of actions can be directly and parsimoniously accounted for in terms of the social-comparison/social-identity/positive-in-group-distinctiveness sequence described here.

The implicit conflicts are those that can be shown to exist despite the absence of explicit institutionalization or even an informal normative acceptance of their existence by the groups involved. The proof of their existence is to be found in the large number of studies (and also everyday occurrences in real life) in which differentiations of all kinds are made between groups by their members although, on the face of it, there are no "reasons" for these differentiations to occur. Examples of this have been provided in several studies mentioned in this chapter in which the introduction by the subjects of various intergroup differentiations directly decreased the objective rewards that could otherwise have been gained by the in-group, or even directly by the individual. Findings of this kind, which can be generalized widely to many natural social situations, provide a clear example of the need to introduce into the complex spiral of social causation the social-psychological variables of the "relational" and "comparative" kind discussed in this chapter.

REFERENCES

Adorno, T. W., Frenkel-Brunswik, E., Levinson, D. J., & Sanford, R. N. (1950). *The authoritarian personality.* New York: Harper. 1950.

Allen, V. L., & Wilder, D. A. (1975). Categorization, belief similarity, and intergroup discrimination. *Journal of Personality & Social Psychology, 32*(6), 971–977.

Aschenbrenner, K. M., & Schaefer, R. E. (1980). Minimal intergroup situations: Comments on a mathematical model and on the research paradigm. *European Journal of Social Psychology, 10*, 389–398.

Bass, B. M., & Dunteman, G. (1963). Biases in the evaluation of one's own group, its allies, and opponents. *Journal of Conflict Resolution, 2*, 67–77.

Baxter, G. W. (1973). Prejudiced liberals? Race and information effects in a two-person game. *Journal of Conflict Resolution, 17*, 131–161.

Berkowitz, L. (1962). *Aggression: A social psychological analysis.* New York: McGraw-Hill.

Berkowitz, L. (1969). The frustration-aggression hypothesis revisited. In L. Berkowitz (Ed.), *Roots of aggression: A reexamination of the frustration-aggression hypothesis.* New York: Atherton Press.

Berkowitz, L. (1974). Some determinants of impulsive aggression: Role of mediated associations with reinforcements for aggression. *Psychological Review, 81*, 165–176.

Berry, J. W., Kalin, R., & Taylor, D. M. (1976). *Multiculturalism and ethnic attitudes in Canada.* Kingston, Ontario: Queen's University.

Billig, M. (1972). *Social categorization in intergroup relations.* University of Bristol, Bristol.

Billig, M. (1973). Normative communication in a minimal intergroup situation. *European Journal of Social Psychology, 3*(3), 339–343.

Billig, M. (1976). *Social psychology and intergroup relations* (Vol. 9). London: Academic Press.

Billig, M., & Tajfel, H. (1973). Social categorization and similarity in intergroup behaviour. *European Journal of Social Psychology, Vol. 3*(1), 27–52.

Blake, R. R., & Mouton, J. S. (1961). Competition, communication and conformity. In I. A. Berg & B. M. Berg (Eds.), *Conformity and deviation.* New York: Harper.

Blake, R. R., & Mouton, J. S. (1962). The intergroup dynamics of win-lose conflict and problem-solving collabo-ration in union-management relations. In M. Sherif (Ed.), *Intergroup relations and leadership.* New York: Wiley.

Bornstein, G., Crum, L., Wittenbraker, J., Harring, K., Insko, C. A., & Thibaut, J. (1983a). On the measurement of social orientation in the minimal group paradigm. *European Journal of Social Psychology, 13*, 321–350.

Bornstein, G., Crum, L., Wittenbraker, J., Harring, K., Insko, C. A., & Thibaut, J. (1983b). Reply to Turner's comments. *European Journal of Social Psychology, 13*, 360–381.

Bourhis, R. Y., Giles, H., & Tajfel, H. (1973). Language as a determinant of Welsh identity. *European Journal of Social Psychology, 3*, 447–460.

Brantwaite, A., Doyle, S., & Lightbown, N. (1979). The balance between fairness and discrimination. *European Journal of Social Psychology, 9*, 149–163.

Brewer, M. B. (1979). In-group bias in the minimal intergroup situation: A cognitive-motivational analysis. *Psychological Bulletin, 86*(2), 307–324.

Brewer, M. B., & Silver, M. (1978). Ingroup bias as a function of task characteristics. *European Journal of Social Psychology, 8*(3), 393–400.

Brigham, J. C. (1971). *Views of White and Black schoolchildren concerning racial differences.* Paper presented at the Midwestern Psychological Association, Detroit, Michigan.

Brown, R. J., Tajfel, H., & Turner, J. C. (1980). Minimal group situations and intergroup discrimination: Comments on the paper by Aschenbrenner and Schaefer. *European Journal of Social Psychology, 10*(4), 399–414.

Brown, R. J., & Turner, J. C. (1981). Interpersonal and intergroup behaviour. In J. C. Turner & H. Giles (Eds.), *Intergroup behaviour.* Oxford: Basil Blackwell.

Caddick, B. (1980). Equity theory, social entity and intergroup relations. *Review of Personality and Social Psychology, 1*, 219–245.

Caddick, B. (1982). Perceived illegitimacy and intergroup relations. In H. Tajfel (Ed.), *Social identity and intergroup relations.* Cambridge: Cambridge University Press.

Campbell, D. T. (1965). Ethnocentric and other altruistic motives. In D. Levine (Ed.), *Nebraska Symposium on Motivation* (pp. 283–311). Lincoln, Nebraska: University of Nebraska Press.

Cederblom, D., & Diers, C. J. (1970). Effects of race and strategy in the prisoner's dilemma. *Journal of Social Psychology, 81*, 275–276.

Commins, B., & Lockwood, J. (1979). The effects of status differences, favoured treatment, and equity on intergroup comparisons. *European Journal of Social Psychology, 9*, 281–290.

Deutsch, M. (1949). A theory of cooperation and competition. *Human Relations, 2*, 129–151.

Diab, L. (1970). A study of intragroup and intergroup relations among experimentally produced small groups. *Genetic Psychology Monographs, 82*, 49–82.

Dizard, J. E. (1970). Black identity, social class, and Black power. *Psychiatry, 33*, 195–207.

Doise, W., & Weinberger, M. (1973). Représentations masculines dans differentes situations de rencontres mixtes. *Bulletin de Psychologie, 26*, 649–657.

Ferguson, C. K., & Kelley, H. H. (1964). Significant factors in overevaluation of own group's products. *Journal of Abnormal & Social Psychology, 69*, 223–228.

Festinger, L. (1954). A theory of social comparison processes. *Human Relations, 7*, 117–140.

Fiedler, F. E. (1967). The effect of inter-group competition on group member adjustment. *Personnel Psychology, 20*(1), 33–44.

Friedman, N. (1969). Africa and the Afro-Americans: The changing Negro identity. *Psychiatry, 32*(2), 127–136.

Giles, H., & Johnson, P. (1981). The role of language in ethnic group relations. In J. C. Turner & H. Giles (Eds.), *Intergroup behavior.* Oxford: Basil Blackwell.

Giles, H., & Powesland, P. F. (1976). *Speech style and social evaluations.* London: Academic Press, European Monographs in Social Psychology.

Gregor, A. J., & McPherson, D. A. (1966). Racial preference and ego identity among White and Bantu children in the Republic of South Africa. *Genetic Psychology Monographs, 73,* 217–254.

Harris, S., & Braun, J. R. (1971). Self-esteem and racial preferences in Black children. *Proceedings of the 79th Annual Convention of the American Psychological Association, 6.*

Harvey, O. J. (1956). An experimental investigation of negative and positive relations between small groups through judgmental indices. *Sociometry, 19,* 201–209.

Hirschman, A. O. (1970). *Exit, voice and loyalty: Responses to decline in firms, organizations and states.* Cambridge, MA: Harvard University Press.

Hogg, M. A. (1983). *The social psychology of group-formation: A cognitive perspective.* Unpublished doctoral dissertation, University of Bristol.

Hraba, J., & Grant, G. (1970). Black is beautiful: A reexamination of racial preference and identification. *Journal of Personality & Social Psychology, 16*(3), 398–402.

Jahoda, G. (1961). *White man.* Oxford, England: Oxford University Press.

Johnson, D. W. (1967). Use of role reversal in intergroup competition. *Journal of Personality & Social Psychology, 7*(2), 135–141.

Julian, J. W. (1968). The study of competition. In W. E. Vinacke (Ed.), *Readings in general psychology.* New York: American Book Company.

Kalin, R., & Marlowe, D. (1968). The effects of intergroup competition, personal drinking habits and frustration in intra-group cooperation. *Proceedings of the American Psychological Association, 3,* 405–406.

Katz, I. (1964). Review of evidence relating to effects of desegregation on the intellectual performance of Negroes. *American Psychologist, 19*(6), 381–399.

Kidder, L. H., & Stewart, V. M. (1975). *The psychology of intergroup relations.* New York: McGraw-Hill.

Klineberg, O., & Zavalloni, M. (1969). *Nationalism and tribalism among African students.* The Hague and Paris: Mouton.

Lefcourt, H. M., & Ladwig, G. (1965). The effect of reference group upon Negroes' task persistence in a biracial competitive game. *Journal of Personality and Social Psychology, 1,* 688–671.

Lemaine, G. (1966). Inegalité, comparaison et incomparabilité: Esquisse d'une theorie de l'originalité socialite. *Bulletin de Psychologie, 252*(20), 1–2, 1–9.

Locksley, A., Ortiz, V., & Hepburn, C. (1980). Social categorization and discrimination behaviour: Extinguishing the minimal intergroup discrimination effect. *Journal of Personality and Social Psychology, 39,* 773–783.

Milner, D. (1975). *Children and race.* Harmondsworth, Middlesex: Penguin.

Milner, D. (1981). Racial prejudice. In J. C. Turner & H. Giles (Eds.), *Intergroup behavior.* Oxford: Basil Blackwell.

Morland, J. K. (1969). Race awareness among American and Hong Kong Chinese children. *American Journal of Sociology, 75*(360–374).

Oakes, P. J., & Turner, J. C. (1982). Social categorization and intergroup behaviour: Does minimal intergroup discrimination make social identity more positive? *European Journal of Social Psychology, 10,* 295–301.

Oberschall, A. (1973). *Social conflict and social movements.* New York: Prentice-Hall.

Peabody, D. (1968). Group judgments in the Philippines: Evaluative and descriptive aspects. *Journal of Personality and Social Psychology, 10,* 290–300.

Rabbie, J. M., & Wilkens, C. (1971). Intergroup competition and its effects on intra- and intergroup relations. *European Journal of Social Psychology, 1,* 215–234.

Rosenberg, M., & Simmons, R. G. (1972). *Black and White self-esteem: The urban school child.* Unpublished manuscript.

Ross, G. F. (1979). *Multiple group membership, social mobility and intergroup relations.* Unpublished doctoral dissertation, University of Bristol.

Runciman, W. G. (1966). *Relative deprivation and social justice.* London: Routledge and Keegan Paul.

Sherif, M. (1967). *Social interaction: Process and products.*

Sherif, M., Harvey, O. J., White, B. J., Hood, W. R., & Sherif, C. W. (1961). *Intergroup cooperation and competition: The Robber's Cave experiment.* Norman, OK: University Book Exchange.

Sherif, M., & Sherif, C. W. (1953). *Groups in harmony and tension; an integration of studies of intergroup relations.* New York: Harper.

Skevington, S. M. (1980). Intergroup relations and social change within a nursing context. *British Journal of Social & Clinical Psychology, 19,* 201–213.

St Claire, L., & Turner, J. C. (1982). The role of demand characteristics in the social categorization paradigm. *European Journal of Social Psychology, 12*(3), 307–314.

Stephenson, G. M. (1981). Intergroup bargaining and negotiation. In J. C. Turner & H. Giles (Eds.), *Intergroup behavior.* Oxford: Basil Blackwell.

Tajfel, H. (1959). A note on Lambert's "Evaluational reactions to spoken languages." *Canadian Journal of Psychology, 13,* 86–92.

Tajfel, H. (1970). Experiments in intergroup discrimination. *Scientific American, 223*(5), 96–102.

Tajfel, H. (1972a). Experiments in a vacuum. In J. Israel & H. Tajfel (Eds.), *The context of social psychology: A critical assessment.* London: Academic Press, European Monographs in Social Psychology.

Tajfel, H. (1972b). La catégorisation sociale. In M. S (Ed: *Introduction à la psychologie sociale* (Vol. 1). Paris: Larousse.

Tajfel, H. (1974a). *lntergroup behavior, social comparison and social change.* Paper presented at the Katz-Newcomb Lectures, University of Michigan, Ann Arbor.

Tajfel, H. (1974b). Social identity and intergroup behaviour. *Social Science Information, 13*(2), 65–93.

Tajfel, H. (1975). The exit of social mobility and the voice of social change: Notes on the social psychology of intergroup relations. *Social Science Information, 14*(2), 101–118.

Tajfel, H. (1978a). The achievement of group differentiation, *Differentiation between social groups: Studies in the social psychology of intergroup relations.* London: Academic Press.

Tajfel, H. (1978b). The psychological structure of intergroup relations. In H. Tajfel (Ed.), *Differentiation between social groups: Studies in the social psychology of intergroup relations.* London: Academic Press.

Tajfel, H. (1981). *Human groups and social categories.* Cambridge, UK: Cambridge University Press.

Tajfel, H. (1982a). Social psychology of intergroup relations. *Annual Review of Psychology, 33*, 1–39.

Tajfel, H. (Ed.). (1982b). *Social identity and intergroup relations.* Cambridge: Cambridge University Press.

Tajfel, H., & Billig, M. (1974). Familiarity and categorization in intergroup behavior. *Journal of Experimental Social Psychology, Vol. 10*(2), 159–170.

Tajfel, H., Billig, M. G., Bundy, R. P., & Flament, C. (1971). Social categorization and intergroup behaviour. *European Journal of Social Psychology, Vol. 1*(2), 149–178.

Thibaut, J. (1950). An experimental study of the cohesiveness of underprivileged groups. *Human Relations, 3*, 251–278.

Tomlinson, T. M. (1970). Contributing factors in Black politics. *Psychiatry, 33*(2), 137–281.

Turner, J. C. (1975a). *Social categorization of social comparison in intergroup relations.* Unpublished doctoral dissertation, University of Bristol.

Turner, J. C. (1975b). Social comparison and social identity: Some prospects for intergroup behaviour. *European Journal of Social Psychology, 5*(1), 5–34.

Turner, J. C. (1978a). Social categorization and social discrimination in the minimal group paradigm. In H. Tajfel (Ed.), *Differentiation between social groups: Studies in the social psychology of intergroup relations* (pp. 101–140). London: Academic Press.

Turner, J. C. (1978b). Social comparison, similarity and ingroup favoritism. In H. Tajfel (Ed.), *Differentiation between social groups: Studies in the social psychology of intergroup relations* (pp. 235–250). London: Academic Press.

Turner, J. C. (1980). Fairness or discrimination in intergroup behavior? A reply to Branthwaite, Doyle and Lightbown. *European Journal of Social Psychology, 10*(2), 131–147.

Turner, J. C. (1981). The experimental social psychology of intergroup behavior. In J. C. Turner & H. Giles (Eds.), *Intergroup behavior.* Oxford: Basil Blackwell.

Turner, J. C. (1982). Towards a cognitive redefinition of the social group. In H. Tajfel (Ed.), *Social identity and intergroup relations* (pp. 15–40). New York: Cambridge University Press.

Turner, J. C. (1983a). A second reply to Bornstein, Crum, Wittenbraker, Harring, Insko and Thibaut on the measurement of social orientations. *European Journal of Social Psychology, 13*(4), 383–387.

Turner, J. C. (1983b). Some comments on … "the measurement of social orientations in the minimal group paradigm." *European Journal of Social Psychology, 13*(4), 351–367.

Turner, J. C. (1984). Social identification and psychological group formation. In H. Tajfel (Ed.), *The social dimension: European developments in social psychology.* New York: Cambridge University Press.

Turner, J. C., & Brown, R. (1978). Social status, cognitive alternatives and intergroup relations. In H. Tajfel (Ed.), *Differentiation between social groups: Studies in the social psychology of intergroup relations* (pp. 201–234). New York: Academic Press.

Turner, J. C., & Brown, R. J. (1976). Social status, cognitive alternatives and intergroup relations. In H. Tajfel (Ed.), *Differentiation between social groups: Studies in the social psychology of intergroup relations.* London: Academic Press.

Turner, J. C., Brown, R. J., & Tajfel, H. (1979). Social comparison and group interest in ingroup favouritism. *European Journal of Social Psychology, 9*(2), 187–204.

Turner, J. C., & Giles, H. (Eds.) (1981). *Intergroup behavior.* Oxford: Basil Blackwell.

Turner, J. C., Sachdev, I., & Hogg, M. A. (1983). Social categorization, interpersonal attraction and group formation. *British Journal of Social Psychology, 22*(3), 227–239.

Van Den Berghe, P. L. (1967). *Race and racism.* New York: Wiley.

Vaughan, G. M. (1978). Social change and intergroup preferences in New Zealand. *European Journal of Social Psychology, 8*, 297–314.

Vinacke, W. E. (1964). Intra-group power differences, strategy, and decisions in inter-triad competition. *Sociometry, 27*, 27–40.

Wilson, W., & Miller, N. (1961). Shifts in evaluations of participants following intergroup competition. *Journal of Abnormal & Social Psychology, 63*, 428–431.

Particularistic and Universalistic Evaluation in the Social Comparison Process

Dale T. Miller, William Turnbull,* and Cathy McFarland*

In this article we argue that people are motivated to evaluate both the universalistic and particularistic standing of their abilities. One's *universalistic* standing is assessed by comparing with others who are similar to oneself on attributes related to the ability being assessed. One's *particularistic* standing is assessed by comparing with reference others, those with whom one shares an identity or bond. In five studies we attempted to distinguish between these two types of evaluation. We manipulated reference closeness by varying the distinctiveness of a shared attribute. In Studies 1 and 2 we gave subjects the choice of comparing a test score with that of either a distinctively similar (reference) other or a nondistinctively similar (nonreference) other. Although the two choices provided equivalent universalistic information, subjects overwhelmingly preferred to compare with the distinctively similar other. Studies 3–5 provided evidence that subjects actually did identify more closely with distinctively similar others than with nondistinctively similar others.

For people to evaluate their abilities and outcomes, they often must compare themselves with others (Festinger, 1954; Merton & Rossi, 1957; Pettigrew, 1967). Not all potential comparison others are equally relevant, however, and considerable social psychological research and theory has addressed the issue of comparison selectivity. Both sociologists working within the tradition of reference group theory (Hyman, 1960) and psychologists working within the tradition of social comparison theory

*Simon Fraser University, Burnaby, British Columbia, Canada.

This research was supported by a Social Sciences and Humanities Research Council Grant (410-85-1347) to Dale T. Miller and by a President's Research Grant from Simon Fraser University to William Turnbull.

We are grateful to John Holmes, John Jemmott, Ned Jones, Ziva Kunda, Mike Ross, Diane Ruble, and Ben Slugowski for their comments on earlier drafts of this article.

Correspondence concerning this article should be addressed to Dale T. Miller, Department of Psychology, Green Hall, Princeton University, Princeton, New Jersey 08544.

(Suls & Miller, 1977) accord perceived similarity a central role in the selection process. The two traditions differ; however, in the conceptualization of similarity and its role in the comparison process.

Social comparison theory (Festinger, 1954) contends that the comparison process is motivated by a drive to evaluate the goodness or badness of one's abilities. This theory postulates that individuals prefer to compare themselves with similar others because others provide the greatest cognitive clarity concerning their abilities. According to Goethals and Darley (1977), the information people gain about their abilities is especially great when they compare themselves with others who are similar to them on attributes that are related to or predictive of the variable they wish to evaluate (see also Suls, Gastorf, & Lawhon, 1978; Wheeler, Koestner, & Driver, 1982; Zanna, Goethals, & Hill, 1975). For example, if people wish to determine how much tennis ability they have, they will prefer to compare themselves with another who is similar in practice time (a variable presumably correlated with tennis performance) than with another who is similar in political ideology (a variable presumably uncorrelated with tennis performance). The logic of Goethals and Darley's (1977) attributional formulation is that by discovering the performance level of another who is similar in practice time, people can confidently attribute their own level of performance to (a) superior ability (if they are better), (b) inferior ability (if they are worse), or (c) average ability (if they are equal).

As this brief summary indicates, social comparison theory (at least contemporary statements of it) conceptualizes the goal of the comparison process to be *universalistic evaluation*: people determining their standing relative to other people in general. It assumes that people do not care where they stand in relation to particular comparison others per se; other people simply provide the highest informational clarity concerning a person's overall standing on an ability dimension. It is true that doing well or poorly relative to those chosen for comparison purposes will have affective consequences for people, but this is not because of their relation to the others; it is because of what their relation to the

others tells them about their *universalistic* standing. For example, if people play tennis more poorly than someone who is similar to them on attributes that are related to tennis performance, this means that they are not very good at tennis and it is presumably this inference, not the antecedent comparison, that leads to any affect they experience (Goethals & Darley, 1977).

Reference group theory offers a different conceptualization of the comparison process (E. Singer, 1981). The focus of this theory is not universalistic evaluation but rather what we term *particularistic evaluation*: people determining their standing relative to those others with whom they identify or feel a bond.[1] Whereas social comparison theory has focused on the process by which individuals assess their *global* status, reference group theory has focused on the process by which people assess their *local* status (Frank, 1985). Reference group theory views comparisons with similar (reference) others as being more than simply the instrumental means by which people achieve the goal of assessing their overall standing on an attribute (e.g., "What is my level of tennis ability?"). Comparisons with reference others are presumed to be of intrinsic interest to people (Tesser, 1986) and affect their feelings of self-worth directly (e.g., "Am I better or worse than my friend?").

The distinction between universalistic and particularistic evaluation has been overlooked by social psychologists. This probably is because of the methodological difficulty of separating comparison choices that reflect a preference for one type of evaluation over the other. Frequently, the individuals with whom a person shares related attributes will also be the individuals with whom the person identifies. For example, other college students from one's home town will serve both as a reference group and as a relevant social comparison group (at least they will if the attribute of home town is believed to be related to abilities pertinent to the college context). In some instances, however, the two types of groups will diverge. Not all of

---

[1] We borrowed the terms *universalistic* and *particularistic* from Parsons (1949; see also Berger 1977).

those who share attributes related to the target task will be reference others and not all reference others will share related attributes. As an example of the first type of divergence, consider how much more distressing it is to do worse than one's friend on an exam than it is to do worse than an anonymous other, even if the two are equally similar to oneself on attributes related to exam performance. The young child who wants to know how his or her task performance compared with that of his or her parent illustrates that reference others need not be individuals who provide people with the greatest cognitive clarity concerning their universalistic standing on ability dimensions.

In our five studies we attempted to demonstrate that people are motivated to evaluate not only their universalistic status but also their particularistic status. We proposed that people will prefer to compare themselves with a reference other than with a nonreference other, even when the reference other cannot provide any more universalistic information.

To test these propositions we first had to devise a means of manipulating the reference closeness of another independently of the other's informational value. The variable we chose for this purpose was the distinctiveness of the attribute that the two individuals shared. Our guiding hypothesis was that people will identify more strongly with others who share a statistically distinctive attribute with them than they will with others who share a statistically nondistinctive attribute with them.

Two sets of empirical findings led us to propose that attribute distinctiveness may contribute to reference closeness. The first of these focuses on the different feelings that members of minorities and majorities have toward their own group. Jellison and Zeisset (1969) found that members of a successful minority were more strongly attracted to one another than were members of a successful majority. Kaplan and Olczak (1971) found that minority subjects cared more than did majority subjects whether in-group members agreed with them. Finally, Gerard and Hoyt (1974) found that members of minority groups evaluated each other more favorably relative to out-group members than did members of majority groups. There is little

theorizing in these articles as to why there is a stronger bond among minority group members than among majority group members. Nevertheless, the pattern of results is consistent with the proposition that the fewer the number of people sharing an attribute, the greater is their reference closeness.

The second set of findings that led us to consider the relation between attribute distinctiveness and reference closeness is that reported by McGuire and his colleagues on the phenomenon of spontaneous self-concept (McGuire & McGuire, 1981). This work does not address the issue of in-group identification directly, but it does provide a plausible account for why the distinctiveness of an attribute may affect the reference closeness of individuals sharing that attribute. In an impressive array of studies, McGuire and his colleagues showed that the attributes that individuals spontaneously identify when asked to describe themselves tend to be ones on which they are statistically distinctive in their social contexts. For example, individuals are more likely to mention their ethnicity, gender, or age if their standings on these variables are distinctive in their social context than if they are not. If distinctive attributes generally are more central to one's self-concept than nondistinctive ones, then it could be argued that individuals who share distinctive (and hence important) attributes will identify more strongly with one another.

In summary, we explored the role of particularistic evaluation in the social comparison process. To do this successfully, we first had to discover how to empirically distinguish between two meanings of similarity: shared related attributes versus reference closeness. The means by which we attempted to operationalize this distinction was through the variable of attribute distinctiveness. The distinctiveness of an attribute is presumed to affect the perceived reference closeness of those sharing it, but not the perceived relatedness of the attribute to the performance dimension.

Study 1

In Study 1 we tested the hypothesis that the desire for particularistic social evaluation can influence an individual's choice of comparison others. The experimenter presented subjects with an opportunity to compare their performance score with the performance score of 1 of 2 other subjects. One of these scores was that of a distinctively similar individual, the other was that of a nondistinctively similar individual. Although both scores provided equivalent information concerning universalistic status, we hypothesized that subjects would prefer to see the score of a distinctively similar (reference) other than the score of a nondistinctively similar (nonreference) other.

Method

Subjects

Subjects were 25 male and female undergraduate volunteers from Simon Fraser University who were recruited by telephone and participated individually.

Procedure

The experimenter told the subjects that the study was concerned with the relation between perceptual style (the way in which a person categorizes and processes information) and social perceptiveness (the ability to make accurate judgments of others' personalities). Subjects first completed the test of social perceptiveness and then two tests of perceptual style.

Social perceptiveness test. The social perceptiveness test required subjects to read a biographical description of a person and then to answer 15 multiple-choice questions regarding the individual's past and present life experiences (e.g., whether his parents were strict or lenient). After completing the test all subjects learned that they had obtained a score of 42 out of 60.

Perceptual style tests. Once subjects received their (bogus) score on the social perceptiveness test, the experimenter elaborated on the alleged purposes of the research. He described perceptual styles as being important characteristics of people because of their relation to a wide variety of social and personality characteristics (e.g., whether a person will

show a consistent tendency either to ignore or notice small details of social interactions). It presumably was for the purpose of determining why each of the two different perceptual style dimensions relate to social perceptiveness that Study 1 was being undertaken. In accord with this fiction, the experimenter told subjects that once they had been categorized on the two perceptual style dimensions they would be asked to describe the strategies that they had used in answering the questions on the social perceptiveness test. The experimenter also told subjects that their responses on these latter measures would allow the researchers to assess whether people with different perceptual styles use different test-taking strategies. The experimenter emphasized that the two perceptual style dimensions were equally related to social perceptiveness.

The first test of perceptual style required subjects to estimate the number of dots appearing on 10 slides that were each projected for approximately 1 s. A feedback sheet informed subjects that people generally tend to either overestimate or underestimate the number of dots. Following the presentation the experimenter told subjects that their estimates indicated that they were *overestimators*, as opposed to *underestimators*. The second test required them to estimate the size of objects presented on each of 10 slides. The feedback sheet informed subjects that people generally tend to judge the objects to be either larger or smaller than they actually are. Following the presentation of these slides, the experimenter told all subjects that their estimates indicated that they were *reducers*, as opposed to *enlargers*.

Distinctiveness manipulation. In addition to informing subjects that they were characterized by the overestimator and reducer perceptual styles, the feedback sheet also informed subjects that one of their perceptual styles was distinctive and that the other was nondistinctive. For the purpose of counterbalancing, half of the subjects learned that overestimators were a distinctive group, with overestimators making up 9% of the population and underestimators the remaining 91%, and that reducers were a nondistinctive group, with reducers making up 88% of the population and enlargers the remaining 12%. The other half of the subjects learned that reducers were a distinctive group, with reducers making up 12% of the population and enlargers the remaining 88%, and that overestimators were a nondistinctive group, with overestimators making up 91% of the population and underestimators the remaining 9%.

Following this feedback the experimenter stated that many participants in the study had requested additional information concerning their score on the social perceptiveness test. These previous participants allegedly had expressed an interest in seeing the scores of others who shared their perceptual style. Accordingly, the experimenter announced to the subjects that he would permit them to see the score of either the last overestimator or the last reducer who had participated in the study. The experimenter then asked subjects to indicate which of the two scores they would prefer to see. Once subjects indicated their preference, the experimenter debriefed them.

Results and Discussion

The experimenter told subjects that the two perceptual styles were related equally to scores on the social perceptiveness test. Consequently, if they were motivated only by the desire to discover how their score compared with people in general, their choice of a comparison other should not have varied with the distinctiveness of the shared attribute. The two scores would be expected to yield equivalent information concerning their universalistic status. On the other hand, if subjects also were motivated to determine how well they compared with reference others, those with whom they shared a bond, then they should have exhibited a preference for the score of the distinctively similar other. This prediction was confirmed. Eighty percent of the subjects chose to see the score of the distinctively similar other, whereas only 20% chose to see the

score of the nondistinctively similar other, $\chi^2(1, N = 25) = 9.0, p < .001.$[2]

The experimenter explicitly told subjects that the two perceptual styles were related equally to social perceptiveness. It is possible, however, that subjects believed that the perceptual style dimension on which their standing was distinctive was more highly correlated with social perceptiveness ability than was the perceptual style dimension on which their standing was nondistinctive. If subjects did believe this, they might also have believed that the score of a distinctively similar other would provide them with greater informational clarity concerning their universalistic status than would the score of a nondistinctively similar other. We conducted Study 2 to rule out the possibility that the subjects in Study 1 preferred to see the score of the distinctively similar other because they expected this score to yield greater universalistic information.

Study 2

Whereas the experimenter told subjects in Study 1 that both styles were related (equally) to social perceptiveness, he told subjects in Study 2 that neither perceptual style was related to the ability being evaluated. This information was designed to ensure that subjects would infer that the scores of the distinctively similar and nondistinctively similar other yielded equivalent information concerning their general standing on the ability dimension. We did not expect the absence of a relation between perceptual style and social perceptiveness to affect the perceived reference or particularistic value of the distinctively similar other's score. Once again, we expected the score of a distinctively similar other to better satisfy a need for knowledge about one's local status than the score of a nondistinctively similar other.

---

[2] In this study and in all subsequent studies, preliminary analyses indicated that there were no gender effects that approached significance. Consequently, the reported analyses collapse across this variable. Also, preliminary analysis in this and all subsequent studies indicated that the perceptual style dimension did not qualify the distinctiveness effect; hence, all reported analyses collapse across this variable.

Method

Subjects

Subjects were 21 male and female undergraduate volunteers from Simon Fraser University who were recruited by telephone and participated individually.

Procedure

The experimenter informed the subjects when they arrived that they were to take part in two brief experiments that were being conducted by different researchers in the psychology department. The alleged purpose of the first experiment was to investigate the strategies people use when taking social perceptiveness tests; the alleged purpose of the second study was to explore the interrelations among perceptual style, age, sex, and family composition.

Subjects began by completing the same social perceptiveness test that was used in Study 1. All subjects learned that they bad received a score of 42 out of 60 on the test. The experimenter subsequently asked subjects to provide a brief description of the strategies that they had used in answering the questions on the test. When they had completed this, the experimenter informed them that the social perceptiveness study was completed and provided them with more information concerning the perceptual style study (see Study 1 for details). The experimenter told subjects that they would take two tests of perceptual style: The first would assess their style on the overestimator–underestimator dimension and the second their style on the enlarger–reducer dimension.

Subjects then completed both the size-estimation and dot-estimation tests (see Study 1), as well as a questionnaire requesting their age, sex, and family size. A feedback sheet subsequently provided them with feedback indicating that they were an overestimator on the first dimension of perceptual style and a reducer on the second dimension. One of these styles was described as being distinctive and the other nondistinctive (see Study 1 for details).

The experimenter continued by telling subjects that many of the previous participants had found their score on the social perceptiveness test difficult to interpret. He stated that even though there was no relation between the dimensions of perceptual style and social perceptiveness ("overestimators perform the same as underestimators; reducers perform the same as enlargers"), people had expressed a desire to see the scores of others who shared their perceptual style. In order to accommodate this desire, the experimenter indicated that he was allowing subjects to see the score of either the last overestimator or the last reducer to have participated in the study. Subjects indicated the score they preferred to see and then were debriefed.

Results and Discussion

The results supported the hypothesis that subjects prefer to compare their score with that of another with a distinctively similar perceptual style than with that of another with a nondistinctively similar style, even when neither of the perceptual style dimensions relates to performance on the target task. Eighty-one percent of the subjects chose to see the score of the distinctively similar other, whereas only 19% chose to see the score of the nondistinctively similar other, $\chi^2(1, N = 21) = 8.04$, $p < .005$.

These results, as do those of Study 1, support the proposition that people's choice of comparison others is not motivated solely by the goal of determining their universalistic standing on the relevant ability dimensions. People also are motivated to determine their local status on attributes, a goal best pursued by comparing with reference others.

Study 3

Studies 1 and 2 showed that people prefer to compare themselves with a distinctively similar other than with a nondistinctively similar other. We argued that this finding demonstrates people's desire to assess their particularistic status. Underlying this argument are two related assumptions: (a) Individuals view their distinctive traits as being more central and important to their personalities; and (b) individuals identify more strongly with those who share their distinctive (central) traits. To date, however, we have no evidence to support either of these assumptions. In Study 3 we attempted to remedy this omission by examining the hypothesis that individuals believe that their distinctive attributes are more central to their personalities than are their nondistinctive attributes.

Method
Subjects

Subjects were 31 male and female undergraduate volunteers who were recruited by telephone and participated individually.

Procedure

The procedure used in this experiment was similar to the one used in Experiment 1. Briefly, the experimenter informed subjects that the purpose of the study was to investigate the relations between two dimensions of perceptual style and social perceptiveness. The experimenter stressed that both perceptual style dimensions were equally related to social perceptiveness and that the major goal of the study was to explore why these relations exist. Consistent with this rationale, the experimenter asked subjects to complete (a) two tests of perceptual style, (b) a social perceptiveness ability test, and (c) a questionnaire assessing their test-taking strategies.

Distinctiveness manipulation. After completing the two perceptual style tests, subjects received a feedback sheet that revealed that they possessed the overestimator style on the dot-estimation test and the reducer style on the size-estimation test. Furthermore, they learned that one of these styles was distinctive and the other nondistinctive (see Experiment 1 for details).

Dependent measures. Following this feedback the experimenter indicated that she had several pamphlets, each containing information about a different perceptual style. She then explained that because she needed a few minutes to prepare the test materials, the subjects could read one of the pamphlets. The experimenter asked subjects to indicate which of their two perceptual styles they would most like

to learn more about and which of their perceptual styles they thought was more central and important in their personality.

Results and Discussion

We predicted that subjects would be more interested in learning about their distinctive characteristic than their nondistinctive characteristic. This prediction was confirmed. Eighty-seven percent of the subjects chose to read the pamphlet containing information about their distinctive perceptual style, whereas only 13% chose to read the pamphlet containing information about their nondistinctive perceptual style, $\chi^2(1, N = 31) = 17.06, p < .001$. We also predicted that subjects would view their distinctive characteristic as being more important and central to their personality than their nondistinctive characteristic. This prediction also was confirmed. Sixty-eight percent of the subjects indicated that their distinctive perceptual style was more central and important in their personality, whereas only 32% of the subjects indicated that their nondistinctive perceptual style was more important in their personality, $\chi^2(1, N = 31) = 3.9, p < .05$.

Study 4

Study 3 demonstrated that people view their distinctive traits as being more central and self-defining than their nondistinctive traits. This finding provides a clue as to why people may feel a stronger particularistic bond with distinctively similar than with nondistinctively similar others: The traits they share with distinctively similar others are more central and important to them. However, do individuals actually perceive a closer bond between themselves and distinctively similar others than between themselves and nondistinctively similar others? In Study 4 we examined this hypothesis.

Method
Subjects

Subjects were 26 male and female undergraduate volunteers from Simon Fraser University who were recruited by telephone and participated individually.

Procedure

The experimenter told subjects that the purpose of the study was to investigate the relation between perceptual style and group decision making. The experimenter allegedly was interested in assessing whether groups composed of people with similar perceptual styles make better decisions than groups composed of people with different perceptual styles. Accordingly, subjects learned that once they had completed a test of perceptual style, they would participate in a decision-making task in which they would communicate with another individual via an intercom system.

The experimenter also told subjects that she was interested in determining whether individuals who have knowledge of their partner's background characteristics and perceptual style perform better than individuals without such knowledge. To accomplish this some participants in the study were to learn of their partner's background characteristics and perceptual style and others were not. The experimenter informed all subjects that they were in the shared information condition.

Distinctiveness manipulation. Following the initial instructions, subjects completed the dot-estimation test that was used in Studies 1 and 2 (see Study 1 for details). The experimenter told all subjects that the test had revealed that their characteristic style was overestimation. In addition, half of the subjects learned that overestimation was a distinctive perceptual style (possessed by only 9% of the population), and the other half learned that overestimation was a nondistinctive perceptual style (possessed by 91% of the population).

The experimenter then gave subjects a background information questionnaire on which they were asked to indicate their age, sex, major, years of education, place of birth, neighborhood, recreational interests, and perceptual style (overestimator or underestimator). After subjects completed this questionnaire, the experimenter took it, explaining that she would give it to their partner. The experimenter returned with a completed questionnaire that she alleged to be that of the other subject. The responses on this questionnaire were generated so as to converge with those of the subjects in some

respects and diverge in others. All subjects learned from the questionnaire that their partner also was an overestimator.

Dependent measures. Once subjects had examined the background information questionnaire, the experimenter asked them to provide their first impressions of their partner. The experimenter informed subjects that she was assessing their first impressions because these may influence the decision-making task. The first impressions questionnaire asked subjects to indicate (a) the degree to which they and their partner were similar in perceptual style (1 = *not at all*, 9 = *extremely similar*); (b) how similar their own score would be to that of their partner if they were both to take another test of perceptual style (1 = *not at all*, 9 = *extremely similar*); (c) the degree to which they and their partner were similar to one another in general (1 = *not at all*, 9 = *extremely similar*); and (d) how likely they thought it was that they and their partner had similar interests and personalities (1 = *not at all*, 9 = *extremely likely*). After subjects had provided their first impressions, the experimenter debriefed them regarding the purposes of the study.

Results and Discussion

We predicted that subjects would indicate greater closeness to a distinctively similar target than to a nondistinctively similar target. This prediction was supported by two findings. First, subjects predicted that the distinctively similar target would be more similar to them in general ($M = 6.77$) than would the nondistinctively similar target ($M = 4.92$), $t(24) = 3.0$, $p < .03$. Second, subjects predicted that the distinctively similar target would be more similar to them in terms of interests and personality traits ($M = 6.69$) than would the nondistinctively similar target ($M = 5.31$), $t(24) = 2.46$, $p < .03$.

That subjects expected distinctively similar others to be more similar to them than nondistinctively similar others in general as well as in terms of interests and personalities raises an interpretational question concerning the findings of Studies 1 and 2.

Specifically, do our findings suggest that the subjects in the earlier experiments might have believed that the distinctively similar other was more similar to them on related attributes? We do not think so. First, subjects in this experiment did not rate the distinctively similar target as being more similar to them in perceptual style ($M = 8.08$) than the nondistinctively similar target ($M = 7.40$), $t(24) = 1.14$, *ns*. Second, subjects did not predict that a distinctively similar target would score more similarly to them on a subsequent measure of perceptual style ($M = 7.15$) than would a nondistinctively similar target ($M \doteq 7.15$), $t(24) < 1$.[3] In short, distinctively similar others did not perceive themselves to be more similar than nondistinctively similar others on attributes related to their performance score, only on ones related to global similarity.

Study 5

The results of the fourth study support the proposition that the distinctiveness of the attribute shared by people affects their perception of in-group similarity, which we used as an index of reference closeness (see Pleban & Tesser, 1981). In Study 5 we pursued the link between distinctive similarity and reference closeness by examining the fraternal component of particularistic evaluation. Previous research has demonstrated that the degree of closeness people acknowledge between themselves and in-group members depends on the accomplishments of the in-group members (Cialdini & Richardson, 1980). The successes or failures of people's in-group can have greater or lesser effects on the individuals' feelings of pride and shame depending on the bond between them. One consequence of this fact is that people can modify their feelings of satisfaction by increasing or decreasing, depending on the circumstances, their perceptions of closeness to

their group (Tesser, 1986). In addition, any variable that affects people's feelings of closeness to in-group members should affect the impact that the in-group members' performance has on the people's self-evaluations. One example of such a variable may be the distinctiveness of the bond that unites the in-group. Specifically, a member of a group should be affected more strongly by the fate of his or her group when the attribute shared by the group is distinctive than when it is nondistinctive. In Study 5 we tested this hypothesis.

Method
Subjects

Subjects were 40 male and female undergraduate volunteers from Simon Fraser University who were recruited by telephone and participated individually.

Procedure

Initially, the experimenter informed subjects that they would be participating in two separate research projects that were being conducted by different researchers in the psychology department. The first experiment allegedly was concerned with social perceptiveness. Specifically, the research was described as attempting to assess the strategies people use to solve social perceptiveness problems. The second experiment allegedly was concerned with the interrelations among perceptual style, age, sex, and family composition.

Subjects began by completing the social perceptiveness test, after which the experimenter asked them to briefly describe the strategies they had used in answering the questions on the test. Once subjects had finished this task, the experimenter indicated that the first experiment was completed.

Distinctiveness manipulation. The researchers involved in the second study presumably were

---

[3] At first glance these findings may appear to be inconsistent with those of Simon and Brown (1987). Those authors found that minority group members perceived their group to be less variable (in terms of the attribute on which they were categorized as a minority–majority) than did majority group members. Our study differs from theirs, however, in that we attempted to convey to subjects that the variable on which they were categorized (perceptual style) was discrete rather than continuous.

interested in whether people of differing ages, sexes, or family composition patterns tend to have different perceptual styles. Accordingly, after subjects described themselves in terms of the demographic categories, they completed the dot-estimation test (see Study 4 for details). The experimenter told all subjects that the test indicated that they were overestimators. In addition, they learned that this style was either distinctive or nondistinctive (see Study 4 for details).

Performance-level manipulation. The experimenter continued by announcing that many previous participants had asked if they could see their score on the social perceptiveness test. He explained he could not do that because the calculations would take too long. However, he indicated that he could allow them to see the average scores of the overestimators and underestimators who had participated in the study thus far. He then reminded subjects that social perceptiveness was unrelated to perceptual style and, consistent with this, told them that the average score of the overestimators and underestimators was the same, either 56 of 60 points or 26 of 60 points.

We described perceptual style as being unrelated to social perceptiveness in order to avoid a potential alternative account of the findings. If the two variables were related, those individuals sharing a distinctive perceptual style would occupy a more extreme relative position (a higher or lower percentile score) in the general distribution of social perceptiveness scores than would the group of individuals sharing a non-distinctive perceptual style. Consequently, stronger affective reactions to the performance scores of a distinctively similar group could be mediated by subjects' inferences concerning the relative position of their group (and hence themselves) rather than by their feelings of a fraternal bond. This alternative interpretation would be obviated if the variables are described as being unrelated because the relative standings of the distinctive and nondistinctive groups in the overall distribution would not be expected to differ.

Dependent measures. Once subjects learned the average score of the previous overestimators and underestimators, they completed a questionnaire that asked them to indicate their current mood. Specifically, they were to indicate on 7-point scales the degree to which they felt satisfied, happy, pleased, disappointed, sad, proud, and competent (1 = *not at all*, 7 = *extremely*).

Once subjects completed the mood questions the experimenter asked them to indicate (a) the score (out of 60) they thought they themselves would receive on the social perceptiveness test and (b) the highest and lowest score they thought would be obtained by those sharing their perceptual style.

We obtained these last 2 measures in order to assess an alternative explanation of the findings. We hypothesized that mood reactions should be more polarized in distinctive than in nondistinctive groups because of the stronger sense of bonding among distinctive individuals. However, it could be argued that the hypothesized effect reflects the differential amount of information subjects in the two groups believe they can deduce about their own score from their knowledge of their group's average score. Specifically, individuals in distinctive groups may be more likely than those in nondistinctive groups to believe that their own score is close to the average score of their group. Such a belief would follow from the assumption that distinctive groups are more homogeneous than nondistinctive groups (see Simon & Brown, 1987). If subjects do engage in this reasoning, they should (a) predict their own score to be closer to the group mean when their group is distinctive than when it is nondistinctive and (b) predict a smaller group range when their group is distinctive than when it is nondistinctive.

Results and Discussion

Because the internal consistency among the seven mood scales was high ($\alpha = .74$), we collapsed the items to yield a single mood index. We performed all subsequent analyses on this index.

Mood. We hypothesized that the performance level of a group would influence the affective responses of group members more when the attribute that the group members shared was distinctive than when it was nondistinctive. A 2 (high vs. low performance) × 2 (distinctive vs. nondistinctive group) analysis of variance (ANOVA) performed on the mood index supported this prediction. In addition to a main effect for performance level, $F(1, 36) = 16.42, p < .001$, there was a significant interaction, $F(1, 36) = 4.24, p < .05$. The means are presented in Table 20.1.

Simple effects analyses provided further support for the hypothesis. Subjects belonging to the group sharing a distinctive attribute reported experiencing a significantly more positive mood when their group performed well ($M = 5.24$) than when it performed poorly ($M = 3.92$), $t(36) = 4.29, p < .001$. In contrast, the mood of the subjects belonging to the group sharing a nondistinctive attribute was not significantly affected by the performance level of their group, $t(36) = 1.55$, ns.

Prediction. Earlier we raised the possibility that individuals may assume that distinctive groups are less variable than nondistinctive groups. One consequence of this assumption in the present context is that subjects might have believed that they had learned more about their own score from the mean score of their group in the distinctive condition than in the nondistinctive condition. Analyses of subjects' predicted scores provided no support for this account. A 2 × 2 ANOVA performed on the prediction scores (see Table 20.2) revealed a main

TABLE 20.1. Mean Mood Ratings as a Function of Group Distinctiveness and Group Performance Level

Group distinctiveness	Low performance	High performance
Nondistinctive	4.45[a]	4.90[b]
Distinctive	3.92[c]	5.24[b]

Note: Higher numbers indicate more positive mood.
[a]$n = 11.$ [b]$n = 10.$ [c]$n = 9.$

TABLE 20.2. Mean Predictions as a Function of Group Distinctiveness and Group Performance Level

Group distinctiveness	Low performance	High performance
Nondistinctive	26.82	47.89
Distinctive	28.67	48.30

Note: Predictions could range from 0 (low) to 60 (high).

effect of group performance, $F(1, 36) = 102.32, p < .001$, but no main effect of group distinctiveness ($F < 1$) and no interaction between group performance level and group distinctiveness ($F < 1$).

It is instructive to examine the relation between subjects' predictions of their own scores and the group averages they received. In the low-performance condition (the group average was 26 of 60), subjects' predictions in both the distinctive and nondistinctive conditions (Ms = 28.67 and 26.82, respectively) closely paralleled the group average. However, in the high-performance condition (the group average was 58 of 60), subjects' predictions in both the distinctive and nondistinctive conditions (Ms = 48.30 and 47.89, respectively) were significantly lower than their group's average, $t(35) = 4.89, p < .01$, and $t(35) = 4.86, p < .01$, respectively. Two inferences can be drawn from this pattern. First, the finding that subjects' estimates, at least in the high-performance condition, deviated from the group average suggests that subjects' estimates were not simply restatements of the group average. This is important because it counters the charge that the experimental constraints were such as to preclude group distinctiveness from having an effect on subjects' predictions even if it was perceived to relate to group variability. The second interesting aspect of these findings is their inconsistency with a self-serving account. In the low-performance condition subjects estimated that they would do just as poorly as the average member of the group, and in the high-performance condition they actually estimated that they would do less well than the average group member.

Finally, it should be noted that the prediction findings support the contention that individuals do not perceive a greater relation between perceptual style and performance when their perceptual style is distinctive. If distinctive individuals perceived a stronger relation between perceptual style and social perceptiveness scores, their predicted scores should have been closer to the group mean than the predicted scores of nondistinctive individuals.

Group range. Analyses of the range estimates (see Table 20.3) also failed to support the hypothesis that subjects believe there is less variability in

TABLE 20.3. Mean Group Range Estimates as a Function of Group Distinctiveness and Group Performance Level

Group distinctiveness	Low performance	High performance
Nondistinctive	28.45	28.00
Distinctive	33.00	21.70

Note: The lowest possible score was 0 and the highest 60.

distinctive than in nondistinctive groups, A 2×2 ANOVA on subjects' estimates of the range of social perception scores in their group revealed no main effects of either group distinctiveness ($F < 1$) or group performance, $F(1, 35) = 1.8$, *ns*, and no interaction between these two variables, $F(1, 35) = 1.61$, *ns*.

General Discussion

When people compare their performances with others they can obtain valuable information. If the others are similar to them on attributes that they perceive to be related to the performance in question, such comparisons can yield information about their universal standing on the performance dimension (Goethals & Darley, 1977). For example, people can acquire valuable information about their ability (or at least potential ability) at tennis by comparing themselves with others who are similar to them on attributes related to tennis performance. Thus, if they have played tennis for 1 year; they will gain a clearer fix on their tennis ability if they compare themselves with someone who also has played tennis for 1 year than if they compare themselves with either someone who has played tennis for 6 months or someone who has played tennis for 2 years. People seek such information, Festinger (1954) argued, because without it their evaluation of their tennis ability would be unstable. Also, without a stable evaluation of their tennis ability they would not be able to answer questions such as "Should I consider turning pro in a few years?" or even "Should I enter the tennis tournament at the next meeting of the Society for Experimental Social Psychology?"

The thesis of this article is that the motive to seek universalistic evaluation can be distinguished from the motive to seek particularistic information. People are not always content to know where their level of performance falls in relation to other people generally, they also want to know how it compares with people with whom they identify or feel a bond: their reference group. It is through comparisons with reference others that people assess their self-worth. Even in contexts in which individuals have stable evaluations of their ability, they will be motivated to compare their performance level with that of their reference group in order to assess how satisfied they should feel with their performance. For example, the golfer who has long ago resigned himself or herself to his or her perennial 36 handicap will still be motivated to discover how a particular golfing performance compares with that of reference others.

It is certainly true that feelings of pride and shame are influenced by people's assessments of their universal standing on performance dimensions, but we propose that these feelings are much more strongly linked to their assessments of their particularistic standing. The feelings of satisfaction or dissatisfaction that people derive from their weekly matches with their tennis partner can hardly be attributable to comparable upward or downward revisions in their assessments of their tennis ability. Fluctuation in the level of self-satisfaction does not derive from the indirect universalistic implications of their victories or defeats but from their direct particularistic implications ("She beat me again!", "I finally beat him," etc.). Just as fraternal feelings of pride and shame derive most strongly from in-group–out-group comparisons involving those in-groups with whom people identify most strongly (see Study 5 and Tesser, 1986), so egoistic feelings of pride and shame may derive most strongly from self-comparisons with those similar others with whom people identify most closely.

Until now, the process of particularistic evaluation has not been distinguished from that of universalistic evaluation. This is probably because the means by which the two types of evaluation are pursued tend to be similar, and in many instances are identical. Whether people are interested in particularistic or universalistic evaluation, they generally engage in comparisons with similar others.

The point is, however, that the role played by similar others is fundamentally different in the two comparison processes. The similar others whom people seek out to help in assessing their universal standing hold no special social significance for them; they simply facilitate computation. If individuals could calculate their universal standing by algorithm or divine it from tea leaves, comparisons with others would not be necessary. The comparisons people make with reference others are qualitatively different. From this perspective, similar others are those with whom people share an identity or sense of "we-ness" (Heider, 1958; Tesser, 1986), not those with whom they share a set of task-specific related attributes. Here people do care about the particular others and their relation to them. It is in relation to them that people define themselves and measure their self-worth. Providing students with Graduate Record Examination or Scholastic Aptitude Test percentile scores, even if they are broken down in terms of related attributes, will not eliminate the students' desire to compare their scores with those of their friends.

We designed Studies 1 and 2 to provide support for the contention that people's choice of similar comparison others can be motivated by the desire for particularistic evaluation as well as universalistic evaluation. We gave subjects in those experiments the opportunity to compare their score on a social perceptiveness test with the score of 1 of 2 other subjects. The others allegedly were similar to them on different perceptual style variables, one of which was shared by many other individuals and one of which was shared by few others. In Study 1 we presented the two perceptual style dimensions as being related equally to social perceptiveness; in Study 2 we presented both dimensions as being unrelated to social perceptiveness. We designed the distinctiveness manipulation to affect the degree of closeness subjects felt toward the similar others, with distinctive bonds being expected to lead to greater closeness than nondistinctive bonds. We did not expect the distinctiveness of the shared bond to influence the comparison choices of subjects if they were being influenced only by the need for cognitive clarity concerning their global or universalistic status. However, we did expect it to influence

subjects' choices if they also were interested in assessing their local status. The results were consistent with this latter prediction. Subjects revealed an overwhelming preference to see the score of the distinctively similar other.

The quest for particularistic evaluation might also have guided certain comparison choices made by subjects in previous social comparison studies. For example, a number of studies have shown that subjects expressed a desire to compare themselves with same-sex others even when they believed that there were no sex differences on the criterion attribute (Feldman & Ruble, 1981; Major & Forcey, 1985; Suls, Gaes, & Gastorf, 1979). These comparisons are puzzling if the subjects were attempting to evaluate their universalistic status, but not if they were attempting to evaluate their particularistic status. This latter possibility seems especially plausible in light of the fact that gender constitutes a common basis for establishing identity.

Implications

Self-validation versus self-evaluation

We are not the first to suggest that the choice of comparison others can reflect more than one motive. Previous theorists have distinguished the motive for *self-evaluation* from the motive for *self-validation* (Hakmiller, 1966; J. Singer, 1966; Tesser, 1986; Wills, 1981). This latter distinction appears to be orthogonal to the distinction proposed here. In the same way that a person can seek self-evaluation in either a particularistic or universalistic sense, a person can seek self-validation in either a particularistic or universalistic sense. For example, people may be motivated to play tennis against their least skilled friend, not because such a comparison will inflate their estimate of their universal standing on the dimension of tennis ability, but because it will make them feel better about their local standing on that dimension (e.g., "At least I'm better than her!").

Multiple reference groups

Both social comparison and reference group theorists have observed that people do not use the same reference groups in all contexts, especially for comparative purposes. Individuals may compare their salaries with one group, their tennis game with another, and their voting behavior with yet another. This attribute-specific pattern of comparison group selection is most likely to occur if universalistic self-evaluation is the goal. The attributes that are perceived to be related to tennis skill will not necessarily be those perceived to be related to voting behavior, and hence the individuals chosen to help evaluate these different aspects of the self need not be the same. On the other hand, particularistic self-evaluations across a wide range of attributes may well derive from the same people. The centrality of certain others in the comparison process has been viewed previously in terms of global similarity (Samuel, 1973; Zanna *et al.*, 1975). However, to the extent that the concept of global similarity refers to the sharing of attributes that tend to be related to or predictive of a great many aspects of the self, it may be misleading. The centrality of certain others in the comparison process may simply reflect their shared identity rather than their global similarity on related attributes. Of course, as we mentioned earlier, the others with whom people identify or share a bond often will be those with whom they share related attributes. The important point, however, is that there will be some circumstances in which people will prefer to compare themselves with reference others than with others who more closely resemble them on related attributes but who are not reference others.

Distinctiveness: The Minimal Reference Group

This research goes beyond demonstrating that people seek comparison information for more than one purpose. Study 3 indicates that people view their distinctive attributes as being more important and central to their personalities than their nondistinctive attributes. Further, Studies 4 and 5 reveal that the distinctiveness of a commonality shared by individuals affects the strength of the bond between the individuals (see also Gerard & Hoyt, 1974; Jellison & Zeisset, 1969; Kaplan & Olczak, 1971). Subjects in Study 4 reported that they would have more in common with others with whom they shared

a distinctive attribute than with others with whom they shared a nondistinctive attribute. Furthermore, the mood of subjects in Study 5 was more strongly influenced by the performance level of a group with whom they shared a distinctive attribute than by the performance level of a group with whom they shared a nondistinctive attribute.

Why should sharing a distinctive attribute create a bond and a sense of we-ness? Earlier we proposed that attribute distinctiveness may influence the group bond through its mediational effect on the self-concept. Specifically, we argued that the more distinctive an attribute is, the more central it may be in an individual's self-concept. The finding of McGuire and his colleagues (McGuire & McGuire, 1981) that individuals are more likely to spontaneously mention distinctive than nondistinctive attributes when asked to describe themselves is consistent with this speculation. What our findings may suggest beyond this is that people may tend to adopt as reference others those who share attributes that are central to their self-concept. This line of reasoning is clearly speculative, but a study by Miller (1984) is suggestive in this regard.

In that study Miller (1984) categorized subjects in terms of self-schemas with respect to gender (defined as organizations of self-related information about masculinity or femininity). Subjects then chose which of several group norms they wanted to see to evaluate their performance. Schematic subjects, those who incorporated masculine or feminine characteristics into their self-concept, made same-sex comparisons regardless of the relation of sex to performance. In contrast, aschematic subjects made same-sex comparisons only when sex was related to performance. Miller's findings are consistent with the hypothesis that when an attribute of the self (e.g., masculinity or femininity) is important to people's self-concept, those sharing that attribute will be reference others and, consequently, a source of particularistic self-evaluation.

One reason to pursue the link between distinctiveness and reference closeness is its potential for providing an alternative conceptualization of numerous group phenomena. Consider the finding that minority groups are more cohesive than majority groups. One account of this is that minority group members are drawn together in response to majority group persecution or oppression (Coser, 1956). In the case of self-selected groups, it also could be argued that more stringent selection criteria play a role in the greater cohesion of minority groups. Our findings, however; suggest that the greater sense of we-ness that emerges in groups sharing distinctive attributes may arise because there is a greater sense of "me-ness" in these groups. Minority group members may be more likely to identify themselves in terms of the attribute that makes them distinctive (e.g., homosexuality) than majority group members are to identify themselves in terms of the attribute that makes them nondistinctive (e.g., heterosexuality). As a consequence of this, the former individuals may identify more strongly with one another than do the latter individuals. Future research should address these and other possible implications of statistical distinctiveness.

REFERENCES

Berger, S. M. (1977). Social comparison, modeling and perseverance. In J. M. Suls & R. L. Miller (Eds.), *Social comparison processes: Theoretical and empirical perspectives* (pp. 209–234). Washington, DC: Hemisphere.

Cialdini, R. B., & Richardson, K. D. (1980). Two indirect tactics of image management: Basking and blasting. *Journal of Personality and Social Psychology, 39*, 406–415.

Coser, L. (1956). *The function of social conflict*. New York: Free Press of Glencoe.

Feldman, N. S., & Ruble, D. N. (1981). Social comparison strategies: Dimensions offered and options taken. *Personality and Social Psychology Bulletin, 7*, 11–16.

Festinger, L. (1954). A theory of social comparison processes. *Human Relations, 7*, 117–140.

Frank, R. (1985). *Choosing the right pond: Human behavior and the quest for status*. London, England: Oxford University Press.

Gerard, H. B., & Hoyt, M. F. (1974). Distinctiveness of social categorization and attitude toward ingroup members. *Journal of Personality and Social Psychology, 29*, 836–842.

Goethals, G. R., & Darley, J. M. (1977). Social comparison theory: An attributional approach, In J. M. Suls & R. L. Miller (Eds.), *Social comparison processes: Theoretical and empirical perspectives* (pp. 259–278). Washington, DC: Hemisphere.

Hakmiller, K. L. (1966). Threat as a determinant of downward comparison. *Journal of Experimental Social Psychology, 2*(Suppl. 1), 32–39.

Heider, E (1958). *The psychology of interpersonal relations*. New York: Wiley.

Hyman, H. (1960). Reflections on reference groups. *Public Opinion Quarterly, 24*, 383–396.

Jellison, J. M., & Zeisset, P. T. (1969). Attraction as a function of the commonality and desirability of a trait shared with another. *Journal of Personality and Social Psychology, 11*, 115–120.

Kaplan, M. F., & Olczak, P. V. (1971). Attraction toward another as a function of similarity and commonality of attitudes. *Psychological Reports, 28*, 515–521.

Major, B., & Forcey, B. (1985). Social comparisons and pay evaluations: Preferences for same-sex and same-job image comparisons. *Journal of Experimental Social Psychology, 21*, 393–405.

McGuire, W. J., & McGuire, C. V. (1981). The spontaneous self-concept as affected by personal distinctiveness. In M. D. Lynch, A. A. Norem-Hebeison, & K. Gergen (Eds.), *Self-concept: Advances in theory and research* (pp. 147–171). New York: Ballinger.

Merton, R. K., & Rossi, A. S. (1957). Contributions to the theory of reference group behavior. In R. K. Merton & P. F. Lazarsfeld (Eds.), *Continuities in social research: Studies in the scope and method of "The American Soldier"* (pp. 40–105). New York: Free Press of Glencoe.

Miller, C. T. (1984). Self-schemas, gender, and social comparison: A clarification of the related attributes hypothesis. *Journal of Personality and Social Psychology, 46*. 1222–1229.

Parsons, T. (1949). *Essays in sociological theory*. New York: Macmillan.

Pettigrew, T. F. (1967). Social evaluation theory: Convergence and applications. In D. Levine (Ed.), *Nebraska symposium on motivation* (Vol. 15, pp. 241–311). Lincoln: University of Nebraska Press.

Pleban, R., & Tesser, A. (1981). The effects of relevance and quality of another's performance on interpersonal closeness. *Social Psychology Quarterly, 44*, 278–285.

Samuel, W. (1973). On clarifying some interpretations of social comparison theory. *Journal of Experimental Social Psychology, 9*, 450–465.

Simon, B., & Brown, R. (1987). Perceived intragroup homogeneity in minority-majority contexts. *Journal of Personality and Social Psychology, 53*, 703–711.

Singer, E. (1981). Reference groups and social evaluations. In M. Rosenberg & R. Turner (Eds.), *Social psychology: Sociological perspectives* (pp. 66–93). New York: Basic Books.

Singer, J. E. (1966). Social comparison: Progress and issues. *Journal of Experimental Social Psychology, 2*(Suppl. 1), 103–110.

Suls, J. M., Gaes, G., & Gastorf, J. (1979). Evaluating a sex-related ability: Comparison with same-, opposite-, and combined-sex norms. *Journal of Research in Personality, 13*, 294–304.

Suls, J. M., Gastorf, J., & Lawhon, J. (1978). Social comparison choices for evaluating a sex- and age-related ability. *Personality and Social Psychology Bulletin, 4*, 102–105.

Suls, J. M., & Miller; R. L. (Eds.). (1977). *Social comparison processes: Theoretical and empirical perspectives.* Washington, DC: Hemisphere.

Tesser, A. (1986). Some effects of self-evaluation maintenance on cognition and action. In R. M. Sorrentino & E. T. Higgins (Eds.), *The handbook of motivation and cognition: Foundations of social behavior* (pp. 435–464).

Wheeler, L., Koestner, R., & Driver, R. E. (1982). Related attributes in the choice of comparison others. *Journal of Experimental Social Psychology, 18,* 489–500.

Wills, T. A. (1981). Downward comparison principles in social psychology. *Psychological Bulletin, 90,* 245–271.

Zanna, M. P., Goethals, G. R., & Hill, J. F. (1975). Evaluating a sex-related ability: Social comparison with similar others and standard setters. *Journal of Experimental Social Psychology, 11,* 86–93.

Received November 17, 1987
Revision received June 17, 1988
Accepted June 23, 1988 ■

Social Contagion of Binge Eating

Christian S. Crandall

A social psychological account of the acquisition of binge eating, analogous to the classic social psychological work, "Social Pressures in Informal Groups" (Festinger, Schachter, & Back, 1950), is suggested and tested in two college sororities. In these sororities, clear evidence of group norms about appropriate binge-eating behavior was found; in one sorority, the more one binged, the more popular one was. In the other, popularity was associated with binging the right amount: Those who binged too much or too little were less popular than those who binged at the mean. Evidence of social pressures to binge eat were found as well. By the end of the academic year, a sorority member's binge eating could be predicted from the binge-eating level of her friends (average $r = .31$). As friendship groups grew more cohesive, a sorority member's binge eating grew more and more like that of her friends (average $r = .35$). The parsimony of a social psychological account of the acquisition of binge eating behavior is shown. I argue that there is no great mystery to how bulimia has become such a serious problem for today's women. Binge eating seems to be an acquired pattern of behavior, perhaps through modeling, and appears to be learned much like any other set of behaviors. Like other behaviors, it is under substantial social control.

Bulimia is rapidly becoming *the* women's psychological disease of our time, rivaling depression in its prevalence. It is receiving a great deal of attention in both the scientific community (Gandour, 1984; Schlesier-Stropp, 1984; Striegel-Moore, Silberstein, & Rodin, 1986) and the popular press (Boskind-Lodahl & Sirlin, 1977). Bulimia is an eating pattern characterized by periodic episodes of

This article is based on my dissertation at the University of Michigan. Financial support came from an NIMH training grant in health and social behavior to the University of Michigan, the Michigan Alumni Fund, University of Michigan Continuing Education for Women, a Society for the Psychological Study of Social Issues Grant-in-Aid, and NSF Grant SES85-07342 to Richard Nisbett.

Special thanks are due to my committee for their helpful comments and encouragement: Eugene Burnstein, Hazel Markus, Andre Modigliani, and especially to the chairman, Richard Nisbett, whose guiding hand can be seen throughout. This version also profited from discussions with and knowledgeable comments from Monica Biernat, Steve Cardoze, Adam Drewnowski, Martin Gold, Norbert Kerr, Adam Lehman, Judith Rodin, Lisa Silberstein, David Smith, and three anonymous reviewers.

Correspondence concerning this article should be addressed to Christian S. Crandall, Department of Psychology, Box 11A Yale Station, Yale University, New Haven, Connecticut 06520.

uncontrolled binge eating alternating with periods of fasting, strict dieting, or purging via vomiting, diuretics, or laxatives. The uncontrolled eating is usually accompanied by negative affect, a sense of loss of control, and guilt. Nearly all of those affected are women (Gandour, 1984).

The evidence is that bulimia is indeed quite prevalent; estimates suggest 4–15% of college women have serious problems with bulimia (Halmi, Falk, & Schwartz, 1981; Sinoway, Raupp, & Newman, 1985; Strangler & Printz, 1980). By contrast, there is little evidence to suggest that bulimia afflicted any more than a handful of people prior to the late 1960s and early 1970s (Rosenzweig & Spruill, 1986).

The sudden and dramatic appearance of bulimia as a set of clinical symptoms has prompted a great deal of psychological and psychiatric theorizing about the roots of the syndrome. Surprisingly little is known about the causes of bulimia. Bulimics seem to be virtually indistinguishable from non-bulimic controls on a surprising number of variables, such as height, weight (Gandour, 1984), sex role orientation (Srikameswaran, Leichner, & Harper, 1984), and even ego involvement with food and eating (Crandall, 1987). There have been three general classes of explanations put forward: a sociohistorical/cultural approach, a clinical/psychiatric approach, and an epidemiological/risk factors approach.

Sociocultural Approach

Sociocultural theorists argue that changing norms in our society, especially those toward thinness for women, have created a cult of dieting (Dwyer, Feldman, & Mayer, 1970; Orbach, 1978). For example, Garner, Garfinkel, Schwartz, and Thompson (1980) have shown that body sizes of the winners of the Miss America Pageant and the Playboy centerfolds have been steadily decreasing over the past 20 years. Apparently, now more than ever, thin is in.

Women have internalized the message that they should care a great deal about how they look and at the same time internalize a thinness norm that is virtually unattainable for most of them (Rodin, Silberstein, & Striegel-Moore, 1984). Initial and subsequent attempts to reach this social rather than biological norm (i.e., dieting) are disruptive to the body's natural balance (Nisbett, 1972), making weight reduction extremely difficult (Bennett & Gurin, 1982; Garrow, 1978). At the same time, because there is a heavy psychological investment in dieting, the success or failure of behaviors related to weight loss attempts are very self-relevant, and strongly affectively tinged.

There is undoubtedly a sociocultural component to bulimia, because severe binge eating accompanied by an emotional roller coaster among women is a new problem, but social history certainly does not contain a complete account of the phenomenon. Thinness norms have come and gone in the past few centuries, and social roles have gone through dramatic changes as well, both apparently without concomitant increases in bulimia. During the Roaring Twenties, for example, although the flappers were as thin as plastic drinking straws, there is no indication that bulimia was a problem then (Bennett & Gurin, 1982). (The exact data to establish this are very difficult to collect; see Rosenzweig & Spruill, 1986, for one attempt.)

More important, however, is that these social pressures operate on all women in the middle-class subculture. Thus, the most difficult problem for the sociocultural perspective is that it fails to specify who is at risk for bulimia and who is not at risk. Although thinness norms and the fear of fatness are everywhere in our society, not all women are in trouble with dieting, binging, and body image. Why beauty norms for thinness work their destruction on only a relative minority of the population is a question that this perspective has a great deal of difficulty in answering.

Clinical/Psychiatric Approach

A wide variety of researchers and clinicians have proposed models of bulimia based on existing psychiatric/clinical models, for example, impulsiveness (Dunn & Ondercin, 1981), feelings of inadequacy or low self-efficacy (Garfinkel & Garner, 1982), borderline personality disorder (Radant, 1986), or parents' psychological health and family structure (Strober, Morell, Burroughs, Salkin, &

Jacobs, 1985). One approach claims that bulimia is simply a variant of major affective disorder (Pope & Hudson, 1984).

The clinical approach provides an answer to the "Why this person?" question, which the sociocultural perspective does not: Women experiencing psychological distress are at risk. However, a serious problem for the clinical perspective is the vagueness with which it specifies predisposing factors. The personality and family predisposing factors that have been linked to bulimia can separate bulimics from the normal population, but they cannot successfully discriminate bulimics from other globally defined kinds of psychological disorders such as depression (Cantwell, 1985). Also, it is not clear how feelings of inadequacy or low self-efficacy, for example, should lead to problems with binge eating. In their 240-page book, Pope and Hudson (1984) made a reasonable case for the role of depression in bulimia, but they fail to say anything about why depression should lead to problems with binge eating in particular, or whether depression is a cause or a consequence of the disorder.

Most important, problems such as feelings of inadequacy and impulsiveness have been around for some time, long before bulimia became a major health problem. Unless one is willing to argue that such things as clinical levels of inadequacy or impulsiveness are exhibiting a huge growth, it is hard to claim that they are the cause of bulimia. The crucial issues are, why should such things as depression, impulsiveness, or inadequacy be linked to binge eating, and why now?

Epidemiological/Risk Factors Approach

An epidemiological approach to bulimia focuses on the various factors that can be expected to predict bulimia (Johnson, Lewis, & Hagman, 1984). It is a statistical approach: What are the independent variables one can use to predict the dependent variable of bulimia?

Rodin and her colleagues (Rodin *et al.*, 1984; Striegel-Moore *et al.*, 1986) have reviewed an impressive amount of literature relating to binge eating and bulimia and have outlined the various factors that put a person at risk for bulimia. The list is long and diverse, including body image, affective instability, family factors, hormones, sex roles, stress, exercise, genetic factors, coping skills, developmental factors, and so forth. It seems certain that a number of the factors on this list can be used to predict bulimia, using as they do factors from the entire range of theoretical perspectives.

Though practical, the approach is not parsimonious; the focus for this group of theorists has been on inclusion rather than exclusion. The result has been a large compendium of likely risk factors for bulimia. It is both descriptive and predictive, but the process of acquiring bulimic behavior remains obscure.

A useful tool at this point would be an account of bulimia that is both plausible and parsimonious. It should be plausible in that it fits the known facts about bulimia, and it should be parsimonious in that the phenomenon is not overexplained by many concomitant, nonindependent forces. An appropriate theory should define the people at risk for the disorder as well as those not at risk. A good theory should also describe the process of acquiring the symptoms themselves.

None of the existing theories can do all of these things. Although the sociocultural approach can define who is at risk, it neither effectively defines who is not at risk nor how bulimics acquire the binge-eating behavior. The clinical perspective is well suited to defining who is at risk and who is not at risk but has not carefully spelled out how it is that the symptoms are acquired. The epidemiological approach, like the clinical approach, is better suited to defining risk factors than to describing processes of symptom acquisition. I wish to propose a model that is well suited to describing the symptom acquisition process, based on social psychological processes.

Social Psychological Factors

There is good reason to think that social processes are implicated in various ways with respect to bulimia and binge eating. Anecdotal evidence suggests that bulimia tends to run in social groups, such as cheerleading squads (Squire, 1983), athletic teams (Crago, Yates, Beutler, & Arizmendi, 1985), and dance camps (Garner & Garfinkel, 1980). There is also indication that the onset of eating disorders follows entrance into the group (e.g., Crago *et al.*, 1985), suggesting that social pressure might be involved.

There is a great deal of speculation about social psychological factors of bulimia by clinicians and the popular press. In *The Slender Balance*, Squire (1983) tells the story of a cheerleader, Laura, who

> explains matter-of-factly "everyone on the [cheerleading] squad binges and vomits. That's how I learned."… Laura considers her behavior frightening and awful, except in one context: before cheerleading a game. "Everybody does it then, so it doesn't seem like the same thing." (p. 48)

One of the most interesting and yet underexamined processes in bulimia is the acquisition of bulimic behavior, particularly binge eating. The few studies that have looked at this problem have focused almost exclusively on particular social groups, for example, dance camps (Garner & Garfinkel, 1980) and athletic teams (Crago *et al.*, 1985).

This focus is not an accident. I wish to argue that social groups are at the very heart of the issue of symptom acquisition. Symptoms are spread from one member to another in these groups, and group membership is at the heart of the transmission. Groups that are most likely to transmit the symptoms of bulimia, most notably binge eating, are groups that are made up almost entirely of women of the same age. This includes dance camps and athletic teams as well as sororities, all-women dormitories, or workplaces comprising mostly women.

Social groups are important to us. They serve to tell us who we are (McGuire & Padawer-Singer, 1976), what to think (Cantril, 1941), and how to behave (Sherif, 1936). The more we value the social group, the more we are willing to be influenced by it.

> The power of a group may be measured by the attractiveness of the group for its members. If a person wants to stay in a group, he will be susceptible to influences coming from the group, and he will be willing to conform to the rules which the group sets up." (Festinger, Schachter, & Back, 1950, p. 91)

Members of the same social group tend to be relatively uniform in the attitudes and behaviors that are important to the group (Festinger, 1954). When a particular individual deviates from the group, social pressures are brought to bear to bring the prodigal back into the fold via direct communication, emotional support, or disapproval. Ultimately, the deviate is rejected if he or she fails to conform (Schachter, 1951).

I wish to argue that social pressures in friendship groups are important mechanisms by which binge eating is acquired and spread. Social groups such as athletic teams, cheerleading squads, dormitories, and sororities develop social norms about what is appropriate behavior for their members. If eating, dieting, and losing weight are important to the members, then norms will arise in the group defining how much, when, and with whom. Deviation from these norms will result in rejection from the group, as evidenced by a reduction in the person's popularity (Schachter, 1951). Thus, not only is there likely to be modeling of the behaviors and attitudes associated with bulimia, but there are likely to be sanctions for counternormative behavior.

People are very motivated to imitate or model attitudes or behaviors that are important, characteristic, or definitional to the social group. The more important the social group, and the more central a behavior is to the group, the greater the pressure toward uniformity and the more likely that members of the group will imitate each other's behavior (Festinger, 1950). Friends should become more like each other as they spend time together and grow closer. If binge eating is an important or meaningful behavior to a social group, then over time within groups, people's binge-eating patterns should grow more similar.

Social Pressures in Informal Groups

A classic investigation of the effects of social norms on group life is the study of *Social Pressures in*

Informal Groups by Festinger *et al.* (1950). Their study provides a template to examine how social influence affects binge eating. Festinger *et al.* were interested in how social norms about attitudes toward a tenant organization were related to popularity and communication patterns within a housing project. Two housing arrangements were studied, Westgate and Westgate West, which were adjoining but physically and architecturally distinct. In Westgate, social groups were defined by courts of grouped houses, ranging from 7 to 13 homes. In Westgate West, social groups were apartment buildings with ten apartments in each.

In Westgate, Festinger *et al.* (1950) found that the different groups had different norms about the attitudes to take toward the tenant organization; some courts were strongly in favor of the organization, and some were strongly against it. When the court's prevailing attitude toward the tenant organization was positive, those who had negative attitudes toward the organization were less well liked, and when the court's prevailing attitude was negative, those who had a positive attitude were less popular than others.

In Westgate West, the normative pattern was different. Tenants of all of the apartment buildings had primarily favorable attitudes toward the tenant organization. (Westgate West was occupied after the tenant organization had already been established, so that the more controversial aspects of the organization were less salient to the occupants of Westgate West.) There was no correlation between attitude and popularity in Westgate West; those who did not share the generally positive attitude toward the organization did not suffer in terms of popularity. Festinger *et al.* (1950) interpreted this to mean that, although the overarching group norm was a positive attitude, local group norms were neither salient nor particularly strong.

Festinger *et al.* (1950) studied existing social groups at one point in time (although the comparison between Westgate and Westgate West is implicitly temporal). But social groups have a dynamic life cycle: Groups form, exert pressures on their members, go up and down in cohesion and uniformity, and eventually disband (Moreland & Levine, 1982). Groups usually do not form with ready-made cohesion; when groups are new, one should not expect pressures toward uniformity to have taken effect. It is only after some amount of time that individuals should become more like the other group members. As more information is shared among members, and as the groups become more cohesive, similarity among group members on binge eating should increase.

Festinger *et al.* (1950) also reasoned that as group pressures increase in strength, characteristics of the person should decrease in importance. They argued that the amount of time one expected to stay in the housing project should be correlated with how much one is concerned with the quality of life there, and so one's expected length of stay would normally be associated with a positive attitude toward the organization. This was true for the Westgate West complex, where norms were weak. However, at Westgate, in the presence of strong local norms about the tenant organization, anticipated length of stay was uncorrelated with attitude.

With respect to binge eating, however, social pressures are not likely to remove completely the importance of personal characteristics, because, in addition to social psychological factors, other psychobiological and psychiatrically relevant variables are likely to affect the behavior. A variety of factors might be important (Striegel-Moore *et al.*, 1986). A woman's weight puts her at risk; the heavier she is, the more likely she is to feel pressure to diet, which puts her at risk for binge eating (Polivy & Herman, 1985). Her general psychological health is also likely to be a factor; the poorer her mental health, the more likely she is to acquire binging. Furthermore, the lower her self-esteem, the more likely she is to be open to social influence (Janis, 1954).

One social group that is ideally suited for studying such questions as they apply to binge eating is the college sorority. There is anecdotal evidence that sororities are breeding grounds for eating disorders (Squire, 1983), so that one is likely to find a range of binging severity in such a group. Second, women in a sorority are, on average, very interested in physical appearance, weight, and body shape (Rose, 1985), which is a risk factor for bulimia (Johnson *et al.*, 1984; Striegel-Moore *et al.*, 1986).

But most important, sorority membership is a very powerful source of social influence. Much of a sorority woman's social and academic life revolves around the living group, in addition to the more mundane aspects of life, such as sleeping, eating, laundry, and so forth.

From the point of view of social impact theory (Latané & Wolf, 1981), a sorority will have a dramatic impact on its members' lives. It is large enough to generate a strong consensus, the strength of the group is high due to its high degree of attractiveness to members, and the continuing closeness of other members in the sorority ensures the immediacy of their impact.

Finally, a sorority has the distinct advantage of being a well-defined social group with clearly discernible boundaries. With such a social group, one can obtain a fairly clear picture of the social influence patterns in a substantial portion of these women's lives.

If social pressures in friendship groups play a role in the acquisition of binge eating, a variety of research questions present themselves. To what extent are there group norms about binge eating? What role does binging play in determining social acceptance or rejection? To what extent are there social pressures toward uniformity in binge eating? Do women come to have binge eating behavior that resembles that of their friends over time? These questions were looked at in two consecutive studies of 163 women living in sororities.

Method

Overview

Two different sororities were investigated during two different academic years. In Study 1, one sorority was studied in the spring only. In Study 2, two sororities were studied in both the fall and spring. Subjects responded to questions of three general sorts: social ties, personal factors, and binge eating. Social ties were measured by having subjects list their friends within the sorority; this served as information to distinguish subgroups or cliques, as well as popularity. Personal factors were used to some

extent to help define those women most at risk for binge eating. These included, among other things, self-esteem as a rough measure of a woman's general psychological health, and height and weight.

In Study 1, Sorority Alpha was contacted. The sorority members filled out questionnaires anonymously, 3 weeks before the summer break. In Study 2, both Sorority Alpha and a second house, Sorority Beta, filled out a modified version of the questionnaire. They filled out the questionnaires both in the fall, shortly after "rush" (when new members are selected by the sorority to move in during the following year) and again the spring (as in Study 1). Because social influence takes some time to operate, it was expected that there would be relatively little evidence of social pressures operating in the fall data collection, after only 6 weeks of contact.[1] In the spring, however, after 7 months of steady and intense contact, ample opportunity for pressures toward uniformity to operate was expected. This two-wave design of Study 2 also allowed for comparison over time. If social pressures were operating, then the individual sorority member's levels of binge eating should change over time, and these changes should be predicted by those social influences. In the presence of social influence, whether it is active social pressure or simply modeling, friends should grow more alike.

Subjects were active members of two different college sororities (all female). The sororities were both popular and highly sought-after houses at the campus of a large state university. The sororities were paid $150 for each wave of the study.

Subjects were given questionnaires, characterized as "a study of community and sorority life." The questionnaires were given out only to those women actually residing in the sorority house (made up of mostly sophomores and juniors). The pledge class (new recruits) and inactives (mostly seniors living outside the house and relatively removed from sorority life) were not included in these analyses. Responses to the questionnaire were completely anonymous. A code sheet was prepared by a member of the sorority's executive council; code

---

[1] Presumably, a substantial portion of the social impact of the sorority on its members dissipates over the summer.

TABLE 21.1. Demographic Description and Design Overview

Variable	Sorority Alpha			Sorority Beta	
	Spring₁	Fall₂	Spring₂	Fall₂	Spring₂
Sorority size	46	52	44	66	61
% response rate	100	98	82	100	92
Mean age (years)	19.8	19.5	19.7	20.4	20.6
Weight (kg)					
M	55.8	54.3	55.8	58.2	58.6
SD	5.8	6.3	6.4	6.9	6.5
Body-mass index					
M	21.0	20.6	21.0	20.9	21.3
SD	1.6	1.7	1.9	2.0	2.7
BES scores					
M	13.9	13.7	11.5	11.8	10.1
SD	6.1	6.9	5.8	8.2	7.1
Height (m)					
M	1.63	1.62	1.62	1.69	1.68
SD	0.05	0.06	0.06	0.06	0.07
% fathers with graduate or professional degree	54	58	—	43	—
% mothers with graduate or professional degree	22	32	—	23	—

Note: Subjects were measured in the spring, and fall. Subscripts on seasons indicate either Study 1 or Study 2. Dashes indicate that parents' educational data were not collected for the second wave of Study 2. BES = Binge Eating Scale.

numbers were used instead of names to investigate the social networks within the sororities.

Design

In Study 1, women from Sorority Alpha filled out a nine-page questionnaire in the spring ($n = 46$), a few weeks before the sorority closed down for the end of the term. In Study 2, members of both Sorority Alpha ($n = 51$) and Sorority Beta ($n = 66$) filled out questionnaires of seven pages in the fall and five pages in the spring, at the same time of year as in Study 1.[2]

Subjects. A general description of the subjects can be found in Table 21.1. Height, weight, and age were included in all forms of the questionnaire. Parents' educational status, as a proxy for social class, was included in Study 2 only on the fall questionnaire. The body-mass index found in Table 21.1 is a measure of overweight, or "fatness" (Sjostrom, 1978), and is calculated by the formula: weight

(kg')/height^2 (m). The body-mass index correlates highly ($>.90$) with other common measures of overweight, such as the ponderal index and deviation from the Metropolitan Life Insurance tabled norms for height and weight.

Questionnaire

The three versions of the questionnaire from the three waves differed slightly from each other, but there was a central, invariant core to all of them. (Across sororities all questionnaires were identical at any given time. Only the core questions are discussed in this article.)

Binge eating. Bulimia was measured by the Binge Eating Scale (BES; Gormally, Black, Daston, & Rardin, 1982). The 16-item BES was designed to assess the criteria for bulimia defined by the *Diagnostic and Statistical Manual (DSM-III)* of the American Psychiatric Association (1980), but has the advantage of providing a continuous measure rather than a classification of bulimic versus not bulimic. All of the *DSM-III* aspects of bulimia were measured: binge eating, purging (either by vomiting or by restrictive dieting), the emotional

---

[2]There is, of course, no one who is in both Sorority Alpha and Sorority Beta. However, there is some degree of overlap (40%) within Sorority Alpha over the two studies.

consequences of binging, inconspicuous eating during a binge, and so forth. Previous research at the same university has found the BES to have a one-factor solution; all items load substantially on the first factor. It has a 2-month test–retest reliability of .84. Further validation materials are available (Gormally, 1984; Gormally *et al.*, 1982).

How severe was binge eating in the sororities? Only a handful of the nearly 160 different subjects had high enough scores on the BES to be worthy of professional attention; almost all of the binge eating described here is at subclinical levels. However, binge eating was significantly higher in the sororities than subjects in two all-women dormitories ($n = 86$) measured at the same time as Study 1, $t(131) = 2.47$, $p < .01$).[3] Women with low BES scores reported that they were able to stop eating when they wanted to; they did not feel they had trouble controlling eating urges, and did not think a great deal about food. Women with high BES scores reported frequent uncontrollable eating urges, they spent a lot of time trying not to eat any more food, and had days where they could not seem to think about anything else but food. Women with moderate BES scores reported a compulsion to eat "every so often"; they spent some of their time trying to control eating urges and had brief periods of total occupation with thoughts of food.

Social networks. To uncover the pattern of social ties within the houses, respondents were asked to list their "ten best friends (within the house), in order." Popularity was defined as the number of times one was chosen by other people on their lists of friends. These data were also used to form friendship clusters or cliques, via cluster analyses. Membership in clusters was nonoverlapping; no woman was assigned membership in more than one social group.

The cluster analyses were performed on a square n by n matrix of friendship choices (the "top ten"). In this matrix, rows represented a subject's friendship choices, and columns represented subjects

being chosen. Choices were weighted from 10 (*top choice*) to 1 (*10th choice*), and then divided by the weighted sum of all of the choices, $n(n + 1)/2$, so that the weighted choices summed to unity for each set. The diagonal of the matrix, which represents self-choice (all zeros, as no one chose herself from her list of friends), was replaced with ones. The result of this is that being chosen by others in the friendship groups was more important to cluster assignment than sharing choices of other people in common. Thus, friends who chose each other and had similar patterns of friendship choices were put into the same cliques by the cluster analysis. Euclidean distances were used as a measure of similarity, and an average linkage criterion was used to join cases to clusters. Using different measures of similarity, different linkage criteria, a different weighting of the variables, or different values along the diagonal had little effect on the solutions. Separate cluster analyses were performed for each sorority at each time period, so that friendship cliques were determined for each wave of the study. These analyses resulted in an average of 10.0 ($SD = 2.9$) friendship clusters in each sorority at each time period, with an average of 5.1 ($SD = 2.3$) persons in each cluster.

Festinger *et al.*'s (1950) study differs from ours in that they were fortunate enough to have relatively equal-sized groups of individuals, whose members were randomly assigned to membership. In this study, groups were uncovered on the basis of friendship choices rather than being independent of them. The drawback to this is that friendship clusters were almost uniformly cohesive, based as they were on the similarity of their friendship choices. No friendship cluster contains a true isolate. Because groups were based in large part on reciprocated friendship choices (mutual popularity), finding group members particularly low in within-group popularity was relatively difficult.

Self-esteem. As a brief global measure of psychological health, a six-item version of the Rosenberg

---

[3] I collected data from two all-women dormitories with a very similar questionnaire at the same time as Sorority Alpha, Study 1, hoping to compare the dormitories to the sororities.

Unfortunately, the response rate was much too low in the dormitories (42%) to study social networks, and so the data are not discussed further here.

TABLE 21.2. Patterns of Popularity and Binge Eating

Variable	Sorority Alpha			Sorority Beta	
	Spring$_1$	Fall$_2$	Spring$_2$	Fall$_2$	Spring$_2$
Popularity and deviation from mean of binging	−.30[†]	.12	−.25	−.02	−.12
Popularity and binging	−.02	−.04	−.06	.28[†]	.32[†]
Prestige of group and group's normative binge level (aggregate)	−.80[††]	.33	−.53	.61[†]	.60[†]
Popularity within-group and within-group level of binge eating	−.10	.16	−.04	.22[*]	.36[††]

Note: Correlations are based on ns of 46, 51, 36, 66, and 55, respectively. Correlations between prestige and group's normative binge level were calculated with groups as the unit of analysis; the numbers of groups were 7, 9, 8, 12, and 14, respectively. Subscripts on seasons indicate either Study 1 or Study 2.
[*] $p < .05$, one-tailed. [†] $p < .05$, two-tailed. [††] $p < .01$, two-tailed.

Self-Esteem Scale (RSE; Rosenberg, 1965) was included. Among college students at the same university, the RSE correlated with the Eysenck Neuroticism Scale at $r = −.55$, with the Beck Depression Inventory at $r = −.62$, and with the Spielberger Trait Anxiety Scale at $r = −.69$.[4] Self-esteem is also likely to be an important factor in that those low in self-esteem are more likely to be open to the influence of their peers, compared with those high in self-esteem (Janis, 1954).

Results

Social Norms

The first issue for understanding how social norms work is to uncover their existence and patterns. To look for social norms, we traced the patterns of popularity within each of the social groups. If there are indeed norms about binge eating within a group, then deviation from those norms should be associated with a reduction in popularity. The less conforming to a binge eating norm one is, the more one is likely to be sanctioned through a reduction in popularity.

By the same token, whatever the most popular people do in any group is defined as normative. If the norm for binge eating is at the mean level of binging in the sorority, with absolute deviations from the mean representing deviations from the norm, then distance from the mean represents social deviance. In Sorority Alpha, this measure of social

deviance correlated with popularity at −.30 in Study 1, and −.25 in Study 2, for spring. In this sorority, the highest levels of popularity were among moderate bingers; binging both too little as well as too much were associated with reductions in popularity. These data are summarized in Table 21.2.

In Sorority Beta, a different pattern emerged. Surprisingly, in this group there was apparently a social norm that promoted binge eating; the more a woman binged, the more popular she was (rs = .28 for fall and .32 for spring). (The actual data peak in popularity was empirically determined to be not at the top of the binging severity distribution, but about 1.3 SDs above the mean, or about 1.2 SDs below the highest end.) Thus, there was evidence for social norms in support of some level of binge eating in both Sorority Alpha and Sorority Beta. The norms appeared to be somewhat different. In Sorority Alpha, a moderate level was associated with greater popularity. In Sorority Beta more binge eating was associated with more popularity.

It is somewhat surprising to find in Sorority Beta that more binging and more popularity went hand-in-hand. It is possible that the popularity of binge eaters was inflated if those women who binged the most in Sorority Beta all chose each other exclusively, whereas the women who did not binge as much spread their choices out among bingers and nonbingers alike. On the other hand, if a higher degree of binge eating was actually associated with greater popularity, then groups with high levels of binging should have been more prestigious within the entire sorority. To test this, average levels of binge eating in the cliques were calculated and correlated with a measure of group prestige: the

---

[4] I am grateful to Jonathan Shedler for making these data available.

percentage of out-group members who chose people within that group (i.e., the average amount of times in-group members were chosen by the out-group). This calculation is presented in the third line of Table 21.2. The prediction was borne out; the groups that binged the most were the most prestigious in Sorority Beta. The companion effect is also shown for Sorority Alpha. The more deviant the group was from the mean level of binge eating, the more it suffered from a reduction in prestige.

Not only were high-binging groups more popular in Sorority Beta, but also within social groups, those who binged more were better liked. In the bottom row of Table 21.2, the correlations between within-group popularity[5] and level of binging (adjusted for each group mean) are described; again, Sorority Beta demonstrated a norm in support of greater binge eating.

Festinger *et al.* (1950) found that, within groups, those who deviated from the local group norm were less popular than those who followed the norm. This suggests that, within friendship clusters, the more a woman deviates from her group mean, the less popular she should be. The patterns of correlations between within-group popularity and within-group deviance did not support this prediction, however, in the spring they ranged from −.15 to .16, and averaged .03 (all *p*s were *n*s). The inability to find the effect was largely due to the manner in which social groups were defined in this study. Because mutual choice and reciprocity were used in the cluster analysis, no social groups could have

had true isolates, and thus the variability among group members was likely to be greatly attenuated.

Pressures Toward Uniformity

In the presence of social norms in a valued social group there will be pressures toward uniformity. If a woman's friends are binge eaters, then the likelihood that she is also a binge eater increases. This is the crux of the social psychological account of the acquisition of bulimic behavior, and it is represented as the contagion coefficient in the top line of Table 21.3.

The contagion coefficient is a calculation based on the social networks analysis previously described. Subjects were sorted into social friendship clusters (cliques) by means of a cluster analysis. The contagion coefficient is the Pearson *r* between a woman's binge-eating level and the average binge-eating level of her closest friends in the sorority (statistically, this is the correlation between her own BES score and the average BES score of her cluster-mates, not including the target subject). The contagion coefficient is a behavior-to-behavior model of influence; it asks the question, To what extent is a woman's binge eating like that of her friends?

The answer, apparent from Table 21.3, is "considerably." In the fall, after only 6 weeks of interaction within the friendship cliques, there was no indication that friends were more like each other than any other sorority member (*r*s = .00 and −.15,

TABLE 21.3. Pressure Toward Uniformity in Social Groups

Variable	Sorority Alpha			Sorority Beta	
	Spring$_1$	Fall$_2$	Spring$_2$	Fall$_2$	Spring$_2$
Contagion coefficient	−.30†	.00	.21*	−.15	.40††
% choices made in group	81.6	87.2	89.4†	82.3	85.4††
Deviation from friends in fall with how binging changed over time	—		−.36†		−.34††

Note: Correlations are based on *n*s of 46, 51, 36, 66, and 55, respectively.
* different from −.08 at *p* < .05, one-tailed. † *p* < .05, two-tailed. †† *p* < .01, two-tailed.

[5] Within-group popularity is based on the percentage of people within a person's group choosing her. Because smaller clusters are likely to have more reciprocal choices just by chance (a group of two is sure to have 100% reciprocation), each person's percentage choice was divided by the group's average percentage within choice. Each group's mean thus becomes 1.00; numbers above that indicate higher within-group popularity, numbers below it, lower popularity.

for Alpha and Beta, respectively). However, after 7 months of interaction, friends had become more uniform (rs ranged from .21 to .40).

It is important to note that the expected value for the contagion coefficient under the null hypothesis is not in fact .00, because when a woman is removed from the population, the mean of that population, and hence the expected value of the sample of friends, is shifted slightly in the opposite direction. To ascertain exactly what size correlation to expect by chance, a Monte Carlo study based on 200 randomly generated data sets was performed for each of the sororities.[6] These analyses yielded, under the null hypothesis, expected contagion coefficients of $-.09$ for Sorority Alpha in Study 1, $-.08$ for Sorority Alpha in Study 2, and $-.07$ for Sorority Beta.

The time difference is probably due to two effects. First, social influence probably would require more than 6 weeks to have any appreciable effect on a woman's binge eating. Second, the more cohesive the group, the more influence it should have over its members.

The second row of Table 21.3 indicates that, in fact, cohesion increased over time. "Percentage choices made within group" is the total number of in-group choices made, divided by the total number of in-group choices possible. Because the subjects made 10 friendship choices, and the average cluster size was 5.1 members (and the members did not choose themselves), 41% of all possible choices could have been made to the in-group. Across all studies, of the possible 4.1 choices, approximately 3.5, or 85% of possible choices, were made in-group. In spite of the relatively high cohesion even in the fall, cohesion did increase over time (daggers represent the significance levels of pairwise t tests). Thus, it is likely that time and increased cohesion worked together to bring friends' binging levels into agreement.

In fact, at the entire group level, there was a decrease in variability on binge eating over the course of the year. The standard deviation shrank from 6.9 to 5.8 in Sorority Alpha, and from 8.2 to 7.1 in Sorority Beta (see Table 21.1). This difference across both sororities was significant at $p < .05$ (test of equality of variances, one-tailed).

Apparently, at both the group level (whole sorority) as well as the friendship level (within clusters), friends became more similar over time. The central question to ask at this point is, Do we have evidence here of social pressure, or is this evidence of assortative friendships (birds of a feather flock together)? Is the behavior-to-behavior correlation found in Table 21.3 evidence of contagion or of assortment? If sorority members were making friends on the basis of how much they binged, then a similar pattern of within-group results would obtain in the absence of any actual social pressures or movement toward uniformity. Several converging lines of evidence suggest that this is a pattern of social influence and not merely differential assortment.

Evidence of Social Influence

First, if the phenomenon observed is merely assortment, then personality-type variables other than binge eating should also correlate among friends. This, however, does not seem to be the case; for example, self-esteem (RSE) correlates were .01, .00, and .04 in the spring for Alpha 1, Alpha 2, and Beta, respectively. Such problems, however, are best handled by data collected over time, and Study 2 provided us with just these sorts of data.

If binge eaters were simply reassorting to be with "birds of a feather," the social cliques uncovered in the spring (which differed significantly on binging) should have differed from each other in their past binging level as well; their fall BES scores should have been significantly different by cluster. However, in neither Sorority Alpha nor Sorority Beta were these differences significant. In fact, friendship choices were quite stable. Because friendship patterns are not continuous but nominal variables, a class measure of association, the *contingency coefficient*, was used to describe stability

[6] For the Monte Carlo analyses, random data were generated with the same mean, standard deviation, and size of cliques for each sorority separately. All other calculations were made as in the actual data set. Observed correlations were in the 99th, 97th, and 99th percentile of their respective null hypothesis distributions.

of friendship patterns.[7] From fall to spring, choices were stable, with contingency coefficients of .87 and .94 in Alpha and Beta, respectively.

If the contagion coefficient were due merely to self-selection into similar groups, then one would expect this correlation to be significant in the fall. Six weeks is probably enough time to learn something about one another's eating habits; however, there is no evidence of contagion in the fall, indicating that 6 weeks was not enough time for social influence to take place.

If one allows the necessary passage of time and the increased group cohesion that accompanies it, then we would expect that pressures toward uniformity should, across the two waves, pressure women to become more like their immediate social groups. To test this, we calculated the distance a woman was from her friends at Time 1 by subtracting her binge-eating level from the average binge-eating level of her friends. This number was then correlated with how her binging level moved over the academic year. If there were social pressures toward uniform levels of binging, then the distance a woman was from her friends at Time 1 should have correlated negatively with the change in her binging level. If she binged much less than her friends, she should have increased her binging level; if she binged much more, she should have decreased.

This is exactly what happened. The bottom row of Table 21.3 describes these correlations. In both sororities Alpha and Beta, women became more like their friends over time. The less each woman was like her friends in the fall, the more she moved toward them over the academic year. Thus, the contagion coefficient seems to be, in sum, a measure of social influence.

One possible interpretation of this finding is that it is regression toward the mean. Certainly,

regression toward the mean is likely to take place. But what is the size of correlations that we would expect to find based merely on chance, and are these correlations significantly larger? To test this, a Monte Carlo study based on the same parameters, but using 325 randomly generated data sets, generated expected correlations of $-.079$ for Sorority Alpha and $-.091$ for Sorority Beta, significantly smaller than the correlations found in Table 21.3 (both $ps < .05$, two-tailed).[8]

Festinger *et al.* (1950) found that in Westgate, social norms overrode personal factors, so that the potential value of the tenants organization to a person was entirely independent of his or her attitude toward it. This does not seem to be the case in the present study. Because the personal factors are essentially risk factors in the epidemiological model, standardized regressions on binge eating by risk factors were computed. Both psychological health, as measured by the RSE, and degree of fatness, as measured by the body-mass index, were independently predictive of binge eating in almost all groups at all times (see Table 21.4). Even as social pressures grew over the course of the year, the correlations between binge eating and the risk factors of fatness and low self-esteem remained relatively stable (no beta weights were significantly different from each other between fall and spring).

To demonstrate the simplicity of this account of the acquisition of the behavior of binge eating, Table 21.5 shows the regressions within each sorority of an overall regression testing the social contagion model of binge eating. Using only the RSE as a measure of general psychological well-being, the average binging level of a woman's friends, and her body-mass index, one can predict a woman's binge-eating score with a multiple correlation of .48 to .57. Although this is a fairly parsimonious account of binge eating, it nonetheless appears to

---

[7] The contingency coefficient is calculated as

$$C = \sqrt{\frac{x^2}{x^2 + N}},$$

where the minimum value of C is for .00, and the maximum value is never greater than 1.00.

---

[8] The same procedure for Monte Carlo analyses was followed as before. Random data were generated with the same mean, standard deviation, and size of cliques for each sorority separately. Furthermore, the randomly generated variables representing fall and spring Binge Eating Scale scores were correlated to the same extent as the observed data. All other calculations were made as in the actual data set. Observed correlations were in the 98th and 99th percentile of their respective null hypothesis distributions.

TABLE 21.4. Risk Factors for Binge Eating in Studies 1 and 2 Expressed as Standardized Beta Weights

Sorority and wave	Body-mass index	Self-esteem
Alpha		
Spring$_1$	.28*	−.46***
Alpha		
Fall$_2$	.41***	−.37**
Spring$_2$	.42**	−.50***
Beta		
Fall$_2$	.37***	−.37***
Spring$_2$	.20	−.46***

Note: Beta weights are based on *n*s of 46, 51, 36, 66, and 55, for each row, respectively. Subscripts on seasons indicate either Study 1 or Study 2.
* $p < .05$. ** $p < .01$. *** $p < .005$.

TABLE 21.5. Social Influence, Body Mass, and Self-Esteem: The Social Contagion Model of Binge Eating

Study	Adjusted R	Adjusted R^2
Sorority Alpha		
Study 1	.51*	.26
Study 2	.57*	.32
Sorority Beta		
Study 2	.48*	.23

Note: Multiple correlations are based on *n*s of 46, 36, and 55 for each row, respectively. The regression model includes social influence, self-esteem, and the body-mass index as predictors, and are based on spring data.
* $p < .005$.

be fairly useful for explaining patterns of binge eating in these sororities.

Discussion

To demonstrate social norms, popularity patterns were traced with respect to binge eating. In Sorority Alpha, deviations from the normative level of binge eating were associated with reductions in popularity. In Sorority Beta, a different normative pattern emerged; the more a woman binged, the more popular she was.

To demonstrate behavior-to-behavior influence on binge eating, sorority members' binge-eating levels were correlated with the binge-eating levels of their friends. This correlation was found in the spring for both sororities. This finding was most likely due to social influence rather than assortment, based on data including the stability of friendship ties, the lack of friend-to-friend correlation of self-esteem and other person variables, and the lack of difference among spring groups in their prior fall binging levels. Most important, however, is the correlation which directly indicates social influence: Women became more like their friends over time.

I have suggested that when a woman experiences distress, she is open to social influence. When the influence she is receiving in terms of social information and approval is in support of binging, she is more likely to become a binge eater. Some sort of interaction between social influence and susceptibility is necessary to explain the problem of binge eating. For example, there is no reason to expect that the significant negative correlations between binge eating and self-esteem reflect a fact of nature. Prior to the sociocultural development of binge eating as a symptom related to psychological distress, binge eating and self-esteem had to be uncorrelated; there was such a low incidence of problem binging prior to the early 1970s that little variability existed in binge eating (Rosenzweig & Spruill, 1986). It is only in the presence of models for and information about binge eating that low self-esteem is likely to lead to binge eating. Because both of these sororities had prescriptive norms about binge eating, the appropriate social group with which to compare the self-esteem to binge-eating correlation—no backdrop of social norms—could not be included here. If it is true that an interaction between social influence and susceptibility is necessary, then individuals who are susceptible to influence (e.g., are low in self-esteem), but are not in groups where there are norms about binge eating, should not binge eat any more than average.

A Social Psychological Integration

The social influence account of binge eating provides a parsimonious bridge among the three accounts of bulimia discussed in the introduction. From the sociocultural perspective, one can discern which kinds of influence are likely to be found among social groups. Currently, one kind of influence is toward binge eating, and a college sorority is likely to reflect current concerns of this sort. From the clinical perspective, one can discern who is at risk for this social influence. In fact, many of the personality characteristics that clinicians have uncovered can be characterized as indicators of susceptibility to social influence: low self-esteem, depression, impulsivity, poor family environment, poorly developed sense of self, etc. For the epidemiological perspective, the social influence model provides a mechanism by which we can describe how symptoms are acquired and spread.

The social influence model works together with the other three approaches to meet the necessary theoretical criteria specified in the introduction. Who is and who is not at risk for binge eating is a function of both the immediate social influence and one's susceptibility to that influence. Influence and susceptibility will be affected by group cohesion, consensus on norms, and the attractiveness of the group as well as the individuals' general susceptibility to influence based on depression, self-esteem, and so forth.

The sorority milieu is likely to be a breeding ground for eating disorders (Squire, 1983); it is a powerful setting for translating cultural influence into direct social influence. The extreme social importance of body size and shape for this population most likely serves to increase the risk of beginning dieting and hence binge eating. It is likely that in other social groups where physical attractiveness and body shape are not weighed so heavily, the sorts of findings reported here would be greatly attenuated or even nonexistent.

It is important to note that a social influence model of binge eating explicitly predicts this possibility. If the group norm is entirely against dieting and binging but rather for, vegetarianism, for example, the correlation between psychological distress and binging should approach zero. Instead, the correlation between distress and vegetarianism should be high. For this reason, the size and direction of correlations should differ between groups, depending on what the norms are for handling personal distress (e.g., Garner & Garfinkel, 1980). The content portion of the social influence model (in this case, binge eating) is a relatively open slot. Distress may be handled in a number of ways, and social pressures could as easily result in

smoking, delinquency, heavy drinking, loss of virginity, drug use, or depression (Jessor & Jessor, 1977; Orford, 1985). It may be in this way that bulimia has replaced depressive symptoms as a primary pathway of expressing psychological distress among younger women. If cultural norms move away from the current over-concern with dieting and thinness, then bulimia and binge eating will disappear with them. The expression of psychological distress will continue to follow cultural norms, wherever they may wander.

These results indicate that a social psychological analysis of eating disorders is warranted and likely to bear fruit. The spread of one important symptom of bulimia—binge eating—through a population is likely to be the result of social influence. Further research in this social psychological vein is necessary to delineate the interrelationship of the variables in the model. The role and development of social norms about binge eating and their importance to friendship ties, the nature of the transfer of behavior from friend to friend, and, especially, whether and how social pressures are applied among friends, are important issues that now face us. What is necessary are longitudinal studies of women at risk for binge eating and bulimia that are begun prior to the development of disordered eating habits. This may mean beginning longitudinal studies as early as junior high school, or even before.

The question remains, what form does social influence take in these sororities? A variety of possibilities exist. It may be that the women are directly teaching each other appropriate binging levels, although several informants indicated that they felt this was unlikely. It may be a case of leadership, where the most popular women set the tone for the rest of the sorority. This would be consistent with an account based on simple imitation or modeling: The high status members' level of binging is transmitted via imitation to the rest of the group. Or members of social groups may be coerced into conforming to a clique's standard. Presumably, the coercion could be based on the giving or withholding of popularity. However, the exact process of acquisition cannot be determined in this study.

Nonetheless, these data do appear to fit the model of behavioral contagion proposed by Wheeler (1966). Wheeler, following Redl (1949), proposed that in cases where a behavior has both some sort of prior restraint to it (as excessive binge eating certainly does) and at the same time has some other strong impulse or urge toward fulfillment of a need, the presence of a model acting out the conflictual behavior increases the likelihood of the behavior being performed (Wheeler, 1966). In a sense, the avoidance gradient in an approach–avoidance conflict is lowered, making approach more likely. The social norms of the sorority, in combination with the presence of models, are likely to make the costs associated with binge eating appear less severe and increase the likelihood of higher levels of binge eating. In this way, observation of binge eating, motivated (or released) in part by social pressures based on popularity, may account for how binge eating as a behavior is acquired and expressed.

A general model of the social influence patterns in psychological distress could be derived from the social psychological model proposed here. It would involve changing the content of the social influence but not its pattern. In general, the pattern of influence is likely to follow the outline described by Kerckhoff and Back (1968) in their study of contagion in a North Carolina garment factory. Whichever symptom is being spread, it still should appear among people experiencing distress, it should spread out along sociometric and communication networks, and the norms about the behavior should change toward acceptance as the behavior becomes more widespread. Thus, the social influence model could apply to as diverse phenomena as the hysterical fainting found in Freud's day, depression, or bulimia. All one would need to change in the model is the type of data made socially available in terms of social norms and modeling of the behavior, and one can predict fainting, rashes, vomiting, depression, or binge eating.

Indeed, the social influence processes described here look strikingly like those described by Newcomb (1943) in his famous Bennington study. A strong social norm in favor of left-wing politics emerged at Bennington College, first among the faculty, and increasingly with age, the students. New students who did not follow the norm, that is, did not espouse left-wing politics, were sanctioned with a reduction in popularity. Newcomb (1943) argued that the process of social influence and attitude change was not specific to political attitudes, but could generalize to almost any expressible attitude or set of behaviors, and these results with respect to binge eating seem to bear out his claim.

An important task remains. Peer influence may account for how behaviors such as binge eating or alcohol use begin (Orford, 1985), but an account of the sort outlined here does not describe how these behaviors can escalate into full-blown bulimia or alcoholism. Although some social factors have been studied, the role of social influence in this process as yet remains far too unexamined.

REFERENCES

American Psychiatric Association. (1980). *Diagnostic and statistical manual of mental disorders* (*3rd ed.*). Washington, DC Author.

Boskind-Lodahl, M., & Sirlin, J. (1977, March). The gorging-purging syndrome. *Psychology Today*, pp. 50–52, 82, 85.

Bennett, W., & Gurin, J. (1982). *The dieter's dilemma*. New York: Basic Books.

Cantril, H. (1941). *The psychology of social movements*. New York: Wiley.

Cantwell, P. (1985). Understanding bulimia. *Contemporary Psychology, 30*, 196–198.

Crago, M., Yates, A., Beutler, L. E., & Arizmendi, T. G. (1985). Height-weight ratios among female athletes: Are collegiate athletics the precursors to an anorexic syndrome? *International Journal of Eating Disorders, 4*, 79–87.

Crandall, C. S. (1987). Do men and women differ in emotional and ego involvement with food? *Journal of Nutrition Education, 19*, 229–236.

Dunn, O. K., & Ondercin, P. (1981). Personality variables related to compulsive eating in college women. *Journal of Clinical Psychology, 37*, 43–49.

Dwyer, J., Feldman, J. J., & Mayer, J. (1970). The social psychology of dieting. Journal of Health and Social Behavior, 11, 269–287.

Festinger, L. (1950). Informal social communication. *Psychological Review, 57*, 271–292.

Festinger, L. (1954). A theory of social comparison processes. *Human Relations, 7*, 117–140.

Festinger, L., Schachter, S., & Back, K. W. (1950). *Social pressures in informal groups*. New York: Harper.

Gandour, M. J. (1984). Bulimia: Clinical description, assessment, etiology, and treatment. *International Journal of Eating Disorders, 3*, 3–38.

Garfinkel, P. E., & Garner, D. M. (1982). *Anorexia nervosa: A multidimensional perspective*. New York: Brunner/Mazel.

Garner, D. M., & Garfinkel, P. E. (1980). Socio-cultural factors in the development of anorexia nervosa. *Psychological Medicine, 10,* 647–656.

Garner; D. M., Garfinkel, P. E., Schwartz, D., & Thompson, M. (1980). Cultural expectations of thinness in women. *Psychological Reports, 47,* 483–491.

Garrow, J. (1978). The regulation of energy expenditure. In G. A. Bray (Ed.), *Recent advances in obesity research* (Vol. 2). London: Newman.

Gormally, J. (1984). The obese binge eater: Diagnosis, etiology and clinical issues. In R. C. Hawkins II, W. J. Fremouw, & P. F. Clement (Eds.), *The binge-purge syndrome*. New York: Springer Publishing.

Gormally, J., Black, S., Daston, S., & Rardin, D. (1982). The assessment of binge eating severity among obese persons. *Addictive Behaviors, 7,* 47–55.

Halmi, K. A., Falk, J. R., & Schwartz, E. (1981). Binge-eating and vomiting: A survey of a college population. *Psychological Medicine, 11,* 697–706.

Janis, I. L. (1954). Personality correlates of susceptibility to persuasion. *Journal of Personality, 22,* 504–518.

Jessor, R., & Jessor, S. (1977). *Problem behavior and psychosocial development: A longitudinal study of youth*. New York: Academic Press.

Johnson, C., Lewis, C., & Hagman, L. (1984). The syndrome of bulimia. *Psychiatric Clinics of America, 7,* 247–274.

Kerckhoff, A. C., & Back, K. W. (1968). *The june bug: A study of hysterical contagion*. Englewood Cliffs, NJ: Prentice-Hall.

Latané, B., & Wolf, S. (1981). The social impact of majorities and minorities. *Psychological Review, 88,* 438–454.

McGuire, W. J., & Padawer-Singer, A. (1976). Trait salience in the spontaneous self-concept. *Journal of Personality and Social Psychology, 33,* 743–754.

Moreland, R. L., & Levine, J. M. (1982). Socialization in small groups: Temporal changes in individual-group relations. In L. Berkowitz (Ed.), *Advances in experimental social psychology* (Vol. 15, pp. 137–189). New York: Academic Press.

Newcomb, T. M. (1943). *Personality and social change*. New York: Dryden.

Nisbett, R. E. (1972). Hunger, obesity and the ventromedial hypothalamus. *Psychological Review, 79,* 433–453.

Orbach, S. (1978). *Fat is a feminist issue*. New York: Berkeley Press.

Orford, J. (1985). *Excessive appetites*. London: Wiley.

Polivy, J., & Herman, C. P. (1985). Dieting and binging: A causal analysis. *American Psychologist, 40,* 193–204.

Pope, H. G., & Hudson, J. I. (1984). *New hope for binge eaters: Advances in the understanding and treatment of bulimia*. New York: Harper & Row.

Radant, S. (1986, May). *Bulimia as a subtype of borderline personality disorder: A comparison study*. Paper presented at the meeting of the Western Psychological Association, Seattle, WA.

Redl, F. (1949). The phenomenon of contagion and "shock effect" in group therapy. In K. R. Eissler (Ed.), *Searchlights on delinquency*. New York: International Universities Press.

Rodin, J., Silberstein, L., & Striegel-Moore, R. (1984). Women and weight: A normative discontent. *Nebraska Symposium on Motivation* (Vol. 27, pp. 267–307). Lincoln: University of Nebraska Press.

Rose, M. A. (1985). *Rush: The girl's guide to sorority success*. New York: Villard.

Rosenberg, M. (1965). *Society and adolescent self-image*. Princeton, NJ: Princeton University Press.

Rosenzweig, M., & Spruill, J. (1986). Twenty years after Twiggy: A retrospective investigation of bulimic-like behaviors. *International Journal of Eating Disorders, 6,* 24–31.

Schachter, S. (1951). Deviation rejection, and communication. *Journal of Abnormal and Social Psychology, 46,* 190–207.

Schlesier-Stropp, B. (1984). Bulimia: A review of the literature. *Psychological Bulletin, 95,* 247–257.

Sherif, M. (1936). *The psychology of social norms*. New York: Harper.

Sinoway, C. G., Raupp, C. D., & Newman, J. (1985, August). *Binge eating and bulimia: Comparing incidence and characteristics across universities*. Paper presented at the meeting of the 93rd Annual Convention of the American Psychological Association, Los Angeles, CA.

Sjostrom, L. (1978). The contribution of fat cells to the determination of body weight. In G. A. Bray (Ed.), *Recent advances in obesity research* (Vol. 2). London: Newman.

Squire, S. (1983). *The slender balance*. New York: Pinnacle.

Srikameswaran, S., Leichner, P., & Harper, D. (1984). Sex role ideology among women with anorexia nervosa and bulimia. *International Journal of Eating Disorders, 3,* 39–43.

Strangler, R. S., & Printz, A. M. (1980). DSM-III: Psychiatric diagnosis in a university population. *American Journal of Psychiatry, 137,* 937–940.

Striegel-Moore, R. H., Silberstein, L., & Rodin, J. (1986). Toward an understanding of risk factors for bulimia. *American Psychologist, 41,* 246–263.

Strober, M., Morell, W., Burroughs, J., Salkin, B., & Jacobs, C. (1985). A controlled family study of anorexia nervosa. *Journal of Psychiatric Research, 19,* 239–246.

Wheeler, L. (1966). Toward a theory of behavioral contagion. *Psychological Review, 73,* 179–192.

Received October 8, 1987
Revision received April 30, 1988
Accepted May 4, 1988 ■

Social Comparisons and Pay Evaluations: Preferences for Same-Sex and Same-Job Wage Comparisons

Brenda Major and Blythe Forcey

This research examined women's and men's social comparison preferences when evaluating the fairness of pay. Subjects were assigned randomly to work on a job described as masculine, feminine, or sex neutral and were told that they would be paid for their work. After working on the job and privately receiving identical payment, subjects rank ordered their preference for seeing the average male, average female, and average combined-sex wage paid in each of the three jobs. Despite the availability of the combined-sex wage, subjects preferred to maximize similarity in their wage comparisons, with the majority choosing to see the pay of a same-sex and same-job group first. Regardless of the sex linkage of their job assignment, subjects selected a same-job comparison first. Sex linkage of job did affect same-sex preferences: whereas subjects in sex-appropriate and sex-neutral jobs showed a significant preference for seeing the pay of same-sex others first, subjects in sex-inappropriate jobs did not. Results also indicated that both men and women assigned to the feminine job expected somewhat less pay and thought their obtained pay was more fair than did those assigned to the masculine job. Furthermore, women thought they deserved less pay for their work than did men, regardless of their job assignment. Implications of these results for gender differences in outcome evaluations are discussed.

This research was supported by a Biomedical Research Support Grant from the State University of New York at Buffalo, 150-H079R. Portions of this research were presented at the 1983 meetings of the Eastern Psychological Association in Philadelphia. Thanks are extended to Dean McFarlin and Carol Miller for their helpful comments on earlier drafts of this manuscript, to Nancy Johnson for her suggestions on design, and to Ann Marie Schmidlin for her assistance with data collection. Requests for reprints should be sent to Brenda Major, Department of Psychology, State University of New York, 4230 Ridge Lea Road, Buffalo, NY 14226.

Social comparison processes are a central construct in most theories of interpersonal justice and outcome evaluations, including equity theory (cf. Adams, 1965; Walster, Berscheid, & Walster, 1973) and relative deprivation theories (cf. Crosby, 1982; Davis, 1959; Pettigrew, 1967; Runciman, 1966). Indeed, according to traditional equity theory (Adams, 1965), we come to know what is fair *only* through comparing our inputs and outcomes to those of others. Despite the importance of social comparison processes in theories of social justice, however, the precise manner in which social comparison information is selected and utilized in justice judgments and outcome evaluations has been ignored by both theory and research.

The typical approach in research on social justice, and equity theory in particular, has been to provide individuals with an explicit comparison other or comparison standard and then to examine their judgments of whether the outcomes they receive (or observe others to receive) are fair, just, or satisfactory. Thus, the question of who individuals freely choose as comparison others is sidestepped. In most situations, however, people do not have one explicit external standard available, but rather have a large number of people available who might potentially serve as comparison others. Under these circumstances, with whom do they choose to compare their inputs and outcomes? Most justice theorists agree that similarity is an important basis on which social comparisons are made (Austin, 1977), but have done little more to specify the precise nature of the comparison others chosen in determinations of fairness.

Examination of who individuals choose to compare with when evaluating their outcomes may clarify individual differences observed in justice-related behaviors. For example, research has found that American university women tend to pay themselves less than men do when allocating monetary rewards between themselves and others (see Kahn, O'Leary, Krulewitz, & Lamm, 1980; Major & Deaux, 1982, for reviews) or to themselves alone (Callahan-Levy & Messé, 1979; Major, McFarlin, & Gagnon, 1984, Experiment 1); women work longer, do more work, and are more efficient than men when given the same amount of pay and instructions to

work as long as they think fair (Major et al., 1984, Experiment 2), and women expect lower salaries than do comparably qualified men in the same field (Major & Konar, 1984). Furthermore, studies of job and pay satisfaction consistently have found that working women do not consider themselves unfairly paid (cf. Crosby, 1982), despite objective evidence that women are paid less than men working in comparable jobs (Treiman & Hartmann, 1981). Crosby (1982) has referred to this as the "paradox of the contented female worker."

The above sex differences may result, in part, from similarity biases in social comparisons that operate to women's disadvantage. Specifically, several authors have suggested that men and women rely on *same-sex* others rather than different-sex others for wage comparisons (Chesler & Goodman, 1976; Crosby, 1982; Major & Konar, 1984; Major et al., 1984). Since women typically are paid less than men for their work (Treiman & Hartmann, 1981), women thus compare their outcomes with a lower wage standard than do men. Several field studies (cf. Crosby, 1982; Oldham et al., 1982) recently have obtained some indirect support for this hypothesis. For example, Crosby (1962) found that working men and women were much more likely to name someone of their own sex than someone of the other sex when asked to name three people who they used as referents in evaluating their jobs.

Similarity biases in social comparison preferences also may result in an overreliance on comparisons with *same-job* others rather than with others in different but comparable jobs (cf. Patchen, 1961). Same-job comparisons, however, also may operate to women's disadvantage. Specifically, since female-dominated jobs tend to be lower paid than comparable male-dominated jobs (Treiman & Hartmann, 1981), comparisons with same-job co-workers may result in women comparing with a lower pay standard than men. Furthermore, since the majority of jobs are highly sex segregated (Treiman & Hartmann, 1981), comparisons with same-job co-workers may result in a de facto comparison with same-sex others. That is, since most men and women work in jobs dominated by their own sex, comparing wages with one's co-workers may be essentially the same as comparing with others of one's own sex.

Although the above hypotheses are suggestive regarding a possible mechanism underlying women's and men's outcome evaluations, research has not, as yet, tested these hypotheses directly. Specifically, social comparison preferences have not been examined in controlled settings where the outcomes of other males and females in one's own job as well as comparable jobs are equally available for comparison. Whether same-sex and/or same-job social comparisons are preferred under such conditions is an open question. One purpose of the current research was to address this question.

A second purpose of this research was to examine whether outcome comparisons follow the same pattern as ability comparisons. In contrast to the limited research on social comparisons of outcomes, a large amount of research has been devoted to the question of who people choose for social comparison of abilities (see Suls & Miller, 1977). A recent advance in this area is the "related attributes hypothesis" (Goethals & Darley, 1977), which proposes that people prefer to compare their abilities with others who are similar on attributes perceived to be related to performance. Although some research is supportive of this hypothesis (Suls, Gastorf, & Lawhon, 1978; Wheeler, Koestner, & Driver, 1982; Zanna, Goethals, & Hill, 1975), other research suggests that there may be a drive to maximize information gain, that is, to acquire information about both similar others and "standard setters" (those who have the highest ability) when comparing one's abilities with others (Feldman & Ruble, 1981). Other recent research, however, suggests that similarity on certain salient attributes, such as sex (Miller, 1984; Suls, Gaes, & Gastorf, 1979) and physical attractiveness (Miller, 1982) may be particularly important in the choice of comparison other, regardless of the relationship between these attributes and performance. Research has not as yet explored whether similar comparison patterns apply when the goal is to evaluate one's outcomes rather than one's abilities.

The current research investigated women's and men's preferences for acquiring information about the pay of same-sex and same-job others when evaluating the fairness of pay. In this experiment, males and females were randomly assigned to work on a job described as masculine, feminine, or sex neutral and were informed that they would be paid according to their performance and job assignment. After working on the job, all subjects were given privately an ambiguous performance score and were paid the same amount of money. They then were given the opportunity to rank order their preferences for seeing the average wage paid to nine different groups of individuals—the average male, average female, and average combined-sex wage for each of the three jobs. Subjects also indicated how fair they thought the wage they received was and how satisfied they were with it.

We hypothesized that individuals would prefer to maximize similarity on their first ranked comparison choice. Specifically, we predicted that both sexes would indicate as their first preference the choice of the same-sex and same-job comparison group. Second comparison choice was examined to determine whether preferences were stronger to compare within sex or within job. The impact of sex linkage of assigned job on social comparisons also was examined. If the related-attributes hypothesis is applicable to outcome comparisons, individuals should prefer to compare outcomes with those of same-sex others only when sex is related to pay, that is, same-sex preferences should occur primarily for subjects assigned to the masculine and feminine jobs, and no same-sex bias should be seen among subjects assigned to the sex-neutral job. In contrast, if sex is a particularly salient attribute for comparison regardless of its link to performance or pay (Miller, 1984; Suls *et al.*, 1979), same-sex comparison preferences should be displayed by subjects across all jobs.

Outcome comparisons, however, may not follow the same principles as ability comparisons. Rather, people may consider the average (combined-sex) wage as the most appropriate standard for pay comparison, since it yields the most general and unbiased information. Alternatively, people may prefer to acquire information about the pay of those others who dominate or excel at their own job. This preference would be compatible with a same-sex choice for those individuals assigned to a sex-appropriate job (i.e., men working on a masculine job or women working on a feminine job). For people assigned to a sex-inappropriate job, however, this pattern would result in social comparison preferences being stronger for opposite-sex others than for same-sex others. For example, a woman working in a male-dominated, "masculine" job may see the pay of other men, rather than other women, as the most appropriate comparison standard for evaluating her own wage. Some evidence consistent with this "standard setter" hypothesis was obtained by Crosby (1982). She found that although the majority of women (60%) working in high-prestige, male-dominated jobs named same-sex others as job referents, these women also were more likely than other groups to name cross-sex others as job referents.

Method

Subjects and Design

Thirty-three male and twenty-four female undergraduates at the University of Buffalo took part in this study in partial fulfillment of a course requirement. Six subjects were excluded from the analysis: 4 because they failed to understand crucial portions of the instructions and 2 because they were not able to remember the sex linkage of their assigned job on the post-task questionnaire. All were aware prior to the experiment that they would be receiving an unspecified amount of pay for their work in the experiment. Approximately equal numbers of males and females were assigned randomly to work on a job labeled as masculine, feminine, or sex neutral, resulting in a 2×3 between-subject factorial design.

Procedure

Subjects participated in mixed-sex groups ranging in size from two to eight persons. A female experimenter and male assistant conducted all sessions. Upon arrival at the laboratory, subjects were escorted to one of eight individual desks. Each desk was separated from all others by barriers, constructed in such a way that subjects could not see the people on either side of them.

Once all of the subjects had arrived, the experimenter informed them that the purpose of the experiment was to examine the performance of college students at several local universities on three specific types of jobs and that they would each be assigned randomly to work on one of the jobs. They were told that "All three jobs require about the same amount of education (a high school degree) to do well, and the three jobs are of comparable difficulty." Furthermore, they were informed that the pay range for the jobs was from $1.25 to $2.75 and that the exact amount of money they would be paid depended on their performance as well as on the particular job to which they were assigned. All three jobs were then described orally, in counterbalanced order, as follows:

> The first job involves *analytical reasoning*. This job requires a person to make a series of decisions on the basis of their analysis of factual and numerical information. United States Department of Labor (USDL, 1981) statistics indicate that about 80% of the people who perform this job in the work force are men and about 20% are women.
>
> The second job involves *interpersonal perceptiveness*. This job requires a person to make a series of decisions on the basis of their intuition and interpersonal judgment. USDL (1981) statistics indicate that about 80% of the people who perform this type of job in the work force are women, and about 20% are men.
>
> The third job involves *predictive ability*. This job requires a person to make a series of decisions on the basis of their analysis of facts as well as intuitive judgments. Current USDL statistics indicate that this type of job is performed about equally often by men and women in the work force.

Following the above three job descriptions, subjects were assigned randomly to work on one of the three jobs. Each subject was given a written description of their assigned job that was identical to one of those previously presented. One third received the masculine job description, one third received the feminine job description, and one third received the neutral job description. Regardless of their assigned job description, however, all subjects actually were given the same job. The job required them to make a series of decisions predicting the success in college of a number of students on the basis of several types of information such as high school grades, SAT scores, and extracurricular activities. This task has been used in previous research (cf. Kahn, Nelson, & Gaeddert, 1980; Major & Adams, 1983) and is perceived as sex neutral when unaccompanied by a sex-linked label. Thus, the only difference between conditions was in the description of the job, that is, whether the job was described in masculine, feminine, or neutrally sex-linked terms. Before performing the task, subjects were given a short questionnaire assessing how well they expected to perform on the job, the amount of money they expected to earn (in a dollar amount), and the average pay they perceived college males and females as earning on the subject's assigned job. All were then given 15 min to work on the 80-item task. Most were unable to complete all of the items.

At the end of 15 min, task sheets were collected by the assistant who took them to another room, ostensibly to score them and determine each person's payment. While waiting for the assistant to return, subjects were asked to evaluate their performance on a 1 (*very poor*) to a 7 (*very good*) scale and to indicate, in monetary terms, how much pay they felt would be fair for their work. When the assistant returned he handed each subject a sealed envelope labeled with his or her seal number. The envelope contained the subject's performance score (which was an ambiguous 114 in all cases) and cash payment, which was $2.35 in all cases. Subjects were asked to examine this information and pocket the money. The anonymity of their score and payment were emphasized, and barriers prevented them from seeing how much money any of the other subjects had earned.

At this point social comparison preferences for seeing the *wages* paid to others were assessed using a rank-order procedure previously used in research on the social comparison of abilities (cf. Miller, 1982; Suls *et al.*, 1978, 1979; Zanna *et al.*, 1975). Subjects were informed

You can, if you wish, find out the average amount of money paid to others who have worked on these

jobs. We have been keeping a running record on the computer of the average amount of money paid to the different groups of people who have worked on the three jobs. The information is organized in various ways, and you can see the average wage paid to any one of the groups. I will give you an order sheet on which you should rank order your preferences for this information in case your first or second choice is unavailable. (The assistant) will then go and get the information you request from the computer.

Subjects then were given a "Wage Order Sheet" listing the nine different groups for whom average pay figures were available. The three jobs were listed across the top of the form with three possible choices listed under each one: average male pay, average female pay, and average male/female pay (combined). Subjects were asked to rank order their preferences for seeing this information from 1 (*most preferred*) to 9 (*least preferred*). The order of presentation of the jobs and the comparison choices was varied on six different forms of the wage order sheet.

While this information ostensibly was being retrieved, subjects were asked to complete a final questionnaire measuring their perceptions of the fairness of the pay they received and their satisfaction with this pay. Manipulation checks investigating whether or not subjects knew the sex linkage of their job and were aware of how much money they had received also were included. Subjects did not actually see the wage information they requested. They were informed during the debriefing that everyone had been paid the same amount.

Results

Social Comparison Preferences

In order to examine subjects' social comparison preferences, the frequency with which the various choices were ranked first and second was analyzed using χ^2 analyses, comparing the obtained frequency against that expected by chance. The prediction that subjects would prefer to maximize similarity on their first comparison choice was confirmed. As can be seen in Table 22.1, subjects

TABLE 22.1. First Choice of Comparison Information Collapsed across Job Assignment

	Sex choice			
Job choice	Same sex	Other sex	Average sex	Total
Same job	36 (63%)	4 (7%)	12 (21%)	52 (91%)
Other job	1 (2%)	2 (3.5%)	2 (3.5%)	5 (9%)
Total	37 (65%)	6 (10.5%)	14 (24.5%)	57 (100%)

TABLE 22.2. First Sex Comparison by Sex Linkage of Assigned Job

First sex choice	Assigned job		
	Sex appropriate	Sex inappropriate	Neutral
Same sex	16 (80%)	9 (47%)	12 (67%)
Other sex	1 (5%)	4 (21%)	1 (6%)
Average sex	3 (15%)	6 (32%)	5 (28%)
Total	20 (100%)	19 (100%)	18 (100%)
$\chi^2(2) =$	19.90***	2.00 n.s.	10.33**

$** p < .01. \quad *** p < .001.$

showed an extremely strong preference for seeing the pay of a same-job comparison group first, with 91% of subjects indicating this preference, $\chi^2(1) = 85.97, p < .0001$. Furthermore, across jobs, 65% of subjects chose to see the pay of a same-sex comparison group first. This also was significantly greater than expected by chance, $\chi^2(1) = 25.58, p < .0001$. Overall, 63% of subjects ranked the same-sex/same-job comparison group first, which was far greater than expected by chance, $\chi^2(1) = 156.54, p < .0001$. No significant sex differences were found in any of the above comparison preferences.

To examine the impact of sex linkage of assigned job on comparison preferences, separate χ^2 analyses were performed on the first choices of those individuals assigned to sex-appropriate (males in the masculine job and females in the feminine job), sex-inappropriate (males in the feminine job and females in the masculine job), and sex-neutral jobs. Sex linkage of job had no impact on the frequency with which subjects chose a same-job comparison group first, with over 89% of subjects in all jobs ranking a same-job comparison first.

Sex linkage of job did have a significant impact, however, on first preferences by sex. Recall that the related attributes hypothesis predicts that people prefer to compare with those who have similar performance-related attributes, for example, same-sex persons on sex-related tasks. As can be seen in Table 22.2, the pattern of choices observed provided mixed support for the related-attributes hypothesis. As would be expected, those individuals assigned to the sex-appropriate jobs showed a significantly greater preference for seeing the pay of a same-sex group first (80%) than either a cross-sex group (5%) or a combined-sex group (15%), $\chi^2(2) = 19.90, p < .001$. However, a strong same-sex bias

also was seen among subjects assigned to the sex-neutral job, $\chi^2(2) = 10.33, p < .01$, with 67% of these choosing a same-sex group first. The only people who did *not* show a significant preference for seeing the pay of a same-sex group first were those assigned to a sex-inappropriate job, $\chi^2(2) = 2.0, p > .25$. Although the largest percentage (47%) of these people chose to compare with a same-sex group first, 21% preferred to compare with a cross-sex group first, and 32% preferred as their first comparison the combined-sex group.

χ^2 analyses were performed on those choices ranked second to determine whether same-job or same-sex comparison preferences were stronger. These analyses revealed a strong preference to compare again within job on the second choice rather than to make a same-sex but different job comparison. Overall, 87.7% of subjects chose a same-job comparison on their second choice, which was significantly greater than expected by chance, $\chi^2(1) = 88.36, p < .001$. In contrast, only 24.5% chose a same-sex comparison group on their second choice, which was not different from chance, $\chi^2(1) = 1.93, p < .50$. Separate analyses performed on the second choices of those 36 individuals who had ranked the same-sex/same-job group first indicated that *none* of these individuals chose a same-sex/different-job group as their second choice. Thus, same-job comparison preferences appeared to be stronger than same-sex preferences. Of the 21 subjects who did not rank the same-sex/same-job comparison group first, 82.4% ranked this choice second. Thus, of those individuals who did not choose to maximize similarity in their first choice, the vast majority chose to maximize similarity in their second choice.

Questionnaire Responses

Separate 2 (Sex of Subject) × 3 (Sex linkage of Job) analyses of variance (ANOVAS) were performed on responses to each of the three questionnaires. Consistent with prior research (cf. Major *et al.*, 1984), women felt that less money ($M = 1.93) was fair pay for their work than did men ($M = 2.31), regardless of job assignment, $F(1, 51) = 4.10, p < .05$. Women, however, also thought they had performed worse on the job ($M = 3.50$) than did men ($M = 4.24$), $F(1, 51) = 5.27, p < .05$. These two variables were positively correlated for both women, $r(22) = .46, p < .02$, and men, $r(31) = .61, p < .001$. No sex differences were found for prejob performance expectations, pay expectations, or ratings of the importance of earning a high wage. In addition, no sex differences were observed for postjob ratings of task difficulty, task enjoyment, pay satisfaction, or perceived fairness of the pay received.

Main effects for sex-linkage of assigned job were observed for both prejob pay expectations, $F(2, 51) = 2.53, p < .09$, and ratings of the fairness of the obtained pay, $F(2, 51) = 3.29, p < .05$. Despite the fact that the jobs were described *and perceived* as comparable in difficulty, individuals assigned to the female sex-linked job tended to expect to earn less prior to doing their job ($M = 2.36) than did those assigned to the male sex-linked job ($M = 2.70). Pay expectations of those assigned to the sex-neutral job fell in between ($M = 2.59). In addition, those assigned to the female sex-linked job perceived their pay as significantly more fair ($M = 6.25$ on a 7-point scale) than did those assigned to the male sex-linked job ($M = 5.22$). Fairness ratings of those assigned to the neutral job fell in between ($M = 5.50$) and did not differ significantly from the fairness ratings of those in the masculine or feminine jobs. A similar, although weaker, trend was observed for pay satisfaction, $F(2, 51) = 1.65, p < .20$. No interactions

were observed between sex of subject and sex linkage of job for any of the questionnaire variables.

As might be expected, postpay ratings of pay fairness and pay satisfaction were positively correlated, $r(55) = .61, p < .001$. Furthermore, consistent with predictions from relative deprivation theory (cf. Crosby, 1982; Runciman, 1966) and theories of pay satisfaction (cf. Lawler, 1973), prejob pay expectations were negatively correlated with postpay ratings of pay fairness, $r(55) = -.37, p < .01$, and pay satisfaction, $r(55) = -.47$. The amount of money subjects perceived as fair pay for their work also was negatively correlated with postpay ratings of pay fairness, $r(55) = -.37, p < .01$, and pay satisfaction, $r(55) = -.38, p < .01$. Thus the more pay people expected and thought they deserved, the less fair and less satisfactory they rated their obtained pay.

Discussion

As predicted, results of this experiment demonstrated that both men and women prefer to maximize similarity in their wage comparisons, with the majority choosing to see the pay of same-sex/same-job others first. Same-sex preferences occurred despite the availability of the average combined-sex wage as a comparison choice. Furthermore, same-sex preferences were observed even in the sex-neutral job, where sex was presumably irrelevant to performance or pay. The only individuals who did not show a significant preference for acquiring same-sex comparison information first were those assigned to a job dominated by the opposite sex. Even so, the largest percentage (47%) of these subjects did rank the same-sex comparison group first. This finding is consistent with Crosby's (1982) finding that although women in male-dominated jobs were more likely than other groups to compare with cross-sex others, these women were still most likely to compare with same-sex others.

The failure of the people in our study to select the combined-sex wage group as their first comparison choice is intriguing, since this choice would presumably yield the most general and unbiased wage information. Our finding that same-sex comparisons were preferred over combined-sex comparisons supports previous speculations that sex may be a fundamental attribute for social comparison purposes, regardless of its stated relationship to the dimension being evaluated (outcomes or abilities) (Miller, 1984; Suls *et al.*, 1979). Alternatively, sex may be perceived as an attribute that is related to performance (and therefore pay) quite generally, across tasks and jobs. It is noteworthy, however, that recent research (Miller, 1984) suggests that sex may be a fundamental attribute for comparison purposes only for those individuals who are schematic with respect to gender. Since this may be characteristic of the majority of individuals, however, same-sex social comparisons may be a prevalent pattern. The link between self-schema and the selection and utilization of comparison information clearly deserves further attention.

In general, same-job comparison preferences appeared stronger than same-sex preferences in this research. Almost everyone selected a same-job wage comparison for their first choice, and this was unaffected by the sex linkage of the assigned job. Furthermore, people were more likely to choose another same-job comparison group for their second choice than to choose a same-sex but different-job group. This suggests that people believe that others in their own job are even more relevant as wage comparisons than are others of their own sex. This seems a reasonable inference, since in this experiment, as well as in the paid work force more generally, pay is explicitly related to job assignment whereas sex is not.

Our finding that people prefer to make same-sex and same-job comparisons, even in a controlled setting where other types of comparisons are equally available, is consistent with previous speculations that similarity biases occur in the acquisition of information about the outcomes of others. Further, our data are consistent with field studies of wage (Goodman, 1974) and job (Oldham *et al.*, 1982) comparisons that have shown similarity biases in the selection of referent others. It has been suggested (Major & Konar, 1984; Major *et al.*, 1984) that these social comparison biases lead women to acquire a lower wage standard than men in typical

work settings. This occurs because women are generally paid less than men and people in female-dominated jobs are generally paid less than those in male-dominated jobs (Treiman & Hartmann, 1981). Furthermore, these different wage standards are hypothesized to affect what women and men feel they deserve to be paid and their evaluations of their pay. Although this experiment did not test these latter hypotheses, recent research (Major & Testa, 1985) provides general support for this process.

Two alternative explanations for sex differences in outcome evaluations also were suggested by this research. First, consistent with prior research (Callahan-Levy & Messé, 1979; Major *et al.*, 1984), women felt they deserved less pay for their work than did men, regardless of job assignment. Women also, however, evaluated their work performance less positively than did men in this study. The positive correlation observed between these two judgments suggests that women's lower sense of personal entitlement with respect to pay may be due, in part, to lower evaluations of their own performance. Whereas some past research has obtained evidence consistent with this hypothesis (e.g., Major *et al.*, 1984, Experiment 2), the majority of past research has not (e.g., Callahan-Levy & Messé, 1979; Major & Adams, 1983; Major *et al.*, 1984, Experiment 1).

A second explanation for the "paradox of the contented female worker" is suggested by our intriguing finding that simply labeling the same job as feminine (female-dominated) or masculine (male-dominated) led people assigned to feminine jobs to expect somewhat less pay and consider their obtained pay as significantly more fair than those assigned to masculine jobs. This occurred despite the fact that the jobs were explicitly described as comparable in difficulty and were *perceived* as such by individuals assigned to them. This finding suggests that individuals are aware of the discrepant wages generally paid to comparable masculine and feminine jobs in the labor market (Treiman & Hartmann, 1981) and adjust their pay expectations accordingly. Thus, the "paradox of the contented female worker" may be due, in part, to the fact that most women work in "feminine" or female-dominated jobs and hence expect less pay for their work than do men. Since expectations are negatively related to pay satisfaction and fairness ratings, given the same wage, those who have lower expectations should be more satisfied with their pay and should perceive their pay as more fair than should those with higher expectations (Lawler, 1973; Major & Konar, 1984). It is noteworthy, however, that although people doing the "feminine" job in this experiment perceived their obtained wage as more fair, they did not feel they *deserved* less pay than those doing the "masculine" job.

In conclusion, this experiment suggests three mechanisms that may underlie observed sex differences in evaluations and distributions of pay: (a) similarity biases in the acquisition of comparison information, (b) evaluations of own performance, and (c) pay expectations based on the sex linkage of one's job. These cognitive explanations are in contrast to frequently cited explanations based on assumed value differences between the sexes, that is, that women are less concerned than men with money, or put a higher priority on interpersonal rather than monetary rewards (cf. Crosby, 1982; Kahn *et al.*, 1980). This research did not examine the validity of these value-based explanations (see Major & Adams, 1983). Rather, it suggests that normal cognitive processes can explain the "paradox" of the contented female worker when these processes occur in an environment where women are paid less than men, female-dominated jobs are paid less than male-dominated jobs, and female performance is evaluated less positively than comparable male performance.

REFERENCES

Adams, J. S. (1965). Inequity in social exchange. In L. Berkowitz (Ed.), *Advances in experimental social psychology* (Vol. 2, pp. 267–299). New York: Academic Press.

Austin, W. (1977). Equity theory and social comparison processes. In J. Suls & R. Miller (Eds.), *Social comparison theory: Theoretical and empirical perspectives* (pp. 279–305). Washington, DC: Hemisphere Publishing.

Callahan-Levy, C. M., & Messé, L. A. (1979). Sex differences in the allocation of pay. *Journal of Personality and Social Psychology*, **37**, 443–446.

Chesler, P., & Goodman, E. J. (1976). *Women, money and power*. New York: Morrow.

Crosby, F. (1982). *Relative deprivation and working women*. New York: Oxford Univ. Press.

Davis, J. A. (1959). A formal interpretation of the theory of relative deprivation. *Sociometry*, **22**, 280–296.

Feldman, N. S., & Ruble, D. N. (1981). Social comparison strategies: Dimensions offered and options taken. *Personality and Social Psychology Bulletin*, **7**, 11–16.

Goethals, G. R., & Darley, J. (1977). Social comparison theory: An attributional approach. In J. M. Suls & R. L. Miller (Eds.), *Social comparison processes: Theoretical and empirical perspectives* (pp. 259–278). Washington, DC: Halsted/Wiley.

Goodman, P. S. (1974). An examination of referents used in the evaluation of pay. *Organizational Behavior and Human Performance*, **12**, 170–195.

Kahn, A., Nelson, R. E., & Gaeddert, W. P. (1980). Equity and equality: Sex and situation as determinants of reward allocation. *Journal of Personality and Social Psychology*, **38**, 737–750.

Kahn, A., O'Leary, V., Krulewitz, J. E., & Lamm, H. (1980). Equity and equality: Male and female means to a just end. *Basic and Applied Social Psychology*, **1**, 173–197.

Lawler, E. E. (1973). *Motivation in work organizations*. Monterey, CA: Brooks/Cole.

Major, B., & Adams, J. B. (1983). The role of gender, interpersonal orientation and self-presentation in distributive justice behavior. *Journal of Personality and Social Psychology*, **45**, 598–608.

Major, B., & Deaux, K. (1982). Individual differences in justice behavior. In J. Greenberg & R. L. Cohen (Eds.), *Equity and justice in social behavior* (pp. 43–76). New York: Academic Press.

Major, B., & Konar, E. (1984). An investigation of sex differences in pay expectations and their possible causes. *Academy of Management Journal*, **27**, 777–792.

Major, B., McFarlin, D., & Gagnon, D. (1984). Overworked and underpaid: On the nature of gender differences in personal entitlement. *Journal of Personality and Social Psychology*, **47**, 1399–1412.

Major, B., & Testa, M. (1985). *The role of social comparison processes in judgments of entitlement and satisfaction.* Manuscript under review. State University of New York at Buffalo, Psychology Department, Buffalo, NY.

Miller, C. T. (1982). The role of performance-related similarity in social comparison of abilities: A test of the related attributes hypothesis. *Journal of Experimental Social Psychology*, **18**, 513–523.

Miller, C. T. (1984). Self-schemas, gender, and social comparison: A clarification of the related attributes hypothesis. *Journal of Personality and Social Psychology*, **46**, 1222–1229.

Oldham, G. R., Nottenburg, G., Kassner, M. W., Ferris, G., Fedor, D., & Masters, M. (1982). The selection and consequences of job comparisons. *Organizational Behavior and Human Performance*, **29**, 84–111.

Patchen, M. (1961). *The choice of wage comparisons*. Englewood Cliffs, NJ: Prentice-Hall.

Pettigrew, T. (1967). Social evaluation theory. In D. Levine (Ed.), *Nebraska symposium on motivation* (Vol. 15). Lincoln, NE: Univ. of Nebraska Press.

Runciman, W. G. (1966). *Relative deprivation and social justice*. Berkeley: Univ. of California Press.

Suls, J., Gaes, G., & Gastorf, J. (1979). Evaluating a sex-related ability: Comparison with same-, opposite-, and combined-sex norms. *Journal of Research in Personality*, **13**, 294–304.

Suls, J. M., Gastorf, J., & Lawhon, J. (1978). Social comparison choices for evaluating a sex- and age-related ability. *Personality and Social Psychology Bulletin*, **4**, 102–105.

Suls, J. M., & Miller, R. L. (Eds.). (1977). *Social comparison processes: Theoretical and empirical perspectives*. Washington, DC: Halsted/Wiley.

Treiman, D. J., & Hartmann, H. I. (1981). *Women, work and wages: Equal pay for jobs of equal value*. Washington, DC: National Academy Press.

Walster, E., Berscheid, E., & Walster, G. W. (1973). New directions in equity research. *Journal of Personality and Social Psychology*, **25**, 151–176.

Wheeler, L., Koestner, R., & Driver, R. E. (1982). Related attributes in the choice of comparison others. *Journal of Experimental Social Psychology*, **18**, 489–500.

Zanna, M. P., Goethals, G. R., & Hill, J. F. (1975). Evaluating a sex-related ability: Social comparison with similar others and standard setters. *Journal of Personality and Social Psychology*, **11**, 86–93.

Received November 14, 1984 ■

Social Identity versus Reference Frame Comparisons: The Moderating Role of Stereotype Endorsement

Hart Blanton, Charlene Christie, and Maureen Dye

Two studies tested the prediction that belief in a negative stereotype about an in-group will cause members to shift from viewing their in-group as a social identity to viewing it as a frame of reference. The stereotype that was the focus of inquiry was the belief that women have less aptitude at math and spatial tasks than do men. In both studies, female participants took a test of math and spatial ability and then received social comparison information about their abilities relative to a male and a female confederate. In Study 1, participants felt enhanced when the two women outperformed the male confederate, even when this meant that the participants themselves performed worse than the other woman. If participants were first reminded of the negative stereotype, however, they felt best when they outperformed the other woman, even if this meant that the two women performed worse than the man. Study 2 showed that the effects of stereotype activation were especially pronounced among female participants who showed moderate to high levels of stereotype endorsement. These findings suggest that belief in stereotypes about the in-group can lead to in-group comparison and contrast, even in contexts in which a group member's ability level challenges the validity of the stereotype.

The authors thank Adam Galinksy, Jim Jaccard, and Mark Muraven for their comments and suggestions. Thanks especially go to Alexander Haslam for providing a signed review that improved the Discussion section and to Judith M. Harackiewicz for a thoughtful and speedy review.

Address correspondence and reprint requests to Hart Blanton, Department of Psychology, State University of New York at Albany, Albany, NY 12222. E-mail: hblanton@ albany.edu.

The social psychological literature points to two ways in which gender might influence the social comparison of abilities. We label these two theoretical perspectives the *social identity view* and the *reference frame view*. First, social identity theory (Tajfel, 1978; Tajfel & Turner, 1979) and its extension, self-categorization theory (Turner, Hogg, Oakes, Reicher, & Wetherell, 1987; Turner, Oakes, Haslam, Haslam, & McGarty, 1994), indicate that increased gender salience might heighten concern for the maintenance of a positive gender identity. When this occurs, individuals will want their "in-group gender" to be positively distinct from their "out-group gender," and they will view their own self-attributes as psychologically interchangeable with the attributes of other in-group members (Turner, 1985). As a result, upward same-gender social comparisons and downward cross-gender social comparisons should have the potential to raise self-esteem, whereas downward same-gender and upward cross-gender social comparisons should have the potential to lower self-esteem (Blanton, Crocker, & Miller, 2000; see also Blanton, 2001). In contrast to this theoretical view, traditional social comparison theory has considered how people treat their gender as a reference frame, against which their personal abilities are then evaluated. This literature indicates that increased gender salience might heighten concern for doing well in relation to same-gender standards of comparison and simultaneously lower concern for doing well in relation to cross-gender standards of comparison. When this occurs, individuals will view same-gender targets as more relevant standards of comparison than cross-gender targets (e.g., Feldman & Ruble, 1981; Major & Forcey, 1985; Miller, 1984; Suls, Gaes, & Gastorf, 1979). As a result, upward social comparisons should threaten self-esteem, and downward social comparisons should enhance self-esteem to greater degrees, when they are made with same-gender targets of comparison than when they are made with cross-gender targets of comparison (Major, Sciacchitano, & Crocker, 1993; see also Blanton, 2001).

The current studies test the prediction that negative gender stereotypes can alter the manner in which gender influences the social comparison of

abilities. Specifically, we predict that the negative stereotype regarding women's math and spatial abilities, when activated, will cause women to shift from treating their gender as a social identity to treating it as a reference frame. The rationale for this prediction is based on the social construction of the stereotype regarding women's math and spatial abilities. We argue that women often show some degree of endorsement of these stereotypes. As a result, they will restrict their definitions of "high" and "low" abilities in these domains to same-gender norms when the stereotypes are activated, which will then cause them to use same-gender standards of comparison when evaluating their own abilities. Moreover, we predict that stereotype activation will cause gender to be treated as a reference frame, even in social contexts where it would be treated as a social identity if stereotypes were not activated.

Endorsement of the Gender and Math Stereotype

Many have noted that the psychological dynamics surrounding gender stereotypes are not typical of the dynamics that surround many other social stereotypes. It appears that women, like men, often have what might be termed a "cooperative relationship" with the stereotypes about their group. As Eberhardt and Fiske (1994) have noted, romantic relationships create incentives for heterosexual men and women to accept stereotypical gender roles (see also Eagly, 1987; Peplau, 1983). Reflective of this, gender stereotypes appear to reinforce social constructions of men and women as two different "groups" that possess complementary strengths and weaknesses (Glick & Fiske, 1996). By comparison, constructions of Blacks and Whites often emphasize antagonistic relationships. The result is that women at times view their diminished status relative to men as legitimate, whereas African Americans more typically view their diminished status relative to Whites as illegitimate (see Major, 1994).

One consequence of legitimating status differences is endorsement of in-group stereotypes, even when they are negative (see Jost & Banaji, 1994). As a specific case, it appears that women show some acceptance of the stereotype that their gender possesses less aptitude for solving math and spatial problems than does the male gender. There is strong developmental evidence, for instance, that parents' gender stereotypical beliefs undermine girls' belief in their math abilities (Eccles, Jacobs, & Harold, 1990; Frome & Eccles, 1998; Jacobs & Eccles, 1992), and there is evidence that socialization contexts that increase the salience of young girls' gender diminishes their aspirations in male-stereotypical ability domains (Abrams, Sparkes, & Hogg, 1985; Abrams, Thomas, & Hogg, 1990). These findings suggest that gender socialization often undermines women's confidence in their math and spatial abilities and that this can flow from informal pressures to adopt gender stereotypes. Admittedly, however, these findings fall short of showing that women often take the next step and internalize beliefs that the stereotypes about their abilities are true. For instance, women may be more likely than men to believe that they have poor math abilities but still reject the stereotype that women *as a group* have less math ability than do men *as a group*.

There is reason to believe, however, that women will often show signs of stereotype endorsement. Laboratory studies suggest, for instance, that young women have at least implicit belief in gender stereotypes. Various research projects have shown that the increased salience of gender stereotypes undermines women's performance on math tests (e.g., Gonzales, Blanton & Williams, 2001; Inzlicht & Ben-Zeev, 2000; Spencer, Steele, & Quinn, 1999). This suggests that women often possess some degree of internalization of the stereotypical view, even if they do not explicitly endorse the stereotype as true. It seems likely, however, that many will take the next step as well and explicitly endorse gender stereotypes. In fact, some theoretical perspectives within the psychological community have suggested that women *should* believe the stereotype related to their abilities. This is because some psychological researchers have argued that gender differences in ability do exist and that they reflect biological

differences in aptitude (e.g., Benbow & Stanley, 1983).

Although most women will not be familiar with the specific reports that take this view, many appear to believe that "research has shown" that women are less able than men in these domains. We became aware of this while running pilot studies that lead to the studies presented here (see Blanton, 2001). In an initial study, female participants interacted with a male experimenter who made an offhand comment that he did not think women were as capable as men at tasks requiring math and spatial ability. When asked during the debriefing whether they had been offended by this statement, many participants stated that they had not been because they had assumed that the statement was accurate. This anecdote certainly is not a systematic demonstration that women often buy into the stereotypes about their math and spatial abilities, but the passive acceptance we observed in this pilot work stands in stark contrast to the response we might expect from members of many other stereotyped groups.

In summary, there is good reason to believe that women often show some degree of belief in or endorsement of the stereotypes that women have worse math and spatial abilities than do men. Although the belief in these in-group stereotypes might not be high in absolute terms, it seems likely that it is higher than would be found for most targets of negative stereotypes. To the extent that women buy into negative gender stereotypes, this should have dramatic consequences for social comparisons of ability.

Stereotype Endorsement and Social Comparison

If a negative ability stereotype about one's own group is true, then in-group members are more relevant standards of comparison than are members of the advantaged out-group (Goethals & Darley, 1977). Indirect evidence that activation of gender stereotypes will narrow comparisons in this way can be found in person perception research by Biernat and Manis (1994; see also

Biernat, Manis, & Nelson, 1991). According to their "shifting standards model," group members are typically evaluated by others on stereotype-relevant dimensions against in-group standards. Thus, perceivers who hold the stereotype "women are less competent than men" will typically evaluate women based on their ability to do well relative to other women and men based on their ability to do well relative to other men (Biernat & Manis, 1994, Study 1). In a similar fashion, we are suggesting that women who believe the stereotype "women are less competent than men at math" will evaluate their *own* math ability relative to the math ability of other women—not the abilities of other men. Moreover, we are predicting that activation of the math stereotype will cause this comparison style, even in contexts that would otherwise promote the treatment of gender as a social identity.

The competing hypotheses are that activation of a negative stereotype will either increase the tendency to view gender as a social identity or leave such tendencies unaffected. In a recent study, Blanton *et al.* (2000) found that Black students showed higher self-esteem following upward as opposed to downward social comparison with another Black student. Although the negative stereotype about Blacks' intellectual abilities was not explicitly activated, the testing situation contained aspects of stereotype threat that should have heightened the salience of negative stereotypes (Steele & Aronson, 1995). It is possible that these stereotypes were responsible for Black students identifying with one another's performance. Such effects of stereotypes are not predicted in Study 1, however, because female participants are expected to show a greater acceptance of the negative intellectual stereotypes about their gender than Black participants typically show for the negative intellectual stereotypes about their race.

Creating an Intragroup/Intergroup Dilemma

The current studies present female participants with comparison information that should increase the salience of intergender (social identity)

comparisons. In evidence of this, we predict that participants will feel enhanced by the superior performance of women relative to men and diminished by the superior performance of men relative to women. This comparison situation will be set up in such a way, however, that *the status of women relative to men improves at the cost of the participant's own status relative to other women.* As a result, any manipulation that shifts attention away from the intergender implications of the comparison information and toward the intragender implications of the comparison information should result in a shift in the contingencies surrounding self-evaluation. When a manipulation causes such a shift, participants should feel diminished by the comparison information that was previously enhancing and enhanced by the comparison information that was previously diminishing. This logic provides the tool we need to determine whether stereotypes about women's math and spatial abilities will cause female participants to shift from viewing their gender as a social identity to viewing it as a reference frame.

STUDY 1

Method

Participants. A total of 61 female college students from introductory psychology classes participated for course credit. Of these participants, 61% were White, 23% were Asian American, 8% were African American, 2% were Latino, and the remaining indicated a multiracial or multiethnic identification. The mean age of the sample was 19 years.

Social comparison procedure. The social comparison manipulation was adapted from a study by Sanders, Gastorf, and Mullen (1979). Participants in all conditions took a test of math and spatial abilities and received identical feedback about their performance. Following this, they were presented with one of two types of social comparison information about both a male and a female confederate. In the *women-up* condition, each participant learned that she and another woman had outperformed a male but that she personally had performed worse than the other woman. An alternative way of stating this is to say that participants were exposed to downward social comparison information regarding a male confederate's performance and to upward social comparison information regarding a female confederate's performance. In the *women-down* condition, each participant learned that she and another woman had performed worse than a male but that she personally had outperformed the other woman. Or, participants were exposed to upward social comparison regarding a male confederate's performance and to downward social comparison regarding a female confederate's performance.

In the absence of a negative stereotype, we predicted higher self-evaluations following social comparison in the women-up condition then in the women-down condition. The rationale for this was based on Turner's (1985) meta-contrast principle. We predicted that our comparison procedure, which simultaneously presents both same-sex and cross-sex comparison information, would heighten the intergroup implications of the comparison information and thereby heighten the desire for positive distinctions between the in-group gender and the out-group gender. As a result, we expected that women would feel best when they outperformed the male confederate.[1] Support for this prediction can be found in a study by Sanders *et al.* (1979). They gave both male and female participants comparison information about both same-sex and cross-sex targets of comparison and then manipulated the relative performance of male versus female targets of comparison. Results showed that participants cued in to the relative standing of same-sex versus cross-sex targets and that they made their highest ability ratings when same-sex targets outperformed cross-sex targets. This finding suggests that study participants will spontaneously

view gender as a social identity if they are presented with feedback about both male and female targets of comparison. The current study attempted to replicate the sort of social identity effect shown in Sanders *et al.* to determine whether the activation of a negative stereotype would shift participants from viewing their gender as a social identity to viewing it as a frame of reference.

Design. Participants were randomly assigned (with cell sizes ranging from 14 to 16) to one of the four experimental conditions based on a 2 (Stereotype Salience: low vs high) × 2 (Social Comparison: women-up vs women-down) between-subjects factorial design. The primary dependent variable was self-ratings of ability after task performance.

Procedure. The procedure in the current study was adapted from Blanton *et al.* (2000). Each participant was met by a female experimenter, who asked her to wait for two other participants. The other participants, actually a male and a female confederate, arrived after the participants had an opportunity to sign the experimental consent form. At this point, the experimenter directed all three individuals to a laboratory, where she explained that the purpose of the study was to "standardize" a new measure of "natural math and spatial ability." She explained that this measure was unlike tests they may have taken in the past. Although the test was based on mathematical and spatial reasoning ability, she said, it was not thought to be contingent on previous level of schooling in math and spatial reasoning. The advantage of this instruction set is that it should minimize stereotypical gender expectations for the task (see Spencer *et al.*, 1999). Participants were then told that most college students could solve these problems regardless of their level of training and that their own scores would be

---

[1] The conditions created by this procedure have conceptual similarity to those that have been of interest in research on the "frog pond effect" (Davis, 1966). The frog pond effect proposes that individuals evaluate personal ability relative to in-groups and pay little attention to out-groups. The prediction we make are the reverse of this. We predict that self-evaluations will be based on intergroup standing, with little concern for in-group standing.

The rationale for our prediction is that participants observe their in-group's performance in the context of salient feedback about the out-group's performance. This is different from what occurs with the frog pond effect. In this research, individuals are aware of in-group performance levels, but they are mostly unaware of performance levels in more distant out-groups (see Marsh & Parker, 1984; McFarland & Buehler, 1995).

based on a combination of their speed and accuracy. The advantage of linking performance to reaction times for an unfamiliar task is that this made it difficult for participants to determine how they had done, increasing the likelihood that they would accept the test feedback when they received it.

For those in the high stereotype salience condition, the experimenter introduced the notion that women might perform worse than men, even on this new task. She stated,

> The point of this study is that we are hoping to standardize this test. What do we mean by standardizing? By standardizing, we hope to determine if different groups perform differently. For instance, some of the men working on this project believe that women will do poorly relative to men, and your performance on this test will help us determine if this is true.

For those in the low salience condition, the experimenter made no mention of gender, although she did mention that the test was being standardized. She stated,

> The point of this study is that we are hoping to standardize this test. What do we mean by standardizing? By standardizing, we hope to determine how most people perform on this test. For instance, since you three are college students, you can thus help us know how college students typically perform.

Participants then took the test on the computer in an isolated terminal. This program presented a straightforward set of computational and spatial problems, with answers presented in a multiple-choice response format. As examples, the test asked participants, "What is the remainder after 72 is divided by 3?" and "When a cube is sitting on a table, what is the maximum number of sides one can view at once?" When participants finished, the computer delivered feedback in the form of speed and accuracy scores, but it did not provide them with any information about what these scores might mean. Instead, it instructed them to meet the experimenter in a neighboring room, where she would help them to code their scores. In all conditions, the participant was the first to return to the

room, where she was told that she had scored a 67 out of 100. The upward and downward social comparison targets then entered the room. The participant thus overheard an upward comparison target of comparison receiving a 99 out of 100 and then a downward target of comparison receiving a 35 out of 100. In half of the conditions (women-up), the upward comparison target was the female confederate and the downward comparison target was the male confederate. In the other half of the conditions (women-down), the upward comparison target was the male confederate and the downward comparison target was the female confederate. After receiving the performance feedback and the social comparison information, participants then completed an ability appraisal. Following this, they were given a full process debriefing.

Ability evaluation. The primary dependent variable was a seven-item ability appraisal adapted from the performance subscale of the Heatherton and Polivy (1991). Participants rated their agreement with statements describing their performance on the task and their competence in general (e.g., "I did well on this task," "I feel confident about my abilities," "I feel as smart as others"). Agreement was made using a 10-point Likert scale, with end points of $1 = $ *strongly disagree* and $9 = $ *strongly agree* (Cronbach's alpha $= .80$).

Predictions. We predicted a crossover interaction between stereotype salience and social comparison. When the stereotype was not activated, we predicted higher ability ratings in the women-up condition than in the women-down condition. This would suggest that the comparison information led women to view their own gender as a social identity, such that their self-evaluations were highest when the two women outperformed the male. When the stereotype was activated, however, we predicted higher ability ratings in the women-down condition than in the women-up condition. This would suggest that the stereotype caused women to view their gender as a frame of reference, such that their self-evaluations were highest when they performed well relative to the other woman.

Social comparison × Stereotype salience

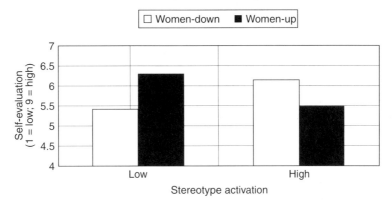

FIGURE 23.1 ■ Ability evaluations in Study 1 as a function of social comparison and stereotype salience.

Results

To test for the predicted interaction, we conducted a 2 (Stereotype Salience) × 2 (Social Comparison) analysis of variance (ANOVA) on ability evaluation. As predicted, and as shown in Figure 23.1, a significant first-order interaction was revealed, $F(1, 57) = 6.37$, $p < .02$. When the stereotype was not activated, participants reported higher ability in the women-up condition ($M = 6.29$, $SD = 1.02$), in which the two women outperformed the one man, than in the women-down condition ($M = 5.41$, $SD = 1.06$), $F(1, 57) = 4.23$, $p < .04$. When the stereotype was activated, participants reported higher ability in the women-down condition ($M = 6.14$, $SD = 1.32$) than in the women-up condition ($M = 5.50$, $SD = 1.28$). Thus, they felt better when they performed better than the other woman, even though this meant that the two women performed worse than the one man. This simple main effect did not reach statistical significance, $F(1, 57) = 2.27$, $p < .14$, but the significant first-order interaction showed that it represented a significant attenuation of the social identity effect occurring when the stereotype was not activated.

Discussion

As predicted, participants appeared most concerned with the intergroup implications of the comparison information when no mention was made of math and spatial ability stereotypes. The

evidence for this is that female participants had higher ability evaluations when the social comparison information indicated that the two women outperformed a male on a test of math and spatial ability. It is important to note that this effect occurred even though participants' *absolute* performances were held at a constant across conditions. Specifically, participants in all conditions received a 67 out of 100 on the test. In addition, this effect occurred even though participants' *relative* performances were held at a constant across conditions. Specifically, participants in all conditions performed 27 points higher than a downward comparison other (who scored a 35 out of 100) and 27 points lower than an upward comparison (who scored a 99 out of 100). It is thus safe to conclude that the differences in self-evaluation occurred as a result of the rank ordering of the male versus female confederate. When the stereotype was not mentioned, self-evaluations were higher when the two women outperformed the man than when the man outperformed the two women. This pattern suggests a concern for the maintenance of a positive social identity.

The effect of the comparison information changed dramatically when the negative gender stereotype was activated. The significant first-order interaction indicated that the previous effect was attenuated by the stereotype activation procedure. Moreover, there was a tendency for participants to have higher ability ratings when the two women performed worse than the man. One might predict that the presence of the negative stereotype would cause women to feel *more* enhanced by the superior performance of other women (e.g., Blanton *et al.*, 2000). Consistent with the notion that the gender and math stereotype is endorsed to some degree by women, however, participants instead appeared to be more focused on their own standing relative to other women. Specifically, they showed a tendency to have more positive self-evaluations when they outperformed the other woman than when they did not.

Although the results lent support to the predictions, there were two primary shortcomings that Study 2 sought to address. First, the results in the stereotype activation condition did not reach statistical significance. Although stereotype activation significantly attenuated the predicted social identity effect and shifted findings in the direction of the predicted reference frame effect, it did not produce a reference frame effect that reached statistical significance using the targeted sample size. Second, the study did not establish that the predicted shift occurred as a result of stereotype endorsement. Study 2 sought to address each of these concerns by determining whether stereotype endorsement moderated reactions to the social comparison feedback. In this way, it was able to determine whether stereotype endorsement was responsible for the observed shift and whether this shift would reach statistical significance among a subsample of women who showed especially high levels of stereotype endorsement.

STUDY 2

Overview

Female participants first completed a questionnaire assessing the extent to which they believed the gender and math stereotype. They then took the measure of natural math and spatial ability under conditions of high stereotype salience and were given social comparison feedback, following the procedure in Study 1. The primary prediction was that level of endorsement would moderate the effect of comparison information on self-evaluations. To the extent participants believed that women have worse math and spatial ability than men, they should show higher ability evaluations when they outperform the other member of their in-group (women-down) than when they do not (women-up). To the extent that the stereotype is not believed, participants should show higher ability evaluations when their in-group outperforms the out-group (women-up) than when it does not (women-down).

The predicted moderating effect of stereotype endorsement was tested against two plausible alternative moderators. It seemed reasonable that the stereotype altered responses not because it was believed but rather because it changed the emotional reaction to the comparison information. For instance, women may have felt offended by mention of the negative stereotype. As a result, those in the women-up condition may have felt that they had let the other woman down when they had done worse than her on the task. Alternatively, participants may have wanted to see the stereotype discredited when it was mentioned but taken it on themselves to be the one doing the discrediting. As a result, those in the women-up condition may have felt frustrated when the other woman—and not them—was the one to discredit the stereotype. Either of these effects could cause stereotype activation to heighten concern for doing well relative to the other woman, but each would reflect a heightened concern among participants for the maintenance of a positive social identity. We thus developed two measures to test for these alternative moderators. The first measure assessed the degree to which participants were offended by the negative stereotype (stereotype offense), and the second one assessed the degree to which participants took it on themselves to challenge the negative stereotype (stereotype personalizing). Both measures, along with stereotype endorsement measure, are described below. All three ratings were tested as potential moderators of the reaction to social comparison information in the context of the gender and math stereotype.

Participants

A total of 196 female students participated for credit in introductory psychology. Of these, 68%

were White, 8% were African American, 5% were Asian American, 5% were Latino, 10% indicated a multiple-group identification, and the remaining students did not respond to the question. The mean age of the sample was 19 years. Ages ranged from 17 to 50, with less than 3% of the sample having ages over 23. Results did not differ if these older individuals were eliminated from the analyses.

Design

Participants were randomly assigned (with cell sizes of $n = 98$) to one of two (Social Comparison Information: women-up vs women-down) experimental conditions. Stereotype endorsement was treated as the focal moderator to determine whether it altered the manner in which comparison direction influenced ability evaluation in the context of the gender and math stereotype.

Procedure

Participants were run in groups of 3 to 10 using a bogus two-study procedure. They first arrived at a laboratory room, where they completed a set of questionnaires that assessed stereotype endorsement, stereotype offense, and stereotype personalizing. To reduce experimenter demand, these three questionnaires were embedded within a larger set of questionnaires that took about 20 min to complete. Once participants were done, they were directed to a second laboratory on the floor above the first study. There, they were met by a woman who told them that they were going to take a math test on the computer. Participants were randomly assigned either to sit in front of a computer that gave them women-up social comparison feedback or to sit in front of a computer that gave them women-down social comparison feedback.

In all conditions, the computer program first had participants list their age, their year in school, and their gender. It then explained that they were about to take a measure of "natural math and spatial ability," using the same description as in Study 1. To increase stereotype salience, it further told them, "A number of researchers at this university have predicted that women will not perform as well as men on this measure. . . . We are now in the

process of standardizing to investigate for the presence of this gender difference." Participants then took the same math test that had been administered in the first study. Afterward, the computer told them that two other students who were their same age and year in school had taken the test on that computer. It then gave them the scores of these students, along with feedback about their own performance. Participants in all conditions learned that they had scored an 82 out of 100. This performance feedback was higher than that which was given in the first study. Participants in Study 1 were told that they scored a 67. During debriefings, however, they often reported that this sounded like a poor score to them. By raising the score to an 82, we hoped to eliminate esteem threat as a potential artifact in our result. Anecdotally, a number of Study 2 participants reported during debriefings that they had been pleased with their own performances. Following this, they then heard that the scores for two other students were a 98 and a 66. Thus, one student scored 16 points worse than they had performed and one student scored 16 points higher than they had performed. When the computer presented the scores of the other two students, it listed their age, their year in school, their gender, and their test scores. This made it possible to manipulate the gender of the upward versus downward social comparison target, as was done in Study 1. It also ensured that the targets of comparison had some degree of comparability with the participant. Once participants viewed the social comparison information, the computer directed them to complete a questionnaire sitting in a folder next to the computer. The seven-item ability evaluation index from Study 1 was included in this questionnaire (Cronbach's alpha = .79).

Measures

Stereotype endorsement. In the initial packet of questionnaires, participants were asked to rate the degree to which different stereotypes were true. This idea was introduced with the statement,

> Below, we have listed some common gender stereotypes. When you read these, you may feel that some are based on gender differences that really do exist.

Or, you may feel that the stereotype has no basis in fact. Please read each of the following stereotypes and rate *the degree to which you feel the stereotype is based on true gender differences.* Please answer each question openly and honestly.

They then read a list of 12 stereotypes. Embedded in this list of 12 stereotypes were 2 statements related to the math and spatial ability stereotype. Participants rated their belief in these stereotypes by answering the questions "How much truth is there to the stereotype that 'Men typically have better math skills than women'?" and "How much truth is there to the stereotype that 'Men typically have better spatial skills than women'?" Responses were made on a unipolar 11-point rating scale ranging from 0 to 10. Underneath the numbers 0, 3, 6, and 9 were centered the labels *not at all true, some truth, a great deal of truth,* and *completely true,* respectively. Responses on these two ratings, $r(194) = .51$, $p < .001$, were then averaged together as a measure of endorsement of the math ability stereotype. For comparison purposes, a measure of general stereotype endorsement was also created by taking an average of all 12 stereotypes. The remaining items tapped beliefs that men are more violent, are more impulsive, are stronger, are more athletic, have better analytic reasoning skills, and have greater intellectual ability, whereas women are more interpersonally sensitive, have better verbal ability, want more children, and are more emotional (Cronbach's alpha = .87).

Stereotype offense. Participants were asked to consider the following:

When another person expresses a stereotypic belief, we at times will get offended. At other times, we may feel less offended. Please rate each stereotype below for how offensive you find it.

Participants then rated how offensive they found each of the 12 stereotypes, using a unipolar 11-point rating scale ranging from 0 to 10. Underneath the numbers 0, 3, 6, and 9 were centered the labels *not at all offensive, somewhat offensive, very offensive,* and *extremely offensive,* respectively. As before, we computed both the average offensiveness rating for the math and spatial stereotypes, $r(194) = .70$, $p < .001$, and the average offensiveness rating for all 12 gender stereotypes (Cronbach's alpha = .88).

Stereotype personalizing. Participants were asked to consider the following:

With some stereotypes, you may feel it is personally important to you to work to see them eliminated. For others, you will feel it is less important to see them eliminated. We would like to know how important it is to you to see each of the stereotypes eliminated from society.

They then rated how important it was to them to help eliminate each of the 12 stereotypes rated for importance, on a unipolar 11-point rating scale ranging from 0 to 10. Underneath the numbers 0, 3, 6, and 9 were centered the labels *not at all important, somewhat important, very important,* and *extremely important,* respectively. As before, we computed the average ratings for the math and spatial ability stereotypes, $r(194) = .68, p < .001$, and we computed the average rating for all 12 stereotypes (Cronbach's alpha = .89).

Results

Descriptive statistics. Table 23.1 provides a sense of how participants viewed the math stereotype. It

TABLE 23.1. Associations between Ratings of the Math and Spatial Ability Stereotypes

Variable	2	3	Mean	SD	Median	MAD
1. Endorsement	−0.27*	−.04	2.52	2.00	2.29	1.45
2. Offense	—	.64*	4.96	2.65	5.01	2.00
3. Personalizing	—	—	4.89	1.83	5.94	1.50

Note: Endorsement, offense, and personalizing were measured on 11-point scales, with high values indicating high degree of endorsement, offense taken, and personal desire to eliminate. *SD*, standard deviation of the mean; *MAD*, median absolute deviation. Asterisk (*) indicates a significant association at $p < .01$.

shows the mean level of stereotype belief, stereotype offense, and stereotype personalizing, along with the correlation matrix between these three measures. The sample as a whole did not show a high degree of belief. The mean ($M = 2.52$, $SD = 2.00$) and median (median = 2.29, median absolute deviation [MAD] = 1.45) both indicate an endorsement just short of the value of 3 (= *some truth*). Inspection of the full distribution suggests, however, that many in the sample did show moderate to high levels of endorsement. Figure 23.2 presents the frequency distribution of the responses to the two stereotype endorsement items. For ease of interpretation, the evaluative anchors for the 11 points of response scales are included along the x axis. Although 19% of the sample rated both the math and spatial stereotypes at the level of 0 (= *not at all true*), 17% gave ratings at a level that was at or above the scale midpoint of 5, and 41% gave ratings at a level that was at or above the level of 3 (= *some truth*). It appears, then, that many in the sample were at least open to the idea that their own gender was at a disadvantage relative to the male gender. Although

these ratings do not suggest strong support for the stereotype in the sample as a whole, it is important to remember that these are ratings of endorsement for a negative stereotype about participants' own gender. These ratings are quite high when compared to the traditional view that people are biased to endorse positive self-views (Taylor & Brown, 1988; cf. Jost & Banaji, 1994).

Despite this possibly counterintuitive level of endorsement, the fact remains that the sample as a whole did not have a degree of endorsement that was high in absolute magnitude. This might explain why the results in Study 1 were weaker than anticipated. The level of endorsement in that study might not have been high enough to reveal reference frame effects in analyses conducted on the entire sample. The full distribution of the current sample indicated, however, that many participants showed moderate to high levels of stereotype endorsement. As a result, significant reference frame effects should be pronounced among this subgroup.

In comparison to stereotype endorsement, the level of stereotype offense was high in an absolute

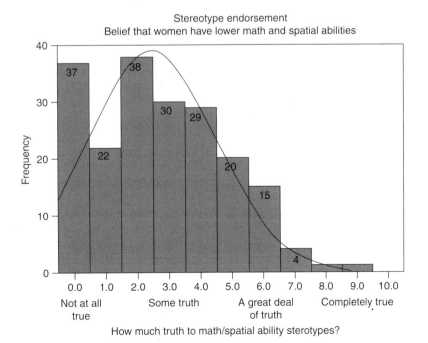

Stereotype endorsement
Belief that women have lower math and spatial abilities

How much truth to math/spatial ability sterotypes?

FIGURE 23.2 ■ Distribution of endorsement of the average endorsement of the math and spatial stereotypes.

TABLE 23.2. Ability Evaluation as a Function of Comparison Information and Stereotype Endorsement

Independent variables	B	t	Significance
Block 1: Main effects			
Constant	7.47	36.11	.00
Comparison information	0.00	0.01	ns
Stereotype endorsement	0.03	0.51	ns
Block 2: Simple main effects and cross-product			
Constant	7.17	30.29	.00
Comparison information	0.67	1.94	.05
Stereotype endorsement	0.15`	2.02	.05
Comparison Information × Stereotype Endorsement	−0.27	2.48	.01

Note: Shown are unstandardized coefficients for equation regressing the ability evaluation on comparison information, average endorsement of the math and spatial ability stereotypes, and the multiplicative cross-product of the two. Comparison information is dummy coded such that 0 = women-down condition and 1 = women-up condition. Endorsement is coded such that higher scores indicate a greater belief in the gender stereotype. Ability evaluation can range from 0 to 10, with higher values indicating more positive self-evaluation. All t values are assessed with degrees of freedom = 190.

sense ($M = 4.96$, $SD = 2.65$; median = 5.01, $MAD = 2.00$), as was the level of stereotype personalizing ($M = 4.89$, $SD = 1.83$; median = 5.94, $MAD = 1.50$). The correlation matrix in Table 23.1 reveals that stereotype offense and stereotype personalizing were highly correlated, $r(194) = .64$, $p < .01$. This suggests that those who were most offended by the math stereotype were also the ones who most wanted to see it eliminated.[2] Stereotype endorsement was reasonably independent of these two constructs, although it did show a negative correlation with stereotype offense, $r(194) = −.27, p < .01$. This indicates that the women who had the highest level endorsement of the math and spatial stereotypes were also the ones who were the least offended by them. Importantly, however, stereotype endorsement showed enough independence from these two alternative moderators that its effects could be disentangled from them.

Stereotype endorsement as moderator. The primary prediction was that endorsement of the stereotype would moderate the effect of the social comparison manipulation on self-evaluation. To test this, ability evaluation was regressed on stereotype endorsement, a dummy code for experimental condition, and the multiplicative cross-product of stereotype endorsement and experimental condition (Jaccard, Turrisi & Wan, 1990). For clarity of presentation, the dummy code for experimental condition was constructed to indicate whether or not the two women outperformed the man. Thus, those in the women-up condition were given a value of 1 and those in the women-down condition were given a value of 0. To first test for the main effects of stereotype endorsement and experimental condition, however, these two variables were entered in the first block of a hierarchical regression, with the cross-product entered in the second step.

The unstandardized regression coefficients are shown in Table 23.2. The first block revealed that there were no main effects of stereotype endorsement or experimental condition, $Fs < 1.0$. The second block revealed that, consistent with predictions, stereotype endorsement moderated the effect of experimental condition on self-evaluation. The direction of the unstandardized regression coefficient for the cross-product indicated that, as stereotype endorsement increased, self-evaluations in the women-up condition diminished relative to

---

[2] In fact, this high degree of association between stereotype offense and stereotype personalizing was roughly equivalent to the interitem correlation in the two scales. This suggests that the they could be viewed as a single construct. As a result, all analyses using these constructs were repeated using the combined average of these two scales. This procedure did not alter the conclusions.

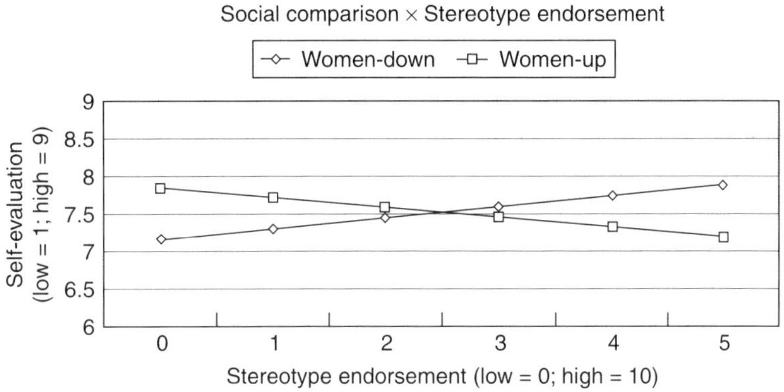

Social comparison × Stereotype endorsement

FIGURE 23.3 ■ Ability evaluations in Study 2 as a function of social comparison and stereotype endorsement.

those in the women-down condition, $B = -.27$, $t(190) = 2.48$, $p < .01$. More specifically, the magnitude of the unstandardized regression coefficient indicated that the mean rating in the women-up condition dropped an additional 0.27 unit below the mean rating in the women-down condition for every 1 unit increase in stereotype endorsement.[3]

The nature of the Social Comparison × Stereotype Endorsement interaction can be further understood by inspecting Figure 23.3. This figure plots the estimated ability rating at different levels of stereotype endorsement, broken down by experimental condition. As predicted, stereotype endorsement determined whether or not self-evaluations increased or decreased in the two conditions. When stereotype endorsement was at its lowest point, or equal to 0, ability evaluations were $B = .67$ unit higher in the women-up condition than in the women-down condition. This indicated a significant difference in ability ratings, $t(190) = 1.94$, $p < .05$. Thus, among women who did not believe the stereotype, ability ratings were higher when the two women outperformed a man, even though this meant that participants themselves performed poorly relative to another woman. When stereotype endorsement was at the scale midpoint of 5, however, ability ratings were .68 unit lower in the

women-up condition than in the women-down condition. This represented a significant difference, $B = -.68$, $t(190) = 1.96$, $p < .05$, and it indicated that, among women showing a moderate degree of belief in the stereotype, ability ratings were higher when they performed well relative to another woman. This was true even though the two women performed worse than the man. Interestingly, when the 2-item math ability stereotype scale was replaced with the full 12-item scale, this interaction remained significant, $B = -.35$, $t(193) = 2.43$, $p < .02$. The slight drop in the magnitude of the effect suggests that the specific belief provided the best prediction.

Alternative moderators. To test for the effects of the two alternative moderators, equivalent regression analyses were run replacing stereotype endorsement with stereotype offense and stereotype personalizing. No main effects or interactions were found for these measures. Follow-up analyses also revealed that the previously uncovered moderating effect of stereotype endorsement remained even when these two constructs and the importance of doing well in math were controlled. Assuming valid measurement, these findings argue against the alternative moderators.

Discussion

Study 2 provided clear evidence that endorsement of negative ability stereotypes moderates reactions to social comparison information when these

---

[3] Inspection of residuals revealed one individual who had self-evaluations that were 3 standard deviations from predicted values. Removal of this individual did not alter the significance level of any of the significant interactions reported.

stereotypes have been activated. Female participants who did not believe that men have better math
and spatial abilities than women showed higher
self-evaluations when they and another woman outperformed a man on a test of math and spatial ability. This occurred even though the other woman had
performed better than the participants had performed. This suggests that participants who were
low in stereotype endorsement based their self-
evaluations on the relative ability of women versus
men. As stereotype endorsement increased, however, participants showed higher self-evaluations
when they outperformed the other woman on the
task. This occurred even though their superior
performance occurred in a comparison context in
which the male confederate outperformed both of
the women. This suggests that participants who
were higher in stereotype endorsement based their
self-evaluations on their own performance relative
to the other woman.

General Discussion

We began this article by contrasting the social
identity view of gender with the reference frame
view of gender. The social identity view argues
that women will base their self-evaluations on the
relative standing of women versus men. The reference frame view argues that women will base
their self-evaluations on their personal standing
relative to other women and that they will be
unconcerned about their own standing relative to
men. We hypothesized that negative ability stereotypes, when believed, would cause women to treat
their gender as a frame of reference, even in a
comparison context that would otherwise encourage them to treat it as a social identity. Our first
task was thus to create a comparison context that
would cause women to treat their gender as a
social identity. This was accomplished by providing female participants with comparison feedback
about how their own performances on a test of
math and spatial ability compared to the performances of both a male and a female confederate. As
predicted, participants had higher ability ratings
when they were led to believe that the two women

outperformed the man than when it suggested the
reverse (see also Sanders *et al.*, 1979). Although
this finding was not the main focus of Study 1, it
provided important evidence that women will
treat their gender as a social identity during comparisons of ability. This adds to a growing experimental literature showing that people often feel
enhanced by the superior performance of others
when they share a meaningful bond or group identity with them (Blanton *et al.*, 2000; Brown,
Novick, Lord, & Richards, 1992; Lockwood &
Kunda, 1997; Pelham & Wachsmuth, 1995; for
relevant reviews, see Blanton, 2001; Buunk &
Ybema, 1997; Tesser, 1988).

As predicted, activation of a negative stereotype altered the contingencies for self-evaluation.
When women in Study 1 were reminded of the
negative stereotypes that women have worse math
and spatial abilities than do men, they showed a
tendency to have higher ability evaluations when
they performed better than another woman, even
if this meant that the two women performed worse
than the man. Although this tendency was not statistically significant, Study 2 offered an explanation for this and revealed a group for which the
trend was significant. This study showed that
belief in the negative math and spatial stereotypes
was low for the entire sample but that a sizable
minority did show moderate to high belief in the
in-group stereotypes. Among this latter group,
stereotype activation led to a significant reference
frame effect. In other words, they had higher self-
evaluations when they performed better than
another woman, even though this meant that the
two women performed worse than the man.

It might seem that the activation of gender
stereotypes would have an opposite effect and that
it would increase the tendency for women to identify with one another during social comparisons.
Negative gender stereotypes could increase attention to the intergender implications of comparisons
and thereby increase concern for maintaining a
positively distinct gender identity. To wit, an
effect such as this was predicted and found in our
earlier work. Blanton *et al.* (2000) showed that
Black students can identify with one another
when they compare with members of their racial

in-group in the context of a negative in-group stereotype. Many other researchers have argued for similar effects for women. It has been suggested, for instance, that strong female role models help women to maintain positive self-views and high aspirations in the face of lowered stereotypical expectations for their gender (e.g., Barak, Feldman, & Noy, 1991; Hackett, Esposito, & O'Halloran, 1989; Nauta, Epperson, & Kahn, 1998). Although the current results challenge our own past research and this line of reasoning, they nevertheless follow from a straightforward application of the relevant attributes hypothesis (Goethals & Darley, 1977). This social comparison principle predicts that people will base their self-evaluations on their personal standing relative to in-group standards when group membership is predictive of ability. It follows from this that a woman who endorses a gender stereotype about an ability will use social comparison information to determine whether her own ability is "good for a woman" (Biernat & Manis, 1994).

Generalization. A reasonable concern with this study is that it used a contrived method that might not generalize to a wide array of social comparison contexts. This concern can be broken into two broad categories. First, the effects might not hold if the nature of the social comparison information were altered. Second, the effects might not hold if the nature of the social stereotype were altered. With respect to the first concern, we admit that the feedback method we developed may have limited generality. Because participants were always given conflicting inter- and intragroup social comparison information, we were not able to ascertain how participants might have responded if one part of the comparison compensated for another. We would argue, however, that the current studies were concerned with demonstrating that negative stereotypes can shift an individual to a reference frame view of the in-group *when a social identity view would otherwise predominate.* Based on self-categorization principles, we predicted that our feedback method would cause a female participant to treat her gender as a social identity because it placed her and another woman in

either a superior or inferior status relative to a man (Turner, 1985). The effects on ability evaluation supported this prediction. The fact that negative stereotypes lead to reference frame effects using this same comparison method suggests that the effects of negative stereotypes will generalize to any number of comparison contexts in which individuals would otherwise identify with one another on the basis of a shared social identity.

The second concern is that our effects might not hold if the nature of the social stereotype were altered. We chose to focus on gender and math stereotypes because we believed that they are often endorsed to some degree, even by their targets. Although we predict that our effects will generalize to other in-group stereotypes when they generate similar levels of endorsement, it is possible that endorsement such as this occurs only rarely. Future research will need to address this question, however. It may be that, contrary to intuition, endorsement of in-group stereotypes is often quite high. In fact, a number of theoretical traditions argue that targets of negative stereotypes do internalize the stereotypes about their groups (see Jost & Banaji, 1994). Still others suggest that the pervasive nature of social stereotypes cause individuals to treat them as if they are true, even if they explicitly reject them (e.g., Steele & Aronson, 1995). If future research indicates common acceptance of many in-group stereotypes, we expect that the reference frame shift we have observed will prove to be quite common as well.

Self-esteem versus stereotype maintenance. These studies point to possible tensions between the desire to see the in-group as positively distinct from the out-group and the competing desire to see the self as positively distinct from the in-group. The current study proposed a resolution to this tension by arguing that people refer back to an underlying belief structure (social stereotypes) to determine which aspect of the comparison situation is the most informative guide for self-evaluation. One surprising implication of this resolution is that participants' belief systems directed their social perceptions in ways that appeared to be quite independent of the ultimate effects on self-evaluation.

A plausible alternative to the resolution we proposed might have been that individuals would resolve the tension in whatever manner was most likely to enhance or maintain self-esteem. It might seem, for instance, that people presented with competing inter- and intragroup comparison information would focus on whichever piece of information put the self in the most favorable light. Thus, participants in the women-up condition could have focused their attention on the intergroup implications of the social comparison feedback and felt good about the superior performance of the women relative to the man. By contrast, participants in the women-down condition could have focused their attention on the intragroup implications of the social comparison feedback and felt good about their own superior performance relative to the other woman.

This alternative to our predictions is consistent with the theoretical view arguing that people typically bias their social perceptions to maintain self-esteem (e.g., Taylor & Brown, 1988). Within the social comparison literature, it is best represented in Buunk and Ybema's (1997) identification contrast model. Like other comparison frameworks (Taylor & Lobel, 1989; Tesser, 1988; Wood & Taylor, 1991), the identification contrast model emphasizes personal freedom to use social comparison information to further perceptual goals, particularly the goal of esteem maintenance. Buunk and Ybema (1997) have shown compelling instances in which people maintain self-esteem by selectively focusing their attention on their similarities with upward targets and on their differences with downward targets. As our two studies demonstrated, however, people can at times be "trapped" by the comparison context to interpret social comparison information in ways that run counter to esteem maintenance goals (see also Wood, 1989). More specifically, it seems that reactions to others will, at times, be determined by the relatively inflexible dictates of social stereotypes.

One compelling aspect of our methodology was that the women in the women-up condition were presented with information showing them that women can outperform men on measures of math and spatial ability. If the participants were so motivated, they might have used this information to justify a strategic suspension of belief in the in-group stereotype. If participants in the women-up condition had done this, they could have benefited in at least two ways. First, they would have been released from a stereotypical belief that puts women at a disadvantage relative to men, making it easier for them to maintain positive self-views (cf. Crocker & Major, 1989). Second, they could have focused attention on their association with the other women who had done well, thereby feeling enhanced by the superior performance of the women relative to the man. Instead of suspending belief, however, participants who were reminded of the stereotype reacted to stereotype-inconsistent feedback as if the stereotype were true. The fact that they did this may show just how pervasive negative stereotypes can be. Once individuals internalize in-group stereotypes, they may rely on them to interpret the very situations that would otherwise suggest to them that the stereotypes are false.

The adaptive view on stereotype retention. This analysis might then suggest that the women who endorsed gender stereotypes responded in a way that was not at all adaptive. They ignored comparison information that argued against the stereotype, even in a context in which stereotype retention put them at risk of diminished self-esteem. Although it is tempting to draw this conclusion, one must be careful about applying such logic. To know what is "adaptive" in this particular situation, one must know whether it is better for these women to retain their prior beliefs or to hold positive self-views. At first blush, it might seem straightforward enough; women should simply drop their stereotypes so that they can hold more positive self-views. This reasoning falls apart, however, if the stereotypes the women are dropping are actually true (see Oakes, Haslam, & Turner, 1994).

We suggest two ways in which the stereotypes can possess "reality," and either one could justify the continued use of the stereotypes, even in the face of contradictory evidence. First, stereotypes can possess some *objective reality.* With respect to math and spatial ability stereotypes, opinion in the psychological community is mixed. Some researchers have argued that there are biological determinants of gender differences in academic performance (e.g., Benbow & Stanley, 1983), whereas others have taken issue with this research (e.g., Bellisari, 1989) or focused greater attention on the social determinants (e.g., Spencer *et al.*, 1999). We could try to argue for one side or the other in this debate. Then, we could use our own opinion to advocate either that women should drop their belief in these stereotypes or that they should not. We do not do this because, independent of any objective reality, these stereotypes can possess a compelling *social reality*.

The study participants who believed the stereotypes about their gender held a belief system that is not entirely uncommon. In fact, some theoretical perspective in psychology would argue that it would not be possible for these women to believe these stereotypes if they had not had some contact in the past with individuals who also held these beliefs (see Hardin & Higgins, 1996). In the case of these particular stereotypes, participants' beliefs probably developed from meaningful social interactions with important reference others (Eccles *et al.*, 1990; Frome & Eccles, 1998; Jacobs & Eccles, 1992). Their stereotypes may therefore serve important social functions among the subset of participants who believe in them, as expressed by tendencies such as the preference for social contact with similarly minded others who share these same beliefs. If so, the response of our participants could be socially adaptive, even if the objective validity of the stereotype is in question.

To illustrate, it is useful to return to the stereotype used to describe the Biernat and Manis (1994) shifting standards model—that women are shorter than men. This particular stereotype is less controversial than the stereotypes about academic abilities, and so most would find it easier to work with the assumption that the stereotype has both an objective and a social reality. If the height stereotype is an accurate statement about the relative stature of men and women, it is arguably adaptive (and justified) for women to restrict their definitions of "tall" and "short" to same-gender norms. It would also seem to be adaptive for them

to retain their height stereotype in the face of isolated instances of disconfirming evidence. Take as a specific illustration a fictitious situation inspired by our feedback methodology. It would not seem adaptive for two women encountering a man who is shorter than they are to abandon their well-learned stereotype that women are typically shorter than men. Doing so would run in the face of their accumulated wisdom about the distribution of height across genders. It would also put their opinion at odds with the opinions of others in their lives who probably endorse the height stereotype. More to the point, if these women live in a society where men truly are taller than women, where height is socially valued, and where height is a common basis for feelings of self-worth, these women should not to allow their one interaction with a short man to initiate a new interest in cross-gender height comparisons. If this were to happen, these women would open themselves up to many future social comparisons in which they would be at a disadvantage relative to men. Instead of abandoning their stereotype, these women would find it easier to maintain positive and socially valid self-views if they restrict their frame of reference to same-gender norms. If they do this, they can take encouragement when they feel "tall for a woman" and be unconcerned when they fail to measure up to men. The downside is that when they encounter tall women, they will feel short.

We point out the distinction between objective and social reality to show that either can justify the use of prior stereotypes to interpret stereotype-inconsistent information, even when doing so causes personal distress. We rush to point out, however, that neither objective nor social reality is sufficient grounds for labeling such responses as "adaptive." One could argue that it is maladaptive, for instance, for individuals to adjust their perceptions to current realities when doing so reinforces the very situations that put them or their groups at a disadvantage (Blanton, George, & Crocker, 2001; see Major, 1994). Although social stereotypes may at times possess compelling realities, this is not to say that these truths may not be open to change. In such instances, it might benefit individuals to look beyond their current arrangements. In the process, they might see how they can help their groups to move to new and more satisfying frames of reference.

REFERENCES

Abrams, D., Sparkes, K., & Hogg, M. A. (1985). Gender salience and social identity: The impact of sex of siblings on educational and occupational aspirations. *British Journal of Educational Psychology, 55*, 224–232.

Abrams, D., Thomas, J., & Hogg, M. A. (1990). Numerical distinctiveness, social identity and gender salience. *British Journal of Social Psychology, 29*, 87–92.

Barak, A., Feldman, S., & Noy, A. (1991). Traditionally of children's interests as related to their parents' gender stereotypes and traditionality of occupations. *Sex Roles, 24*, 511–524.

Bellisari, A. (1989). Male superiority in mathematical aptitude: An artifact. *Human Organization, 48*, 273–279.

Benbow, C. P., & Stanley, J. C. (1983). Sex differences in mathematical reasoning ability: More facts. *Science, 222*, 1029–1030.

Biernat, M., & Manis, M. (1994). Shifting standards and stereotype based judgments. *Journal of Personality and Social Psychology, 66*, 5–20.

Biernat, M., Manis, M., & Nelson, T. E. (1991). Stereotypes and standards of judgment. *Journal of Personality and Social Psychology, 60*, 485–499.

Blanton, H. (2001). Evaluating the self in the context of another: The three-selves model of social comparison assimilation and contrast. In G. B. Moskowitz (Ed.), *Cognitive social psychology: The Princeton Symposium on the Legacy and Future of Social Cognition* (pp. 75–87). Mahwah, NJ: Erlbaum.

Blanton, H., Crocker, J., & Miller, D. T. (2000). The effects of in-group versus out-group social comparison on self-esteem in the context of a negative stereotype. *Journal of Experimental Social Psychology, 36*, 519–530.

Blanton, H., George, G., & Crocker, J. K. (2001). Contexts of system justification and system evaluation: Exploring the social comparison strategies of the (not yet) contented female worker. *Group Processes and Intergroup Relations, 4*, 127–138.

Brown, J. D., Novick, N. J., Lord, K. A., & Richards, J. M. (1992). When Gulliver travels: Social context, psychological closeness, and self-appraisals. *Journal of Personality and Social Psychology, 62*, 717–727.

Buunk, B. P., & Ybema, J. F. (1997). Social comparison and occupational stress: The identification-contrast model. In B. P. Buunk & F. X. Gibbons (Eds.), *Health, coping, and social comparison* (pp. 359–388). Hillsdale, NJ: Erlbaum.

Crocker, J., & Major, B. (1989). Social stigma and self-esteem: The self-protective properties of stigma. *Psychological Review, 96*, 608–630.

Davis, J. A. (1966). The campus as a frog pond: An application of the theory of relative deprivation to career. *American Journal of Sociology, 72*, 17–31.

Dixon, J., & Seron, C. (1995). Stratification in the legal profession: Sex, sector, and salary. *Law and Society Review, 29*, 381–412.

Eagly, A. H. (1987). *Sex differences in social behavior: A social role interpretation.* Hillsdale, NJ: Erlbaum.

Eberhardt, J. L., & Fiske, S. T. (1994). Affirmative action in theory and practice: Issues of power, ambiguity, and gender versus race. *Basic and Applied Social Psychology, 15*, 201–220.

Eccles, J. S., Jacobs, J. E., & Harold, R. D. (1990). Gender role stereotypes, expectancy effects, and parents' socialization of gender differences. *Journal of Social Issues, 46*, 183–201.

Feldman, N. S., & Ruble, D. N. (1981). Social comparison strategies: Dimensions offered and options taken. *Personality and Social Psychology Bulletin, 7*, 11–16.

Frieze, I. H., Olson, J. E., & Good, D. C. (1990). Perceived and actual discrimination in the salaries of male and female managers. *Journal of Applied and Social Psychology, 20*, 46–67.

Frome, P. M., & Eccles, J. S. (1998). Parents' influence on children's achievement-related perceptions. *Journal of Personality and Social Psychology, 74*, 435–452.

Glick, P., & Fiske, S. T. (1996). The ambivalent sexism inventory: Differentiating hostile and benevolent sexism. *Journal of Personality and Social Psychology, 76*, 491–512.

Goethals, G. R., & Darley, J. M. (1977). Social comparison theory: An attributional approach. In J. M. Suls & R. L. Miller (Eds.), *Social comparison processes: Theoretical and empirical perspectives* (pp. 259–278). New York: Hemisphere.

Gonzales, P. J., Blanton, H., & Williams, K. J. (in press). *The effects of stereotype threat and double-minority status on the test performance of Latino women. Personality and Social Psychology Bulletin.*

Hackett, G., Esposito, D., & O'Halloran, M. S. (1989). The relationship of role model influences to the career salience and educational and career plans of college women. *Journal of Vocational Behavior, 35*, 164–180.

Hagan, J. (1990). The gender stratification of income inequality among lawyers. *Social Forces, 68*, 835–855.

Hardin, C. D., & Higgins, E. T. (1996). Shared reality: How social verification makes the subjective objective. In R. M. Sorrentino & E. T. Higgins (Eds.), *Handbook of motivation and cognition* (Vol. 3, pp. 28–84). New York: Guilford.

Heatherton, T. F., & Polivy, J. (1991). Development and validation of a scale for measuring state self-esteem. *Journal of Personality and Social Psychology, 60*, 895–910.

Inzlicht, M., & Ben-Zeev, T. (2000). A threatening intellectual environment: Why females are susceptible to experiencing problem-solving deficits in the presence of males. *Psychological Science, 11*, 365–371.

Jaccard, J., Turrisi, R., & Wan, C. K. (1990). *Interaction effects in multiple regression* (Sage University Paper series on Quantitative Applications in the Social Sciences, No. 07–072). Newbury Park, CA: Sage.

Jacobs, J. E., & Eccles, J. S. (1992). The impact of mothers' gender-role stereotypic beliefs on mothers' and children's ability perceptions. *Journal of Personality and Social Psychology*, *63*, 932–944.

Jost, J. T., & Banaji, M. R. (1994). The role of stereotyping in system-justification and the production of false consciousness. *British Journal of Social Psychology*, *33*, 1–27.

Lockwood, P., & Kunda, Z. (1997). Superstars and me: Predicting the impact of role models on the self. *Journal of Personality and Social Psychology*, *73*, 91–103.

Major, B. (1994). From social inequality to personal entitlement: The role of social comparisons, legitimacy appraisals, and group membership. In M. P. Zanna (Ed.), *Advances in experimental social psychology* (Vol. 26, pp. 293–348). San Diego: Academic Press.

Major, B., & Forcey, B. (1985). Social comparisons and pay evaluations: Preferences for same-sex and same-job image comparisons. *Journal of Experimental Social Psychology*, *21*, 393–405.

Major, B., Sciacchitano, A., & Crocker, J. (1993). In-group versus out-group comparisons and self-esteem. *Personality and Social Psychology Bulletin*, *19*, 711–721.

Marsh, H., & Parker, J. (1984). Determinants of students' self-concept: Is it better to be a relatively large fish in a small pond even if you don't learn to swim as well? *Journal of Personality and Social Psychology*, *47*, 213–231.

McFarland, C., & Buehler, R. (1995). Collective self-esteem as a moderator of the frog-pond effect in reactions to performance feedback. *Journal of Personality and Social Psychology*, *68*, 1055–1070.

Miller, C. T. (1984). Self-schemas, gender, and social comparison: A clarification of the related attributes hypothesis. *Journal of Personality and Social Psychology*, *46*, 1222–1228.

Nauta, M. M., Epperson, D. L., & Kahn, J. H. (1998). A multiple-groups analysis of predictors of higher level career aspirations among women in mathematics, science, and engineering majors. *Journal of Counseling Psychology*, *45*, 483–496.

Oakes, P. J., Haslam, A., & Turner, J. C. (1994). *Stereotyping and social reality*. Oxford, UK: Blackwell.

Pelham, B. W., & Wachsmuth, J. O. (1995). The waxing and waning of the social self: Assimilation and contrast in social comparison. *Journal of Personality and Social Psychology*, *69*, 825–838.

Peplau, L. A. (1983). Roles and gender. In H. H. Kelley, E. Berscheid, A. Christensen, J. H. Harvey, T. L. Huston, G. Levinger, E. McClintock, L. A. Peplau, & D. R. Peterson (Eds.), *Close relationships* (pp. 220–264). New York: Freeman.

Sanders, G. S., Gastorf, J. W., & Mullen, B. (1979). Selectivity in the use of social comparison information. *Personality and Social Psychology Bulletin*, *5*, 377–380.

Spencer, S. J., Steele, C. M., & Quinn, D. M. (1999). Stereotype threat and women's math performance. *Journal of Experimental Social Psychology*, *35*, 4–28.

Steele, C. M., & Aronson, J. (1995). Stereotype threat and the intellectual test performance of African Americans. *Journal of Personality and Social Psychology*, *69*, 797–811.

Suls, J. M., Gaes, G. G., & Gastorf, J. W. (1979). Evaluating a sex-related ability: Comparison with same-opposite and combined-sex norms. *Journal of Research in Personality*, *13*, 294–304.

Tajfel, H. (1978). *Differentiation between social groups: Studies in the social psychology of intergroup relations*. London: Academic Press.

Tajfel, H., & Turner, J. C. (1979). An integrative theory of intergroup conflict. In S. Worchel & W. G. Austin (Eds.), *The social psychology of intergroup relations* (pp. 33–47). Pacific Grove, CA: Brooks/Cole.

Taylor, S. E., & Brown, J. D. (1988). Illusion and well-being. A social psychological perspective on mental health. *Psychological Bulletin*, *103*, 193–210.

Taylor, S. E., & Lobel, M. (1989). Social comparison activity under threat: Downward evaluation and upward contacts. *Psychological Review*, *96*, 569–575.

Tesser, A. (1988). Toward a self-evaluation maintenance model of social behavior. In L. Berkowitz (Ed.), *Advances in experimental social psychology* (Vol. 20, pp. 181–227). New York: Academic Press.

Turner, J. C. (1985). Social categorization and the self-concept: A social cognitive theory of group behavior. In E. J. Lawler (Ed.), *Advances in group processes* (Vol. 2, pp. 77–122). Greenwich, CT: JAI.

Turner, J. C., Hogg, M. A., Oakes, P. J., Reicher, S., & Wetherell, M. S. (1987). *Rediscovering the social group: A self-categorization theory*. Oxford, UK: Basil Blackwell.

Turner, J. C., Oakes, P. J., Haslam, S., Haslam, A., & McGarty, C. (1994). Self and collective: Cognition and social context. *Personality and Social Psychology Bulletin*, *20*, 454–463.

Wood, J. V. (1989). Theory and research concerning social comparisons of personal attributes. *Psychological Bulletin*, *106*, 231–248.

Wood, J. V., & Taylor, K. L. (1991). Serving self-relevant goals through social comparison. In J. Suls & T. A. Wills (Eds.), *Social comparison: Contemporary theory and research* (pp. 23–49). Hillsdale, NJ: Erlbaum.

Received March 29, 2001
Revised September 17, 2001
Accepted September 19, 2001
Published online February 11, 2002 ■

PART 7

Social Cognition

When it concerns new, revolutionary, earth-shattering events or breakthroughs, it is often difficult to indicate an exact starting date. Many of us learned in school or in college that the Russian Communist revolution reached its climax in 1917 and that the French revolution came to full flourish in 1789. But it is difficult even for cognitive psychologists to say when exactly the "cognitive revolution" changed the face of psychology (Baars, 1986; Gardner, 1987). Some might argue that the cognitive revolution started on 11 September 1956 in Boston. On that day several researchers came together to talk about the Information Theory during a conference organized at the Massachusetts Institute of Technology. At this event, the linguist Chomsky presented his new anti-behaviorist theory of verbal learning, Newell and Simon presented their work on artificial intelligence with the "Logic Theory Machine," a computer that could solve mathematical problems, and Miller presented his now famous work on the limits of short-term memory, "The magic number 7." With the advantage of history, we can now say that these three presentations became the core of what could be called "the cognitive perspective in psychology." The fact that these papers were all presented at the same symposium on the same day makes it tempting to say that that day (11 September 1956) is the birthday of the cognitive revolution in psychology.

Of course, others may point to other important symposia and conferences that may be seen as revolutionizing the field. For example, on 17 March 1957 a symposium at Harvard University was convened that counted among its speakers Solomon Asch, Fritz Heider, Iggy Hastorf, and

Jerome Bruner. Interestingly all these psychologists stressed in their talks that studies on the accuracy of (social) perception ("How good are people at seeing what is really there?") should be replaced by the study of the process of (social) perception ("What psychological mechanisms determine the contents of subjective perception?"). This move away from prescriptive and outcome-oriented studies to more descriptive, process-oriented studies can also be marked as the advent of the cognitive movement in (social) psychology. The fact that several influential psychologists pleaded for a more process-oriented approach in psychological science on the same day, perhaps can be taken to mean that 17 March 1957 is the actual beginning of cognitive psychology. After all, cognitive psychology is about the mental processes and mechanisms that are underlying people's thoughts, emotions, and behaviors (see Baars, 1986; Gardner, 1987).

Trying to find a proper starting date may be one way to find out what exactly the "cognitive revolution" did to the study of social psychology. Such a historical approach is likely to paint a lively and romantic picture of (social) psychologists (i.e., they come together in Ivy League institutions and present controversial and thought-provoking papers). One can also try to define the cognitive revolution in social psychology by looking more closely at what it did to social psychology on a content level. This approach is perhaps a little less romantic, but probably somewhat more informative. Thus, one could argue that the cognitive revolution in psychology was much more one that was method driven than a theory-driven change of topics. That is, psychologists have always been interested in mentalistic constructs and mechanisms. However,

not until the invention of the computer, and thus computer-aided experiments, did psychologists have the tools to study people's minds in a relatively sophisticated way or at least to make rather informed guesses about them. In other words, in addition to behavioristic, non-mentalistic, stimulus-response psychology (that focused on observable behavior), cognitivistic, mentalistic, stimulus-organism-response studies became an important paradigmatic branch of psychology, with the advent of the computer metaphor and with the availability of the tools and techniques to tap and study human information processing.

Thus, since the early 1970s the computer metaphor of mental life has been an inspiring perspective that has sparked an enormous amount of process-oriented theorizing and paradigm building, mostly along the lines of the maxim that "people are information processors with limited information capacity. They have learned to make shortcuts to process information as efficiently as possible" (see, e.g., Stapel, 2000). Interestingly (and fortunately), the behaviorist approach to the study of social psychology never dwindled (see, e.g., studies in applied social psychology). In fact, nowadays behaviorist and cognitivist approaches to social psychology can best be seen as cohabiting the same domain of scientific study.

Although there may be some debate over whether the cognitive revolution in psychology started in the late 1950s or early 1970s, interestingly it was not until the mid 1990s that social comparison papers started to be published in which a more cognitive-oriented, process-driven approach to the study of social comparison processes was advocated. As may be seen in the readings in the other sections of this book, social comparison research has excelled in studying "when" questions ("When do people engage in social comparisons?"), "who" questions ("Who do people select to compare themselves with?"), and "what" questions ("What is the effect of social comparisons on self-evaluations?"). Less attention has been given to "how" questions ("How do people process social comparison information and how does this affect the outcome of social comparisons?"). Kruglanski and Mayseless (1990) were the first to note, in a review article on the epistemic bases of social comparison effects, that there were surprisingly few articles taking full advantage of theories and methods from cognitive (social) psychology. The past decade, however, has seen an interesting wave of "social cognition/social comparison" studies, a few of which we present here.

What distinguishes the articles in this section from the articles in the previous ones is that, in a sense, all the articles included in this social cognition section could be seen as "applied social cognition" articles. In each of the articles presented here, the authors make innovative, clever use of methods from social cognition. Thus, in this section you will find articles that use implicit rather than explicit self-evaluation measures. The implicit measures are used as cognitive activation measures, mood measures that are designed to tap the impact of social comparison in an unobtrusive way. Furthermore, you will see in these readings the use of cognitive load manipulations (to study the automatic versus controlled effects of social comparison information), and priming manipulations (to study the impact of processing modes on the effects of social comparison information): techniques

and methods that are the stock in trade of social cognition research (see Hamilton, 2005).

The first article in this section is by Gilbert, Giesler, and Morris (1995). In this article, Gilbert and his colleagues show that people do not always restrict their social comparisons to sources of relevant information. Gilbert *et al.* show that the relevance or diagnosticity of social comparison information is often considered only after comparisons are made. Gilbert *et al.* (1995) conducted two studies that support this perspective. In each of these studies they examined participants' self-evaluations after they performed a "schizophrenia detection" task and were shown a videotape of a confederate (i.e., a stranger they had never seen before) performing the same task. The results showed that when the confederate's performance was *irrelevant* and either high (i.e., the confederate had been given the right answers) or low (i.e., the confederate was purposely misled), a contrastive social comparison effect occurred when participants were cognitively busy (when they were rehearsing an eight-digit number). No effects were found when participants were not cognitively busy. Thus, Gilbert *et al.* (1995) conclude that irrelevant social comparisons might not always show their real impact when people have sufficient mental resources. Null effects may sometimes be *corrected* comparison effects.

Interestingly, until the publication of Gilbert *et al.*'s (1995) study of relatively "mindless" social comparison effects, the vast majority of social comparison studies had been focusing on the impact of social comparisons in situations that allow for relatively mindful and effortful processing. Only recently have studies been published that explicitly investigate relatively "mindless" social comparison effects. These recent studies have shown that social comparison effects are ubiquitous: They may occur unbidden and without awareness (e.g., Mussweiler, Rüter, & Epstude, 2004; Stapel & Blanton, 2004). Stapel and Blanton (2004), for example, exposed participants to a picture of Albert Einstein or to a picture of a clown. The exposure time of these pictures was so short that picture presentation was "subliminal": Participants saw flashes but were not aware of the actual content of these flashes. Stapel and Blanton found that the unconscious presentation of pictures influenced an unobtrusive measure of people's self-esteem, namely signature size. That is, they found that participants' signatures "shrank" after subliminal exposure to a picture of Einstein, whereas their signatures "grew" after subliminal exposure to a clown.

It is important to note, as Gilbert *et al.* write in the general discussion section of their paper, that the fact that social comparison effects may occur relatively automatically should not be taken to mean that any comparison standard will yield self-evaluative effects (which then need or need not be corrected). The fact that automatic social comparison effects can occur does not mean that they always occur. One of the important questions for future research is to find out what types of comparison targets automatically yield comparison effects and what types of target do not (see also Stapel & Blanton, 2004).

In the second reading in this section, Stapel and Koomen (2001) show in a number of experiments that one of the primary determinants of assimilation and contrast effects in social comparison is the "level" on which people "construe" themselves.

Stapel and Koomen show that when people think of themselves in more inclusive, collective, groupy terms (i.e., when they think about themselves in terms of "we"), they are more likely to assimilate to others. Conversely, when people take or have a more exclusive, distinctive perspective on the self (i.e., when they think about themselves in terms of "I"), they are more likely to compare and contrast to others. Recently, Stapel and Koomen (2005) showed that a similar effect holds true for cooperative versus competitive orientations. People who work in competitive situations or who have a "competitive personality" are more likely to contrast themselves to others, whereas people who work in cooperative situations or who have a "cooperative personality" are more likely to assimilate with others.

An important message of the Stapel–Koomen paper that is included in this section is the notion that social comparison effects are more likely to show a defensive pattern (such that self-serving effects of social comparisons are incorporated and self-threatening effects are ignored) when the self is made especially salient. That is, they show that *I*-activation leads to defensive contrast effects and *we*-activation leads to defensive assimilation effects, whereas when only the "cold" or "cognitive" mindsets are activated, which are thought to be driving contrast and assimilation, "differentiate" and "integrate", symmetric or non-defensive social comparison effects occur. That is, when subtly priming the construct of differentiation, upward as well as downward targets lead to contrast, and when subtly priming the construct of integration, upward as well as downward targets lead to assimilation. The difference between "I" and "differentiation" priming and "we" and "integration" priming addresses the important and relatively under-researched question of what determines whether or not social comparisons are defensive. It shows that defensive, self-maintenance processing is especially likely when the self is cognitively activated, and that nondefensive processing typically occurs when the self is not activated (see also Part 2 of this volume).

In the third and final paper of this section, Mussweiler and Strack (2000) apply their well-known work on anchoring to the study of social comparison processes. In the anchoring paradigm, people are asked to make two consecutive judgments about the same target object: a comparative judgment and an objective judgment. For example, when applied to the realm of social comparison, one may be asked to compare one's intellectual abilities to those of Albert Einstein and then be asked "How intelligent are you?". As Stapel and Suls (2004) recently pointed out, it is interesting to investigate to what extent this anchoring paradigm (in which explicit comparisons are made) affects the outcome of social comparison processes compared to other methodologies (i.e., ones in which comparison information is implicitly activated, see e.g., Gilbert *et al.*, 1995). Some research suggests that method matters (see Stapel & Suls, 2004), whereas other studies suggest that it does not (Mussweiler, 2003; Mussweiler & Bodenhausen, 2002). Using their anchoring methodology, Mussweiler and Strack present a number of well-designed experiments in which they show that comparison information often has two types of consequences: Presenting people with information about a comparison standard activates standard-consistent information (when you are asked to compare yourself to Einstein, you ponder

the ways in which you are similar to Einstein). At the same time, however, such comparison information may be used as a reference frame and thus activate standard-inconsistent information ("I am no Einstein"). Mussweiler and Strack demonstrate the accessibility of both types of information. Interestingly, they also show that whether the informational, standard-consistent information or the judgmental, standard-inconsistent information is weighed more heavily depends on the type of judgment. That is, in the Mussweiler–Strack studies, standard-consistent inferences typically "win" on objective measures (e.g., performance on a general knowledge task), whereas standard-inconsistent inferences typically "win" in subjective measures ("How intelligent are you?").

REFERENCES

(Asterisks indicate Key Readings in this section.)

Baars, B. J. (1986). *The cognitive revolution in psychology.* New York: Guilford Press.
* Gardner, H. (1987). *The mind's new science.* New York: Basic Books.
Gilbert D. T., Giesler, R. B., & Morris, K. A. (1995). When comparisons arise. *Journal of Personality and Social Psychology, 69,* 227–236.
Hamilton, D. L. (Ed.). (2005). *Key readings in social psychology: Social psychology.* New York: Psychology Press.
Kruglanski, A. W., & Mayseless, O. (1990). Classic and current social comparison research: Expanding the perspective. *Psychological Bulletin, 108,* 195–208.
Mussweiler, T. (2003). Comparison processes in social judgment: Mechanisms and Consequences. *Psychological Review, 110,* 472–489.
Mussweiler, T., & Bodenhausen, G. V. (2002). I know you are but what am I? Self-evaluative consequences of judging ingroup and outgroup members. *Journal of Personality and Social Psychology, 82,* 19–32.
Mussweiler, T., Rüter, K., & Epstude, K. (2004). The man who wasn't there – subliminal social standards influence self-evaluation. *Journal of Experimental Social Psychology, 40,* 689–696.
* Mussweiler, T., & Strack, F. (2000). The "relative self": Informational and judgmental consequences of comparative self-evaluation. *Journal of Personality and Social Psychology, 79,* 23–38.

Stapel D. A. (2000). Moving from fads and fashions to integration: Illustrations from knowledge accessibility research. *European Bulletin of Social Psychology, 12,* 4–27.

Stapel, D. A., & Blanton, H. (2004). From seeing to being: Subliminal social comparisons affect implicit and explicit self-evaluations. *Journal of Personality and Social Psychology, 87,* 468–481.

∗ Stapel, D. A., & Koomen, W. (2001). I, we, and the effects of others on me: How self-construal level moderates social comparison effects. *Journal of Personality and Social Psychology, 80,* 766–781.

Stapel, D. A., & Koomen, W. (2005). Competition, cooperation, and the effects of others on me. *Journal of Personality and Social Psychology, 88,* 1029–1038.

Stapel, D. A., & Suls, J. (2004). Method matters: Effects of implicit versus explicit social comparisons on activation, behavior, and self-views. *Journal of Personality and Social Psychology, 87,* 860–875.

Discussion Questions

1. How has the use of cognitive techniques furthered our understanding of social comparison processes and effects?
2. Social cognition studies of social comparison processes have been accused of being overly artificial and "unreal." Do you agree? Is it a problem?
3. Social comparisons often arrive unbidden, as research in this section shows. Often, social comparison effects show a defensive pattern (see Part 3). What may determine whether spontaneous social comparison effects show a defensive pattern?

Suggested Readings

Brown, J. D., Novick, N. J., Lord, K. A., & Richards, J. M. (1992). When Gulliver travels: Social context, psychological closeness, and self-appraisals. *Journal of Personality and Social Psychology, 62,* 717–727.

Gibbons, F. X., & Gerrard, M. (1997). Health images and their effects on health behavior. In B. P. Buunk & F. X. Gibbons (Eds.), *Health, coping, and social comparison* (pp. 63–94). Hillsdale, NJ: Lawrence Erlbaum Associates Inc.

Kruglanski, A. W., & Mayseless, O. (1990). Classic and current social comparison research: Expanding the perspective. *Psychological Bulletin, 108,* 195–208.

Mussweiler, T. (2003). Comparison processes in social judgment: Mechanisms and consequences. *Psychological Review, 110,* 472–489.

McFarland, C., Buchler, R., & Mackay, L. (2001). Affective responses to social comparisons with extremely close others. *Social Cognition, 19,* 547–586.

Roese, N. J. (1997). Counterfactual thinking. *Psychological Bulletin, 121,* 133–148.

Stapel, D. A., & Marx, D. M. (2006). Hardly thinking about others: On cognitive busyness and target similarity in social comparison effects. *Journal of Experimental Social Psychology, 42,* 397–405.

Wedell, D. H. (1994). Contextual contrast in evaluative judgments: A test of pre- versus post-integration models of contrast. *Journal of Personality and Social Psychology, 66,* 1007–1019.

When Comparisons Arise

Daniel T. Gilbert, R. Brian Giesler, and Kathryn A. Morris

People acquire information about their abilities by comparison, and research suggests that people restrict such comparisons to those whom they consider sources of diagnostic information. We suggest that diagnosticity is often considered only *after* comparisons are made and that people do not fail to make nondiagnostic comparisons so much as they mentally undo them. In 2 studies, participants made nondiagnostic comparisons even when they knew they should not, and quickly unmade them when they were able. These results suggest that social comparisons may be relatively spontaneous, effortless, and unintentional reactions to the performances of others and that they may occur even when people consider such reactions logically inappropriate.

If we say that a thing is great or small by its own standard of great or small, then there is nothing in all creation which is not great, nothing which is not small.

—Chuang Tzu (circa 400−300 BC), *Autumn Floods*

If we tried to describe the world in absolute terms we would probably find ourselves with little to say. Although some properties of objects can be considered absolutely (the numerosity of grapes, the mortality of people), many more can be considered only as relations. A haiku is short, a pizza is hot, and an African elephant is slightly lumpy, but only in the context of other poems, pies, and

Daniel T. Gilbert and Kathryn A. Morris, Department of Psychology, University of Texas at Austin; R. Brian Giesler, Baylor College of Medicine and Houston Veterans Affairs Medical Center, Houston, Texas.

This research was supported by a research grant (R01-MH49613) and a Research Scientist Development Award (KO2-MH00939) from the National Institute of Mental Health (NIMH). The support of NIMH is gratefully acknowledged.

We thank Brett Pelham and Abraham Tesser for their comments on an earlier version of this article, and Susan Brupbacher, Rebecca Pratt, Leah Shimatsu, and Michelle Skeen for their help with the execution of these experiments.

Correspondence concerning this article should be addressed to Daniel T. Gilbert, Department of Psychology, University of Texas, Austin, Texas 78712. Electronic mail may be sent via the Internet to GILBERT@PSYVAX.PSY.UTEXAS.EDU.

pachyderms. As it is with physical characteristics such as size and temperature, so it is with our own psychological characteristics such as our dispositions and capacities. Indeed, the things we most want to know about ourselves—Am I attractive? Am I smart? Am I likable?—can often be known only by comparing our thoughts, feelings, and behaviors with those of the people around us. We are intelligent and interesting precisely because others are so dim and dull.

Social psychologists have long been interested in these sorts of comparisons. Festinger (1954a) described the causes and consequences of social comparison and, in the four decades that followed, researchers refined and extended his theoretical effort, generated considerable empirical evidence for and against specific hypotheses, and ultimately came to agree on a number of fundamental truths. (For recent reviews see Kruglanski & Mayseless, 1990; Olson, Herman, & Zanna, 1986; Suls & Wills, 1991; Taylor, Buunk, & Aspinwall, 1990; Wood, 1989.) One of these fundamental truths is that people do not compare themselves with just anyone, but rather only with particular others. A professor may compare her salary with that of a colleague and feel angry, embarrassed, or overjoyed, but she is unlikely to compare her salary with a seven-year-old child's weekly allowance or to an oil baron's annual income. The first comparison is rich with diagnostic information, the subsequent comparisons are not, and because "people engage in social comparison for one reason, and that is to gain information" (Gibbons & Gerrard, 1991, p. 317), they seek the former and avoid the latter.

What is the evidence for this fundamental truth? How do we know that people avoid making non-diagnostic comparisons? The answer is simple. Social comparisons have both cognitive and affective consequences (e.g., Brickman & Bullman, 1977; Morse & Gergen, 1970; Salovey & Rodin, 1984; Taylor & Lobel, 1989; Tesser, 1991; Tesser, Millar, & Moore, 1988), and when people are provided with nondiagnostic comparison information they appear to experience neither of these. A professor who learns that a colleague of the same rank earns twice as much as she does may experience changes in her beliefs ("I must not be as good a teacher as he is") and her emotions ("I think I'll weep"), but a professor who learns that the president of Exxon earns several times her salary probably will not. This lack of cognitive and affective consequences is taken as evidence that the professor did not compare herself with the executive. When self-evaluations are unchanged by nondiagnostic comparison information, it is reasonably assumed that no comparison was made.

Although this assumption is indeed reasonable, we suspect that it is often wrong, and that what appears to be a failure to engage in social comparison may instead be a rapid and deliberate repudiation of its effects. We suggest that people cannot always avoid nondiagnostic comparisons, and that they often consider factors such as diagnosticity only after having made comparisons whose effects they must then work to reverse.

Mental Control of Social Comparisons

Festinger (1954b) introduced his insights about social comparison this way: "We have made the following derivations about the conditions under which a social comparison process arises" (p. 217). Festinger did not say that he had determined when, how, or why people choose to compare themselves with others; rather, he specifically used language that made the process, and not the processor, the active agent—as though he was thinking of social comparison as a reaction to the environment rather than as an action played on it. Although later theorists have generally eschewed explicit claims about the degree to which the social comparison process is under the conscious control of the individual, the literature can sometimes give one the sense that comparisons are mental operations that people choose to perform or not to perform, rather than natural, effortless, or even inevitable reactions to the behavior of others. As Wood (1989, p. 232) correctly noted, "By emphasizing the individual's ability to select comparisons, the literature has largely reflected the view that the social environment is in the background," and thus the literature has given "little attention to situations in which the environment imposes comparisons on the individual."

The not-so-tacit message is that social comparison is indeed a choice that people make rather than a reaction they have (cf. Brickman & Bullman, 1977; Taylor *et al.*, 1990; Wood, 1989).

Such a view of social comparison is somewhat odd in light of what we know about the ease and spontaneity of other forms of mental comparison. Pelham and Wachsmuth (1994) noted that social comparisons are essentially contrast effects ("Tom's perfect score on the civil service exam made me feel particularly bad about mine"), and contrast effects in both the perceptual and cognitive domains often "occur at an early stage in cognitive processing, require minimal resources, and are therefore beyond the subject's control" (Wedell, 1994, p. 1007). On some occasions contrast effects do result from deliberate processing (Martin, Seta, & Crelia, 1990; Schwarz & Bless, 1992; Wedell, 1990), but there is little doubt that on other occasions they simply arrive unbidden. Petty and Wegener (1993) argued that such unwanted contrast effects can bedevil judgment and decision making (a job opportunity in Columbus may seem especially unappealing to an executive who had hoped to relocate to Paris) and that individuals must therefore make post hoc corrections for these unwanted influences ("The Columbus job is probably a great opportunity for me, and I shouldn't let pictures of the Eiffel Tower color my opinion").

Similar reasoning underlies a host of recent *correction models* which, taken together, suggest that people's thoughts and feelings may be uncontrollably influenced in a variety of undesirable ways and that people often exert control over their thoughts and feelings by "undoing" or correcting these undesirable effects after they have happened rather than by avoiding them in the first place (see Gilbert, 1991; Wilson & Brekke, 1994). Because social comparisons are the products of more general inferential mechanisms (Kruglanski & Mayseless, 1990), it seems reasonable to suspect that, like many inferences, they may arise spontaneously and be undone subsequently and with effort. Although it may be logically inappropriate to compare one's backhand with a tennis pro's or one's standing in polite society with a prisoner's, it may be that such logical considerations affect our thoughts and

feelings only after the inappropriate comparisons have arisen. Unfortunately for the social comparison theorist, people who avoid comparisons and people who mentally undo them ultimately look alike; that is, neither appears to have been affected by the performances of others. The individual who decides that a friend's perfect score on a civil service exam is irrelevant to a reasonable assessment of his own ability will look exactly like the individual who never learned how his friend scored in the first place. So how can one tell whether a particular individual avoided making a comparison or made a comparison and then mentally undid its effects?

The Telltales of Correction

Two research strategies have been particularly useful in distinguishing between people who have not changed their minds and people who have changed their minds and then quickly changed them back again. Imagine the simple case in which an office manager encounters a piece of information whose effects she would rather avoid—for example, a nasty rumor about a new employee. A correction model of belief (e.g., Gilbert, Krull, & Malone, 1990) suggests that hearing the rumor necessarily changes the manager's belief about her employee and that only after experiencing this change in belief may the manager remind herself that the rumor is unsubstantiated and thus make an effort to recover her original opinion. Although the manager may report the same opinion both before and after hearing the rumor, and may therefore appear to have been unaffected by it, there are at least two ways in which the researcher can demonstrate that belief change and correction did, in fact, take place in the interim.

First, the researcher may show that when the office manager's ability to correct her beliefs is impaired, the rumor-induced belief remains. For example, if the manager is mentally preoccupied with her quarterly reports at the moment she hears the rumor, then the likelihood that she will later hold a negative opinion of the employee should be substantially increased. This increase may be taken as evidence for a correction model of belief.

Second, the researcher may show that even when the manager is ultimately able to correct her rumor-induced belief, she may still show signs of having briefly held it. For example, if the manager momentarily believed the rumor that the employee was a recovering ax murderer, she may have felt a transient rush of fear. Thoughts and beliefs can be changed quickly ("Mabel starts that silly ax-murderer rumor every time I hire a new typist. Probably no reason to believe it this time"), but emotions subside rather more slowly ("Gosh, my palms are all sticky"). Thus, the office manager's fear may linger measurably even after her belief has evaporated, and such lingering affect may also be taken as evidence for a correction model of belief.

In the following experiments we used these two general strategies to show that what appears to be a failure to make a nondiagnostic social comparison may actually be a success at correcting one. We attempted to show that people do indeed compare themselves with others even when they realize that such comparisons will be nondiagnostic, and that they then "uncompare" themselves if they can. In Experiment 1 we impaired our participants' ability to perform mental corrections by placing them under cognitive load, and we tried to show that the nondiagnostic comparisons they made remained. In Experiment 2 we tried to show that even when participants are able to make mental corrections, they still experience the affective consequences of the nondiagnostic comparisons they made and then corrected.

Experiment 1

Method
Overview

Female participants viewed an instructional videotape in which a female confederate was shown 18 pairs of photographs of target persons and was asked to determine which of the target persons in each pair was schizophrenic. The confederate cither performed poorly (i.e., she responded correctly on 4 trials) or performed well (she responded correctly on 16 trials). When the confederate did

well, participants were told that she had been given instructions about how to detect schizophrenia prior to her videotaped performance. When the confederate did poorly, participants were told that she had been deliberately misled about how to detect schizophrenia prior to her videotaped performance. After viewing the videotape, half the participants were made cognitively busy with a digit-rehearsal task, and the remaining participants were not. All participants then performed the schizophrenia detection task themselves and were given bogus feedback indicating that they had responded correctly on 10 of the 18 trials. Participants then rated their own and the average student's competence at the task.

Participants

Participants were 68 female undergraduates at the University of Texas at Austin who took part in exchange for credit in their introductory psychology course.

Procedure

The schizophrenia detection task. On arrival at the laboratory, participants were greeted by a male experimenter who explained that he was studying the effects of concentration on pattern learning and that the participant would be asked to perform a "schizophrenia detection task" under conditions of either full or impaired concentration. This task was similar to one developed by Aronson and Carlsmith (1962).

The experimenter explained that the schizophrenia detection task required the participant to view 18 pairs of photographs, 1 pair at a time. Each of the 36 photographs showed the face and upper torso of a male or female undergraduate at the University of Texas at Austin who had previously agreed to allow his or her photograph to be used in the experiment. The photographs in each pair were matched for gender and roughly matched for general appearance and attractiveness. The experimenter explained that one target person in each pair of photographs had a normal psychiatric history and that the other target person had been diagnosed as schizophrenic or had a family member who had been so diagnosed and thus was at risk for schizophrenia. The experimenter explained that on each trial he would hold one photograph in each hand and ask the participant to point to the photograph of the target person whom she felt was most likely to have (or be at risk for) schizophrenia, at which time the experimenter would indicate whether or not the participant had chosen correctly. Ostensibly, participants would learn by trial and error to detect the subtle patterns of facial features that indicated the presence of schizophrenia.

Manipulation of cognitive busyness. The experimenter explained that to discover how concentration affected pattern learning, he would ask some participants to perform the schizophrenia detection task while rehearsing an 8-digit number. Half the participants were randomly assigned to the busy condition, were shown an 8-digit number just prior to performing the task, and were told to keep the number in mind throughout the task and to be prepared to report the number when the task was finished. The remaining participants were assigned to the non-busy condition and were not given a number to rehearse.

Manipulation of confederate's performance. Before participants performed the task, they were shown a short "instructional" videotape ostensibly to illustrate the task procedures. The videotape showed the experimenter and a female confederate performing the schizophrenia detection task. Participants were told that the confederate in the videotape had been a participant in a previous experiment and that she was performing precisely the same task that the present participant would be asked to perform. Participants in the good-performance condition saw the videotaped confederate give correct responses on 16 of 18 trials, and participants in the poor-performance condition saw the videotaped confederate give correct responses on 4 of the 18 trials.

Participants in the good-performance condition were told that, prior to performing the task, the videotaped confederate had been taught to recognize the pattern of facial features that indicated schizophrenia, and thus they should expect her performance to be particularly good. Participants in the poor-performance condition were told that, prior to performing the task, the videotaped confederate had been purposely misled about the pattern of facial features that indicated schizophrenia, and thus they should expect her performance to be particularly poor.

It is important to note that participants in the busy condition saw a version of the instructional videotape in which the experimenter gave the confederate an 8-digit number to rehearse as she performed the schizophrenia detection task. This was done so that busy participants would not conclude that their own score differed from the confederate's score because they (but not the confederate) had performed the task under difficult conditions. As such, participants in both the busy and nonbusy conditions saw the confederate perform the schizophrenia detection task under precisely the same conditions that they would encounter themselves.

After seeing the videotaped confederate perform poorly or well, and after receiving or not receiving an 8-digit number to rehearse, all participants performed the schizophrenia detection task. Participants were given feedback indicating that they had given the correct response on 10 of the 18 trials. Participants then completed the dependent measures.

Dependent measures

Participants were asked to recall their own and the videotaped confederate's score on the schizophrenia detection task. Participants were then asked to estimate their own and the average student's ability to detect people at risk for schizophrenia on a 7-point scale that was anchored at the endpoints with the phrases *detect people at risk very poorly* and *detect people at risk very well*. At the conclusion of the experimental session, participants were probed for suspicion and understanding of basic information, thoroughly debriefed, thanked, and dismissed.

Results and Discussion
Excluded data

Two participants reported misunderstanding the instructions, 1 participant misremembered the confederate's score by more than two correct responses, and 4 participants did not recall or reported not understanding that the confederate had been given training or had been misled about how to detect schizophrenia. Data from these 7 participants were excluded from all analyses.

Self-perceived competence

Did participants compare themselves with a confederate whose performance was known to have been shaped by prior training? The difference between a participant's rating of her own ability and her rating of the average student's ability was taken as an index of her self-perceived competence.[1] We submitted this index to a 2 (confederate's performance: good or poor) × 2 (busyness: busy or nonbusy) analysis of variance (ANOVA), which revealed a main effect of confederate's performance, $F(1, 60) = 15.19$, $p < .0003$. This effect was qualified by the predicted Confederate's Performance × Busyness interaction, $F(1, 60) = 4.32$, $p < .04$. As Table 24.1 shows, the self-perceived competence of nonbusy participants was not reliably affected by the confederate's performance, $F(1, 60) = 1.81$, $p = .18$, but the self-perceived competence of busy participants was affected, $F(1, 60) = 16.47, p < .0002$. It is important to keep in mind that busy participants learned that the confederate's performance was nondiagnostic *before* they became busy and before they performed the task themselves. As such, they were just as aware of the nondiagnosticity of the

TABLE 24.1. Self-Perceived Competence as a Function of Confederate Performance and Cognitive Busyness in Experiment 1

| | Confederate's performance | | |
Rating of	Good	Poor	Difference
	Busy		
Self	2.46	3.23	−0.77
Average person	2.60	2.00	0.60
Self-perceived competence	0.14	1.23	−1.37[a]
	Not busy		
Self	2.63	3.00	−0.37
Average person	2.69	2.65	0.04
Self-perceived competence	−0.06	0.35	−0.41

Note: Self-perceived competence was computed by subtracting the rating of the average person from the rating of the self. Larger values indicate greater self-perceived competence.
[a] Significant at $p < .05$ or less by simple effects tests.

performance as were nonbusy participants, who demonstrated that awareness by using it later to correct their inferences.

Finally, an inspection of Table 24.1 reveals that the statistical interaction was driven largely by the condition in which the confederate performed poorly. This suggests either that ratings in the nonbusy condition are already at the psychological floor (i.e., participants simply will not rate themselves as much less capable than the average person) or that busyness caused a slight and inexplicable elevation of ratings. In either case, the important point is that the ratings of busy participants were reliably affected by changes in the confederate's performance, whereas the ratings of nonbusy participants were not.

Exactly what does busyness do?

Although all participants seemed to realize that the confederate's prior training made her a source of nondiagnostic comparison information, busy participants were apparently unable to use this fact to undo the comparison they seemed unable to avoid making. This finding is consistent with our contention that the diagnosticity of a comparison may be taken into account only after a comparison is made.

---

[1] We considered it important to measure self-perceived competence as a perceived deviation of the self from the norm. Observing a good or a poor performance can affect a participant's ratings by affecting her interpretation of particular scale values rather than by changing her self-perceived competence (see Krantz & Campbell, 1961), but this problem is virtually eliminated when one defines self-perceived competence not simply as "a high scale value" but as "a higher scale value than one gives the average person." There is ambiguity in the statement "A Ford is a good car" but not in the statement "A Ford is better than a Chevrolet." Ratings of both the self and the average person are shown in Table 24.1 but, by our logic, it is the difference between these ratings and not the component ratings themselves that is critical.

The interpretation of busyness effects, however, is always tricky business. Past research suggests that busyness truncates sequential mental operations, or "stops people in their mental tracks," so to speak (e.g., Gilbert & Hixon, 1991; Gilbert, Pelham, & Krull, 1988; Kantowitz, 1974; Martin, Seta, & Crelia, 1990). As such, busy participants are generally thought of as having "gotten stuck" at a stage through which nonbusy subjects have successfully passed, and their reports are thought to be identical to the reports that nonbusy participants *would have made* had it been possible to interrogate them in the moments before they changed their minds. Although this is a viable interpretation, it is not the only viable interpretation. One might argue, for example, that busyness did not truncate the information processing sequence that nonbusy participants normally follow, but rather that it caused busy participants to follow an entirely different sequence. In other words, busyness may have caused participants to make comparisons that they would not have made had they not been busy. If busyness gives rise to an abnormal information processing sequence rather than simply interrupting a normal information processing sequence, then the reports of busy participants may say little about the mental life of nonbusy participants.

The busyness technique simply cannot overcome these ambiguities, and thus we felt it important to generate converging evidence for our hypothesis by using a very different technique. As we mentioned earlier, cognitions are often fleeting, but they may leave affective traces that take somewhat longer to decay. Because emotions have a greater half-life than do thoughts, they may be taken as relatively enduring evidence of the transient cognitions that generated them, just as fossil imprints may be taken as evidence of the transient life forms that left them behind. As Tesser (1991, p. 116) noted, emotion "serves as a marker. Its presence provides information about whether social comparison and reflection processes are engaged." In Experiment 2 we attempted to find the affective fossils left by very brief social comparisons. The basic plan was to expose nonbusy participants to diagnostic or nondiagnostic social comparison information and then measure their cognitive and affective reactions. We expected that cognitive measures would suggest that nonbusy participants had used the diagnostic information and ignored the nondiagnostic information but that affective measures would clearly show that in both cases they had, in fact, made social comparisons.

Experiment 2

Method

Overview

Female participants were connected by electrode to a machine that could ostensibly detect the valence of their affect. Participants were shown 18 pairs of photographs and were asked to determine which of the male target persons in each pair was expressing insincere emotions. Participants were asked to report the valence of their affect at several points during the task. After performing the task, participants watched a female confederate perform the task. Participants were then told that they had responded correctly on 10 of 18 trials and that the confederate had responded correctly on either 16 of 18 trials or 4 of 18 trials. Participants knew that the confederate was either performing a different task than the participant had performed or the same task that the participant had performed. Finally, all participants rated their ability and the average woman's ability to detect the sincerity of men's emotional expressions.

Participants

Participants were 53 female undergraduates at the University of Texas at Austin who participated in exchange for credit in their introductory psychology course.

Procedure

Participants arrived at the laboratory, where they met another female college student (a confederate) who had ostensibly arrived a bit earlier. The experimenter told the participant and confederate that the experiment consisted of two unrelated tasks.

The primary task involved reading "insincerity in men's emotional expressions," and the secondary task involved "validating some new lie-detection machinery."

Emotion-reading task. The participant and confederate were told that the purpose of the primary task was to determine how well women can distinguish between men's sincere and insincere emotional expressions. The experimenter explained that the participant and confederate would view a series of photographs of men who had ostensibly undergone a mood induction procedure in which they had been made to feel either happy or sad. The experimenter had then ostensibly instructed each man to smile for the camera as she photographed him. Thus, the men who were in good moods as a result of the mood induction procedure were ostensibly expressing sincere emotions when they smiled for the camera, whereas the men who were in bad moods as a result of the mood induction procedure were ostensibly expressing insincere emotions when they smiled for the camera. (In fact, the photographs used for the emotion-reading task were of male college students who had not undergone any mood induction procedure and who had simply been asked to smile. These students all gave permission for their photographs to be used in later experiments.) The participant and the confederate were told that they would be shown 18 pairs of photographs and that in each pair one man would be expressing sincere emotions and one man would be expressing insincere emotions. They were told that their primary task was to view each pair of photographs and determine which of the two men pictured was expressing insincere emotions (i.e., which one was smiling while actually feeling sad).

Manipulations of confederate's performance. The participant performed the emotion-reading task and then watched the confederate perform the task. After both the participant and the confederate had performed the task, the experimenter announced the participant's score and then the confederate's score. All participants were told that they had responded correctly on 10 of the 18 trials.

Half the participants were randomly assigned to the same-task condition. These participants and the confederate were told that the confederate would be shown the same photographs that the participant had just seen and would thus perform the same emotion-reading task that the participant had just performed. Half these participants saw the confederate perform well (i.e., they heard the experimenter tell the confederate that she had responded correctly on 16 of 18 trials), and half saw the confederate do poorly (i.e., they heard the experimenter tell the confederate that she had responded correctly on only 4 of 18 trials).

The remainder of the participants were assigned to the different-task condition. These participants and the confederate were told that the confederate would be shown the same photographs that the participant had seen but that in each photograph the left side or the right side of the man's face would be covered by a piece of paper. The experimenter explained that prior research had shown that all men have a "strong and a weak side to their faces" and that the confederate would be seeing only the strong side of each man's face. Half the participants in the different-task condition were told that women who see only the strong side of a man's face tend to make very few errors on the emotion-reading task (ostensibly because false cues from the weak side are not present to confuse them). These participants then saw the confederate perform well (i.e., they heard the experimenter tell the confederate that she had responded correctly on 16 of 18 trials). The remaining participants in the different-task condition were told that women who see only the strong side of a man's face tend to make many errors on the emotion-reading task (ostensibly because useful cues from the weak side are not present to help them). These participants then saw the confederate perform poorly (i.e., they heard the experimenter tell the confederate that she had responded correctly on only 4 of 18 trials). In short, participants in the different-task condition saw the confederate perform poorly or well, and in both cases the confederate's performance was easily explained by the relative difficulty or ease of the task that the confederate had been assigned to perform.

Equipment-validation task. The purpose of this experiment was to determine whether participants' thoughts and feelings were affected by the confederate's performance. We expected that participants in the different-task condition would recognize that social comparisons would be nondiagnostic under these circumstances and thus might be particularly reluctant to admit that their affective states had been influenced by the confederate's performance. As such, we employed a bogus pipeline procedure (Jones & Sigall, 1971) to increase the veracity of participants' self-reports (see Roese & Jamieson, 1993, for a review of this technique).

Prior to performing the detection task, the experimenter pointed to an aggregation of interconnected electronic machinery (e.g., a computer, signal light, transfer box, wires and cables, etc.). The experimenter told the participant and confederate that this was a new, sophisticated device that could reliably detect the valence of a person's current affective state. The participant and confederate were asked to participate in a "validation trial" that would help confirm the accuracy of the affect-detection device. The experimenter pointed to a signal light that was visibly connected to the affect-detection device and told the participant and confederate that at several times during the detection task the signal light would flash and that when it did, they were to report their current affective state. They were told that these written reports would later be compared with the affect-detection device's readings and that this would enable the experimenter to validate the accuracy of the affect-detection device. Before the participant and confederate performed the emotion-reading task, the experimenter cleaned their middle and index fingers with rubbing alcohol and fastened electrodes to those fingers with Velcro straps. These electrodes were visibly attached to the affect-detection device.

Summary of procedure. Participants were connected to a bogus affect-detection device and were signaled to report their current affective states at several points throughout the experiment. Participants performed the emotion-reading task and then watched the confederate perform either the same task or a different task. The experimenter then announced

both the participant's score (10 of 18 correct) and the confederate's score (either 16 of 18 correct or 4 of 18 correct). Finally, participants were asked to complete a questionnaire that contained several dependent measures.

Dependent measures

The signal light flashed 20 times throughout the experiment, and thus the participant made 20 written reports of her current affective state. Each report was made on a 9-point Likert-type scale that was anchored at the endpoints with the words *positive* and *negative*. Two of these reports were considered critical. The first critical report was made immediately after the participant learned how she had performed on the primary task. We refer to this as the *self-feedback measure*. The second critical report was made immediately after the participant learned how the confederate had performed on the primary task. We refer to this as the *other-feedback measure*.

After the participant and confederate had completed the emotion-reading task and received their scores, the experimenter asked them to complete a questionnaire. The participant's questionnaire asked her to recall her own score and the confederate's score, to rate her own ability to detect sincerity in men's faces (on a 9-point scale anchored with the phrases *very bad* and *very good*), and to rate the average University of Texas student's ability to detect sincerity in men's faces (on the same scale). After completing the questionnaire, the participant and confederate were instructed to remove the electrodes from their fingers. The participant was probed for suspicion, debriefed, thanked, and dismissed.

Results and Discussion
Excluded data

Of the 53 participants who took part in the experiment, 2 participants reported extreme suspicion, 1 participant was unable to understand the instructions, 1 participant was unable to concentrate on the task, and 1 participant's age made her inappropriate for the experiment. The data from these

TABLE 24.2. Self-Perceived Competence and Changes in Affective State as a Function of Confederate's Task and Performance in Experiment 2

Dependent measure	Confederate's performance		
	Good	Poor	Difference
	Same task		
Rating of self	4.69	6.31	−1.62[a]
Rating of average person	5.84	5.38	0.46
Self-perceived competence	−1.15	0.93	−2.08[a]
Other feedback measure (Time 2)	4.69	6.30	−1.61[a]
Self-feedback measure (Time 1)	5.31	5.77	0.46
Change in affective state	−0.62	0.53	−1.15[a]
	Different task		
Rating of self	5.50	5.17	0.33
Rating of average person	5.40	4.92	0.48
Self-perceived competence	0.10	0.25	−0.15
Other feedback measure (Time 2)	5.30	5.58	−0.28
Self-feedback measure (Time 1)	5.80	4.67	1.13[a]
Change in affective state	−0.50	0.91	−1.41[a]

Note: Self-perceived competence was computed by subtracting the rating of the average person from the rating of the self. Changes in affective state were computed by subtracting the self-feedback measure from the other-feedback measure. Higher values indicate (a) greater self-perceived competence or (b) changes toward more positive affect states over time.
[a] Significant at $p < .05$ or less by simple effects tests.

5 participants were excluded from all analyses, leaving 48 participants in the data set.[2]

Recall of scores

All participants correctly recalled their own scores and the confederate's score.

Self-perceived competence

Did participants compare themselves with a confederate whose performance was known to have been a function of the ease or difficulty of the task she had been assigned? The difference between a participant's rating of her own ability and her rating of the average student's ability was taken as an index of her self-perceived competence. We submitted this index to a 2 (confederate's performance: poor or good) × 2 (confederate's task: same or different) ANOVA. The analysis revealed a main effect of confederate's performance, $F(1, 44) = 7.91, p < .01$,

but this effect was qualified by the predicted Confederate's Performance × Confederate's Task interaction, $F(1, 44) = 5.93, p < .02$. As Table 24.2 shows, participants' self-perceived competence was affected by the confederate's performance when the confederate performed the same task that the participant had performed, $F(1, 44) = 15.09, p < .001$, but not when she performed a different task than the participant had performed ($F < 1$).

Change in affective state

Ratings of self-perceived competence suggest that participants did not engage in social comparison when the confederate's performance was determined by the ease or difficulty of her task. If participants in the different-task condition did not engage in social comparison, then their affective state should not have been influenced by the confederate's performance. The influence of the confederate's performance on the participant's affective state was operationalized as the difference between the self-feedback measure (the participant's report of her affective state after she received feedback about her performance) and the other-feedback measure

[2] The excluded participant was 36 years old (8.92 sigma units from the mean participant age of 18.83 years) and was thus considered a demographic outlier. Including her data would not change the pattern or significance level of any result.

(the participant's report of her affective state after she heard the confederate receive feedback about the confederate's performance). We submitted this index to a 2 × 2 ANOVA (as above) that revealed only the predicted main effect of confederate's performance, $F(1, 44) = 14.44$, $p < .001$. As Table 24.2 shows, participants experienced more positive changes in their affective states when the confederate did poorly than when she did well. Importantly, this was true in both the same-task condition, $F(1, 44) = 6.38$, $p < .02$, and the different-task condition, $F(1, 44) = 8.06$, $p < .001$. Clearly, participants in the different-task condition were affected by the performance of the confederate, despite their claims of immunity. It is worth noting that, by the end of the experiment, the affective consequences of social comparison had entirely faded. Analysis of the participants' last affective ratings showed absolutely no effects of any manipulation (all Fs < 1).

General Discussion

If an insurance salesman from Wichita compares himself with Charles Manson, he will probably learn little about his own moral character. Although ordinary people seem to realize that such comparisons are not worth the bother, our research suggests that making them may not be much of a bother at all. In fact, social comparisons can sometimes be so natural and easy that people may make them even when they don't really want to, and when that happens, they may have little choice but to mentally undo the comparisons they made. Such efforts are not always successful, and when they are, the unwanted comparisons may continue to have emotional effects even after their cognitive effects have been reversed. In short, sometimes we choose to compare ourselves with others, but sometimes such comparisons are thrust upon us. When they are, we may not be able to escape their unwanted influence.

This view of the social comparison process raises three important questions. First, if social comparisons are relatively automatic responses to the performances of others, does this mean that people have no choice about which comparisons

they will or won't make? Second, when people are not consciously choosing to compare themselves with one person rather than another, then what factors will determine the object of their comparisons? And third, if comparison is a relatively automatic response to the performance of another, then what does this say about other responses, such as reflection? We address each issue in turn.

The Role of Choice in Social Comparison

Although our work suggests that the decision to compare or not to compare is not always ours to make, conscious choice does play an important role in a correction model of social comparison. Correction models are based on the assumption that people lack complete control over their processing of information—in other words, the mind often responds to information in ways that the mind's owner might wish it would not. But a lack of complete control is not a complete lack of control. Indeed, even a person who spontaneously compares himself with those whom he encounters can control his conclusions by (a) choosing which others to encounter, and (b) choosing which conclusions to revise. Perhaps a small-town mayor cannot avoid comparing her political stature with that of the President when she meets him, but she may be able to avoid meeting him, and if not, then she may be able to correct her ill-advised comparison after it has been made. Even when people are unable to control directly their processing of information, the two strategies of *exposure control* (determining the information to which one will be exposed in the future) and *unbelieving* (consciously repudiating the conclusions that one has reached in the past) allow them exceptional authority over the contents of their own minds (Gilbert, 1992).

These two strategies are key to understanding how a correction model of the social comparison process fits with more traditional conceptualizations. Previous work has been largely concerned with articulating the "rules" of social comparison—that is, describing the factors that determine when and with whom people consciously choose to compare—and these rules constitute the naive psychology of social comparison. Although our data suggest that such rules do not necessarily determine when people make mental comparisons, we suspect that they do indeed determine when people will engage in the more deliberate strategies of exposure control and unbelieving. For example, one of the most well-established social comparison rules is that people who are uncertain of their standing on an ability-linked dimension (and who wish to gain accurate, rather than merely flattering, information about themselves) tend to think of dissimilar others as nondiagnostic sources of comparison information and thus do not compare with them. Although our research suggests that this "similarity rule" is sometimes wrong inasmuch as people *do*, in fact, compare with dissimilar others, we suspect it is quite right inasmuch as accuracy-driven people probably do not seek encounters with dissimilar others (exposure control) and, when such encounters occur, may repudiate the thoughts and feelings that the encounter produced (unbelieving). In short, the well-established rules of social comparison may not predict when we will compare with those whom we encounter, but they probably do predict whom we will encounter and whether we will work to undo the effects of that encounter after it has taken place. Our conceptualization represents a departure from previous conceptualizations of the social comparison process, but it does not do so by rejecting previous work but rather by relocating it.

The Object of Comparison

If social comparisons were thoroughly reflexive responses to the real or simulated presence of others, then people would mentally compare themselves with every person whom they encountered or imagined on a particular day. Given the sizable number of people with whom we have some form of social commerce, it seems logically absurd to suggest that social comparison is an inevitable consequence of observing another's performance. What, then, determines which performances will spark a comparison and which will not?

This problem in the study of social comparison is very much like the "context problem" in the study of psychophysical contrast. A librarian may consider *Totem and Taboo* especially light if he moved *The Rise and Fall of the Roman Empire* in order to reach it, but why was the first book judged in the context of the second book rather than in the context of books lifted hours before, groceries lifted last month, grandchildren lifted last year, or for that matter, every object ever lifted during the librarian's lifetime? Decades of psychophysical research suggest some answers to this question. Contextual stimuli are most likely to become the objects of comparison when (a) they have been recently encountered, (b) they are explicitly judged, and (c) their values are especially extreme (Parducci, 1992; Parducci & Wedell, 1990). In other words, the librarian is more likely to experience contrast when he lifts the heavy book just moments before the lighter one, when he explicitly mutters, "That book is the heaviest damn thing I've lifted today," and when the book *is* in fact, the heaviest damn thing he lifted today.

These three principles may provide clues about when social comparisons will and will not arise. In our studies, the confederate's performance was in close spatial and temporal proximity to the participant's, it was the most extreme performance the participant had ever observed, and its value was explicitly judged. As noted, these are the very factors that encourage contextual effects. Indeed, we would have been surprised if our participants had spontaneously compared themselves with a confederate whose moderate performance they had incidentally witnessed a year earlier. We suspect that these three factors—recency, extremity, and explicit judgment—created just the sort of climate in which comparisons are most likely to arise. Our research demonstrates that under some circumstances comparisons may arise without conscious effort, but future research must determine when they will and when they will not arise. These three principles seem to provide a reasonable point of departure.

Reflection and Correction

As every proud parent knows, another person's performance can evoke reactions other than social comparison. When a close other's performance provides evidence of abilities that are irrelevant to an observer's own cherished identity, the self-evaluation maintenance model (Tesser & Campbell, 1983) suggests that observers engage in *reflection* rather than comparison and that they react to the other's performance as if it were their own (Tesser, 1984). Indeed, it would be a strange mother who was steaming rather than beaming when her daughter won first prize in the third grade math competition, and the odd coach who felt smugly self-satisfied when his star sprinter placed last in the 50-yard dash. A variety of experiments have shown that when those with whom we share special bonds perform in domains that are not relevant to our own sense of self-worth, we share in the thrill of their victories and the agony of their defeats (Tesser, 1986; 1991). How does our theorizing relate to this important work?

The self-evaluation maintenance model is a dual-process model. In other words, comparison and reflection are thought to be different processes that produce different cognitive and emotional responses, and the closeness of the other and the relevance of the other's behavior determine which of these processes is (or is most strongly) evoked. Of course, just because people show different responses does not mean that these responses are necessarily produced by different processes. Correction models provide an alternative to dual-process models by suggesting that different responses are sometimes the result of a single, multistage process, and that what appear to be the products of two separate processes may actually be the initial and updated outputs of one. This suggests that, at least in some cases, the jealousy of comparison and the pride of reflection could be the early and late results of a single psychological operation. Just as participants in our studies presumably corrected their spontaneous comparisons by reminding themselves that they should not have been affected by another's performance ("I feel pretty stupid. But then again, the other participant had prior training at schizophrenia detection, so I guess I shouldn't feel stupid after all"), it is conceivable that under other circumstances correction might involve reminding oneself that one *should* have been affected by another's performance, but in a different way than

one was affected ("Gosh, Fred's Academy Award makes me feel jealous. But I'm a plumber, not a producer, so I guess I should feel proud to be Fred's brother"). In this case, the sense of self-worth and feelings of pride that appear to be the products of a reflection process are actually the products of a corrected comparison.

We do not wish to suggest that *all* reflections are merely revisions of comparisons, but it may be useful to distinguish between two kinds of reflections—those produced when one regards another's irrelevant behavior as an extension of one's own and thus initially has positive reactions to success and negative reactions to failure, and those produced when one regards another's relevant behavior as belonging to the other, initially compares the other's performance with one's own, experiences positive reactions to the other's failure and negative reactions to the other's success, and finally, engages in the cognitive work necessary to reverse or undo these early reactions. In both cases one may ultimately take pride in the other's achievements and suffer the humiliation of the other's failures, but such conclusions may be achieved by distinctly different means. It is not unreasonable to suppose that the latter sort of reflection may produce weaker changes in and greater discontinuity between cognition and emotion. These issues are surely worthy of investigation.

Coda

Bertrand Russell (1930) suggested that envy is one of the fundamental causes of human suffering, and he counseled his readers to avoid it:

> The habit of thinking in terms of comparison is a fatal one . . . which consists in seeing things never in themselves but only in their relations. . . . You can get away from envy by enjoying the pleasures that come your way, by doing the work that you have to do, and by avoiding comparisons with those whom you imagine, perhaps quite falsely, to be more fortunate than yourself" (pp. 87–88).

Is it possible to break the fatal habit of social comparison? Russell (1930) thought so. After all, he argued, "Beggars do not envy millionaires, though of course they will envy other beggars who are more successful" (p. 90). In other words, because people clearly do not compare themselves with everyone they must therefore be capable of controlling their comparisons and hence of avoiding the envy that informs their daily misery. Alas, the fact that comparisons are less than ubiquitous does not mean they are under the voluntary control of the individual. We have argued that people can *indirectly* control their thoughts and feelings by avoiding the situations that give rise to unwise comparisons or by undoing those comparisons once they have been made. But our studies also suggest that when ordinary people are deprived of such indirect control—and when certain environmental factors that encourage comparison are in place—they may well experience the very comparisons they wish to avoid. A life without envy would itself be an envious life, but our research suggests that the injunction to live one may be somewhat impractical advice.

REFERENCES

Aronson, E., & Carlsmith, J. M. (1962). Performance expectancy as a determinant of actual performance. *Journal of Abnormal and Social Psychology, 65,* 178–182.

Brickman, P., & Bullman, R. J. (1977). Pleasure and pain in social comparison. In J. M. Suls & R. L. Miller (Eds.), *Social comparison processes: Theoretical and empirical perspectives* (pp. 149–186). Washington, DC: Hemisphere.

Festinger, L. (1954a). A theory of social comparison processes. *Human Relations, 7,* 117–140.

Festinger, L. (1954b). Motivation leading to social behavior. In M. R. Jones (Ed.), *Nebraska symposium on motivation* (Vol. 2, pp. 191–218). Lincoln: University of Nebraska Press.

Gibbons, F. X., & Gerrard, M. (1991). Downward comparison and coping with threat. In J. Suls & T. A. Wills (Eds.), *Social comparison: Contemporary theory and research* (pp. 317–346). Hillsdale, NJ: Erlbaum.

Gilbert, D. T. (1991). How mental systems believe. *American Psychologist, 46,* 107–119.

Gilbert, D. T. (1992). The assent of man: Mental representation and the control of belief. In D. M. Wegner & J. Pennebaker (Eds.), *The handbook of mental control* (pp. 57–87). New York: Prentice-Hall.

Gilbert, D. T., & Hixon, J. G. (1991). The trouble of thinking: Activation and application of stereotypic beliefs. *Journal of Personality and Social Psychology, 60,* 509–517.

Gilbert, D. T., Krull, D. S., & Malone, P. S. (1990). Unbelieving the unbelievable: Some problems in the rejection of false information. *Journal of Personality and Social Psychology, 59,* 601–613.

Gilbert, D. T., Pelham, B. W., & Krull, D. S. (1988). On cognitive busyness: When person perceivers meet persons perceived. *Journal of Personality and Social Psychology, 54,* 733–740.

Jones, E. E., & Sigall, H. (1971). The bogus pipeline: A new paradigm for measuring affect and attitude. *Psychological Bulletin, 76,* 349–364.

Kantowitz, B. H. (1974). Double stimulation. In B. H. Kantowitz (Ed.), Human information processing: *Tutorials in performance and cognition* (pp. 83–132). Hillsdale, NJ: Erlbaum.

Krantz, D. L., & Campbell, D. T. (1961). Separating perceptual and linguistic effects of context shifts upon absolute judgments. *Journal of Experimental Psychology, 62,* 35–42.

Kruglanski, A. W., & Mayseless, O. (1990). Classic and current social comparison research: Expanding the perspective. *Psychological Bulletin, 108,* 195–208.

Martin, L. L., Seta, J. J., & Crelia, R. A. (1990). Assimilation and contrast as a function of people's willingness and ability to expend effort in forming an impression. *Journal of Personality and Social Psychology, 59,* 27–37.

Morse, S., & Gergen, K. J. (1970). Social comparison, self-consistency, and the concept of self. *Journal of Personality and Social Psychology, 40,* 624–634.

Olson, J. M., Herman, C. P., & Zanna, M. P. (Eds.). (1986). *Relative deprivation and social comparison: The Ontario symposium* (Vol. 4). Hillsdale, NJ: Erlbaum.

Parducci, A. (1992). Elaborations upon psychophysical contexts for judgment: Implications of cognitive models. In H. G. Geissler, S. W. Link, & J. T. Townsend (Eds.), *Cognition, information processing, and psychophysics: Basic issues* (pp. 207–224). Hillsdale, NJ: Erlbaum.

Parducci, A., & Wedell, D. (1990). The context of evaluative judgments: Psychophysics and beyond. In H. H. Geissler (Ed.), *Psychophysical explorations of mental structures* (pp. 94–103). Göttingen, Germany: Hogrefe & Huber.

Pelham, B. W., & Wachsmuth, J. O. (1994). *Feeling tall in the land of giants: A theory of social assimilation processes.* Unpublished manuscript, University of California at Los Angeles.

Petty, R. E., & Wegener, D. T. (1993). Flexible correction processes in social judgment: Correcting for context-induced contrast. *Journal of Experimental Social Psychology, 29,* 137–165.

Roese, N. J., & Jamieson, D. W. (1993). Twenty years of bogus pipeline research: A critical review and meta-analysis. *Psychological Bulletin, 114,* 363–375.

Russell, B. (1930). *The conquest of happiness.* New York: Liveright.

Salovey, P., & Rodin, J. (1984). Some antecedents and consequences of social comparison jealousy. *Journal of Personality and Social Psychology, 47,* 780–792.

Schwarz, N., & Bless, H. (1992). Constructing reality and its alternatives: An inclusion/exclusion model of assimilation and contrast effects in social judgment. In L. L. Martin &

A. Tesser (Eds.), *The construction of social judgments* (pp. 217–245). Hillsdale, NJ: Erlbaum.

Suls, J., & Wills, T. A. (1991). (Eds.). *Social comparison: Contemporary theory and research*. Hillsdale, NJ: Erlbaum.

Taylor, S. E., Buunk, B. P., & Aspinwall, L. G. (1990). *Social comparison, stress, and coping. Personality and Social Psychology Bulletin, 16*, 74–89.

Taylor, S. E., & Lobel, M. (1989). Social comparison activity under threat: Downward evaluation and upward contacts. *Psychological Review, 96*, 569–575.

Tesser, A. (1984). Self-evaluation maintenance processes: Implications for relationships and development. In J. C. Masters & K. Yarkin-Levin (Eds.), *Boundary areas in social and developmental psychology* (pp. 271–299). San Diego, CA: Academic Press.

Tesser, A. (1986). Some effects of self-evaluation maintenance on cognition and action. In R. M. Sorrentino & E. T. Higgins (Eds.), *Handbook of motivation and cognition* (pp. 435–464). New York: Guilford Press.

Tesser, A. (1991). Emotion in social comparison and reflection processes. In J. Suls & T A. Wills (Eds.), *Social comparison: Contemporary theory and research* (pp. 117–148). Hillsdale, NJ: Erlbaum.

Tesser, A., & Campbell, J. (1983). Self-definition and self-evaluation maintenance. In J. M. Suls & A. Greenwald (Eds.), *Social psychological perspectives on the self* (Vol. 2, pp. 1–31). Hillsdale, NJ: Erlbaum.

Tesser, A., Millar, M., & Moore, J. (1988). Some affective consequences of social comparison and reflection processes: The pain and pleasure of being close. *Journal of Personality and Social Psychology, 54*, 49–61.

Wedell, D. H. (1990). Methods for determining the locus of context effects in judgment. In J. P. Caverni, J. M. Fabre, & M. Gonzalez (Eds.), *Cognitive biases* (pp. 285–302). New York: Elsevier Science.

Wedell, D. H. (1994). Contextual contrast in evaluative judgments: A test of pre- versus postintegration models of contrast. *Journal of Personality and Social Psychology, 66*, 1007–1019.

Wills, T. A. (1981). Downward comparison principles in social psychology. *Psychological Bulletin, 90*, 245–271.

Wilson, T D., & Brekke, N. (1994). Mental contamination and mental correction: Unwanted influences on judgments and evaluations. *Psychological Bulletin, 116*, 117–142.

Wood, J. V. (1989). Theory and research concerning social comparisons of personal attributes. *Psychological Bulletin, 106*, 231–248.

Received September 14, 1994
Revision received February 2, 1995
Accepted February 2, 1995 ■

I, We, and the Effects of Others on Me: How Self-Construal Level Moderates Social Comparison Effects

Diederik A. Stapel and Willem Koomen

In 5 studies, the authors investigate the impact of self-activation on the occurrence and direction of social comparison effects. They show that self-evaluative comparison effects are more likely to occur when self-related cognitions are made cognitively accessible. Contrast occurs when personal self-construals ("I") are accessible, whereas assimilation occurs when social self-construals ("we") are activated. These effects of self-construal activation are similar to the impact of self-unrelated information processing styles that are often associated with personal and social self-accessibility (i.e., differentiation and integration mind-sets). However, whereas self-construal activation elicits self-serving social comparisons, activation of self-unrelated processing styles results in non-self-serving social comparison effects. Implications of these results for understanding the cognitive processes underlying social comparison effects are discussed.

One of social psychology's central missions has been to offer a view of how social factors affect the ways people come to define themselves. In the past century, the burgeoning literature on the social psychology of the self focused on how individuals' self-perceptions are created and shaped by the social world they inhabit. Self-perceptions depend not only on the absolute nature of one's features

---

Diederik A. Stapel and Willem Koomen, Department of Social Psychology, University of Amsterdam, Amsterdam, the Netherlands.

This research was supported by a fellowship from the Royal Netherlands Academy of Arts and Sciences.

Correspondence concerning this article should be addressed to Diederik A. Stapel, who is now at the Department of Social and Organizational Psychology, University of Groningen, Grote Kruisstraat 2/1, 9712 TS Groningen, the Netherlands. Electronic mail may be sent to d.a.stapel@ppsw.rug.nl.

(e.g., "I am 6 ft 5 in.") but even more so on the way one measures up to relevant others (e.g., "I am tall—for a Portuguese-born male psychologist"). In fact, when we want to find out how attractive, smart, or likable we are, objective, non-social standards are often not available. We are then likely to obtain self-knowledge by relating our thoughts, feelings, and behaviors to those of the people around us (Festinger, 1954; see also Blanton, in press; Wood, 1989).

Others therefore constitute an important input for the construction of self-evaluations. We engage in social comparison to evaluate, enhance, verify, or improve ourselves (see, e.g., Gibbons & Buunk, 1999; Taylor & Lobel, 1989). Hence, social comparison information should be especially likely to affect self-evaluations in situations that promote a need for self-information. Research suggesting that social comparison information may affect self-evaluations in circumstances associated with uncertainty (e.g., "Who am I?", "How am I doing?") supports this notion. Social comparison effects are strongest when the need for self-related information is particularly salient: in situations that are competitive (e.g., Morse & Gergen, 1970) or performance-oriented (Tesser & Paulhus, 1983), under circumstances that emphasize comparative evaluations (e.g., Gilbert, Giesler, & Morris, 1995; Mussweiler & Strack, 2000; Taylor & Lobel, 1989), and in periods of stress, novelty, or change (see Wills & Suls, 1991).

Given that there is a need for self-information and that one engages in social comparison and uses information about others to construct self-evaluations, what determines the direction of the self-evaluative consequences of this information? If social comparison exerts effects, what determines whether these effects are assimilative or contrastive? Real-life experience, anecdotal evidence, and, more important, empirical research suggest that the impact of both upward and downward social comparisons on self-evaluation may be assimilative as well as contrastive. When contrast occurs, another person's success (i.e., upward comparison) is a source of envy and frustration (e.g., "I am worse"), whereas a person's failure (i.e., downward comparison) is felt as a boost to one's

sense of relative worth or status (e.g., "I am better"). When assimilation is the effect of social comparison, another person's success functions as a source of inspiration (e.g., "I may become like her") and may trigger elation (e.g., "I am similar to her"), whereas another person's failure (i.e., downward comparison) is felt as depressing (e.g., "I am similar to her") or threatening, because it may suggest that one's own status is likely to deteriorate (e.g., "I may become like her"). Recently, several studies have identified a number of potent constructs that moderate which of these effects is more likely to occur (for reviews, see Blanton, in press; Stapel & Koomen, 2000; Taylor, Wayment, & Carillo, 1996). Specifically, the personal importance of the focal comparison dimension (e.g., Tesser, 1988), the similarity (e.g., Brewer & Weber, 1994), shared distinctiveness (e.g., Brown, Novick, Lord, & Richards, 1992), or psychological closeness (Pelham & Wachsmuth, 1995) of the comparison other, and the extremity or attainability (e.g., Lockwood & Kunda, 1997) of his or her performance appear to be important moderators of whether the impact of a comparison other on self-evaluation is likely to be assimilative or contrastive.

In sum, it is clear that an impressive array of social comparison studies have focused on the "when" question and investigated the conditions under which social comparison information is selected as a basis for self-evaluation (see Blanton, in press; Wood, 1989). One important conclusion of this type of research is that social comparison information is more likely to be used in the construction of self-evaluations when there is a need to acquire information about the self (see Gibbons & Buunk, 1999). More recently, the focus has shifted to the "what" question, and more attention has been given to what determines the outcome of social comparison. This research has identified a number of potent moderators of whether social comparisons result in assimilation or contrast (see Stapel & Koomen, 2000).

In the present research, we set out to find answers to the what as well as the when question by approaching social comparison from a perspective that, to date, has been given surprisingly little attention. In a series of studies, we examine the impact of self-activation on the occurrence and direction of social comparison effects. Specifically, we investigate whether self-evaluative comparison effects are more likely to occur when self-related cognitions are made cognitively accessible. In addition and more important, we test the hypothesis that the direction of social comparison effects is more likely to be contrastive when personal self-construals ("I") are accessible, whereas assimilation is more likely when social self-construals ("we") are activated. Furthermore, we compare the effects on social comparison of this type of self-construal activation with the impact of self-unrelated information processing styles (i.e., differentiation and integration mind-sets) that are often associated with personal and social self-accessibility.

When it concerns the when of social comparison effects, previous research has shown that social comparison effects occur more readily when comparison others are perceived as self-relevant. Most of this research, however, has studied how differences in features or circumstances affect the perceived relevance of others for the purpose of social comparison, such as gender, occupation, education, or relevant training (see Goethals & Darley, 1977; Tesser, 1988; Wood, 1989). In the present studies, we keep such variables constant and investigate the hypothesis that whether social comparison occurs may be a function of the way the mind attends to and processes social comparison information. That is, when the mind is set on seeing others as relevant to obtaining self-knowledge, social comparison information is more likely to exert self-evaluative effects than when others are not perceived as relevant for the construction of self-evaluations. In other words, social comparison effects occur when the mind is set so that others matter.

One goal of the present studies, therefore, is to assess the ways self-accessibility, be it personal or social, increases the perceived relevance of social comparison information, such that this information results in self-evaluative consequences. Our thinking concerning this issue follows directly from Festinger's (1954) notion that the primary goal of social comparison is to acquire information about the self (see, also, Gibbons & Buunk, 1999). This need for self-information is likely to be stronger in conditions in which self-related cognitions are especially accessible or salient. One is probably more motivated to seek information about the self (and engage in social comparison) when self-concepts are on the top of one's mind than when the mind is otherwise engaged. Self-activation increases interest in and attention to social comparison information (Stapel & Tesser, 2000). Therefore, under circumstances in which self-cognitions are highly accessible, exposure to social comparison information is more likely to affect self-evaluations than when one's mind is occupied with other thoughts.

Self-activation may activate an *others-are-relevant* processing style and, thus, increase the probability that information about others is related to the self, such that social comparison effects are likely to occur. But what determines the direction (contrast or assimilation) of such effects? We test the hypothesis that the level of activated self-construals (personal self, or *I*, versus social self, or *we*) is important in determining the direction of social comparison effects, such that contrast is more likely when "*I*-ness" is activated and assimilation when "*we*-ness" is activated.

This hypothesis is grounded in the notion that there are two kinds of self-construals that are especially powerful in influencing one's relation to the social world and available to be activated at different times or in different contexts, the personal self and the social self (see Aron, Aron, Tudor, & Nelson, 1991; Brewer, 1991; Markus & Kitayama, 1991; Trafimow, Triandis, & Goto, 1991; Triandis, 1989; Turner, 1987). The personal self represents those aspects of the self-concept that differentiate the self from others. The social self represents those aspects of the self-concept that reflect integration and inclusion of the self in the social world (cf. Brewer & Gardner, 1996).

When this information is viewed in relation to the present concerns, it seems safe to draw the general conclusion that activating self-related cognitions— be they personal or social—increases the likelihood that others are perceived as relevant to the construction of self-evaluations. More specifically, however, the level of activated self-construals may affect the way information about others is processed (cf. Brewer & Gardner, 1996, pp. 91–92).

When an individual's personal self is activated, he or she is in an *I* frame of mind and is likely to value being distinct and, thus, accentuate differences from others. When a person's social self becomes activated, he or she shifts into a *we* frame of mind and is likely to value being part of a social unit and, thus, accentuate similarities to others (see Abelson, Dasgupta, Park, & Banaji, 1998; Hoyle, Kernis, Leary, & Baldwin, 1999; cf. Aron, Aron, & Smollan, 1992; Aron *et al.*, 1991). Thus, changes in self-construal level affect whether information about others is processed with a mind that is set on differentiating the self from others or with a mind that is set on including others in the self or conforming the self to others. Changes in self-construal level may thus reflect differences in self-definition (e.g., Hogg & Turner, 1987; Trafimow *et al.*, 1991; cf. Aron *et al.*, 1991) as well as differences in information processing style, in the way in which information about others is attended to and processed (Brewer, 1991; Brewer & Gardner, 1996; Turner, 1987). This latter characteristic of the differences between personal and social self-construals, especially, provides the background for our hypothesis that social comparison is likely to result in contrast when the personal self is made salient, whereas assimilation occurs when the social self is activated. *I* priming is likely to activate a *differentiation mind-set*, in which self-distinctiveness is emphasized, such that self-perceptions are contrasted away from relevant comparison targets. Conversely, *we* priming is likely to activate an *integration mind-set*, in which similarities between the self and others are emphasized, such that self-perceptions are assimilated toward those others (cf. Carnevale & Probst, 1998; Gollwitzer, Heckhausen, & Steller, 1990; Schwarz & Bless, 1992; Stapel & Koomen, 1999, 2000).

In sum, then, in the present research we test the hypothesis that self-activation is an important determinant of whether social comparison information leads to no effects, contrast effects, or assimilation effects on self-evaluations. Specifically, self-activation increases the perceived relevance of others to self-evaluation and, thus, activates an others-are-relevant processing style. The level of the activated self-construals determines the direction of social comparison effects. When the personal self is accessible, a differentiation mind-set is likely to be activated, and contrast is more likely. When the social self is accessible, an integration mind-set is likely to be activated, such that assimilation is more likely.

This latter line of reasoning suggests that activating the (self-unrelated) differentiation (i.e., "attend to differences between stimuli") and integration (i.e., "attend to similarities between stimuli") mind-sets or processing styles should yield social comparison effects that are similar to priming personal (*I*) and social (*we*) self-construals. That is, priming a processing style (see Chartrand & Bargh, 1996) that emphasizes either differentiation or integration should result in contrastive or assimilative social comparison effects, respectively.

This raises the question of whether the impact of priming differentiation versus integration is identical to the impact of priming *I* versus *we*. One may argue that increased accessibility of self-cognitions is more likely to instigate self-serving processing of social comparison information. The need to maintain a positive self-evaluation may be especially strong when self-cognitions, values, and concepts are relatively accessible (see Stapel & Tesser, 2000; Tesser, 1988). Therefore, increased accessibility of self-cognitions is more likely to instigate self-serving processing of social comparison information than is increased accessibility of self-unrelated processing styles. Thus, the predicted social comparison effects probably resemble more of a self-serving pattern when self-construals are relatively accessible. Specifically, contrast occurs when the personal self is activated, but this effect is especially strong when its impact on self-evaluation is positive (i.e., downward comparison information). Similarly, assimilation occurs when the social self is activated, but this effect is especially strong when its impact on self-evaluation is positive (i.e., upward comparison information).

Research Overview

We present five experiments in which we test our predictions concerning the relation between self-activation and social comparison effects. In the first experiment, we put to a first test our general hypothesis that *I* accessibility leads to contrastive self-evaluative comparisons, whereas *we* accessibility results in assimilative self-evaluations. In the second experiment, we further test the validity of this general hypothesis by using a different method to activate personal versus social selves.

In Experiments 2–4, we investigate whether the activation of the self-unrelated information processing styles that are often associated with personal self- and social self-accessibility (differentiation and integration mind-sets) yield social comparison effects that are similar to the effects of priming self-related mind-sets. Moreover, we test whether such self-unrelated mind-set priming is likely to show less of a self-serving pattern than when the corresponding self-construal levels have been activated.

In Experiment 5, we further address the issue of self-servingness of social comparison effects after personal versus social self-priming. In that study, we investigate the impact of personal self-versus social self-accessibility on self-evaluative comparisons in situations in which the focal comparison dimension is either important or unimportant. We predict that assimilation and contrast effects are more likely to show a self-serving pattern when the comparison situation deals with an important dimension than when it is relatively trivial.

Experiment 1

In our first study, we exposed participants to a description of an upward or a downward comparison other, either under conditions in which self-activation was low or under conditions in which either personal or social self-construals had been made accessible. Social comparison information should be relatively likely to affect self-evaluation in the self-activation conditions, as compared with the conditions in which self-activation was low. The level of the activated self-construal should determine the direction of the effect, such that contrast occurs under *I* priming conditions and assimilation occurs under *we* priming conditions. These contrast

and assimilation effects are most likely to surface when they are self-serving—that is, when they are positive. Specifically, under *I* priming conditions, the positive effect of downward comparison information should be stronger than the negative effect of upward comparison information. Conversely, under *we* priming conditions, the positive effect of upward comparison information should be stronger than the negative effect of downward comparison information.

Method
Participants and design

Ninety students were randomly assigned to the conditions of a 2 (valence other: positive, negative) × 3 (self-activation: *I*, *we*, control) between-subjects design. Participants received partial course credit for their participation.

Procedure and materials

Participants were told they would participate in a series of studies.[1] First, they would participate in a reading comprehension task, then in a study of journalistic styles, and, finally, they would fill out a self-evaluation questionnaire. They were told that the experimenter would time them through each of these studies.

Self-activation priming. The priming task was modeled after Brewer and Gardner (1996, p. 87). Participants read paragraphs describing a trip to the city. They were instructed to carefully circle all the pronouns that appeared in the text, as part of a proofreading and word search task. In each of the three conditions, the paragraph contained 19 pronouns, but the text was varied so the same materials were presented with almost all of the pronouns referring to *I* or *me* (*I* priming condition), *we* or *us* (*we* priming condition), or *it* (control condition). Brewer and Gardner (1996; see also Gardner, Gabriel, & Lee, 1999) showed that this priming task is successful in eliciting responses

---

[1] Experiments 1–4 were conducted in Dutch. Throughout the article, examples of materials used are the English equivalent of the Dutch materials used in those experiments.

associated with personal versus social self-activation as well as independent (*I* oriented) versus interdependent (*we* oriented) cultures.

Social comparison information. This task was modeled after Lockwood and Kunda (1997, p. 94). Participants read an invented one-page newspaper article describing a psychology student from their university (the University of Amsterdam). Their task was to guess in which Dutch daily newspaper or weekly magazine the article could have been published. The student described in the article was very successful or rather unsuccessful. The successful (positive) comparison target had finished his undergraduate studies in only 3 years, had won an award for his honor's thesis, was attractive, had many friends, had started his own business while he was still enrolled at the university, had recently sold his business to a small company to be able to have free time and travel around the world with some of his friends, and afterward would perhaps enroll in a PhD program. The unsuccessful (negative) comparison target was described as being not particularly intelligent. He had never completed his undergraduate studies because he got involved in a fight with his advisor and was unemployed most of the time but sometimes worked odd shifts at a bar. He did not have many friends, was often tired, felt somewhat depressed, and hoped he would become more successful in the future but had no idea how to achieve that. Pretest participants indicated that they saw commonalities as well as differences between themselves and the positive as well as the negative comparison target and indicated that they could differentiate themselves from as well as identify themselves with the protagonists in the stories.

Self-evaluation. After having read the newspaper article and having written down their answers to the media source question, participants answered some questions about themselves, ostensibly to determine whether their personality had any impact on their perceptions of the article. All participants rated themselves on the following adjectives: *attractive, kind, happy, bright, friendly, ambitious, frustrated, successful, sincere, undetermined, lucky,*

incompetent, balanced, promising, tense. These items were rated on 7-point scales ranging from 1 (*not at all*) to 7 (*very*).

Target person ratings. Next, participants rated the target person on the following adjectives: *intelligent, arrogant, successful, likable.* These items were also rated on 7-point scales ranging from 1 (*not at all*) to 7 (*very*).

Debriefing. On completion of the questionnaire, participants were carefully debriefed about the goal and purpose of the experiment. None of the participants spontaneously indicated suspicion of the actual goal of the study. Furthermore, when explicitly asked, none of the participants felt their self-evaluation ratings might have been influenced by either the word search or the journalist style task. After the debriefing, participants were thanked and dismissed.

Results and Discussion

Manipulation check

First, we checked whether the participants indeed judged the positive comparison target more positively on the relevant dimensions than they judged the negative target. After reverse scoring the negative item (*arrogant*), we averaged the four items into a single index (Cronbach's $\alpha = .89$). A Valence Other $\times$ Self-Activation analysis of variance (ANOVA) revealed the predicted main effect of valence other, $F(1, 84) = 194.32$, $p < .01$ (other $Fs < 1$). Participants judged the positive target more positively ($M = 6.23$) than they judged the negative target ($M = 2.71$).

Self-evaluation

We averaged the self-evaluation items into a single index after reverse scoring the negative items (Cronbach's $\alpha = .82$). An ANOVA on this index revealed the predicted Valence Other $\times$ Self-Activation interaction, $F(2, 84) = 4.99$, $p < .01$, and a main effect of self-activation, $F(2, 84) = 3.39$, $p < .05$ (effect self-activation, $F < 1$). Table 25.1 presents the mean self-evaluations for each of the conditions. As can be seen in Table 25.1, simple

TABLE 25.1. Mean Self-Evaluations as a Function of Valence Comparison Other (Positive, Negative) and Self-Activation (I, We, Control)

Comparison other	Self-activation		
	I	We	Control
Positive			
M	5.33ₐ	6.29	5.31
SD	0.82	0.61	1.08
Negative			
M	6.00_{b,c}	5.54_{a,c,d}	5.25_{a,d}
SD	0.82	0.88	1.55

Note: Scale range is from 1 (*negative*) to 7 (*positive*). Higher numbers indicate more positive self-evaluations. Means that do not share subscripts differ significantly at $p < .05$.

comparisons revealed that social comparison information showed effects after *I* priming as well as after *we* priming, but only when these effects were self-serving. When the personal self was activated, contrast occurred. Downward comparison information led to self-evaluations that were more positive ($M = 6.00$) than in the downward control condition ($M = 5.25$), $F(1, 84) = 4.25$, $p < .05$, whereas upward comparison information led to self-evaluations ($M = 5.33$) that were similar to those in the upward control condition ($M = 5.31$; $F < 1$). When the social self was activated, assimilation occurred. Upward comparison information led to self-evaluations that were more positive ($M = 6.29$) than in the upward control condition ($M = 5.31$), $F(1, 84) = 8.69$, $p < .05$, whereas downward comparison information led to self-evaluations ($M = 5.54$) that were similar to those in the control condition ($M = 5.25$; $F < 1$). It is interesting to note that in the control (*it* priming) conditions, the social comparison information with which we presented participants had no effect on self-evaluations ($M = 5.31$ when comparison target was positive, and $M = 5.25$ when comparison target was negative). Thus, by itself, this information did not possess the characteristics necessary to yield either assimilation or contrast. Only when self-activation was relatively high did such effects occur.

These findings nicely fit our predictions and, thus, provide the first support for our hypotheses.

Self-evaluation was affected by social comparison information only when personal or social self-construals were made accessible. Contrast occurred when personal self-construals were activated. Assimilation was found when the self-construal level was social. It is interesting to note that, as predicted, these effects showed a self-serving pattern and only surfaced in conditions in which they were likely to reflect positively on participants' self-worth.

Experiment 2

In our first experiment, self-construal level was manipulated through a rather subtle priming procedure (participants circled pronouns such as *I* or *we* in a word search task). In the present experiment, we investigate the generalizability of the findings of Experiment 1 by using a more blatant priming procedure: We had participants write a short (7 lines) paragraph about *I* or *we*.

More important, however, in the present experiment we make a comparison between the impact on social comparison effects of personal versus social self-accessibility and the impact of the processing styles (cf. Gollwitzer *et al.*, 1990) often associated with these two self-construal levels (see Brewer, 1991; Turner, 1987), *differentiation* and *integration*, respectively. If *I* priming leads to contrast because personal self-accessibility means that one's mind is focused on self-distinctiveness and concerned with self–other differentiation and contrast and if *we* priming leads to assimilation because social self-accessibility means that one's mind is focused on integration and concerned with self–other similarity and assimilation, then activation of these processing styles per se (without increasing self-construal accessibility) should lead to similar effects. Priming differentiation should yield contrast. Priming integration focus should lead to assimilation. Moreover, because self-evaluation maintenance or enhancement concerns are likely to be less of an issue when the self is not particularly accessible (see Steele, 1988; Tesser, 1988), these processing styles should lead to contrast and assimilation effects, respectively, that show less of a self-serving pattern.

In the present experiment, we put this line of reasoning to a first test. In the *unique* condition, a simple priming task activated the words *unique, special, unusual*. In this way, we hoped to increase the likelihood that participants would attend to the ways they are unique and, thus, differentiate themselves from the comparison target. In the *integration* condition, the priming words were *together, integrate, harmonize*. In this way, we hoped to activate a way of thinking that focuses participants on the ways they are similar to the comparison target. A number of recent studies have now shown that the subtle (and even subliminal) priming of words resembling goals (e.g., Chartrand & Bargh, 1996), mind-sets (e.g., Gollwitzer *et al.*, 1990), or processing styles (e.g., Stapel & Koomen, 1999) is sufficient to have participants subsequently behave in line with the associated knowledge structures.

As a final extension of the first experiment, in the present experiment we included a measure tapping the extent to which participants perceived the comparison target as being similar to themselves. On this measure, we predicted that in the *we* and integration conditions, the comparison target would be perceived as more similar than in the *I* and unique conditions.

Method

Participants and design

One hundred ninety-six students were randomly assigned to the conditions of a 2 (valence other: positive, negative) × 5 (mindset: *I*, *we*, unique, integration, control) between-subjects design. Participants received partial course credit for their participation.

Procedure and materials

The procedure was identical to the one used in Experiment 1.

Mindset priming. In the priming task, participants were instructed to write a short paragraph (7 lines) on a particular topic. In the present experiment, we not only replicate the design of Experiment 1 but also put our processing style hypotheses to a first test by extending the design. In the *I* priming condition, participants were asked to write a story about themselves, describing themselves in neutral, descriptive terms. Furthermore, they were instructed that every sentence they wrote should include one of the following words: *I, me, myself, mine.* In the *we* priming condition, the topic was *we,* and participants were asked to write a story about "who we are," using the words *we, our, ourselves, ours.* In the unique and the integration conditions, we asked participants to write a short (7 lines) paragraph about a (real or fictional) product of their choice. In the unique condition, participants were instructed to use the words *unique, special, unusual.* In the integration condition, they were instructed to use the words *together, integrate, harmonize.*[2] In the control condition, participants were asked to write a short paragraph about the Dutch economy, using the words *water, trade, tulips, tourism.*

---

[2]Our integration manipulation was designed to activate an "inclusive" processing style and thus differed from our *we* priming manipulation, which was designed to activate social (and inclusive) self-construals. To check whether our integration manipulation was indeed successful in merely activating a processing style and not increasing the accessibility of social self-construals (because, e.g., the primes used to activate an integration focus—*together, integrate, harmonize*—indirectly activated social self-construals), we performed a study in which we measured the impact of these manipulations on the extent to which individuals identify with a salient in-group. We asked University of Georgia students ($N = 60$) how much they identified with the Georgia Bulldogs (the university football team) after exposing them to our *we* priming, integration priming, and control priming manipulations. Following Jetten, Spears, and Manstead (1996), we measured identification with four items (e.g., "I identify with the Georgia Bulldogs"). An ANOVA, $F(2, 57) = 5.18$, $p < .01$, revealed that on a 7-point identification index ranging from 1 (*low*) to 7 (*high identification*), *we* priming increased the level of identification ($M = 5.0$) compared with the control group ($M = 4.0$, $p < .05$), whereas integration priming ($M = 4.2$) did not ($p > .20$). This suggests, as intended, that our *we* priming manipulation was successful in making the social self accessible (see Brewer & Gardner, 1996), whereas our integration manipulation does not increase the accessibility of social self-construals.

Social comparison information, dependent measures, and debriefing. After the priming task, participants were presented with an upward or downward comparison target and were asked to give self-evaluations. These tasks were identical to the ones used in Experiment 1. After the self-evaluation task, participants were asked to indicate how similar the target was to them on a 7-point scale with endpoints labeled 1 (*very dissimilar*) and 7 (*very similar*). Then they rated the target person on several items and were debriefed (for details, see Experiment 1).

Results and Discussion

Manipulation check

A Valence Other × Mindset ANOVA on the composite (see Experiment 1) comparison target ratings (Cronbach's $\alpha = .81$) revealed the predicted main effect of valence other, F (l, 186) = 427.14, $p < .01$ (other effects, Fs < 1). Participants judged the positive target more positively ($M = 5.88$) than they judged the negative target ($M = 3.62$).

Self-evaluation

As in Experiment 1, we averaged the self-evaluation items into a single index (Cronbach's $\alpha = .88$). An ANOVA on this index revealed the predicted Valence Other × Mindset interaction, $F(4, 186) = 9.52$, $p < .01$, a main effect of valence other, $F(1\ 186) = 7.64$, $p < .01$, and a marginally significant effect of mind-set, $F(4, 186) = 2.20, p = .07$. Table 25.2 presents the mean self-evaluations for each of the conditions. As can be seen in Table 25.2, similar to Experiment 1, social comparison information had no effect on self-evaluations in the control conditions ($M = 5.00$ when comparison target was positive and $M = 4.86$ when comparison target was negative; $F < 1$). Social comparison information again showed self-serving contrast effects when the personal self was activated. Downward comparison information led to self-evaluations that were more positive ($M = 5.61$) than in the downward control condition ($M = 4.86$), $F(1, 186) = 5.69$, $p < .05$, whereas upward comparison information led to self-evaluations ($M = 4.96$) that were

TABLE 25.2. Mean Self-Evaluations as a Function of Valence Comparison Other (Positive, Negative) and Mind-Set (I, We, Unique, Integration, Control)

Comparison other	Self-activation				
	I	We	Unique	Integration	Control
Positive					
M	4.96$_a$	5.75$_b$	4.88$_a$	5.71$_b$	5.00$_a$
SD	1.07	0.91	0.89	0.82	0.83
Negative					
M	5.61$_b$	4.94$_a$	5.04$_a$	4.10$_c$	4.86$_a$
SD	0.76	1.00	0.98	0.87	1.04

Note: Scale range is from 1 (*negative*) to 7 (*positive*). Higher numbers indicate more positive self-evaluations. Means with different subscripts differ significantly at $p < .05$.

similar to those in the upward control condition ($M = 5.00$). When the social self was activated, assimilation occurred. Upward comparison information led to self-evaluations that were more positive ($M = 5.75$) than in the upward control condition ($M = 5.00$), $F(1, 186) = 5.14, p = <.05$, whereas downward comparison information led to self-evaluations ($M = 4.94$) that were similar to those in the downward control condition ($M = 4.86$; $F < 1$).

The self-unrelated uniqueness manipulation was not successful in activating a differentiation mindset that yielded non-self-serving, symmetric contrast effects. Comparison information had no effect in the uniqueness conditions ($M = 4.88$ when comparison target was positive, and $M = 5.04$ when comparison target was negative; $F < 1$). However, the self-unrelated integration manipulation was successful and yielded non-self-serving, symmetric assimilation effects. Upward comparison information led to more positive ($M = 5.71$) self-evaluations than in the upward control condition ($M = 5.00$), $F(1, 186) = 5.45, p < .05$, and downward comparison information led to less positive self-evaluations ($M = 4.10$) than in the downward control condition ($M = 4.86$), $F(1, 186) = 6.55, p < .05$.

Similarity ratings

An ANOVA on the perceived similarity measure revealed a main effect of valence other, $F(1, 186) = 26.17$, $p < .01$, and a main effect of mind-set,

$F(4, 186) = 43.49$, $p < .01$. There was no interaction effect ($F < 1$). The valence effect indicated that participants exposed to positive comparison information reported themselves as being more similar to the target ($M = 3.84$) than did those exposed to negative comparison information ($M = 3.03$). This should not be surprising, given that it is more self-enhancing to perceive similarities to an upward comparison target than to a downward comparison target. More important, the pattern of the mind-set effect on similarity was in line with our expectations: The tendency to perceive similarity was stronger ($ps < .05$) in the *we* ($M = 4.64$) and integration ($M = 4.71$) conditions than in the *I* ($M = 2.78$), unique ($M = 2.03$), and control ($M = 2.88$) conditions. It is interesting to note that in the unique conditions, similarity ratings were even lower than in the *I* and control conditions ($ps < .05$).

These findings nicely corroborate the data of Experiment 1. Self-evaluations were affected by social comparison information only when personal or social self-construals were made accessible. The level of the activated self-construal determined the direction of the social comparison effects. Self-evaluations showed self-serving contrast effects when personal self-construals were made accessible and self-serving assimilation effects when social self-construals were made accessible.

In extension to the first experiment, we were successful in showing that activating a self-unrelated integration mind-set could yield symmetric, non-self-serving assimilation effects. This is the first evidence in support of the hypothesis that not only self-activation but also the activation of certain processing styles may increase the likelihood that social comparison information yields self-evaluative effects. When constructs like *together, integrate*, and *harmonize* were on the top of participants' minds, not only positive comparison information but also negative comparison information resulted in assimilation. This suggests that whereas social self-activation leads to assimilative social comparison effects that reflect self-evaluation maintenance strategies, self-unrelated mind-set activation results in social comparisons

in which such strategies are less likely to come into play. Put differently, integrative self-construals are likely to lead to assimilation, but not when this hurts. Integration mind-sets are likely to yield assimilation, independent of whether this feels good or bad.

Unfortunately, our uniqueness manipulation did not yield the predicted effect. Social comparison effects did not occur when constructs such as *special* and *unique* were on the top of our participants' minds. The similarity measure did reveal that this manipulation was especially successful in leading to perceptions that "you and I are dissimilar," more so than was the personal self-construal manipulation—which did result in contrastive social comparison effects. The null effect in the uniqueness conditions is especially interesting, because the same type of manipulation did work in the integration conditions. It is therefore unlikely that the lack of effects in the uniqueness conditions was due to a tragic flaw in our priming method, such that a different priming technique would be more likely to yield uniqueness effects. The finding that other-self similarity ratings were particularly low in the uniqueness conditions suggests that perhaps a uniqueness focus elicits a processing style in which the emphasis on the differences between others and the self is so strong that information about others is perceived as irrelevant and uninformative for the construction of self-evaluations. In the following two experiments, we further investigate this issue.

Experiment 3

Why did the uniqueness manipulation not yield the predicted contrast effects in Experiment 2? The answer to this question may be relatively simple. It is possible that our uniqueness manipulation was not successful (whereas our integration manipulation was) because it activated a uniqueness mind-set rather than a differentiation mind-set. Through a uniqueness lens, objects are likely to be seen as unique, autonomous entities that can be defined without reference to other objects (a rose is a rose is a rose). In other words, when a uniqueness mind-set is activated, the self is likely to be perceived as such—as a unique, autonomous entity—and the self-relevance of comparison information is low (as is evidenced by the low similarity ratings in the uniqueness conditions of Experiment 2). Hence, social comparison effects are less likely to occur. Because such effects (i.e., contrast) do occur when personal self-construals have been activated, it seems safe to conclude that the contrast effects following *I* priming do not occur because this type of priming activates feelings of personal uniqueness (e.g., "I am a unique person").

The discrepancy between our *I* priming and uniqueness priming findings suggests that personal self-accessibility cannot always be equated to the activation of egocentric, (Schweder & Bourne, 1984), individualist, (Triandis, 1989) or independent (Markus & Kitayama, 1991) self-construals that define the self as an "autonomous and unique individual" (Gardner *et al.*, 1999). In fact, the findings of Experiments 1 and 2 suggest that in situations of social self-accessibility as well as in situations of personal self-accessibility, self-evaluations may be constructed in relation to others. An important distinction between personal and social self-construal levels may thus not only be the extent (see Markus & Kitayama, 1991; Schweder & Bourne, 1984; Triandis, 1989) but also the way the self is defined in relation to others. When the social self is accessible, others may affect the self but do so in an inclusive, assimilative manner. When the personal self is accessible, others affect the self but do so in a differentiative, contrastive manner. Thus, the impact of personal self-accessibility is perhaps best likened to the activation of feelings of relational distinctiveness or differentiation (e.g., "I am different from others") rather than to feelings of autonomous distinctiveness or uniqueness (e.g., "I am a unique person") that make information about others irrelevant for self-evaluations.

In sum, then, in the previous experiment, the activation of a uniqueness mind-set was probably unsuccessful in instigating social comparison effects because it focused participants on the uniqueness of objects and, thus, on the ways information

about others is not only different from but also irrelevant to the self. If this is indeed the case, then a processing style that emphasizes relational distinctiveness should be more successful in obtaining contrastive social comparison effects than is a processing style that emphasizes autonomous distinctiveness.

In the present experiment, we address the question of whether we are right in assuming that social comparisons are less likely to result in contrast when feelings of autonomous distinctiveness have been activated, whereas such an effect is more likely when feelings of relational distinctiveness have been activated. In the "I-am-unique" condition, the focus is on the self as an autonomous entity, and the ways the personal self is unique and special are emphasized. We expect that in this condition, comparison information will have no impact on self-evaluations. In the "I-am-different" conditions, the ways the personal self can be differentiated from others are emphasized. Here, we expect comparison information to yield contrast effects.

It is important to note that compared with the self-unrelated manipulations in Experiment 2, in the current experiment, we did not investigate the impact of self-unrelated (uniqueness or differentiation) processing styles (but see Experiment 4). The goal of the current experiment was to assess whether the occurrence of social comparison effects is dependent on whether personal self-construals emphasize autonomous self-distinctiveness or relational self-distinctiveness. Thus, a fortunate by-product of the current experiment is that it allows us to investigate whether the null findings in the uniqueness conditions in Experiment 2 were due to the self-unrelated nature of this manipulation or (as we have argued) to the fact that a uniqueness focus leads to the notion that comparison information is irrelevant to the self. If self-related uniqueness yields social comparison effects (which is not in line with our predictions), whereas self-unrelated uniqueness does not, then the null findings in the uniqueness conditions of Experiment 2 may be interpreted as pointing to an artifact of the self-unrelated nature of that manipulation.

Method

Participants and design

One hundred twenty-six students were randomly assigned to the conditions of a 2 (valence other: positive, negative) × 3 (mind-set: I am unique, I am different, control) between-subjects design. Participants received partial course credit for their participation.

Procedure and materials

The procedure and materials were identical to those in Experiment 2, except for the mind-set priming manipulation.

In the *I-am-unique* condition, participants were asked to write down five personality traits in response to the statement, "I am who I am. I am a unique and special individual because I am…" In the *I-am-different* condition, participants were asked to write down five short sentences in response to the statement, "I am who I am because I am different from others. I am different from most people because…" In the control condition, participants were asked to write down five short, descriptive sentences about the room in which the experiment was performed.

Results and Discussion

Manipulation check

A Valence Other × Mind-Set ANOVA on the composite (see Experiment 1) comparison target ratings (Cronbach's $\alpha = .83$) revealed the predicted main effect of valence other, $F(1, 120) = 278.80$, $p < .01$ (other effects, $Fs < 1$). Participants judged the positive target more positively ($M = 6.02$) than they judged the negative target ($M = 3.48$).

Self-evaluation

As in Experiments 1 and 2, we averaged the self-evaluation items into a single index (Cronbach's $\alpha = .79$). An ANOVA on this index revealed the predicted Valence Other × Mind-Set interaction, $F(2, 120) = 7.62$, $p < .01$, and a main effect of valence other, $F(1, 120) = 8.53$, $p < .01$. There was no mind-set effect ($F < 1$). Table 25.3 presents the mean self-evaluations for each of the conditions.

TABLE 25.3. Mean Self-Evaluations as a Function of Valence Comparison Other (Positive, Negative) and Mind-Set (I Am Unique, I Am Different, Control)

| Comparison other | Self-activation | | |
	I am unique	I am different	Control
Positive			
M	4.88_a	4.21_b	4.94_a
SD	1.00	0.99	0.97
Negative			
M	$5.10_{a,c}$	5.60_c	4.81_a
SD	0.60	0.85	1.05

Note: Scale ranges from 1 (*negative*) to 7 (*positive*). Higher numbers indicate more positive self-evaluations. Means that do not share subscripts differ significantly at $p < .05$.

As can be seen in Table 25.3, social comparison information had no effect on self-evaluations in the control conditions ($M = 4.94$ when comparison target was positive, and $M = 4.81$ when comparison target was negative; $F < 1$). Furthermore, there was no social comparison effect in the I-am-unique conditions ($M = 4.88$ when comparison target was positive, and $M = 5.10$ when comparison target was negative; $F < 1$). Social comparison information did show an effect when an I-am-different focus was activated. In those conditions, contrast occurred in the negative-other as well as in the positive-other conditions. Downward comparison information led to self-evaluations that were more positive ($M = 5.60$) than in the downward control condition ($M = 4.81$), $F(1, 120) = 6.42$, $p < .05$. Upward comparison information led to self-evaluations that were less positive ($M = 4.21$) than they were in the upward control condition ($M = 4.94$), $F(1, 120) = 5.73$, $p < .05$.

Similarity ratings

An ANOVA on the perceived similarity measure revealed a main effect of valence other, $F(1, 120) = 12.69$, $p < .01$, and a main effect of mind-set, $F(2, 120) = 6.70$, $p < .01$. There was no interaction effect ($F < 1$). Similar to Experiment 2, the valence effect indicates that participants exposed to positive comparison information reported themselves as being more similar to the target ($M = 3.52$) than did those exposed to negative comparison information ($M = 2.73$). More interesting is the pattern of the mind-set effect: The tendency to perceive similarity was stronger ($ps < .05$) in the I-am-different conditions ($M = 3.68$), in which the self was defined in relation to others, than in the I-am-unique ($M = 2.72$) and the control ($M = 2.89$) conditions.

These findings support our hypothesis concerning the differences between relational distinctiveness and autonomous distinctiveness and their relevance for the occurrence of social comparison effects. In the I-am-unique conditions, social comparison information did not affect subsequent self-evaluations, whereas in the I-am-different conditions, contrastive comparison effects occurred. This is in line with the view that in the I-am-unique conditions, participants' focus was on the self as an autonomous, unique entity. This focus makes information about others irrelevant when it concerns the construction of self-evaluations. Conversely, in the I-am-different conditions, the ways the personal self can be differentiated from others were emphasized. This focus makes information about others more relevant for self-evaluations. The similarity ratings support this. Participants rated themselves as more similar to the comparison other in the I-am-different conditions than in the I-am-unique conditions. This seems to suggest that although both mind-sets emphasize individuality and activate focus on personal self-construal, the more relational nature of the differentiation focus emphasizes that others are at the same time different from as well as relevant to the self. The autonomous nature of the uniqueness focus seems to emphasize that the differences between others and the self are such that information about others is completely irrelevant to the self. For comparison information to yield contrast effects, one needs to perceive others as relevant to self-evaluation as well as be in a state of mind that emphasizes other-self differentiation over other–self integration or inclusion.

The present findings clearly show that I-am-different thinking is more likely to yield contrastive comparisons to another than is I-am-unique thinking. It is interesting to note that these contrast effects were symmetric in the positive and negative conditions (see Table 25.3). Not only did downward comparison information lead to relatively positive self-evaluations, upward comparison information resulted in relatively negative self-evaluations. On the face of it, this non-self-serving pattern of results is somewhat surprising. After all, our I-am-different manipulation is a self-related manipulation designed to activate (a certain type of) personal self-accessibility. As evidenced by the findings of Experiments 1 and 2, personal self-accessibility is likely to yield self-serving comparison effects. Why does self-serving contrast occur when *I* has been activated (see Experiments 1 and 2), whereas non-self-serving contrast occurs when one is focused on the ways in which "I am different"? In Experiment 4, we address this question by investigating the differences between self-related differentiation and self-unrelated differentiation information processing styles.

Experiment 4

Why does the activation of an I-am-different focus yield symmetric social comparison effects, whereas these effects are asymmetric and self-serving after the mere activation of *I*? We think the answer to this question may be found in the differences between the impact on social comparison effects of mere personal-level accessibility (*I* priming), a differentiation focus (differentiation priming), and the combination of these (*I* + differentiation priming). When one's thoughts are engaged in thinking about the ways one is different from others (I-am-different focus), what is activated is a certain type of self-concept—a personal-level self-construal—and a certain processing style—a differentiation mind-set. The finding that the impact of this combination of self-construal and mind-set activation results in symmetric rather than asymmetric social comparison effects (see Experiment 3) suggests that the processing effects of the mind-set activation are sufficiently powerful to overshadow the self-protective effects of self-activation. This, in turn, suggests that the mere activation of such a mind-set may also yield symmetric social comparison effects. That is, when a self-unrelated differentiation mind-set is activated, social comparison information should lead to symmetric contrast effects. Put differently, just like priming words like *together, integrate, harmonize* leads to symmetric assimilation effects (Experiment 2), priming words like *differ, compare, distinguish* may lead to symmetric contrast effects.

In sum, then, in the present experiment, we test the hypothesis that whereas social comparison information is more likely to result in self-serving contrast after self-related *I* priming, such information results in non-self-serving, symmetric contrast after self-unrelated differentiation priming. Furthermore, a combination of *I* and differentiation priming episodes mirrors the impact of I-am-different thinking on social comparison effects (Experiment 2) and also results in symmetric contrast effects.

Method

Participants and design

One hundred six students were randomly assigned to the conditions of a 2 (valence other: positive, negative) × 4 (mind-set: I, differentiation, *I* + differentiation, control) between-subjects design. Participants received partial course credit for their participation.

Procedure and materials

The procedure and materials were identical to those in Experiments 2 and 3, except for the mind-set priming manipulation.

In the control and *I* priming conditions, participants performed the same word search task as did participants in Experiment 1 (see also Brewer & Gardner, 1996). Control participants were instructed to circle neutral words in a page-long text. *I* priming participants were instructed to circle all pronouns referring to *I* or *me*. Participants in the differentiation condition were given a version of the Scrambled Sentence Test used by Chartrand and Bargh (1996) to nonconsciously activate information processing mind-sets. This task was titled "Language Comprehension" and included 20 items, each requiring the participant to form a grammatically correct five-word sentence from six words presented in a scrambled order. Words related to

differentiation and comparison (e.g., *compare, distinguish, differ, opposition*) were embedded in 10 of the items. An example of a test item is "table the he compares books." The remaining items contained only neutral words. Participants in the *I* + differentiation condition were first given the same task as participants in the differentiation condition. After they had completed this language comprehension task, they were immediately given the *I* priming word search task.

Results and Discussion

Manipulation check

A Valence Other × Mind-Set ANOVA on the composite (see Experiment 1) comparison target ratings (Cronbach's $\alpha = .84$) revealed the predicted main effect of valence other, $F(1, 98) = 341.35, p < .01$ (other effects, $Fs < 1$). Participants judged the positive target more positively ($M = 6.22$) than they judged the negative target ($M = 3.51$).

Self-evaluation

As in Experiments 1–3, we averaged the self-evaluation items into a single index (Cronbach's $\alpha = .83$). An ANOVA on this index revealed the predicted Valence Other × Mind-Set interaction, $F(3, 98) = 5.51, p < .01$, and a main effect of valence other, $F(1, 98) = 28.68, p < .01$. There was no mind-set main effect, $F(3, 98) = 1.36, p = .26$. Table 25.4 presents the mean self-evaluations for each of the conditions. As can be seen in Table 25.4, social comparison information had no effect on self-evaluations in the control conditions ($M = 5.00$ when comparison target was positive, and $M = 4.79$ when comparison target was negative; $F < 1$). As predicted, social comparison information did show a self-serving contrast effect in the *I* priming conditions. In those conditions, downward comparison information led to self-evaluations that were more positive ($M = 5.82$) than in the downward control condition ($M = 4.79$), $F(1, 98) = 6.30, p < .05$, whereas upward comparison information led to self-evaluations ($M = 4.88$) that were similar to those in the upward control condition ($M = 5.00; F < 1$).

TABLE 25.4. Mean Self-Evaluations as a Function of Valence Comparison Other (Positive, Negative) and Mind-Set (I, Differentiation, I + Differentiation, Control)

	Self-activation			
Comparison other	I	Differentiation	I + Differentiation	Control
Positive				
M	$4.88_{a,d}$	$4.19_{b,d}$	4.02_b	5.00_a
SD	1.03	0.83	1.12	1.15
Negative				
M	5.82_c	5.71_c	5.79_c	4.79_a
SD	0.61	0.99	0.87	0.87

Note: Scale ranges from 1 (negative) to 7 (positive). Higher numbers indicate more positive self-evaluations. Means that do not share subscripts differ significantly at $p < .05$.

As predicted, in both the differentiation and I + differentiation conditions, symmetric, non-self-serving contrast occurred. In those conditions, contrast occurred in the negative-other as well as in the positive-other conditions. Specifically, in the I + differentiation conditions, downward comparison information led to self-evaluations that were more positive ($M = 5.79$) than they were in the control condition ($M = 4.79$), $F(1, 98) = 5.87$, $p < .05$. Upward comparison information led to self-evaluations that were less positive ($M = 4.02$) than in the upward control condition ($M = 5.00$), $F(1, 98) = 5.23$, $p < .05$. Similarly, in the differentiation conditions, downward comparison information led to self-evaluations that were more positive ($M = 5.71$) than in the downward control condition ($M = 4.79$), $F(1, 98) = 4.68$, $p < .05$. Upward comparison information led to self-evaluations that were less positive ($M = 4.19$) than in the upward control condition ($M = 5.00$), $F(1, 98) = 3.97$, $p < .05$.

Similarity ratings

An ANOVA on the perceived similarity measure revealed a main effect of valence other, $F(1, 98) = 21.50$, $p < .01$, and a main effect of mind-set, $F(3, 98) = 6.73$, $p < .01$. There was no interaction effect ($F < 1$). The valence effect again indicates that participants exposed to positive comparison information reported themselves as being more similar to the target ($M = 3.72$) than did those exposed to negative comparison information ($M = 2.78$).

More interesting is the mind-set pattern: The tendency to perceive similarity was stronger ($ps < .05$) in the I + differentiation ($M = 3.68$) and differentiation ($M = 3.72$) conditions than in the I priming ($M = 2.73$) and control ($M = 2.77$) conditions. Thus, participants felt relatively similar to comparison targets when thinking about the ways they were different from others. At one level, differentiative thinking focuses on other–self differences (leading to contrast on the focal comparison dimension), but at another level, it recognizes other–self similarities (resulting in medium, not low, similarity ratings). We think this paradox may be resolved by recognizing that a differentiation mind-set is likely to activate thinking about the ways one differs from others in distinctive, salient ways. After all, differences become more meaningful when there is also common ground (saying that X is taller than Y is especially meaningful when X and Y are similar on all other dimensions). A differentiation mind-set may thus instigate a search for *distinctive* differences rather than a search for differences per se (cf. Brewer, 1991; McGuire & McGuire, 1981). This implies that such a focus is likely to increase recognition of the ways one is different from others in a specific sense (e.g., on focal dimensions) as well as the ways one is similar to others in a general sense (i.e. on background characteristics; cf. Goethals & Darley, 1977).

Together, these findings support the hypothesis that whereas social comparison information is more likely to result in self-serving contrast after self-related *I* priming, non-self-serving contrast effects occur when this kind of personal self-accessibility is accompanied with a differentiation focus or when only such a focus is activated. Thus, similar to the finding of Experiment 2 that activating a self-unrelated integration mind-set yields symmetric, non-self-serving assimilation effects, a self-unrelated differentiation mind-set yields non-self-serving contrast effects. A processing style that focuses on differentiation is likely to yield contrast, independent of whether this reflects well or badly on one's self-worth.

Experiment 5

In the previous experiments, we found support for the hypothesis that social comparison effects are likely to show a self-serving pattern when (personal or social) self-construals are cognitively accessible. In the present study, we further address the issue of self-servingness of social comparison effects in situations of personal or social self-accessibility. We investigate the impact of *I* versus *we* priming on self-evaluative comparisons in situations in which the focal comparison dimension is perceived as either important or unimportant. In Experiments 1–4, we studied the self-evaluative consequences of comparison information that was either positive or negative on an important dimension. In those studies, we presented participants with a comparison target who was described either as relatively successful and intelligent or as relatively unsuccessful and unintelligent. In such conditions, self-construal activation is likely to lead to social comparison effects that have a self-serving pattern. The notion that these effects are indeed explained best in terms of self-protective, self-evaluation maintenance strategies would be strengthened if we could show that this self-serving pattern would disappear when the focal dimension has low importance. There is less reason to protect the self against negative evaluations when these evaluations are unimportant. Finding out that one is very similar to someone who has done very badly on a task that measures a trivial, unimportant personality characteristic is less threatening than

when this task taps a trait that is diagnostic for future success. Similarly, comparing and differentiating oneself from someone who has performed extremely well on an unimportant dimension is less frustrating than when the comparison dimension is important (Steele, 1988; Tesser, 1988; Wood, 1989). Thus, in the present experiment, our hypotheses are as follows: Social comparison information results in contrast when personal self-construals (*I*) have been primed. Assimilation occurs when social self-construals (*we*) have been primed. When the focal dimension is important, these effects show an asymmetric, self-serving pattern. When the focal dimension is unimportant, these effects show a symmetric, non-self-serving pattern.

Method

Participants and design

Two hundred fourteen students were randomly assigned to the conditions of a 2 (valence other: positive, negative) $\times$ 2 (self-activation: *I, we*) $\times$ 2 (importance: high, low) between-subjects design or to one of the two control conditions, in which social comparison information but no importance information was given (positive-other control, negative-other control). Participants received 10 Dutch guilders (approximately \$4) for their participation.

Procedure and materials

Participants were told they would participate in a series of tasks. First they would participate in a reading comprehension task, then they would perform the Remote Associates Task (RAT). The experimenter timed them through each of these studies.

Self-activation priming. The priming task was identical to the one used in Experiment 1. Participants in the *I* priming, *we* priming, and control priming conditions completed a word search task designed to activate the relevant cognitions.

Social comparison information and importance. After they had completed the word search task, participants were given a booklet titled "Remote Associates Task." On the first page, the task was introduced, and participants were instructed how to complete the tasks in the booklet. Participants were told that they would be given six RAT items. These items were based on McFarlin and Blascovich (1984). A RAT item consists of three words that have something in common. Respondents' task is to figure out the one thing these three words have in common. For example, the remote associate of the words *car, swimming, cue* is *pool* (see McFarlin & Blascovich, 1984).

In the *important* conditions, the RAT was described as an important device in selection batteries, useful for predicting important abilities, one of the best predictors of managerial success that exists, and as a test that correlates surprisingly well with interpersonal skills. In the *unimportant* conditions, the RAT was described as an interesting yet rather useless test that had met with very limited success in the testing industry. Participants were told that the RAT does not correlate with managerial success or interpersonal skills.

On the next page, participants were given 5 min to complete the six RAT items. When these 5 min were over, the participants were instructed to turn to the next page in the booklet, on which the answers to the six items were given. They were instructed to rate their own performance and write down the number of correct answers (0–6) in a small box on the page. Then they could turn the page to the next phase of the task, called impression formation. On this page, they were given some brief information ("for the purposes of this study," they were told) about another student who had recently completed the RAT. They were told that they had 3 min to read the person information carefully and that they should try to form an impression of this other person. The person information contained neutral information such as participant number (231), age (21), gender (male), hair color (red–brown), and, more important, the person's RAT score. The valence of the comparison target's score (positive, negative) was manipulated as follows.

In the positive conditions, the comparison target's score was very high (5). Because the six RAT items that participants were given before they were exposed to the comparison information were almost impossible to solve (in fact, most participants scored 1 or 2), the comparison target was likely to be perceived as an upward comparison other.

In the negative conditions, the comparison target's score was very low (2). Because the six RAT items participants were given were very easy and could easily be completed in 5 min, participants' scores were likely to be high (in fact, all participants scored 5 or 6). In this way, the comparison target would be perceived as a downward comparison other.

Self-evaluation. After the comparison information, participants were given a filler task (unscrambling bird names). Then they were given the self-evaluation task. This task was introduced as measuring background characteristics. All participants rated themselves on the following adjectives: *intelligent, tense, special, incompetent, socially skilled, slow, creative,* and *self-confident*. These items were rated on 7-point scales ranging from 1 (*not at all*) to 7 (*very*).

Target person ratings. Next, participants rated the target person on the following adjectives: *intelligent, creative, socially skilled, interesting, creative*. These items were rated on 7-point scales ranging from 1 (*not at all*) to 7 (*very*).

Importance. Next, participants rated the importance of the RAT task on a dimension that was anchored at 1 (*not measuring an important ability*) and 7 (*measuring an important ability*).

Debriefing. On completion of the questionnaire, participants were carefully debriefed about the goal and purpose of the experiment. None of the participants spontaneously indicated suspicion of the actual goal of the study or indicated that either the word search task or the comparison target might have influenced their self-evaluations. After the debriefing, participants were thanked, paid, and dismissed.

Results and Discussion

Manipulation check

First, we checked whether the positive comparison target was indeed judged more positively on the relevant dimensions than the negative target was. We averaged the five items into a single index (Cronbach's $\alpha = .77$). A Valence Other $\times$ Self-Activation $\times$ Importance ANOVA on this index revealed the predicted main effect of valence other, $F(1, 161) = 129.84, p < .01$ (other effects, $Fs < 1$). Participants judged the positive target as more positive ($M = 4.92$) than they judged the negative target ($M = 2.89$). For a check on the effects of the importance manipulation, see below.

Self-evaluation

We averaged the self-evaluation items into a single index after reverse scoring the negative items (Cronbach's $\alpha = .80$). A Valence Other $\times$ Self-Activation $\times$ Importance ANOVA on this index revealed the predicted Valence Other $\times$ Self-Activation $\times$ Importance interaction, $F(1, 161) = 6.55, p < .01$, a Self-Activation $\times$ Valence Other interaction, $F(1, 161) = 69.73, p < .01$, and a main effect of importance, $F(1, 161) = 12.44, p < .01$ (other $Fs < 1$). Table 25.5 presents the mean self-evaluations for each of the conditions. As can be seen in Table 25.5 and as predicted, I priming led to contrast, and we priming led to assimilation

effects; this pattern was self-serving in the important conditions but not in the unimportant conditions. Simple comparisons further corroborate the support for our hypothesis, as the following analyses (which used the error term of the complete design—that is, including the two control conditions) show.

Important conditions. Important social comparison information resulted in a self-serving contrast effect in the I priming conditions. In those conditions, downward comparison information led to self-evaluations that were more positive ($M = 5.67$) than those in the downward control condition ($M = 5.13$), $F(1, 204) = 4.90, p < .05$, whereas upward comparison information led to self-evaluations ($M = 5.10$) that were similar to those in the upward control condition ($M = 5.22$; $F < 1$). Similarly, *important* social comparison information resulted in a self-serving assimilation effect in the *we* priming conditions. In those conditions, upward comparison information led to self-evaluations that were more positive ($M = 5.89$) than those in the upward control condition ($M = 5.22$), $F(1, 204) = 6.79, p < .05$, whereas downward comparison information led to self-evaluations ($M = 4.94$) that were similar to those in the downward control condition ($M = 5.13$; $F < 1$). These effects nicely correspond with the personal and social self-accessibility effects in the previous studies.

TABLE 25.5. Mean Self-Evaluations as a Function of Valence Other (Positive, Negative) and Self-Activation (I, We), and Importance (Important, Unimportant) and Positive and Negative No-Self-Activation, No-Importance Control Groups

| | Self-activation | | | | |
| | I | | We | | |
Comparison other	Important	Unimportant	Important	Unimportant	Control
Positive					
M	$5.10_a{}^*$	4.17_c	5.89_b	5.71_b	5.22_a
SD	0.94	0.90	0.87	0.82	0.98
Negative					
M	$5.67_b{}^*$	5.59_b	4.94_a	4.28_c	5.13
SD	0.80	0.63	0.99	0.67	1.07

Note: Scale ranges from 1 (*negative*) to 7 (*positive*). Higher numbers indicate more positive self-evaluations. Means with different subscripts differ significantly at $p < .05$, except the a*–b* comparison, which differs at $p < .08$.

Unimportant conditions. *Unimportant* social comparison information resulted in a symmetric, non-self-serving contrast effect in the *I* priming conditions. In those conditions, downward comparison information led to self-evaluations that were more positive ($M = 5.59$) than those in the downward control condition ($M = 5.13$). This effect was marginally significant, $F(1, 204) = 3.42$, $p < .07$. Upward comparison information led to self-evaluations that were less positive ($M = 4.17$) than were those in the upward control condition ($M = 5.22$), $F(1, 204) = 13.18$, $p < .05$. *Unimportant* social comparison information resulted in a symmetric, non-self-serving assimilation effect in the *we* priming conditions. In those conditions, upward comparison information led to self-evaluations that were more positive ($M = 5.71$) than were those in the upward control condition ($M = 5.22$). This effect was marginally significant, $F(1, 204) = 3.64$, $p < .06$. Downward comparison information led to self-evaluations that were less positive ($M = 4.28$) than were those in the downward control condition ($M = 5.13$), $F(1, 204) = 7.75$, $p < .05$.

Importance ratings

A Valence Other $\times$ Self-Activation $\times$ Importance ANOVA on the importance measure revealed a Valence Other $\times$ Self-Activation interaction, $F(1, 161) = 25.80$, $p < .01$, and a main effect of importance, $F(1, 161) = 62.65$, $p < .01$ (other $Fs < 1$). The importance effect indicated, as intended, that participants who were told that the RAT was an important and diagnostic test indeed perceived the task as more important ($M = 4.72$), compared with participants who were told that the task measured rather trivial abilities ($M = 3.53$). The Valence Other $\times$ Self-Activation interaction points to a self-repair pattern: In conditions in which

social comparison had a relatively negative impact on self-evaluation, participants rated the importance of the comparison dimension lower (*I* priming, upward $M = 3.69$; *we* priming, downward $M = 3.91$) than in conditions in which social comparison information had a relatively positive impact on self-evaluation (*I* priming, downward $M = 4.63$; *we* priming, upward $M = 4.72$). Thus, the importance ratings mirror nicely the positivity of the self-evaluative consequences of social comparisons.[3]

These findings provide clear support for the hypothesis that self-serving social comparison effects are most likely to occur when the focal dimension is perceived as important. The self-serving asymmetry of the effects of personal and social self-accessibility that we reported in Experiments 1–4 turns into symmetry when the comparison dimension is perceived as unimportant. This finding strengthens the notion that the asymmetric assimilation and contrast effects we found earlier were, indeed, the effect of self-serving mechanisms and not an artifact of the experimental paradigm. Self-construal accessibility instigates defensive processing of social comparison information, but only when important aspects of the self are at stake, such that negative self-evaluations indeed reflect negatively on the self. The need for defensive processing is dormant when comparison information is less important. In that case, the effects of self-construal accessibility mainly reflect particular styles (i.e., differentiation, integration) with which social comparison information is attended to and processed.

General Discussion

Previous studies of the self-evaluative consequences of social comparisons focused primarily on how

---

[3] It is important to note the distinction between the perceived importance of social comparison information and its perceived relevance for constructing self-evaluative judgments. As the results throughout this article indicate, social comparison information is more easily related to the self and self-evaluation effects are more likely to occur when an others-are-relevant processing style has been activated (e.g., through *I*, *we*, integration, or differentiation priming). As the results of Experiment 5 show, whether comparison information is related to the self and is used to inform self-evaluations may be independent from the perceived importance of this information. Social comparison effects may occur when information is unimportant (see Table 25.5).

individuals' motives (e.g., self-evaluation, self-enhancement, self-improvement) or features of the comparison target (e.g., self-relevance, attainability, closeness, similarity, extremity) moderate the occurrence and direction of social comparison effects (for reviews see Blanton, in press; Wood, 1989). In the present studies, each of these variables was kept constant, such that we could test the hypothesis that beyond these variables, important determinants of the when (occurrence) and what (direction) of social comparison effects concern the accessibility and level of self-construals and the knowledge structures they are thought to activate (see Brewer, 1991). Together, the most important findings of our studies may be summarized as follows.

1. Social comparison effects are more likely to occur when the activation level of the self-related cognition (i.e., personal or social self-construals) is high rather than low.

2. The level of activated self-construals determines the direction of social comparison effects. Contrast occurs when the personal self is activated. Assimilation occurs when the social self is activated.

3. These effects of self-construal activation show a self-serving pattern. That is, they are stronger when they reflect positively on important aspects of the self. Specifically, downward comparison others yield contrast effects when the personal self is accessible, whereas upward comparison others yield assimilation effects when the social self is accessible. This self-serving use of social comparison information is especially strong when the focal comparison dimension is perceived as important and diagnostic for future performance. It is important to note that the finding that self-activation resulted in self-serving assimilation as well as self-serving contrast effects indicates that it is a genuine effect of self-activation, not an artifact of a particular comparison direction (cf. Tesser, 1988).

4. Priming self-unrelated information processing styles that are often associated with personal self- and social self-accessibility yields more

symmetric, non-self-serving social comparison effects. That is, both upward and downward comparison information result in contrast when a differentiation mind-set is activated. Similarly, both upward and downward comparison information result in assimilation when an integration mind-set is activated.

When it concerns the when of social comparison effects, these findings suggest that activating self-related cognitions (personal self and social self) as well as priming self-unrelated processing styles (differentiation and integration) increases the likelihood that social comparison information is perceived as relevant and informative to the construction of self-evaluations, such that self-evaluation effects occur. The finding that no social comparison effects resulted after uniqueness priming gives extra credence to the claim. For social comparison effects to occur, a processing style is needed in which the focus is on how knowledge about an object (e.g., the self) is relative to other objects (e.g., different from or similar to others). A pure uniqueness focus emphasizes autonomous distinctiveness (e.g., "I am unique") over relational distinctiveness (e.g., "I am different from others") and is therefore less likely to instigate a processing style that bases self-evaluations on information about others.

Previous studies have also shown that perceived relevance is often a precondition for the occurrence of social comparison effects. For example, in a series of studies on the effects of role models on self-evaluations, Lockwood and Kunda (1997) showed that superstars only affect self-evaluations when they are perceived as relevant to one's own domain of expertise. Specifically, self-evaluations of aspiring accountants were affected by a description of a superstar accountant but not by a similar description of a superstar high school teacher. In the present studies, the perceived relevance of social comparison information was manipulated not by changing structural features defining other–self relations, such as closeness or similarity (e.g., Goethals & Darley, 1977; Lockwood & Kunda, 1997; Tesser, 1988), but merely by increasing the activation level of self-related cognitions or certain processing styles. Thus, the present studies are the first to suggest that perceived relevance is also a matter of how one approaches social comparison information in addition to what this information is about. Information about others that is otherwise ignored may be perceived as relevant and used to inform self-evaluations when the mind is set as such.

When it concerns the what of social comparison effects, the present findings provide strong evidence for the notion that the self-evaluative consequences of social comparison depend less on its direction than on the manner of its use (see also Brewer & Weber, 1994; Gilbert *et al.*, 1995). The present studies clearly show that each direction has its "ups and downs" (cf. Buunk, Collins, Taylor, VanYperen, & Dakof, 1990).

The starting point for our studies was the notion that people have available to them a range of self-construals that are linked together to form a general self-concept. At any given point in time, however, only a subset of these self-construals is activated. Two types of self-construals are especially powerful in influencing one's relation to the social world and, thus, likely to affect the outcome of social comparisons, the personal self (representing those aspects that differentiate the self from others) and the social self (representing those aspects of the self-concept that reflect integration in the social world). Previous research demonstrated how self-construal level contributes to a large range of group phenomena as well as cognitive, emotional, and motivational differences associated with intercultural differences (see Abelson *et al.*, 1998; Brewer & Gardner, 1996; Trafimow *et al.*, 1991; Triandis, 1989; Turner, 1987). We investigated the impact of self-construal levels on how information about others is processed and used in a social comparison context. We reasoned that when an individual's personal self is activated, the mind is set on differentiating the self from others. When a person's social self becomes activated, that person shifts into a frame of mind in which he or she values being part of a social unit and, thus, accentuates similarities to others. Thus, changes in self-construal level (personal or social) are likely to affect the way (differentiation

or integration) information about others is processed and used in the construction of self-evaluations. The pattern of the present assimilation and contrast findings clearly supports this perspective. When the personal self or a differentiative processing style was activated, social comparison was used to differentiate and contrast the self, whereas assimilation occurred when the social self or an integrative processing style was activated. The difference between self-construal and mind-set activation seems to lie mainly in the pattern of these contrast effects. Personal and social self-accessibility result in relatively asymmetric social comparison effects, whereas when self-unrelated differentiation and integration mind-sets are activated, social comparison effects show a more symmetric, less self-serving pattern of results.

In the present studies, the focus was on interpersonal rather than intergroup social comparisons as a basis for self-evaluations. Future studies may investigate how differences in self-construal level affect the outcome of social comparisons in intergroup contexts—that is, in which the relation in terms of group membership between comparison target and self is made salient. On the one hand, one may argue that in such a context, by default, the social self is accessible and that attempts to increase the personal self-accessibility are obsolete. In this case, information about in-group members results in assimilation, and information about out-group members yields contrast effects (see Brewer & Weber, 1994). On the other hand, one may argue that self-construal level should be an important determinant of the extent to which individuals focus either on their personal identity or on their social identity and engage in interpersonal or intergroup comparisons. That is, following Brewer's (1991) optimal distinctiveness theory, one may argue that personal self-accessibility increases an individual's need for differentiation from other in-group members and, hence, makes interpersonal comparison and contrast effects more likely than intergroup comparison effects such as out-group differentiation and in-group assimilation (see also Turner, 1987).

The present studies show the importance of self-construal level and the associated processing styles for both the occurrence and the direction of social comparison effects. They suggest that given the presence of relevant situational features, self-concepts or processing styles may become active and operate on presented information. In these studies, as in the great majority of priming studies, we used somewhat artificial techniques to activate the relevant representations (see Brewer & Gardner, 1996; Chartrand & Bargh, 1996; Stapel & Koomen, 1999). We used priming instructions that were directly relevant to the representation they were supposed to activate. For example, we used words such as *I* and *me* to increase personal self-accessibility and words such as *distinguish* and *differ* to prime a differentiation mind-set. Although this may seem to be a rather artificial proxy for the activation of particular self-construals or processing styles, we note that earlier studies have successfully used similar priming techniques (see Stapel & Koomen, 1999). Following Chartrand and Bargh (1996), we are therefore confident that the present findings will also be obtained when more natural priming manipulations are used, especially because it is relatively easy to imagine naturalistic settings in which personal or social self-construals may be activated relatively spontaneously by environmental cues. Under circumstances in which one's individual performance or responsibility is stressed, the personal self is activated, whereas situations that stress communal feelings, consensus, and togetherness activate the social self. In fact, differences in self-construal level may be caused by a number of divergent variables.

One such variable is personality. Cheek (1989) has suggested that there are individual differences in the extent to which one's personal or social self is chronically accessible. For some people, personal identity is more readily accessible, whereas for others, social identity is what is most important and what drives most of their thoughts and actions. Cheek developed a scale to assess individual differences in the chronic accessibility of the personal versus the social self (see Brown, 1998, p. 31). Related to this individual-differences perspective on level of self-construal accessibility is the notion that cultural differences may contribute to differences in the level of self-construal accessibility. As we noted before, culture is thought to be an important determinant of whether the personal or the social self is more accessible. In independent (Western) cultures, the personal self is thought to be more readily accessible than in interdependent (Eastern) cultures, in which the social or collective self seems to be the driving force behind people's emotions, judgments, and behaviors (see Markus & Kitayama, 1991).

Research by Driskell, Salas, and Johnston (1999) suggests that stress is another important determinant of whether the personal or the social self is accessible. These investigators showed that group members working under stress adopted a narrower, more individual perspective of task activity. Compared with group members who were not working under stress, their cognitions shifted from a broader, team perspective to an individualistic focus. In other words, they shifted their thinking from *we* to *I*. Similarly, Carnevale and Probst (1998) reported findings suggesting that competition increases the salience of personal self-construals, whereas cooperation makes the social self more accessible. That is, they showed that competition reduces the tendency to perceive relationships among items and to group things together (similar to a differentiation set), whereas cooperation increases the use of broader and more integrated mental categories and a tendency to see relationships among items and to group things together (similar to an integration set). Future research may investigate to what extent our findings concerning the relation between self-construal level and the direction of social comparison effects generalize to situations and circumstances in which certain self-construal levels are argued to be "naturally" or "chronically" accessible.

Phillips and Ziller (1997) have recently published findings that suggest that our distinction between differentiation and integration mind-sets may distinguish prejudiced and nonprejudiced people, respectively. These authors developed a Universal Orientation Scale to tap the differences between prejudiced and nonprejudiced thinking. Their results reliably indicate that differentiative thinking is more prominent in prejudiced people, whereas an inclusive integration focus is what defines the nonprejudiced mind. Nonprejudiced perceivers selectively attend to, accentuate, and interpret similarities rather than differences between the self and others (cognitive integration vs. differentiation). When viewed in relation to the present findings, this provocative perspective on prejudice suggests that prejudice level (high, low) may be related to the manner in which one attends to and processes social comparison information (differentiation, integration). It is interesting to note that the present social comparison paradigm may allow one to test the universality of the prejudiced style of processing social information. By manipulating relevant features of the comparison target (race, gender, age) as well as the focal comparison dimension (stereotype related or unrelated; important or unimportant), one can test whether prejudice results in differentiative thinking (and thus contrast) per se or only in situations in which comparison information is likely to elicit prejudiced thinking.

In conclusion, with the current approach to the when (occurrence) and what (direction) of social comparison effects, the search for possible determinants of these effects has at the same time widened as well as narrowed. As we have seen, on the one hand, our perspective seems to open Pandora's box: All kinds of psychological phenomena may be relevant in furthering our understanding of the psychology of social comparison. Group processes (e.g., Brewer & Weber, 1994), individual differences (Cheek, 1989), cultural differences (e.g., Markus & Kitayama, 1991), stress level (Driskell et al., 1999), social value orientation (e.g., Carnevale & Probst, 1998), and prejudice (Phillips & Ziller, 1997)—each of these variables could affect the result of social comparison processes and thus further our understanding of these processes in ways that are important but underresearched. On the other hand, however, there is a common denominator to describe the way these divergent psychological states are thought to impinge on the processing of social comparison information. They all affect the style with which social comparison information is processed (cf. Schwarz & Bless, 1992; Stapel & Koomen,

2000). Activating the personal self or a differentiation-oriented processing style yields contrast, whereas assimilation occurs when the social self is made salient or an integration mind-set has been primed. Any variable that directly or indirectly activates one of these self-construal levels or the associated processing style should therefore have the corresponding consequences for self-evaluations. In a sense, then, our assessment of how personal and social self-accessibility may affect the when and what of social comparison effects has provided us with a perspective on understanding social comparison effects that is grounded in relatively general cognitive processes—namely, whether social comparison information is attended to with a mind that is focused on differentiation or with a focus on inclusion and integration. Similar to a previous investigation of social comparison effects (Stapel & Koomen, 2000) in which we examined the impact of structural features influencing the other–self relation on the way comparison information is processed, the current findings suggest that an important determinant of the self-evaluative consequences of social comparison information is the manner of its use during the self-evaluation process. To date, social comparison research has given little attention to the idea that the occurrence and direction of social comparison effects may be influenced by the style with which comparison information is attended to and processed. We hope that the current demonstration of how self-construal activation influences the impact of social comparison information on self-evaluation will instigate similar investigations of the basic cognitive processes underlying social comparison effects.

REFERENCES

Abelson, R. P., Dasgupta, N., Park, J., & Banaji, M. R. (1998). Perceptions of the collective other. *Personality and Social Psychology Review, 2,* 243–250.

Aron, A., Aron, E. N., & Smollan, D. (1992). Inclusion of Other in the Self Scale and the structure of interpersonal closeness. *Journal of Personality and Social Psychology, 63,* 596–612.

Aron, A., Aron, E. N., Tudor, M., & Nelson, G. (1991). Close relationships as including other in the self. *Journal of Personality and Social Psychology, 60,* 241–253.

Blanton, H. (in press). Evaluating the self in the context of another: Assimilation and contrast effects in social comparison. In G. Moskowitz (Ed.), *The tenure of social cognition*. Mahwah, NJ: Erlbaum.

Brewer, M. B. (1991). The social self: On being the same and different at the same time. *Personality and Social Psychology Bulletin, 17*, 475–482.

Brewer, M. B., & Gardner, W. (1996). Who is this "we"? Levels of collective identity and self representations. *Journal of Personality and Social Psychology, 71*, 83–93.

Brewer, M. B., & Weber, J. G. (1994). Self-evaluation effects of interpersonal versus intergroup social comparison. *Journal of Personality and Social Psychology, 66*, 268–275.

Brown, J. D. (1998). *The self*. Boston: McGraw-Hill.

Brown, J. D., Novick, N. J., Lord, K. A., & Richards, J. M. (1992). When Gulliver travels: Social context, psychological closeness, and self-appraisals. *Journal of Personality and Social Psychology, 62*, 717–727.

Buunk, B. P., Collins, R. L., Taylor, S. E., VanYperen, N. W., & Dakof, G. A. (1990). The affective consequences of social comparison: Either direction has its ups and downs. *Journal of Personality and Social Psychology, 59*, 1238–1249.

Carnevale, P. J., & Probst, T. M. (1998). Social values and social conflict in creative problem solving and categorization. *Journal of Personality and Social Psychology, 74*, 1300–1309.

Chartrand, T. L., & Bargh, J. (1996). Automatic activation of impression formation and memorization goals: Nonconscious goal priming reproduces effects of explicit task instructions. *Journal of Personality and Social Psychology, 71*, 464–478.

Cheek, J. M. (1989). Identity-orientations and self-interpretation. In D. Buss & N. Cantor (Eds.), *Personality psychology: Recent trends and emerging directions* (pp. 275–285). New York: Springer-Verlag.

Driskell, J. E., Sales, E., & Johnson, J. (1999). Does stress lead to a loss of team perspective? *Group Dynamics, 3*, 291–302.

Festinger, L. (1954). A theory of social comparison processes. *Human Relations, 7*, 117–140.

Gardner, W. L., Gabriel, S., & Lee, A. Y. (1999). "I" value freedom, but "we" value relationships: Self-construal priming mirrors cultural differences in judgment. *Psychological Science, 10*, 321–326.

Gibbons, F. X., & Buunk, B. P. (1999). Individual differences in social comparison: The development of a scale of social comparison orientation. *Journal of Personality and Social Psychology, 76*, 129–142.

Gilbert, D. T., Giesler, R. B., &, Morris, K. A. (1995). When comparisons arise. *Journal of Personality and Social Psychology, 69*, 227–236.

Goethals, G. R., & Darley, J. (1977). Social comparison theory: An attributional approach. In J. Suls & R. L. Miller (Eds.), *Social comparison processes: Theoretical and empirical perspectives* (pp. 259–278). Hillsdale, NJ: Erlbaum.

Gollwitzer, P. M., Heckhausen, H., & Steller, B. (1990). Deliberative and implemental mind-sets: Cognitive tuning toward congruous thought and information. *Journal of Personality and Social Psychology, 58*, 1119–1127.

Hogg, M., & Turner, J. C. (1987). Intergroup behaviour, self-stereotyping, and the salience of social categories. *British Journal of Social Psychology, 26*, 325–340.

Hoyle, R. H., Kernis, M. H., Leary, M. R., & Baldwin, M. W. (1999). *Selfhood: Identity, esteem, regulation*. Boulder, CO: Westview.

Jetten, J., Spears, R., & Manstead, A. S. R. (1996). Defining dimensions of distinctiveness: Group variability makes a difference to differentiation. *Journal of Personality and Social Psychology, 74*, 1481–1492.

Lockwood, P. L., & Kunda, Z. (1997). Superstars and me: Predicting the impact of role models on the self. *Journal of Personality and Social Psychology, 73*, 91–103.

Markus, H. R., & Kitayama, S. (1991). Culture and the self: Implications for cognition, emotion, and motivation. *Psychological Review, 98*, 224–253.

McFarlin, D. B., & Blascovich, J. (1984). On the Remote Associates Test (RAT) as an alternative to illusory performance feedback: A methodological note. *Basic and Applied Social Psychology, 5*, 223–229.

McGuire, W. J., & McGuire, C. V. (1981). The spontaneous self-concept as affected by personal distinctiveness. In M. D. Lynch, A. A. Norem-Hebeisen, &. K. J. Gergen (Eds.), *Self-concept: Advances in theory and research* (pp. 147–171). Cambridge, MA: Balinger.

Morse, S., & Gergen, K. J. (1970). Social comparison, self-consistency, and the concept of the self. *Journal of Personality and Social Psychology, 16*, 148–156.

Mussweiler, T., & Strack, F. (2000). The "relative self": Informational and judgmental consequences of comparative self-evaluation. *Journal of Personality and Social Psychology, 79*, 23–38.

Pelham, B. W., & Wachsmuth, J. O. (1995). The waxing and waning of the social self: Assimilation and contrast in social comparison. *Journal of Personality and Social Psychology, 69*, 825–838.

Phillips, S. T., & Ziller, R. C. (1997). Toward a theory and measure of the nature of nonprejudice. *Journal of Personality and Social Psychology, 72*, 420–432.

Schwartz, N., & Bless, H. (1992). Constructing reality and its alternatives: An inclusion/exclusion model of assimilation and contrast effects in social judgment. In L. L. Martin & A. Tesser (Eds.), *The construction of social judgments* (pp. 217–245). Hillsdale, NJ: Erlbaum.

Schweder, R. A., & Bourne, L. (1984). Does the concept of the person vary cross-culturally? In R. A. Schweder & R. A. Levine (Eds.), *Culture theory: Essays on mind, self, and emotion* (pp. 158–199). New York: Cambridge University Press.

Stapel, D. A., & Koomen, W. (1999). Let's not forget the past when we go to the future: On our knowledge of knowledge accessibility effects. In G. Moskowitz (Ed.), *The tenure of social cognition* (pp. 229–246). Mahwah, NJ: Erlbaum.

Stapel, D. A., & Koomen, W. (2000). *Distinctness of others, mutability of selves: Their impact on self-evaluations.* Unpublished manuscript, University of Amsterdam, Amsterdam, the Netherlands.

Stapel, D. A., & Tesser, A. (2000). *Self-activation and interest in social comparison information.* Unpublished manuscript, University of Amsterdam, Amsterdam, the Netherlands.

Steele, C. M. (1988). The psychology of self-affirmation: Sustaining the integrity of the self. In L. Berkowitz (Ed.), *Advances in experimental social psychology* (Vol. 20, pp. 261–302). New York: Academic Press.

Taylor, S. E., & Lobel, M. (1989). Social comparison activity under threat: Downward evaluation and upward contacts. *Psychological Review, 96,* 569–575.

Taylor, S. E., Wayment, H. A., & Carillo, M. (1996). Social comparison, self-regulation, and motivation. In R. M. Sorrentino & E. T. Higgins (Eds.), *Handbook of motivation and cognition* (pp. 3–27). New York: Guilford.

Tesser, A. M. (1988). Toward a self-evaluation maintenance model of social behavior. In L. Berkowitz (Ed.), *Advances in experimental social psychology* (Vol. 20, pp. 181–227). New York: Academic Press.

Tesser, A., & Paulhus, D. (1983). Self-definition of self: Private and public self-evaluation strategies. *Journal of Personality and Social Psychology, 44,* 672–682.

Trafimow, D., Triandis, H. C., & Goto, S. C. (1991). Some tests of the distinction between the private self and the collective self. *Journal of Personality and Social Psychology, 60,* 649–655.

Triandis, H. C. (1989). The self and social behavior in differing cultural contexts. *Psychological Review, 96,* 506–520.

Turner, J. C. (1987). *Rediscovering the social group: A self-categorization theory.* Oxford, England: Blackwell.

Wills, T. A., & Suls, J. (1991). Commentary: Neo-social comparison theory and beyond. In J. Suls & T. A. Wills (Eds.), *Social comparison: Contemporary theory and research* (pp. 395–412). Hillsdale, NJ: Erlbaum.

Wood, J. V. (1989). Theory and research concerning social comparison of personal attributes. *Psychological Bulletin, 106,* 231–248.

Received May 8, 2000
Revision received July 24, 2000
Accepted September 13, 2000 ■

The "Relative Self": Informational and Judgmental Consequences of Comparative Self-Evaluation

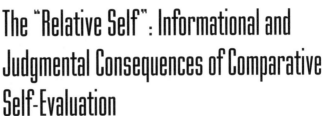

Thomas Mussweiler and Fritz Strack

Results of 5 studies demonstrated that self-evaluative comparisons have 2 distinct informational consequences with opposing judgmental effects: They selectively increase the accessibility of standard-consistent self-knowledge and provide an evaluative reference point. The first informational consequence produces assimilation in self-evaluative judgments, whereas the latter yields contrast. Using a lexical decision task, Study 1 demonstrated that a social comparison selectively increases the accessibility of standard-consistent self-knowledge. Study 2 showed that this effect also holds for comparisons with objective standards. Studies 3 and 4 revealed that the same comparison may lead to assimilation on objective and contrast on subjective self-judgments. Finally, Study 5 demonstrated that assimilation results for comparisons with relevant and irrelevant standards, whereas contrast occurs only for relevant standards.

Who am I? How do people answer this question? How do they know themselves? How do they acquire an identity? For centuries, these issues have occupied the minds of philosophers (e.g., Hume, 1739/1890; Kant, 1787/1956) and psychologists (e.g., James, 1892) alike. Obtaining knowledge about the self, however, appears to be a difficult task to master because the self cannot be

Thomas Mussweiler and Fritz Strack, Department of Psychology, Universität Würzburg, Würzburg, Germany.

This research was supported by a grant from the Deutsche Forschungsgemeinschaft. We thank Birte Englich, Hans-Peter Erb, Jens Förster, Roland Neumann, and Lioba Werth for discussions of the issue; Simon Finkeldei, Cornelia Florig, Daniela Meiser, Iris Müller, Markus Schuhmacher, Anke Siebers, and Sabine Wolfrath for their assistance in data collection and questionnaire construction; and Christopher Müller for the computer programming. We also thank Galen V. Bodenhausen, Brett Pelham, and Robert S. Wyer Jr. for their insightful comments on a draft of this article.

Correspondence concerning this article should be addressed to Thomas Mussweiler, Psychologie II, Universität Würzburg, Röntgenring 10, 97070 Würzburg, Germany. Electronic mail may be sent to mussweiler@psychologie.uni-wuerzburg.de.

perceived directly but has to be inferred from its activities (Kant, 1787/1956; see Baumeister, 1998, for a discussion). These activities do not take place in some isolated ether; rather, they are situated in social contexts and thus relate the self to other objects in the world. As a consequence, the self can only be perceived—and its attributes can only be inferred—in a relative manner. Stated differently, self-perception is inherently relative in nature. This reasoning suggests that people know themselves (i.e., obtain self-knowledge) through a process of relating their inferred attributes to those of the surrounding world.

This relational perspective on the acquisition of self-knowledge is quite consistent with a host of classic psychological approaches to the self (Higgins, Strauman, & Klein, 1986; Miller & Prentice, 1996). For example, James (1892) proposed that people evaluate their attributes relative to their aims and pretensions, and Lewin (1951) suggested that one's performances are evaluated in comparison to a particular frame of reference. Similarly, Festinger (1954) claimed that there is a drive to evaluate one's opinions and abilities and that people use salient comparison standards to do so. More recently, elaborate models have been developed that describe how such standards are constructed (e.g., Miller & Prentice, 1996) and what the consequences of their use in the self-evaluation process are (e.g., Higgins et al., 1986; Higgins, 1987, 1989; Tesser, 1988). These different perspectives on the self converge on the assumption that people do not evaluate their attributes and abilities in an absolute sense. Rather, they use salient comparison standards as a basis for self-evaluation. For example, the evaluation of one's athletic abilities does not take place in an absolute manner. It is relative in nature and is made in comparison with salient standards. In fact, the very statement "I am athletic" already implies that one is more athletic than others and is thus essentially comparative (Huttenlocher & Higgins, 1971).

Although the notion that self-evaluation is comparative in nature has thus always played a central role in psychological reasoning, little is known about the informational consequences of comparative self-evaluation. What self-knowledge do people gain when comparing themselves with a given standard? How do such comparisons change one's self-perceptions and self-evaluations? For example, what knowledge about your athletic abilities would you gain by comparing yourself with either a social or an objective standard? How would comparing your athletic abilities with those of current U.S. President Bill Clinton, for example, change the knowledge you have about your own physical fitness? How would determining whether you can or cannot meet an objective standard of performance (e.g., 50 push-ups) change the evaluation of your athletic abilities?

Informational Consequences of Comparative Self-Evaluation

To answer these questions about the informational consequences of self-evaluative comparisons, it may be fruitful to explore their commonalities with other instances of comparison processes. Doing so may enable us to apply our knowledge about the informational consequences of these comparisons to the realm of self-evaluation. One classic psychological paradigm in which we (Mussweiler & Strack, 1999a, 2000; Strack & Mussweiler, 1997; for an overview, see Mussweiler & Strack, 1999b) have recently examined the informational consequences of comparisons is the anchoring paradigm (Tversky & Kahneman, 1974). In this paradigm, judges make two consecutive judgments about the same target object: a *comparative* and an *objective judgment*. For example, they may first be asked to compare the average price of a German car with an arbitrary numerical standard (the anchor) and indicate whether this price is higher or lower than the standard (Mussweiler & Strack, 2000). Judges are then asked to give their best estimate of the average price (i.e., make an objective judgment).

What are the informational consequences of the comparative anchoring judgment? Our previous research (for an overview, see Mussweiler & Strack, 1999b) indicated that comparing the target with the given standard selectively increases the accessibility of *standard-consistent* knowledge about the target.[1] That is, making the comparison renders knowledge indicating that the target's value is similar to the given standard more accessible. For example, comparing the average price for a German car with a high standard (e.g., DM 40,000) increases the accessibility of knowledge indicating that the price is fairly high. Similarly, comparing the average price with a low standard (e.g., DM 20,000) increases the accessibility of knowledge indicating that the price is fairly low (Mussweiler & Strack, 2000).

Applying these insights to self-evaluative comparisons suggests their first informational consequence. Specifically, comparing oneself to a given standard may selectively increase the accessibility of standard-consistent knowledge about the self. That is, the accessibility of knowledge indicating that one's standing on the judgmental dimension is similar to the standard may be increased. Thus, after a comparison with a high standard, knowledge indicating a high standing of the self should be more accessible. Similarly, after a comparison with a low standard, knowledge indicating a low standing should be more accessible. For example, comparing one's athletic abilities with those of Bill Clinton (showed by our study to be considered a low standard) should render knowledge suggesting a low level of athletic ability for the self more accessible.[2] This analysis suggests selective accessibility as a first informational consequence of self-evaluative comparisons (see also, Mussweiler, in press; Mussweiler & Strack, in press-b).

However, there is reason to believe that evaluating the self in comparison to a salient standard not only renders a specific (standard-consistent) subset of self-knowledge more accessible, it also provides a reference point against which the implications of this knowledge can be evaluated. This assumption is consistent with sample evidence in psychophysical

(e.g., Brown, 1953; Helson, 1964) and social judgment (e.g., Eiser, 1990; Ostrom & Upshaw, 1968; Sherif & Hovland, 1953), which suggests that making a comparison provides participants with a reference point against which the target can be evaluated. For example, in the realm of psychophysical judgment, judges may use salient context stimuli as reference points for their evaluation of the properties of the target stimulus (e.g., Brown, 1953). Similarly, in social judgment, one's own attitude may be a reference point against which the attitudes of others can be evaluated (e.g., Sherif & Hovland, 1953). In much the same way, people may use the standard of a self-evaluative comparison as a reference point against which they evaluate their own abilities. In our example, they may thus use Bill Clinton as a reference point for the evaluation of their athletic abilities.

Taken together, this analysis suggests that comparing oneself with a given standard may have two distinct informational consequences. For one, it selectively increases the accessibility of standard-consistent knowledge about the self. In addition, it suggests a reference point against which the implications of this knowledge can be evaluated.

Judgmental Consequences of Self-Evaluative Comparisons

How will these two informational consequences of self-evaluative comparisons influence self-evaluative judgments? How does comparing one's athletic abilities to those of Bill Clinton, for example, influence subsequent self-evaluations? How does such a comparison affect one's answer to the question, "How athletic are you?" As any judgment, such self-evaluative judgments are likely to be based on judgment-relevant information that is accessible at the time the judgment is made (Higgins, 1996). Thus, self-evaluations are likely to reflect both informational consequences of comparing oneself to a given standard.

Notably, both informational consequences are likely to influence self-evaluative judgments in opposite directions. Research on knowledge accessibility effects (for a recent review, see Higgins,

---

[1] For a discussion of the judgmental processes that are responsible for this selective accessibility effect, see Mussweiler and Strack (1999a, 1999b).

[2] Note that the accessibility of standard-consistent knowledge about the self can be increased only if such knowledge is available. Given the abundance of self-knowledge, however, this is likely to be the case for most comparison domains.

1996) has repeatedly demonstrated that using easily accessible knowledge as a basis for a given judgment typically produces an *assimilation effect*. For instance, increasing the accessibility of the trait construct "recklessness" leads participants to judge an ambiguously described target person as more reckless (Higgins, Rholes, & Jones, 1977). This research suggests that using the standard-consistent self-knowledge that was rendered easily accessible during a comparison for a subsequent self-evaluative judgment should induce this judgment to be standard-consistent as well. For our example, this implies that comparing one's athletic abilities to those of Bill Clinton (i.e., a low standard) would produce lower judgments of one's own athletic abilities. Thus, the selective accessibility mechanism is likely to produce an assimilation effect on self-evaluative judgments. This assumption is also consistent with the fact that assimilation is the standard effect in the anchoring paradigm (see Strack & Mussweiler, 1997, for an exception).

Using the comparison standard as a reference point for self-evaluation, however, is likely to produce a *contrast effect*. Consistent with this assumption, the standard effect of reference-point use in psychophysical and social judgment is contrast (for a detailed discussion, see Wyer & Srull, 1989). For instance, evaluating the weight of a target stimulus in the context of a heavy stimulus leads to "lighter" judgments than evaluating the very same target in the context of a light stimulus (e.g., Brown, 1953). For our example, this implies that using Bill Clinton as a reference point for the evaluation of one's athletic abilities may also lead to higher judgments of one's abilities (i.e., a contrast effect). Taken together, these findings suggest that making the very same comparison may have two opposing consequences for subsequent self-evaluative judgments: assimilation resulting from selective accessibility and contrast resulting from reference point use.

Which of these two opposing effects manifests itself is likely to depend on how relevant the two respective types of information (i.e., self-knowledge and reference point) are for the given judgment. Research on knowledge accessibility effects has repeatedly shown that easily accessible knowledge is used only if it provides relevant information (i.e., information that can appropriately be used to make a good judgment) for the judgment at hand (for discussions, see Higgins, 1996; Strack, 1992; Wyer & Srull, 1989).[3] For example, an easily accessible trait construct is only used to characterize an ambiguous behavior if the trait is applicable to the described behavior (Higgins *et al.*, 1977). Similarly, the self-knowledge and the reference point that are made accessible during the comparison process will only influence a subsequent self-evaluative judgment if they provide relevant information for this judgment and are consequently judged to be usable (Higgins, 1996). Thus, whether the assimilative consequences of selective accessibility or the contrastive consequences of reference point use dominate self-judgments depends on how relevant their respective informational bases are for the critical judgment.

This perspective on assimilation and contrast holds one notable and counterintuitive implication. Unlike previous conceptualizations (e.g., Brown, Novick, Lord, & Richards, 1992; Buunk, Collins, Taylor, VanYperen, & Dakof, 1990; Tesser, 1988), the current perspective suggests that assimilation and contrast are not necessarily mutually exclusive consequences of self-evaluative comparisons. Rather, to the extent that the relevance of its two informational consequences varies for different self-evaluative judgments, the very same comparison may indeed lead to assimilation and contrast. This assumption is quite consistent with previous work by Manis and colleagues (e.g., Manis, Biernat, & Nelson, 1991; Manis & Paskewitz, 1984a, 1984b) showing that assimilation and contrast can be simultaneous effects in social judgment.

In fact, the judgmental relevance of a given reference point is likely to depend on whether the critical judgment takes the form of a subjective judgment along a given rating scale (e.g., "How athletic are you?," 1 = *little athletic*, 9 = *very athletic*) or an objective judgment about physical

---

[3] This notion of judgmental relevance is closely related to Higgins' (1996) concept of "judged usability" and can thus be seen as the "judged appropriateness ... of applying ... knowledge to a stimulus" (p. 136).

quantities (e.g., miles per hour, pounds; Biernat, Manis, & Nelson, 1991). It has been suggested (Biernat & Manis, 1994; Biernat, Manis, & Kobrynowicz, 1997; Biernat et al., 1991) that reference points only provide relevant information for subjective judgments. Note that in order to make such a subjective judgment, judges first have to interpret the given scale labels. Specifically, they have to infer what target quantity each of the given scale labels represents (e.g., What level of athletic ability does a scale label of "1" imply?). To do so, judges are likely to use a salient reference point to "anchor" (Ostrom & Upshaw, 1968; Parducci, 1965) the given response scale (for a more elaborate discussion of this process, see Wyer & Srull, 1989). For example, judges who are asked whether they are more or less athletic than Bill Clinton are likely to use this low reference point to anchor the lower end of the response scale. Specifically, they are likely to assume that the lower scale labels refer to a level of ability that is comparable to that of Bill Clinton. Including such a low standard shifts the response scale in its direction (e.g., Biernat et al., 1991; Ostrom & Upshaw, 1968; Parducci, 1965) so that the value ascribed to one's own level of ability is higher (a contrast effect). Thus, subjective judgments are likely to capture the contrastive effects of using the comparison standard as a reference point.[4]

Objective judgments, however, are unlikely to be influenced by a salient reference point. Because such judgments are externally anchored by consensual standards, the underlying scale cannot be shifted to include or exclude a specific reference point. Consequently, the mechanism that is responsible for the contrast effects that result from reference-point use is not operating. In this situation, judgments are likely to reflect the implications of accessible knowledge. That is, objective judgments are likely to show the assimilation effect that results from selective accessibility. Consistent

with this assumption, our previous research on judgmental anchoring (for an overview, see Mussweiler & Strack, 1999b) has repeatedly demonstrated that objective judgments reflect the consequences of selective accessibility.

This reasoning suggests that judgments on objective and subjective scales are differentially responsive to the two informational consequences of comparative self-evaluation. Because a salient reference point is only relevant for subjective judgments, its contrastive consequences are likely to be limited to this judgment type. Objective judgments, however, are likely to be based on the implications of easily accessible self-knowledge and should thus capture the assimilative consequences of a preceding comparison. Thus, using both judgment types to assess the consequences of comparative self-evaluation may enable us to demonstrate that the very same comparison may lead to assimilation and contrast in self-judgments.

The Present Research

The above reasoning suggests that self-evaluative comparisons provide people with two distinct types of information that are relevant for subsequent self-evaluative judgments. Specifically, comparing oneself with a given standard selectively increases the accessibility of a standard-consistent subset of self-knowledge. Using this knowledge has an assimilative influence on subsequent self-evaluations. In addition, the comparison provides a reference point against which the implications of this knowledge can be evaluated. Using this reference point typically produces a contrast effect. The present research was designed to test the core assumptions of this conceptualization along with some of its implications. Following Festinger's (1954) fundamental distinction, we examined the effects of objective as well as social standards. We assumed

---

[4] To be sure, as previous research (e.g., Higgins et al., 1977) has demonstrated, subjective judgments are also sensitive to the implications of accessible knowledge and may thus show assimilation in situations that prevent a shift of the response scale by holding the judgmental context constant. In a comparative judgment situation, however, in which the source of accessibility (i.e., the comparison) also suggests the use of a different scale anchor, such assimilation is likely to be overridden by the contrast that results from reanchoring the scale.

the described psychological mechanisms underlie the process of comparing oneself with any kind of standard. Consequently, we expected to obtain similar findings for objective and social standards.

In the first two studies, we focused primarily on the consequences that self-evaluative comparisons have for the accessibility of self-knowledge. Specifically, in Study 1, we attempted to demonstrate that social comparisons render standard-consistent information about the self more accessible. In Study 2, we tested for the generality of this mechanism by examining the consequences of comparisons with objective standards. At the same time, in the latter study, we attempted to provide an initial demonstration of the effects of reference point use. Again using objective and social standards, respectively, in Studies 3 and 4 we further explored the existence of two distinct informational consequences and attempted to show that both may have opposing judgmental effects. Finally, we designed Study 5 to examine the different rules that govern the use of accessible self-knowledge and reference points and thus lend further credence to their assumed distinctiveness. At the same time, in Study 5, we explored the behavioral consequences of self-evaluative comparisons.

Study 1

To assess the accessibility of self-related knowledge subsequent to making a social comparison, we used a lexical decision task (see Neely, 1991, for a review). Specifically, we had participants compare themselves with either a moderately athletic (the former Formula 1 champion Nicki Lauda) or a moderately unathletic (U.S. President Bill Clinton) celebrity.[5] After making this comparison, they received a lexical decision task that included words associated with being athletic (e.g., *dynamic, athletic*), words associated with being unathletic (e.g., *weak, heavy*), neutral words (e.g., *purify, cow*),

---

[5] Although Nicki Lauda may not be familiar to most Americans, he is very popular in Germany. The general image and the level of athletic ability that he represents is similar to the one associated with the race car driver Mario Andretti in the United States.

and nonwords. For each of the presented words, participants' task was to determine whether the word does or does not constitute a German word.

On the basis of the above analysis, we expected that lexical decisions for standard-consistent words would be faster than for standard-inconsistent words. For example, participants should be faster in recognizing words that are associated with being athletic after comparing themselves with the high standard (i.e., Nicki Lauda) than after comparing with the low standard (i.e., Bill Clinton). It is important to note, however, that this pattern of response latencies would allow for a plausible alternative interpretation. Rather than reflecting differences in the accessibility of self-related knowledge, this effect may well be caused by a simple priming mechanism (Herr, 1986). Specifically, participants may be faster in responding to standard-consistent words not because they generated evidence that indicates that they are similar to the standard, but because the process of thinking about the standard increases the accessibility of concepts that are closely associated with it. That is, after comparing themselves with Bill Clinton, participants may be faster in responding to words associated with being unfit because Bill Clinton is strongly associated with this characteristic and thus primes the respective concept (Herr, 1986).

Thus, to put our hypothesis to a strict test, we had to distinguish the accessibility of self-related knowledge (i.e., evidence suggesting that one is similar to the standard) from the accessibility of semantic knowledge in general. To do so, we followed a procedure developed by Dijksterhuis *et al.* (1998). Specifically, half of the lexical decisions were preceded by the subliminal presentation of a word that is closely associated with the self-concept (*I, my, me*). The other half was preceded by a word unrelated to the self (*and, or, when*). Subliminal presentation of self-related words has been demonstrated to activate the self-concept, so that lexical decision trials that are preceded by such primes assess the specific accessibility of self-related knowledge (Dijksterhuis *et al.*, 1998).

If the selective accessibility mechanism plays a role in social comparison, then the accessibility of self-related knowledge indicating that the self is similar to the standard should be increased. Specifically, after comparing themselves with the upward standard, participants should be faster in responding to words that are associated with being athletic than to words that are associated with being unathletic. By the same token, after comparing themselves with the downward standard, participants should be faster in responding to words that are associated with being unathletic. Furthermore, to the extent that this effect is driven by the accessibility of self-related knowledge rather than semantic knowledge in general, it should primarily occur if the lexical decision trials are preceded by the self-primes (i.e., the self-concept is activated).

Method

Participants. We recruited 41 students at the University of Würzburg as participants and randomly assigned them to experimental conditions. They were contacted by phone, asked to take part in a study on cognitive performance, and offered DM 7 (U.S. $4) as compensation.

Materials. The social comparison standards were pretested using a different group of 21 participants. Using 9-point rating scales that ranged from 1 (*not at all athletic*) to 9 (*very athletic*), these participants rated how athletic they themselves and a total of 19 celebrities are. On the basis of these ratings, we selected U.S. President Bill Clinton ($M = 3.9$) as the moderately unathletic standard and the former race car driver Nicki Lauda ($M = 6.8$) as the moderately athletic standard. Ratings for these two standards were at about an equal distance from participants' mean self-rating ($M = 5.2$).

In the lexical decision task, we used four sets of stimulus words as targets: 4 words that are associated with being athletic (*fit* [fit], *athletisch* [athletic], *dynamisch* [dynamic], *trainiert* [in good shape]), 4 words that are associated with being unathletic (*steif* [stiff], *schwach* [weak], *schwerfällig* [heavy], *plump* [plump]), 10 neutral words (e.g., *läutern* [purify], *Kuh* [cow]), and 9 nonwords (e.g., *molen*, *schonzem*). Moreover, we used two sets of primes:

words that are closely associated with the self (*Ich* [I], *mein* [my], *mir* [me]) and words that are not associated with the self (*und* [and], *oder* [or], *aber* [but]). From these primes and targets we constructed two lists of 27 prime–target combinations. In the first list, the one half of each target category was preceded by a self-prime, whereas the other half was preceded by a neutral prime. For the second list, this assignment was reversed, so that across the two lists each word was preceded once by a self-prime and once by a neutral prime. Within the two prime categories, the individual primes were randomly assigned to the specific targets. Moreover, the order of the prime–target combinations was randomly determined for both lists. Thus, for each list, 2 of the words that are associated with being athletic were preceded by a self-prime, and 2 were preceded by a neutral prime. Similarly, 2 of the words that are associated with being unathletic were preceded by a self-prime and 2 were preceded by a neutral prime. Moreover, 5 of the neutral words and 4 of the nonwords were preceded by a self-prime, whereas 5 of the neutral and nonwords were preceded by a neutral prime.

In sum, participants compared themselves with either a moderately high or a moderately low standard of athletic performance and then made lexical decisions about words associated with being athletic and words associated with being unathletic. Half of these lexical decisions were preceded by a subliminal self-prime, and the other half were preceded by a control prime. Study 1 was thus based on a 2 (high vs. low standard) × 2 (athletic vs. unathletic target word) × 2 (self vs. control prime) design. The first factor was manipulated between, the final two factors within participants.

Procedure. The procedure closely followed the one used by Dijksterhuis *et al.* (1998). On arrival, participants were greeted by the experimenter, led to separate booths and seated in front of a 70-Hz computer monitor at a predetermined distance. Then, instructions were presented on the computer screen. Here, participants were informed that the current study was concerned with the extent to which cognitive performance is influenced by preceding comparisons with others. To examine this question, we first asked them to compare themselves with a celebrity and then presented them a number of letter strings for which they had to decide whether these letter strings constitute German words. Half of the participants were told to press the *x* key to indicate that the presented letter string was a word and the "period" key to indicate that it was not a word. For the other half, this assignment was reversed. To reduce variance in response latencies, participants were told to position their forefingers on the two keys and to keep this position throughout the lexical decision task. Moreover, participants were instructed to solve this task as quickly and as accurately as possible. Finally, it was pointed out that participants should concentrate on the fixation point that occurred in the center of the screen, and that the letter strings would be presented at the same position.

After reading the instructions, about half of the participants were asked to compare themselves with Bill Clinton. The other half were asked to compare themselves with Nicki Lauda. Specifically, they were instructed to bring the respective comparison standard to mind and compare themselves with him regarding how athletic they are. They were then asked to indicate whether they are more or less athletic than the standard.

Subsequently, participants worked on the lexical decision task. A total of 37 trials were presented. The first 10 were practice trials, whereas Trials 11 through 37 were the critical ones that were included in the analysis. Each of the two lists of prime–target combinations described above was administered to about half of the participants. At the beginning of each individual trial, a fixation stimulus (*XXXX*) was presented at the center of the screen for 1,000 ms. The prime was then presented at the same location for 15 ms and was immediately masked by a letter string (*XXXX*) that was presented for 500 ms. It has been demonstrated that words presented for such a brief period of time activate their representation in memory outside of conscious awareness (Bargh & Chartrand, in press). Then, the target word was presented, overwriting the masking stimulus, and remained on the screen until participants had made the lexical decision. After 2 s, the same sequence was repeated with the next trial.

After completion of the lexical decision task, participants answered a final questionnaire, which tested for awareness of the priming manipulation. First, they were asked whether they had recognized anything extraordinary in the experiment. Then they were informed that before the presentation of the target words, we had presented them with other words for very brief periods of time and instructed them to list any of the words they had recognized.

Results

Awareness check. None of the participants realized that prime words had been presented prior to the target words. Moreover, no participant was able to list any of the prime words.

Lexical decisions. As suggested by Fazio (1990), we conducted logarithmic transformations (*ln*) of the response latencies for the lexical decisions in order to reduce the skewness of the response distribution. Our analysis is based on these logarithmic transformations. For ease of interpretation, however, we report the nontransformed means.

In our main analysis, we compared response latencies for standard-consistent words (i.e., athletic words for the high standard and unathletic words for the low standard) and standard-inconsistent words (i.e., unathletic words for the high standard and athletic words for the low standard).[6] Inspection of Table 26.1 reveals that standard-consistent words were recognized faster ($M = 578.5$ ms) than standard-inconsistent words ($M = 600.0$ ms). This, however, was only the case if the target words were preceded by a self prime, $t(40) = 2.56$, $p < .01$ (one-tailed) and not if the target words were preceded by a neutral prime, $t(40) = .15$, *ns*. In a 2 (standard-consistent vs. standard-inconsistent target word) × 2 (self vs. control prime) repeated measure analysis of variance (ANOVA), this pattern yielded a significant interaction effect, $F(1, 40) = 4.32$,

---

[6] Similar patterns of response latencies to the standard-consistent and standard-inconsistent words resulted for comparisons with the high and the low standards ($F < 1.8$, $p > .2$) for all effects including standard. Consequently, we did not include this factor in our main analysis.

TABLE 26.1. Response Latencies for Standard-Consistent and Standard-Inconsistent Words by Prime (Study 1)

	Prime	
Target word	Self	Control
Standard consistent	573 (115)	584 (128)
Standard inconsistent	614 (142)	586 (119)

Note: N = 41. Response latencies are given in milliseconds. Standard deviations are in parentheses.

$p < .04$. In this analysis the main effect for target also proved to be significant, $F(1, 40) = 4.48$, $p < .04$, whereas the main effect for prime was not significant ($F < 1$).

Discussion

As is apparent from the above analysis, after comparing with the low standard, Bill Clinton, participants recognized words associated with being unathletic faster than words associated with being athletic. After comparing with the high standard, Nicki Lauda, however, the reverse was true. Importantly, this facilitation effect only held for those lexical decision trials that assessed the specific accessibility of self-related knowledge. The latter finding renders a simple semantic priming explanation (e.g., Herr, 1986) implausible. Instead, these data support the current conceptualization. They suggest that making a social comparison selectively increases the accessibility of standard-consistent knowledge about the self. For example, after comparing with Bill Clinton, participants appear to have knowledge indicating that they are relatively unathletic more accessible than knowledge indicating that they are athletic.

Study 2

In Study 2, we examined whether such a selective increase in standard-consistent knowledge about the self also results from comparisons with objective standards (Festinger, 1954). To assess the assumed accessibility increase, we used a different method than the one applied in Study 1. Specifically, we asked participants to describe themselves after they had made the comparison. Consistent with the findings of Study 1, we expected that these self-descriptions would show a selective increase in the accessibility of standard-consistent knowledge about the self. After comparing with a high standard of athletic ability, participants should describe themselves as more athletic than after comparing with a low standard.

Thus, one of our goals for Study 2 was to examine the generality of the selective accessibility effect demonstrated in Study 1. In addition, in Study 2, we attempted to provide initial support for the assumption that self-evaluative comparisons not only influence the accessibility of self-related knowledge but also provide a reference point against which the implications of this knowledge can be evaluated. As outlined before, using this reference point is likely to produce a contrast effect on self-evaluative judgments along subjective judgment scales. Consequently, we included a subjective judgment scale to assess the consequences of reference point use. Specifically, after comparing their athletic abilities with a series of objective standards, half of the participants were asked to describe their athletic abilities (our measure of selective accessibility) whereas the other half was asked to judge their athletic abilities along a subjective rating scale (our measure of reference point use).

Method

Participants. We recruited 76 students at the University of Würzburg as participants and randomly assigned them to one of four experimental conditions. As a compensation for their participation they were offered a chocolate bar.

Materials. The questionnaire included two comparative judgments pertaining to different behaviors that are related to athletic abilities. In the first question, participants were instructed to evaluate whether they would be able to perform a given number of push-ups. In the second question they were asked to evaluate whether they would be able to run 110-m hurdles in a given time. Specifically, they were told to take a few minutes and evaluate whether they would be able to perform the critical behavior and were then asked to judge how difficult this evaluation had been. They were given a 9-point rating scale that ranged from 1 (*not at all difficult*) to 9 (*very difficult*) to make this judgment.

Again the high and low standards were set at one standard deviation above and below the mean estimate of a different group of pretest participants (*N* = 20) who made objective judgments only. For the number of push-ups, the high standard (i.e., standard for high athletic abilities) was 37, whereas the low standard was 8. For the time needed to run 110-m hurdles, the high standard was 15 s and the low standard was 25 s. Half of our participants received standards of high athletic abilities for both comparisons; the other half consistently received standards of low athletic abilities.

After the two comparisons, about half of the participants were asked to describe themselves. Specifically, they were told that we would like them to tell us a little about themselves and that our foremost interest was in their athletic abilities. These participants were further instructed to take a few minutes and write down everything that came to their minds when trying to evaluate their athletic abilities. The other half were asked to judge how athletic they are along a 9-point rating scale that ranged from 1 (*not at all athletic*) to 9 (*very athletic*). Thus, the type of measure (self-report vs. subjective judgment) was manipulated between participants.

In sum, Study 2 was based on a 2 (high vs. low standard) × 2 (self-report vs. subjective judgment) factorial design. Both factors were manipulated between participants.

Procedure. Participants were recruited in the university cafeteria. They were asked to take part in a pretest for the construction of a questionnaire assessing self-evaluations and were led to a separate room where they participated in groups of up to 10. On arrival, they were greeted by the experimenter, led to their seat, handed the questionnaire, and told to read instructions carefully. The instructions indicated that the purpose of the study was to help determine which questions are

best suited to assess self-evaluations. To do so, they were told, we would use different question formats. Some of the questions would require them to evaluate their abilities relative to a given numeric comparison standard. Participants were further instructed to answer all the questions in the questionnaire in the given order and to do so as accurately as possible. After finishing the questionnaire, participants were thanked, debriefed, and given their candy.

Results

Two independent judges who were blind to conditions rated participants' self-reports of their athletic abilities (e.g., "I do work out regularly," "I was never good at track and field"). For each self-report, judges rated how athletic participants described themselves using 9-point rating scales that ranged from 1 (*not at all athletic*) to 9 (*very athletic*). Ratings of the two judges were highly correlated ($r = .90$, $p < .001$), so they were combined into one single score.

As is apparent from Table 26.2, comparing themselves with high versus low standards of athletic abilities had differential effects on self-reports and subjective judgments. On the self-reports, participants described themselves to be more athletic after comparing with high rather than low standards, $t(72) = 1.51$, $p < .07$ (one-tailed). On the subjective judgment, however, the reverse pattern occurred. Here, participants judged themselves to be less athletic after comparing with the high rather than the low standard, $t(72) = 1.63$, $p < .05$

TABLE 26.2. Self-Descriptions and Subjective Judgments of Athletic Ability by Standard (Study 2)

	Athletic ability	
Standard	Self-description	Subjective judgment
High	5.92 (1.88)	5.05 (1.93)
Low	4.89 (2.37)	6.10 (1.97)

Note: *N* = 18 (self-description) and 20 (subjective judgment). Ratings and judgments were given on 9-point scales that ranged from 1 (*not at all athletic*) to 9 (*very athletic*). Standard deviations are in parentheses.

(one-tailed). In a 2 (high vs. low standard) × 2 (self-report vs. subjective judgment) ANOVA, this pattern produced a significant interaction effect, $F(1, 72) = 4.9$, $p < .03$. None of the remaining effects was significant ($F < 1$).

Discussion

Clearly, the results of Study 2 are consistent with our hypotheses. First, self-descriptions showed a selective accessibility effect. That is, after comparing themselves with high standards of athletic ability, participants described themselves as more athletic than after comparing with low standards. Thus, making the comparison appears to increase the accessibility of standard-consistent self-knowledge. This finding demonstrates that just as comparisons with social standards (see Study 1), comparisons with objective standards selectively increase the accessibility of standard-consistent knowledge about the self.

Although the self-descriptions were thus assimilated to the standard, subjective self-evaluative judgments were contrasted away from the standard. Here, participants judged themselves to be less athletic after comparing themselves with the high standard than after comparing with the low standard. These findings provide the first evidence suggesting that although comparing oneself with a salient standard renders standard-consistent knowledge about the self more accessible, self-evaluative judgments may be contrasted away from the standard. Because this contrast effect is opposed to the implications of easily accessible self-knowledge, it is unlikely to result from using this knowledge. Rather, it suggests that in addition to selective accessibility, self-evaluative comparisons also suggest a reference point that may be used for subsequent judgments. Because reference-point use typically leads to contrast and is primarily apparent on subjective judgment scales, the obtained contrast effect is likely to be caused by this second informational consequence of self-evaluative comparisons.

As we have pointed out before, however, the direction of influence that a comparison has on self-evaluative judgments is likely to depend on the form this judgment takes. Because objective judgment scales do not have to be anchored with a given reference point, they are likely to reflect the implications of accessible knowledge about the self. As the first two studies demonstrated, this knowledge is likely to indicate that the self is similar to the standard, so that using this knowledge should produce an assimilation effect on self-evaluations. This suggests that by using objective and subjective judgment scales, we may be able to demonstrate that the very same comparison can produce assimilation and contrast effects on subsequent self-evaluative judgments. To the extent that assimilation results for objective judgments (which are sensitive to selective accessibility) and contrast occurs on subjective judgments (which are sensitive to reference point use), such a finding would also lend further credence to the assumption that self-evaluative comparisons have two distinct informational consequences. Focusing on objective and social standards respectively, we examined this possibility in Studies 3 and 4.

Study 3

We asked participants to compare themselves with either a high or a low objective standard with respect to three abilities that are related to intelligence. For example, they were asked whether they would be able to perform more or less than either 62 or 10 simple mathematical calculations within 1 min. We then assessed the consequences of these comparisons on self-evaluations using objective (e.g., "How many simple mathematical computations can you perform in one minute?") and subjective (e.g., "How intelligent are you on a scale from 1 to 7?") judgments. Consistent with the above analysis, we expected objective self-evaluations to be assimilated to the standard and subjective evaluations to be contrasted away from the standard. That is, on the objective judgment participants should evaluate themselves to be more intelligent after the comparisons with high standards than after the comparisons with low standards, whereas the reverse should be true on the subjective judgments.

Method

Participants. Twenty students at the University of Würzburg were recruited as participants for what was ostensibly a pretest for the construction of a questionnaire assessing self-evaluations. Participants were randomly assigned to one of two experimental conditions. They received a chocolate bar as compensation.

Materials. The questionnaire contained a total of 26 questions. The first 16 consisted of eight pairs of comparative and objective judgment questions. Among those were the 3 critical questions, which assessed intelligence-related abilities. In particular, these questions assessed participants' evaluations of how many simple mathematical computations (e.g., $2 + 5 = 7$) they would be able to perform in 1 min, how long it would take them to read the front page of a newspaper in a manner that would allow them to reproduce its content, and how many telephone numbers they could report spontaneously. For each of these abilities, participants were first asked the comparative and then the objective judgment question. For example, they were first asked whether they would be able to perform more or less than 62 simple computations in 1 min. Then they were asked how many computations they would be able to perform. For half of the participants, all of the three critical comparative questions included high standards of performance. For the other half, all three included low standards.

We determined the standard values on the basis of the results of a pretest that included a different group of 20 participants. These participants received objective judgment questions only (e.g., "How many simple mathematical computations can you do in 1 minute?"). The high and low numeric standards for the main study were selected to be one standard deviation higher or lower than the mean estimate of the pretest participants. The resulting values are 62 and 10 for the number of mathematical computations, 10 and 30 min for the time needed to read the front page of a newspaper, and 48 and 10 for the number of telephone numbers.

Subsequent to the eight pairs of comparative and objective questions, we asked participants how difficult answering these questions was, using a 7-point rating scale that ranged from 1 (*not at all difficult*) to 7 (*very difficult*). Then, participants answered a final set of questions. Eight of these questions were unrelated to the critical dimension of intelligence (e.g., "What is your profession?" "How old are you?" "How thrifty are you?"), and one was the critical subjective judgment question, which assessed participants' general evaluation of their intelligence ("How intelligent do you take yourself to be?") along a 7-point rating scale that ranged from 1 (*little intelligent*) to 7 (*very intelligent*). The questions were always presented in the same order. The critical comparative and objective judgment questions constituted the 2nd, 3rd, and 5th question pairs, and the critical subjective judgment question was at the 21st position of the questionnaire.

In sum, each of the questionnaires included either high or low standards of performance for the three critical comparative questions pertaining to the intelligence-related abilities. Moreover, each questionnaire assessed the effects of these standards on three objective and one subjective judgment. Thus, Study 3 was based on a 2 (high vs. low standard) × 2 (objective vs. subjective judgment) mixed factorial design. The first factor (i.e., Standard) was manipulated between participants; the second factor (i.e., Judgment) was manipulated within participants.

Procedure. The procedure was identical to Study 2.

Results

Preliminary analysis. Ratings of the difficulty of the questions were similar for participants who received the high ($M = 2.5$) versus low standard ($M = 2.4$), $t(18) = .19, p > .8$.

Objective and subjective judgments. To allow for a combination of the three objective judgments into a single score and for a comparison of objective and subjective judgments, all judgments were z transformed. As inspection of the means given in Table 26.3 reveals, objective judgments ($\alpha = .74$) were higher when the comparative questions included a high rather than a low standard,

TABLE 26.3. Objective and Subjective Judgments of Intelligence by Standard (Study 3)

Standard	Intelligence	
	Objective judgment	Subjective judgment
High	0.22 (0.34)	−0.33 (0.83)
Low	−0.22 (0.43)	0.33 (1.09)

Note: N = 10. *z*-transformed values are given. Standard deviations are in parentheses.

$t(18) = 2.53, p < .01$ (one-tailed). For the subjective judgment, however, the reverse pattern occurred. Here, lower estimates were given when high rather than low standards were present, $t(18) = 1.52, p < .07$ (one-tailed). In a 2 (high vs. low standard) $\times$ 2 (objective vs. subjective judgment) mixed model ANOVA, this pattern of means produced a significant interaction effect, $F(1, 18) = 5.84, p < .03$. All other effects failed to reach significance ($Fs < 1$).

Study 4

To examine the judgmental consequences of social comparisons, we asked participants to compare the magnitude of their drug consumption with either a high (i.e., the musician Frank Zappa) or a low (i.e., the tennis professional Steffi Graf) social standard. Again, self-evaluative judgments were assessed using objective and subjective scales.

Method

Participants. We recruited 32 students at the University of Würzburg as participants, randomly assigned them to one of two experimental conditions, and offered them a chocolate bar as compensation.

Materials. The questionnaire consisted of two sets of three questions pertaining to different content domains. The first set of questions was a practice trial, whereas the second set was the critical one that was included in the analysis. Each set consisted of a comparative, an objective, and a subjective judgment. In the critical set, half of the participants were first asked whether they consumed drugs and

alcohol more or less often per month than Frank Zappa (i.e., the upward standard). The other half were asked whether they consumed drugs and alcohol more or less often than Steffi Graf (i.e., the downward standard). In the subsequent objective judgment, participants were asked to estimate the number of times they consumed drugs and alcohol per month. Finally, using a 9-point rating scale that ranged from 1 (*not at all extensive*) to 9 (*very extensive*) participants were then asked to indicate how extensive their drug consumption is.

The standards were selected based on the results of a pretest in which a different group of participants ($N = 20$) had estimated how often they and a number of celebrities would engage in a variety of behaviors. The critical questions pertained to the number of times a specific target would consume drugs and alcohol within 1 month. On average, participants reported consuming drugs about eight times per month. The estimates for the selected standards deviated from this number by about the same extent. Specifically, participants estimated that Frank Zappa (i.e., the upward standard) would consume drugs about 15 times a month, whereas Steffi Graf (i.e., the downward standard) would consume drugs about once a month.

In sum, Study 4 was based on a 2 (high vs. low standard) $\times$ 2 (objective vs. subjective judgment) mixed factorial design. The first factor (i.e., Standard) was manipulated between participants; the second factor (i.e., Judgment) was manipulated within participants.

Procedure. The procedure was identical to that of Studies 2 and 3.

Results

Again, objective and subjective judgments were transformed into *z* scores for each question. As inspection of Table 26.4 reveals, on the objective judgment, participants tended to estimate their drug consumption to be higher after comparing themselves with the upward standard than after comparing with the downward standard. For the subjective judgment, however, the reverse pattern occurred. Here, there was a tendency for participants to judge

TABLE 26.4. Objective and Subjective Judgments of Drug Consumption by Standard (Study 4)

Standard	Drug consumption	
	Objective judgment	Subjective judgment
High	0.19 (1.27)	−0.06 (0.93)
Low	−0.19 (0.61)	0.06 (1.10)

Note: $N = 16$. z-transformed values are given. Standard deviations are in parentheses.

their drug consumption to be lower after comparing themselves with the upward standard than after comparing with the downward standard.[7] A 2 (upward vs. downward standard) × 2 (objective vs. subjective judgment) mixed model ANOVA using the z-transformed objective and subjective judgments as dependent variables yielded a significant interaction effect, $F(1, 30) = 4.49, p < .04$. None of the main effects proved to be significant ($Fs < 1$).

Discussion

Consistent with our reasoning, the results of Studies 3 and 4 demonstrate that self-evaluative comparisons can indeed have two opposing judgmental consequences. Specifically, objective self-evaluations tended to be assimilated to the standards, so that participants evaluated their intelligence and their drug consumption to be higher after comparing themselves with the high standard than after comparing with the low standard. Subjective self-evaluations, however, tended to be contrasted away from the standard. Here, participants evaluated their intelligence and their drug consumption to be higher after comparing with the low rather than the high standard.

We have suggested so far that the assimilation and the contrast effects that we have obtained in the preceding studies were caused by the differential use of two different informational bases for the respective judgments. Specifically, we assume that the assimilation effect obtained on objective judgments results because these judgments are based on the implications of easily accessible

knowledge about the self. The contrast effect we obtained for subjective judgments, however, is assumed to result because participants used the comparison standard as a reference point to anchor the judgment scale. The findings we have presented so far are consistent with this assumption. First, the fact that the objective judgments (see Studies 3 and 4) point in the same direction as the implications of easily accessible self-related knowledge (see Studies 1 and 2) suggests that participants based these judgments on the implications of easily accessible knowledge. Moreover, the fact that assimilation and contrast were obtained on those judgment scales that are typically responsive to selective accessibility and reference-point use suggests that these two informational consequences of self-evaluative comparisons are indeed responsible for the divergent effects. To provide further support for this claim, however, we set out to demonstrate that the assimilation and the contrast effects we obtained depend on those factors that have been found to be critical for the respective mechanisms. One factor that seems crucial in this respect is the relevance of the given standard.

Standard Relevance in Selective Accessibility and Reference-Point Use

As we pointed out in the introduction, the informational consequences of self-evaluative comparisons only yield judgmental consequences if they provide relevant information for the critical judgment. That is, they only influence judgment if they are judged as providing useable information (Higgins, 1996) for the judgment at hand. The fact that the reference points suggested in self-evaluative comparisons produced contrast effects only on subjective but not on objective judgments constitutes one example of this principle. Specifically, because the response scales used for objective judgments are clearly defined and anchored by consensual norms, a reference point that is suggested in a given comparison does not provide relevant information for these judgments. Consequently, it is not used for an objective judgment and does not produce a contrastive effect.

---

[7] An analysis of the individual contrasts revealed that both tendencies failed to reach significance ($t < 1$).

To give a subjective judgment, however, participants have to interpret the given response scale and are likely to use salient standards to do so. Notably, a given standard will only be used to anchor the response scale if it is seen as relevant for the judgment to be made. That is, to be used as a scale anchor, a reference point has to provide information that can be appropriately used to interpret and disambiguate the response scale. This is likely to be the case only if the standard provides information about the target's relative standing on the judgmental dimension. This suggests that contrast effects on subjective judgments, which result from reference-point use, are likely to occur only for such relevant standards. Consistent with this reasoning, previous research has repeatedly demonstrated that judges use only relevant standards as reference points (e.g., Brown, 1953; Cash, Cash, & Butters, 1983; Stapel, Koomen, & van der Pligt, 1997). In the realm of psychophysical judgment, Brown (1953) provided a particularly informative demonstration of this dependency. He had participants judge a series of target weights in the presence of some context weights. In one of his conditions, the context weight was a tray of weights. To manipulate the relevance of this context weight, the experimenter either introduced the tray as another target stimulus or he simply asked participants to hold the tray as a favor to him. In the first case, the tray of weights was a part of the stimulus set so that it helped to evaluate the relative standing of the targets along the judgmental dimension. That is, the tray of weights was relevant for judgments of the targets. Consequently, Brown found that the context stimulus produced a contrast effect on judgments of the target stimuli. The heavier the tray was, the lighter the target weights were judged to be. However, if the tray was seen as irrelevant for the critical judgment, because it was not a part of the stimulus set, this contrast effect did not hold. This suggests that a given standard is only used as a reference point and consequently only produces a contrast effect if it is seen as relevant for the critical judgment.

Similar effects have been obtained in research examining the effects of social comparison on self-evaluation. For example, Cash *et al.* (1983) demonstrated that participants contrasted evaluations of their physical attractiveness away from a very attractive standard only if this standard provided relevant information for evaluations of their relative attractiveness. If this were not the case, because the standard was introduced as a supermodel and thus belonged to a particularly attractive subgroup of people, no contrast occurred. Thus, the judgmental consequences of reference-point use appear to critically depend on the perceived relevance of the standards.

This dependency, however, does not exist for the second informational consequence of self-evaluative comparisons, namely, selective accessibility. To the extent that participants use a given standard to make a comparison—which is a requirement in the current experimental paradigm—this comparison process is likely to increase the accessibility of standard-consistent self-knowledge. Notably, the relevance of this knowledge for subsequent self-evaluative judgments does not depend on the perceived relevance of the standard. Even if the standard is irrelevant, the knowledge that was generated during the comparison with this standard still pertains to the target of the self-evaluative judgment (i.e., the self) and is likely to be used to make this judgment. As a result, the assimilation effect that results from selective accessibility is likely to occur for comparisons with relevant as well as irrelevant standards.

Research on judgmental anchoring—a phenomenon mediated by selective accessibility—is consistent with this assumption. Here, it has repeatedly been demonstrated that objective judgments are assimilated to the standard, even if this value is randomly determined. For example, Tversky and Kahneman (1974) provided their participants with standards that were ostensibly selected by spinning a wheel of fortune. Although the standards were thus clearly irrelevant for the judgment, they had a strong assimilative influence (see also Cervone & Peake, 1986; Mussweiler & Strack, in press-a). These findings suggest that the judg-mental consequences of selective accessibility do not depend on the relevance of the comparison standard.

Taken together, this research suggests that the extent to which the two informational consequences of self-evaluative comparisons affect subsequent self-evaluative judgments are differentially influenced by changes in the relevance of the comparison standard. That is, the respective judgmental consequences of selective accessibility and reference-point use should be differentially responsive to changes in standard relevance. These differing dependencies allow for an additional test of our conceptualization. If the assimilation effects we have obtained are caused by selective accessibility, they should occur for relevant as well as irrelevant standards. Furthermore, if the contrast effects are produced by reference-point use, they should occur only for relevant and not for irrelevant standard. We tested these predictions in our final study.

Study 5

In Study 5, we examined the role of standard relevance for self-evaluations in cognitive performance tests. Specifically, participants were given a test (attention load in Study 5a and intelligence in Study 5b) that consisted of a number of individual tasks and received a comparison standard against which they were to evaluate their prospective performance. Half of our participants ostensibly determined this standard themselves by rolling dice; the other half were given a standard and told that this standard represented the average students' performance in the task. This manipulation is conceptually equivalent to the one used by Brown (1953) and has clear implications for the relevance of the respective standards. Specifically, whereas a standard that informs participants of the average performance of their peers helps them evaluate their relative standing on the judgmental dimension, a randomly determined standard does not do so. In this respect, the latter standard is less relevant for evaluations of one's performance than the first. Consistent with the above reasoning, we expected that objective evaluations would be assimilated to the relevant as well as the irrelevant standard. Subjective evaluations, however, should only be contrasted away from relevant but not irrelevant standards.

In addition to assessing the comparison effects on self-evaluations, we examined their effects on participants' performance in the respective tasks. Researchers have suggested (e.g., Atkinson, 1957; Cervone & Peake, 1986; Seta, 1982; Taylor, Wayment, & Carrillo, 1996) that task performance may be influenced by comparisons with salient standards. For example, Seta (1982) demon-strated that participants' performance in a pattern-recognition task improved in the presence of a social comparison standard who did slightly better. Similarly, Cervone and Peake (1986) demonstrated that participants performed better in a problem-solving task after evaluating their prospective performance in comparison to a high rather than a low numeric standard. Taken together, this research suggests that participants should perform better after evaluating their prospective performance in comparison with a high rather than a low standard.

We tested these predictions in two separate studies that used different performance tasks. We used an attention-load task in Study 5a, whereas we used parts of an intelligence test in Study 5b.

Study 5a

Method

Participants. Sixty-four students at the University of Würzburg were recruited as participants and were randomly assigned to one of four experimental conditions. They were asked to participate in a study with the ostensible purpose of evaluating different methods of assessing people's ability to concentrate. Participants received an ice-cream cone as compensation.

Materials. We used an adaptation of the d2 attention-load test (Brickenkamp, 1962) as a measure of ability to concentrate. Our adaptation of the test consisted of a matrix of 16×47 letters (d or p) with one to four dashes located above and below the letters. Participants' task was to circle all the ds that were marked with a total of two dashes. The respective number of each line of the matrix was given in the first column. The cumulative number of letters (i.e., 47 to 752) for each of the consecutive lines was given in the last column. A pretest using a different set of 21 participants had revealed that participants processed an average of 459 ($SD = 87.88$) letters in 5 min. The high and low standards of 562 and 365 were selected to deviate from the mean of pretest participants' performance by about one standard deviation.

Procedure. Participants were recruited in the university cafeteria and were led to a separate room where they participated in groups of up to 4. On arrival, they were greeted by one of the experimenters. Participants who were to receive irrelevant comparison standards (i.e., standards ostensibly determined at random) were first led to a separate room in which they were given three dice to determine a number they would later need in the study. They were told to roll the dice one after another and were informed that the numbers would be combined in the order in which they were rolled to form their personal number. The dice were manipulated (i.e., loaded) so that they would always indicate the number "365" in the low standard condition and "562" in the high standard condition. The respective numbers were noted on a sheet of paper with which participants were sent to the main experiment. None of the participants expressed any skepticism concerning this "random" selection of the standards.

Participants who were to receive the relevant standard were directly led to the room in which the main experiment was conducted. Here, all participants were escorted to a separate booth. They received a folder that included written instructions as well as experimental materials and were told to read instructions carefully. The instructions explained that the purpose of the study was to evaluate different methods that are used to determine the difficulty of tests that assess people's ability to concentrate. Specifically, we told them we would ask them whether they are able to solve more or less than a given number of tasks, have them estimate the number of tasks they think they can solve, and assess how many tasks they actually can solve. To make the random standard selection plausible, participants who had received

an irrelevant standard were further informed that to minimize the influence of the number used in the first question type, this number was randomly determined by rolling dice.

The next page of the instructions explained the d2 task. Participants were told that we would ask them to work on a matrix of 16×47 *d*s and *p*s, which were marked by one to four dashes, and that their task would be to circle as many *d*s marked with two dashes as they could within 5 min. Examples of the letters they should and should not circle were given. Then, participants were asked to have a close look at the d2 test that was included in their folder before answering the following questions. The first question was the comparative judgment. Participants in the high relevance condition were told that the average student processed 365 (in the low standard condition) or 562 (in the high standard condition) letters within 5 min.[8] Participants in the low relevance condition were told to complete the comparative question with the number they had rolled. All participants were then asked to indicate whether they would be able to process more or fewer letters.

The objective judgment ("What do you think, how many letters will you be able to process within 5 minutes?") followed the comparative judgment. Subsequently, participants were given 5 min to solve as many of the tasks as possible and then answered a final set of questions. The first question was the subjective judgment of their ability to concentrate. On a 9-point rating scale that ranged from -4 (*very poorly*) to $+4$ (*very well*), participants were asked to indicate how well they are able to concentrate.[9] The subsequent questions assessed how intelligent (1 = *little intelligent*,

---

[8] Although participants are unlikely to use the average student's performance to anchor the endpoint of the response scale, they are likely to align the midpoint of the scale with the given value. This yields the same kind of scale shift produced by the more extreme standards used in Studies 2 through 4.

[9] Note that the objective, behavioral, and subjective measures were always administered in the same order, so we cannot rule out for certain that the expected effects partly depend on this specific sequence. Studies 2 through 4, however, suggest that this is unlikely to be the case. For one, manipulating the judgment type between participants, Study 2 demonstrates that subjective

9 = *very intelligent*) participants judged themselves to be and how content they were with their performance (1 = *not at all content*, 9 = *very content*). Two additional questions assessed the perceived relevance of the standards. Here, participants were asked how strongly they thought their judgments had been influenced by the given numbers (1 = *not at all influenced*, 9 = *strongly influenced*) and how helpful they found the standards in making their judgments (1 = *not at all helpful*, 9 = *very helpful*).

In sum, Study 5a was based on a 2 (high vs. low standard) × 2 (relevant vs. irrelevant standard) × 3 (objective judgment vs. task performance vs. subjective judgment) mixed factorial design. Half of the participants received the high standard, and the other half received the low standard. For one half of the participants the standard was relevant, but for the other half it was irrelevant. Thus, standard and relevance were manipulated between participants. In addition, all participants received the objective judgment, the behavioral task, and the subjective judgment, so that task was manipulated within participants.

Results

Preliminary analysis. An analysis of the two questions that assessed the perceived relevance of the standards revealed that they were highly correlated ($r = .61$, $p < .001$). Consequently, we combined them into one relevance score. Participants saw the standards to be more relevant if they were introduced as representing the average student's performance ($M = 4.9$) than if they were randomly determined ($M = 3.5$), $F(1, 58) = 5.4$, $p < .02$.[10]

Objective judgments. As inspection of Table 26.5 reveals, objective judgments were assimilated to

judgments show contrast even if they are not preceded by another task. Moreover, Studies 2 through 4 demonstrate that these contrast effects also result if the subjective judgment is not preceded by a performance task. Taken together, these findings suggest that the expected effects do not depend on the specific sequence of tasks we used in Study 5.

[10] Two of the participants did not answer one of the questions assessing relevance. As a result, this analysis is based on the responses of 62 participants.

TABLE 26.5. Objective Judgments of Ability to Concentrate by Standard and Relevance (Study 5a)

Standard	Relevance	
	High	Low
High	526.56 (80.51)	429.13 (117.41)
Low	373.94 (102.95)	338.00 (134.05)

Note: $N = 16$. Estimates for number of letters to be processed are reported. Standard deviations are in parentheses.

TABLE 26.6. Task Performance for Ability to Concentrate by Standard and Relevance (Study 5a)

Standard	Relevance	
	High	Low
High	492.19 (87.09)	484.88 (110.64)
Low	442.50 (53.79)	429.81 (107.43)

Note: $N = 16$. Numbers of correctly processed letters are reported. Standard deviations are in parentheses.

the standard of comparison. Participants who received the high standard estimated the number of letters they could process to be higher ($M = 477.84$) than those who received the low standard ($M = 355.97$), $F(1, 60) = 19.47$, $p < .001$, for the main effect of Standard. Although higher estimates were given when the standard was relevant ($M = 450.25$) rather than irrelevant ($M = 383.56$), $F(1, 60) = 5.83$, $p < .02$, for the main effect of Relevance, the effect of Standard was similar at both levels of Relevance, $F(1, 60) = 1.24$, $p > .2$, for the interaction.

Task performance. As the means in Table 26.6 indicate, participants processed more letters correctly if they had received the high standard ($M = 488.53$) than if they had received the low standard ($M = 429.91$), $F(1, 60) = 6.81$, $p < .01$. This effect remained uninfluenced by the relevance of the standard, $F(1, 60) < 1$, for all effects including Relevance. Notably, similar effects are obtained if the total number of processed letters rather than the number of correctly identified letters is used as the behavioral measure.

TABLE 26.7. Subjective Judgments of Ability to Concentrate by Standard and Relevance (Study 5a)

Standard	Relevance	
	High	**Low**
High	0.25 (1.34)	1.31 (1.48)
Low	1.38 (1.63)	0.75 (1.29)

Note: N = 16. Ratings were made along a 9-point scale that ranged from −4 (*very poor*) to 4 (*very good*). Standard deviations are in parentheses.

Subjective judgments. The mean subjective judgments are provided in Table 26.7. Clearly, the effect of comparisons with the standard on the subjective judgments depended on the relevance of the standard. If the standard was introduced as representing the average student's performance, participants judged their ability to concentrate to be lower when given the high standard than when given the low standard, $t(60) = 2.22, p < .02$ (one-tailed). If the standard was randomly determined, however, this contrast effect did not hold. In this case, there is even a tendency in participants to judge their ability to concentrate to be higher when given the high standard than when given the low standard, $t(60) = 1.16, p < .13$ (one-tailed). In a 2 (high vs. low standard) × 2 (high vs. low relevance) ANOVA using the subjective judgments as the dependent variable, this pattern of means produced a significant interaction effect, $F(1, 60) = 5.55, p < .02$ (all other Fs < 1).

Combined analysis of objective judgments, task performance, and subjective judgments. The results of a combined analysis of the objective, behavioral, and subjective measure are consistent with those of the separate analyses. Specifically, we conducted a mixed model ANOVA including the z-transformed objective judgments, behavioral measure, and subjective judgments as dependent variables. In this analysis, the three-way interaction of Standard × Relevance × Measure proved to be significant, $F(2, 120) = 4.91, p < .01$.

Additional analyses. Participants' subjective judgments of their intelligence were parallel to those of their ability to concentrate. Specifically, if the standard was relevant, they judged themselves to

be less intelligent when given the high standard ($M = 5.94$) than when given the low standard ($M = 6.63$), $t(60) = 1.77, p < .04$ (one-tailed). Again, this contrast effect did not hold when the standard was irrelevant. Here, participants judged themselves to be more intelligent when given the high standard ($M = 6.44$) rather than the low standard ($M = 5.69$), $t(60) = 1.94, p < .03$ (one-tailed). The corresponding interaction effect proved to be significant in a 2 (high vs. low standard) × 2 (high vs. low relevance) ANOVA, $F(1, 60) = 6.88$, $p < .01$, for the interaction effect (all other Fs < 1).

A similar pattern of means also holds for participants' judgments of how content they were with their task performance. Once more, the contrast effect ($M = 5.44$ for the high standard; $M = 6.75$ for the low standard) only held when the standard was relevant, $t(60) = 2.64, p < .01$ (one-tailed) not when it was irrelevant ($M = 5.75$ for the high standard; $M = 5.80$ for the low standard), $t(60) = .1, ns, F(1, 60) = 3.18, p < .08$, for the interaction effect.

Study 5b

Method

Participants. We recruited 63 students of the University of Würzburg as participants and randomly assigned them to one of four experimental conditions. We offered participants an ice-cream cone as compensation.

Materials. Participants received a booklet with 90 standard nonverbal intelligence tasks of increasing difficulty as a behavioral measure. In each individual task, participants were given a series of three figures, which they were to continue with a fourth figure that logically supplemented the series. Six options were presented for each task of which only one constituted a correct answer.

Procedure. For the most part the procedure was identical to Study 5a, so we will only describe deviations from this procedure. Participants were asked to participate in a study evaluating different measures of intelligence. About half of the participants

TABLE 26.8. Objective Judgments, Task Performance (Number of Tasks Solved Correctly), and Subjective Judgments for Intelligence by Standard and Relevance (Study 5b)

Standard	Relevant standard			Irrelevant standard		
	Objective	Behavioral	Subjective	Objective	Behavioral	Subjective
High	1.07 (0.56)	0.10 (1.31)	−0.28 (1.33)	0.10 (1.02)	0.25 (1.0)	0.36 (0.75)
Low	−0.83 (0.48)	−0.31 (0.94)	0.07 (0.79)	−0.33 (0.69)	−0.03 (0.60)	−0.18 (1.0)

Note: $N = 16$ (high relevant and irrelevant standard), 17 (low relevant standard), and 14 (low irrelevant standard). z-transformed values are reported. Standard deviations are in parentheses.

ostensibly determined the standards by throwing dice, whereas the other half were told that the standards represented the average students' performance. The high standard was set at one standard deviation above the mean performance of a different set of pretest participants ($N = 20$). The low standard was set at one standard deviation below this value. Specifically, about half of the participants received the low standard of 23 tasks, and the other half received the high standard of 56 tasks.

In the instructions, participants were informed that the purpose of this study was to evaluate different tasks that are typically used to assess intelligence. To do so, they were told we would give them one task that is often used to assess intelligence and would ask them a number of questions about it. They were then instructed to inspect the test that was included in their folder before answering the questions concerning this test. In the questionnaire, participants were first asked to indicate whether, in 10 min, they would be able to solve more or fewer tasks than the respective standard value. They were then asked to make an objective judgment about the number of tasks they would be able to solve, were given 10 min to solve as many tasks as possible, and then answered a final set of questions. Among those was the critical subjective judgment in which they were asked to indicate how intelligent they took themselves to be on a 9-point rating scale that ranged from 1 (*not at all intelligent*) to 9 (*very intelligent*). Moreover, the same questions assessing the perceived relevance of the standard as in Study 5a were included. After completing the questionnaire, participants were thanked, debriefed, and dismissed.

In sum, Study 5b was based on the same 2 (high vs. low standard) × 2 (relevant vs. irrelevant standard) × 3 (objective judgment vs. behavioral task vs. subjective judgment) mixed factorial design as was used in Study 5a.

Results

Preliminary analysis. As in Study 5a, responses to the questions that assessed the perceived relevance of the standards were highly correlated ($r = .58$, $p < .001$), so that they were combined into one single score. Participants judged the standards to be less relevant if they were randomly selected ($M = 3.57$) rather than introduced as representing the average student's performance ($M = 4.71$), $F(1, 59) = 4.74$, $p < .03$, for the main effect of Relevance.[11]

Combined analysis of objective judgments, task performance, and subjective judgments. To examine the effects on the objective judgment, the task performance, and the subjective judgment, the respective responses were z transformed and analyzed in a mixed model ANOVA, which used these z values as dependent measures. As inspection of Table 26.8 reveals, a similar pattern as in Study 5a was obtained. In particular, objective judgments were assimilated to relevant as well as irrelevant standards. Similarly, for relevant and irrelevant standards alike, task performance was better for the high than for the low standard. That

---

[11] One participant did not answer both of the critical questions and was excluded from the analysis. Consequently, the reported analysis is based on the answers of 62 participants.

is, no matter whether the standard was introduced as a random number or as representing the average student's performance, participants expected to solve more tasks, and actually solved more tasks correctly, when they had received the high rather than the low standard. In contrast, the subjective judgments were clearly influenced by the relevance of the standards. For relevant standards, participants judged themselves to be less intelligent after comparing with a high rather than a low standard. For irrelevant standards, however, they judged themselves to be more intelligent after comparing with a high rather than a low standard. This pattern produced a significant three-way interaction of Standard × Relevance × Task, $F(2, 118) = 9.23, p < .001$.

Discussion

Taken together, the results of Studies 5a and 5b clearly support our reasoning. Consistent with the previous studies, they indicate that the very same comparison can lead to assimilation and contrast in subsequent self-evaluations. Specifically, comparing their prospective task performance with a given standard led participants to assimilate their objective estimates for their performance to this standard. Thus, participants expected to concentrate better or perform more intelligently if a high standard rather than a low standard was given. Moreover, their actual performance was consistent with this expectation. That is, participants did in fact concentrate better or perform more intelligently after comparing themselves with the high rather than the low standard. Despite their better performance, however, subjective judgments were contrasted away from the standard. Here, participants judged their ability as worse after having compared with the high standard.

Importantly, this contrast effect only holds if the standard was relevant, because it was introduced as representing the average performance of participants' peers. If the standard was irrelevant because it was randomly determined, however, subjective judgments were not contrasted away from the standard, but also tended to show assimilation.[12] This reversal of the standard contrast effect for subjective judgments was quite consistent with our conceptualization. To the extent that the mechanism that is responsible for contrast (i.e., reference-point use) is not operating, subjective judgments should also reflect the implications of easily accessible self-knowledge and thus show assimilation (cf. Higgins *et al.*, 1977). In fact, this assimilative influence was likely to operate for relevant as well as irrelevant standards. For relevant standards, however, it appears to be superimposed by the apparently stronger contrast effect that results from reference-point use.

These findings hold several important implications. For one, once again they demonstrate that assimilation and contrast can both be consequences of the same self-evaluative comparison. Moreover, they show that the assimilative consequences are not limited to self-evaluative judgments. Rather, the behavioral expectancies that were apparent in the objective judgments translated into differences in task performance that were consistent with these expectancies (for a similar finding see, Sherman, Skov, Hervitz, & Stock, 1981).[13] Most important, however, the current results lend further credence to our conceptualization of the informational and judgmental consequences of self-evaluative comparisons. Specifically, the fact that—just as other manifestations of selective accessibility (e.g., Tversky & Kahneman, 1974)—the assimilative judgmental consequences occurred for relevant as well as irrelevant standards suggests that they are

---

[12] Notably, the fact that irrelevant standards did not produce a contrast effect cannot be explained by assuming that participants simply ignored irrelevant standards. The fact that these standards influenced objective judgments as well as task performance clearly argues against this possibility.

[13] Several mechanisms may be responsible for these behavioral effects. For one, comparing with a high standard may have

motivated participants to exert more effort and thus perform better. Alternatively, these effects may constitute an example of behavioral priming (Bargh, Chen, & Burrows, 1996) and may be directly driven by the knowledge that was rendered accessible during the comparison. The present research was not designed to distinguish between both possibilities.

indeed caused by the use of standard-consistent self-knowledge that was rendered easily accessible during the comparison. Moreover, the fact that—just as other manifestations of reference-point use (e.g., Brown, 1953)—the contrastive judgmental consequences only occurred for relevant standards suggests that these effects are in fact produced by the use of the suggested reference point to anchor the subjective response scale.

General Discussion

In the present set of studies, we examined the informational and judgmental consequences of self-evaluative comparisons. We hypothesized that comparing oneself to a given objective or social standard has two distinct informational consequences. First, it selectively increases the accessibility of standard-consistent knowledge about the self. Using this knowledge for subsequent self-evaluations is likely to produce an assimilation effect. Second, it provides a reference point against which the implications of this knowledge can be evaluated. Using this reference point is likely to produce a contrast effect on subsequent self-evaluations. Thus, the judgmental effects produced by the two informational consequences go in opposite directions. Which of these opposing consequences dominates a given self-evaluative judgment depends on how relevant their informational bases are for the respective judgment.

The present data provide substantial support for this conceptualization. Studies 1 and 2 demonstrated that after a self-evaluative comparison with either a social (Study 1) or an objective standard (Study 2), standard-consistent knowledge about the self is more accessible than standard-inconsistent knowledge. Furthermore, Study 2 provided some initial evidence for the existence of the second informational consequence of self-evaluative comparisons, namely the suggestion of an evaluative reference point. Studies 3 and 4 demonstrated that the judgmental effects of both informational consequences go in opposite directions. Selective accessibility produces an assimilation effect, whereas reference-point use leads to contrast. The

fact that these opposing effects appear on those judgment types that are typically responsive to selective accessibility and reference-point use, respectively, suggests that they are indeed produced by these two mechanisms. This assumption is further supported by the fact that—as is true for reference-point and selective accessibility effects in other research paradigms—contrast only occurs if the standard is relevant for the given judgment, whereas assimilation results for relevant as well as irrelevant standards.

The present findings hold several novel implications concerning the judgmental, behavioral and affective consequences of self-evaluative comparisons. First, assimilation and contrast do not appear to be mutually exclusive consequences of self-evaluative comparisons. Unlike previous conceptualizations (e.g., Brown et al., 1992; Buunk et al., 1990; Tesser, 1988), the current framework acknowledges that the very same comparison can lead to both assimilation and contrast. Which of these effects occurs depends on how relevant the respective informational bases are for the self-evaluative judgment at hand. This suggests an important determinant of the direction of influence a comparison has. In addition to such classic factors as self-esteem (see, e.g., Buunk et al., 1990; Gibbons & Gerrard, 1989), psychological closeness (see, e.g., Brewer & Weber, 1994; Brown et al., 1992; Pelham & Wachsmuth, 1995; Tesser, Millar, & Moore, 1988) and the relevance of the comparison dimension (see, e.g., Lockwood & Kunda, 1997; Tesser, 1988), the type of the self-evaluative judgment (e.g., objective vs. subjective) appears to play a crucial role.

Furthermore, the present research suggests that the effects of self-evaluative comparisons are not limited to self-evaluative judgments. Consistent with earlier findings (e.g., Seta, 1982; Taylor et al., 1996), the current results demonstrate that comparisons may also have strong behavioral effects. Finally, our conceptualization affords a novel perspective on the affective consequences of comparing oneself with a given standard. Recent conceptualizations of the affective consequences of social comparisons (e.g., Buunk et al., 1990) typically assume that affect is determined by the target's relative standing on the comparison dimension. Specifically,

> learning that another is better off than yourself provides at least two pieces of information: (a) that you are not as well off as everyone and (b) that it is possible for you to be better than you are at present. (Buunk *et al.*, 1990, p. 1239)

From this perspective, the affective consequences of a comparison depend on which piece of information judges focus. Specifically, a person may feel worse if he or she focuses on the fact that the comparison standard is better off, and this person may feel better if he or she focuses on the fact that the superior state of the standard may be obtained. Consistent with this assumption, researchers have demonstrated that people who are able to focus on the possibility of self-improvement (e.g., because of their high self-esteem) are more likely to experience positive affect after an upward comparison (see, e.g., Buunk *et al.*, 1990).

From a selective accessibility perspective, however, there appears to be an additional mechanism that contributes to the affective consequences of social comparison. Specifically, independent of the implications a specific comparison has for one's relative standing on the comparison dimension, self-related knowledge that is generated to make this comparison has its own affective qualities. For example, thinking about one's athletic achievements when comparing oneself with a high standard is likely to elicit more positive affect than thinking about one's failures when comparing with a low standard (e.g., Bill Clinton in our studies). Consequently, more positive affect is likely to be elicited by an upward than by a downward comparison. The affective consequences of the implications concerning one's relative standing on the judgmental dimension, however, are likely to go in the opposite direction. Specifically, realizing that one is less athletic than, for example, Nicki Lauda produces more negative affect than realizing that one is better than, for example, Bill Clinton. This suggests that generating standard-consistent knowledge about the self and assessing one's position along the judgmental dimension relative to the standard may yield opposing affective consequences.

Conclusion

We started out with a simple question—*Who am I?*—and proposed that to answer this fundamental question people often compare their attributes and abilities with objective and social standards (Festinger, 1954). The present work has demonstrated that doing so, in fact, provides valuable self-evaluative information. However, our findings also suggest that the implications of this information may not always be clear-cut. Rather than providing one simple answer, the comparison process affords different pieces of information with differing, and even contradicting, implications. In light of the fact that generations of psychologists and philosophers have contemplated the roots of self-knowledge and identity, however, it seems hardly surprising that simple answers are difficult to find.

REFERENCES

Atkinson, J. W. (1957). Motivational determinants of risk-taking behavior. *Psychological Review, 64,* 359–372.

Bargh, J. A., & Chartrand, T. L. (in press). A practical guide to priming and automaticity research. In H. Reis & C. Judd (Eds.), *Handbook of research methods in social psychology.* New York: Cambridge University Press.

Bargh, J. A., Chen, M., & Burrows, L. (1996). Automaticity of social behavior: Direct effects of trait construct and stereotype activation on action. *Journal of Personality and Social Psychology, 71,* 230–244.

Baumeister, R. F. (1998). The self. In D. T. Gilbert, S. T. Fiske, & G. Lindzey (Eds.), *The handbook of social psychology* (Vol. 1, pp. 680–740). New York: McGraw-Hill.

Biernat, M., & Manis, M. (1994). Shifting standards and stereotype-based judgments. *Journal of Personality and Social Psychology, 66,* 5–20.

Biernat, M., Manis, M., & Kobrynowicz, D. (1997). Simultaneous assimilation and contrast effects in judgments of self and others. *Journal of Personality and Social Psychology, 73,* 254–269.

Biernat, M., Manis, M., & Nelson, T. E. (1991). Stereotypes and standards of judgment. *Journal of Personality and Social Psychology, 60,* 485–499.

Brewer, M. B., & Weber, J. G. (1994). Self-evaluation effects of interpersonal versus intergroup social comparison. *Journal of Personality and Social Psychology, 66,* 268–275.

Brickenkamp, R. (1962). *Test d2: Aufmerksamkeits-Belastungs-Test* [Test d2: Attention-Load Test]. Göttingen, Germany: Hogrefe.

Brown, D. R. (1953). Stimulus similarity and the anchoring of subjective scales. *American Journal of Psychology, 66,* 199–214.

Brown, J. D., Novick, N. J., Lord, K. A., & Richards, J. M. (1992). When Gulliver travels: Social context, psychological closeness, and self-appraisals. *Journal of Personality and Social Psychology, 62,* 717–727.

Buunk, B. P., Collins, R. L., Taylor, S. E., VanYperen, N. W., & Dakof, G. A. (1990). The affective consequences of social comparison: Either direction has its ups and downs. *Journal of Personality and Social Psychology, 59,* 1238–1249.

Cash, T. F., Cash, D., & Butters, J. W. (1983). "Mirror, mirror, on the wall…?': Contrast effects and self-evaluations of physical attractiveness. *Personality and Social Psychology Bulletin, 9,* 351–358.

Cervone, D., & Peake, P. K. (1986). Anchoring, efficacy, and action: The influence of judgmental heuristics on self-efficacy judgments and behavior. *Journal of Personality and Social Psychology, 50,* 492–501.

Dijksterhuis, A., Spears, R., Postmes, T., Stapel, D. A., Koomen, W., van Knippenberg, A., & Scheepers, D. (1998). Seeing one thing and doing another: Contrast effects in automatic behavior. *Journal of Personality and Social Psychology, 75,* 862–871.

Eiser, J. R. (1990). *Social judgment.* Milton Keynes, United Kingdom: Open University.

Fazio, R. H. (1990). A practical guide to the use of response latency in social psychological research. In C. Hendrick & M. S. Clark (Eds.), *Research methods in personality and social psychology* (pp. 74–97). Newbury Park, CA: Sage.

Festinger, L. (1954). A theory of social comparison processes. *Human Relations, 7,* 117–140.

Gibbons, F. X., & Gerrard, M. (1989). Effects of upward and downward social comparison on mood states. *Journal of Social and Clinical Psychology, 8,* 14–31.

Helson, H. (1964). *Adaptation level theory: An experimental and systematic, approach to behavior.* New York: Harper.

Herr, P. M. (1986). Consequences of priming: Judgment and behavior. *Journal of Personality and Social Psychology, 51,* 1106–1115.

Higgins, E. T. (1987). Self-discrepancy: A theory relating self and affect. *Psychological Review, 94,* 319–340.

Higgins, E. T. (1989). Self-discrepancy theory: What patterns of self-beliefs cause people to suffer? In L. Berkowitz (Ed.), *Advances in experimental social psychology* (Vol. 22, pp. 93–136). San Diego, CA: Academic Press.

Higgins, E. T. (1996). Knowledge activation: Accessibility, applicability, and salience. In E. T. Higgins & A. W. Kruglanski (Eds.), *Social psychology: Handbook of basic principles* (pp. 133–168). New York: Guilford Press.

Higgins, E. T., Rholes, W. S., & Jones. C. R. (1977). Category accessibility and impression formation. *Journal of Experimental Social Psychology, 13,* 141–154.

Higgins, E. T., Strauman, T., & Klein, R. (1986). Standards and the process of self-evaluation: Multiple affects from multiple stages. In R. M. Sorrentino & E. T. Higgins (Eds.), *Handbook of motivation and cognition: Foundations of social behavior.* New York: Guilford Press.

Hume, D. (1890). *A treatise of human nature.* Cleveland, OH: Langmans, Green, & Co. (Original work published 1739)

Huttenlocher, J., & Higgins, E. T. (1971). Adjectives, comparatives, and syllogisms. *Psychological Review, 78,* 487–504.

James, W. (1892). *Psychology.* New York: Henry Holt.

Kant, I. (1956). *Kritik der reinen vernunft* [Critique of pure reason]. Frankfurt, Germany: Verlag. (Original work published 1787)

Lewin, K. (1951). *Field theory in social science.* New York: Harper.

Lockwood, P., & Kunda, Z. (1997). Superstars and me: Predicting the impact of role models on the self. *Journal of Personality and Social Psychology, 73,* 91–103.

Manis, M., Biernat, M., & Nelson, T. F. (1991). Comparison and expectancy processes in human judgment. *Journal of Personality and Social Psychology, 61,* 203–211.

Manis, M., & Paskewitz, J. R. (1984a), Judging psychopathology: Expectancy and contrast. *Journal of Experimental Social Psychology, 20,* 363–381.

Manis, M., & Paskewitz, J. R. (1984b). Specificity in contrast effects: Judgments of psychopathology. *Journal of Experimental Social Psychology, 20,* 217–230.

Miller, D. T., & Prentice, D. A. (1996). The construction of social norms and standards. In E. T. Higgins & A. W. Kruglanski (Eds.), *Social psychology: Handbook of basic principles* (pp. 133–168). New York: Guilford Press.

Mussweiler, T. (in press). Focus of comparison as a determinant of assimilation versus contrast in social comparison. *Personality and Social Psychology Bulletin.*

Mussweiler, T., & Strack, F. (1999a). Hypothesis-consistent testing and semantic priming in the anchoring paradigm: A selective accessibility model. *Journal of Experimental Social Psychology, 35,* 136–164.

Mussweiler, T., & Strack, F. (1999b). Comparing is believing: A selective accessibility model of judgmental anchoring. In W. Stroebe & M. Hewstone (Eds.), *European review of social psychology* (Vol. 10, pp. 135–167). Chichester, England: Wiley.

Mussweiler, T., & Strack, F. (2000). The use of category and exemplar knowledge in the solution of anchoring tasks. *Journal of Personality and Social Psychology, 78,* 1038–1052.

Mussweiler, T., & Strack, F. (in press-a). Numeric judgment under uncertainty: The role of knowledge in anchoring. *Journal of Experimental Social Psychology.*

Mussweiler, T., & Strack, F. (in press-b). Consequences of social comparison: Selective accessibility, assimilation, and contrast. In J. Suls & L. Wheeler (Eds.), *Handbook of social comparison: Theory and research.* New York: Plenum.

Neely, J. H. (1991). Semantic priming effects in visual word recognition: A selective review of current findings and theories. In D. Besner & G. W. Humphreys (Eds.), *Basic processes in reading* (pp. 264–337). Hillsdale, NJ: Erlbaum.

Ostrom, T. M., & Upshaw, H. S. (1968). Psychological perspectives and attitude change. In A. G. Greenwald, T. C. Brock, & T. M. Ostrom (Eds.), *Psychological foundations of attitudes* (pp. 217–242). New York: Academic Press.

Parducci, A. (1965). Category judgment: A range–frequency model. *Psychological Review, 72,* 407–418.

Pelham, B. W., & Wachsmuth, J. O. (1995). The waxing and waning of the social self: Assimilation and contrast in social comparison. *Journal of Personality and Social Psychology, 69,* 825–838.

Seta, J. J. (1982). The impact of comparison processes on coactors' task performance. *Journal of Personality and Social Psychology, 42,* 281–291.

Sherif, M., & Hovland, C. I. (1953). Judgmental phenomena and scales of attitude measurement: Placement of items with individual choice of number of categories. *Journal of Abnormal and Social Psychology, 48,* 135–141.

Sherman, S. J., Skov, R. B., Hervitz, E. F., & Stock, C. B. (1981). The effects of explaining hypothetical future events: From possibility to probability to actuality and beyond. *Journal of Experimental Social Psychology, 17,* 142–158.

Stapel, D., Koomen, W., & van der Pligt, J. (1997). Categories of category accessibility: The impact of trait versus exemplar priming on person judgments. *Journal of Experimental Social Psychology, 33,* 44–76.

Strack, F. (1992). The different routes to social judgments: Experiential versus informational strategies. In L. L. Martin & A. Tesser (Eds.), *The construction of social judgment* (pp. 249–275). Hillsdale, NJ: Erlbaum.

Strack, F., & Mussweiler, T. (1997). Explaining the enigmatic anchoring effect: Mechanisms of selective accessibility. *Journal of Personality and Social Psychology, 73,* 437–446.

Taylor, S. E., Wayment, H. A., & Carrillo, M. (1996). Social comparison, self-regulation, and motivation. In R. M. Sorrentino & E. T. Higgins (Eds.), *Handbook of motivation and cognition* (pp. 3–27). New York: Guilford Press.

Tesser, A. (1988). Toward a self-evaluation maintenance model of social behavior. In L. Berkowitz (Ed.), *Advances in experimental social psychology* (Vol. 20, pp. 181–227). New York: Academic Press.

Tesser, A., Millar, M., & Moore, J. (1988). Some affective consequences of social comparison and reflection processes: The pain and pleasure of being close. *Journal of Personality and Social Psychology, 54,* 49–61.

Tversky, A., & Kahneman, D. (1974, September 27). Judgment under uncertainty: Heuristics and biases. *Science, 185,* 1124–1130.

Wyer, R. S., & Srull, T. K. (1989). *Memory and cognition in its social context.* Hillsdale, NJ: Erlbaum.

Received April 27, 1999
Revision received November 4, 1999
Accepted November 29, 1999 ■

How to Read a Journal Article in Social Psychology

Christian H. Jordan and Mark P. Zanna

When approaching a journal article for the first time, and often on subsequent occasions, most people try to digest it as they would any piece of prose. They start at the beginning and read word for word, until eventually they arrive at the end, perhaps a little bewildered, but with a vague sense of relief. This is not an altogether terrible strategy; journal articles do have a logical structure that lends itself to this sort of reading. There are, however, more efficient approaches—approaches that enable you, a student of social psychology, to cut through peripheral details, avoid sophisticated statistics with which you may not be familiar, and focus on the central ideas in an article. Arming yourself with a little foreknowledge of what is contained in journal articles, as well as some practical advice on how to read them, should help you read journal articles more effectively. If this sounds tempting, read on.

Journal articles offer a window into the inner workings of social psychology. They document how social psychologists formulate hypotheses, design empirical studies, analyze the observations they collect, and interpret their results. Journal articles also serve an invaluable archival function: They contain the full store of common and cumulative knowledge of social psychology. Having documentation of past research allows researchers to build on past

findings and advance our understanding of social behavior, without pursuing avenues of investigation that have already been explored. Perhaps most importantly, a research study is never complete until its results have been shared with others, colleagues and students alike. Journal articles are a primary means of communicating research findings. As such, they can be genuinely exciting and interesting to read.

That last claim may have caught you off guard. For beginning readers, journal articles may seem anything but interesting and exciting. They may, on the contrary, appear daunting and esoteric, laden with jargon and obscured by menacing statistics. Recognizing this fact, we hope to arm you, through this paper, with the basic information you will need to read journal articles with a greater sense of comfort and perspective.

Social psychologists study many fascinating topics, ranging from prejudice and discrimination, to culture, persuasion, liking and love, conformity and obedience, aggression, and the self. In our daily lives, these are issues we often struggle to understand. Social psychologists present systematic observations of, as well as a wealth of ideas about, such issues in journal articles. It would be a shame if the fascination and intrigue of these topics were lost in their translation into journal publications. We don't think they are, and by the end of this paper, hopefully you won't either.

Journal articles come in a variety of forms, including research reports, review articles, and theoretical articles. Put briefly, a *research report* is a formal presentation of an original research study, or series of studies. A *review article* is an evaluative survey of previously published work, usually organized by a guiding theory or point of view. The author of a review article summarizes previous investigations of a circumscribed problem, comments on what progress has been made toward its resolution, and suggests areas of the problem that require further study. A *theoretical article* also evaluates past research, but focuses on the development of theories used to explain empirical findings. Here, the author may present a new theory to explain a set of findings, or may compare and contrast a set of competing theories, suggesting why one theory might be the superior one.

This paper focuses primarily on how to read research reports, for several reasons. First, the bulk of published literature in social psychology consists of research reports. Second, the summaries presented in review articles, and the ideas set forth in theoretical articles, are built on findings presented in research reports. To get a deep understanding of how research is done in social psychology, fluency in reading original research reports is essential. Moreover, theoretical articles frequently report new studies that pit one theory against another, or test a novel prediction derived from a new theory. In order to appraise the validity of such theoretical contentions, a grounded understanding of basic findings is invaluable. Finally, most research reports are written in a standard format that is likely unfamiliar to new readers. The format of review and theoretical articles is less standardized, and more like that of textbooks and other scholarly writings, with which most readers are familiar. This is not to suggest that such articles are easier to read and comprehend than research reports; they can indeed be quite challenging. It is simply the case that, because more rules apply to the writing of research reports, more guidelines can be offered on how to read them.

The Anatomy of Research Reports

Most research reports in social psychology, and in psychology in general, are written in a standard format prescribed by the American Psychological Association (1994). This is a great boon to both readers and writers. It allows writers to present their ideas and findings in a clear, systematic manner. Consequently, as a reader, once you understand this format, you will not be on completely foreign ground when you approach a new research report—regardless of its specific content. You will know where in the paper particular information is found, making it easier to locate. No matter what your reasons for reading a research report, a firm understanding of the format in which they are written will ease your task. We discuss the format of research reports next, with some practical suggestions on how to read them. Later, we discuss how this format reflects the process of scientific investigation, illustrating how research reports have a coherent narrative structure.

Title and Abstract

Though you can't judge a book by its cover, you can learn a lot about a research report simply by reading its title. The title presents a concise statement of the theoretical issues investigated, and/or the variables that were studied. For example, the following title was taken almost at random from a prestigious journal in social psychology: "Sad and guilty? Affective influences on the explanation of conflict in close relationships" (Forgas, 1994, p. 56). Just by reading the title, it can be inferred that the study investigated how emotional states change the way people explain conflict in close relationships. It also suggests that when feeling sad, people accept more personal blame for such conflicts (i.e., feel more guilty).

The abstract is also an invaluable source of information. It is a brief synopsis of the study, and packs a lot of information into 150 words or less. The abstract contains information about the problem that was investigated, how it was investigated, and the major findings of the study, and hints at the theoretical and practical implications of the findings. Thus, the abstract is a useful summary of the research that provides the gist of the investigation. Reading this outline first can be very helpful, because it tells you where the report is going, and gives you a useful framework for organizing information contained in the article.

The title and abstract of a research report are like a movie preview. A movie preview highlights the important aspects of a movie's plot, and provides just enough information for one to decide whether to watch the whole movie. Just so with titles and abstracts; they highlight the key features of a research report to allow you to decide if you want to read the whole paper. And just as with movie previews, they do not give the whole story. Reading just the title and abstract is never enough to fully understand a research report.

Introduction

A research report has four main sections: introduction, method, results, and discussion. Though it is not explicitly labeled, the introduction begins the main body of a research report. Here, the researchers set the stage for the study. They present the problem under investigation, and state why it was important to study. By providing a brief review of past research and theory relevant to the central issue of investigation, the researchers place the study in an historical context and suggest how the study advances knowledge of the problem. Beginning with broad theoretical and practical considerations, the researchers delineate the rationale that led them to the specific set of hypotheses tested in the study. They also describe how they decided on their research strategy (e.g., why they chose an experiment or a correlational study).

The introduction generally begins with a broad consideration of the problem investigated. Here, the researchers want to illustrate that the problem they studied is a real problem about which people should care. If the researchers are studying prejudice, they may cite statistics that suggest discrimination is prevalent, or describe specific cases of discrimination. Such information helps illustrate why the research is both practically and theoretically meaningful, and why you should bother reading

about it. Such discussions are often quite interesting and useful. They can help you decide for yourself if the research has merit. But they may not be essential for understanding the study at hand. Read the introduction carefully, but choose judiciously what to focus on and remember. To understand a study, what you really need to understand is what the researchers' hypotheses were, and how they were derived from theory, informal observation, or intuition. Other background information may be intriguing, but may not be critical to understand what the researchers did and why they did it.

While reading the introduction, try answering these questions: What problem was studied, and why? How does this study relate to, and go beyond, past investigations of the problem? How did the researchers derive their hypotheses? What questions do the researchers hope to answer with this study?

Method

In the method section, the researchers translate their hypotheses into a set of specific, testable questions. Here, the researchers introduce the main characters of the study—the subjects or participants—describing their characteristics (gender, age, etc.) and how many of them were involved. Then, they describe the materials (or apparatus), such as any questionnaires or special equipment, used in the study. Finally, they describe chronologically the procedures of the study; that is, how the study was conducted. Often, an overview of the research design will begin the method section. This overview provides a broad outline of the design, alerting you to what you should attend to.

The method is presented in great detail so that other researchers can recreate the study to confirm (or question) its results. This degree of detail is normally not necessary to understand a study, so don't get bogged down trying to memorize the particulars of the procedures. Focus on how the independent variables were manipulated (or measured) and how the dependent variables were measured.

Measuring variables adequately is not always an easy matter. Many of the variables psychologists are interested in cannot be directly observed, so they must be inferred from participants' behavior. Happiness, for example, cannot be directly observed. Thus, researchers interested in how being happy influences people's judgments must infer happiness (or its absence) from their behavior—perhaps by asking people how happy they are, and judging their degree of happiness from their responses; perhaps by studying people's facial expressions for signs of happiness, such as smiling. Think about the measures researchers use while reading the method section. Do they adequately reflect or capture the concepts they are meant to measure? If a measure seems odd, consider carefully how the researchers justify its use.

Oftentimes in social psychology, getting there is half the fun. In other words, how a result is obtained can be just as interesting as the result itself. Social psychologists often strive to have participants behave in a natural, spontaneous manner, while controlling enough of their environment to pinpoint the causes of their behavior. Sometimes, the major contribution of a research report is its presentation of a novel method of investigation. When this is the case, the method will be discussed in some detail in the introduction.

Participants in social psychology studies are intelligent and inquisitive people who are responsive to what happens around them. Because of this, they are not always initially told the true purpose of a study. If they were told, they might not act naturally. Thus, researchers frequently need to be creative, presenting a credible rationale for complying with procedures, without revealing the study's purpose. This rationale is known as a *cover story*, and is often an elaborate scenario. While reading the method section, try putting yourself in the shoes of a participant in the study, and ask yourself if the instructions given to participants seem sensible, realistic, and engaging. Imagining what it was like to be in the study will also help you remember the study's procedure, and aid you in interpreting the study's results.

While reading the method section, try answering these questions: How were the hypotheses translated into testable questions? How were the variables of interest manipulated and/or measured?

Did the measures used adequately reflect the variables of interest? For example, is self-reported income an adequate measure of social class? Why or why not?

Results

The results section describes how the observations collected were analyzed to determine whether the original hypotheses were supported. Here, the data (observations of behavior) are described, and statistical tests are presented. Because of this, the results section is often intimidating to readers who have little or no training in statistics. Wading through complex and unfamiliar statistical analyses is understandably confusing and frustrating. As a result, many students are tempted to skip over reading this section. We advise you not to do so. Empirical findings are the foundation of any science and results sections are where such findings are presented.

Take heart. Even the most prestigious researchers were once in your shoes and sympathize with you. Though space in psychology journals is limited, researchers try to strike a balance between the need to be clear and the need to be brief in describing their results. In an influential paper on how to write good research reports, Bem (1987) offered this advice to researchers:

> No matter how technical or abstruse your article is in its particulars, intelligent non-psychologists with no expertise in statistics or experimental design should be able to comprehend the broad outlines of what you did and why. They should understand in general terms what was learned. (p. 74)

Generally speaking, social psychologists try to practice this advice.

Most statistical analyses presented in research reports test specific hypotheses. Often, each analysis presented is preceded by a reminder of the hypothesis it is meant to test. After an analysis is presented, researchers usually provide a narrative description of the result in plain English. When the hypothesis tested by a statistical analysis is not explicitly stated, you can usually determine the hypothesis that was tested by reading this narrative description of the result, and referring back to the introduction to locate an hypothesis that corresponds to that result. After even the most complex statistical analysis, there will be a written description of what the result means conceptually. Turn your attention to these descriptions. Focus on the conceptual meaning of research findings, not on the mechanics of how they were obtained (unless you're comfortable with statistics).

Aside from statistical tests and narrative descriptions of results, results sections also frequently contain tables and graphs. These are efficient summaries of data. Even if you are not familiar with statistics, look closely at tables and graphs, and pay attention to the means or correlations presented in them. Researchers always include written descriptions of the pertinent aspects of tables and graphs. While reading these descriptions, check the tables and graphs to make sure what the researchers say accurately reflects their data. If they say there was a difference between two groups on a particular dependent measure, look at the means in the table that correspond to those two groups, and see if the means do differ as described. Occasionally, results seem to become stronger in their narrative description than an examination of the data would warrant.

Statistics *can* be misused. When they are, results are difficult to interpret. Having said this, a lack of statistical knowledge should not make you overly cautious while reading results sections. Though not a perfect antidote, journal articles undergo extensive review by professional researchers before publication. Thus, most misapplications of statistics are caught and corrected before an article is published. So, if you are unfamiliar with statistics, you can be reasonably confident that findings are accurately reported.

While reading the results section, try answering these questions: Did the researchers provide evidence that any independent variable manipulations were effective? For example, if testing for behavioral differences between happy and sad participants, did the researchers demonstrate that one group was in fact happier than the other? What were the major findings of the study? Were the researchers' original hypotheses supported by their observations? If not, look in the discussion section for how the researchers explain the findings that were obtained.

Discussion

The discussion section frequently opens with a summary of what the study found, and an evaluation of whether the findings supported the original hypotheses. Here, the researchers evaluate the theoretical and practical implications of their results. This can be particularly interesting when the results did not work out exactly as the researchers anticipated. When such is the case, consider the researchers' explanations carefully, and see if they seem plausible to you. Often, researchers will also report any aspects of their study that limit their interpretation of its results, and suggest further research that could overcome these limitations to provide a better understanding of the problem under investigation.

Some readers find it useful to read the first few paragraphs of the discussion section before reading any other part of a research report. Like the abstract, these few paragraphs usually contain all of the main ideas of a research report: What the hypotheses were, the major findings and whether they supported the original hypotheses, and how the findings relate to past research and theory. Having this information before reading a research report can guide your reading, allowing you to focus on the specific details you need to complete your understanding of a study. The description of the results, for example, will alert you to the major variables that were studied. If they are unfamiliar to you, you can pay special attention to how they are defined in the introduction, and how they are operationalized in the method section.

After you have finished reading an article, it can also be helpful to reread the first few paragraphs of the discussion and the abstract. As noted, these two passages present highly distilled summaries of the major ideas in a research report. Just as they can help guide your reading of a report, they can also help you consolidate your understanding of a report once you have finished reading it. They provide a check on whether you have understood the main points of a report, and offer a succinct digest of the research in the authors' own words.

While reading the discussion section, try answering these questions: What conclusions can be drawn from the study? What new information does the study provide about the problem under investigation? Does the study help resolve the problem? What are the practical and theoretical implications of the study's findings? Did the results contradict past research findings? If so, how do the researchers explain this discrepancy?

Some Notes on Reports of Multiple Studies

Up to this point, we have implicitly assumed that a research report describes just one study. It is also quite common, however, for a research report to describe a series of studies of the same problem in a single article. When such is the case, each study reported will have the same basic structure (introduction, method, results, and discussion sections) that we have outlined, with the notable exception that sometimes the results and discussion section for each study are combined. Combined "results and discussion" sections contain the same information that separate results and discussion sections normally contain. Sometimes, the authors present all their results first, and only then discuss the implications of these results, just as they would in separate results and discussion sections. Other times, however, the authors alternate between describing results and discussing their implications, as each result is presented. In either case, you should be on the lookout for the same information, as outlined above in our consideration of separate results and discussion sections.

Reports including multiple studies also differ from single study reports in that they include more general introduction and discussion sections. The general introduction, which begins the main body of a research report, is similar in essence to the introduction of a single study report. In both cases, the researchers describe the problem investigated and its practical and theoretical significance.

They also demonstrate how they derived their hypotheses, and explain how their research relates to past investigations of the problem. In contrast, the separate introductions to each individual study in reports of multiple studies are usually quite brief, and focus more specifically on the logic and rationale of each particular study presented. Such introductions generally describe the methods used in the particular study, outlining how they answer questions that have not been adequately addressed by past research, including studies reported earlier in the same article.

General discussion sections parallel discussions of single studies, except on a somewhat grander scale. They present all of the information contained in discussions of the single studies, but consider the implications of all the studies presented together. A general discussion section brings the main ideas of a research program into bold relief. It typically begins with a concise summary of a research program's main findings, their relation to the original hypotheses, and their practical and theoretical implications. Thus, the summaries that begin general discussion sections are counterparts of the summaries that begin discussion sections of single study reports. Each presents a digest of the research presented in an article that can serve as both an organizing framework (when read first), and as a check on how well you have understood the main points of an article (when read last).

Research Reporting as Story Telling

A research report tells the story of how a researcher or group of researchers investigated a specific problem. Thus, a research report has a linear, narrative structure with a beginning, middle, and end. In his paper on writing research reports, Bem noted that a research report:

> . . . is shaped like an hourglass. It begins with broad general statements, progressively narrows down to the specifics of [the] study, and then broadens out again to more general considerations. (1987, p. 175)

This format roughly mirrors the process of scientific investigation, wherein researchers do the following: (1) start with a broad idea from which they formulate a narrower set of hypotheses, informed by past empirical findings (introduction); (2) design a specific set of concrete operations to test these hypotheses (method); (3) analyze the observations collected in this way, and decide if they support the original hypotheses (results); and (4) explore the broader theoretical and practical implications of the findings, and consider how they contribute to an understanding of the problem under investigation (discussion). Though these stages are somewhat arbitrary distinctions—research actually proceeds in a number of different ways—they help elucidate the inner logic of research reports.

While reading a research report, keep this linear structure in mind. Though it is difficult to remember a series of seemingly disjointed facts, when these facts are joined together in a logical, narrative structure, they become easier to comprehend and recall. Thus, always remember that a research report tells a story. It will help you to organize the information you read, and remember it later.

Describing research reports as stories is not just a convenient metaphor. Research reports *are* stories. Stories can be said to consist of two components: A telling of what happened, and an explanation of why it happened. It is tempting to view science as an endeavor that simply catalogues facts, but nothing is further from the truth. The goal of science, social psychology included, is to *explain* facts, to explain *why* what happened happened. Social psychology is built on the dynamic interplay of discovery and justification, the dialogue between systematic observation of relations and their theoretical explanation. Though research reports do present novel facts based on systematic observation, these facts are presented in the service of ideas.

Facts in isolation are trivia. Facts tied together by an explanatory theory are science. Therein lies the story. To really understand what researchers have to say, you need consider how their explanations relate to their findings.

The Rest of the Story

> There is really no such thing as research. There is only search, more search, keep on searching. (Bowering, 1988, p. 95)

Once you have read through a research report, and understand the researchers' findings and their explanations of them, the story does not end there. There is more than one interpretation for any set of findings. Different researchers often explain the same set of facts in different ways.

Let's take a moment to dispel a nasty rumor. The rumor is this: Researchers present their studies in a dispassionate manner, intending only to inform readers of their findings and their interpretation of those findings. In truth, researchers aim not only to inform readers, but also to *persuade* them (Steinberg, 1995). Researchers want to convince you their ideas are right. There is never only one explanation for a set of findings. Certainly, some explanations are better than others; some fit the available data better, are more parsimonious, or require fewer questionable assumptions. The point here is that researchers are very passionate about their ideas, and want you to believe them. It's up to you to decide if you want to buy their ideas or not.

Let's compare social psychologists to salesclerks. Both social psychologists and salesclerks want to sell you something; either their ideas, or their wares. You need to decide if you want to buy what they're selling or not—and there are potentially negative consequences for either decision. If you let a salesclerk dazzle you with a sales pitch, without thinking about it carefully, you might end up buying a substandard product that you don't really need. After having done this a few times, people tend to become cynical, steeling themselves against any and all sales pitches. This too is dangerous. If you are overly critical of sales pitches, you could end up foregoing genuinely useful products. Thus, by analogy, when you are too critical in your reading of research reports, you might dismiss, out of hand, some genuinely useful ideas—ideas that can help shed light on why people behave the way they do.

This discussion raises the important question of how critical one should be while reading a research report. In part, this will depend on why one is reading the report. If you are reading it simply to learn what the researchers have to say about a particular issue, for example, then there is usually no need to be overly critical. If you want to use the research as a basis for planning a new study, then you should be more critical. As you develop an understanding of psychological theory and research methods, you will also develop an ability to criticize research on many different levels. And *any* piece of research can be criticized at some level. As Jacob Cohen put it, "A successful piece of research doesn't conclusively settle an issue, it just makes some theoretical proposition to some degree more likely" (1990, p. 1311). Thus, as a consumer of research reports, you have to strike a delicate balance between being overly critical and overly accepting.

While reading a research report, at least initially, try to suspend your disbelief. Try to understand the researchers' story; that is, try to understand the facts—the findings and how they were obtained—and the suggested explanation of those facts—the researchers' interpretation of the findings and what they mean. Take the research to task only after you feel you understand what the authors are trying to say.

Research reports serve not only an important archival function, documenting research and its findings, but also an invaluable stimulus function. They can excite other researchers to join the investigation of a particular issue, or to apply new methods or theory to a different, perhaps novel, issue. It is this stimulus function that Elliot Aronson, an eminent social psychologist, referred to when he admitted that, in publishing a study, he hopes his colleagues will "look at it, be stimulated by it, be provoked by it, annoyed by it, and then go ahead and do it better. . . . That's the exciting thing about science; it progresses by people taking off on one another's work" (1995, p. 5). Science is indeed a cumulative enterprise, and each new study builds on what has (or, sometimes, has not) gone before it. In this way, research articles keep social psychology vibrant.

A study can inspire new research in a number of different ways, such as: (1) it can lead one to conduct a better test of the hypotheses, trying to rule out alternative explanations of the findings; (2) it can lead one to explore the limits of the findings, to see how widely applicable they are, perhaps exploring situations to which they do not apply; (3) it can lead one to test the implications of the findings, furthering scientific investigation of the phenomenon; (4) it can inspire one to apply the findings, or a novel methodology, to a different area of investigation; and (5) it can provoke one to test the findings in the context of a specific real-world problem, to see if they can shed light on it. All of these are excellent extensions of the original research, and there are, undoubtedly, other ways that research findings can spur new investigations.

The problem with being too critical, too soon, while reading research reports is that the only further research one may be willing to attempt is research of the first type: Redoing a study better. Sometimes this is desirable, particularly in the early stages of investigating a particular issue, when the findings are novel and perhaps unexpected. But redoing a reasonably compelling study, without extending it in any way, does little to advance our understanding of human behavior. Although the new study might be "better," it will not be "perfect," so *it* would have to be run again, and again, likely never reaching a stage where it is beyond criticism. At some point, researchers have to decide that the evidence is compelling enough to warrant investigation of the last four types. It is these types of studies that most advance our knowledge of social behavior. As you read more research reports, you will become more comfortable deciding when a study is "good enough" to move beyond it. This is a somewhat subjective judgment, and should be made carefully.

When social psychologists write up a research report for publication, it is because they believe they have something new and exciting to communicate about social behavior. Most research reports that are submitted for publication are rejected. Thus, the reports that are eventually published are deemed pertinent not only by the researchers who wrote them, but also by the reviewers and editors of the journals in which they are published. These people, at least, believe the research reports they write and publish have something important and interesting to say. Sometimes, you'll disagree; not all journal articles are created equal, after all. But we recommend that you, at least initially, give these well-meaning social psychologists the benefit of the doubt. Look for what they're excited about. Try to understand the authors' story, and see where it leads you.

Acknowledgments

Preparation of this paper was facilitated by a Natural Sciences and Engineering Research Council of Canada doctoral fellowship to Christian H. Jordan. Thanks to Roy Baumeister, Arie Kruglanski, Ziva Kunda, John Levine, Geoff MacDonald, Richard Moreland, Ian Newby-Clark, Steve Spencer, and Adam Zanna for their insightful comments on, and appraisals of, various drafts of this paper. Thanks also to Arie Kruglanski and four anonymous editors of volumes in the series, Key Readings in Social Psychology, for their helpful critiques of an initial outline of this paper.

Correspondence concerning this article should be addressed to Christian H. Jordan, Department of Psychology, University of Waterloo, Waterloo, Ontario, Canada N2L 3G1. Electronic mail can be sent to chjordan@watarts.uwaterloo.ca

REFERENCES

American Psychological Association (1994). *Publication manual* (4th ed.). Washington, DC: APA.

Aronson, E. (1995). Research in social psychology as a leap of faith. In E. Aronson (Ed.), *Readings about the social animal* (7th ed., pp. 3–9). New York: W. H. Freeman & Company.

Bem, D. J. (1987). Writing the empirical journal article. In M. P. Zanna & J. M. Darley (Eds.), *The complete academic: A practical guide for the beginning social scientist* (pp. 171–201). New York: Random House.

Bowering, G. (1988). *Errata*. Red Deer, Alberta, Canada: Red Deer College Press.

Cohen, J. (1990). Things I have learned (so far). *American Psychologist, 45*, 1304–1312.

Forgas, J. P. (1994). Sad and guilty? Affective influences on the explanation of conflict in close relationships. *Journal of Personality and Social Psychology, 66*, 56–68.

Sternberg, R. J. (1995). *The psychologist's companion: A guide to scientific writing for students and researchers* (3rd ed.). Cambridge, UK: Cambridge University Press.

Author Index

Subject Index